D1058315

CHEMISTRY & BIOCHEMISTRY OF MARINE FOOD PRODUCTS

Chemistry & Biochemistry of Marine Food Products

edited by
Roy E. Martin
National Fisheries Institute
Washington, DC

George J. Flick
Chieko E. Hebard
Department of Food Science and Technology
Virginia Polytechnic Institute and
State University
Blacksburg, Virginia

Donn R. Ward
Seafood Processing Research and
Extension Laboratory
Department of Food Science and Technology
Virginia Polytechnic Institute and
State University
Hampton, Virginia

AVI PUBLISHING COMPANY
Westport, Connecticut

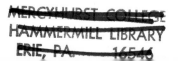

© Copyright 1982 by
THE AVI PUBLISHING COMPANY, INC.
Westport, Connecticut

Library of Congress Cataloging in Publication Data
Main entry under title:

Chemistry & biochemistry of marine food
  products.

  Includes bibliographies and index.
  1. Fish as food—Analysis.   2. Seafood—
Analysis.   I. Martin, Roy E.
TX556.5.C47   1982   664'.94   82-11486
ISBN 0-87055-408-5

Printed in the United States of America

Contents

List of Contributors

JERRY K. BABBITT, Northwest and Alaska Fisheries Center, National Marine Fisheries Service, National Oceanic and Atmospheric Administration, Seattle, Washington 98112

W. DUANE BROWN, Institute of Marine Resources, Department of Food Science and Technology, University of California, Davis, California 95616

C.L. CHOU, Fisheries and Environmental Sciences, Department of Fisheries and Oceans, Halifax, Nova Scotia, Canada B3J 2S7

JOHN A. DASSOW, Utilization Research Division, Northwest and Alaska Fisheries Center, National Marine Fisheries Service, National Oceanic and Atmospheric Administration, Seattle, Washington 98112

RONALD R. EITENMILLER, Department of Food Science, University of Georgia, Athens, Georgia 30602

MICHAEL FEY, Departments of Poultry Science and Food Science and Institute of Food Science, Cornell University, Ithaca, New York 14853

GUNNAR FINNE, Seafood Technology Section, Department of Animal Science, Texas A&M University, College Station, Texas 77843

GEORGE J. FLICK, Department of Food Science and Technology, Virginia Polytechnic Institute and State University, Blacksburg, Virginia 24061

H.C. FREEMAN, Fisheries and Environmental Sciences, Department of Fisheries and Oceans, Halifax, Nova Scotia, Canada B3J 2S7

DENNIS T. GORDON,* Seafoods Laboratory, Oregon State University, Astoria, Oregon 97103

CHIEKO E. HEBARD, Department of Food Science and Technology, Virginia Polytechnic Institute and State University, Blacksburg, Virginia 24061

---

*Present address: Department of Food Science and Nutrition, University of Missouri, Columbia, Missouri 65211

JANIS A. HUBBARD, Department of Food Science and Technology, Virginia Polytechnic Institute and State University, Blacksburg, Virginia 24061

H.O. HULTIN, Massachusetts Agricultural Experiment Station, Department of Food Science and Nutrition, Marine Foods Laboratory, University of Massachusetts Marine Station, Gloucester, Massachusetts 01930

LORI F. JACOBER, Department of Food Science and Technology, Nutrition and Dietetics, University of Rhode Island, Kingston, Rhode Island 02881

E. LEE JOHNSON, Kypro Company, 808 16th Avenue, N. E., Bellevue, Washington 98004

S.D. KELLEHER, Massachusetts Agricultural Experiment Station, Department of Food Science and Nutrition, Marine Foods Laboratory, University of Massachusetts Marine Station, Gloucester, Massachusetts 01930

SHOJI KONOSU, Laboratory of Marine Biochemistry, Faculty of Agriculture, The University of Tokyo, Tokyo, Japan

JACK LAVÉTY, Ministry of Agriculture, Fisheries and Food, Torry Research Station, Aberdeen AB9 8DG, Scotland

MICHAEL G. LEGENDRE, Southern Regional Research Center, USDA-SEA, New Orleans, Louisiana 70179

JOSEPH J. LICCIARDELLO, Gloucester Laboratory, Northeast Fisheries Center, National Marine Fisheries Service, National Oceanic and Atmospheric Administration, Gloucester, Massachusetts 01930

J. LISTON, College of Fisheries, Institute for Food Science and Technology, University of Washington, Seattle, Washington 98195

R. MALCOLM LOVE, Ministry of Agriculture, Fisheries and Food, Torry Research Station, Aberdeen AB9 8DG, Scotland

R.E. McDONALD, Massachusetts Agricultural Experiment Station, Department of Food Science and Nutrition, Marine Foods Laboratory, University of Massachusetts Marine Station, Gloucester, Massachusetts 01930

ROY E. MARTIN, National Fisheries Institute, Inc., Washington, D.C. 20036

TERUSHIGE MOTOHIRO, Laboratory of Food Environmental Engineering, Faculty of Fisheries, Hokkaido University, Hakodate, Hokkaido, Japan

JOSEPH H. ORR, Department of Food Science, University of Georgia, Athens, Georgia 30602

ROBERT L. ORY, Southern Regional Research Center, USDA-SEA, New Orleans, Louisiana 70179

KIRK L. PARKIN, Institute of Marine Resources, Department of Food Science and Technology, University of California, Davis, California 95616

Q.P. PENISTON,* Kypro Company, 808 16th Avenue, N. E., Bellevue, Washington 98004

GEORGE M. PIGOTT, College of Fisheries, Institute for Food Science and Technology, University of Washington, Seattle, Washington 98195

ARTHUR G. RAND, JR., Department of Food Science and Technology, Nutrition and Dietetics, University of Rhode Island, Kingston, Rhode Island 02881

JOE M. REGENSTEIN, Departments of Poultry Science and Food Science and Institute of Food Science, Cornell University, Ithaca, New York 14853

LOUIS J. RONSIVALLI,† Gloucester Laboratory, Northeast Fisheries Center, National Marine Fisheries Service, National Oceanic and Atmospheric Administration, Gloucester, Massachusetts 01930

A. J. ST. ANGELO, Southern Regional Research Center, USDA-SEA, New Orleans, Louisiana 70179

ALLAN SAMSON, Departments of Poultry Science and Food Science and Institute of Food Science, Cornell University, Ithaca, New York 14853

MARY ANNE SCHLOSSER, Departments of Poultry Science and Food Science and Institute of Food Science, Cornell University, Ithaca, New York 14853

KENNETH L. SIMPSON, Department of Food Science and Technology, Nutrition and Dietetics, University of Rhode Island, Kingston, Rhode Island 02881

G.R. SIROTA, Fisheries and Environmental Sciences, Department of Fisheries and Oceans, Halifax, Nova Scotia, Canada, B3J 2S7

JOHN SPINELLI, Utilization Research Division, Northwest and Alaska Fisheries Center, National Marine Fisheries Service, National Oceanic and Atmospheric Administration, Seattle, Washington 98112

*Deceased

†Present address: 336 Howard St., Lawrence, MA 01840

MAURICE E. STANSBY, Northwest and Alaska Fisheries Center, National Marine Fisheries Service, National Oceanic and Atmospheric Administration, Seattle, Washington 98112

PAUL M. TOOM, Department of Chemistry, University of Southern Mississippi, Hattiesburg, Mississippi 39401

J.F. UTHE, Fisheries and Environmental Sciences, Department of Fisheries and Oceans, Halifax, Nova Scotia, Canada B3J 2S7

FRANÇOISE VELLAS, Ministry of Agriculture, Fisheries and Food, Torry Research Station, Aberdeen AB9 8DG, Scotland

WAYNE W. WALLIS, Department of Food Science, University of Georgia, Athens, Georgia 30602

CHERYL F. WARD, Department of Chemistry, University of Southern Mississippi, Hattiesburg, Mississippi 39401

JAMES R. WEBER, Department of Chemistry, University of Southern Mississippi, Hattiesburg, Mississippi 39401

KATSUMI YAMAGUCHI, Laboratory of Marine Biochemistry, Faculty of Agriculture, The University of Tokyo, Tokyo, Japan

Preface

Although the food of aquatic and marine origin is this country's earliest food supply and the base for its oldest commercial industry, over the past many decades we, as a nation, have given up this heritage to a land-based protein economy.

With the congressional passage of the "Fishery Conservation and Management Act of 1976", today known as the 200-mile bill, this nation is being given a renewed opportunity to use and manage more than 20% of the world's seafood resources that happen to live within this 200-mile zone.

Twenty years ago, our food resources seemed inexhaustible. With today's technology, we know they are not. The demand for food protein will continue to grow as population expands. Food from the sea will provide an alternate source of this nourishment.

This volume represents the first attempt to draw together in one forum what we presently know about the chemistry and biochemistry of marine food products. The book is an expansion of a symposium held in 1979 during the American Chemical Society's Washington meeting.

This book is an attempt to emphasize the importance of chemistry and biochemistry to the complexities of fisheries technology and to provide a deeper understanding of those changes occurring in this resource. Fisheries are unique in our domestic food system because we have potentially some 250 species to work with, each with its own set of characteristics. When we expand our subject to include species from other parts of the world, we increase our matrix to more than 1000 kinds of fish and shellfish.

It is understandable, then, that we should attempt to bring together that basic body of knowledge upon which others can continue to expand.

This book also includes data and references translated from foreign sources that have not appeared elsewhere in U.S. scientific literature.

The scope of the book will give to the fisheries scientist and food technologist an immense appreciation for the complexities called fish as food and their by-products.

Acknowledgment

The authors are indebted to National Fisheries Institute, Inc., and the Sea Grant Program at Virginia Polytechnic Institute and State University for providing funds for making the publication possible.

Related AVI Books

Lipid Oxidation in Fish Muscle Microsomes

H.O. Hultin, R.E. McDonald, and S.D. Kelleher

INTRODUCTION

Lipid oxidation is a major cause of spoilage in fish muscle. This is due to the highly unsaturated nature of the fatty acids in fish tissue. Fatty-type fish, such as mackerel and herring, can undergo lipid oxidation rapidly at refrigerator temperatures. It is generally not as significant a problem with nonfatty fish stored in the round or as fillets, since mircobial spoilage usually develops more rapidly than lipid oxidation. This occurs even though tissue enzymes are considered to be the principal problem in stored fish until approximately 6 days after storage, after which microbial deterioration becomes dominant. Lipid oxidation may become a problem in nonfatty fish which are minced, because of the incorporation of oxygen into the tissue or the disruption and intermixing of tissue components.

Although the general importance of lipid oxidation in fish tissue has been recognized, the mechanisms of the oxidative processes are not well understood. It is known that metals such as iron (Fe) catalyze lipid oxidation in fish (Castell 1971). The involvement of an enzyme system in lipid oxidation has not been confirmed.

It was first observed in 1963 that the microsomal fraction from liver was capable of catalyzing the oxidation of the microsomal lipids in the presence of reduced nicotinamide adenine dinucleotide phosphate (NADPH), O_2, and Fe (Hochstein and Ernster 1963). The oxidation was enhanced in the presence of adenosine diphosphate (ADP) or other pyrophosphates and appeared to be coupled to the NADPH oxidase system of the microsomes. Wills (1969) demonstrated that liver microsomes formed lipid peroxides when incubated with ascorbate or NADPH but not with NADH. Pfeifer and McCay (1971) reported the generation of free radicals during the oxidation of NADPH by

Massachusetts Agricultural Experiment Station, Department of Food Science and Nutrition, Marine Foods Laboratory, University of Massachusetts Marine Station, Gloucester, Massachusetts 01930 liver microsomes which caused rapid lysis of erythrocytes incubated with the peroxidation system. Chen and McCay (1972) showed that the oxidation of NADPH by liver microsomes *in vitro* produced a factor that caused the release of hydrolases from lysosomes. It was suggested that this factor was a free radical.

Svingen *et al.* (1979) suggest that the lipid peroxidation reaction can be broken down into two steps: initiation and propagation. In the first step, the flavoprotein, NADPH-cytochrome P-450 reductase, catalyzes the reduction of ADP-Fe^{3+} to ADP-Fe^{2+}. This interacts with molecular oxygen to produce the ADP-perferryl ion (ADP-Fe^{3+}-O_2^-) which interacts with lipid to form lipid hydroperoxide. The lipid hydroperoxide may then be converted to a variety of free radicals by the ferric form of cytochrome P-450, a process which also results in the degradation of the cytochrome. The free radicals can then participate in typical lipid propagation steps by interacting with other fatty acid molecules.

Although most of the studies of the microsomal system have dealt with NADPH, it has been shown that lipid peroxidation of microsomes can also be activated by NADH at reduced levels (Pederson *et al.* 1973; Jansson and Schenkman 1975, 1977). Pederson and Aust (1972) found that microsomal lipid oxidation was inhibited by the addition of superoxide dismutase, suggesting O_2^- was involved in the reaction or some reductant derived from O_2^-. Fong *et al.* (1973) reported the disruption of lysosomal membranes by a free radical-like factor produced during NADH oxidation by rat liver microsomes. They suggested that peroxidation of the lysosomal membrane lipids was initiated by the hydroxyl free radical derived from the activity of certain flavoenzymes. Three different hydroxyl free radical scavengers protected the membrane from degradation. Lai and Piette (1977) also presented evidence using free radical spin traps that the hydroxyl radical was generated in liver microsomes during NADPH-catalyzed lipid peroxidation.

Although Hochstein *et al.* (1964) did not observe formation of thiobarbituric acid-reactive substances in the presence of NADPH and NADH with microsomes from skeletal muscle, and Hrycay and O'Brien (1974) found no NADH-driven lipid oxidation in the microsomal fraction from skeletal muscle, we have shown in our laboratory that there is a lipid peroxidation system in the microsomal fraction of chicken muscle. The peroxidation can be catalyzed by either NADPH or NADH, although the latter is less effective in that less peroxidation occurred and much higher concentrations of NADH were required for maximal results (Lin and Hultin 1976). We have demonstrated that the lipid peroxidation system can catalyze the oxidation of myoglobin to metmyoglobin and that this oxidation can be inhibited by antioxidants and by reduced glutathione and glutathione peroxidase (Lin and Hultin 1977). Superoxide dismutase inhibited the lipid peroxidation, but catalase had no effect (Player and Hultin 1977).

We report here some characteristics of an enzyme-catalyzed lipid oxidation in a microsomal fraction isolated from fish muscle.

METHODS

Two sources of fish were used in the study: red hake *(Urophycis chuss)* and winter flounder *(Pseudopleuronectes americanus)*. The choice was based principally on availability. The red hake was received iced from day fishing boats and the microsomal fraction prepared from the fish as received or after storage at $-90°C$. In the latter case, the fish was first thawed in a plastic bag immersed in water at about 30°C. No major differences were observed between microsomes prepared from the iced fish and those from the frozen fish. Flounders were kept alive in seawater fish tanks and processed within approximately 5 min after dispatching. Effects of refrigerated and frozen storage of the fish and microsomes on the characteristics of the isolated microsomes were examined. The lipid peroxidative activity survived well and was affected little by either treatment, supplementing the information that we had observed with the red hake. Additionally, no differences were observed between the microsomes from red hake and flounder.

The microsomes were prepared by differential centrifugation after homogenization in a Brinkmann Polytron homogenizer with a PT20ST generator (McDonald *et al.* 1979). The fraction which was collected sedimented between 14,800 g for 30 min and 105,000 g for 60 min. Before utilization, the preparation was taken up in 0.6 M KCl$-$5 mM histidine buffer (pH 7.3) and recentrifuged to remove actomyosin. Thiobarbituric acid (TBA)-reactive materials measured are reported as nanomoles of malondialdehyde (MDA) per milligram of protein-time. Trichloracetic acid was used to stop the reaction. NADH disappearance was measured at 340 nm after stopping the reaction with ethanol.

RESULTS AND DISCUSSION

Liver microsomes utilize NADPH in lipid oxidation to a greater extent than NADH (the latter has usually been found to be effective only under certain special conditions), and the microsomal fraction from chicken skeletal muscle also prefers NADPH as the cofactor in microsomal lipid peroxidation. This is not the case, however, with the microsomal fraction prepared from fish skeletal muscle (Fig. 1.1). It is clear from the data presented that NADH is the preferred substrate for fish microsomes in the range of 0 to 2.5 mM. In addition, NADH exhibits an optimal concentration for the catalysis of lipid peroxidation. NADPH, on the other hand, presents a more typical hyperbolic-type response. Consequently, the difference between the two nucleotides is much greater at lower concentrations than at 2.5 mM. The pH optimum for the production of TBA-reactive substances was approximately 6.5 with NADH. The reaction in the presence of NADPH had a broad optimal pH range of 7 to at least 8 (we did not measure activity at a higher pH than this), but the activity at 6.5 was essentially 0.

Most investigators agree that the first step in microsomal lipid peroxidation is the reduction of Fe from the Fe^{3+} to the Fe^{2+} state. Figure 1.2

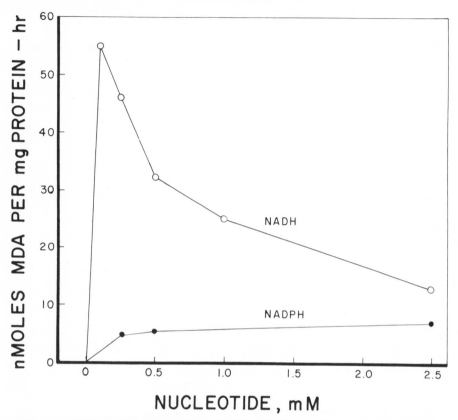

FIG. 1.1.   EFFECT OF NUCLEOTIDE CONCENTRATION ON MALONDIALDEHYDE PRODUCTION BY FISH SKELETAL MUSCLE MICROSOMES
The reaction was carried out at 5°C, and the assay medium contained 0.015 mM FeCl$_3$, 0.1 mM ADP, and 5 mM histidine buffer, pH 7.1.

shows the rate of malondialdehyde formation in the presence of increasing concentrations of Fe^{2+} and Fe^{3+}. These reactions were carried out at 5°C in the presence of 0.5 mM NADH and in the absence of ADP. It can be seen that Fe^{2+} is approximately twice as effective as Fe^{3+} over the range of concentrations used. The cross in Fig. 1.2 is a point at which equal molar amounts of Fe^{2+} and Fe^{3+} were mixed, and the rate of MDA production is approximately the arithmetic mean of the reactions run with the individual ions. Fe^{2+} was added as the sulfate and Fe^{3+} as the chloride. Control experiments indicated there was no effect on the rate of MDA production by either sulfate or chloride ions. The enzyme system can apparently reduce Fe^{3+} in the uncomplexed state.

Table 1.1 shows the effect of inhibition by heat and ADP. Certain conclusions can be drawn from these data. The lower peroxidation after heating

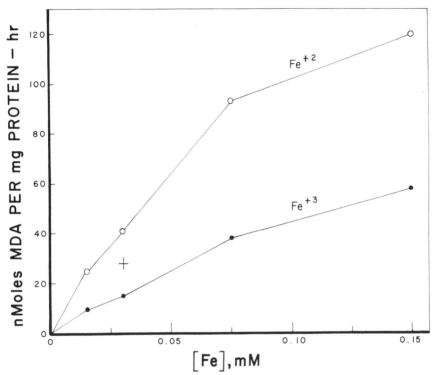

FIG. 1.2. EFFECT OF TYPE AND CONCENTRATION OF Fe SALT ON MALONDIAL-
DEHYDE PRODUCTION BY FISH SKELETAL MUSCLE MICROSOMES
The reaction was carried out at 5°C and pH 7.1, 5 mM histidine buffer. The concentration of
NADH used was 0.5 mM. No ADP was used in these experiments. The datum represented by
the "+" was obtained by adding equal parts of Fe(SO$_4$) and FeCl$_3$ to obtain the desired
concentration of Fe.

TABLE 1.1. INHIBITION OF MICROSOMAL LIPID OXIDATION BY HEAT
AND ADP[1]

Treatment	nmoles MDA per mg protein—30 min	
	30°C	1°C
NADH, Fe^{+3}	70.0	8.1
NADH, Fe^{+3}, ADP	6.7	1.3
NADH, Fe^{+3} (microsomes heated)	30.7	1.7
NADH, Fe^{+2}	—	21.1
NADH, Fe^{+2}, ADP	—	1.9
NADH, Fe^{+2} (microsomes heated)	—	5.4

[1]The assay medium contained 0.015 mM Fe(SO$_4$) or FeCl$_3$, 0.5 mM NADH,
and where used, 4.0 mM ADP. Heating was done at 80°C for 5 min.

would indicate the enzymic nature of the reaction, if only partially. The nonenzymic portion of the reaction may be considered as that which exists after heating. This is probably a good first approximation, although it may not be exactly correct. For example, the process of heating could be exposing more reactive sites in the membrane and/or more of the phospholipid to nonmembrane components. This hypothesis is supported by the fact that, when the nonenzymatic reaction is obtained by omitting NADH from the reaction medium, the rate of oxidation is less than that of the membranes after they have been heated. The nonenzymic portion of the reaction increases more rapidly than the enzymic portion as the temperature is increased. It is clear that ADP inhibits the Fe^{2+}-catalyzed reaction as well as the Fe^{3+}-catalyzed reaction. It is probable that ADP inhibits the nonenzymic oxidation as well as the enzymic oxidation. This is based on the lower level of MDA production in the presence of ADP than that of the heated samples. If the reaction in the heated samples were due only to nonenzymic processes and if ADP only inhibited the enzymic processes, then the value of the heated samples should be as low as the samples treated with ADP. They are not. Therefore, the tentative conclusion is that ADP inhibits the nonenzymic reaction as well as the enzymic reaction. This conclusion is further supported by the effect of 4 mM ADP on the production of MDA in the absence of NADH. Under these circumstances, 53% of MDA production was inhibited in the presence of 0.15 mM $FeCl_3$, 38% in the presence of 0.015 mM $FeSO_4$, and 66% in the presence of 0.15 mM $FeSO_4$.

The effect of the concentration of ADP on the lipid peroxidation reaction of fish muscle microsomes is shown in Fig. 1.3. There is an optimal level of ADP. When the reaction is carried out at 4 mM ADP (not shown in the figure), the activity is reduced to extremely low levels under the conditions of assay used in these experiments, i.e., 0.015 mM Fe^{3+}. The optimal level of ADP is shifted to higher levels with higher concentrations of Fe. The shift appears to be roughly linear: a tenfold increase in the concentration of Fe shifts the optimal level of ADP by a factor of approximately 10. Thus, it appears that it is the ADP : Fe ratio which is the critical factor. Over the range tested, ATP produced a similar response to ADP, whereas the effect of AMP was relatively slight.

The inhibitory effect of phosphate is demonstrated in Fig. 1.4, where the reaction was carried out at two pH values using histidine and phosphate as buffers. The stimulatory effect of low concentrations of ADP is not observed in the presence of 5 mM phosphate.

In Table 1.2, the effect of several substances on lipid peroxidation in the microsomal system is shown. Mannitol, benzoate, dimethylsulfoxide (DMSO), and thiourea are free hydroxyl radical scavengers. Superoxide dismutase (SOD) catalyzes the dismutation of superoxide ions, and catalase catalyzes the disproportionate of hydrogen peroxide to oxygen and water. All of these substances inhibited malondialdehyde production, indicating that, in our system, hydrogen peroxide, O_2^-, and ˙OH are involved in the reaction. It is interesting also to note the potent inhibitory effect of sodium

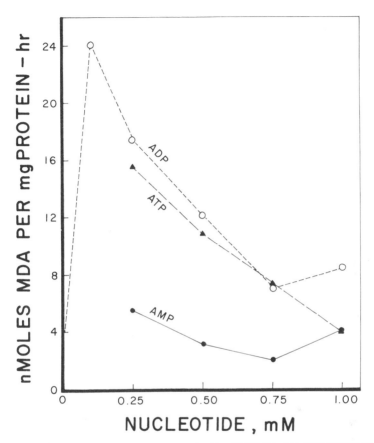

FIG. 1.3. EFFECT OF NUCLEOTIDE CONCENTRATION ON MALONDIALDEHYDE PRODUCTION BY FISH SKELETAL MUSCLE MICROSOMES
The reaction was carried out at 5°C; the assay medium contained 0.015 mM FeCl$_3$, 0.5 mM NADH, and 5 mM histidine buffer, pH 7.1.

TABLE 1.2. EFFECT OF VARIOUS INHIBITORS ON MICROSOMAL LIPID PEROXIDATION[1]

Inhibitor	nmoles per mg protein-hr (% of control)	
	MDA	NADH
Mannitol, 100 mM	66	109
Catalase, 50 μg/ml	62	80
Sodium benzoate, 100 mM	58	17
Dimethylsulfoxide, 50 mM	48	97
Superoxide dismutase, 50 μg/ml	41	99
Thiourea, 20 mM	28	74
Sodium tripolyphosphate, 0.2 mM	0	84

[1] The assay medium contained 0.015 mM FeSO$_4$, 0.1 mM ADP, and 0.5 mM NADH. The reaction was carried out at 5°C.

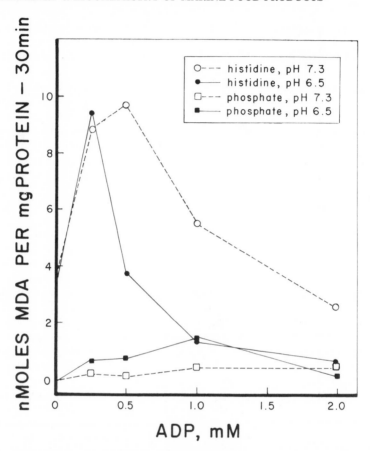

FIG. 1.4.   EFFECT OF PHOSPHATE ON MALONDIALDEHYDE PRODUCTION BY FISH
SKELETAL MUSCLE MICROSOMES
The reaction was carried out at 5°C; the assay medium contained 0.015 mM FeCl$_3$, 0.2 mM
NADH, and 5 mM buffer at the indicated pH values.

tripolyphosphate (STPP), which is a very good antioxidant in muscle food
systems. This compound at 0.2 mM completely eliminated production of
TBA-reactive substances. Most of these substances had only a slight effect
on NADH oxidation. The one exception was sodium benzoate which inhibited some 80% of NADH oxidation. The differential effect of these inhibitors on the disappearance of NADH versus the production of malondialdehyde implies that there probably is more than one NADH oxidation
system in the microsomal fraction and that not all of these systems are
involved with lipid oxidation. This conclusion was also supported by the
observation that the ability of the microsomes to utilize NADH frequently
decreased rapidly with time postmortem, while there was little or no effect

on the capacity of the microsomal fraction to catalyze the production of malondialdehyde.

It is interesting that we have observed essentially no difference in behavior between the microsomes prepared from flounder recently killed and those prepared from red hake that has been stored frozen at $-90°C$. These observations are consistent with our previous data with chicken skeletal muscle microsomes in which very little loss of lipid peroxidative activity was observed over a storage period of 7 days whether stored at neutral pH or pH 5.6 (Player and Hultin 1977). In addition, preliminary studies have indicated that similar microsomal preparations can be made from other species including yellow tail flounder, whiting (silver hake), and sculpin.

CONCLUSIONS

Several species of fish contain in the muscle an NADH-dependent lipid peroxidation system which utilizes NADPH relatively poorly. The system requires Fe, most probably in the Fe^{2+} state. The reaction rate *in vitro* depends on several factors. ADP can both stimulate and inhibit the reaction depending on the concentration used. The optimal concentration of ADP is dependent on the concentration of Fe. The concentrations of NADH, ADP, ATP, and Fe which inhibit or stimulate the reaction are in the physiological range. Thus, the system may represent an important means of lipid peroxidation in the tissue. Of these factors, Fe appears to be the only one which does not show an optimal level; increasing Fe concentrations gives increasing reaction rates.

Relatively low concentrations of inorganic phosphate also inhibit the system. The pH optimum for the production of malondialdehyde is somewhere between 6 and 7, which again is in the range of pH of postmortem fish muscle. The relative extent of the enzymic versus the nonenzymic oxidation of the microsomal lipids is temperature dependent. As the temperature increases, the relative proportion of the nonenzymic catalyzed reaction increases. The reduction products of molecular oxygen—i.e., O_2^- H_2O_2, and $·OH$—appear to be involved in some way in the reaction.

ACKNOWLEDGMENTS

This work was supported in part by Massachusetts Experiment Station Projects 197 and 345 and by the Graduate School of the University of Massachusetts at Amherst.

REFERENCES

CASTELL, C.H.   1971.   Metal-catalyzed lipid oxidation and changes of proteins in fish.   J. Am. Oil Chemists Soc. *48*, 645–649.

CHEN, K.L., and MCCAY, P.B.   1972.   Lyosome disruption by a free radical-like component generated during microsomal NADPH oxidase activity. Biochem. Biophys. Res. Commun. *48*, 1412–1418.

FONG, K.-L., MCCAY, P.B., POYER, J.L., KEELE, B.B., and MISRA, H. 1973. Evidence that peroxidation of lysosomal membranes is initiated by hydroxyl free radicals produced during flavin enzyme activity. J. Biol. Chem. *248*, 7792–7797.

HOCHSTEIN, P., and ERNSTER, L. 1963. Adenine diphosphate (ADP)-activated lipid peroxidation coupled to the reduced triphosphopyridine nucleotide (TPNH) oxidase system of microsomes. Biochem. Biophys. Res. Commun. *12*, 388–394.

HOCHSTEIN, P., NORDERBRAND, D., and ERNSTER, L. 1964. Evidence for the involvement of iron in the ADP-activated peroxidation of lipids in microsomes and mitochondria. Biochem. Biophys. Res. Commun. *14*, 323–328.

HRYCAY, E.G., and O'BRIEN, P.J. 1974. Microsomal electron transport. II. Reduced nicotinamide adenine dinucleotide–cytochrome b_5 reductase and cytochrome $P450$ as electron carriers in microsomal NADH-peroxidase activity. Arch. Biochem. Biophys. *160*, 230–245.

JANSSON, I., and SCHENKMAN, J.B. 1975. Three microsomal electron transfer enzyme systems. Effects of alteration of component enzyme levels *in vivo* and *in vitro*. Mol. Pharmacol. *11*, 450–461.

JANSSON, I., and SCHENKMAN, J.B. 1977. Studies on three microsomal electron transfer enzyme systems. Specificity of electron flow pathways. Arch. Biochem. Biophys. *178*, 89–107.

LAI, C.-S., and PIETTE, L.H. 1977. Hydroxyl radical production involved in lipid peroxidation of rat liver microsomes. Biochem. Biophys. Res. Commun. *78*, 51–59.

LIN, T.-S., and HULTIN, H.O. 1976. Enzymic lipid peroxidation in microsomes of chicken skeletal muscle. J. Food Sci. *41*, 1488–1489.

LIN, T.-S., and HULTIN, H.O. 1977. Oxidation of myoglobin *in vitro* mediated by lipid oxidation in microsomal fractions of muscle. J. Food Sci. *42*, 136–140.

MCDONALD, R.E., KELLEHER, S.D., and HULTIN, H.O. 1979. Membrane lipid oxidation in a microsomal fraction of red hake muscle. J. Food Biochem. *3*, 125–134.

PEDERSON, T.C., and AUST, S.D. 1972. NADPH-dependent lipid peroxidation catalyzed by purified NADPH-cytochrome c reductase from rat liver microsomes. Biochem. Biophys. Res. Commun. *48*, 789–795.

PEDERSON, T.C., BUEGE, J.A., and AUST, S.D. 1973. Microsomal electron transport. Role of reduced nicotinamide adenine dinucleotide phosphate–cytochrome c reductase in liver microsomal lipid peroxidation. J. Biol. Chem. *248*, 7134–7141.

PFEIFER, P.M., and MCCAY, P.B. 1971. Reduced triphosphopyridine nucleotide oxidase-catalyzed alterations of membrane phospholipids: V. Use of erythrocytes to demonstrate enzyme-dependent production of a component with the properties of a free radical.   J. Biol. Chem. *246*, 6401−6408.

PLAYER, T.J., and HULTIN, H.O. 1977. Some characteristics of the NAD(P)H-dependent lipid peroxidation system in the microsomal fraction of chicken breast muscle.   J. Food Biochem. *1*, 153−171.

SVINGEN, B.A., BUEGE, J.A., O'NEAL, F.O., and AUST, S.D. 1979. The mechanism of NADPH-dependent lipid peroxidation. The propagation of lipid peroxidation. J. Biol. Chem. *254*, 5892−5899.

WILLS, E.D. 1969. Lipid peroxide formation in microsomes. General considerations. Biochem. J. *113*, 315−324.

2

Fish Proteins: Their Modification and Potential Uses in the Food Industry

John Spinelli and John A. Dassow

INTRODUCTION

In the past 20 years, three major developments in world fisheries have influenced the importance of fish proteins in the food industry and have created a need for their use in both natural and modified forms. First, the world commercial catch increased from 36.9 million metric tons in 1959 to 73.5 million metric tons in 1977. Second, the expansion of world fisheries showed that we are increasingly dependent on nontraditional and formerly underutilized marine resources to maintain the upward curve of fishery landings. Third, the major fishing nations of the world accepted the principle of exclusive 200-mile coastal fishery zones off each fishery nation. The United States promulgated the Fishery Conservation and Management Act in 1976 and established regulations for the control of domestic and foreign fishing in a fisheries zone from 3 to 200 miles off the coasts of the United States effective March 1, 1977. All fish except tuna were covered by the act.

Foremost among the species in the U.S. fishery zone that contributed to the increasing world fish catch after 1960 were two previously under-utilized species, the walleye or Alaska pollock *(Theragra chalcogramma)* of the Southeastern Bering Sea, and Pacific whiting[1] *(Merluccius productus)* of the Northeast Pacific. These and other species of bottomfish were harvested during the 1960s almost exclusively off Alaska and the Pacific Northwest by the great fishing fleets of the Soviet Union and Japan. Annual foreign harvest of bottomfish from the Bering Sea and the Aleutian Islands region peaked in 1972 with catches totaling 2.3 million metric

Utilization Research Division, Northwest and Alaska Fisheries Center, National Marine Fisheries Service, National Oceanic and Atmospheric Administration, Seattle, Washington 98112
[1] Pacific whiting (also known as Pacific hake) was approved as the common name by the U.S. Food and Drug Administration, August 3, 1979.

tons (5.1 billion pounds), an amount exceeding the total U.S. catch for that year of 2.2 million tons. Of this enormous bottomfish catch by foreign fleets, over 80% or 1.8 million metric tons consisted of Alaska pollock. During these same years, Pacific whiting harvest off Oregon and Washington by foreign fleets increased to over 200,000 metric tons, making it second only to pollock as a high-volume trawl species in the Northeast Pacific. In comparison, the total U.S. landings of six traditional species of trawl fish (rockfish, flounders, sablefish, Pacific cod, lingcod, ocean perch) on the Pacific Coast was 79,100 metric tons in 1978.

Obviously there is a lot of room for expansion by the Pacific Coast and Alaska trawl fisheries in Alaska pollock and Pacific whiting as well as in the traditional trawl species in some areas. The potential for expanded pelagic fisheries is also impressive according to resource specialists. However, the development of the U.S. bottomfish industry is clearly the major program for industry in cooperation with government for the next decade or two.

TECHNOLOGICAL POTENTIALS OF BOTTOMFISH EXPANSION

The act establishing the 200-mile fishery zone provided for continuing foreign fishing under certain conditions. The primary intent of the law is to give U.S. fishermen the first chance at all fisheries and to allocate to foreign fishermen only the portion of the optimum yield that U.S. fishermen do not plan to harvest. Since Alaska pollock and Pacific whiting are the major bottomfish species, but are currently harvested to a small extent by U.S. fishermen, the major job for industry and government in the Northeast Pacific is clear: Develop a large trawl-fish industry for pollock in Alaska where none exists, and expand the trawl fishery for whiting off the Pacific Coast. At the outset, most fishery experts said the major problems were economic; large investments in vessels and processing facilities were necessary, especially in Alaska; furthermore, high operating costs and uncertain market conditions meant that the profit potential was questionable. Of major concern were the technological problems imposed by such species characteristics as size, fillet quality, preservation problems, the need for high volume production of quality food products, and a competitive world price.

Although some of the figures presented for potential volume of a U.S. pollock fishery are impressive, what is often overlooked is that, in marine commercial fisheries, a large percentage of the total catch may not be suitable (by current processing methods) for processing into human foods. For example, one-third to one-half of the Bering Sea catch of pollock are 35 cm in length or less and not suitable with present economics and technology for processing into fillets.

Alternative uses of smaller pollock as food are production of *surimi* for use in *kamaboko* in Japan, headed and gutted fish frozen for later marketing, and minced flesh blocks frozen for use as a raw material in processed foods.

At present, production costs and market prices in these areas are not favorable. Alternatives for industrial use include production of frozen animal feed and reduction to fish meal. Although 35% of the world's catch and 50% of the U.S. catch are reduced to fish meal and oil, production costs of fish meal, freight rates to markets, and selling price do not appear to justify these operations in Alaska.

From a technological viewpoint, the best way to improve prospects for food use is to develop processes and products that can utilize fish muscle in a frozen, heat-treated, or modified form as a significant ingredient in high-value processed foods. Stabilized low-fat proteins in both dry and moist forms are needed in high volume for food uses. With fish proteins, the retention of valuable nutrition and functional values is essential. As we examine some aspects of composition and protein modification in the following sections, it will be seen that the task is not as easy as might be expected.

COMPOSITION OF FISH

Because of its extreme perishability and compositional variations, the utilization of fish as a basic raw food material presents difficult processing problems. Its composition varies not only among species but also within the same species. For example, anchovies caught off the coast of Southern California have an average fat composition ranging from 2 to 12%, depending on the season in which they are caught. Pacific whiting caught off the coasts of Washington and Oregon vary in fat content from 1 to 4%. Fish composition is also dependent on age, maturity, feeding conditions, location of catch, and water temperature. To further complicate matters, fish come in all sizes and shapes, and the color of the flesh ranges from almost pure white to red. In between, there are various shades of yellow, brown, and gray.

For purposes of this chapter, fish can be classified into lean and fat species. The muscle of lean fish, such as cod, pollock, rockfish, and flounder, contain approximately 78–83% moisture, 15–20% protein, 1–4% fat, and 1–1.3% mineral matter. The component proteins of fish muscle contain from 20 to 30% sarcoplasmic proteins that are soluble in water and dilute buffers, 70–80% structural proteins most of which are soluble in cold neutral salt solutions of fairly high ionic strength (i.e., 0.5 M), and about 2–3% connective tissue. Under a microscope, myofibrils have a striated appearance like that of mammalian muscle and contain the same major myofibril proteins such as myosin, actin, actomyosin, and tropomyosin. In contrast to most proteins of mammalian origin, the loss of ATPase activity and aggregation occurs at a faster rate in fish muscle (Arai et al. 1973).

Fish muscle comprises both red and white muscles. Figure 2.1 shows the transverse sections of several species of fish. The red meat fraction varies from a low of 1–2% in lean fishes such as whiting, pollock, cod, and flounder, to a high of 10% or over in the fat species such as salmonids. The muscle in some fish, such as the elasmobranch (sharks), is distinctly differ-

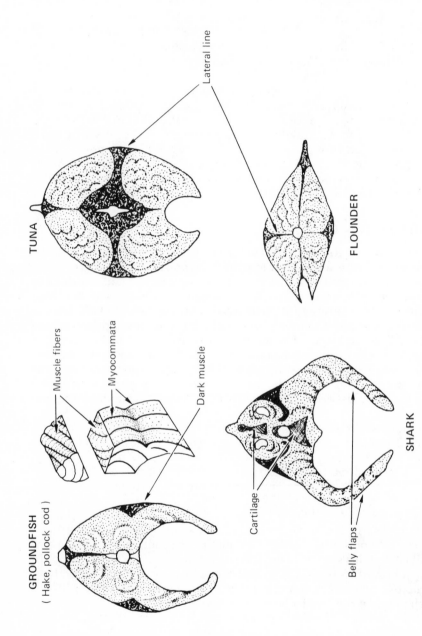

TUNA

FLOUNDER

Lateral line

GROUNDFISH
(Hake, pollock cod)

Muscle fibers

Myocommata

Dark muscle

SHARK

Cartilage

Belly flaps

FIG. 2.1.   TRANSVERSE SECTIONS OF VARIOUS FISH SPECIES

ent in character from most other fish. It contains up to 10% collagen and lacks the characteristic flaky texture of most other finfish.

Although it is the light muscle of the fish that is primarily used as food, the red muscle is very important to the physiology and biochemistry of the fish. A higher concentration of fats, fatty acids, myoglobin, and enzymes such as succinic dehydrogenase, lecithinase, and respiratory enzymes are found in the dark muscle of the fish (Buttkus and Tomlinson 1966). From the food technologist's point of view, these compounds present a formidable processing problem because they give rise to postmortem spoilage problems induced by these enzymes, such as the production of free fatty acids and oxidation reactions that severely affect the organoleptic properties of the fish. Canned tuna, for example, does not contain red meat which possesses a very strong flavor. It is carefully removed during packing and utilized only in the pet food industry.

Nonprotein Nitrogen

Nitrogenous constituents not classified as proteins (components in the tissue that are not precipitable by 5% trichloroacetic acid protein) comprise between 0.5 and 1% of total weight of the muscle. The major components are trimethylamine oxide, urea, taurine, peptides, amino acids, nucleotides, and related purine-based compounds (Konosu et al. 1974). Many of these compounds have been related to the flavor of fish (Jones 1963), and the degradation products of muscle ATP such as inosine monophosphate and hypoxanthine have been correlated with the flavor and freshness of fish (Spinelli 1971). Trimethylamine oxide (TMAO) can be degraded to trimethylamine (TMA), dimethylamine (DMA), and formaldehyde (FA), and the contents of these amines in fish have been used as spoilage indices for many years.

Postmortem Changes

This discussion is confined to postmortem changes and remarks that are related to alteration of the muscle proteins and how these changes affect the processing and subsequent organoleptic alterations of muscle tissue. Aside from attack by microorganisms and oxidative rancidity, the most conspicuous change that affects the quality of fish is an alteration of textural characteristics. In most instances this change is reflected by a significant change in the water-holding capacity (WHC), generally accompanied by a corresponding toughness of the muscle tissue. There are divergent theories and different explanations in the literature as to the root of these muscle changes.

Protein–Lipid Interactions

In 1961 Dyer and Dingle, studying the protein alteration in frozen fish, observed that the proteins in fatty fishes were more resistant to denaturation (expressed as salt-soluble proteins) than those of lean fishes. They postulated that (1) the lipids associated with the protein stabilized the protein molecule against denaturation and that this protection is lost when the lipid is hydrolyzed, or (2) fatty acids hydrolyzed from the lipids modify the surface of the protein and make it subject to denaturation. Working with cod, halibut, lemon sole, and spiny dogfish, King *et al.* (1962) did not find an absolute correlation between free fatty acids that were enzymically liberated at −14°C and protein insolubilization. Anderson and Steinberg (1964) shed light on some of the divergent observations by showing that competition between protein and neutral lipids for the liberated free fatty acids influence the amount of proteins that are insolubilized. They also postulated that other compounds such as lipoproteins were involved in protecting proteins.

DEGRADATION OF TRIMETHYLAMINE OXIDE TO DIMETHYLAMINE AND FORMALDEHYDE

Until about 1960 the only relation demonstrated between free amines and the condition or quality of fish was that between free TMA and fish spoilage. The origin of TMA was TMAO. TMAO was shown to be degraded by enzymes produced by certain spoilage microorganisms such as the pseudomonads. Little attention was given to DMA as a spoilage index because very little was found in spoiling fish and because its formation was rather species-related, forming primarily in the gadoids. In 1965 Amano and Yamada wrote a rather comprehensive paper on the formation of DMA in cod. They suggested that TMAO was degraded to DMA and FA by an enzyme. They also postulated that the liberated formaldehyde reacted with the structural proteins causing textural alterations. Subsequent work by many investigators has shown some evidence that formaldehyde can react with the structural proteins to reduce protein extractability and cause related texture changes (Tokunaga 1964, 1965; Castell *et al.* 1973). Work at our laboratory using carbon-14 has not convincingly demonstrated the role formaldehyde plays in the alteration of structural proteins. As might be expected, we found that formaldehyde reacted with the sarcoplasmic as well as the structural proteins but that about 60% of the formaldehyde reacted with the sarcoplasmic protein, 30% with the structural proteins, and 10% remained unreacted (H. Groninger 1980, personal communication).

Some of the interpretations relating to textural changes and their causes are complicated by the fact that many investigators often correlate salt-soluble protein or extractable protein nitrogen (EPN) with changes in the organoleptic properties of muscle. In their recent paper on the deterioration of frozen whiting and haddock muscle, Gill *et al.* (1979) showed the error of using EPN as an index in this manner. They pointed out that, whereas cooking decreased EPN by 95%, poor frozen storage caused a much higher degree of toughening with only a small change in EPN. This, of course, is an extreme example but does illustrate that decreases in EPN can be induced by a variety of reactions, not all of which correlate with organoleptic changes. What we generally find is that EPN correlates very well with organoleptic properties when the fish is held under poor frozen storage conditions (e.g., $-10°C$), and not under more favorable storage conditions (e.g., $-26°C$).

Aitken and Connell (1977) reasoned that changes in water-holding capacity and concomitant textural changes should be readily detected by measuring changes in the interfilament distance of the muscle fibers. What they found, however, was that loss of WHC and toughening occurred with no significant alterations in interfilament distances. They concluded that the protein change was due to an increase in hydrophobic properties.

Current work at our laboratory indicates that the proposed mechanism of TMAO degradation to DMA and FA is certainly open to question. In recent years the presence of secondary amines in foods has assumed a new significance in relation to potential formation of the carcinogen dimethylnitrosamine. Therefore the mechanism(s) for DMA formation in fresh and processed fish needs clarification.

Since Amano and Yamada (1965) published their paper, the theory that the formation of DMA and FA is enzymically catalyzed has been almost taken for granted. But as early as 1958, Tarr, in an excellent review on the biochemistry of fish, speculated that the degradation of TMAO in fish muscle could result from a nonenzymic reaction. Spinelli and Koury (1979) have shown that DMA is produced in very significant quantities in both drum- and freeze-dried fish, and that its formation is neither species-related nor enzymically induced. They also showed that compounds such as EDTA, SO_2, and phytic acid in the presence of Fe^{2+} accelerate this reaction. More recent work shows that the addition of catabolic intermediates of cysteine, such as cysteinesulfinic acid, hypotaurine, and taurine in nongadoid species will result in the degradation of TMAO to DMA. Although our work does not disprove the existence of the so-called TMAOase enzyme in the tissue, it definitely establishes that at least an alternate pathway can be operative and lends support to Tarr's hypothesis of 22 years ago.

MODIFIED PROTEINS

In the early 1960s, some very serious attempts were made to prepare and market relatively pure fish proteins. At that time the primary efforts in this direction were being made in the United States, Canada, and Sweden. The end-product of this effort was, of course, fish protein concentrate (FPC). FPC never became a viable commercial product and the FPC story need not be retold here. For those interested in the FPC story, we respectfully refer to an article that appeared in *Food Technology* (1977) by Roland Finch "Whatever Happened to FPC" and another "FPC and Fish Protein Concentrate: Panacea for Protein Malnutrition" by Pariser *et al.* (1978). Simply put, FPC was not needed in the industrialized countries and its merits were never demonstrated in third world countries. What about FPC today? It would appear that the technology to produce an inert FPC, solely a protein supplement, is too sophisticated and probably economically unsound. New approaches based on relatively old technology are beginning to show that fish can be used to supplement cereal proteins in a much simpler fashion than as a solvent-extracted powder.

MECHANICAL DEBONING

Flesh separators or deboners are probably the most significant development in the direct utilization of fish flesh from undervalued fishes. The machines were developed in Japan and have been in common use in that country for some 40 years for the production of bone-free minced flesh used in the preparation of a variety of Japanese fish products. The deboning machine produces more minced flesh than is possible either by hand or machine cutting. They are now ubiquitous in all industrial countries, and their design and operation have been described in detail by Steinberg and Spinelli (1976). The advantages of using the deboning machine are threefold: they (1) permit the processor to process fish that are too small to fillet, (2) produce high yields of edible flesh, and (3) permit the recovery of edible flesh from what would otherwise be waste from filleting operations. Yields of flesh ranging from 65 to 92.6% were reported (King and Carver 1970) on 19 different species of fish processed with flesh-separating machines. With mechanical deboning, minced flesh is now considered a raw material that can be used as an intermediate for the preparation of a variety of products as depicted in Fig. 2.2.

Since the FPC experience, the use of fish as a raw material for the preparation of functional protein ingredients has been the subject of a modest research effort. That it is possible to make these products has been amply demonstrated (Groninger 1973; Miller and Groninger 1976; Spinelli et al. 1977).

Probably the biggest stumbling block in preparing functional isolates from fish muscle is that organic polar solvents are necessary to remove residual lipids that are associated with the muscle. Solvent extraction is particularly necessary to remove the phospholipids which are insoluble in nonpolar solvents. Polar solvents, of course, insolubilize the proteins, and thus put you back on square one. Spinelli et al. (1972) showed that the basic properties of natural fish proteins could be maintained during hot-solvent extraction with solvents such as IPA if they were first hydrolyzed mildly and then reacted with sodium hexametaphosphate at pH 2.0–3.5. Cobb et al. (1972) reported that they prepared functional isolates by solvent-extracting fish protein at low pH in the presence of high salt concentrations. Although these processes produced functional proteins, their functional stability rapidly decreased during storage. Koury and Spinelli (1975) showed that the decrease in functional stability during storage could be significantly improved by co-drying the isolate in the presence of disaccharides or sorbitol. They also showed that functional stability was closely

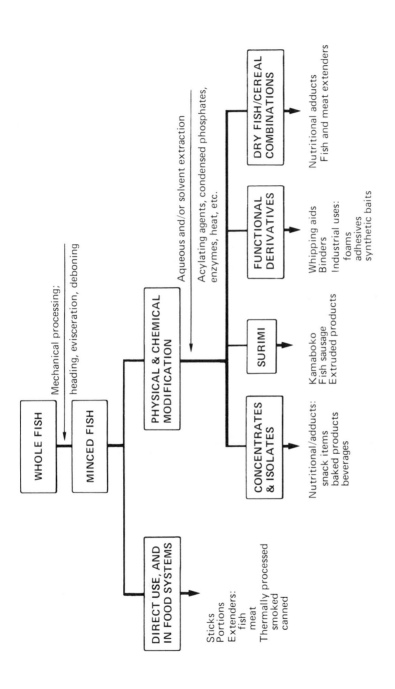

FIG. 2.2. PROCESSING WHOLE FISH INTO MINCED FISH FOR DIRECT USE OR AS AN INTERMEDIATE INGREDIENT IN FOOD SYSTEMS

related to water activity (a_w), the maximum stability being exhibited at $a_w = 12$.

Groninger (1973) and Groninger and Miller (1979) have made extensive studies on the preparation and functional and nutritional properties of acylated fish proteins. Acylation is accomplished in a slightly alkaline medium using either acetic or succinic anhydride as the acylating agent. Basically, acylation involves the reaction of a nucleophilic group, such as an amino group, with reactants that are electrophilic, such as the anhydrides, to form amide products. In contrast to some of the functional preparations previously mentioned, acylated derivatives not only are extremely functional but also require no protection to maintain this stability during storage at ambient temperatures. The functional properties of acylated fish proteins have been demonstrated by Miller and Groninger (1976) in such food systems as confections, whipped desserts, and baked products. Acylated proteins can also serve as excellent binders in nonfood systems and have been evaluated as a nutrient component of aquaculture diets for shellfish larvae and synthetic baits (Groninger and Miller 1974).

The nutritional properties of acylated products have been the subject of study for quite some time (Gounaris and Perlmann 1967; Groninger and Miller 1979; Creamer et al. 1971). As might be expected, the PER of acylated proteins is related to its degree of acylation (Groninger and Miller 1979). Also of concern are the side reactions that occur during acylation, e.g., the reaction of the OH of tyrosine, serine, and threonine and the SH group of cysteine.

Drum-Dried Fish Muscle

A simplified method of enhancing the nutritional properties of cereal proteins might be to co-dry the muscle with the cereal. This approach was described by Spinelli et al. (1977). Fish–cereal mixtures can be dried in any ratio of combinations. The organoleptic stability of the product can be enhanced by first removing sarcoplasmic proteins and some of the interstitial lipids by extraction with 0.1 M NaCl. Stability can also be enhanced by the addition of combinations of TBHQ and EDTA and pelletizing. Drum-dried Pacific whiting has one important functional property—that of rehydration. It readily rehydrates with four parts of water, and the rehydrated product has been used successfully as a meat extender (Spinelli et al. 1977).

Work in Venezuela (G. Luna 1977, personal communication), indicates that rice paste containing 5% fish (dry basis) can be successfully dried into a product called chi-cha. Chi-cha forms a base for a popular drink: it is mixed with sugar and appropriate flavorings, then reconstituted with water. It strongly resembles a milk shake.

Use of Wet Muscle

Minced fish muscle can be used directly to make sticks and portions, thermally processed products, and extruded products. Minced flesh, depending on the species, often has an unattractive appearance because of color. It has been reported that the use of H_2O_2 not only improves color but also favorably modifies some of the physical and organoleptic properties. Our own experience is that H_2O_2 seems to remove some of the objectionable flavors associated with minced whiting. The treatment of mince with H_2O_2 does not seem to accelerate rancidity during storage. This is probably attributable to the strong catalase activity in the muscle that can reduce fairly high concentrations of H_2O_2 to nondetectable levels in less than 30 min.

It has often been asked if there are any commercially viable industries based on the use of modified fish proteins. At present, some success is beginning to be reported in the United States, particularly with the use of minced muscle. Work sponsored by the National Marine Fisheries Service (Anon. 1978) shows the potential of substituting between 15 and 30% of the meat portion of frankfurters with walleye pollock muscle. The protein content of these frankfurters is 20–30% higher than the commercial product and the fat 30–40% lower. Pilot plant lots of these frankfurters with 15% fish rated equal or better in acceptance than commercial all-meat frankfurters (Miyauchi et al. 1979). On a worldwide basis, we find an industry based on modified fish muscle—the kamaboko industry in Japan. It has a retail value in excess of one billion dollars, a larger dollar volume than the entire retail value of tuna in the United States.

With the price of fish continuing to climb, we are beginning to think that perhaps we have overlooked the obvious target in our attempt to increase the value of fish protein. If we consider that the pollock industry of the eastern Bering Sea can provide over 100 million pounds of purified proteins from the fish too small for filleting, then we realize the problem is not volume but market value. Perhaps we should be thinking of extending fish with fish or developing products that exemplify the virtues of fish. Then our technological problems would be simplified, and the goal of optimally utilizing the marine environment to produce food for the world will be nearer.

REFERENCES

AITKEN, A., and CONNELL, J.J. 1977. The effect of frozen storage on muscle filament spacing in fish. Bull. Int. Inst. Refrig. Ann. 1, 187–191.

AMANO, K., and YAMADA, K. 1965. Biological formation of formaldehyde in cod fish. In Technology of Fish Utilization. R. Kreuzer (Editor), pp. 73–79. Fishing News (Books) Ltd, London, Great Britain.

ANDERSON, M.L., and STEINBERG, M.A. 1964. Effect of lipid content on protein–sodium linolenate interaction in fish muscle homogenates. J. Food Sci. 29, 327–330.

ANON. 1978. Fish/meat sausage moves toward commercialization. Food Process. (Chicago) Oct., 39–40.

ARAI, K., KAWAMURA, K., and HAYASHI, C. 1973. The relative thermo-stabilities of the actomyosin-ATPase from the dorsal muscles of the various fish species. Bull. Jpn. Soc. Sci. Fish. *39*, 1077–1085.

BUTTKUS, H., and TOMLINSON, N. 1966. Some aspects of post-mortem changes in fish muscle. *In* The Physiology and Biochemistry of Muscle as a Food. E. Briskey, R.G. Cossers and T.C. Trautman (Editors), pp. 197–203. University of Wisconsin Press, Madison, Wisconsin.

CASTELL, C.H., SMITH, B., and DYER, W.J. 1973. Effects of formaldehyde on salt extractable proteins of gadoid muscle. J. Fish Res. Board Can. *30*, 1205–1213.

COBB, B.F., III, and HYDER, K. 1972. Development of a process for preparing a fish protein concentrate with rehydration and emulsifying capacities. J. Food Sci. *37*, 743–749.

CREAMER, L.K., ROEPER, J., and LOHREY, E.H. 1971. Preparation and evaluation of some acid soluble casein derivatives. N. Z. J. Dairy Sci. Technol. *6*, 107–111.

DYER, W.J., DINGLE, J.R. 1961. Fish proteins with special reference to freezing. *In* Fish as a Food. I.G. Borgstrom (Editor), pp. 275–327. Academic Press, New York.

FINCH, R. 1977. Whatever happened to fish protein concentrate? Food Technol. *31*, 44–53.

GILL, T.A., KEITH, R.A., and SMITH-LALL, B.S. 1979. Textural deterioration of red hake and haddock muscle in frozen storage as related to chemical parameters and changes in the myofibrillar proteins. J. Food Sci. *44*, 661–667.

GOUNARIS, A.D., and PERLMANN, G. 1967. Succinylation of pepsinogen. J. Biol. Chem. *242*, 2739–2745.

GRONINGER, H.S., JR. 1973. Preparation and properties of succinylated myofibrillar protein. J. Agric. Food Chem. *21*, 978–981.

GRONINGER, H.S., JR., and MILLER, R. 1974. Preparation and use of a modified protein binder in the fabrication of feed for post-larval aquacultural animals. J. Fish Res. Board Can. *31*, 477–479.

GRONINGER, H.S., JR., and MILLER, R. 1979. Some chemical and nutritional properties of acylated fish protein. J. Agric. Food Chem. *27*, 949–955.

JONES, N.R. 1963. Chemical changes in fish muscle during storage. Proc. Nutr. Soc. *22*, 172–176.

KING, F.J., and CARVER, S.H. 1970. How to use nearly all the ocean's food. Commer. Fish. Rev. *32*, 12–21.

KING, F.J., ANDERSON, M.L., and STEINBERG, M.A. 1962. Reaction of actomyosin with linoleic and linolenic acids. J. Food Sci. *27*, 363–366.

KONOSU, S., WATANABE, K., and SHIMIZU, T. 1974. Distribution of nitrogenous constituents in the muscle extracts of eight species of fish. Bull. Jpn. Soc. Sci. Fish. *40*, 909–915.

KOURY, B., and SPINELLI, J.   1975.   Effect of moisture, carbohydrate, and atmosphere on the functional stability of fish protein isolates.   J. Food Sci. *40*, 58–61.

MILLER, R., and GRONINGER, H.S.   1976.   Functional properties of enzyme-modified acylated fish protein derivatives.   J. Food Sci. *41*, 268–272.

MIYAUCHI, D., KUDO, G., and PATASHNIK, M.   1979.   Minced fish as meat extender gets go-ahead in school test.   Nat. Provis. *39*, 12–14.

PARISER, E., WALLENSTEIN, M.B., CORKERY, C.J., and BROWN, N.L. 1978. Fish protein concentrate: Panacea for protein malnutrition?   p. 266. MIT Press, Cambridge, Massachusetts.

SPINELLI, J.   1971.   Biochemical basis of fish freshness.   Process Biochem. *6*, 36–37, 54.

SPINELLI, J., and KOURY, B.J.   1979.   Nonenzymic formation of dimethylamine in dried fishery products.   J. Agric. Food Chem. *27*, 1104–1108.

SPINELLI, J., KOURY, B., and MILLER, R.J.   1972.   Approaches to the utilization of fish for the preparation of protein isolates.   Enzymic modifications of myofibrillar fish proteins.   J. Food Sci. *37*, 604–608.

SPINELLI, J., KOURY, B., GRONINGER, H., and MILLER, R.   1977.   Expanded uses for fish protein from underutilized species.   Food Technol. *31*, 184–187.

STEINBERG, M.A., and SPINELLI, J.   1976.   Some developing trends for the use of fishery resources.   *In* Industrial Fishery Technology, p. 274. M. Stansby (Editor). Robert E. Krieger Publ. Co., Huntington, New York.

TARR, H.L.A.   1958.   Biochemistry of fishes.   Annu. Rev. Biochem. *27*, 2223–2239.

TOKUNAGA, T.   1964.   Development of dimethylamine and formaldehyde in Alaskan pollack muscle during frozen storage.   Hokkaido-ku Suisan Kenkyusho Kenkyu Hokoku *29*, 108–122.

TOKUNAGA, T.   1965.   Studies on the development of dimethylamine and formaldehyde in Alaska pollack muscle during frozen storage.   II.   Factors affecting the formation of dimethylamine and formaldehyde.   Hokkaido-ku Suisan Kenkyusho Kenkyu Hokoku *30*, 90–97.

3

Recent Advances in the Chemistry of Iced Fish Spoilage

J. Liston

The spoilage of fish held in ice is a bacteriological phenomenon, and the chemical changes that take place are mainly due to bacterial enzymes. The only major exceptions to this are (1) when digestive enzymes from heavily feeding fish penetrate the belly wall and cause softening of the adjacent musculature, or (2) in certain physiological conditions when softening may apparently be due to endogenous enzymes (Partmann 1965). Of course, the complex series of changes involving glycolysis, lactic acid production, and protein change which are associated with rigor mortis are due to fish muscle enzymes as, too, is the progressive breakdown of nucleotides and nucleosides (Kassensarm *et al.* 1963). But these do not lead, in the absence of bacterial activity, to the characteristic signs and symptoms of spoilage. This has been clearly demonstrated by experiments in which aseptically excised—and therefore sterile—fish flesh has been held under sterile conditions at low temperature for periods of up to 6 weeks without becoming spoiled (Shewan 1977).

Fish held without such precautions support a rapidly increasing population of psychrotrophic bacteria (Table 3.1). These bacteria appear to remain dominantly at the surface of the fish but secrete enzymes into the tissues, bringing about a complex series of chemical changes (Shewan 1977).

Investigations in recent years have shown that in most cases the bacterial population shifts toward a spoilage population composed of *Pseudomonas* and *Pseudomonas*-like bacteria (Table 3.2). Organisms of the newly defined genus *Alteromonas* probably make up a major part of the spoilage flora (Van Spreekens 1977). Interestingly enough, the same type of bacteria has been shown to be important in the spoilage of meat and poultry held at low temperatures (McMeekin *et al.* 1978).

College of Fisheries, Institute for Food Science and Technology, University of Washington, Seattle, Washington 98195

TABLE 3.1. BACTERIAL COUNTS ON ICED PACIFIC OCEAN FISH[1,2]

Days in ice	Hake (Merluccius productus)	Rockfish (Sebastodes spp.)	English sole (Parophrys vetulus)
0	1.18	2.08	1.80
3	2.49	1.38	2.30
7	6.33	5.54	4.97
10	6.27	4.92	6.26
24	7.27	7.16	7.18

[1] All counts were on trypticase soy agar (BBC) incubated at 10°C for 21 days.
[2] Count expressed as $\log_{10}$ per cm^2 skin.

TABLE 3.2. GENERIC DISTRIBUTION OF THE MICROBIAL FLORA OF ENGLISH SOLE STORED IN ICE[2]

	Days in ice					
	3 days		9 days		16 days	
	Skin	Flesh	Skin	Flesh	Skin	Flesh
Pseudomonas	28	0	72	83	98	87
Achromobacter	18	50	5	3	1	1
Flavobacterium	3	25	3	2	0	0
Alcaligenes	3	0	7	2	1	4
Cocci (gram +)	33	0	0	0	0	0
Rods (gram +)	10	25	13	3	0	7
Yeasts	5	0	0	0	0	1
Total %	100	100	100	100	100	100
Total no. of isolates	39	4	64	68	85	82

Source: Bannerjee (1967).
[1] Values given in percentage.

For many years, it has been recognized that spoilage is a chemically complex process. Until relatively recently, however, attention has been focused on the substances that accumulate in large amounts in fish tissues during spoilage and can be readily measured. This is because of a dominant interest in practical methods for determining the degree of spoilage so that fish caught in offshore waters can be graded for processing and distribution. Moreover, much of the work on spoilage has been done with gadoid species, such as cod and haddock, which are of major importance in Arctic and North Atlantic fisheries (Shewan 1977). Consequently, there has been much concern with the well-known (though not necessarily well-understood) reduction of trimethylamine oxide to trimethylamine and, to a lesser extent, dimethylamine and the production of ammonia and volatile fatty acids.

The reduction of trimethylamine oxide was shown quite early to be associated with bacterial enzyme action and was postulated by Tarr to be coupled to the oxidation of lactic acid produced during rigor mortis (Reay and Shewan 1949). Ammonia was assumed to come from the breakdown of nitrogen-containing compounds and, in the case of elasmobranchs, of urea. Volatile fatty acids were believed to be derived from amino acids and lactic acid (Shewan 1977). The presence of other compounds in small amounts has been recognized in spoiling fish from time to time, but the limitations of the analytical methods available prior to the development of chromatographic and spectrophotometric procedures limited work on these substances.

Work by a number of technologists and microbiologists during the 1960s showed that not all bacteria occurring in spoiling fish are capable of producing typical objectionable spoilage odors when grown in pure culture on sterile fish muscle or muscle press juice at low temperatures ($0-10°C$) (Adams et al. 1964; Laycock and Regier 1970; Lerke et al. 1963, 1965). In many cases the organisms would produce trimethylamine and other volatile bases causing a fishy odor but failed to cause the more repulsive odors. A portion of the microflora mainly consisting of Pseudomonas (types I and II) and Alteromonas (Pseudomonas putrefaciens) types did produce objectionable odors (Shaw and Shewan 1968).

Modern analytical procedures have revealed a wide range of odorous compounds present in spoiling fish at low concentration, and some are shown in Table 3.3. Attention has been focused on volatile sulfur-containing compounds which at a suitable concentration have been shown to yield the characteristic objectionable odor of spoilage. Moreover, as illustrated in Table 3.4, these substances have been shown to be commonly produced by the spoilers when tested in pure culture (Herbert et al. 1975; Miller et al. 1972, 1973; Wong et al. 1967). An overview of some current concepts of the chemical changes is provided in Tables 3.5, 3.6, and 3.7 adapted from an important review by Shewan (1977).

TABLE 3.3. PARTIAL LIST OF VOLATILE COMPOUNDS PRESENT IN SPOILING FISH MUSCLE IN SMALL AMOUNTS

Ethyl mercaptan	Ethanol
Methyl mercaptan	Methanol
Dimethyl sulfide	Acetone
Dimethyl disulfide	Acetoin
Hydrogen sulfide	Butanal
Diacetyl	Ethanal
Acetaldehyde	Methyl butanal
Propionaldehyde	

It is a consistent view of scientists studying spoilage that proteolysis is not a process of major significance in the early stages of bacterial spoilage. The primary substrate for bacterial growth and the main source of spoilage products is the dissolved material in the muscle. Studies of spoilage in meat and poultry have suggested that bacterial proteolysis may be necessary to facilitate penetration of the upper layers of tissue (Gill and Renny 1977), but there is no evidence for this in fish. The meat studies have also indicated that Pseudomonas preferentially use carbohydrate and then lactic acid and selected amino acids for growth (Gill 1976; Gill and Newton 1977). This also is almost certainly true in fish although, since free carbohydrate is very low in fish, amino acids seem to provide a primary substrate. Pseudomonas rapidly utilize most amino acids and peptides found in the nonprotein nitrogen (NPN) fraction of muscle, and this is a major reason for their rapid

TABLE 3.4. PROPERTIES OF FISH SPOILAGE BACTERIA

Test	Group			
	Pseudomonas putrefaciens	Alteromonas I[1]	Alteromonas II[2]	Pseudomonas[3]
Fish Spoilage	Strong odors	Strong odors (D)[4]	Odors (D)	Strong odors
Shrimp Spoilage	Mostly strong odors	Strong odors (D)	Strong odors (R)	Strong odors
H$_2$S Cysteine	+	$\mp$ (2/10)	$\pm$	−
Gelatin liquefied	+	+	+	+
TMAO reduced	+	+	−	−
Hypoxanthine from IMP	+	+	+	−

Modified from Van Spreekens (1977).
[1] "Non-defined" spoilers.
[2] Pseudomonas-like shrimp spoilers.
[3] Pseudomonas Groups I and II.
[4] D = delayed, R = rapid.

TABLE 3.5.   BACTERIAL PRODUCTS RESPONSIBLE FOR ODORS IN SPOILING
FISH AND THEIR SOURCES

Compound	Perceived odor	Probable source
H_2S	Characteristic odor	Cysteine
$(CH_3)_2S$	Cabbage-like; strong sulfide	Methionine
CH_3SH	Musty, sour, cabbage-like	Methionine

Adapted from Shewan (1977).

TABLE 3.6.   BACTERIAL PRODUCTS RESPONSIBLE FOR ODORS IN SPOILING
FISH AND THEIR SOURCES

Compound	Perceived odor	Probable source
Acetic, butyric, propionic and hexanoic acid esters	Fruity	Glycine, serine leucine
$(CH_3)_3N, (CH_3)_2NH$	Fishy, ammoniacal	$(CH_3)_3NO$
NH_3	Ammoniacal, fishy	Amino acids, urea

Adapted from Shewan (1977).

TABLE 3.7.   TENTATIVE SCHEME OF THE CHEMICAL CHANGES OCCURRING
DURING SPOILAGE OF FISH

Substrate	Compound produced by bacterial action
Inosine	Hypoxanthine
Carbohydrates and lactate	Acetic acid, CO_2 and H_2O
Methionine and cyst(e)ine	Hydrogen sulfide, methyl mercaptan, and dimethyl sulfide
Glycine, leucine, serine	Esters of acetic, propionic, butyric, and hexanoic acids
Trimethylamine oxide	Trimethylamine
Urea	Ammonia

Adapted from Shewan (1977).

domination of the microflora during spoilage. The utilization of common NPN constituents by a fish spoilage *Pseudomonas* is shown in Fig. 3.1. Creatine was found to be utilized vigorously by adapted cells of *Pseudomonas* (Bannerjee 1967). The primary mode of utilization seems to be oxidative deamination, which could explain the accumulation of ammonia and volatile fatty acids.

Some proteolysis seems to occur even in the early stages of spoilage, but there is evidence that protease enzyme production by bacteria is initially repressed. The lag in onset of proteolysis in fresh English sole fillets which lasted between 7 and 11 days is clearly shown in Fig. 3.2 taken from Chung (1968). This appears to be due to the presence of free amino acids at a high level. It has been shown experimentally that NPN extracts from fresh fish depress proteinase production in pure cultures of a proteolytic *Pseudomonas* (Fig. 3.3), and Chung (1968) experimentally established that this is probably due to free amino acids. Proteolysis becomes more vigorous in the later stages of spoilage, which appears to be due to derepression as the amino acids are utilized. The increased supply of amino acids to the NPN pool resulting from proteolysis supports greater production of ammonia and volatile acids in the later stages of spoilage.

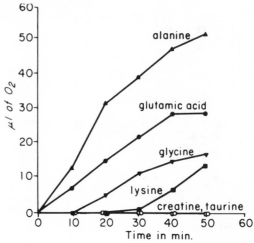

FIG. 3.1. UTILIZATION OF FISH
NPN COMPONENTS BY *Pseu-*
domonas

From Bannerjee (1967)

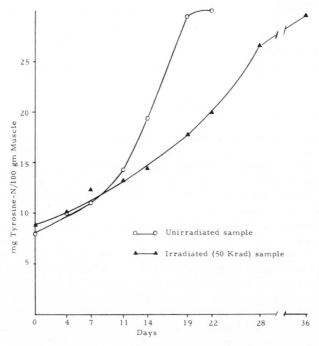

From Chung (1968)

FIG. 3.2. TYROSINE-N IN ENGLISH SOLE FILLETS STORED IN POLYMYLAR BAGS AT
0–2°C
Each point represents the four separate determinations.

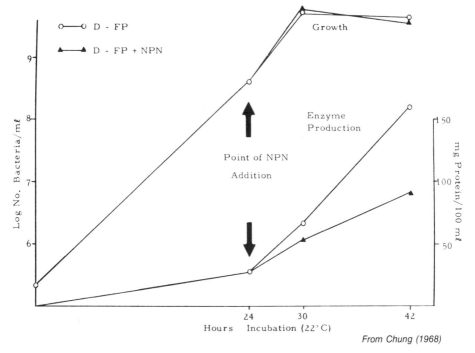

From Chung (1968)

FIG. 3.3.   REPRESSIVE EFFECT OF NPN ON PROTEINASE PRODUCTION BY D-62 IN
DIAZOTIZED FISH PROTEIN MEDIUM
Each point of growth represents four counts and that of enzyme production a duplicate
determination.

A number of authors have reported actual increases in some free amino
acids in cod during the early stages of ice storage. However, some amino
acids have been reported to decrease when bacterial activity increases
(Bramstedt 1962; Shewan and Jones 1957).

Recent work in our laboratory has established that, in the case of Pacific
hake *(Merluccius productus)*, nearly all amino acids showed a sharp reduction between 4 and 7 days of storage in ice (Table 3.8) at the time of rapid
increase in bacterial counts to above 10^6 per square centimeter. The fish
were judged to be clearly spoiled at 7 days. During later storage the amino
acids increased in quantity, suggesting significant proteolytic activity,
particularly since the number of bacteria continued to increase (to
$10^8/cm^2$). Amino acid breakdown also proceeded but at a higher level related to the more numerous bacteria.

There was a correlation between these events and the occurrence of
volatile sulfur compound producing bacteria. In an earlier study it had been
shown that spoilage of hake (and other species) was obvious when the
population of sulfide producers exceeded 10^6 per gram (Table 3.9). Report-
ing a similar observation with Australian fish, Gillespie (1977) suggested

that when the sulfide producers reach 40% of the population, overt spoilage occurs. The sulfur compounds most commonly encountered are H_2S, $(CH_3)_2S$, and CH_3SH, and these have been shown to have organoleptic thresholds well below the level occurring in spoiling fish (Table 3.10). Herbert and Shewan (1975) have shown that H_2S is produced primarily from cysteine, and $(CH_3)_2S$ and CH_3SH from methionine. Their data showed an increase of the two S-containing amino acids in cod during early storage followed by a drop during the period of maximum production of volatile sulfide compounds.

TABLE 3.8.   CHANGES IN FREE AMINO ACIDS IN HAKE DURING ICE STORAGE[1]

Days storage	Percentage
0	100%
7	31−59%
	(Except tyrosine 5%)
21	73−89%
	(Except cyst(e)ine 58% and tyrosine, arginine, proline and histidine > 100%)

Source: Ayinla (1979).
[1] Tryptophan not included.

TABLE 3.9.   CHANGES[1] IN TMAO-REDUCING AND H_2S-PRODUCING BACTERIA ON STORED FISH

Days stored	Hake		Rockfish		English sole	
	TMAO[2]	H_2S[3]	TMAO	H_2S	TMAO	H_2S
0	1.18	1.28	1.20	0	0	0
3	2.46	1.53	0.63	0	0.81	0.81
7	6.40	6.15	4.60	4.30	5.48	5.18
10	5.69	5.37	4.67	4.61	5.08	0
14	6.98	6.66	6.18	6.15	6.24	6.06
18	—	—	6.67	0	7.06	7.06
22	—	—	7.97	0	8.02	0

[1] Calculated by extrapolation from properties of isolates.
[2] Estimated log count per gram of organisms able to reduce TMAO to TMA.
[3] Estimated log count per gram of organisms producing H_2S.

TABLE 3.10.   THRESHOLD VALUES FOR DETECTION OF VOLATILE SULFUR COMPOUNDS

Compound	Threshold value (ppb)	Conc. in spoiling fish (ppb)
H_2S	40	150
$(CH_3)_2S$	0.50	20
CH_3SH	0.05	120

Adapted from Shewan (1977).

In hake no increase of these acids was noted in the early stages, but a sharp decrease coincided with production of the volatile sulfides in the fish flesh (Table 3.11) as measured by 5,5,-dithio-*bis*-(2-nitrobenzoic acid) (DTNB), which turns yellow on reaction with sulfhydryl compounds. The S-containing amino acids later showed an increase during extended storage, presumably due to proteolysis. But cysteine did not recover to the extent of methionine, which may have been due either to greater bacterial activity on cysteine or to a smaller recruitment because it is less abundant in fish protein.

TABLE 3.11.   CHANGES IN SULFUR CONTAINING AMINO ACIDS DURING ICE STORAGE OF HAKE *(Merluccius productus)*

Days storage	Cyst(e)ine	Methionine
0	14.77[1]	9.03[1]
4	13.32	10.17
7[2]	5.37	4.02
11	6.95	5.20
15	7.22	5.76
21	8.51	7.92

Source: Ayinla (1979).
[1] Values as nanomoles per 50 µl homogenate.
[2] Spoilage organoleptically apparent here.

Testing bacteria isolated from the spoiling hake revealed that while only one out of 20 isolates from hake 0 and 4 days old (unspoiled) was DTNB positive, 100% of isolates from 7 and 11 days were positive. Thus recent studies of fish spoilage suggest the following pattern in most cases:

a. *Pseudomonas* and related types rapidly dominate the microflora as numbers increase.
b. Initially, lactic acid and NPN compounds, particularly TMAO and amino acids, are attacked with the resultant production of TMA, DMA, NH_3, and volatile acids, while proteolysis is negligible.
c. Capable of growing actively at temperatures near 0°C and of attacking methionine and cysteine with production of H_2S, $(CH_3)_2S$, and $(CH_3)SH$, *Alteromonas* and *Pseudomonas* become dominant in the microflora.
d. When the number of the above bacteria exceeds $10^6/cm^2$ (or /g) or 40% of the microflora, significant amounts of the volatile S-containing compounds are produced and spoilage becomes organoleptically evident. [Note that Gillespie (1977) reported that, by mixing spoiled minced fish with mercuric chloride solution to remove H_2S and CH_3SH, "almost all foul odors were removed and only 'fishy' odors remained."]
e. (Tentative) As amino acids decrease due to bacterial oxidation, bacterial protease enzyme production is derepressed. Amino acid concentrations begin to increase again as fish protein is hydrolyzed, even

though there is increased utilization of the amino acids for bacterial growth.

   f. Spoilage bacteria accelerate the conversion of inosine to hypoxanthine.

REFERENCES

ADAMS, R., FARBER, L., and LERKE, P.   1964.   Bacteriology of spoiling fish muscle II.   Incidence of spoilers during spoilage.   Appl. Microbiol. *12*, 277–279.

AYINLA, O.A.   1979.   Relationship between biochemical and bacteriological changes in iced Pacific hake *(Merluccius productus)*.   M.S. Thesis, University of Washington, Seattle, Washington.

BANNERJEE, D.   1967.   Oxidative metabolism of non-protein nitrogen components by fish spoilage bacteria and their physiology of psychrotrophic growth during storage of fish (English sole).   Ph.D. Dissertation, University of Washington, Seattle, Washington.

BRAMSTEDT, F.   1962.   Amino acid composition of fresh fish and influence of storage and processing.   *In* Fish in Nutrition.   E. Heen and R. Kreuzer (Editors), pp. 61–67.   Fishing News (Books) Ltd., London.

CHUNG, J.R.   1968.   Post mortem degradation of fish muscle proteins: The role of proteolytic *Pseudomonas* spp. and their mechanism of action.   Ph.D. Dissertation, University of Washington, Seattle, Washington.

GILL, C.O.   1976.   Substrate limitation of bacterial growth at meat surfaces.   J. Appl. Bacteriol. *41*, 401–410.

GILL, C.O., and NEWTON, K.G.   1977.   The development of aerobic spoilage flora on meat stored at chill temperatures.   J. Appl. Bacteriol. *43*, 189–195.

GILL, C.O., and RENNY, H.   1977.   Penetration of bacteria into meat.   Appl. Environ. Microbiol. *33*, 1284–1286.

GILLESPIE, N.C.   1977.   A bacteriological and chemical examination of fish spoilage.   Rep. Proc. Fish Expo '76 Seminar, pp. 301–315. Dept. of Primary Industry, Canberra, Australia.

HERBERT, R.A., and SHEWAN, J.M.   1975.   Precursors of the volatile sulfides in spoiling North Sea Cod *(Gadus morhua)*.   J. Sci. Food Agric. *26*, 1195–1202.

HERBERT, R.A., ELLIS, J., and SHEWAN, J.M.   1975.   Isolation and identification of the volatile sulphides produced during chill storage of North Sea Cod *(Gadus morhua)*.   J. Sci. Food Agric. *26*, 1187–1194.

KASSENSARM, B., SANZ PEREZ, B., MURRAY, J., and JONES, N.R.   1963.   Nucleotide degradation in the muscle of iced haddock *(Gadus aeglifinus)*, lemon sole *(Pleuronectes microcephalus)* and plaice *(Pleuronectes platesa)*.   J. Food Sci. *28*, 28–37.

LAYCOCK, R.A., and REGIER, L.W.   1970.   Pseudomonads and Achromobacters in the spoilage of irradiated haddock of different pre-irradiation quality. Appl. Microbiol. *20*, 333–341.

LERKE, P., ADAMS, R., and FARBER, L.   1963.   Bacteriology of spoiling fish muscle I.   Sterile press juice as a suitable experimental medium.   Appl. Microbiol. *11*, 458–462.

LERKE, P., ADAMS, R., and FARBER, L.   1965.   Bacteriology of spoiling fish muscle III.   Characterization of spoilers. Appl. Microbiol. *13*, 625–630.

MCMEEKIN, T.A., GIBBS, P.A., and PATTERSON, J.T.   1978.   Detection of volatile sulfide producing bacteria isolated from poultry processing plants. Appl. Environ. Microbiol. *35*, 1216–1218.

MILLER, A., III, SCANLAN, R.A., LEE, J.S., and LIBBEY, L.M.   1972. Volatile compounds produced in ground muscle tissue of canary rockfish *(Sebastes pinniger)* stored on ice.   J. Fish Res. Board Can. *29*, 1125–1129.

MILLER, A., III, SCANLAN, R.A., LEE, J.S., and LIBBEY, L.M.   1973.   Volatile compounds produced in sterile fish muscle *(Sebastes melanops)* by *Pseudomonas putrefaciens, Pseudomonas fluorescens* and an *Achromobacter* species.   Appl. Microbiol. *26*, 18–21.

PARTMANN, W.   1965.   Changes in proteins, nucleotides and carbohydrates during rigor mortis.   *In* The Technology of Fish Utilization. R. Kreuzer (Editor) pp. 4–13 Fishing News (Books) Ltd., London, England.

REAY, G.A., and SHEWAN, J.M.   1949.   The spoilage of fish and its preservation by chilling.   Adv. Food Res. *11*, 343–398.

SHAW, B.G., and SHEWAN, J.M.   1968.   Psychrophilic spoilage bacteria of fish.   J. Appl. Bacteriol. *31*, 89–96.

SHEWAN, J.M.   1977.   The bacteriology of fresh and spoiling fish and the biochemical changes induced by bacterial action.   *In* Handling, Processing and Marketing of Tropical Fish, pp. 51–66.   Tropical Products Institute, London, England.

SHEWAN, J.M., and JONES, N.R.   1957.   Chemical changes occurring in cod muscle during chill storage and their possible use as objective indices of quality.   J. Sci. Food Agric. *8*, 491–498.

VAN SPREEKENS, K.J.A.   1977.   Characterization of some fish and shrimp spoiling bacteria.   Antonie van Leeuwenhoek *43*, 283–303.

WONG, N.P., DAMICO, J., and SALWIN, H.   1967.   Investigation of volatile compounds in cod fish by gas chromatography and mass spectrometry.   J. Assoc. Off. Anal. Chem. *50*, 8–15.

4

Histamine Formation in Fish: Microbiological and Biochemical Conditions

Ronald R. Eitenmiller, Joseph H. Orr, and Wayne W. Wallis

INTRODUCTION

The word "scombroid" is derived from the families of fish, *Scomberescidae* and *Scombridae* (Arnold and Brown 1978). Many commonly consumed fish species including tuna, mackerel, bonito, and skipjack are scombroid fish. These fish characteristically contain large amounts of free -histidine in the muscle, which can give rise to toxic levels of histamine under conditions leading to histidine decarboxylation.

Although scombroid food poisoning (histamine intoxication) is usually manifested as a discomfort for a period of hours and very rarely proves fatal, it is not to be taken lightly. Worldwide incidences of scombroid food poisoning indicate the potential for a variety of foodstuffs to induce the intoxication. By the nature of its dissemination—often via commercial products—it is frequently widespread before it can be arrested. During one well-documented outbreak in the United States, 232 persons in four states were poisoned from the consumption of commercially canned tuna. Two lots of tuna constituting some 170,000 cans were recalled (Merson *et al.* 1974).

Ferencik (1970) cites several authors who have reported cases of scombroid food poisoning involving tuna in the United States, Japan, Indonesia, and in European countries such as Czechoslovakia. Occurrence of this type of food poisoning is significant but is much lower on a per capita basis in the United States than in those countries that depend more on fish in their diet yet rely less on refrigeration. The consumption of certain dried fish products popular in Japan has resulted in many outbreaks. Kawabata *et al.* (1967) described 14 outbreaks involving 1215 people during a 4-year period.

Undoubtedly, the major causative agent of scombroid food poisoning is histamine. It is one of the most potent capillary dilators known to man. The

Department of Food Science, University of Georgia, Athens, Georgia 30602 physiological effects of histamine are basically hypotension and hemocon-centration. The major symptoms are headache, nausea, cramps, diarrhea, vomiting, thirst, hives, swelling of the lips, and a burning sensation in the throat. The association between histamine and the toxic syndrome is con-clusive evidence for the assumption that histamine plays a major role. Goodman and Gilman (1965) provided incriminating evidence against his-tamine by virtually duplicating the symptoms of scombroid food poisoning by intravenous injections of histamine into human subjects. Further verifi-cation was the success in treating outbreaks with antihistamines. There are many factors to be considered when histamine is taken orally; i.e., what is consumed with it and its passage through the intestinal wall. Henry (1960) formulated three quantitative groups of histamine intoxications: (1) mild poisoning due to consumption of 8–40 mg of histamine, (2) moderate inten-sity disorders (70–1000 mg histamine), and (3) severe incidents (1500–4000 mg histamine). The moderate 70- to 1000-mg histamine range which causes mild poisoning merits the most concern because severe incidents are less common.

The question of a synergist for histamine in food-related illness is still unanswered. Arnold and Brown (1978), after an extensive review of the literature concerning histamine, concluded that histamine alone is not responsible for scombroid food poisoning. They believe that histamine to-gether with some accompanying synergist or potentiating condition leads to the toxic syndrome. Ferencik (1970) pointed out that other biologically active substances must be considered. While other biologically active amines may be consumed at the same time, they scarcely alter the clinical symptoms of scombroid food poisoning. Even tyramine, which has physio-logical effects opposite to those of histamine, provides little relief unless administered in large quantities.

Ienistea (1973) pointed out that diamines such as putrescine, cadaverine, and spermine may facilitate the transport of histamine through the intesti-nal wall and increase its toxicity. Parrot and Nicot (1966) noted that putrescine, if administered prior to histamine, could increase histamine toxicity. Bjeldanes et al. (1978), in an article on the etiology of scombroid poisoning, put the question of a synergist for histamine in proper perspec-tive. They pointed out that, to exhibit synergism, investigators have used completely unrealistic ratios of putrescine to histamine. They demon-strated that cadaverine is synergistic in quantities only twice that found in vivo. They also demonstrated that optimal cadaverine synergism is ob-tained by simultaneous administration with histamine to guinea pigs. Unlike cadaverine, putrescine required a time lag before histamine was administered.

BACTERIAL HISTAMINE PRODUCTION

Table 4.1 gives several bacterial genera that have the capacity to decar-boxylate histidine to form histamine. Of these, only a limited number of histidine decarboxylating bacteria have actually been isolated and identified from fishery products incriminated in scombroid poisoning. *Proteus morganii* has been most frequently mentioned in relation to histamine formation in fish muscle (Ferencik 1970; Kawabata and Suzuki 1959; Omura *et al.* 1978; Taylor *et al.* 1978). Other bacteria isolated from tuna containing large levels of histamine include *Hafnia alvei* (Ferencik 1970) and *Klebsiella pneumoniae* (Taylor *et al.* 1979).

Recent studies have shown that *P. morganii* is a common contaminant of fish tissue during spoilage and that few other bacteria have as great a capacity to form histamine. Omura *et al.* (1978) examined bacterial isolates from spoiled skipjack tuna and jack mackerel for their ability to produce histamine in tuna infusion broth. Forty-four strains of histamine formers were identified. Twenty-one isolates produced large amounts of histamine and were identified as *P. morganii*. Thirteen weak histamine formers were identified as *Hafnia alvei*. Three other species of *Proteus*, one of *Klebsiella*, and six unidentified bacteria were included in the group of histamine-forming bacteria.

Taylor *et al.* (1978B) studied 112 bacterial strains from a variety of sources. Twenty-three strains produced greater than 50 nmoles of histamine per milliliter in trypticase soy–histidine broth. Thirteen of 15 *P. morganii* strains and three of three *Enterobacter aerogenes* strains produced histamine at this level. In tuna fish infusion broth, the *P. morganii* and *E. aerogenes* cultures produced histamine at much higher levels than any of

TABLE 4.1. BACTERIA THAT DECARBOXYLATE HISTIDINE

Hafnia sp.	Gram-negative rods Facultatively anaerobic *Hafnia alvei*
Klebsiella sp.	Gram-negative rods Facultatively anaerobic *Klebsiella pneumoniae*
Escherichia coli	Gram negative rods Facultatively anaerobic
Clostridium sp.	Gram-positive rods Anaerobic *Clostridium perfringens*
Lactobacillus sp.	Gram-positive rods Facultatively anaerobic *Lactobacillus* 30a
Enterobacter spp.	Gram-negative rods Facultatively anaerobic *Enterobacter aerogenes*
Proteus sp.	Gram-negative rods Facultatively anaerobic *Proteus morganii*

the other cultures, including 12 strains of *Hafnia alvei*. The authors indicated that the *H. alvei* cultures would have limited ability to precipitate scombroid poisoning in comparison to the histamin-forming capacity of *P. morganii* and *E. aerogenes*. The incidence of *E. aerogenes* as a contaminant of fishery products is unknown. The *E. aerogenes* cultures utilized by Taylor *et al.* (1978B) were from non-marine sources.

The above studies demonstrate that *P. morganii* is a powerful histidine-decarboxylating bacteria. Furthermore, the relationship of *P. morganii* to products incriminated in scombroid poisoning episodes and the fact that the organism has been isolated by several investigators from spoiled tuna clearly indicate that it plays a role in scombroid fish poisoning. Further studies need to be completed to identify the frequency of occurrence and sources of *P. morganii* on marine fish.

Recently, a study of 22 *P. morganii* strains was completed in our laboratory (Orr 1978). The remainder of this chapter presents results of this study, which was designed to determine factors influencing the production and activity of *P. morganii* histidine decarboxylase. The *P. morganii* strains were acquired from the Department of Microbiology, University of Leicester, LE1 7RH, England. The cultures were used by McKell and Jones (1976) in a taxonomic study of the *Proteus-Providence* bacteria.

FACTORS INFLUENCING HISTIDINE DECARBOXYLASE PRODUCTION

Examination of the 22 *P. morganii* strains revealed that each possessed histidine decarboxylase activity and formed histamine in tuna fish infusion broth and 1% tryptone – 1% yeast extract broth (Table 4.2). Strain GRMO 6 was chosen for studies to determine the effects of incubation temperature, medium pH, culture age, and histidine concentration on enzyme production. Histamine was determined by the method of Shore (1971) as modified by Taylor *et al.* (1978A). Histidine decarboxylase activity was measured by the method of Levine and Watts (1966).

Incubation Temperature

The test cultures was incubated at 24°, 30°, 37°, and 42°C for 24 hr at pH 6.5 in 1% tryptone – 1% yeast extract broth (Fig. 4.1). Highest specific activity of histidine decarboxylase (nanomoles CO_2/mg cells/hr) was obtained when strain GRMO 6 was grown at ambient temperature. The activities decreased from 98 nmoles CO_2/mg cells/hr at 24°C to 12 nmoles CO_2/mg cells/hr at 42°C. As first observed by Bellamy and Gunsalus (1944), it appears that conditions maximizing enzyme synthesis, histidine decarboxylation, and cell growth are different. The culture at 24°C grew the least, whereas maximal growth occurred at 37°C. The drop in enzyme activity, especially evident at 42°C, was probably the result of histidine decarboxylase thermolability.

TABLE 4.2. HISTIDINE DECARBOXYLASE AND HISTAMINE PRODUCTION BY 22 STRAINS OF *Proteus morganii* (12 HR GROWTH)

Culture[1]		Tuna fish infusion		Tryptone–Yeast Extract[2]	
		Enzyme[3]	Histamine[4]	Enzyme[3]	Histamine[4]
GRMO	1	902	133.4	62	8.9
GRMO	2	638	116.7	80	10.0
GRMO	3	708	177.8	51	5.0
GRMO	4	629	166.7	32	13.3
GRMO	5	870	235.6	47	6.1
GRMO	6	723	266.8	94	11.7
GRMO	7	408	146.7	186	6.1
GRMO	8	682	95.6	28	8.3
GRMO	9	1106	164.5	107	9.5
GRMO	10	689	157.8	57	7.8
GRMO	11	802	37.8	83	8.9
PHL	253	611	88.9	75	10.0
PHL	378	606	80.0	47	3.4
HG	114	14	61.1	9	4.5
NCTC	232	799	115.6	38	5.0
NCTC	1707	1250	111.1	147	6.7
NCTC	2815	1164	163.4	61	11.2
NCTC	2818	406	126.7	37	7.2
NCTC	5845	19	25.6	7	5.6
NCTC	7381	1291	143.4	99	6.1
NCTC	10041	870	132.3	6	11.2
NCTC	10375	844	136.7	50	15.0

[1] Culture designations, used by McKell and Jones (1976).
[2] Supplemented with 0.05% L-histidine.
[3] Histidine decarboxylase activity (nanomoles CO_2 released/hr/mg cells).
[4] Histamine (mg/100 ml).

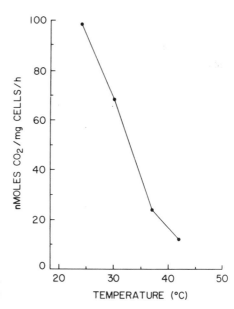

FIG. 4.1. HISTIDINE DECARBOXYLASE PRODUCTION AT VARIOUS TEMPERATURES

Medium pH

Eight levels of pH at increments of 0.5 were used, ranging from 5.0 to 8.5 by aseptic adjustment of the media with sterile 1.0 N NaOH or 1.0 N HCl (Fig. 4.2). Maximal specific activity was obtained at pH levels that tended to inhibit growth, suggesting the protective action theory postulated by Koessler *et al.* (1928). This theory deals with the induction of certain enzymes whose end products remedy the low pH microenvironmental condition which threatens the microorganism. Specific activity was highest at pH 5.0, but growth of the culture was very poor. At all other pH levels examined, growth was good. Ienistea (1973) found that the optimal pH for histidine decarboxylase induction in most bacterial species was between 5.0 and 5.5. Very little histidine decarboxylase activity was noted when the culture was grown at pH 8.5. The protective action theory has been demonstrated with other decarboxylases. Gale (1943) observed that *Streptococcus fecalis* possessed the most active tyrosine decarboxylase system in trypsin-digested casein glucose medium when cells were grown at pH 5.0.

Culture Age

The influence of incubation time of the culture on histidine decarboxylase activity at 30°C and pH 6.5 was examined for 10, 14, 17, and 21 hr. Histidine decarboxylase activity decreased as the age of the culture increased (Fig. 4.3). The rapid decrease from 388 to 104 nmoles CO_2/mg cells/hr between 10 and 21 hr of growth, respectively, was approximately

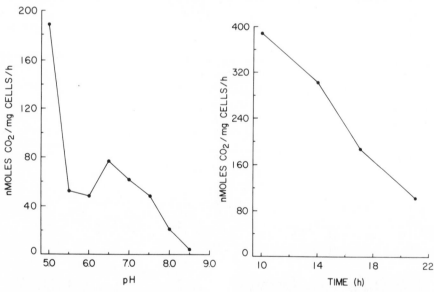

FIG. 4.2. EFFECT OF pH ON HISTIDINE DECARBOXYLASE PRODUCTION

FIG. 4.3. EFFECT OF CULTURE AGE ON HISTIDINE DECARBOXYLASE ACTIVITY linear. A rise in pH with growth may be responsible for the decrease in activity. Gale (1941) reached a similar conclusion for other decarboxylases and went so far as to plot decarboxylase activity not against the age of the culture but against the pH of the medium during growth. In most cases the activity decreased as the pH increased above 6.5.

Histidine Concentration

Concentrations of 0.025, 0.05, 0.07, 0.10, 0.25, and 0.50% L-histidine were added to tryptone–yeast extract broth. The cultures were incubated at 30°C and pH 6.5 for 24 hr following inoculation. Increased specific activity was observed when free histidine was included in the medium, indicating that *P. morganii* histidine decarboxylase is inducible. Specific activity of the cultures increased rapidly up to 0.07% added L-histidine and decreased slowly between 0.07 and 0.50% (Fig. 4.4).

Effect of Reaction Temperature on Histidine Decarboxylation

Reaction mixtures were incubated at 25°, 30°, 37°, 45°, and 55°C. The measurement of the activity of histidine decarboxylase indicated an incubation temperature optimum of 37°C (Fig. 4.5). Gale (1941) demonstrated a

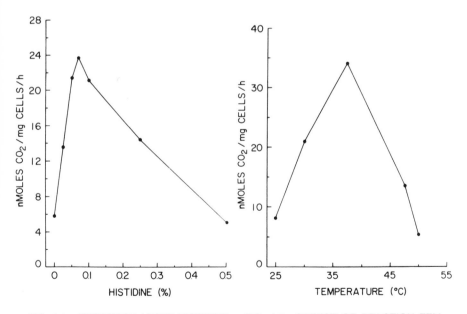

FIG. 4.4. EFFECT OF ADDED HISTIDINE ON DECARBOXYLASE PRODUCTION BY *Proteus morganii*

FIG. 4.5. EFFECT OF REACTION TEMPERATURE ON HISTIDINE DECARBOXYLATION BY *Proteus morganii* general decline in activity of most bacterial decarboxylases at incubation temperatures above 40°C. The rate of decarboxylation increases gradually with temperature and starts to fall when the higher temperature begins to affect adversely the tertiary structure of the enzyme. In the study of the effect of incubation temperature on enzyme production, the activity at 37°C was approximately 25% of that found at 24°C. Since both enzyme induction and activity are significant to the production of histamine, the optimum temperature for histamine production in tuna must be a compromise between the two parameters.

Reaction pH

The reaction medium was adjusted from pH 5.0 to 7.5 in increments of 0.5. Optimal activity of the enzyme was obtained at pH 6.5. Histidine decarboxylase activity decreased rapidly on both sides of the optimum with little activity at pH 5.0 (Fig. 4.6). As previously mentioned, pH 5.0 provided maximum induction of synthesis of histidine decarboxylase during culture growth. However, the minimal enzyme activity at this pH would greatly inhibit histamine accumulation in the media. The affinity of the active site for histidine is low at a pH of 7.0 and above (Rescei and Snell 1970). Kimata (1961) found a pH optimum of 6.0 for histidine decarboxylase of *P. morganii*. Histidine decarboxylase isolated from gastric tissue had a pH optimum of 6.8 (Levine and Watts 1966).

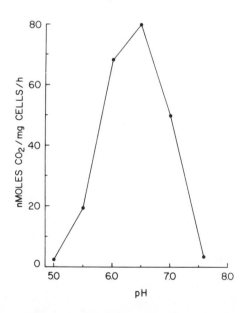

FIG. 4.6. EFFECT OF pH ON HISTIDINE DECARBOXYLATION BY *Proteus morganii*

Histamine Formation and Histidine Decarboxylase Production in Tuna

Fresh yellowfin tuna was obtained at a seafood market in San Francisco, frozen and shipped with dry ice to the University of Georgia (courtesy of Ms. Ellen Lieber, FDA, San Francisco). This tuna was used to determine effects of storage time and temperature on decarboxylase development and histamine formation. Fillets were stored at 15°, 24°, and 30°C. Storage trials consisted of uninoculated fillets and fillets inoculated by dipping in a suspension of *P. morganii* (strain GRMO 6) containing approximately 10^4 cells per milliliter.

Results of the study are shown in Fig. 4.7–4.9. Storage at 15°C (Fig. 4.7) resulted in negligible build-up of decarboxylase and histamine in the uninoculated fillets. The *P. morganii* inoculated samples showed histidine decarboxylase development that reached 12.1 nmoles/hr/g after 24 hr incubation. At this temperature, histamine content increased slightly. After 48 hr, the inoculated fillets contained 43.7 mg of histamine per 100 g. Decarboxylase activity and histamine content remained low in the uninoculated tuna stored at 24°–30°C. Rapid enzyme production and histamine formation occurred in the inoculated samples stored at 24° and 30°C (Fig. 4.8 and 4.9, respectively). At both temperatures, enzyme activity was maximal after storage for 12 hr. Histamine concentrations were 520 mg/100 g and 608 mg/100 g after 24 hr at 24° and 30°C, respectively.

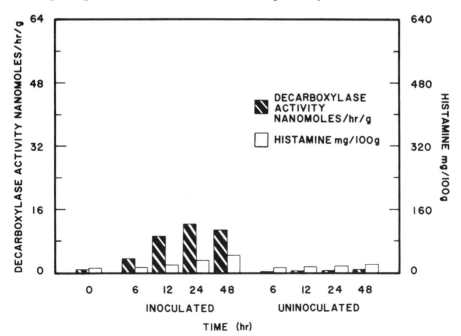

FIG. 4.7. FORMATION OF HISTIDINE DECARBOXYLASE AND HISTAMINE IN TUNA MUSCLE AT 15°C

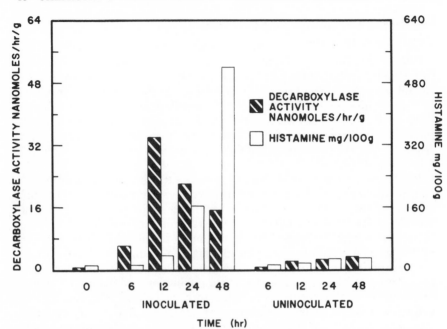

FIG. 4.8.   FORMATION OF HISTIDINE DECARBOXYLASE AND HISTAMINE IN TUNA MUSCLE AT 24°C

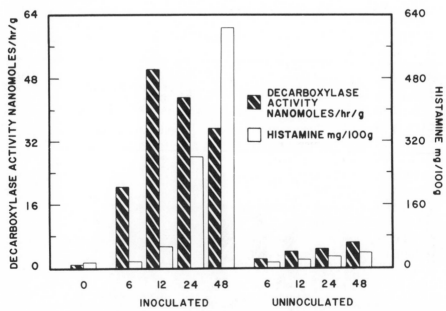

FIG. 4.9.   FORMATION OF HISTIDINE DECARBOXYLASE AND HISTAMINE IN TUNA MUSCLE AT 30°C

CONCLUSION

The data demonstrate that storage temperature is a critical factor influencing the formation of histamine in tuna. Tuna or other scombroid fish that are caught in tropical waters are particularly vulnerable to build-up of histamine. The requirement for rapid and uninterrupted refrigeration after catch cannot be overemphasized. Normal muscle pH conditions correspond closely to pH levels required for optimal activity of the enzyme (pH 6.5) and are low enough to permit rapid enzyme synthesis. The ready availability of free histidine in the muscle to act as both an inducer and substrate makes scombroid fish muscle an ideal environment for histamine formation. As shown with tuna muscle, *P. morganii*, if given the opportunity to grow, can rapidly synthesize histidine decarboxylase and cause histamine accumulation to levels that can be toxic. Although the literature does not give a completely clear understanding of the frequency of occurrence of *P. morganii* on marine fish, its implication in several outbreaks of scombroid food poisoning indicates that it is a fairly common contaminant.

REFERENCES

ARNOLD, S.H., and BROWN, W.D. 1978. Histamine (?) toxicity from fish products. Adv. Food Res. *24*, 113.

BELLAMY, W.D., and GUNSALUS, I.C. 1944. Tyrosine decarboxylation by *Streptococci:* Growth requirements for active cell production. J. Bacterial. *48*, 191–199.

BJELDANES, L.F., SCHUTZ, D.E., and MORRIS, M.M. 1978. On the aetiology of scombroid poisoning: Cadaverine potentiation of histamine toxicity in the guinea pig. Food Cosmet. Toxicol. *16*, 157.

FERENCIK, M. 1970. Formation of histamine during bacterial decarboxylation of histidine in the flesh of some marine fishes. J. Hyg. Epidemiol. Microbiol. Immunol. *14*, 52.

GALE, E.F. 1941. Production of amines by bacteria. Decarboxylation of amino acids by organisms of the groups *Clostridium* and *Proteus*. Biochem. J. *35*, 66.

GALE, E.F. 1943. Factors influencing the enzymic activities of bacteria. Bacteriol. Rev. *7*, 139.

GOODMAN, L.S., and GILMAN, A. 1965. The Pharmacological Basis of Therapeutics. Macmillan, London.

HENRY, M. 1960. Dosage biologique de l'histamine dans les aliments. Ann Falsif. Expert. Chim. *53*, 24.

IENISTEA, C. 1973. Significance and detection of histamine in food. *In* The Microbiological Safety of Food, p. 327. Academic Press, New York.

KAWABATA, T., and SUZUKI, S. 1959. Studies on the food poisoning associated with putrefaction of marine products. VIII. Distribution of

L(−)histidine decarboxylase among *Proteus* organisms and the specificity of decarboxylation activity with washed cell suspensions.   Bull. Jpn. Soc. Sci. Fish. *25*, 473.

KAWABATA, T., ISHIZAKA, K., and MIURA, T.   1967.   Studies on the food poisoning associated with putrefaction of marine products.   *In* Poisonous and Venomous Marine Animals of the World.   B.W. Halstead and D.A. Courville (Editors), p. 639.   U.S. Government Printing Office, Washington, DC.

KIMATA, M.   1961.   The histamine problem.   *In* Fish as Food.   G. Borgstrom (Editor), p. 329. Academic Press, New York.

KOESSLER, K.K., HANKE, M.T., and SHEPPARD, M.S.   1928.   Production of histamine, tyramine, bronchospastic and arteriospastic substances in blood broth by pure cultures of microorganisms.   J. Infect. Dis. *43*, 363.

LEVINE, R.J., and WATTS, E.D.   1966.   A sensitive and specific assay for histidine decarboxylase activity.   Biochem. Pharmacol. *15*, 841.

MCKELL, J., and JONES, D.   1976.   A numerical taxonomic study of *Proteus-Providence* bacteria.   J. Appl. Bacterial. *41*, 143.

MERSON, M.H., BAINE, W.B., GANGAROSA, E.J., and SWANSON, R.C.   1974.   Scombroid fish poisoning: Outbreak traced to commercially canned tuna fish.   J. Am. Med. Assoc. *228*, 1268.

OMURA, Y., PRICE, R.J., and OLCOTT, H.S.   1978.   Histamine-forming bacteria isolated from spoiled skipjack tuna and jack mackerel.   J. Food Sci. *43*, 1779.

ORR, J.H.   1978.   Histidine decarboxylase in *Proteus morganii*.   M.S. Thesis. University of Georgia, Athens, Georgia.

PARROT, J., and NICOT, G.   1966.   Pharmacology of histamine.   *In* Handbuch der Experimentellen Pharmakologie, p. 148.   Springer-Verlag, New York.

RESCEI, P.A., and SNELL, E.A.   1970.   Histidine decarboxylase of *Lactobacillus 30a*.   VI.   Mechanism of action and kinetic properties.   Biochemistry *7*, 1492.

SHORE, P.A.   1971.   The chemical determination of histamine.   *In* Methods of Biochemical Analysis: Supplementary Volume.   D. Glick (Editor), p. 89. Wiley (Interscience) New York. 89.

TAYLOR, S.L., LIEBER, E.R., and LEATHERWOOD, M.   1978A.   A simplified method for histamine analysis of foods.   J. Food Sci. *43*, 247−250.

TAYLOR, S.L., GUTHERTZ, L.S., LEATHERWOOD, M., TILLMAN, F., and LIEBER, E.R.   1978B.   Histamine production by food-borne bacterial species.   J. Food Safety *1*, 173.

TAYLOR, S.L., GUTHERTZ, L.S., LEATHERWOOD, M., and LIEBER, E.R.   1979.   Histamine production by *Klebsiella pneumoniae* and an incident of scombroid fish poisoning.   Appl. Environ. Microbiol. *37*, 274.

5

Identification of Fish Species by Isoelectric Focusing

Paul M. Toom, Cheryl F. Ward, and James R. Weber

INTRODUCTION

Although a number of electrophoretic techniques have been used to speciate fish, the identification of fish fillets and minced fish products continues to be a difficult procedure. Connel (1953) was the first to apply electrophoretic techniques to obtain "fingerprint" patterns for the speciation of fishery products. Thompson (1960) found that fish species could be identified more easily by the use of starch gel electrophoresis, since zonal techniques such as this resulted in higher resolution and reproducibility of protein patterns.

Subsequent studies by Payne (1963), Mancuso (1964), Thompson (1967), Cowie (1968), Corduri (1972), Corduri and Rand (1972), and Mackie and Jones (1978) utilizing polyacrylamide gels and a study by Hill *et al.* (1966) using agar gels all found that the use of these supports resulted in shorter analysis time and easier staining, handling, and storing than the starch gels used by Thompson (1960). In addition, both of these supports produced better resolution of protein zones, facilitating species identification. Although cellulose acetate electrophoresis (Lane *et al.* 1966; Learson 1969, 1970) does not exhibit the resolving power of other stabilizing media, it has found widespread use in quality control laboratories. This acceptance of cellulose acetate is based on both the speed with which electrophoretic separations can be achieved and the relative simplicity of the technique as compared to other stabilizing media.

While each of these techniques is still used to speciate fish, none exhibits the resolving capability necessary to differentiate closely related species. Furthermore, variations in sample application, stabilizing media composition, and various analysis parameters are such that reproducibility is a major problem (Thompson 1967; Learson 1970).

Department of Chemistry, University of Southern Mississippi, Hattiesburg, Mississippi 39401

The use of an equilibrium technique—thin layer polyacrylamide gel isoelectric focusing—to speciate fish was recently reported by Lundstrom (1977). Unlike other forms of electrophoresis in which proteins migrate at a constant rate through a gel of a given pH, isoelectric focusing employs a pH gradient. Hence, proteins migrate through the electric field until they reach the pH corresponding to their isoelectric point, at which time they lose their charge and no further migration takes place. As a result, the proteins become concentrated in very sharp bands whose isoelectric points differ by as little as 0.02 pH units.

It is the purpose of this paper (1) to compare the technique of isoelectric focusing to other electrophoretic techniques commonly used to speciate fish; (2) to optimize extracting, staining, and isoelectric focusing conditions to produce optimum resolution of protein fingerprints; and (3) to evaluate the reproducibility and suitability of the technique for routine speciation of fishery products.

MATERIALS AND METHODS

Sample Preparation

Muscle extracts were prepared either from freshly caught fish that had been cleaned and skinned or from fish that had been frozen immediately following capture and maintained at $-20°C$. One gram of tissue was placed in a glass tissue homogenizer with 5 ml of a 0.01 M phosphate buffer (pH 7.0) containing 0.6 M NaCl. Following homogenization, the sample was centrifuged at 31,000 g for 20 min at 4°C. The supernatant was then removed and enough sucrose added to bring the sucrose concentration to 30% (w/v).

Optimum Extraction Procedures

For those studies designed to determine the optimum ionic strength of the extraction medium, a 0.01 M phosphate buffer was employed. The ionic strength was adjusted by the addition of varying amounts of NaCl, ranging in concentration from 0.1 to 6.0 M. Protein was determined by the technique of Lowry as modified by Hartree (1972). To determine the optimum pH for extraction, a buffer consisting of 0.01 M acetate, 0.01 M phosphate, 0.01 M Tris and 0.6 M NaCl was used. Aliquots of this buffer were then removed and adjusted with 0.5 M NaOH or 0.5 M HCl to selected pH values ranging from pH 3.0 to pH 10.0.

Electrophoresis

Cellulose acetate electrophoresis was performed according to the method of Learson (1969). Polyacrylamide disc electrophoresis was carried out by the method described by Thompson (1967).

Isoelectric Focusing in Polyacrylamide Gel (IF)

Five percent acrylamide gels containing 2% Ampholine (pH 3.5–10) were polymerized in 5 mm × 75 mm glass tubes. Following light polymerization at 4°C (catalyzed by riboflavin), the tubes were inserted into a Canalco disc electrophoresis apparatus with 0.004 N ethylenediamine added to the anode compartment (upper bath) and 0.001 N phosphoric acid placed in the cathode compartment (lower bath). A pH gradient was established by passing 0.1 watt per tube through the gels for 30 min. All separations were carried out at 4°C.

Samples (approximately 25 μl) were then gently layered on the top of each gel and covered with a protective Ampholine–sucrose solution as described by Wrigley (1968). Separations were carried out by passing 0.20 to 0.22 watt per tube through the gels for approximately 90 min. Gels were then immediately removed from the tubes and stained. By use of a Beckman surface membrane combination electrode and a Sargent–Welch NX Digital pH meter, the pH of the gel was determined at 3 mm intervals. A plot of pH as a function of gel length thus permitted the subsequent assignment of isoelectric points to separated proteins following staining.

Staining of Gels

Those gels stained with amido black were incubated for 30 min in a methanol–water–acetic acid (5:5:1) solution containing 0.2% amido black. Excess stain was then removed electrophoretically (40 volts) in the same solution less amido black.

The bromphenol blue staining procedure employed a 12-hr incubation of gels in methanol–H_2O–acetic acid (5:5:1) containing 0.7% bromphenol blue. Destaining was accomplished by repeatedly rinsing gels over a 12-hr period in the same solution less dye.

A modification of the Coomassie brilliant blue system described by Vesterberg (1971) was used in staining separated proteins with Coomassie brilliant blue R250. Gels were incubated at 60°C for 30 min in a solution of methanol (75 ml), H_2O (185 ml), trichoroacetic acid (30 g), sulfosalicyclic acid (9 g), guanidinium hydrochloride (35 g), and Coomassie brilliant blue R250 (275 mg). Background stain was removed by placing the gels in an ethanol–H_2O–glacial acetic acid solution (25:65:8) for 1 to 2 hr. Quantification of gel rods following staining was achieved using a Transidyne General RFT Scanning Densitometer (600 nm).

Inter- and Intrasample Variations in Protein Composition

Variations in protein composition within a specimen were evaluated by taking six tissue samples. The samples taken were anterior dorsal, anterior ventral, mid-dorsal, mid-ventral, posterior dorsal, and posterior ventral. The extraction buffer was 0.6 M NaCl in 0.01 M phosphate, pH 7.0.

Also included within this portion of the study was a reproducibility–age/sex study. Samples were taken from Atlantic croakers, which were collected at various times from different locations. These samples included both juveniles and adults, males and females.

Seasonal Change Study

Effects of seasonal changes on the muscle protein of fish were determined by examining specimens collected during different seasons. For the study, samples were collected monthly for 1 year. The 0.01 M phosphate, pH 7.0 buffer containing 0.6 M NaCl was again used for the extractions.

RESULTS AND DISCUSSION

Effect of Extraction Buffers

As the ionic strength of the extracting buffer was increased, more protein bands were obtained, up to an ionic strength of 0.6. However, when the ionic strength was further increased from 0.7 to 6.0, protein bands not only became fewer in number but also lost their sharpness (Fig. 5.1). Protein determinations from tissue extracts (Fig. 5.2) supported these findings by demonstrating that maximum protein was extracted with buffers containing 0.6 M NaCl. A pH of 7.0 was found to extract the most protein (Fig. 5.3). This pH also resulted in the sharpest and largest number of protein bands following isoelectric focusing (Fig. 5.4).

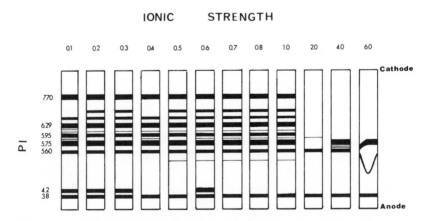

FIG. 5.1.   EFFECT OF IONIC STRENGTH OF EXTRACTION BUFFER ON SUBSEQUENT ISOELECTRIC FOCUSING PROFILES OF FISH MUSCLE
(Atlantic Croaker, *Micropogon undulatus*).

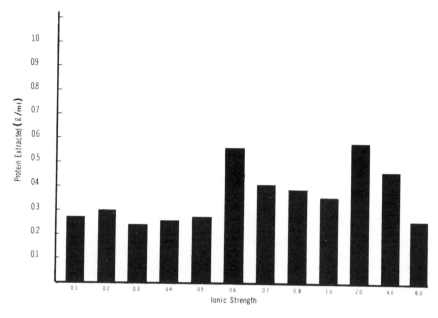

FIG. 5.2.   EFFECT OF IONIC STRENGTH OF EXTRACTION BUFFER ON TOTAL PRO-
TEIN EXTRACTED FROM FISH MUSCLE
(Atlantic Croaker, *Micropogon undulatus*).

Comparison of Protein Stains

Following both electrophoresis and isoelectric focusing on polyacrylamide, gels were stained for soluble protein using the stains amido black,
bromphenol blue, and Coomassie brilliant blue R250. Both visual observation and densitometer scans suggested that there were no significant
differences in the staining capabilities of these three protein stains (Fig.
5.5). However, amido black required 10–12 hr for staining, followed by at
least 24 hr of destaining. Bromphenol blue gave comparable results to
amido black although only 3–4 hr were required for maximum protein
staining. Unfortunately, the stained protein zones quickly faded and were
almost completely invisible within 72 hr. Coomassie brilliant blue R250 required only 30 min for staining and 1–2 hr for removal of unwanted background stains. The protein zones so stained were found to be stable for
several weeks at room temperature and up to 6 months in the refrigerator.
Thus, Coomassie brilliant blue R250 was chosen as the stain for all subsequent studies.

Electrophoretic Separation of Fish Protein Extracts

When extracts of Atlantic croaker, brown shrimp, and silver perch were
applied to cellulose acetate, 2–4 protein bands were obtained following

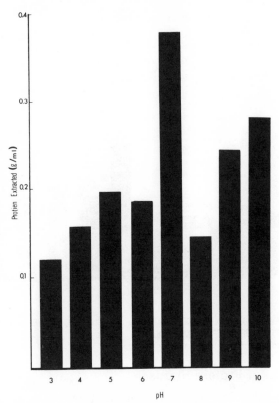

FIG. 5.3.   EFFECT OF pH OF EXTRACTION BUFFER ON TOTAL PROTEIN EXTRACTED
FROM FISH MUSCLE
(Atlantic Croaker, *Micropogon undulatus*).

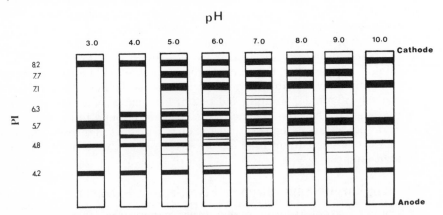

FIG. 5.4.   EFFECT OF pH OF EXTRACTION BUFFER ON SUBSEQUENT ISOELECTRIC
FOCUSING PROFILES OF FISH MUSCLE
(Atlantic Croaker, *Micropogon undulatus*).

electrophoretic separation and staining (Fig. 5.6). However, all protein bands stained only very lightly and faded considerably during the fixing and clearing steps. In addition, due to the limited resolution of this electrophoretic system, species identification based solely on electrophoretic patterns from this technique was difficult.

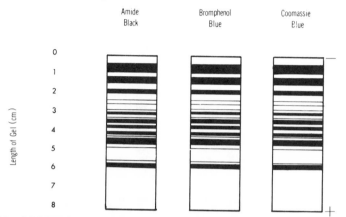

FIG. 5.5. PROTEIN PATTERNS OF ATLANTIC CROAKER (*Micropogon undulatus*) SEPARATED BY ISOELECTRIC FOCUSING AND STAINED WITH AMIDO BLACK, BROMPHENOL BLUE, AND COOMASSIE BRILLIANT BLUE R250

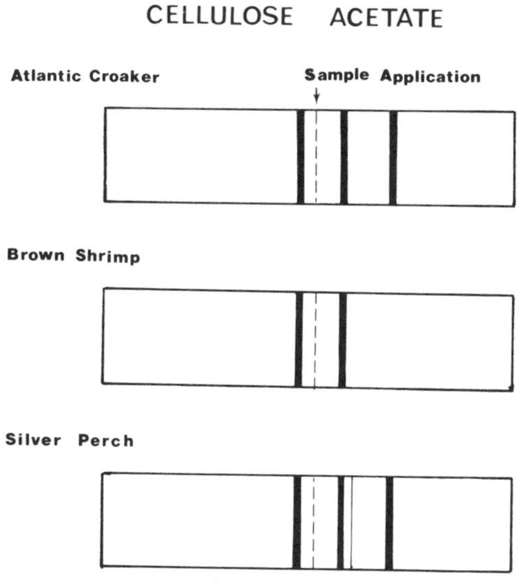

CELLULOSE ACETATE

FIG. 5.6. PROTEIN PATTERNS OF ATLANTIC CROAKER (*Micropogon undulatus*) BROWN SHRIMP (*Penaeus aztecus*), AND SILVER PERCH (*Bairdella chrysura*) SEPARATED BY CELLULOSE ACETATE ELECTROPHORESIS

When one of the species (Atlantic croaker) was run on polyacrylamide gel, 11 protein zones were visible following staining with Coomassie brilliant blue R250 (Fig. 5.7). As shown in Fig. 5.8, results obtained with Atlantic croaker are typical of results obtained with a number of species of fish, where one typically observes 5–14 protein zones following polyacrylamide gel electrophoresis.

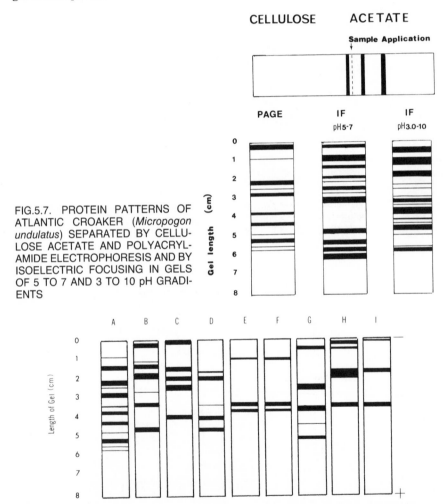

FIG.5.7. PROTEIN PATTERNS OF ATLANTIC CROAKER (*Micropogon undulatus*) SEPARATED BY CELLU-LOSE ACETATE AND POLYACRYL-AMIDE ELECTROPHORESIS AND BY ISOELECTRIC FOCUSING IN GELS OF 5 TO 7 AND 3 TO 10 pH GRADI-ENTS

FIG. 5.8. PROTEIN PATTERNS OF FISH SEPARATED BY POLYACRYLAMIDE GEL ELECTROPHORESIS
(A) Atlantic Croaker (*Micropogon undulatus*), (B) spotted seatrout (*Cynoscion mebulosus*), (C) southern flounder (*Paralichthys lethostigma*), (D) sand seatrout (*Cynoscion arenarius*), (E) brown shrimp (*Penaeus aztecus*), (F) white shrimp (*Peneaus setiferus*), (G) redfish (*Sebastes marinus*), (H) bluefish (*Promatomus salatrix*), (I) American eel (*Anguilla rostrate*).

Isoelectric Focusing Separation of Fish Protein Extracts

Isoelectric focusing was carried out in gels covering the pH range of 3–10 and 5–7. As shown in Fig. 5.7, 15 protein zones were obtained with Atlantic croaker in the pH 3–10 gel, while 12 protein zones were obtained with the same species in the pH 5–8 gel. The effect of different pH gradients within the gel is further illustrated in Fig. 5.10 for four additional species. As illustrated in this figure, the use of a narrower range pH gradient often results in a greater number of protein bands and makes positive identification of an unknown species easier than if a broad range 3–10 pH gradient is used.

Figure 5.9 not only illustrates the diagrammatic representation of five additional fish extracts separated by isoelectric focusing but also gives a direct comparison of the results obtained using isoelectric focusing and polyacrylamide gel electrophoresis to separate fish protein extract. As can be seen in this figure, isoelectric focusing routinely results in approximately four times as many protein zones as polyacrylamide gel electrophoresis. This greater resolution is extremely important when one needs to

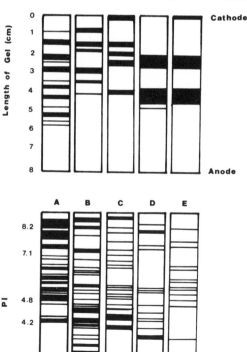

FIG. 5.9. COMPARISON OF POLYACRYLAMIDE GEL ELECTROPHORESIS AND ISOELECTRIC FOCUSING PROFILES OF FISH MUSCLE EXTRACTS
(A) Atlantic croaker (*Micropogon undulatus*), (B) red snapper (*Lutjanus blackfordi*), (C) southern flounder (*Paralichrhys lethostigma*), (D) cod (*Gadus callarias*), (E) haddock (*Melanogrammus aeglifinus*)

distinguish between two or more closely related species. This facet of isoelectric focusing is clearly illustrated when one compares the polyacrylamide gel electrophoresis patterns of samples D and E to the isoelectric focusing patterns of the same two species.

Since the most difficult and time-consuming steps in the isoelectric focusing separation of fish homogenates involves gel preparation, experiments were undertaken to prepare and store gels prior to isoelectric focusing of fish homogenates. Isoelectric focusing gels were prepared and prefocused in batch quantities. These gels were then stored in a refrigerator for up to 60 days. At the end of 60 days the pH gradients on gels were measured and compared to gradients on gels which had been freshly focused. In addition, samples were run on both freshly prepared and stored gels. In these experiments no differences could be found between freshly prepared gels and those gels which had been stored for 60 days.

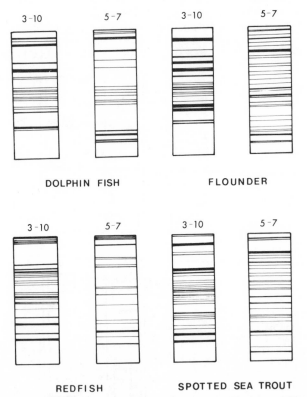

FIG. 5.10.   COMPARISON OF pH 3–10 AND pH 5–7 GRADIENTS FOR THE ISOELECTRIC FOCUSING SEPARATION OF MUSCLE PROTEIN FROM DOLPHIN FISH (*Coryphaena hippurus*), SOUTHERN FLOUNDER (*Paralichthys lethostigma*), REDFISH (*Sebastes marinus*), AND SPOTTED SEATROUT (*Cynoscion mebulosus*)

Quantification of Isoelectric Focusing Results

In order to identify an unknown fish fillet, it is necessary that a data bank of isoelectric profiles of a large number of fish species be on file for comparison purposes. In order to establish such a data bank, it is necessary to convert the visual isoelectric focusing profiles into quantitative data. This can best be done by densitometer scans, an example of which is illustrated in Fig. 5.11. From such a densitometer scan, one can assign the relative percentage of each protein band by measuring the area under the densitometer curve corresponding to that band. Furthermore, the isoelectric point of each protein can be measured by means of a surface membrane electrode prior to final Coomassie brilliant blue staining. Thus, data as shown in Table 5.1, the isoelectric point, and the relative percentage of protein for each major protein, can be filed for future species identification.

Sample Variation

To utilize such data as shown in Table 5.1, it is necessary to establish that (1) differences do not exist between different specimens of the same species; (2) differences do not exist between the muscles obtained from the anterior and posterior regions of the same species; and (3) protein patterns for a species are not season-dependent. As shown in Table 5.2, there were no appreciable differences in protein profiles with respect to point of sample

SILVER   PERCH

5-7

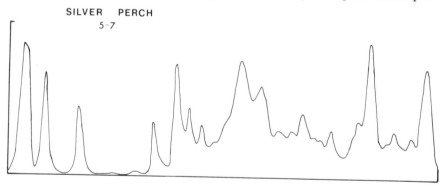

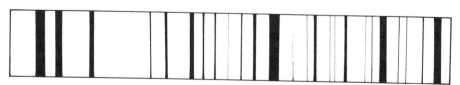

FIG. 5.11. DENSITOMETER SCAN OF MUSCLE EXTRACT FROM SILVER PERCH (*Bairdella chrysura*) SEPARATED BY ISOELECTRIC FOCUSING ON A pH 5−7 GEL

TABLE 5.1.   PROTEIN DISTRIBUTION OF FISH MUSCLE EXTRACTS SEPARATED BY ISOELECTRIC FOCUSING AND QUANTIFIED BY DENSITOMETRY

Silver perch (Bairdella chrysura)		Redfish (Sebastes marinas)		Catfish (Galeichthys felis)	
PI	% Protein	PI	% Protein	PI	% Protein
3.9	6.5	4.2	7.0	4.3	5.2
4.1	6.5	4.3	5.5	4.4	5.2
4.4	5.9	4.5	12.5	5.0	9.8
4.9	3.2	4.6	2.1	5.2	2.2
5.4	1.8	4.7	5.1	5.5	4.2
5.6	3.9	4.8	3.2	5.6	7.2
5.7	6.1	5.3	2.5	5.7	5.9
5.8	2.4	5.4	1.5	5.8	2.8
5.9	10.0	5.5	4.5	6.2	2.2
6.0	6.2	5.6	3.0	6.5	5.0
6.2	5.6	5.7	4.1	6.6	12.9
6.3	3.8	5.8	6.1	6.7	5.2
6.5	7.9	5.9	2.0	6.8	2.2
6.7	2.6	6.0	4.1	7.0	8.9
6.8	1.5	6.1	3.6	7.3	6.0
7.0	8.5	6.2	5.1	7.5	5.5
7.3	1.8	6.4	5.2	7.6	6.5
7.9	3.5	6.5	5.2		
8.2	10.0	6.8	6.7		
		7.0	6.2		
		7.1	4.1		

TABLE 5.2.   EFFECT OF INTER- AND INTRASAMPLE VARIATIONS IN PROTEIN PROFILES OF ATLANTIC CROAKER (Micropogon undulatus) MUSCLE[1]

PI ($\pm.05$)	AD[2] (%)	AV (%)	MD (%)	MV (%)	PD (%)	PV[2] (%)
8.20	17	16	16	17	17	17
7.71	5	6	6	5	6	6
7.10	3	3	3	4	4	3
6.87	1	1	1	1	1	1
6.80	1	1	1	1	1	1
6.58	1	1	1	1	1	1
6.30	5	5	5	5	5	5
6.21	1	1	1	1	1	1
5.72	19	18	19	19	18	19
5.50	4	3	4	3	3	3
5.11	6	7	6	7	7	7
5.00	1	1	1	1	1	1
4.79	20	20	19	19	20	19
4.50	1	1	1	1	1	1
4.31	1	1	1	1	1	1
4.20	19	19	19	19	19	19

[1] Key to abbreviations: AD, anterior dorsal; AV, anterior ventral; MD, mid dorsal; MV, mid ventral; PD, posterior dorsal; PV, posterior ventral.
[2] Same fish—all other samples were obtained on different dates and locations.

TABLE 5.3. EFFECT OF SEASON ON PROTEIN PROFILE OF ATLANTIC CROAKER (*Micropogan undulatus*) MUSCLE EXTRACTS SEPARATED BY ISOELECTRIC FOCUSING

PI (±.05)	Jan.	Feb.	Mar.	Apr.	May	June	July	Aug.	Sept.	Oct.	Nov.	Dec.
8.20	16	16	17	17	17	17	17	17	17	17	16	17
7.71	6	6	5	7	6	6	6	7	5	6	6	5
7.10	3	3	4	4	4	3	3	3	4	3	3	3
6.87	1	1	1	1	1	1	1	1	1	1	1	1
6.80	1	1	1	1	1	1	1	1	1	1	1	1
6.58	5	5	5	5	5	5	5	5	5	5	5	6
6.30	1	1	1	1	1	1	1	1	1	1	1	1
6.21	1	1	1	1	1	1	1	1	1	1	1	1
5.72	20	18	19	19	18	19	19	19	19	18	18	19
5.50	4	4	4	3	3	3	4	3	4	4	3	3
5.11	6	8	7	8	7	7	7	7	6	8	8	7
5.00	1	1	1	1	1	1	1	1	1	1	1	1
4.79	19	20	19	19	20	19	19	20	20	20	20	21
4.50	1	1	1	1	1	1	1	1	1	1	1	1
4.31	1	1	1	1	1	1	1	1	1	1	1	1
4.20	19	19	19	19	19	20	19	19	19	19	19	19

extraction. Nor was there any significant sample-to-sample variation in isoelectric focusing profiles. As shown in Table 5.3, no seasonal variability was found when Atlantic croaker was sampled and analyzed over a 12-month period. Similar results for blue crab, Southern flounder, brown shrimp, and red snapper were found when these four species were sampled and analyzed over the same 12-month period. From these studies it can be concluded that data such as those shown in Table 5.1 can be filed for future species identification with little or no variability expected due to either seasonal change or specimen variability within a given species.

CONCLUSIONS

The results of this study indicate that both electrophoretic and isoelectric focusing techniques are viable methods for the speciation of unknown fish fillets and minced fish products. While both cellulose acetate and polyacrylamide electrophoretic methods can be used to speciate fishery products, better results are obtained using the technique of isoelectric focusing. Furthermore, the method of extracting protein is critical for subsequent speciation. It is thus the conclusion of this study that the best experimental conditions for the identification of fish muscle include (1) extraction of muscle protein with a 0.01 M, pH 7.0 buffer containing 0.6 M NaCl; (2) separation of extracted proteins by isoelectric focusing using gels of pH gradient 3−10 and 5−7; and (3) staining of gels following isoelectric focusing with Coomassie brilliant blue R250.

ACKNOWLEDGMENTS

This work is a result of research sponsored by NOAA, Office of Sea Grant, Department of Commerce, under grant MS GP-78-049, and by NOAA, National Marine Fishery Service, Department of Commerce. The U.S. Government is authorized to produce and distribute reprints for governmental purposes not withstanding any copyright notation that may appear herein.

REFERENCES

CONNEL, J.J.   1953.   Studies on the proteins of fish skeletal muscle.   Electrophoretic analysis of low ionic strength extracts of several species of fish. Biochem. J. *55*, 378−388.

CORDURI, R.J.   1972.   Vertical plate gel electrophoresis for the differentiation of fish and shellfish species.   J. Assoc. Off. Anal. Chem. *55*, 464−466.

CORDURI, R.J., and RAND, A.G.   1972.   Vertical plate gel electrophoresis for the differentiation of meat species.   J. Assoc. Off. Anal. Chem. *55*, 461−463.

COWIE, W.P.   1968.   Identification of fish species by thin-slab polyacrylamide gel electrophoresis of the muscle myogens.   J. Sci. Food Agric. *19*, 226−229.

HARTREE, E.F.   1972.   Determination of protein, a modification of the Lowry method that gives a linear photometric response.   Anal. Biochem. *48*, 422–427.

HILL, W.S., LEARSON, R.J., and LANE, J.P.   1966.   Identification of fish species by agar gel electrophoresis.   J. Assoc. Off. Anal. Chem. *49*, 1245–1247.

LANE, J.P., HILL, W.S., and LEARSON, R.J.   1966.   Identification of species in raw processed fishery products by means of cellulose polyacetate strip electrophoresis.   Commer. Fish. Rev. *28*, 10–13.

LEARSON, R.J.   1969.   Collaborative study of a rapid electrophoresis method for fish species identification.   J. Assoc. Off. Anal. Chem. *52*, 703–707.

LEARSON, R.J.   1970.   Collaborative study of a rapid electrophoresis method for fish species identification. II.   Authentic flesh standards.   J. Assoc. Off. Anal. Chem. *53*, 7–9.

LUNDSTROM, R.C.   1977.   Identification of fish species by thin-layer polyacrylamide gel isoelectric focusing.   Fish. Bull. *75*, 571–576.

MACKIE, I.M., and JONES, B.W.   1978.   The use of electrophoresis of the water soluble (sarcoplasmic) proteins of fish muscle to differentiate the closely related species of hake (*Merluccius* sp.).   Comp. Biochem. Physiol. B *59*, 95–98.

MANCUSO, V.M.   1964.   Protein typing of some authentic fish species by disc electrophoresis.   J. Assoc. Off. Anal. Chem. *47*, 841–844.

PAYNE, W.R.   1963.   Protein typing of fish, pork, and beef by disc electrophoresis.   J. Assoc. Off. Anal. Chem. *46*, 1003–1005.

THOMPSON, R.R.   1960.   Species identification by starch gel zone electrophoresis of protein extracts. I.   Fish. J. Assoc. Off. Anal. Chem. *43*, 763–764.

THOMPSON, R.R.   1967.   Disc electrophoresis method for the identification of fish species.   J. Assoc. Off. Anal. Chem. *50*, 282–285.

VESTERBERG, O.   1971.   Staining protein zones after isoelectric focusing in polyacrylamide gels.   Biochem. Biophys. Acta *243*, 345–348.

WRIGLEY, C.   1968.   Gel electrofocusing—a technique for analyzing multiple protein samples by isoelectric focusing.   Sci. Tools. *15*, 17–23.

6

Unusual Properties of the Connective Tissues of Cod (*Gadus morhua* L.)

R. Malcolm Love, Jack Lavéty, and Françoise Vellas

Muscle tissue in animals is held together by strands or sheets of connective tissue, which also serve to transmit the force of muscular contraction to the skeleton. Connective tissue consists of fibers of the specialized proteins collagen and elastin, a "ground substance" which contains polysaccharides, and various soluble organic and inorganic compounds. In this chapter we shall consider the collagen, which makes up the greater part of connective tissue.

Historically, the connective tissues, being inert and almost insoluble in neutral aqueous solutions, received much less attention then the more immediately attractive contractile proteins actin and myosin. However, the tissue makes up 2–10% of the dry weight of vertebrate skeletal muscle (Mohr 1971), and reports on its properties now make up an increasing proportion of protein literature.

Collagen has an unusual amino acid composition. About one-third of the amino acids are glycine, 6–10 residues per 100 are hydroxyproline (unique to collagen), and 10–12 residues are proline (Eastoe 1967). It is these amino acids, proline and hydroxyproline, which give the collagen its thermal stability (Gustavson 1953; Piez and Gross 1960), and fish collagens differ from mammalian collagens in having less of them. Fish collagens therefore shrink or denature at lower temperatures than those of mammals.

Takahashi and Yokoyama (1954) found a clear linear relationship between the shrinkage temperature of fish skin and its hydroxyproline content, each point on their curve relating to a different species. Fish skins with more hydroxyproline and higher shrinkage temperatures came from fish that tolerate relatively high water temperatures, such as the goldfish

Ministry of Agriculture, Fisheries and Food, Torry Research Station, Aberdeen AB9 8DG, Scotland

(Carassius auratus) and carp *(Cyprinus carpio)*, while thermally unstable collagens, denaturing at low temperatures, were found in cold-water species such as Alaska pollock *(Theragra chalcogramma)*.

The thermal shrinkage temperature of the collagen of *Ophicephalus striatus*, which can spend part of its time on land in a warm climate, is 57°C (Gowri and Joseph 1968), almost as high as that of calf skin (60°C).

It now seems likely that, within a single fish species, certain properties of the collagen also change with the habitat temperature. The skin collagen of *Ophicephalus punctatus* from cooler waters is more soluble (less cross-linked) than that from warmer water (Gantayat and Patnaik 1975). In addition, the thermal shrinkage temperatures of the collagens of *Merlangius merlangus* and *Gadus morhua* are slightly higher in fish from warmer waters (Andreeva 1971).

The role and significance of connective tissue in the texture of edible muscle from warm-blooded animals is well known: as cattle, for example, age, the connective tissues become increasingly insoluble as the number of intermolecular and intramolecular crosslinks increases, and after cooking, even long cooking, the older animal is much tougher than the younger. Everyone knows the problems of eating the muscle of aged cattle, and an old hen needs to be boiled for a very long time before it can be eaten.

In fish, the connective tissue assumes a different significance, being concerned with the integrity of the fillet rather than with its cooked texture. Indeed, its influence on the texture after cooking is negligible (Love *et al.* 1974). But changes in the mechanical strength of the "binding" sheets of connective tissue markedly influence the appearance of the fillet. If the connective tissue weakens, as can result from a number of different causes, the fillet "gapes" or falls to pieces, so that it cannot be skinned mechanically and is difficult to sell because of its unattractive appearance. The factors which weaken the connective tissues, apart from obvious ones such as rough handling, are as follows.

1. Freezing the whole fish, as distinct from the fillets (Love and Robertson 1968).
2. Freezing in rigor mortis, as distinct from before rigor mortis (Love *et al.* 1969).
3. Freezing stale fish (after rigor mortis), which gape more than those frozen in rigor mortis (Love *et al.* 1969). The mechanism is thought to be a progressive hydration of the connective tissue after death, which permits increasing quantities of ice to form within it, exacerbating the disruption caused by freezing (Love and Lavéty 1972).
4. The temperature at which the whole fish enters rigor mortis, higher temperatures simultaneously increasing the force of the rigor contraction while weakening the connective tissue (Love and Haq 1970).
5. The pH of the muscle, small falls in which markedly weaken the connective tissue (a reversible effect) (Love *et al.* 1972).

There are also pronounced differences between species (Love *et al.* 1969; Yamaguchi *et al.* 1976).

Systematic observations have shown that fish in poor condition (post-spawning, semistarved) do not gape (Love and Robertson 1968). This is logical enough on the face of it, because the postmortem pH of the muscle of such fish is always high (usually over 6.9), so the strength of the connective tissue will be maximal. In addition, the disruptive pulling of rigor mortis is likely to be weaker in a starving specimen.

However, the main reason is a curious one. Dissecting the sheets of connective tissue (myocommata) from the muscle of cod, we suddenly became aware that there seemed to be much more myocommata in the starving fish than in normally fed specimens. Direct measurements showed that the myocommata were indeed several times thicker, proportionate to the severity of the depletion (Lavéty and Love 1972). The relationship was still true when the size of the fish was taken into account (Love *et al.* 1976). Studies of the physicochemical properties of the myocommata from fed and starving cod showed that there was a marked similarity between the two as regards molecular shape, intramolecular crosslinking, amino acid composition, and thermal denaturation temperature. However, the collagen from the myocommata contained more intermolecular crosslinks when the fish were starved, having greater mechanical strength per unit thickness.

Experiments on collagen turnover in fed and starving cod were carried out by one of us (F.V.). Radioactive proline was injected into the body cavities of the living fish, and the degree of its incorporation into myocommata and skin was assessed after 24 hr.

The experiment was inconclusive because of the scatter between individual fish. But it raised the important questions: Was the increase in thickness therefore an artifact? and How could such a result have come about?

Studies of the anatomy of cod suggest that any pair of parallel myocommata are joined together by thin tubes of connective tissue, which in nourished fish are filled with contractile tissue (Love 1970). Micrographs of tissue sections published by Love and Lavéty (1977) show that a fair proportion of these tubes at a given point is emptied of their contractile contents in extremely starved cod. Suppose the emptying process were to start near the junction with a myocomma and proceed inward through the body of the myotome as starvation continues. It is then conceivable that the "thickening" of any myocomma results from millions of empty collagenous tubes adding their substance to the surface as the muscle cells are scraped from it during its isolation.

Two experiments have been done to investigate this. The results of the first are illustrated in Fig. 6.1, where musculature from a starving fish has been sectioned as parallel as possible with a myocomma. Just beyond the edge of the myocomma in this picture, we therefore see the ends of muscle cells where they touch the myocomma. While a number of cells are depleted of contractile material, it is clearly inconceivable that the connective tissue

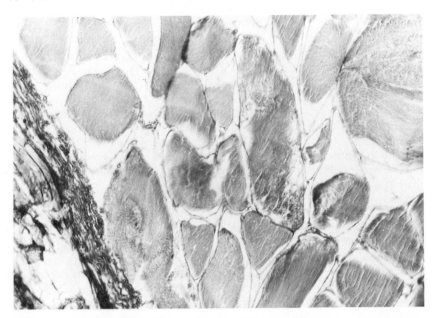

FIG. 6.1. SECTION MADE ALMOST PARALLEL TO A MYOCOMMA OF COD MUSCLE
The darker part is the myocomma, which has been severed along the boundary between the
two types of tissue. Consequently the muscle cells nearest to it are shown at the point where
they touch the myocomma (in cross section). Fixed in buffered formaldehyde, stained with
trichrome collagen stain, and photographed through an orange filter to intensify the color in the
connective tissue. Water content of the cod muscle: 85%.

"tubes" are able to add to the thickness of the myocomma by a whole order of
thickness, if indeed at all.

As a second test, the hydroxyproline, as a measure of collagen, was
measured in a number of complete fish (minus the contents of the alimentary
canal). The results are shown in Fig. 6.2. It is clear beyond reasonable
doubt that actual synthesis of collagen has occurred in the larger fish. The
probable reason for the collagen contents of all smaller fish being similar—
both starved and fed—is that smaller fish cannot be depleted to the same
extent as the large, and in our experience they die when the water content of
the musculature has reached 85–86%. Large cod are able to mobilize more
of their resources, however, and the water contents of the two specimens
with high collagen contents in Fig. 6.2 were close to 90%. The single gram of
musculature removed from each fish for this determination was the only
part not rendered down for hydroxyproline analysis, a minute error in fish
of that size.

The collagen of cod therefore appears to differ from that of mammals,
where it is laid down at birth and becomes more insoluble as the animal
grows older. Bakerman (1962) measured the amount of human skin that
would dissolve in citric acid according to age. He found that about 1.3 mg of

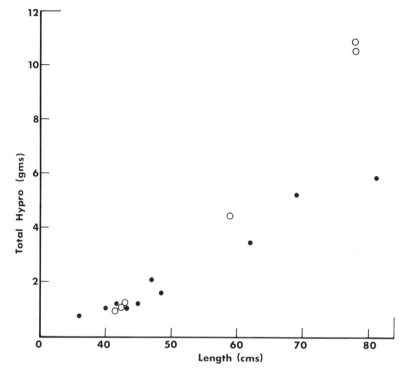

FIG. 6.2.   TOTAL HYDROXYPROLINE IN COD
The values are for the complete fish with the gut emptied and with about 1 g of white muscle removed for water determination. Solid symbols: fed fish; hollow symbols: starving.

soluble collagen was obtained from each gram of dermis of a newborn baby. Beyond about 40 years of age this value was reduced to about 0.2 mg, less than one-sixth of the value at birth.

In our experiment, using conditions similar to those of Bakerman, we found that 51% of the collagen of the myocommata of young cod would dissolve in citric acid. Samples were taken equally from 12 cod of average length 40 cm (1−2 years old). In three very large cod (average length 107 cm, over 7 years old, the largest easily obtainable around Aberdeen), 44% of the total was soluble in citric acid: a small reduction compared with that in man, though the time scale is shorter. In a repeat experiment, 60% of the myocomma collagen was found to be citric acid-soluble in the small fish and 49% in the large.

The collagen of the biggest cod therefore shows little sign of aging over almost the complete life span. The oldest fish used in these experiments were as old as commonly found, and would soon die from "over-reproduction" (Love 1970). Cod are never seen with wrinkled skins or other signs of collagen aging, and it seems at least possible that the synthesis of new collagen every year and, presumably, its resorption on refeeding, keeps the connective tissue of fish in a state approaching youth.

Figure 6.2 suggests that our inability to detect any change in collagen turnover in starving cod stems from the fact that the fish used then were too small, ranging as they did from 59 to 70 cm only. It would be useful to repeat the work with really large fish.

Summarizing the conclusions of this chapter in the context of food science, we can say that connective tissue contributes little if anything to the eating texture of cooked fish. The interest lies in the way in which the musculature is held together. Fish connective tissue is much less stable than that of mammals and can often fail so that the fillet gapes. We here have presented further evidence that collagen is actually synthesized during starvation, and this would help to keep the depleted, watery tissues from falling apart. It is a phenomenon seen mainly in larger fish.

ACKNOWLEDGMENTS

The work described in this paper formed part of the program of the Ministry of Agriculture, Fisheries and Food.

REFERENCES

ANDREEVA, A.P. 1971. Thermostability of the cutaneous collagen of some species and subspecies of the cod family. Tsitologiya *13*, 1004–1008.

BAKERMAN, S. 1962. Quantitative extraction of acid-soluble human skin collagen with age. Nature (London) *196*, 375–376.

EASTOE, J.E. 1967. Composition of collagen and allied proteins. *In* Treatise on Collagen 1. G.N. Ramachandran (Editor), pp. 1–72. Academic Press, New York.

GANTAYAT, S.C., and PATNAIK, B.K. 1975. Collagen in some species of Indian fishes. I. Influence of sex and temperature on the collagen content of the skin and muscle of *Ophiocephalus punctatus*. Sci. Cult. *41*, 404–406.

GOWRI, C., and JOSEPH, K.T. 1968. Characterization of acid-soluble collagen from a live fish or air-breathing fish of India group. Leather Sci. *15*, 300–305.

GUSTAVSON, K.H. 1953. Hydrothermal stability and intramolecular organization of collagens from mammalian and teleost skins. Sven. Kem. Tidskr. *65*, 70–76.

LAVÉTY, J., and LOVE, R.M. 1972. The strengthening of cod connective tissue during starvation. Comp. Biochem. Physiol. *41A*, 39–42.

LOVE, R.M. 1970. The Chemical Biology of Fishes. Academic Press, New York.

LOVE, R.M., and HAQ, M.A. 1970. Connective tissue of fish. III. The effects of pH on gaping in cod entering rigor mortis at different temperatures. J. Food Technol. *5* , 241–248.

LOVE, R.M., and LAVÉTY, J. 1972. The connective tissues of fish. VII. Postmortem hydration and ice crystal formation in myocommata and their influence on gaping. J. Food Technol. *7*, 431–444.

LOVE, R.M., and LAVÉTY, J. 1977. Wateriness of white muscle: A comparison between cod (*Gadus morhua*) and jelly cat (*Lycichthys denticulatus*). Mar. Biol. *43*, 117–121.

LOVE, R.M., and ROBERTSON, I. 1968. The connective tissue of fish. I. The influence of biological condition on gaping in frozen-thawed muscle. J. Food Technol. *3*, 215–221.

LOVE, R.M., LAVÉTY, J., and STEEL, P.J. 1969. The connective tissue of fish. II. Gaping in commercial species of frozen fish in relation to rigor mortis. J. Food Technol. *4*, 39–44.

LOVE, R.M., LAVÉTY, J., and GARCIA, N.G. 1972. The connective tissues of fish. VI. Mechanical studies on isolated myocommata. J. Food Technol. *7*, 291–301.

LOVE, R.M., ROBERTSON, I., SMITH, G.L., and WHITTLE, K.J. 1974. The texture of cod muscle. J. Texture Stud. *5*, 201–212.

LOVE, R.M., YAMAGUCHI, K., CRÉAC'H, Y., and LAVÉTY, J. 1976. The connective tissues and collagens of cod during starvation. Comp. Biochem. Physiol. *55B*, 487–492.

MOHR, V. 1971. On the constitution and physico-chemical properties of the connective tissue of mammalian and fish skeletal muscle. Ph.D. Thesis, University of Aberdeen, Aberdeen, Scotland.

PIEZ, K.A., and GROSS, J. 1960. The amino acid composition of some fish collagens: The relation between composition and structure. J. Biol. Chem. *235*, 995–998.

TAKAHASHI, T., and YOKOYAMA, W. 1954. Physico-chemical studies on the skin and leather of marine animals—XII. The content of hydroxyproline in the collagen of different fish skins. Bull. Jpn. Soc. Sci. Fish. *20*, 525–529.

YAMAGUCHI, K., LAVÉTY, J., and LOVE, R.M. 1976. The connective tissue of fish. VIII. Comparative studies on hake, cod and catfish collagens. J. Food Technol. *11*, 389–399.

7

Properties of Fish Oils and Their Application to Handling of Fish and to Nutritional and Industrial Use

Maurice E. Stansby

INTRODUCTION

In this review, fish oils will be considered both as a component of fish and as a commodity after extraction from fish tissues. The material will be discussed under three main headings: (1) chemical composition and properties, (2) nutritional and pharmaceutical properties, and (3) applications to (a) handling of fish, (b) pharmaceutical applications, and (c) other industrial applications. No treatment will be included in this review on matters concerning the metabolic role of fats and oils in living fish. Primary consideration will be given to oil associated with species important in North America and with only peripheral attention given to fish and fish oil important in other parts of the world.

CHEMICAL COMPOSITION AND PROPERTIES

In most cases, fish oils occur as triglycerides, less frequently as phospholipids. The central focus from the point of view of either handling of the fish or utilization of the fish oils is on the properties of the fatty acids. Initial discussion here will, therefore, relate to the fatty acids. This will be followed by a consideration of the classes of compounds in which the fatty acids occur. In addition to triglycerides and phospholipids, they can include other forms in special instances. The location of these various kinds of lipids in different tissues of fish and the variation in amounts of total lipids will then be discussed. Finally in this section will be included a brief discussion of oxidation of fish oils.

Northwest and Alaska Fisheries Center National Marine Fisheries Service, National Oceanic and Atmospheric Administration, Seattle, Washington 98112

Fatty Acids in Fish Oils

Fish oils contrasted to other oils contain (1) a greater variety of fatty acids than other oils or fats, and (2) a considerably greater amount of fatty acids (a) of 20 or 22 carbon chain length, (b) of a highly polyunsaturated type (five and six double bonds), and (c) of long carbon chain omega-3 type as compared to the usual omega-6 variety. Most fish oils from different species possess the properties which differ markedly from vegetable or other oils. The long chain acids (primarily C_{20} and C_{22}) generally make up one-fourth up to one-third of all the fatty acids in fish oils and, in a few species, may approach one-half of the total fatty acid content. This contrasts sharply to the proportion of long chain fatty acids in most vegetable oils, which seldom exceeds 5% and frequently is less than 1%. Likewise, five and six double-bonded fatty acids of fish oils generally occur to an extent of 15–30% in fish oils, yet they almost never total even 1% in vegetable oils.

Most of the polyunsaturated fatty acids of fish oils occur as the omega-3 type which are of the linolenic acid family as contrasted to the more usual linoleic acid family (omega-6 type) fatty acids in most other oils. The oil within the fish tissue occurs as fat deposits or may be mixed with other tissues in the form of light and dark (red) meat. The polyenoic fatty acids are preferentially attached at the 2 positions of the glycerol (Brockerhoff et al. 1963), and this follows the same pattern as occurs in most land animals. However, marine mammals seem to have most of their highly polyunsaturated fatty acids attached at the 1 and 3 positions (Brockerhoff and Hoyle 1963).

All fish have a small amount of their lipid occurring at the cellular level in the form of phospholipids. Most of these phospholipids in marine fish occur as either phosphatidyl cholines (lecithins) or as phosphatidyl ethanolamines (cephalins). In most fish about half of the phospholipids are lecithins and about one-quarter are cephalins. To a lesser extent fish phospholipids occur in other forms including inositol phosphatides, cerebrosides, and sphingomyelins (Silk and Koning 1964).

Several sharks such as the common dogfish (Squalus acanthias) contain diacyl glyceryl ethers (Malins et al. 1965; Mangold and Malins 1968). These substances have at their 1 and 2 positions esterified fatty acids with an alcohol (usually chimyl, batyl, or selachyl alcohol) combined through an ether linkage at the 3 position. The fatty acids have high proportions of polyenoic C_{20} and C_{22} fatty acids when the glycerol ether occurs in the flesh; but if it resides in the liver, instead of a high proportion of the long chain polyenoic fatty acid, the corresponding C_{20} and C_{22} monenes are present.

In a few species of fish, fish oil occurs as wax esters. Thus, Agawa et al. (1953) found such compounds in the liver of a cod (Lotella phycis). Nevenzel and co-workers (1965) have studied in some depth the occurrence of wax esters in both the flesh and liver lipids of the castor oil fish. The content of omega-6 fatty acids in most fish oils is under 10%, often below 5%. The content of omega-3 type is somewhat higher, about 10%, in the oils of freshwater fish.

Fish oils also contain more fatty acids of odd carbon chain length (C_{15}, C_{17}, C_{19}) than most other oils or fats. The usual range of the total odd carbon chain fatty acids is 1–3%, but at least one species, the mullet, contains as much as 10% or more.

Two fatty acids, palmitic (C16:0) and oleic (C18:1), occur in considerable quantities in nearly all fish oils, ordinarily totaling 30% or more of the total fatty acids. In some fish oils these two fatty acids may make up half or more of the fatty acid content, and in only a few oils do they amount to less than 20% of the total.

Other fatty acids that are often but not always contained in considerable amounts include three monoenes C16:1, C20:1, and C22:1; one other saturated fatty acid, myristic (C14:0); and two polyunsaturates, C20:5 and C22:6. The latter two compounds are characteristic of fish oils and ordinarily do not occur in other oils in more than trace amounts.

For many years there has been a prevailing belief that oil made from any particular species of fish has a fatty acid pattern that will vary only a little from one sample to another. This idea goes back to the late nineteenth century and the early years of the present century before fatty acids were determined in oils and when the oils were characterized by such fat constants as iodine number or saponification numbers. It was believed that each oil had a series of fat constants by which it could be characterized. Any deviations from these constants were believed to be errors primarily in the determination of the constants by a particular analyst. While it is possible that certain vegetable oils, for example, may have a reasonably close chemical composition from one sample to another, fish oils do not possess such a property, as we have seen. Eventually it became customary to establish the various fat constants for each species of fish oil. The values were usually reported to two places past the decimal point, (e.g., iodine number = 129.07), and it was then understood that the oil for which such a value was reported would always give the same value when the analysis was conducted correctly.

After Hilditch, Lovern, and others carried out fatty acid analyses using the laborious early gravimetric techniques available during the first 60 years of the twentieth century, there became prevalent a general idea that fish oils made from a given species might vary, at least to a small extent, from one sample to another. However, even after the much more rapid gas chromatographic procedures became available, very inadequate attention was paid by most workers in the field to procuring anything like representative fish oil samples that were used for fatty acid analyses of oils from a given species of fish.

Actually, the correlation between fatty acid composition and the species of fish from which the oil is made is a very loose one. Many species of fish tend to modify the fatty acids that they consume in their feed so as to lay down, in some cases, fatty acids different from those in the food they eat.

This aspect, however, is overridden to a considerable extent by the laying down in the fish's flesh of the same fatty acids as those occurring in their feed. The feed available to fish differs considerably from place to place and from one season of the year to another. Furthermore, the type and amount of available feed may change from year to year. These various factors tend to result in fish of the same species containing oil with highly variable fatty acid content. The fatty acid pattern should not be thought of as changing from species to species or from season to season or from one geographical location to another; but rather the patterns conform to a large extent to the type and amount of feed available and its fatty acid content.

That the fatty acid content of fish of a given species is completely independent of the species is not true. Most species have metabolic pathways that tend to produce fat of a pattern at least somewhat typical of that species. These metabolic processes cannot, however, prevail against the constantly changing feed availability pattern. The resulting fatty acid make-up of the oil in a fish at a given point is modified from that most typical of the species to the actual pattern, which is highly dependent on the fatty acid composition of the feed ingested in recent periods of time by that fish.

Analyses of commercially prepared fish oil in large batches show these concepts to be correct. In this case, thousands or sometimes millions of fish are rendered at a fish reduction plant and the resulting oil deposited in huge tanks. The oil in such tanks is representative of not just a few fish of a given species but rather of thousands or even millions of fish. Yet, when the fatty acid contents of such large batches of fish made at different places, at different seasons, or during different years are compared, they are often quite different.

Results of such analyses of menhaden and herring are shown in Tables 7.1 and 7.2. There are relatively large differences in fatty acid patterns of each of these species when comparing differences in fatty acid contents among large batches of oil. For example, in Table 7.2, the content of C22:6 fatty acid in commercial herring oil sample No. 1 was just 2.0%; yet the average content of C22:6 in the 12 commercial samples was 4.6%. Now, the number of fish from which the No. 1 commercial batch of herring oil was made was undoubtedly very large, far larger than it ordinarily has been the

TABLE 7.1. RANGES OF CONTENTS OF FATTY ACIDS IN LARGE COMMERCIAL BATCHES[1] OF MENHADEN OIL[2]

Fatty acid	C14:0	C16:0	C16:1	C18:1	C20:5	C22:6
Minimum	7	19	11	10	10	3
Maximum	16	24	18	23	15	11
Average	10	21	12	12	13	8

[1] By a "large commercial batch" is meant one derived from many thousands, sometimes millions, of fish.
[2] Data in this table based largely on analyses provided by Anthony Bimbo, Technical Director, Zapata Haynie Co., Reedville, Virginia, consisting of fatty acid content analyses of large, composited samples of menhaden oil taken from production of this concern throughout the fishing season and at different locations during 1976, 1977, and 1978.

TABLE 7.2. RANGE OF CONTENT OF MOST ABUNDANT FATTY ACIDS IN LARGE
COMMERCIAL BATCHES[1] OF NORTH AMERICAN HERRING OIL[2]

Fatty acid	C14:0	C16:0	C16:1	C18:1	C20:1	C20:5	C22:1	C22:6
Minimum	5	10	6	9	11	4	15	2
Maximum	8	15	12	21	20	9	31	6
Average	7	12	9	13	16	7	22	5

[1] By a "large commercial batch" is meant one derived from many thousands, sometime millions, of fish.
[2] Data in this table taken from analyses of commercial herring oil samples from Nova Scotia and Alaska.

practice to employ in a study of the fatty acids content of oil. Thus, if the determination of the fatty acid content of oil in herring had been based on this one oil even though it was representative of many fish, a value far too low would have been obtained for the C22:6 fatty acid.

A considerable portion of the values for the fatty acid content of oils from a variety of species of fish was obtained during the early 1960s, when the gas chromatography technique largely displaced the older, more time-consuming methods. It was believed at that time by many investigators that there were only minor differences in fatty acid composition of the oil from fish of the same species. As a result, a large number of values frequently suspected to be quite erroneous are used today as if they related to all oil samples of the same species, even when the authors implied that the average fatty acid pattern of a species could be quite different from the values for the limited number of fish used in their experiments. There has been a tendency to ignore these warnings and to accept the values reported in the tables or summary as a true measure of the average for all oil samples of that species.

In most of the reports on fatty acid content of oils of stipulated species during the 1960s, the number of individual fish used has been less than 10. Frequently, samples have comprised less than five fish. Accordingly, if one wants to have any confidence in the validity of the results, it is necessary to examine the original papers to find out what sampling procedure was used. Unless many large batches of commercial fish oil have been analyzed, the sampling ordinarily is inadequate. Actually, it is often impractical to carry out the necessary compositing of oil from a sufficient number of individual fish to obtain meaningful average values. For the most part, not only has this not been attempted, but also most of the investigators in this field are, it appears, quite unaware of this problem.

Even though the lack of adequate data does not permit a statement as to average values or even ranges of fatty acid patterns of fish oils, some information can generally be obtained. With many fish oils, a few of the fatty acids will be so much greater or less than those in other species that some general differences between certain fish oils and the average fish oil can be delineated. For example, herring contain a great deal more C_{20} and C_{22} monoenes than most fish oils, and the total long chain fatty acids may exceed 50%, whereas they usually run from 20 to 35% in most other fish oils. Mullet oils often contain up to 10% of odd chain length fatty acids (mostly

C15:0 and C17:0) as contrasted to other fish oils which seldom have more than 1–3%. Menhaden oils contain somewhat more C14:0 and less C22:6 fatty acids than the majority of other fish oils. We can make such statements only with fish oils that have been studied fairly extensively. When something as unusual as the high incidence of odd chain length fatty acids occur, however, it can be indicated if only a few analyses confirm it.

Classes of Lipids

Combined partly as triglycerides and partly as phospholipids, fatty acids occur in all fish oils. Other classes of lipids such as glyceryl ethers or wax esters also occur in a few species.

Other substances that occur in or are associated with fish oils include hydrocarbons, sterols, vitamins, and pigments. Hydrocarbons are a principal component of the liver oils of some sharks. For example, Heller *et al.* (1957) found that squalene made up about 90% of the liver oil of a shark *Centrophorus uyato*. Lesser quantities of pristane and zymene have also been found in this and other sharks (Christensen and Sörensen 1951). The body oils of herring have been found to contain very small amounts of hydrocarbons. Lambersten and Holman (1963) reported 0.05% of hydrocarbons in herring oil. This was separated into 21 straight chain and 8 branched chain hydrocarbons. Of the branched chain hydrocarbons 70% was pristane.

Sterols are another important component of fish oils. Of the sterols, cholesterol is the most widespread, occurring in the oil of nearly all fish, shellfish, and crustaceans with the amount in crustaceans, especially shrimp, being the highest, up to 200 mg per 100 g of shrimp. Quantities in the flesh of finfish are considerably less, generally well under 100 mg per 100 g of flesh.

Vitamins A and D occur in the oil of most fish, with by far the highest concentrations occurring in the liver oils of certain species including halibut and tuna. Body oils of fish generally contain small amounts of vitamins A and D.

Amount and Occurrence of Oil in Fish

Intracellular lipids of fish occur primarily as phospholipids associated with cells and to an extent of about 0.2–0.3%. In addition to such cellular lipids the fish may contain only a very small amount of triglyceride lipid, sometimes under 0.1%. But, ordinarily, the amount of triglycerides greatly exceeds that of phospholipids. Fish such as cod and haddock with 0.5% or less total oil have very little triglycerides in their flesh, often with most of the oil occurring as phospholipids. Species of fish that often contain 10% or considerably more oil, such as herring and salmon, have a large proportion of their lipids occurring as triglycerides.

The oil in fish flesh occurs in light and dark (or red) muscles. In most but not all instances, the oil content of the dark flesh is higher (sometimes ten times or more) than that of the light flesh. The dark muscle (often of a dark red color) occurs predominantly as a "V" shaped strip beneath the lateral line, and also, to a lesser extent, in other areas such as along the dorsal region.

A comprehensive discussion of the anatomy and function of the red and light muscle of fish has been given by Barets (1961). The red muscle is described as "slow" muscle because it is believed to function as a means of propelling the fish through the water during slow, steady swimming. The light muscle sometimes referred to as "rapid" muscle is believed to function primarily when bursts of speed of short duration are needed.

In addition to its occurrence in differing amounts in the flesh of fish, oil also occurs in certain organs, particularly in the liver, in highly variable proportions. In fish like cod, in which almost all of the flesh oil occurs in the form of phospholipids associated with the cells, the liver is large (about 10% of body weight), is very oily (up to 80%), and consists largely of triglycerides. In species of fish such as salmon and herring, which contain a preponderance of their flesh lipids as triglycerides occurring in depot fats, the livers are small (1–3% of body weight) and relatively nonoily (under 5%).

The oil content of the flesh of fish varies over very wide limits from minimum values of about 0.3% up to maximum values of nearly 90%. Not only does this wide variability occur from species to species, but also the oil content of different fish of a single species varies over a range of ten times or more. It is not, therefore, possible to present any meaningful data on average oil content of the different species of fish.

Stansby (1962) has proposed a system for classifying composition of the flesh based on a purely arbitrary consideration of oil and protein content. The five categories in this classification system are shown in Table 7.3. Oil content ranges in categories A, B, and C are under 5%, 5–15%, and over 15%, respectively. Most fish come under categories A or B. Category A includes both bottomfish (e.g., cod), which possess little or no depot fats, and a number of species that have only modest quantities of depot fat. Category B includes most species that contain fairly large quantities of depot fats. Since many of these species vary widely in oil content from season to season, they may at one season or another have so little oil as to drop down temporarily to category A or so much as to occasionally lap over into category C. Most crustaceans and shellfish (except shrimp) with very low protein content and low oil content fall into category E and a few special species with very high protein as well as low oil content (e.g., tuna and halibut) fall into category D. Some of the most important species of fish are classified by this system in Table 7.4.

TABLE 7.3. TYPES OF FISH BASED ON OIL AND PROTEIN CONTENT OF THE FLESH

Category	Type of fish	Prototype species	Moisture (%)	Protein (%)	Oil (%)	Ash (%)
A	Low oil – high protein (under 5%) (15–20%)	Pacific cod *Gadus macrocephalus*	81.5	17.9	0.6	1.6
B	Medium oil – high protein (5–15%) (15–10%)	Mackerel *Scomber scrombrus*	67.5	18	13	1.5
C	High oil – low protein (over 15%) (under 15%)	Siscowet lake trout *Cristivomer namacush siscowet*	52.5	11.3	36.0	0.53
D	Low oil – very high protein (under 5%) (over 20%)	Skipjack tuna[1] *Katsuwonus pelamis*	72.4	26.2	0.7	1.5
E	Low oil – low protein (under 5%) (under 15%)	Butter clams *Saxidomus nuttalli*	83.0	13.3	1.3	1.9

[1] Analysis of light meat only. This part is the only one that is ordinarily canned.

TABLE 7.4.   TYPE OF COMPOSITION OF THE FLESH OF SOME IMPORTANT SPECIES OF FISH

Species	Category[1]	Remarks
Anchovies	B	Some caught at certain seasons or in certain localities may fall in category C
Carp	A	Some caught at certain seasons or in certain localities may fall in category B
Cod	A	
Flounder	A	
Haddock	A	
Hake	A	
Halibut	D	
Herring	B	Some caught at certain seasons or in certain localities may fall in category C
Mackerel	B	Some caught at certain seasons or in certain localities may fall in category C
Mullet	A	Borders on category B
Ocean perch	A	
Pollock	A	
Rockfishes	A	
Salmon	B	Some species of salmon—chum *(Oncorhynchus keta)*, Atlantic *(Salmo salar)*, and pink *(Oncorhynchus gorbuscha)*—may border on category A
Sardines	B	Some caught at certain seasons and in certain localities may be category C
Tuna	D	Albacore tuna *(Germo alalunga)* when caught in certain areas is in category B. Bluefin tuna *(Thunnus thynnus)* borders on category B
Whiting	A	
Clams	E	
Crabs	A	
Oysters	E	
Scallops	A	
Shrimp	A	

[1] Category A = oil <5%, protein 15–20%; category B = oil 5–15%, protein 15–20%; category C = oil >15%, protein <15%; category D = oil <5%, protein >20%; and category E = oil <5%, protein <15%.

Stability Toward Oxidation

In this section only a brief discussion of chemical oxidation of fish oils is presented. The reader is referred to Section III, Stability and Deterioration, in the book "Fish Oils" (Stansby 1967) for greater detail.

Fish oils, although differing chemically to a considerable extent from animal and vegetable oils, oxidize by the same general mechanism as most lipids, the theoretical basis for which was developed during the 1940s by Farmer (1946), Bolland (1946), and others. Fish oil fatty acids, however, have up to six double bonds where oxidation can take place. Compared to linoleic acid with only two double bonds or linolenic acid with three, many of the fish oil fatty acids are far more vulnerable to oxidation, and their rate of oxidation is far in excess of that of the fatty acids in most other oils.

With most polyunsaturates of fish oils of the omega-3 type the kind of oxidation products resulting may vary from those obtained from the more usual omega-6 variety.

Fish oils generally oxidize in a manner that results in a less distinct break in the induction curve, and antioxidants are less effective in prolonging the induction period than is the case with the same antioxidants applied to animal or vegetable fats and oils (Stansby 1976). Oxidation in the oil of fish is very markedly affected by the presence of hematin compounds acting as prooxidants. The hematin compounds occur in fish primarily in the dark muscle, and oxidation in this dark or red muscle may occur at a rate up to 100 times as rapid as that in the light muscle (Brown *et al.* 1957).

Fish oils with their high content of polyunsaturates can oxidize to a very great extent. Extensive oxidation takes place, for example, when paint and other protective coatings containing fish oil oxidize. However, the extent of oxidation that takes place in fish used for human food and stored under ordinary handling conditions (e.g., in ice or frozen) is very small. The extent of oxidation in oil of iced fish is in fact almost imperceptible, and there appears to be some relationship between the presence of growing bacteria in fish and the reduction in oxidation rate. When frozen fish is stored at usual temperatures (e.g., −20°C), oxidation proceeds more rapidly. But the degree of oxidation at which obnoxious oxidative rancidity flavors develop—peroxide values of 5 or less—occurs at a very early stage of oxidation, often still in the induction period, as compared to the extreme oxidation occurring when fish oils thoroughly oxidize.

The types of odors that develop with the oxidation of a highly purified menhaden oil have been described by Stansby and Jellinek (1965). These follow through a pattern of the loss of the initial normal, fresh, species characteristic flavor or odor, to a particular "fishy" type flavor or odor, and later to the usual rancidity found in most oxidized oils. A more thorough discussion of odors and flavors in oxidizing fish oils has been given by Stansby (1971).

NUTRITIONAL AND PHARMACEUTICAL PROPERTIES

General Nutritional Properties

Most oils contain fatty acids described as essential fatty acids (EFA) which eliminate various dermal symptoms and promote growth. Although, in most instances, the growth promoting effect has more practical value, EFA effects are ordinarily assessed by measurement of their dermal curing effects. As I have previously pointed out (Stansby 1967), when EFA effects are measured by dermal curing symptoms, fish oils appear to be very low, if not deficient, in them. Yet from the standpoint of growth promoting effects for animals, fish oils are equivalent to any animal or vegetable fats or oils.

There is a voluminous literature on growth effects of fish oils on various farm animals (Karrick 1967). In almost all such tests, fish oils have been shown to act as good growth promoters. But unless proper care is taken either to limit the amount of fish oil in the diet or to eliminate the fish oil near the end of the feeding period, the possibility exists that the meat of the animals or poultry may acquire a fishy flavor. Eggs from hens on a fish oil diet, however, are not affected in this way. Fish oil when used properly can also result in production of satisfactory meat or poultry without undesirable off-flavor problems. The high polyunsaturates of fish oil have sometimes caused toxic problems when fish is used in feed for cats or mink where the diseases steotitis and yellow fur disease, respectively, can occur. Generally these conditions can be eliminated by supplementing the diet with tocopherol.

Pharmaceutical Properties

Probably the most important pharmaceutical effect of fish oils is the very effective serum cholesterol depressant effect which is brought about by the highly polyunsaturated fatty acids contained in fish oils. Apparently, owing to the presence of the five and six double-bonded fatty acids and perhaps also to the abundance of omega-3 fatty acids, fish oils have a much greater effect weight for weight, than other polyunsaturated oils such as vegetable oils. Furthermore, Peifer (1967) has shown that in experiments with rats, fish oils bring about an immediate decline of serum cholesterol, whereas vegetable oils such as corn oil have little or no effect until after the feeding has been underway for at least two weeks. Tuna or menhaden oil bring about the maximum lowering within 2 weeks whereas the polyunsaturated vegetable oils only begin to reduce serum cholesterol *after* 2 weeks. Even after 4 weeks of feeding, the decline in serum cholesterol level is only about one-half as much as that achieved with the fish oils.

That the highest polyunsaturated fatty acids in the fish oil are responsible for this effect is shown by the fact that animals under stress from feeding diets with a resulting increase in their serum cholesterol levels tended to build up in their heart tissue high levels of C20:5 and especially C22:6. When fish oil with high proportions of these fatty acids was fed, levels of these fatty acids in the heart increased from values near zero (too small to detect by gas chromatographic analytical methods) to a range of 4.5 to 5 mg per gram of tissue for the hexaenes and 2.5 to 3.5 mg per gram for the pentaenes. Of considerable significance, however, is the fact that, in animals on a linoleic acid diet (analogous to corn oil) where almost no C22:6 or C22:5 fatty acids were present, the heart level of hexaenes and pentaenes increased to about 0.7 mg per gram of heart tissue. This indicates a possible need for these hexaene and pentaene fatty acids by the heart when serum cholesterol levels are high, causing a mobilization of insignificant levels of these fatty acids in the ingested feed to raise the heart tissue levels as much as possible.

Human feeding tests involving polyunsaturated fatty acids of fish oil have been of such a short term nature—mostly limited to only a few weeks in duration—as to be almost meaningless. The one exception is the work of Dr. Averly Nelson (1972) who induced a portion of his patients, all of whom had suffered a heart attack, to go on a diet in which the principal fat came from high oil content fish, which was consumed at least three times per week. Among patients, 80 patients consumed the special diet over a period of 16–19 years; 116 did not and served as controls. At the end of the 19-year period of the experiment, 36% of the dieted patients (29 individuals) were still alive as opposed to only 8% of the undieted controls (10 individuals). Furthermore, of those who followed the diet, but eventually died of a subsequent heart attack, the average survival time was 109 months as compared to only 58 months among the control, undieted individuals. Much of Dr. Nelson's success in this work can be attributed to his ability to keep the patients who followed the diet from deviating from it. He achieved this by allowing them to ignore their diet for four consecutive meals once each week. In addition, he conducted initial weekly class sessions for an extended period of time to explain the need for such a regime, had a full time nutritionist on his staff, and worked out a diet whereby once a week his patients could ignore their special diet. Even with all of these efforts, only 39% of his patients adopted the diet and remained upon it for the many years of the experiment.

In addition to cholesterol depressant activity of fish oil fatty acids, several other pharmaceutical effects are found either in the fatty acids or in other components of the oil. For example, work of Bernsohn and Stephanides (1967) has suggested that one cause of multiple sclerosis may well be a deficiency of long chain omega-3 fatty acids in the diet. These workers have proposed that even though the average American diet contains very little such long chain omega-3 fatty acids, there is sufficient short chain omega-3 acids to provide a basis upon which metabolism can provide the longer chain acids such as docosohexaenoic acid. They suggest that those individuals who develop multiple sclerosis do so because of faulty metabolism which reduces the formation of sufficient long chain omega-3 polyunsaturates. Fish oils are the only food source of the long chain polyunsaturated omega-3 fatty acids in the American diet. As such they might reduce risk of multiple sclerosis when used as part of the diet, or form the basis for preparation of an omega-3 source for therapeutic use.

Several other components of some fish oils such as alkoxydiglycerides have been proposed for various pharmaceutical uses. In most of these cases the pharmaceutical effect is not sufficiently documented to assure that the effect is a real one. For example, the glyceryl ethers derived from some sharks, according to the work of Brohult (1963), can be used to minimize undesirable side effects of extensive radiation therapy. Mixed concentrates of selachyl and chimyl alcohols derived from shark liver oils have been used in Sweden on a routine basis for patients suffering irradiation leukopenia. These results were also confirmed by workers in two other laboratories (Linman et al. 1958; Suki and Grollman 1960). On the other hand, workers in Canada and the United States (Carlson 1966; Snyder 1969) have been unable to confirm these results and found no such results at all. Glyceryl ethers have also been claimed to heal deep-seated wounds and burns (Bodman and Maisin 1958) and have been used in medical lotions and salves for this purpose. Tests at the Mayo Clinic using hairless mice, however, could find no such effect whatever (Stansby et al. 1967).

Some workers (Heller et al. 1963) have found in lipid fractions of shark oil a reticuloendothelial effect that might increase the phagocytic effect. Yet other workers (Ringle et al. 1966), when repeating this work, obtained negative results. For further details on these and other pharmaceutical applications of fish oils, see the review of Stansby (1969).

APPLICATIONS

Handling of Fish

Problems in handling of fish involving oil relate almost entirely to oxidation, whereby adverse changes in flavor and color develop. In this regard, species containing considerable quantities of oil generally present the most problems, but fish having only a small amount of oil, even as little as 1% can, under some circumstances, alter adversely due to oil oxidation.

Species of fish conventionally stored with little or no refrigeration such as salted fish and some smoked fish may alter considerably through oxidation and yet face no severe marketing problems. Salted fish may develop, as a result of oxidation, a flavor which is acceptable, or considered to be desirable for that particular product even though, in fact, the flavor may be a rancid one. Frozen fish which often remain in cold storage from many months to over a year are affected by oxidation to the greatest extent. Unfrozen fish held in ice at a temperature considerably higher than frozen fish nevertheless seldom have rancidity problems. This is the case not only because the storage period usually is only a few days as compared to many months for the frozen product, but also because, as has been mentioned, changes brought about by bacterial spoilage apparently have a retarding effect on the rate of oxidation of the oil in the fish.

By far the best way to slow down or even stop oxidation of oils in fish is to keep air away from the fish. In order to prevent oxidation of such products as frozen fish, it is necessary to keep all air away. This includes not only air which may slowly pass through even the best of conventional packaging materials, but also the air entrapped within the package, which often is of sufficient amount to cause some oxidation, resulting in mildly rancid flavor or discoloration. If fish is stored inside tin cans and the air evacuated, oxidation will be prevented for many years. Samples of frozen salmon packaged in this way in laboratory experiments have remained for 10 years without any changes that could be detected by sensory examination when stored at 0°F.

Another way which seems more acceptable to the fishing industry is the use of an ice glaze on whole fish, fillets, or steaks which are also packaged. As long as an intact ice glaze remains upon fish, almost no air penetrates through the glaze and very little oxidation occurs. The main problem is brought about by loss of the glaze through evaporation during cold storage. Addition of protective packaging on the outside of glazed fish greatly alleviates this problem.

Use of antioxidants, which may be quite effective for the oils in food products other than fish, usually is of only marginal value for frozen fish. The storage life can certainly be extended to a small degree by such treatment, but the extension so obtained is often of such a short duration as to render such treatment of questionable value.

Introduction of some newer methods of processing fish can greatly increase the extent of oxidation of the oil within the flesh of fish. Irradiation accelerates the rate of oxidation of oils in fish considerably (Stansby and Kudo 1964). Preparation of deboned minced fish also may accelerate rancidity formation. This adverse effect may be considerably diminished by washing the minced fish in cold water immediately after deboning. The rancidity acceleration is caused not merely by the greater exposure of a minced product to air but also by pick-up of iron from the deboning machine and, to a lesser extent, by the heating caused by the mincing.

Pharmaceutical Applications

During the early 1960s one fish oil manufacturing concern put up on a trial basis capsules of fish oil and fish oil fatty acid concentrates for use by heart patients. At that time there was no real documentation that such a product would have any value. What evidence existed was based mostly on animal tests with only a few human feeding experiments of only a few weeks. With the lack of confirmation that such a product would be of any benefit, there was no market established for this product. Today with the long-term studies previously cited of Nelson (1972), the value of highly polyunsaturated fatty acids in fish oil has been established for prolonging the life of heart patients who have suffered a heart attack.

There have been almost no follow-up studies subsequent to publication in 1969 of Nelson's investigation (1972). Recently, however, there has been a renewed interest in this field. At least one long-term investigation is currently under way. With the documented experiment of Nelson (1972) as a basis, it would appear that a successful marketing of a drug capsule consisting of fish oil fractionated to achieve a highly concentrated polyunsaturate product should now be successful. Such a product could mean that a much less rigid diet, one which most patients would adhere to, could be used. Availability of such a product would also encourage research on other potentially promising applications of omega-3 fish oil fatty acids for multiple sclerosis as previously mentioned.

Other Industrial Applications

Worldwide, the vast proportion of commercial fish oil is hydrogenated and used as a component of shortening or margarine. About 90% of the fish oil produced in the United States also ends up in a hydrogenated form in edible fats. None of the processing takes place, however, in this country. Our Food and Drug Administration regulations do not include fish oil as a component for margarine in its "Standards of Identity," and other problems concerned with sanitation in American fish oil plants restrict its use in shortening (Stansby 1973). There is currently considerable interest in getting regulations changed so that fish oils can be used in this country as a legal additive in food products. It is apparent, however, that such action could be taken only after conducting detailed feeding tests upon effects of incorporation of fish oils in this way. This would undoubtedly require very expensive projects to be carried out. It is unfortunate that provision for use of fish oil was not made when food standards were first adopted for margarine. In all probability hydrogenated fish oils would have been acceptable at that time under the GRAS provision without need for carrying out expensive research testing.

Thus most of the American-produced fish oil is shipped abroad for hydrogenation. Much of the rest is used as a component in paint and varnish. The remainder is either used directly for a large variety of industrial uses or processed into fatty acids most of which, in turn, are used to synthesize other chemicals.

There are several areas in the production of industrial chemicals where an expansion in the use of fish oils could occur. At present, the supply of rapeseed oil of the type containing abundant quantities of long chain saturated fatty acids is declining. A review of this situation (Stansby 1979) shows that several fish oils could supplement existing rapeseed oil to provide a raw material for manufacture of long chain saturated fatty acids.

There may also be a market for fish oils as a raw material for production of unique, long chain polyunsaturated fatty acids. More research, however, will be required on practical and efficient fat-splitting methods to use with the highly unstable fish oils (Stansby 1979) before this market can be developed.

FISH OIL RESEARCH

During the first part of this century most of the research on fish oils was carried out in Great Britain, particularly by Hilditch at the University of Liverpool and Lovern at Torry Research Station. Research on fish oils in North America first began in Canada in the 1920s at the federally operated Fisheries Research Board of Canada's Prince Rupert, British Columbia, laboratory, later transferred to Vancouver with much of the work directly by H.N. Brocklesby. In the United States, an extensive government-sponsored program began in the early 1950s at the Seattle Technological Laboratory of the Bureau of Commercial Fisheries (now National Marine Fisheries Service). Considerable research on the chemistry and nutritional properties of fish oils continued until about 1965. Although this program was discontinued in 1965, several universities that had participated on a contract basis have continued an interest in such work. Today nearly all the fish oil research carried out in the United States is done at universities. The Canadian fish oil research was eventually transferred from the Vancouver laboratory to the Halifax laboratory of the Fisheries Research Board of Canada. For the past 15 years it has been the center of the active fish oils research programs in North America. During recent years this program has been headed by Dr. Robert Ackman. The program was discontinued by the Canadian government in 1979, but Dr. Ackman is now continuing this research at Nova Scotia Technical College in Halifax.

Over the past several decades, a considerable amount of research has been carried out on fish oils in a number of different laboratories in Japan. This includes work done in both universities and in government laboratories.

Research on fish oils during the first half of this century dealt mainly with chemical characterization of fish oils, first as to carbon chain length and approximate degree of unsaturation, then as analytical techniques improved, to studies of specific fatty acids occurring in fish oils. Beginning in about 1940 interest in oxidation of fish oils in fish accelerated. Soon many investigations to learn how this deteriorative change could be controlled were underway in both university and governmental laboratories. Since no really satisfactory solution to the problem has been developed, such research continues unabated. Meanwhile, coming to the forefront of fish oil research has been the interest in biochemical changes in living fish, which today makes up a considerable portion of such research. Research on characterization of fish oils also continues, but with more attention being paid to such aspects as classes of compounds and positional isomers. Research on nutritional aspects of fish oils which reached a peak of interest in the 1960s has since declined in activity, although during the past two or three years, a slight increase in interest in this field has occurred.

REFERENCES

AGAWA, T., HIRAO, Y., and KOMORI, S. 1953. The liver oil of a cod, *Lotella phycis*. J. Jpn. Oil Chem. Soc. *2*, 246–249.

BARETS, A. 1961. Contribution to the study of slow and rapid motor systems in the lateral muscle of teleosts. Arch. Anat. Microsc. Morphol. Exp. Suppl. *50*, 91–187.

BERNSOHN, J., and STEPHANIDES, L.M. 1967. Aetiology of multiple sclerosis (human, mammal, chick). Nature (London) *215*, 821–823.

BODMAN, J., and MAISIN, J.H. 1958. The α-glycerylesters. Clin. Chim. Acta *3*, 253–274.

BOLLAND, J.L. 1946. Kinetic studies in the chemistry of rubber and related materials. I. The thermal oxidation of ethyl linoleate. Proc. R. Soc. (London) Ser. A *186*, 218–236.

BROHULT, A. 1963. Alkoxyglycerols and their use in radiation treatment. Acta Radiol., Suppl. *223*, 7.

BROCKERHOFF, H., and HOYLE, R. 1963. On the structures of the depot fats of marine fish and mammals. Arch. Biochem. Biophys. *102*, 452–455.

BROCKERHOFF, H., ACKMAN, R.G., and HOYLE, R.J. 1963. Specific distribution of fatty acids in marine lipids. Arch. Biochem. Biophys. *100*, 9–12.

BROWN, W.D., VENOLIA, A.W., TAPPEL, A.L., OLCOTT, H.S., and STANSBY, M.E. 1957. Oxidative deterioration in fish and fishery products. II. Progress on studies concerning mechanism of oil in fish tissues. Commer. Fish. Rev. *19*, 27–31.

CARLSON, W.E. 1966. Some nutritional studies of the naturally occurring α-glycerylethers. Rep. Faculty Agric. Univ. Brit. Columbia, Vancouver, BC, Canada, pp. 1–128.

CHRISTENSEN, P.K., and SÖRENSEN, N.A. 1951. Studies related to pristane. V. The constitution of zamene. Acta Chem. Scand. *5*, 751–756.

FARMER, E.H. 1946. Peroxidation in relation to olefinic structure. Trans. Faraday Soc. *42*, 228–236.

HELLER, J.H., HELLER, M.S., SPRINGER, S., and CLARK, E. 1957. Squalene content of various shark livers. Nature (London) *179*, 919–920.

HELLER, J.H., PASTERNAK, V.Z., RANSOM, J.P., and HELLER, M.S. 1963. New reticuloendothelial system-stimulating agent from shark livers. Nature (London) *199*, 904–905.

KARRICK, N.L. 1967. Nutritional value as animal feed. *In* Fish Oils. M.E. Stansby (Editor), Chapter 24, pp. 363–382. AVI Publishing Co., Westport, CT.

LAMBERTSEN, G., and HOLMAN, R.T. 1963. Partial characterization of the hydrocarbons of herring oil. Acta Chem. Scand. *17*, 281–282.

LINMAN, J.W., BETHEL, F.H., and LONG, M.J. 1958. Erythropoietic stimulatory activity of batyl alcohol. J. Lab. Clin. Med. *52*, 596–604.

MALINS, D.C., WECKELL, J.C., and HOULE, C.R. 1965. Composition of the diacylglyceryl ethers and triglycerides of the flesh and liver of the dogfish *(Squalus acanthias)*. J. Lipid Res. *6*, 100–105.

MANGOLD, H.K., and MALINS, D.C. 1960. Fractionation of fats, oils and waxes on thin layers of silicic acid. J. Am. Oil Chem. Soc. *37*, 383–385.

NELSON, A.M. 1972. Diet therapy in coronary disease: Effect on mortality of high-protein, high-seafood, fat-controlled diet. Geriatrics *27*, 103–116.

NEVENZEL, J.C., RODEGKER, W., and MEAD, J.F. 1965. The lipids of *Ruvettus pretiosus* muscle and liver. Biochemistry *4*, 1589–1594.

PEIFER, J.J. 1967. Hypocholesterolemic effects of marine oils. *In* Fish Oils. M.E. Stansby (Editor), Chapter 23, pp. 223–261. AVI Publishing Co., Westport, CT.

RINGLE, D.A., HERNDON, B.L., and BULLIS, H.R. 1966. Effects of RES-stimulating lipids and zymosan on shock. Am. J. Physiol. *210*, 1041–1047.

SILK, M.H., and KONING, A.J.   1964.   Phospholipids of the South African pilchard *(Sardina ocellata).*   J. Am. Oil Chem. Soc. *41*, 619–622.

SNYDER, F.   1969.   Biochemistry of lipids containing ether bonds.   Progr. Chem. Fats Other Lipids *10*, 287–335.

STANSBY, M.E.   1962.   Proximate composition of fish.   *In* Fish in Nutrition.   E. Heen and R. Kreuzer (Editors), pp. 55–60. Fishing News (Books) Ltd., London.

STANSBY, M.E. ed.   1967.   Fish Oils.   AVI Publishing Co., Westport, CT.

STANSBY, M.E.   1969.   Nutritional properties of fish oils.   World Rev. Nutr. Diet. *11*, 46–105.

STANSBY, M.E.   1971.   Flavors and odors of fish oils.   J. Am. Oil Chem. Soc. *48*, 820–823.

STANSBY, M.E.   1973.   Problems discouraging use of fish oil in American-manufactured shortening and margarine.   J. Am. Oil Chem. Soc. *50*, 220A.

STANSBY, M.E.   1976.   Industrial Fishery Technology, p. 357.   Robert E. Krieger Publishing Co., Huntington, New York.

STANSBY, M.E.   1979.   Marine-derived fatty acids or fish oils as raw material for fatty acids manufacture.   J. Am. Oil Chem. Soc. *56*, 793A–796A.

STANSBY, M.E., and JELLINEK, G.   1964.   Flavor and odor characteristics of fishery products with particular reference to early oxidative changes in menhaden oil.   *In* The Technology of Fish Utilization.   R. Kreuzer (Editor), pp. 171–176. Fishing News (Books) Ltd., London.

STANSBY, M.E. and KUDO, G.   1964.   Effects of ionizing radiation on lipids of fish.   U.S. Atomic Energy Commission Report, Contract AT-(49-11)-2508. TID-21405. 33 pp.

STANSBY, M.E., ZOLLIMAN, P.E., and WINKELMANN, R.K.   1967.   Efficacy of fish oils in healing wounds and burns.   Fish. Ind. Res. *3*, 25–27.

SUKI, W.N., and GROLLMAN, A.   1960.   The effect of batyl alcohol and related alkoglycerols on hemopoiesis in the rat.   Tex. Rep. Biol. Med. *18*, 662–669.

8

Steroids in Mollusks and Crustacea of the Pacific Northwest

Dennis T. Gordon

Liberty is requested in paraphrasing the words of Werner Bergmann (1962) whose work and review on the subject of sterols is highly recommended. In 1816, the isolation of a fatty (ine) solid (stereos) of bile (chole), which was the organic matrix of gallstones, was first reported. The name cholesterine was changed to cholesterol after this material was found to be an alcohol in 1859. As other compounds closely related to cholesterol were discovered they were grouped under the term sterol. Identification of newer compounds and synthesis of synthetic analogs derived from sterols resulted in the use of the more encompassing term steroids.[1] When dealing with mollusks, the term steroid seems most appropriate, but it might slightly overstate the complex mixture found in these bivalves. No matter what term is used, mollusks have a diversity of these lipid components not found in other foods.

A fascinating aspect of steroids is the role they play in the evolution and function of living cells. However, cholesterol is ubiquitous in all animals. It is probably the best known but least understood dietary component believed to affect man's health. Cholesterol is generally thought of negatively, as possibly distracting from health and well being. Food containing cholesterol receive the same adverse comments. Thus the level of cholesterol in foods is of extreme interest.

Two classes of seafoods containing questionably large amounts of cholesterol are mollusks and, to a lesser extent, crustacea. The reader is reminded that mollusks and crustacea contain a mixture of steroids. Concentrating on one geographical region, this paper presents the relationship between cholesterol and other steroids in invertebrates of the Pacific Northwest.

Seafoods Laboratory, Oregon State University, Astoria, Oregon 97103
[1] An alternative definition for steroid is any substance which is a derivative of the condensed ring system cyclopentanoperhydrophenanthrene. Members of the steroid class which contain a hydroxy group capable of forming an ester are called sterols.

TABLE 8.1. TOTAL STEROID LEVELS IN OYSTERS
(Crassostrea gigas) AS DETERMINED BY VARIOUS ANALYTICAL
PROCEDURES

Method	Total steroid level (mg/100 g)[1]
Total steroids by Liebermann–Burchard (LB) reaction	191
Digitonin precipitated steroids by LB reaction	148
Total steroids by gas–liquid chromatography (GLC)	148
Total steroids combining GLC and modified LB reaction	170[2]

[1] Mean value of 20 composite samples, 12 oysters per composite, quantitated by various analytical procedures; wet weight.
[2] Sum of Δ^5 steroids by GLC analysis and Δ^7 steroids by modified LB reaction.

Portions of this work have previously been reported (Gordon 1979; Gordon and Collins 1982).

Methodology plays an important part in determining any food or cellular constituent. The classical method still routinely used for cholesterol measurements is the Liebermann Burchard (LB) reaction (Schoenheimer and Sperry 1952). It is accurate and precise (Abell et al. 1952). However, the LB reaction cannot differentiate between various steroids in a mixture. Only 26–43% of the total steroids of mollusks has been found to be cholesterol. The various steroids produce different chromogens during the LB reaction, which gives an inaccurate total steroid level. While having its limitations, the LB reaction can provide some useful information.

Conducting this colorimetric reaction on an aliquot of the total unsaponifiable fraction of oysters (Crassostrea gigas), a mean level of 191 mg steroid per 100 g wet weight was found using cholesterol as the standard (Table 8.1). This value is dependent on many substrate chemical reactions, some of which are shown in Fig. 8.1. The color intensity over 30 min at 620 mm for three steroids representative of those in oysters is illustrated. Identification of the steroids in marine invertebrates has largely been accomplished by such pioneers as Bergmann (1962) and especially Idler and Wiseman (1971A,B, 1972).

Among the three representative compounds selected in Fig. 8.1, cholesterol, desmosterol, and 7-dehydrocholesterol, there are extreme differences in extinction molar coefficients. The $\Delta^{5,7}$ steroid[2], 7-dehydrocholesterol, gives a much higher absorbance reading per unit mass than cholesterol.[2] The same is true with Δ^7 steroids. The opposite is found with desmosterol, but the difference is not as great. Brassicasterol and desmosterol appear to

_____
[2] $\Delta^{5,7}$ refers to double bonds in the 5, 6 and 7, 8 position of the B-ring.

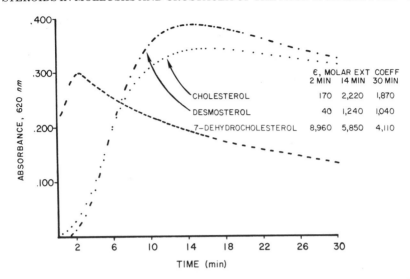

FIG. 8.1.   CHANGE IN ABSORBANCE (620 nm) VERSUS TIME DURING THE LIEBER-
MANN–BURCHARD REACTION FOR THREE STEROIDS PRESENT IN MOLLUSKS
Cold reagent (OC) added at time 0 and reaction allowed to proceed in spectrophotometric cell
maintained at 25°C. Molar extinction coefficient (ε) values indicated at various time periods.

be very similar in this regard (Kritschevsky and DeHoff 1978). The net result of these reactions is an overestimation of the total steroid content. A
common procedure prior to measuring steroids is to first isolate them by
precipitation with digitonin after saponification (Sperry and Webb 1950).
This results in near total loss of the $\Delta^{5,7}$ steroids (Matsumoto $et\ al.$ 1955,
cited by Bergmann 1962) which do not complex with this saponin.
   Measuring the precipitated steroids by the LB reaction gave a value of
148 mg/100 g (Table 8.1). Because of the early (i.e., fast acting) color
development and high extinction molar coefficient of the Δ^7 steroids versus
the Δ^5 steroids (Fig. 8.1), advantage was taken of this property (Moore and
Baumann 1952; Idler and Baumann 1953) to estimate the level of the Δ^7
compounds. The details of this procedure, presented here as the modified LB
reaction, have been described elsewhere (Gordon 1979). Combining the
level of Δ^7 steroids, determined by the modified LB reaction, with the Δ^5
steroids measured by gas–liquid chromatography (GLC), a steroid level of
170 mg/100 g (22 mg Δ^7 plus 148 mg Δ^5) is proposed as a realistic mean
value in Pacific Coast oysters. The mean Δ^5 steroid levels in 20 composite
oyster samples determined by the LB reaction after digitonin precipitation
were 148 ± 19 mg/100 g while the levels determined by GLC analysis were
148 ± 16 mg/100 g. Digitonin was also used to first precipitate and then
quantify the nonesterified steroids in oysters before saponification. Forty-
six percent was found with free hydroxy groups. This level of nonesterifica-
tion appears less than that normally found in specific organs of higher
animals.

A list of the steroids believed to be present in mollusks of the Pacific Northwest are indicated in Table 8.2. Some of these are of questionable occurrence as will be discussed, and still others, not listed, may exist only in trace amounts. The mean and range of each steroid found in Pacific oysters over a 9-month period are indicated in Table 8.3. These data are discussed in relation to a typical gas–liquid chromatogram (Fig. 8.2) and the modified LB reaction. The compound, 5α-cholestane, is used as a qualitative and quantitative standard. Both brassicasterol and desmosterol have been reported in mollusks but could not be separated with the GLC system employed (Gordon 1979) and modeled after the GLC techniques of Miettinen et al. (1965).

Idler and Wiseman (1971A) found 28.1% of the total steroids in Eastern oysters (Crassostrea virginica) to be brassicasterol. They found no desmosterol. In this same report, mussels (Mytilus edulis) were reported to have 8.1% of their total steroids as desmosterol and 9.6% as brassicasterol. Teshima and Kanazawa (1974) showed that the same species of mussels could synthesize desmosterol from mevalonate.

For the determination of steroids in Pacific Coast invertebrates presented here, a purification step by thin-layer chromatography (TLC) was employed (Gordon 1979) prior to GLC analysis. Because the $\Delta^{5,7}$ steroid, 7-dehydro-

TABLE 8.2.   PREDOMINANT STEROIDS IN MOLLUSKS

	Empirical formula	Systematic nomenclature
C$_{26}$-Sterol	C$_{26}$H$_{42}$O	22-trans-24-Norcholesta-5,22-dien-3β-ol
22-Dehydrocholesterol	C$_{27}$H$_{44}$O	22-cis/trans-Cholesta-5,22,dien-3β-ol
Cholesterol	C$_{27}$H$_{46}$O	Cholesta-5-en-3β-ol
Brassicasterol	C$_{28}$H$_{46}$O	24-Methylcholesta-5,22-dien-3β-ol
Desmosterol	C$_{27}$H$_{44}$O	Cholesta-5,24-dien-3β-ol
Lathosterol (Δ^7-cholesterol)	C$_{27}$H$_{46}$O	5α-Cholest-7-en-3β-ol
7-Dehydrocholesterol	C$_{27}$H$_{44}$O	Cholesta-5,7-dien-3β-ol
24-Methylenecholesterol	C$_{28}$H$_{46}$O	24-Methylenecholesta-5-en-3β-ol
Stigmasterol	C$_{29}$H$_{48}$O	24-Ethyl-cholesta-5,22-dien-3β-ol
β-Sitosterol	C$_{29}$H$_{50}$O	24-Ethyl-cholesta-5-en-3β-ol

TABLE 8.3.   MEAN STEROID LEVELS IN OYSTERS (Crassostrea gigas) OVER A 9-MONTH PERIOD (SEPTEMBER 1978–MAY 1979)

Steroid	Mean ± SD[1,2] (mg/100 g)	Range (mg/100 g)
C$_{26}$-Sterol	15.9 ± 4.2	9.4 – 28.6
22-Dehydrocholesterol	14.5 ± 1.2	11.2 – 17.1
Cholesterol	50.7 ± 9.5	36.4 – 69.2
Brassicasterol; desmosterol	26.7 ± 4.0	20.4 – 32.6
Lathosterol (Δ^7-cholesterol); 7-dehydrocholesterol	21.8 ± 8.2[3]	11.1 – 41.8[3]
24-Methylenecholesterol	26.3 ± 4.3	18.9 – 33.8
Stigmasterol	0.7 ± 1.2	0.1 – 3.5
β-Sitosterol	15.5 ± 4.2	5.5 – 21.3
Totals	169.8 ± 20.5	133.5 – 202.4

[1] Twenty composite samples, 12 oysters per composite.
[2] All values determined by GLC; for exception see Table 8.5.
[3] Quantitation by modified Liebermann–Burchard reaction.

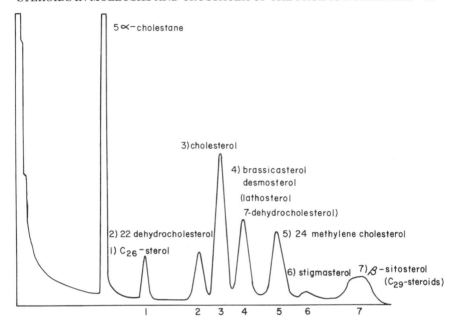

FIG. 8.2. GAS–LIQUID CHROMATOGRAPHIC SEPARATION OF OYSTER *(Crassostrea gigas)* STEROIDS
Trimethylsilyl ether derivations, on 3% SE-30.

cholesterol, is prone to air oxidation (Bergmann 1962), this compound is believed to be totally lost and thus not quantified by GLC. A trace (<0.1 mg/100 g) of 7-dehydrocholesterol, or possibly lathosterol (Δ^7-cholesterol), was found to remain in the mixture isolated by TLC based on the early and positive chromogen formed in the LB reaction. The presence of lathosterol in any mollusk of the Pacific Northwest is, for the time being, conjecture.

Just the opposite is true of the $\Delta^{5,7}$ steroids, provitamins D, which have been shown to be very abundant in mollusks (Bergmann 1962). The presence of lathosterol and desmosterol should not be considered unrealistic. Both are intermediates in the biosynthesis of cholesterol (Heftmann 1970). In retrospect, the $\Delta^{5,7}$ steroids, if adequately protected from oxidation, could have been quantified by ultraviolet analysis. The amount of these steroids could then be subtracted from the total $\Delta^{5,7}$ plus Δ^7 steroids determined by the modified LB reaction to estimate any possible Δ^7 components. All steroids were separated by GLC as their trimethylsilyl ether derivatives. Brassicasterol, desmosterol, lathosterol, and 7-dehydrocholesterol have the same retention volume by the GLC system used (Fig. 8.2) and thus could not be individually quantified. Other compounds present as well as numerous other standards separate, thus neatly preventing the problems previously discussed.

The analytical procedures and discussion described for oysters are applicable to the other mollusks and crustacea examined.

The monthly levels of total lipid, steroids, and cholesterol for oysters are shown in Fig. 8.3. A pronounced seasonal change is depicted, and this is believed to be related to reproductive cycling. Total steroids and cholesterol appear to correlate with total lipid stores. All samples were obtained from the same location, Willipa Bay, Washington.

Remaining questions are "To what extent are the steroids in oysters of dietary origin?" and "What might be their physiological function?" Only a small contribution is offered in response. If the steroids were of dietary origin, they would be expected to be more concentrated in the gills or digestive cavity (i.e., visceral mass). After dissecting the oyster into its five major organ components (Fig. 8.4), total steroids were determined as previously described (Gordon and Collins 1982). The result was that these steroids were distributed in proportion to their component body mass (Table 8.4). In addition, the same distribution of all steroids was found in each organ previously observed in the whole body (Table 8.3). Although not unequivocal, these observations would suggest that each steroid may have a necessary function in these animals compared to only cholesterol in higher animals. This may be especially true for membrane activity.

The steroids and their concentration in seven other mollusks common to the Pacific Northwest are reported in Table 8.5. As with oysters, the same steroids were identified to be approximately in the same proportion. In some mollusks 24-methylenecholesterol approached cholesterol as being the pre-

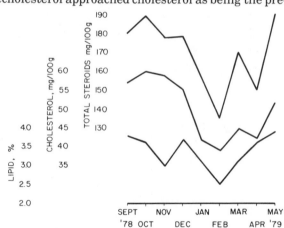

FIG. 8.3. SEASONAL VARIATION OF TOTAL LIPID, CHOLESTEROL, AND TOTAL STEROIDS IN OYSTERS *(Crassostrea gigas)*

TABLE 8.4.   ANATOMICAL DISTRIBUTION OF STEROIDS IN OYSTERS *(Crassostrea gigas)*

	Body mass[1] (%)	Total steroids (%)
Mantle	44.1	41.4
Visceral mass	30.2	36.7
Gills	13.2	11.7
Adductor muscle	8.3	3.7
Labial palps	4.2	6.5

[1]Mean value of 3 oysters; average weight 66 ± 1 g.

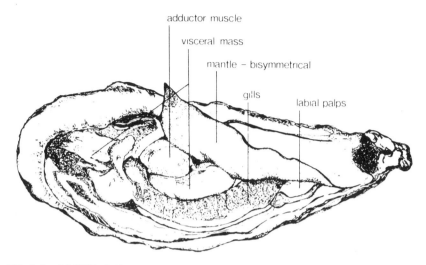

FIG. 8.4.   PACIFIC OYSTER *(Crassostrea gigas)*

dominant steroid. The ratio of desmosterol to brassicasterol remained unre-
solved as previously discussed. In mussels, Idler and Wiseman (1971A)
found that a ratio of 1:1.2 existed between these two steroids. Additional
information that $\Delta^{5,7}$ steroids, and not lathosterol (i.e., Δ^7 steroids), are
predominant in mollusks including Pacific oysters is reported by Kind and
Meigs (1955). They observed that lathosterol (Δ^7-cholesterol) was unique
and only to be found in the class *Amphineura* (chitons) of the phylum
Mollusca. The total amount of steroid observed in any one of the mollusks
examined from the Pacific Northwest (Table 8.5) was lower than any value
found in oysters examined over nine months (133 mg/100 g, Table 8.2).
Steroid levels in two cockle and two butter clam samples are reported in
Table 8.5. Size appeared to have little effect on the amount of steroids in
cockles, while season and/or geographical location changed their levels in
butter clams.

Pacific shrimp *(Pandalus jordani)* and Dungeness crab *(Cancer magister)*
are abundant and of prime economic importance in the Pacific Northwest.
In both of these crustacea, the major steroid is cholesterol. The increase in
cholesterol observed in the three different, fully processed, shrimp products
reported in Table 8.6 is attributed to moisture loss (i.e., mg/100 g wet
weight). Without additional information, it cannot be stated if a difference
exists between the cholesterol levels in cooked crab body and cooked crab
leg. One part of the crab that is often consumed is the material under the
carapace, commonly referred to as gurry (intestine). This material, obtained from a fully cooked crab, is no higher in cholesterol on a wet basis,
than crab meat itself. No Δ^7 steroids could be detected in any of the
crustacea examined by the modified LB test.

TABLE 8.5. STEROID LEVELS IN MOLLUSKS OF THE PACIFIC NORTHWEST (mg/100 g)[1]

	Horse clam	Little neck	Geoduck	Mussel	Razor clam	Cockles[2] No. 1	Cockles[2] No. 2	Butter clams[3] No. 1	Butter clams[3] No. 2
C_{26}-Sterol	2.8	2.9	2.3	3.1	3.6	3.7	3.6	2.2	5.4
22-Dehydrocholesterol	7.0	7.0	4.9	7.2	8.0	8.8	8.2	7.1	13.3
Cholesterol	42.4	35.7	32.1	25.8	19.8	19.9	18.1	31.9	47.9
Brassicasterol, desmosterol	9.5	7.2	6.4	8.9	7.9	7.6	8.8	10.6	11.6
Lathosterol (Δ^7-cholesterol), 7-dehydrocholesterol	6.8	7.6	13.3	27.0	2.5	5.6	5.7	6.5	16.5
24-Methylenecholesterol	27.4	21.8	15.8	10.4	18.0	18.8	20.0	31.3	29.2
Stigmasterol	0.1	0.8	2.4	tr[4]	tr	tr		0.1	tr
β-Sitosterol	3.7	4.7	6.9	2.4	8.7	0.9	5.7	4.0	8.0
Total	99.7	87.7	84.1	84.8	68.5	65.3	70.1	93.7	131.9

[1] Horse clam, *Tresus capax*; Little neck clam, *Venerupis staminea*; Geoduck, *Panope generosa*; Mussel, *Mytilus edulis Linnaeus*; Razor clam, *Siliqua patula*; Cockles *Chinocardium nuttallii*; Butter clams, *Saxidomus giganteus*.
[2] No. 1 composite of 12 cockles 28 ± 4 g; No. 2 composite of 12 cockles 53 ± 6 g.
[3] No. 1 obtained from Paulsbo, WA, September 12, 1978; No. 2 obtained from Tillamook Bay, OR, March 11, 1979.
[4] tr = trace.

TABLE 8.6. STEROIDS IN CRUSTACEA OF THE PACIFIC NORTHWEST (mg/100 g)

	Shrimp Cooked[1]	Shrimp IQF[2]	Shrimp Canned	Crab Body[3]	Crab Leg[3]	Crab Intestine[3]
C_{26}-Sterol	0.1	—	0.3	0.2	0.1	0.9
22-Dehydrocholesterol	0.2	0.1	0.2	0.5	0.4	2.1
Cholesterol	128.9	142.4	160.5	54.2	45.9	55.9
24-Methylenecholesterol	0.1	0.1	0.5	0.2	0.1	2.5
Stigmasterol	tr[4]	tr	tr			
β-Sitosterol	0.1	0.1	tr	tr	—	0.3
Total	129.4	142.7	161.5	55.1	46.5	61.7

[1] Sample commercially cooked and peeled.
[2] Same as cooked shrimp sample, after being further washed, having salt added, and individually quick frozen (IQF).
[3] Analysis of one crab.
[4] tr = trace.

Idler and Wiseman (1968) reported that Alaskan king crab *(Paralithodes camtschatica)* contain 62.3 and 31.1% of their total steroids as cholesterol and desmosterol, respectively. Yasuda (1973) found similar values. Neither report indicated total steroid levels. In reviewing the steroids in crustacea, Idler and Wiseman (1971B) stated that cholesterol was the principal steroid and that desmosterol was second in abundance when present. The metabolism and ultimate distribution of steroids in eight crustacea common to the waters of Japan was studied by Teshima (1972). Cholesterol was the main steroid in all eight species, ranging from 78 to 100%. Other steroids detected, but not in every species, included 22-dehydrocholesterol, brassicasterol, desmosterol, and 24-methylenecholesterol.

Gagosian (1975) found that shrimp *(Pandalus borealis)* contained 130 ± 5 mg steroid/100 g wet weight. Cholesterol accounted for 94.3% and desmosterol 4.2% of the total.

Finally, a few references dealing with the steroid levels in crustacea and mollusks are cited. Sidwell *et al.* (1974) provide a comprehensive review of cholesterol levels, with references, in crustaceans, finfish and mollusks. The work of Thompson (1964) reports cholesterol levels in shellfish as determined by a colorimetric procedure. Even though this analytical method cannot separate or quantify cholesterol alone, the values reported for cholesterol appear realistic in comparison to recent studies. Kritschevsky *et al.* (1967) appear to have been the first to quantify steroids in seafoods employing GLC procedures. This work of Kritschevsky is often quoted in studies dealing with fish steroids. The steroids in British shellfish were measured by Goad (1976). Cholesterol was found to be 47 mg/100 g in oysters and 40 mg/100 g in cockles. Total steroids (mg/100 g) in oysters were 90, 107 in cockles, 198 in shrimp, 167 in crab abdomen "paste," and 69 in crab claw meat.

ACKNOWLEDGMENT

This work was supported in part by the USDC, NOAA, Institutional Sea Grant, and the National Fisheries Institute. Appreciation is extended to Miss Connie Moorehouse, Oregon State University Sea Grant, for the free-hand illustration of the oyster in Fig. 8.4.

REFERENCES

ABELL, L.L., LEVY,B.B., BRODIE, B.B., and KENDALL, F.E. 1952. A simplified method for the estimation of total cholesterol in serum and determination of its specificity. J. Biol. Chem. *195*, 357–366.

BERGMANN, W. 1962. Sterols: their structure and distribution. *In* Comparative Biochemistry. M. Florkin and H.S. Mason (Editors), pp. 103–162. Academic Press, New York.

GOAD, L.J. 1976. Sterols in British shellfish. Proc. Nutr. Soc. *36*, 25A.

GAGOSIAN, R.B. 1975. Sterols of the lobster *(Homarus americanus)* and the shrimp *(Pandalus borealis)*. E. Perientia *31*, 878–879.

GORDON, D.T. 1979. Quantification of steroids in mollusks. Presented at the 1979 American Oil Chemists Society Meeting. San Francisco, Calif. April 29–May 3.

GORDON, D.T., and COLLINS, N. 1982. Anatomical distribution of steroids in oysters *(Crassostrea gigas)*. Lipids. Submitted for publication.

HEFTMAN, E. 1970. Steroid Biochemistry, p. 10. Academic Press, New York.

IDLER, D.R., and BAUMANN, C.A. 1953. III. Sterol structure and the Liebermann–Burchard reaction. J. Biol. Chem. *203*, 387–396.

IDLER, D.R., and WISEMAN, P. 1968. Desmosterol and other sterols of the Alaskan King Crab and the North Atlantic Queen Crab. Comp. Biochem. Physiol. *26*, 1113–1117.

IDLER, D.R., and WISEMAN, P. 1971A. Sterols of molluscs. Int. J. Biochem. *2*, 516–518.

IDLER, D.R., and WISEMAN, P. 1971B. Sterols of Crustacea. Int. J. Biochem. *2*, 91–98.

IDLER, D.R., and WISEMAN, P. 1972. Molluscan sterols: A review. J. Fish Res. Board Can. *29*, 385–398.

KIND, C.A., and MEIGS, R.A. 1955. Sterols of marine mollusks. IV. Δ^7-cholesterol, the principal sterol of *Chiton tuberculatus L.* J. Org. Chem. *20*, 1116–1118.

KRITSCHEVSKY, D., and DEHOFF, J.L. 1978. Sterol content of seafood as a function of analytical method. J. Food Sci. *43*, 1786–1787.

KRITSCHEVSKY, D., TEPPER, S.A., DITULLO, N.W., and HOLMES, W.H. 1967. The sterols of seafood. J. Food Sci. *32*, 64–66.

MATSUMOTO, T., TAMURA, T., and ITO, S. 1955. Nippon Kagaku Zasshi *76*, 953–956.

MIETTINEN, T.A., AHRENS, E.H., JR., and GRUNDY, S.M. 1965. Quantitative isolation and gas-liquid chromatographic analysis of total dietary and fecal neutral steroids. J. Lipid Res. *6*, 411–424.

MOORE, P.R., and BAUMANN, C.A. 1952. I. Colorimetric determination of cholesterol and other sterols in skin. J. Biol. Chem. *195*, 615–621.

SCHOENHEIMER, R., and SPERRY, W.M. 1934. A micro-method for determining of free and combined cholesterol. J. Biol. Chem. *106*, 745–760.

SIDWELL, V.D., FONCANNON, P.R., MOORE, N.S., and BONNET, J.C. 1974. Composition of the edible portion of raw (fresh or frozen) crustaceans, finfish and mollusks. I. Protein, fat, moisture, ash, carbohydrate, energy value, and cholesterol. Mar. Fish. Rev. *36*, 21–35.

SPERRY, W.M., WEBB, M.   1950.   A revision of the Schoenheimer-Sperry method for cholesterol determination.   J. Biol. Chem. *187*, 97–106.

TESHIMA, S.   1972.   Studies on the sterol metabolism in marine crustaceans. Mem. Fac. Fish., Kagoshima Univ. *21*, 69–147.

TESHIMA, S., and KANAZAWA, A.   1974.   Biosynthesis of sterols in abalone, *Haliotis gurneri*, and mussel, *Mytilus edulis*.   Comp. Biochem. Physiol. B *47*, 555–561.

THOMPSON, M.H.   1964.   Cholesterol content of various species of shellfish. 1. -Method of analysis and preliminary survey of variables.   Fish. Ind. Res. *2*, 11–15.

YASUDA, S.   1973.   Sterol compositions of crustaceans–I.   Marine and freshwater decapods.   Comp. Biochem. Physiol. B *44*, 41–46.

9

Studies on the Chemical Nature of and Bioavailability of Arsenic, Cadmium, and Lead in Selected Marine Fishery Products

J.F. Uthe, H.C. Freeman, G.R. Sirota, and C.L. Chou

During the past few decades concern about the presence of natural and anthropogenic toxic chemicals in fisheries products used as human food-stuffs has increased markedly. The anthropogenic chemicals that have had the major impact on fisheries to date are undoubtedly organochlorine materials (including pesticides such as dieldrin and the DDT group and industrial materials such as the polychlorinated biphenyls) and methyl mercury. The requirements for accurate and rapid analytical methodology for ensuring a safe food supply are obvious. In the case of the organ-ochlorines and other pesticides, specific analytical methodologies for each chemical compound and metabolites have been developed to a large degree. The situation with respect to metals is far less advanced and, in most cases, tolerances are based on measuring the total amount of an element present in the foodstuff. This approach is, of course, toxicologically nonsensical unless the chemical nature of the element in the product is known and does not vary from foodstuff to foodstuff.

Alternately the assumption can be made that all forms of an element are equitoxic due to metabolic interconversion following ingestion. Probably the best case in which this philosophy is realistic is that associated with the presence of mercury in fish products. Studies by Westöö (1966, 1969) and others (Uthe *et al.* 1972) showed that the bulk of the mercury present in fin fish muscle preparations could be accounted for by methyl mercury. As can be seen from Table 9.1, this assumption does not hold in every case, and ratios of methyl mercury to total mercury of far less than unity are found in

Fisheries and Environmental Sciences, Department of Fisheries and Oceans, Halifax, Nova Scotia, Canada B3J 2S7 certain edible marine products. Rational assessment of these products would demand use of methodology for selectively determining methyl mercury either through tedious gas chromatography (Westöö 1966; Uthe et al. 1972), selective reduction (Magos 1971), or furnace atomic absorption spectrophotometry graphite furnace coupled assay following selective extraction (Shum et al. 1979). The last technique can be semiautomated to enhance speed of analysis which would then yield a methyl mercury method that is as fast as the current total mercury techniques (e.g., Armstrong and Uthe 1971).

In this chapter we wish to review our studies relative to chemical speciation analysis and bioavailability of three other toxic heavy metals that occur in fishery products, namely, cadmium, arsenic, and lead. These investigations were carried out as part of the Technological Program, Halifax Laboratory, Fisheries and Oceans Canada, between 1973 and 1979.

METHODS OF ANALYSIS

Cadmium. The determination of total and "free" levels of cadmium in fishery products has been described by Chou et al. (1978). Analysis of the total cadmium was carried out by graphite furnace coupled-atomic absorption spectrophotometry of mineral acid digests. "Free"cadmium was determined by differential pulse polarography on solvent washed 1 M ammonium sulfate extracts. "Free" cadmium was defined by its polarographic peak potential of -0.62 ± 0.02 V (saturated calomel electrode).

Arsenic. The determination of total arsenic levels in fishery products has been described by Uthe et al. (1974) and Freeman et al. (1976). Determination of arsenite and arsenate levels have been described by Reinke et al. (1975). Analysis of total arsenic was carried out by graphite furnace coupled-atomic absorption spectrophotometry of vanadium pentoxide catalyzed mineral acid digests. Benzene with concentrated hydrochloric acid

TABLE 9.1. METHYL MERCURY/TOTAL MERCURY RATIOS FOUND IN VARIOUS ANIMAL TISSUES

Species/Tissue	Methyl mercury (μg/g)	Total mercury (μg/g)	Ratio (%)
Northern pike/15 major tissues	0.30−5.77	0.30− 5.80	100
Tuna/muscle	0.33−0.88	0.33− 0.84	100
Mink/muscle	0.29	0.30	97
Mink/liver	0.16	0.39	41
Harp seal/blood	0.14−0.16	0.12− 0.16	100
Harp seal/muscle	0.56−1.67	0.78− 1.80	72−92
Harp seal/liver	0.16−2.63	25.8 − 387	1
American eel/muscle	0.11−0.79	0.42− 1.3	38−65
Black marlin/muscle	0.09−0.50	0.11− 0.77	53−96
Blue marlin/muscle	0.23−1.79	0.35−14.0	5−70
Man/brain	0 −0.19	2.34−14.5	0−5
Man/liver	0 −0.4	0.14−24.1	0−2

and cuprous ion, the latter of which reduces arsenate to arsenite, was used to extract the inorganic arsenic present in the tissue. The arsenite ion was determined by differential pulse polarography using 1 M hydrochloric acid extracts of the previously described mixture. Fish tissue itself is generally capable of carrying out this reduction (Uthe and Reinke 1975).

Lead. The determination of total lead and tetraalkyl lead compounds has been described by Sirota and Uthe (1977). Analysis of total lead was carried out by graphite furnace coupled-atomic absorption spectrophotometry of mineral acid digests. Tetraalkyl lead was determined by graphite furnace coupled-atomic absorption spectrophotometry of mineral acid extracts and digests of the benzene layers from benzene–aqueous EDTA tissue extracts.

All total metal analyses have been supported by check sample studies carried out under the auspices of the International Council for the Exploration of the Sea (Charlottenlund, Denmark) utilizing fish flours as a sample matrix.

STUDIES ON CADMIUM

Certain foodstuffs, especially liver, kidney, and shellfish, contain higher-than-average amounts of total cadmium (Frieberg et al. 1974), with levels in excess of 1 μg of cadmium per gram wet weight being commonly found. In particular, the digestive gland of shellfish which is commonly eaten contain the highest natural amounts of cadmium (Table 9.2).

Lobster *(Homarus americanus)* digestive gland can be seen to contain by far the highest levels of cadmium. This tissue is commonly eaten by individuals served whole boiled lobster, is utilized in lobster-based sauces, and is commercially available as a major ingredient in a canned, relatively cheap "lobster paste" product. Table 9.3 shows the geographical distribution of cadmium in lobster in Canada's western Atlantic region. There is no evidence that the source of this cadmium is anthropogenic (Freeman and Uthe 1974). Although lobster is a delicacy foodstuff in general, an individual eating a single meal a week would exceed the FAO/WHO recommended allowable tolerable intake (FAO/WHO Expert Committee on Food Additives 1972). These recommendations do not, however, allow for the existence of significant difference in the bioavailability of cadmium from

TABLE 9.2.   CADMIUM LEVELS (μg/g WET WEIGHT) IN SHELLFISH

Species/tissue	Cadmium
Blue Mussel/shucked	0.08– 2.0
Lobster/digestive gland	2.8 –68
Lobster/white meat	0.03– 0.58
Scallop/adductor muscle	0.06– 0.39
Rock Crab/digestive gland	0.54–20.58
Rock Crab/white meat	0.06– 0.16
Oyster/shucked	0.11– 1.14

TABLE 9.3.   CADMIUM IN LOBSTER DIGESTIVE GLAND (μg/g WET WEIGHT)

Catch location	Number of animals	Mean[1]
Arnold's Cove, Newfoundland	50	8.82
Comfort Cove, Newfoundland	21	2.82
Beach Point, Prince Edward Island	26	17.2
Caraquet, New Brunswick	17	3.47
Richibucto, New Brunswick	26	6.26
Cape Tormentine, New Brunswick	25	10.9
Shippegan, New Brunswick	26	3.79
Meat Cove, Nova Scotia	26	6.32
Arichat, Nova Scotia	25	7.87
Liverpool, Nova Scotia	26	5.19
Pubnico, Nova Scotia	24	10.42
Grand Manan Island, New Brunswick	26	6.93

[1]Geometric mean.

various foodstuffs, though the effects of various pure dietary constituents on raising or lowering cadmium uptake has been shown. In addition, several authors (Sakamoto 1976; Spivey Fox et al. 1979; Welch et al. 1978) have shown that cadmium naturally present in a variety of foodstuffs differs in bioavailability compared to the uptake of cadmium salts from the usual spiked purified experimental diet.

We decided to determine the bioavailability of cadmium from canned lobster digestive gland, canned porcine liver/kidney prepared from animals injected with cadmium to induce metallothionein synthesis and to compare them with two cadmium chloride-spiked casein diets. All four diets were isocaloric, and contained 20.9 μg cadmium per gram wet weight and 10% protein (except one casein-based diet which contained 20% protein). The diets, for all practical purposes, had the same coefficient of digestibility. In addition, by analysis and fortification all diets contained the same levels of zinc, calcium, and selenium. Young female rats were fed individually the diets for 90 days. At the end of this time cadmium levels were determined in liver, kidney, spleen, and brain (Uthe and Chou 1979).

Although all rats appeared healthy at death and did not show marked differences in growth or organ weights (at autopsy), marked differences were found in the amounts of cadmium taken up from the lobster digestive gland or the liver/kidney mixture and the amounts taken up from the casein diets (Table 9.4). No differences in liver and kidney cadmium uptake were found between the 10 and 20% protein casein-based diets, showing that

TABLE 9.4.   CADMIUM UPTAKE BY RATS FED VARIOUS FORMS OF DIETARY CADMIUM (20.9 μg/g) FOR 90 DAYS (MEAN ± STANDARD DEVIATION)

	Control[1] No added Cd	Casein (CdCl$_2$) 10% protein	Casein (CdCl$_2$) 20% protein	Lobster digestive gland	Porcine liver/kidney
Kidney	0.037 ± .013	3.84 ± .53	3.78 ± 1.13	1.78 ± .29[1]	2.14 ± .32[1]
Liver	0.067 ± .031	1.04 ± .17	1.10 ± .12	0.66 ± .07[1]	0.80 ± .12[1]
Spleen	0.067 ± .031	0.39 ± .14	0.71 ± .17	0.24 ± .036	0.24 ± .64
Brain	0.014 ± .006	0.034 ± .013	0.037 ± .014	0.032 ± .018	0.046 ± .011

[1]Significantly different from casein diet (10%) protein $p \leq 0.001$.

diets containing 10% protein were adequate in preventing the increased cadmium uptake observed with low protein diets (Suzuki *et al.* 1969). Unfortunately, due to reasons discussed by Uthe and Chou (1979), the statistical analysis of spleen and brain could not be carried out. Relative to the casein (10% protein) diet, the cadmium uptake for the lobster hepatopancreas or porcine liver/kidney were 46% and 55%, respectively, for kidney and 64% and 77%, respectively, for liver.

   Interestingly the amount of free cadmium in lobster digestive gland and porcine liver/kidney were 45% and 43% of the total cadmium present in the canned preparation. It is tempting to speculate that the majority of the absorbed cadmium originates from this free cadmium component with a minor amount from the bound component. The bound component is probably metallothionein bound since this protein has been identified in mammals (Cherian and Goyer 1978) and shellfish (Talbot and Magee 1978), and Cherian (1979) has demonstrated that cadmium bound to metallothionein is not taken up by mice as efficiently as cadmium chloride. In addition, metallothionein-bound cadmium appears to be absorbed intact by the gut, which suggests that ingested metallothionein-bound cadmium may not be degraded by proteolytic enzymes and the low pH of the gastric contents. It has also been shown (Cherian and Goyer 1978) that metallothioneins are heat-stable proteins which could, therefore, be expected to survive the canning process to some degree.

STUDIES ON ARSENIC

   Relatively high levels of arsenic are known to occur in fish and shellfish from certain marine areas (Uthe *et al.* 1974; Chapman 1926). Levels over 100 μg arsenic per gram wet weight have been found in fish by our laboratory. In spite of the demonstration that most of this arsenic is present in an organic form (Edmonds *et al.* 1977; Freeman *et al.* 1979) and is rapidly eliminated (Chapman 1926; Coulson *et al.* 1935) in the urine following ingestion, we were concerned that, especially in highly loaded fish, significant amounts of toxic forms of arsenic such as inorganic arsenicals might be present. Concern was heightened following the demonstration (Uthe and Reinke 1975) that dead tissue rapidly reduces arsenate to arsenite, a more toxic form of the element (Uthe and Reinke 1975). To investigate this possibility a specific method for determining arsenate ion levels in fishery products was determined (Reinke *et al.* 1975) and a variety of fishery products analyzed (Table 9.5). During these investigations recovery studies utilizing organic arsenicals indicated that older methods of analysis such as dry ashing yielded low recoveries. Satisfactory recoveries were obtained with inorganic arsenicals by dry ashing. A wet digestion technique based upon vanadium pentoxide-catalyzed acid digestion was developed. By this method arsenic levels in fishery products averaged about 7% higher than those determined by dry ash techniques.

TABLE 9.5. DRY ASH VS. WET ASH METHODOLOGY FOR ARSENIC IN FISHERY PRODUCTS (μg As/g WET WEIGHT)

Species/tissue	Dry ash	Wet ash	Difference	(%)
Clams/shucked	2.51	2.70	0.19	(8)
Cod/muscle	3.60	3.75	0.15	(4)
Halibut/muscle	4.35	4.55	0.20	(8)
Lobster/tail muscle	4.65	4.95	0.30	(7)
Lobster/digestive gland	8.08	9.57	1.63	(20)
Haddock/muscle	6.25	6.67	0.42	(7)
Shrimp/tail muscle	34.8	37.3	2.5	(7)
Skate/muscle	32.6	34.0	1.4	(5)
Sole/muscle	13.0	13.1	0.1	(1)
Swordfish/muscle	0.95	1.04	0.09	(9)
Brook trout/muscle	1.17	1.26	0.09	(8)

Table 9.6 shows inorganic (arsenite + arsenate) arsenic levels in a variety of fish species. Generally, the levels of inorganic arsenic were below a predetermined detection level of 0.5 μg arsenic per gram wet weight, demonstrating that fishery products do not pose a serious threat based on the presence of inorganic arsenic. Only lobster digestive gland had measurable inorganic arsenic, and this at a level of less than 1 μg arsenic per gram wet weight. The elimination of arsenic in the urine following consumption of a normal fish meal was determined in six volunteers (Freeman *et al.* 1979). While we could demonstrate the rapid excretion of the bulk of the ingested arsenic (54–79% after 3 days), even after 9 days only 64–90% of the ingested arsenic was recovered in the urine. The large differences from individual to individual should be noted and warrants further careful investigation (e.g., to determine fecal excretion, respiratory excretion, etc.). We do not know that the arsenic is excreted in an unchanged form during the period of most concentrated excretion.

TABLE 9.6. TOTAL AND INORGANIC ARSENIC CONTENT OF FISHERY PRODUCTS (μg As/g WET WEIGHT)

Species tissue	Total arsenic	Inorganic arsenic
Clams shucked	1.8	0.5
Shrimp/tail muscle	3.9	0.5
Haddock/muscle	10.0	0.5
Crab/white meat	3.7	0.5
Mackerel/muscle	1.5	0.5
Herring/muscle	1.4	0.5
Lobster/tail muscle	40.5	0.5
Lobster/digestive gland	22.5	0.9

STUDIES ON LEAD

Large amounts of lead are introduced into the biosphere each year from anthropogenic sources. While the bulk of this is probably inorganic lead, tetraalkyl lead compounds have found widespread use as antiknock agents in gasolines. Airborne tetraalkyl lead levels in urban air have been determined (Purdue *et al.* 1973), and a recent study (Nielson and Jensen 1978) has demonstrated higher trialkyl lead levels (from tetraalkyl lead metabolism) in brains of individuals residing in lower floors of buildings in Copenhagen than those from individuals residing on upper floors or in the suburbs. This, coupled with the discovery of microbial methylation of lead to tetramethyl lead (Wong *et al.* 1975), led us to conclude that measurements of tetraalkyl lead concentrations in fish tissue were needed. Also the toxicity of alkyl leads in general is greater than that of inorganic lead (National Academy of Sciences 1972). Fish meal preparations containing bone and viscera residues could be expected to have relatively greater levels of lead than fish fillets, so these preparations were also investigated (Sirota and Uthe 1977) (Table 9.7).

TABLE 9.7.   TETRAALKYL LEAD/TOTAL LEAD RATIOS IN FISH AND SHELLFISH SAMPLES (μg Pb/g WET WEIGHT)

Species/tissue	R_4Pb	Pb total	Ratio (%)
Cod/liver	0.03 – 0.13	0.21 – 0.52	9 – 24
Mackerel/muscle	0.05	0.14	39
Lobster/digestive gland	0.16	0.20	80
Flounder/meal	4.8	5.3	91
Yellow perch/muscle (Lake Erie, Ontario)	0.01 – 0.22	0.07 – 0.48	13 – 77

Much to our surprise, rather large percentages of the total lead content of fishery product or tissue were often accounted for as tetraalkyl lead compounds. The amount of lead present as tetraalkyl lead compounds varied from 9 to 91%. Since the methodology for tetraalkyl lead does not determine the lower alkyl leads (Sirota and Uthe 1977), the total organolead levels in these tissues may be much higher. We have not determined bioavailability of leads in these fishery products in a manner analogous to cadmium. The degree of methylation of lead and the potential for alkylation of lead in the environment can be judged from the work of Harrison and Laxen (1978) who believe the high airborne tetraalkyl lead levels (percent of total) were associated with methylation occurring in coastal and estuarine mud flats containing anthropogenic lead.

CONCLUSION

What does all of this mean from the point of view of health regulatory agencies? These results illustrate that tolerances based on total elemental concentrations present in a foodstuff probably are no longer to be trusted. While historically such an approach can be justified due to advances in total elemental methodology compared to chemical speciation analysis, this rationale loses ground as better methods for chemical speciation become available. We have referred to techniques for determining certain species or classes of compounds of mercury, cadmium, arsenic, and lead. The methodologies described are not complicated nor overly tedious. They require instruments which find widescale applications in total elemental determination and are widely found in analytical laboratories (atomic absorption spectrophotometry and polarography, for example). We believe that regulatory agencies can now consider tolerances for certain chemical forms of toxic elements. This is especially demanding in such cases as certain fisheries products, where, although the total amount of a toxic element exceeds a set tolerance, research has demonstrated that the element is acting in a manner quite different than the elemental form and diet used in toxicological assessment.

REFERENCES

ARMSTRONG, F.A.J., and UTHE, J.F. 1971. At. Absorpt. Newsl. *10*, 101-103.

CHAPMAN, A.C. 1926. Analyst (London) *51*, 548–563.

CHERIAN, M.G. 1979. Environ. Health Persp. *28*, 127–130.

CHERIAN, M.G., and GOYER, R.A. 1978. Life Sci. *23*, 1–10.

CHOU, C.L., UTHE, J.F., and ZOOK, E.G. 1978. J. Fish. Res. Board Can. *35*, 409–413.

COULSON, E.J., REMINGTON, R.E., and LYNCH, K.M. 1935 J. Nutr. *10*, 255–270.

EDMONDS, J.S., FRANCESCONI, K.A., CANNON, J.R., RASTON, G.L., SKELTON, B.W., and WHITE, A.H. 1977. Tetrahedron. Lett. *18*, 1543–1546.

FAO/WHO Expert Committee on Food Additives. 1972. WHO Tech. Rep. Ser. No. 505.

FREEMAN, H.C., and UTHE, J.F. 1974. Geographical distribution of cadmium and arsenic in lobster *(Homarus americanus)* digestive gland *(hepatopancreas)*. ICES 62nd Statutory Meet., Copenhagen, International Council for the Exploration of the Sea, Charlottenlund, Denmark. Document E:16/1974.

FREEMAN, H.C., UTHE, J.F., and FLEMING, B. 1976. At. Absorpt. Newsl. *15*, 49–51.

FREEMAN, H. C., UTHE, J.F., FLEMING, R.B., ODENSE, P.H., ACKMAN, R.G., LANDRY, G., and MUSIAL, C. 1979. Bull. Environ. Contam. Toxicol. *22*, 224–229.

FRIEBERG, L., PISCATOR, M., NORBERG, G.F., and KJELLSTROM, T. 1974. Cadmium in the Environment, 2nd Edition. CRC Press, Cleveland, Ohio.

HARRISON, R.M., and LAXEN, D.P.H. 1978. Nature *275*, 738–740.

MAGOS, L. 1971. Analyst (London) *96*, 847–853.

NATIONAL ACADEMY OF SCIENCES. 1972. Lead: Airborne Lead in Perspective. National Academy of Sciences, Washington, DC.

NIELSON, T., and JENSEN, K.A. 1978. Nature *274*, 602–603.

PURDUE, L.J., ENRIONE, R.E., THOMPSON, R.J., and BONFIELD, B.A. 1973. Anal. Chem. *45*, 527–530.

REINKE, J., UTHE, J.F., FREEMAN, H.C., and JOHNSTON, J.R.   1975. Environ. Lett. *8*, 371–380.

SAKAMOTO, J.   1976.   Juzen Igakkai Zasshi *83*, 533–542.   (Fisheries and Marine Service Transl. Ser. No. 3674, Regional Library, Fisheries and Oceans, Canada, Halifax, Canada.)

SHUM, G.T.C., FREEMAN, H.C., and UTHE, J.F.   1979.   Anal. Chem. *51*, 414–416.

SIROTA, G.R., and UTHE, J.F.   1977.   Anal. Chem. *49*, 823–825.

SPIVEY FOX, M.R., JACOBS, R.M., LEE JONES, A.O., and FRY, B.E. 1979.   Environ. Health. Persp. *28*, 107–114.

SUZUKI, S., TAGUCHI, T., and YOKAHASI, G.   1969.   Ind. Health 7, 155–164.

TALBOT, V., and MAGEE, R.J.   1978.   Arch. Environ. Contam. Toxicol. 7, 73–81.

UTHE, J.F., and CHOU, C.L.   1979.   J. Environ. Sci. Health. A14, 117–134.

UTHE, J.F., FREEMAN, H.C., JOHNSTON, J.R., and MICHALIK, P.   1974. J. Assoc. Off. Anal. Chem. *57*, 1363–1365.

UTHE, J.F., and REINKE, J.   1975.   Environ. Lett. *10*, 83–88.

UTHE, J.F., SOLOMON, J., and GRIFT, B.   1972.   J. Assoc. Off. Anal. Chem. *55*, 583–589.

WELCH, R.M., HOUSE, W.A., and VAN CAMPEN, D.R.   1978.   Nutr. Rep. Int. *17*, 35–39.

WESTÖÖ, G.   1966.   Acta. Chem. Scand. *20*, 2131–2142.

WESTÖÖ, G.   1969.   *In* Chemical Fallout.   M.W. Miller and G.G. Berg (Editors), Chapter 5.   Elsevier, New York.

WONG, P.T.S., CHAU, Y.K., and LUXON, P.L.   1975.   Nature *253*, 263–264.

10

Carotenoid Pigments in Seafood

Kenneth L. Simpson

The quality of marine food products is the sum total of a number of factors. Of these, flavor would undoubtedly rank high on most consumers' lists. While flavor could be defined in terms of taste and aroma, in actual practice, it is defined much more broadly. Texture and color have always played a major role in the overall organoleptic properties which are, in practice, collectively termed "flavor." The color of a seafood product is the first characteristic noted by the consumer and is directly related to the subsequent acceptance or rejection of the product. In general, products have a standard of identity and must match what is expected. This is true of color as well as any of the other attributes of the seafood. The usual terms here are off-color, off-taste, and off-odor, which simply mean they are not "natural." Of course "natural" is defined by the consumer as what is natural to that consumer. Red duck egg yolks are natural to a consumer in the Philippines but would be considered off-color by some who expect a yellow or orange egg yolk.

Likewise, the consumer preference for a white- or yellow-skinned chicken, a white or brown eggshell, etc., rests on national or regional tradition and not on nutritional considerations. If the product is to be accepted in the market place, it must meet the consumer's expectations for color as well as other attributes.

The carotenoids are a group of pigments that contribute to the beautiful yellow, orange, and red colors found in the skin, shell, or exoskeleton of aquatic animals, and therefore in seafood products. Actually, they are the most widespread pigments found in nature, as they occur in bacteria, yeasts, mold, all green plants, and many animals. Our interest in this paper is the occurrence of carotenoids in the Mollusca (clam, oyster, scallop), Crustacea (crayfish, lobster, crab, shrimp), and fish (salmon, trout, sea bream, red snapper, tuna).

Department of Food Science and Technology, Nutrition and Dietetics, University of Rhode Island, Kingston, Rhode Island 02881

While the carotenoids are perhaps the most spectacular, they are certainly not the only pigments found in marine animals. The melanins are a broad group of pigments that are the end products of phenolic oxidation and polymerization and are responsible for the brown to black pigmentation found in the eyes, peritoneal lining, and exposed skin of aquatic animals. A list of fish-related pigments should also include the porphyrins, flavines, pterins, quinones, and omnochromes.

With the rapid increase of the world population and the limitation of the world's land resources, more thought has been given to the sea for added harvest, including the aquaculture of shrimp, lobster, salmon, and oysters, in impoundments rather than tracking and capturing them from boats. In many ways this aquaculture resembles agriculture more closely than it does fisheries in the sense that it depends on a management of the variables of production. In the fishery product the fisherman/processor is limited to minimizing quality losses of the product once fish are caught. In the case of the aquacultural product, many of the quality factors are directly related to diet. Thus the consumer expects a salmon to be some shade of red. However, salmon are red because they have consumed carotenoid-containing fish or shellfish and would be white without them. Likewise, salmon raised in aquaculture must also be fed these pigments in order to be pink or red.

One of the characteristics of animals is that they are unable to perform a *de novo* synthesis of the carotenoids. Bacteria, yeasts, molds, and higher plants can form these from acetate according to the scheme shown in Fig.10.1

Some important carotenoids are shown in Fig. 10.2. β-Carotene is a very common carotenoid, which is fortunate since it is a major source of

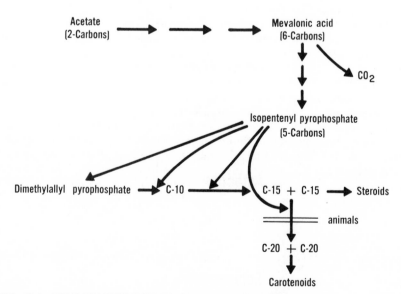

FIG. 10.1   BIOSYNTHETIC FORMATION OF CAROTENOIDS

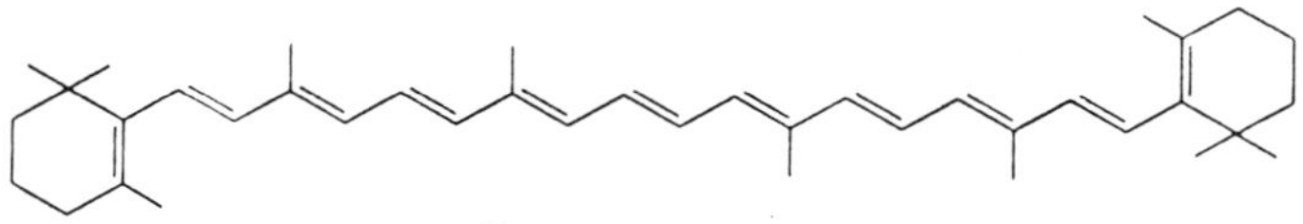

β-carotene

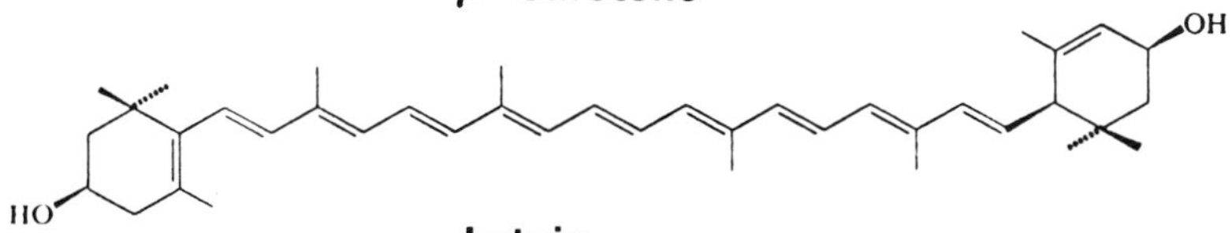

Lutein

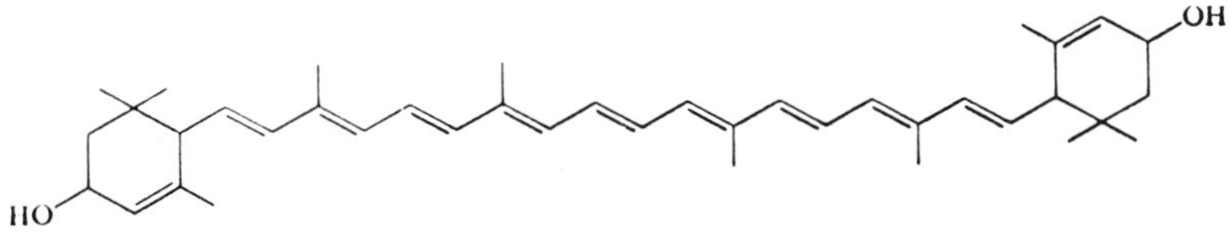

Tunaxanthin

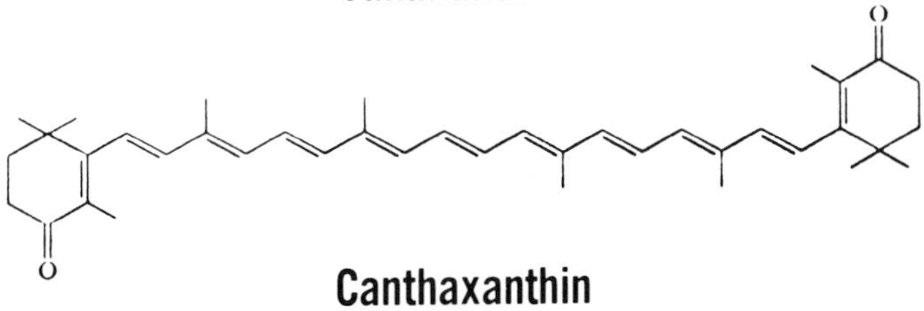

Canthaxanthin

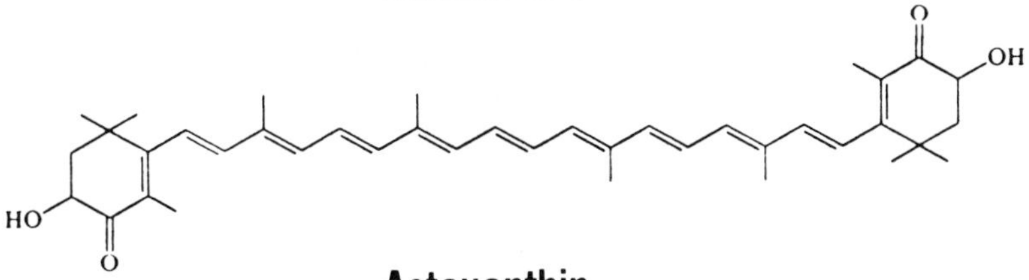

Astaxanthin

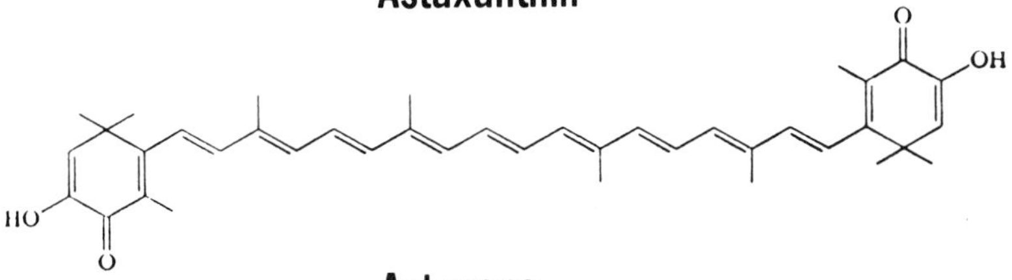

Astacene

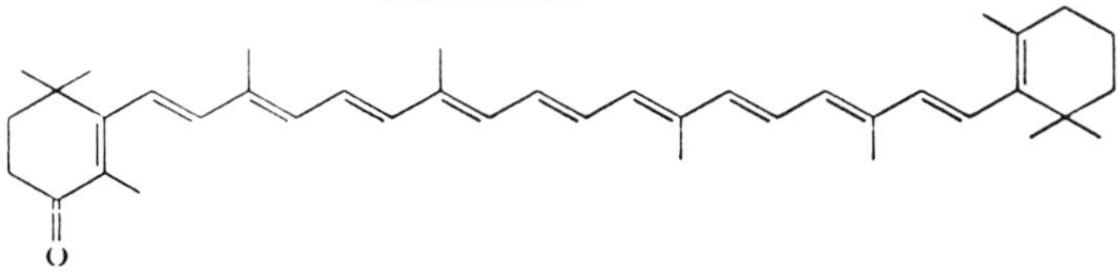

Echinenone

FIG. 10.2.   STRUCTURES OF SOME SEAFOOD CAROTENOIDS

vitamin A for animals. It is constructed from eight isoprene units, has two rings and is all trans. It is yellow in color and is the major pigment in such foodstuffs as butter and carrots. Lutein, also yellow, is widely found in green plants. It has no vitamin A activity to higher animals but may replace the vitamin A requirement of β-carotene in some fish. Lutein is a characteristic pigment of freshwater fish such as trout and carp. Tunaxanthin, first isolated from tuna, is more or less a characteristic pigment of marine fish. Astaxanthin is perhaps the most important marine pigment and is found in a very diverse group of sea animals, some of which are table items such as lobster, crab, shrimp, salmon, red snapper, and others.

Astacene is generally thought to be a breakdown product of astaxanthin. It has, however, been reported to occur in some fish and shellfish. Canthaxanthin has been isolated from a number of aquatic animals; it is available commercially and is widely used in food. With proper declaration, canthaxanthin can be included in the diet for salmon, trout, and other fish.

Carotenoids are named according to a trivial name system and an IUPAC system. The former usually describes the source of isolation and whether it contains (an) oxygen or is a hydrocarbon (i.e., tunaxanthin, isolated from tuna fish, contains oxygen; β-zeacarotene, isolated from corn, is a hydrocarbon). The IUPAC system is structurally based and best describes the 400 or so carotenoids that have been identified to date. In the case of a complicated structure such as fucoxanthin (brown from algae), however, two lines are required to define the structure.

It is necessary to consider the biosynthetic capability of the animal in aquaculturally raised seafood because of the fact that these animals vary significantly in their abilities to transform and deposit ingested carotenoids. As was mentioned above, animals are thought not to be capable of a de novo synthesis, thus any discussion of biosynthesis must, of necessity, be limited to alterations of the ingested carotenoids. These changes may involve conversion of one pigment to another or minor changes such as esterification of an alcohol with a fatty acid. Katayama et al. (1973) proposed that fish and shellfish be divided on the basis of their biosynthetic capabilities as follows.

1. Red carp type: can convert lutein, zeaxanthin or intermediates to astaxanthin, but β-carotene is not an efficient precursor of astaxanthin. Astaxanthin can be stored directly (goldfish, red carp, fancy red carp).

2. Sea bream type: cannot convert β-carotene, lutein or zeaxanthin to astaxanthin. Can transfer pigments from the diet to tissue pigments as free form or esterified (sea bream, red sea bream).

3. Prawn type: β-carotene is converted to astaxanthin. Generally crustaceans belong to this group.

Figure 10.3 shows the carotenoid conversions that have been postulated for red carp. Trout and salmon would best be listed under the sea bream type. Figure 10.4 shows the conversions that have been postulated for prawn.

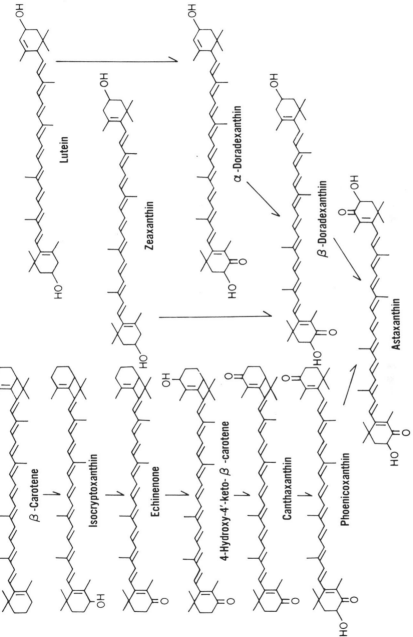

FIG. 10.3. POSTULATED CONVERSIONS FOR RED CARP TYPE FISH

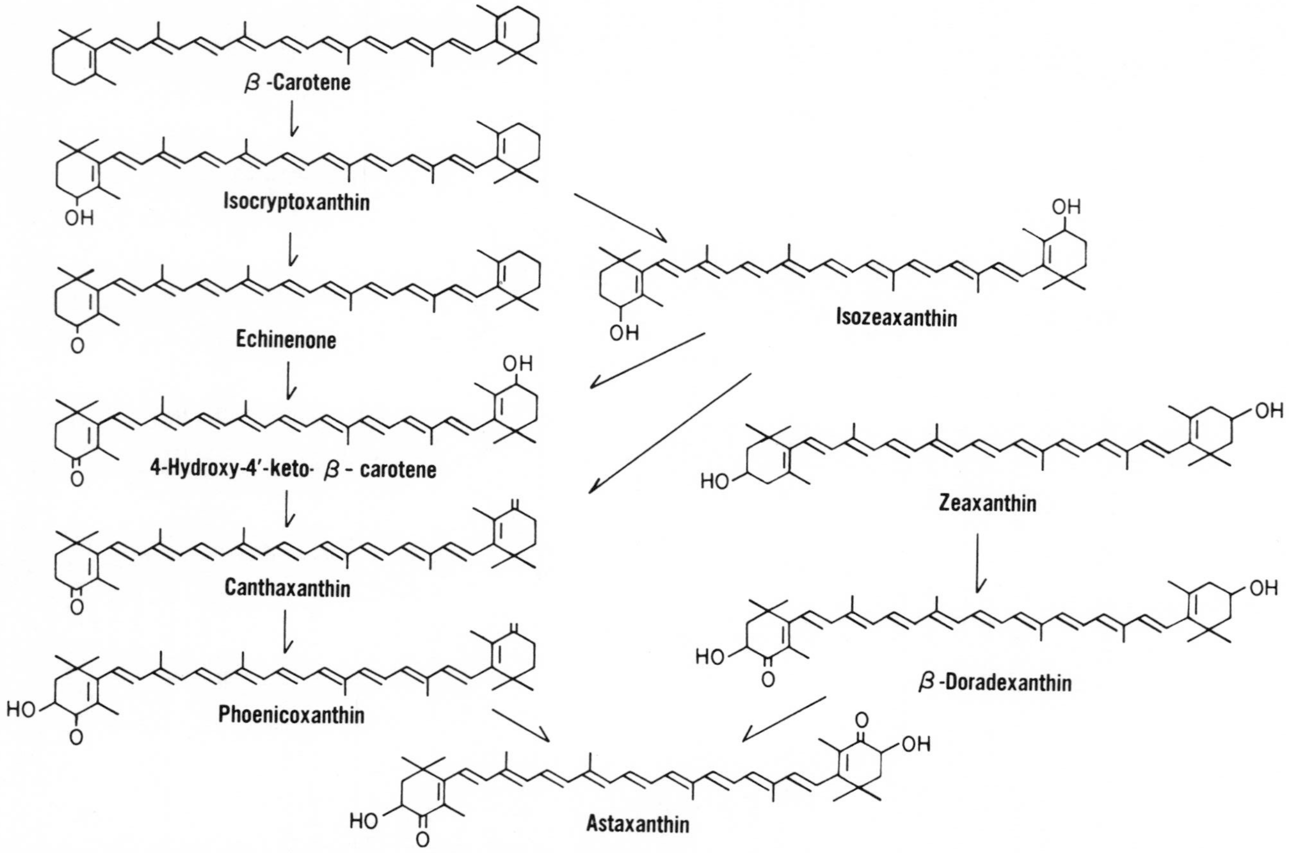

FIG. 10.4. POSTULATED CONVERSIONS FOR PRAWN TYPE FISH

It is important to consider the diet of the animal before concluding a biosynthetic capability since many carotenoids are deposited directly from the diet. The brine shrimp, while not currently a commercial seafood, illustrates the confusion that can arise in the literature over whether pigmentation is due to diet or biosynthesis.

The composition of brine shrimp has been reported to vary considerably depending on the investigator. Only echinenone and canthaxanthin were isolated by some authors (Krinsky 1965; Hata and Hata 1969; Hsu et al. 1969), while others (Czeczuga 1971; Czygan 1968) reported a much more complex carotenoid composition. It would appear to be clear, from the reports of Davis et al. (1970) and Hsu et al. (1969), that brine shrimp can convert β-carotene to echinenone to canthaxanthin. Yet Czeczuga (1971) reported the isolation of β-carotene, γ-carotene, echinenone, canthaxanthin, lutein, violaxanthin, and astaxanthin from brine shrimp cysts. More recently, Soejima et al. (1980) investigated the Artemia obtained from seven geographical areas. In all cases, only canthaxanthin and echinenone were isolated. The total pigment level varied, but the basic ratio of canthaxanthin:echinenone was about 95:5. When Artemia nauplii were fed various extracts or pure pigments, a combination of biosynthesis and pigment absorption became apparent.

Table 10.1 shows the relative carotenoid composition of Rhodotorula yeast. Table 10.2 shows the effect of feeding these pigments to brine shrimp. Torularhodin, a pigment characteristic of red yeast but never reported in brine shrimp, was isolated from the shrimp. The increase in echinenone and canthaxanthin was probably due to the β-carotene in the extract. Table 10.3 shows the effect of feeding pure astaxanthin. The only effect noted is the appearance of astaxanthin in the shrimp. Table 10.4 shows the composition of the algae, Spirulina. The extract was fed to brine shrimp (Table 10.5) and led to an increase in β-carotene, echinenone, and zeaxanthin in the shrimp. On removal of the pigments from the diet, it can be seen that the precursors to canthaxanthin were quickly metabolized. Several generalizations can be made to illustrate the situation in seafood. Artemia accumulate a number of xanthophylls which they cannot biosynthesize. These pigments tend to be lost at a higher rate than natural pigments. Other pigments such as β-carotene can be absorbed and converted to more complex compounds. Thus, care should be exercised in the construction of biosynthetic pathways

TABLE 10.1.   THE CAROTENOID COMPOSITION OF THE YEAST (Rhodotorula)

Carotenoids	Relative abundance (%)
β-Carotene	8.51
γ-Carotene	0.92
Torulene	30.54
Torularhodin	57.87
Unknown	2.16
Total: 69.3 μg/g dry wt.	

Source: Soejima et al. (1980).

TABLE 10.2. THE AMOUNTS OF ECHINENONE, CANTHAXANTHIN, AND TORULARHO-
DIN PRESENT IN *Artemia* AFTER FEEDING WITH PIGMENTS OF THE YEAST *(Rhodotorula)*

Feeding program[1]	Concentration of carotenoids present (µg/g fresh wt.)			
	Echinenone	Canthaxanthin	Torularhodin	Unknown
Group 1	0.11	5.87		
Group 2	0.86	6.25	1.20	0.40
Group 2'	0.82	6.04	0.96	

Source: Soejima *et al.* (1980).
[1]Group 1: rice bran only (12 days); group 2: rice bran + pigments of *Rhodotorula* (6 days);
group 2': same as group 2, then rice bran only (6 days).

TABLE 10.3. THE AMOUNTS OF ECHINENONE, CANTHAXANTHIN, AND ASTAXAN-
THIN PRESENT IN *Artemia* AFTER FEEDING WITH ASTAXANTHIN

Feeding program[1]	Concentration of carotenoids present (µg/g fresh wt.)		
	Echinenone	Canthaxanthin	Astaxanthin
Group 1	0.11	5.87	
Group 3	0.20	5.92	2.11
Group 3'	0.16	5.80	1.80

Source: Soejima *et al.* (1980).
[1]Group 1: rice bran only (12 days); group 3: rice bran + astaxanthin (6 days); group
3': same as group 3, then rice bran only (6 days).

TABLE 10.4. THE CAROTENOID COMPOSITION OF
THE ALGAE *(Spirulina)*

Carotenoids	Relative abundance (%)
β-Carotene	25.38
Echinenone	3.08
β-Cryptoxanthin	2.03
Zeaxanthin	65.30
Unknown	4.21
Total: 547.2 µg/g dry wt.	

Source: Soejima *et al.* (1980).

TABLE 10.5. THE AMOUNTS OF β-CAROTENE, ECHINENONE, CANTHAXANTHIN,
AND ZEAXANTHIN PRESENT IN *Artemia* AFTER FEEDING WITH PIGMENTS OF
Spirulina

Feeding program[1]	Concentrations of carotenoids present (µg/g fresh wt.)				
	β-Carotene	Echinenone	Canthaxanthin	Zeaxanthin	Unknown
Group 1		0.11	5.87		
Group 4	0.71	3.16	6.97	2.71	0.13
Group 4'	0.19	1.48	6.58	1.99	

Source: Soejima *et al.* (1980).
[1]Group 1: rice bran only (12 days); group 4: rice bran + pigments of *Spirulina* (6 days);
group 4': same as group 4, then rice bran only (6 days).

based on simple isolations. It is not surprising that on occasion we see a
yellow trout or salmon. They may be considered "unnatural" but can be
explained by diet studies.

The degradation of carotenoids is of extreme importance to seafood. In the case of aquaculturally raised fish, the quantity and quality of the carotenoids in the diet are of importance, as is the maintenance of color in the product. Figure 10.5 diagrams some changes which can occur in carotenoids. These changes can range from slight shifts in color, in the case of cis/trans isomerization, to loss of color in the presence of strong light, lipoxygenase, or drying conditions.

The carotenoids have long been known to be a substrate for lipoxygenase-type enzymes. Tsukuda and Amano (1966, 1967, 1968) observed that discoloration of red fish occurred at refrigeration temperatures in the dark, and that homogenates from the skin muscle and liver were able to degrade astaxanthin, tunaxanthin, and β-carotene to colorless compounds. These authors isolated and partially purified a heat-labile lipoxygenase-like enzyme from the skin of red fish, *Sebastes thompsoni* and *Chelidonichthys kumu*. The enzyme discolored tunaxanthin in the presence of linoleic and linolenic acids.

Figure 10.6 shows the effect of irradiating β-carotene with a sun lamp with and without added antioxidants. Fortunately, natural antioxidants occur in seafood and the effect seen in a pure solution of β-carotene is more dramatic than it would be, for example, in a salmon steak.

The major degradation step in industry is that of the drying of fish or fish meals and subsequent storage. Lambertsen and Braekkan (1971) analyzed the astaxanthin content of some shrimp meals (Table 10.6). It can be seen that the astaxanthin content ranged from 76 μg/g for a vacuum-dried sample to complete destruction for some industrial samples. Simpson *et al.* (1976) (Table 10.7) reported on the composition of the carotenoids in shrimp meal before and after tray drying (70°C, 12 hr). Again, there is a very dramatic reduction in all carotenoids. While the shrimp meal was red, it contained only small amounts of astaxanthin and astacene.

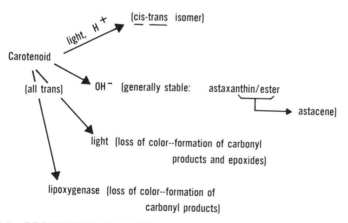

FIG. 10.5.   DEGRADATION OF CAROTENOIDS

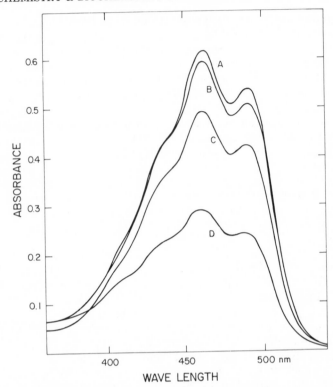

FIG. 10.6.   IRRADIATION OF β-CAROTENE WITH AND WITHOUT ANTIOXIDANTS
A, β-carotene in toluene; B, β-carotene with 0.1% BHA irradiated for 30 minutes with a 275 watt sunlamp 8–12 inches away; C, same with 0.1% BHT; D, same without antioxidant.

Spinelli (1978) gives a graphic presentation of the co-drying under vacuum of euphausids with shrimp waste. The carotenoid retention at 100 min was greatest (ca. 40 mg/100 g) with added soy oil and ethoxyquin, less with only oil (25 mg/100 g), and still lower with just the crustacean mixture (20 mg/100 g). The co-dried mixture with soy oil containing ethoxyquin produced a product that was described as free flowing and easy to mill.

TABLE 10.6.   ASTAXANTHIN CONTENT OF SOME SHRIMP MEALS

Sample	Astaxanthin (μg/g)	% as diester
Industrial meals		
A	8.9	82.0
B	3.9	82.8
C	0.0	
Unknown, of foreign origin		
A	24.5	84.9
B	16.3	89.9
C	12.8	86.8
Vacuum dried		
A	76.2	77.0

Source: Lambertsen and Braekkan (1971).

TABLE 10.7. COMPOSITION OF CAROTENOIDS IN SHRIMP MEAL BEFORE AND AFTER DRYING

Carotenoids	Before drying (μg/g dry basis)	After drying
3,3'-Dihydroxy-ε-carotene	1.36	
Echinenone	0.25	
Isocryptoxanthin	0.38	
Canthaxanthin	0.39	
4-Keto-4'-hydroxy-β-carotene	0.74	
Dihydroxypiradixanthin (?)	4.66	
Lutein	trace	
Zeaxanthin	trace	
Astaxanthin ester	66.1	10.3
Astacene	55.4	6.26
Astaxanthin	7.19	trace

Source: Simpson et al. (1976).

The carotenoids in seafood products or feed for aquaculturally raised products need to be protected from excessive heat and pH conditions, and exposure to light, oxygen, and lipid degrading enzymes. Astaxanthin is perhaps the major pigment in seafood and also one that is very unstable. It is interesting that it occurs in so many diverse species in nature. Table 10.8 shows some selected examples of the appearance of astaxanthin in representative species.

Table 10.9 lists the carotenoid content of some selected fish and shellfish of economic or potential economic value as seafood. A few generalizations can be made. (1) Lutein is a common pigment in freshwater fish and tunaxanthin is usually isolated from marine fish. (2) Although the tissue was not listed for each species, astaxanthin was often reported as occurring as the mono- or diester in the skin, and in the free form in the flesh. (3) The listings are, in some cases, a composite from several authors. (4) In common with other animals, the occurrence of a carotenoid may or may not indicate biosynthetic activity.

Within recent years there has been an upsurge of interest in the commercial culture of marine and freshwater animals. In some countries the need exists for a good protein source while in others the demand for luxury items such as trout, salmon, and shrimp exceeds the supply. It is a mistake to think of fish farming or aquaculture as a recent invention. Fish farming has been practiced for many generations, and carp raising, in particular, has been known for centuries and is now practiced in Europe, Israel, and Asian countries. In addition, milk fish, catfish, trout, prawn, and shrimp are being produced in fish farms.

In Japan there are some very impressive prawn cultures as well as research facilities.Since 1963 more than 15 farms have been established using over 100 hectares of discarded salt beds or sandy inlets (Deshimaru and Shigeno 1972). It has been estimated that more than 100,000 tons of aquatic animals are produced each year including trout, sea bream, prawn, red sea bream, crab, lobster, goldfish, carp, and fancy red carp.

Pan-sized salmon are now being produced in floating pens off the coast of the northwestern United States, Maine, and elsewhere.

TABLE 10.8. THE OCCURRENCE OF ASTAXANTHIN IN NATURE

Sources	Species
Bacteria	*Micrococcus erythromyxa, M. rhodochrous, Mycobacterium lacticola*
Yeast	*Phaffia phodozyma*
Algae	*Haemotoccus pluvialis, Sphaerella nivalis, Euglena heliorubescens, Trachelomonas volvocina*
Plant	*Adonis aestivalis*
Spongiaria	*Axinella crista-galli*
Coelenterates	
1. Scyphomedusae	*Aurelia aurita*
2. Anthozoa	*Paragorgia aborea, Primnoa resedae formis, Lophelia petusa, Alcyonium digitatum, Pennatula phosphorea, Allopora californica, Distichopora coccinea, Stylaster elegans, Actina equina, Metridium senile*
Polychaetes	*Branchiomna vesiculosum, Nereis zonata, Eudistylia polymorpha, Megalomma vesiculosum, Protula intestinum, Sabella pavonina*
Mollusca	*Lima excavata*
Crustacea	
1. Branchipoda	*Branchinecta packardi, B. paludosa, Daphnia magna, Branchipus stagnalis, Chirocephalus diaphanus, Tanymasti lucunae*
2. Copepoda	*Artodaptomus salinus, Diaptomus castor, Hemidiaptomus amblyodon, Argulus foliaccus, Labidocera acutifrons*
3. Cirripeda	*Chthamalus fragilis, Elimius modestus, Lepas anatifera, L. fascicularis, L. pectinata, Pollicipes polymerus*
4. Malacostraca	*Aristeus antennatus, Astacus astecus, A. leptodactylus, Betaeus harfordi, Carcinus manenas, Clibanarius misanthropus, Hyale perieri, Nephrops norvegicus, Orconectes limosus, Pachygrapus marmoratus, Panulirus japonicus, Penaeus japonicus, P. setiferus, Portunus trituberculatus, Potamon edulis*
Echinoderma	
1. Asteroidea	*Asterias rubens, Asterina panceri, Asteropectin auranticus, Echinaster sepositus, Marthasterias glacialis*
2. Holothuroidea	*Psolus fabrichii*
Tunicata	*Pendrodoa grossularia, Halocynthia papillosa*
Fish	*Carassius auratus, Salmo salar, S. trutta, S. gairdneri, Oncorhynchus gorbuscha, O. keta, O. masou, O. tschawytscha, Clupea harengus, Evynnis japonica, Chrysophrys major, Cyprinus carpio Linne, Epinephelus fasciatus, Parasilurus asotus, Sebastes baramenuke, Salmo alpinus, Salvelinus fontinalis, Perca fluviatilis*
Insects	*Locusta migratoria, Nomadacris septemfasiata, Schistocea gregaria*
Reptiles	*Clemmys insculpata retina*
Birds	*Bombycilla cedrorum, Phasianus colchius, Coconia ciconia, Larus sidibundus*
Mammals	*Balaenoptera musculus*

Source: Karrer and Jucker (1950); Brinchmann (1967); Simpson *et al.* (1981).

TABLE 10.9.   CAROTENOID CONTENT OF SEAFOOD SPECIES

Source	Common name	Carotenoids
CRUSTACEA		
Carcinus maenas	Green crab	β-Carotene, γ-carotene, lutein, zeaxanthin, echinenone, canthaxanthin, astaxanthin
Crangon crangon	Sand shrimp	β-Carotene, lutein, zeaxanthin, canthaxanthin, astaxanthin
Geryon quinquidens	Red crab	Astaxanthin, zeaxanthin, β-doradexanthin
Homarus gramarus	Lobster	Astaxanthin
Panulirus japonicus	Spiny lobster	β-Carotene, β-zeacarotene, isocryptoxanthin, 4-hydroxy-echinenone, echinenone, astaxanthin, 3-hydroxy-canthaxanthin, β-doradexanthin
Penaeus japonicus	Shrimp	β-Carotene, echinenone, canthaxanthin, astaxanthin, phoenicoxanthin, tunaxanthin, lutein, zeaxanthin, dihydroxy-piradixanthin
P. setiferus	White shrimp	Cryptoxanthin, astaxanthin
Pleuroncodes planipes	Red crab	β-Carotene, astaxanthin
Portunus trituberculatus	Blue Crab	Canthaxanthin, 4-hydroxy-echinenone, 3-hydroxy-canthaxanthin, astaxanthin, β-carotene, echinenone, isocryptoxanthin
Procambarus clarkii	Red crayfish	β-Carotene, echinenone, astaxanthin, phoenicoxanthin
MOLLUSCA		
Veneus japonica	Short-necked clam	β-Carotene
Meretrix lusoria	Hard clam	β-Carotene, lutein, zeaxanthin
Mytilus edulis	Mussel	β-Carotene, lutein, zeaxanthin, astaxanthin, mytiloxanthin, isomytiloxanthin
Octopus vulgaris	Octopus	Tunaxanthin
FINFISH		
Ambloplites rupestris	Sunfish	Lutein
Auxis thazard	Mackerel	Tunaxanthin, zeaxanthin
Centrophorus squamosus	Shark	Carotenoids present
Chrysophrys major	Sea bream	Zeaxanthin, α-carotene, tunaxanthin, lutein, α-doradecin, astaxanthin, β-carotene
Clupea hargenus	Atlantic herring	Astaxanthin, canthaxanthin, lutein
C. pallasii	Pacific herring	Tunaxanthin, lutein, zeaxanthin, α-cryptoxanthin
Cyprinus carpio	Red carp	Lutein, astaxanthin
Engraulis japonica	Anchovy	Zeaxanthin, diatoxanthin, cynthiaxanthin, lutein
Etrumeus micropus	Sardine	Tunaxanthin, lutein
Evynnis japonica	Red sea bream	Canthaxanthin, lutein, astaxanthin
Lepomis cyanellus	Sun fish	Lutein
Oncorhynchus gorbuscha	Pink salmon	Astaxanthin
O. keta	Chum or dog salmon	Astaxanthin

(Continued)

TABLE 10.9.   *(Continued)*

Source	Common name	Carotenoids
O. kisutch	Coho salmon	Astaxanthin
O. masou	Cherry salmon	Astaxanthin
O. nerka	Sockeye salmon	Astaxanthin
O. tschawytscha	Chinook salmon	Astaxanthin
Parasilurus asotus	Catfish	Lutein, astaxanthin
Plecoglossus altirelis	Sweet smelt	Lutein, astaxanthin
Salmo gairdneri= S. irideus	Rainbow trout	Astaxanthin, canthaxanthin, β-carotene, lutein
S. trutta= S. fario	Sea trout Brown trout	β-carotene, canthaxanthin, astaxanthin, lutein
S. salar	Atlantic salmon	Astaxanthin, canthaxanthin, lutein, zeaxanthin
Salvelinus fontinalis	Brook trout	Lutein, astaxanthin, canthaxanthin
Sardinops melanosticta	Sardine	Tunaxanthin, lutein, zeaxanthin
Scomber japonicus	Japanese mackerel	Tunaxanthin, lutein
Sabastes tompsoni	Rock fish	Astaxanthin, tunaxanthin
Sabastodes eos	Sabastodes	Astaxanthin, zeaxanthin, tunaxanthin
Spirinchus lanceolatus	Smelt	Zeaxanthin, cryptoxanthin, diatoxanthin, lutein
Sprattus sprattus	Sprat	Astaxanthin, canthaxanthin, tunaxanthin,
Theragra chalcogramma	Alaska pollock	Tunaxanthin, lutein, zeaxanthin
Thunnus albacares	yellowfin tuna	Tunaxanthin
T. thynnus orientalis	Pacific bluefin tuna	Tunaxanthin

Source: Simpson *et al.* (1981).

Growing shrimp and crayfish in ponds is now practiced in some countries and shrimp are grown from egg to market size. Intensive lobster culture has not yet become a reality because of the problems associated with high density rearing. The shrimping industry in the United States commands about a quarter of the value of the catch of the fishing industry and the consumption in the United States has averaged about one million pounds per day.

The U.S. crayfish industry, located mainly in southern Louisiana, produces about 10 million pounds valued in excess of 5 million dollars. While it is probable that pond-reared crustaceans will not replace the natural harvest, they certainly will be a valuable supplement, particularly during certain times of the year.

As was stated above, all of these organisms, if they are to be cultured, must have carotenoids in their diet if their standard of identity involves pigmentation. The type of pigmentation would depend on the biosynthetic capability of the organism and the hue of the pigments. For example, Meyers and Rutledge (1971) discussed the value of using shrimp meal as a crustacean food and stressed the importance of quality control in its production if the pigments are to be utilized by crustaceans. A number of authors have reported on the use of various carotenoid sources for the pigmentation of freshwater and marine fish and shellfish. Some selected references are presented in Table 10.10. It can be seen that this selected list shows a wide variety of carontenoid preparations that have been tried in an effort to obtain the proper pigmentation. In actual fact, none of these carotenoid sources is entirely satisfactory. In many cases, the hue was incorrect, the sample was not stable, inert material was included or the mineral balance was altered.

I would like to describe three feeding experiments in some detail because of some points that need to be stressed. Deufel (1965) described a trout feeding study with canthaxanthin. Table 10.11 details these studies. It can be seen that canthaxanthin is readily absorbed by the trout and the flesh takes on a red hue. The feeding was at a rate of 40 mg/kg of feed. A beneficial spawning and fertilization rate was noted for the inclusion of canthaxanthin in the diet. There are, however, problems with canthaxanthin. First, the hue is redder than salmon color and the color tends to cook out. Second, although canthaxanthin is approved for food usage, it still must be declared. While canthaxanthin is commonly used in Europe for salmonids, its use is

TABLE 10.10.   SOURCES OF CAROTENOIDS FED TO FISH AND SHELLFISH

Organism	Carotenoid source	Author
Trout	*Pleuroncodes planipes*, red crab	Spinelli (1975)
	Shrimp waste, crab waste	Saito and Regier (1971)
	Crayfish	Peterson *et al.* (1966)
	Euphausia pacifica	Spinelli (1978)
	Geryon quinquidens, red crab	Kuo *et al.* (1976)
	Shrimp protein coagulum	Simpson *et al.* (1976)
	Paprika pepper	Peterson *et al.* (1966)
	Aesculus sp., pollen	Neamtu *et al.* (1976)
	Synthetic canthaxanthin	cf. Simpsim *et al.* (1981)
	Natural and synthetic astaxanthin	Simpson and Kamata (1978); Torrissen and Braekkan (1978)
	Tagetes erecta, marigold	Lee *et al.* (1978)
	Cucurbita maxima, squash flower	Lee *et al.* (1978)
	Hyppophae rhamnoides oil	Kamata *et al.* (1977)
	Adonis flowers	T. Kamata and K.L. Simpson (unpublished)
Salmon	*Phaffia rhodozyma*, yeast	Johnson *et al.* (1977)
	Shrimp waste	*Ellis (1978); Steel (1971)*
	Pleuroncodes planipes	Spinelli (1975)
Macrobrachium rosenbergii	Shrimp oil	Joseph and Williams (1975)
Penaeus japonicus	Corn gluten, alfalfa	
	Spirulina	
	Zeaxanthin	Tanaka *et al.* (1976)
Lobster	*Phaffia rhodozyma*	Johnson *et al.* (1977)
Sea Bream	*Haematococcus*, algae	Nakazoe and Hata (1978)

TABLE 10.11. TISSUE CAROTENOID CONTENT OF CONTROL AND
CANTHAXANTHIN FED FISH

Feeding period (weeks)	Carotenoid content (mg/100 g)	
	Canthaxanthin	Total carotenoids
Control series		
8	0.0	0.067
16	trace	0.078
24	trace	0.078
Canthaxanthin series		
8	0.034	0.126
16	0.080	0.209
24	0.124	0.238

Source: Deufel (1965).

somewhat restricted in the United States due to the fact that fish must be labeled "artificially colored."

The problems associated with the pigments of crustacean wastes have been discussed above. In 1975, a Sea Grant project was initiated at the University of Rhode Island to work with a deep sea red crab processing plant. Whole crab waste diets and crab waste extracts were prepared.

Kuo et al. (1976) fed rainbow trout on a diet composed of 20% freeze-dried crab waste and a 0.2 mg/g of carotenoid extract diet for various periods. The crab waste was obtained from a plant processing deep sea red crab, *Geryon quinquidens*.

Fish were sacrificed after 15- and 23-week feeding periods (small fish) and 4-week feeding periods (large fish). The fish fed on the 20% crab meal diet had a red rainbow streak and faintly pink-colored flesh, whereas the control fish had a grayish-white flesh and no clear rainbow streak. The nutrient contents of the commercial feed were not the same as those of the 20% crab meal diet. These diets could only be compared on the basis of color since initial efforts to feed the casein control diet failed. The control fish were found to be slightly bigger than the crab meal-fed fish. Crab meal-fed fish as well as the controls exhibited similar mortality rates over the feeding period.

In the control fish, small amounts of lutein ester, trace amounts of α-cryptoxanthin and a few unidentified carotenoids were found. The experimental fish had a mean weight of 34 g per fish after 15 weeks (2.21 g total carotenoids per fish) and 51 g per fish after 23 weeks (3.162 g total carotenoids per fish) of feeding on the 20% crab meal diet (15.4 g crude pigment per gram of diet). Astaxanthin ester, free astaxanthin, and astacene were isolated from these fish. In addition, the plant pigment lutein ester was also isolated (Table 10.12). The amount of total carotenoids per gram of fish was almost the same in the fish after 15- and 23-week feeding periods (0.065 and 0.062 μg total carotenoids per gram, respectively). Larger fish (132 g) were fed the 20% crab meal diet to assess the effect of size on the uptake of carotenoids from the crab meal. After 4 weeks the control (167 g) and the crab meal-fed fish (165 g) had increased in size, but the level of astaxanthin was the same as in the smaller fish (Table 10.12). A strict comparison

TABLE 10.12. CAROTENOID CONTENT OF FISH FED 20% CRAB WASTE DIET

	Concentration of Carotenoids (μg/g)				
Pigments	Control[1] diet 15 weeks	Crabmeal diet 15 weeks	Crabmeal diet 23 weeks	Control[2] diet 4 weeks	Crabmeal diet 4 weeks
Total astaxanthin	—	0.051	0.052	—	0.056
Zeaxanthin	—	—	—	0.26	0.23
Lutein	0.052	0.014	0.01	0.33	0.26
Canthaxanthin	—	—	—	0.01	trace

[1] 25 g fish at the beginning of the experiment.
[2] 132 g fish at the beginning of the experiment.

between the two lots of fish is difficult because of the residual levels of plant carotenoids contained in the fish. It was apparent that this whole red crab meal was not a good source of carotenoids for trout (Spinelli 1978).

Large fish (85 g and 132 g) were fed commercial trout pellets on which pigment extracts (0.1 and 0.2 mg/g diet) were adsorbed. After 4 or 7 weeks (Table 10.13) on this experimental diet, the trout had strong orange-pink flesh and fins and a vivid red streak on the skin, whereas the control trout flesh remained grayish-white in color and only a faint yellow-orange streak was present on the skin. The pigmented diet-fed fish as well as the controls exhibited a similar mortality rate over the feeding periods.

The fish in this study were of a nearly uniform size at the start of the feeding experiments. After a 4-week adaption period on a control diet and a 7-week period on the pigmented diet, the fish went from an average weight of 85 g to a range of 90 to 172 g. The color of the flesh ranged from a faint pink to a strong orange-pink. The large fish contained the greatest concentration of pigment. The fish clearly obtained astaxanthin from the diet.

The ratios of astaxanthin and astaxanthin ester were different in three sets of pigmented trout analyzed (Table 10.13). This suggested that rainbow trout *(Salmo gairdneri)* had the ability not only to absorb the crab pigment but also to make some changes in the pigment with regard to esterification, and then deposit it depending on their own genetic characteristics.

A second experiment was run with larger fish (132 g with 0.1 mg/g diet) over a 4-week period (Table 10.14). The final average weights of the five fish sets were 167 g for the control and 169 g for the extract-fed fish. The larger fish were found to be rapidly pigmented over the 4-week period with 0.1 mg/g of carotenoid content added to the feed.

TABLE 10.14. CAROTENOIDS IN THE RAINBOW TROUT FED ON 0.1 mg/g DIET FOR 4 WEEKS[1]

	Concentration (μg carotenoid/g)	
	Control	0.1 mg/g
Total astaxanthin	—	0.88
Zeaxanthin	0.26	0.21
Lutein	0.33	0.27
Canthaxanthin	0.013	0.008
α-Cryptoxanthin	trace	trace

[1] Initial weight: 132 g; final weight: 167−169 g.

TABLE 10.13. CAROTENOIDS OF RAINBOW TROUT WHICH WERE FED ON PIGMENTED DIET (0.2 mg CAROTENOIDS/g DIET) FOR SEVEN WEEKS

Experiment	No. of fish	Wt. per fish (g)	Color of flesh	Astaxanthin ester	Main carotenoids (μg/g fish)[1]				
					Astaxanthin	Astacene	Lutein ester	Lutein
1	2	91.5	Faint pink	0.5	0.3	0.18	1	trace
2	2	115	Pink	1.1	0.39	0.20	0.1	0.08
3	1	172	Strongly orange-pink	0.61	1.57	0.09	0.56	0.02

[1]The concentration of carotenoids was calculated in saponified forms.

A third study compared the effect of using marigold flowers and squash flowers as carotenoid sources for rainbow trout (Lee *et al.* 1978). Rainbow trout were fed diets consisting of 10 mg% pigment extracts from marigold flowers *(Tageta erecta)* and squash flowers *(Cucurbita maxima)* for 8 weeks. The squash flower was selected because it is an underutilized pigment source whose value had been compared to marigold meal, a current source of pigment for poultry. Lutein represented over 90% of the carotenoid distribution of the marigold flower and zeaxanthin, lutein, and cryptoxanthin over 75% of the carotenoid content of the squash flower. Although the quantity of pigment was much greater in the marigold flower, both extracts were fed at the same level of carotenoids.

During the 8-week period, weight gain between the three treatments was similar and histological examinations showed no adverse or pathological effects on the control or meal-fed fish.

The marigold-fed fish developed a golden yellow color, whereas the squash flower-fed fish were pale like the controls. It was noted, however, that the level of chlorinated hydrocarbons in the squash flower was very high (Table 10.15), and so was that found in the fish fed squash flowers (Table 10.16). The squash flower was imported into the United States from areas where DDT and other chemicals are used. The high level of chlorinated hydrocarbons would limit its use as a pigment source for trout as well as for poultry. This illustrates the need to consider critically all aspects of the food in any feeding program. The color and taste are important, but attention also needs to be drawn to adventitious compounds that may be added to food.

In 1979, Coduri *et al.* (1979) applied vertical plate gel electrophoresis to the separation of the sarcoplasmic extracts of pigmented and nonpigmented trout and salmon species. The fish included brown, brook, and rainbow trout and chinook and coho salmon. It was shown that the trout and salmon species could easily be distinguished regardless of the pigmentation levels. Thus a pink trout could be readily identified as trout and not as pink salmon.

Ostrander *et al.* (1976) compared the preference of a trained sensory panel and a consumer panel for trout and pen-reared, pan-sized salmon. The

TABLE 10.15.   PESTICIDES AND PCB CONTENT (ppm) IN DIETS

Pesticides and PCBs	Control	*Tagetes*	*Cucurbita*
HCB	—	—	—
PCBs	0.07	0.02	0.11
trans-Chlordane	—	—	—
cis-Chlordane	0.01	—	—
Aldrin	—	—	—
o,p'-DDE	—	—	0.02
p,p'-DDE	0.03	0.03	0.37
o,p'-DDT	—	0.01	2.01
p,p'-DDD	—	0.1	0.35
p,p'-DDT	—	0.02	3.89
Dieldrin	0.01	—	—
Toxaphene	—	—	—

Source: Lee *et al.* (1978)

results indicated that without such clues as color and size, a trained panel could not distinguish the taste of trout and pen-raised, pan-sized salmon. A consumer panel listed color by itself or in conjunction with other factors such as size and shape as the most important difference between salmon and trout flesh (Table 10.17).

TABLE 10.16. PESTICIDE AND PCB CONTENT (ppm) IN RAINBOW TROUT FED WITH CONTROL AND TEST DIETS FOR EIGHT WEEKS

Pesticides and PCBs	Control	*Tagetes*	*Cucurbita*
HCB	—	—	—
PCBs	0.08	0.03	0.04
trans-Chlordane	0.02	0.01	0.03
cis-Chlordane	0.04	0.02	0.04
Aldrin	—	—	—
o,p-DDE	—	—	—
p,p-DDE	0.04	0.02	0.03
o,p-DDT	—	0.02	0.43
p,p-DDD	0.01	0.01	0.03
p,p-DDT	0.02	0.03	0.66
Dieldrin	—	—	—
Toxaphene	—	—	—

Source: Lee *et al.* (1978).

TABLE 10.17. FACTORS LISTED BY CONSUMERS AS IMPORTANT DIFFERENCES IN SALMON AND TROUT SAMPLES

Factor	% of Responses
None given	39.8
Color	22.6
Flavor	14.1
Size	6.3
Color, size, and shape	6.2
Others (e.g., shape, texture)	11.0

Source: Ostrander *et al.* (1976).

CONCLUSION

We have established that food standards of identity are very real in the minds of consumers. Of the "flavor" characteristics, color plays a major role in whether a food is accepted or rejected and often serves to identify that food. In many cases, the price of the seafood is directly related to the color; salmon is often priced according to the intensity of its hue, whereas blue prawn (or red prawn on the Japanese market) is judged according to the hue itself. The seafood marketing procedures must be such that the color is maintained in quality and quantity since the carotenoid pigments are easily destroyed. The aquaculturist seeking to market products competing with the "caught" product must provide the right pigments for the organism in order to satisfy the consumer's expectation.

ACKNOWLEDGMENT

This work was supported by grant No. 04-6-158-44085 of the National Oceanic and Atmospheric Administration, Office of Sea Grant, U.S. Department of Commerce, and Rhode Island Agricultural Experiment Station contribution No. 1934.

REFERENCES

BRINCHMANN, H.J.   1967.   Pigmentation of pond-reared fish. Tech. Univ. Norway, Inst. for Tech. Biochem. Rep. Translated by P.M. Jangaard, Fisheries and Environmental Sciences, Halifax Laboratory, Halifax, Nova Scotia, Canada, 1976.

CODURI, R.J., JR., BONATTI, K., and SIMPSON, K.L.   1979.   J. Assoc. Off. Anal. Chem. 62, 269−271.

CZECZUGA, B.   1971.   Comp. Biochem. Physiol. B 40, 47−52.

CZYGAN, F.C.   1968.   Z. Naturforsch. Teil B 23, 1367−1368.

DAVIES, B.H., HSU, W-J., and CHICHESTER, C.O.   1970.   Comp. Biochem. Physiol. 33, 601−615.

DESHIMARU, O., and SHIGENO, K.   1972.   Aquaculture 1, 115−133.

DEUFEL, J.   1965.   Arch. Fischereiwiss. 16, 125−132.

ELLIS, J.N.   1978.   Proc. World Symp. Fin Fish Nutrition and Feed Technology II, 353−364, Hamburg, West Germany.

HATA, M., and HATA, M.   1969.   Comp. Biochem. Physiol. 29, 985−994.

HSU, W-J., CHICHESTER, C.O., and DAVIES, B.H.   1969.   Comp. Biochem. Physiol. 32, 69−79.

JOHNSON, E.A., CONKLIN, D.E., and LEWIS, M.J.   1977.   J. Fish. Res. Board Can. 34, 2417−2421.

JOSEPH, J.D., and WILLIAMS, J.E.   1975.   Proc. Annu. Meet. World Maric. Soc. 6, 147−155.

KAMATA, T., NEAMTU, G.G., and SIMPSON, K.L.   1977.   Rev. Roum. Biochim. 14, 253−258.

KARRER, P., and JUCKER, E.   1950.   Carotenoids. Elsevier Publ. Co., New York. 384 pp.

KATAYAMA, T., KUNISAKI, T., SHIMAYA, M., SIMPSON, K.L., and CHICHESTER, C.O.   1973.   Comp. Biochem. Physiol. B 46, 269−272.

KRINSKY, N.I.   1965.   Comp. Biochem. Physiol. 16, 181−187.

KUO, H.-C., LEE, T.-C., KAMATA, T., and SIMPSON, K.L.   1976.   Alimenta 15, 47−51.

LAMBERTSEN, G., and BRAEKKAN, O.R.   1971.   J. Sci. Food Agric. 22, 99−101.

LEE, R.G., NEAMTU, G., LEE, T.-C., and SIMPSON, K.L.   1978.   Rev. Roum. Biochim. 15, 287−293.

MEYERS, S.P., and RUTLEDGE, J.E.   1971.   Feedstuffs 43(49), 31−32.

NAKAZOE, J., and HATA, M.   1978.   Proc. 53rd Meet. Jpn. Soc. Sci. Fish. Abstr. 558.

NEAMTU, G., WEAVER, C.M., WOLKE, R.E., and SIMPSON, K.L.   1976. Rev. Roum. Biochim. *13*, 25–30.

OSTRANDER, J., MARTINSEN, C., LISTON, J., and MCCULLOUGH, J. 1976.   J. Food Sci. *41*, 386–390.

PETERSON, D.H., JÄGER, H.K., SAVAGE, G.M., WASHBURN, G.N., and WESTERS, H.   1966.   Trans. Am. Fish Soc. *95*, 408–414.

SAITO, A., and REGIER, L.W.   1971.   J. Fish Res. Board Can. *28*, 509–512.

SIMPSON, K.L., and KAMATA, T.   1978.   Proc. World Symp. Fin Fish Nutrition and Fish Feed Technology *II*, 415–424. Hamburg, West Germany.

SIMPSON, K.L., KAMATA, T., COLLINS, J.G., and COLLINS, J.H.   1976. Proc. Trop. and Subtrop. Fish. Tech. Conf., Corpus Christi, Texas, pp. 395–411.

SIMPSON, K.L., KATAYAMA, T., and CHICHESTER, C.O.   1981.   Carotenoids in fish feeds. *In* Carotenoid Color Technology. J.C. Bauernfeind (Editor). Academic Press, New York.

SOEJIMA, T., KATAYAMA, T., and SIMPSON, K.L.   1980.   *In* The Brine Shrimp—Artemia, Vol. 2. G. Persoone, P. Soorgeloos, O. Roels, and E. Jaspers (Editors). pp. 613–622. Universa Press, Wetteren, Belgium.

SPINELLI, J.   1975.   Improved fish feed. Pacific Technologist Meeting, Portland, Oregon.

SPINELLI, J.   1978.   Proc. World Symp. Fin Fish Nutrition and Fish Feed Technology *II*, 383–392. Hamburg, West Germany.

STEEL, R.E.   1971.   M.S. Thesis, Oregon State University, Corvallis, Oregon.

TANAKA, Y., MATSUGUCHI, H., KATAYAMA, T., SIMPSON, K.L., and CHICHESTER, C.O.   1976.   Bull. Jpn. Soc. Sci. Fish. *42*, 197–202.

TORRISSEN, O., and BRAEKKAN, O.R.   1978.   Proc. World Symp. Fin Fish Nutrition and Fish Feed Technology *II*, 377–382. Hamburg, West Germany.

TSUKUDA, N., and AMANO, K.   1966.   Bull. Jpn. Soc. Sci. Fish. *32*, 344–345.

TSUKUDA, N., and AMANO, K.   1967.   Bull. Jpn. Soc. Sci. Fish. *33*, 962–969.

TSUKUDA, N., and AMANO, K.   1968.   Bull. Jpn. Soc. Sci. Fish. *34*, 633–639.

11

Chemical Changes of Trimethylamine Oxide During Fresh and Frozen Storage of Fish

Joe M. Regenstein, Mary Anne Schlosser,
Allan Samson, and Michael Fey

With the extension of jurisdiction for fishing along our coast to 200 miles, it is hoped the United States has begun a new era of fisheries development. In the past few years, the United States has finally begun to recognize the full potential of our coastal fishing resources. Unfortunately, many of the most common food fish found along the coasts of the United States and Canada have been overfished. Only with proper management will these waters again provide abundant harvests of these fish. But even now, these waters are not devoid of fish; many other species of fish inhabit these waters—the so-called underutilized species. (They used to be called "trash" fish, but one cannot ask a person to eat "trash" fish.)

Why are these fish underutilized? The problems are numerous, but among the major underlying reasons are poor names and lack of consumer familiarity, special handling and processing problems, and a large number of bones, or bones in places that make traditional filleting of these fish difficult. The first problem is being dealt with by the National Marine Fisheries Service (NMFS) through a special program to have fish identified for the consumer both by a regular species name and by terms that indicate the organoleptic characteristics of the fish. Attempts are also being made to standardize nationwide the name for each species of fish.

The last problem can be dealt with by the use of mechanical deboners which separate the meat from the bones to produce a product called "minced fish." This can be used as the starting material for many fine fish and meat

[1]Departments of Poultry Science and Food Science and Institute of Food Science, Cornell University, Ithaca, New York 14853

products. Our research group has been actively involved in this area of research. One of us (J.M.R.) reviewed our work in this area at the Torry Jubilee Conference in Aberdeen, Scotland, in July 1979 (Regenstein 1979) and some research findings presented by others at that meeting will also be reported in this chapter.

In dealing with minced flesh of certain saltwater species of fish (particularly red hake), we encountered special handling and processing problems. Deboning accelerates unfavorable changes that, occurring in both fresh and frozen fish, seem to be related to the chemistry of trimethylamine oxide. Solution to this problem is especially necessary if some of the underutilized species are to be more widely used for further processed products. The chemistry of the TMAO breakdown products, then, is the topic of this chapter.

Red hake *(Urophycis chuss)* is widely available in the northwestern Atlantic and has been identified by the New York fishing industry as a major underutilized fish of concern. Other hakes such as white hake, silver hake (whiting), and pacific hake also are all relatively underutilized. They belong to the larger family of gadoid fish *(Gadidae)*, which include such commercially important species as cod, haddock, and pollock. Like their more popular cousins, the underutilized gadoid fish have white flesh that could, in principle, be used for fish sticks, portions and cakes, and possibly even fresh and frozen fillets. Red hake has the species-specific problem of softening relatively rapidly compared with other gadoids which also show this problem during fresh storage. It leads to a particularly stringent requirement for good handling of the fish before processing. The exact cause of this change is not known.

The TMAO chemistry of all gadoid fish in both fresh and frozen storage seems to be similar. (We will not deal with smoking, pickling, etc.) The structure of trimethylamine oxide (TMAO) is shown in Fig. 11.1. The breakdown of TMAO has been implicated in the spoilage of both fresh and frozen fish. There are a number of different ways of expressing the concentration of TMAO and its various breakdown compounds such as trimethylamine (TMA), dimethylamine (DMA), and formaldehyde (FA). For this paper we have tried to convert all of the data to millimoles or μmoles of the

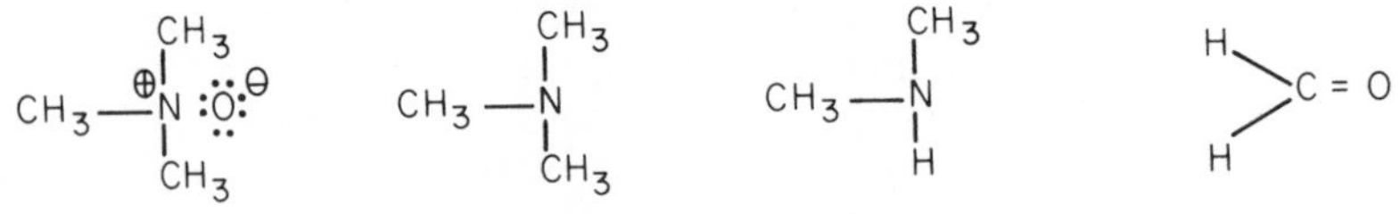

	Trimethylamine Oxide (TMAO)	Trimethylamine (TMA)	Dimethylamine (DMA)	Formaldehyde (FA)
M.W.	75	59	45	30
%N	18.6	23.7	31.1	0

FIG. 11.1. TRIMETHYLAMINE OXIDE AND ITS BREAKDOWN PRODUCTS

compound per 100 grams of fish tissue. By dealing in μmoles, the amounts of all compounds can be compared directly. These points are listed in Table 11.1. Typical values for the TMAO content of various fish are shown in Table 11.2.

Found in most species of marine fish, TMAO is particularly high in the gadoid and the elasmobranch (sharks, etc.) families. TMAO apparently is a part of the system used for osmoregulation of these fish (Love 1970). TMAO is not found in freshwater fish to any great extent, and those species of marine fish that can migrate into freshwater lower their TMAO content to almost zero when in freshwater. The amount of this compound present in the fish seems to show all of the biological variability so common in fish chemistry, i.e., changes due to species, stock area, time of year. Thus, reported levels of TMAO in fish may only be indicative of the state of the fish at the time of analysis.

Apparently, TMAO also is a part of the body's normal buffer system (Farber 1965). It is water-soluble and a part of the nonprotein nitrogen fraction. Caution should be exercised here because, analytically, it is counted as part of the total nitrogen in a crude protein determination by the Kjeldahl method. The high nitrogen content of TMAO and its breakdown products can lead to a serious overestimation of the protein content of the fish meat.

The amount of TMAO present in various tissues of cod, Alaska pollock, and Japanese hake have been measured (Amano and Yamada 1965). Table 11.3 shows the values for some cod muscle tissues. Unfortunately, the table does not include a value for either blood or kidneys, both of which appear to be important for the reactions of interest, though it is not clear whether these tissues supply the enzyme, cofactors, and/or the substrate. Some researchers (e.g., Tokunaga 1974) have found that dark muscle has a higher TMAO level, as well as a higher lipid content, than light muscle. Others claim TMAO is higher in white muscle.

TABLE 11.1.   VARIOUS WAYS TO EXPRESS TMAO AND ITS BREAKDOWN PRODUCTS

1 mg TMAO-N	= 5.38 mg TMAO	= 72 μmoles
1 mg TMA-N	= 4.22 mg TMA	= 72 μmoles
1 mg DMA-N	= 3.22 mg DMA	= 72 μmoles
	2.16 mg FA	= 72 μmoles

TABLE 11.2.   TMAO CONTENT OF VARIOUS SPECIES OF FISH

Fish	millimoles TMAO/100 grams
Cod	7.9−10.8
Haddock	4.3− 5.8
Hake	10.0−13.3
Pollock	5.8− 6.8
Mackerel	2.9− 3.9
Flounder	3.2− 7.2

TABLE 11.3.   TMAO CONTENT OF VARIOUS ORGANS
OF COD

	millimoles TMAO/100 grams
Skin	3.0
Surface Muscle	7.6
Deep Muscle	13.2
Stomach	0.9
Ovary	1.6

Once a fish is slaughtered or dies, various postmortem changes take place due to the breakdown of the cellular structure and biochemistry, and to the growth of microorganisms that are either associated naturally with the fish or that become part of the flora because of contamination during handling.

With fresh fish, the microbiological changes are often the most important. Cold-water fish have a largely naturally occurring population of cold-loving (psychrotrophic) bacteria. Since these are the major organisms responsible for spoilage of flesh foods, cold-water fish are considered particularly prone to spoilage, especially if cooled improperly. In addition, because of the lower sanitation standards for fish as compared with other flesh foods, especially aboard ship, the possibilities of contamination are quite great. Again psychrotrophic bacteria are a major part of the flora involved in spoilage.

Many gram-negative psychrotrophic bacteria have the capability of using TMAO. Watson (1939) suggested that, below the surface and even within rapidly growing bacterial colonies, conditions are anaerobic. Whether these organisms are only able to use TMAO under anaerobic conditions remains to be proved. Certainly many of these organisms are facultative anaerobes and can grow in the absence of molecular oxygen. It should also be noted that, in general, iron tends to stimulate the growth of these gram-negative bacteria (Weinberg 1978). The bacterial reaction using TMAO is

$$AH_2 + (CH_3)_3NO \longrightarrow A + (CH_3)_3N + H_2O$$

One explanation for spoilage indicates that the major species of bacteria initially present on fish and capable of reducing TMAO to TMA is *Achromobacter* (cf. Laycock and Regier 1970; Lee *et al.* 1967). However, the production of significant amounts of TMA from TMAO does not occur immediately, suggesting that the *Achromobacter* are not using TMAO at that time. Rather there is a lag period of 3–4 days until a rapid production of TMA is observed. By the time this spoilage reaction occurs, the dominant organism apparently is *Pseudomonas putrefaciens*, which may represent as much as 80% of the TMA-producing flora. Some authors (cf. Reay and Shewan 1949) have suggested that the initial lack of spoilage is due to an inhibition of the bacteria by rigor mortis. However, it might be more useful to try to understand what specific factors permit the pseudomonads to take over from the achromobacters and what factors (conditions) are necessary for pseudomonads to use TMAO.

Trimethylamine is a volatile compound and has a very low odor threshold. Ikeda (1979) at the Torry Conference presented a table that included odor thresholds, and part of that table is shown in Table 11.4. TMA is associated with the fishy odor of spoilage and is clearly a part of the spoilage pattern of many fish species. However, the bacterial flora and the cellular processes produce other odoriferous compounds that are also a part of the total spoilage picture (cf. Shaw and Shewan 1968; Castell and Greenough 1957).

TABLE 11.4. ODOR THRESHOLDS

	ppb
Ammonia	110,000
DMA	30,000
TMA	600

What do we know about the bacterial enzymes involved in producing TMA?

1. The enzyme involved will also use compounds such as triethylamine oxide, $(CH_3CH_2)_3NO$, and tripropylamine oxide, $(CH_3CH_2CH_2)_3NO$, as substrates, and thus has been called a triamineoxidase.
2. The apparent function of the enzyme is to activate the substrate so that a dehydrogenase in the bacterial cell can then act on the substrate.
3. A number of compounds can serve as a hydrogen source. Two compounds that probably are physiologically important are lactic acid and pyruvic acid:

$$CH_3CHOHCO_2H + TMAO \longrightarrow CH_3COCO_2H + TMA + H_2O$$
Lactic Acid   Pyruvic Acid
$$CH_3COCO_2H + TMAO + H_2O \longrightarrow CH_3CO_2H + CO_2 + TMA + H_2O$$
       Acetic Acid

(It should be noted that the normal end-product of glycolysis in postmortem flesh is lactic acid, which does accumulate in the fish tissues.)

Interestingly enough, following the spoilage of the fish, the pseudomonads decrease to a fraction of the total flora and the *Achromobacter* return to be the dominant culture. The rise in pH and the possible inhibitory effect of TMA may both be part of the cause for a decrease in the pseudomonads. It certainly seems that a further study of the interactions (ecology) of *Achromobacter* and pseudomonads might give valuable insights into fish spoilage.

From the practical point of view, how do we maintain fresh fish quality? Certainly, the inhibition of microbial growth is critical. With longer shelf life, one then may have to do something about the many other biochemical changes that might be taking place in the fish itself.

Many methods and principles have been applied to the maintenance of fresh fish quality. One of the most successful technically was the use of antibiotics. However, antibiotics were never approved by the regulatory agencies. Certainly in light of the problems associated with their use, even in animal feed, hindsight suggests that the fish industry was lucky they were not used. Other chemicals have been used to lower the pH of the fish surface to discourage bacterial growth. A number of such acid treatments have been patented. Psychrotrophs grow best in the pH 6.5–7.5 range (Reay and Shewan 1949). Temperature itself can decrease bacterial growth. Bacteria have been reported to grow at as low as −6.5°C on fish (Reay and Shewan 1949). Yet, if freezing is to be avoided, fish cannot be cooled to more than −1 to −2°C. However, Castell et al. (1973) have suggested that bacteria do not produce TMA below 0°C. Others suggest minimum temperatures for TMA production are between 0 and −6°C.

Another approach to bacterial control has been to change the atmosphere surrounding the fish either by continuous control of the atmosphere (controlled atmosphere), by adding a specific atmospheric mixture to a sealed container (modified atmosphere), or by lowering the total amount of atmosphere present (i.e., vacuum or hypobaric storage). Carbon dioxide has been a particularly effective compound for reducing the growth of most spoilage bacteria. However some bacteria such as the lactobacillus have been reported to grow and to cause a sweet–sour type of spoilage in chicken.

Other compounds such as potassium sorbate may also be tested. Potassium sorbate may play a significant role in the future of the meat and poultry industry as a partial replacement for nitrite. It has recently been reviewed and again designated as a "generally recognized as safe (GRAS)" compound. It is antimicrobial as well as antimycotic. Its specific properties of interest to us in fisheries are its activity against Clostridium botulinum, pseudomonads, and lactobacillus. We have found that the combination of 1°C, 60% CO_2, and ice containing potassium sorbate significantly extends the shelf life of both red hake and salmon. These conditions could be maintained during commercial shipping. A detailed presentation of these results was given at the Atlantic Fisheries Technological Conference at Danvers, Massachusetts (cf. Fey and Regenstein 1982). We have kept fish using the carbon dioxide–potassium sorbate mixture and served them successfully to our taste panel after as much as 1 month of storage.

One experimental note: In comparing hypobarics, controlled and modified atmospheres, and other possible forms of shelf-life extension, we think that it is important that we compare, with the same fish samples, the various techniques against each other rather than just against controls. The costs of the various shelf-life extension procedures will also have to be evaluated before selecting the best conditions for a particular application.

Turning now to freezing, we see that TMAO again undergoes chemical changes that affect the keeping quality of the fish. The reaction is

$$TMAO \longrightarrow DMA + FA$$

There apparently is an enzyme present in some species of fish (Watson 1939; Amano and Yamada 1964; Yamada and Amano 1965) that is able to carry out this reaction. Spinelli and Koury (1979) have also observed that this reaction takes place nonenzymatically at higher temperatures. Spinelli believes that some free amino acids (e.g., cysteine) and their breakdown products may be substrates for the nonenzymatic reaction. They are found in large quantities in gadoids. Heat may destroy the enzymes producing the substrates for this reaction. Red hake seems to produce the highest levels of DMA and FA (Castell et al. 1971) among the fish species studied. The amount produced seems to be higher in the dark muscle than in the white muscle (Dyer and Hiltz 1974).

Unfortunately, the actual enzyme for the reaction has not been isolated to date. Thus, many of the enzyme's properties are extrapolated from analyses of crude preparations. We are assuming in this discussion that both enzymatic and nonenzymatic pathways can exist at low temperatures, but it is clear that more work is needed to clarify this important area, and certainly isolation of the enzyme would be a big step forward.

The kidneys seem to be particularly rich in this enzyme (or the components for this reaction), and the presence of the enzyme in muscle (flesh) tissue is weakly documented. Interestingly, haddock does not seem to have this enzyme (Gill et al. 1979). TMA appears to inhibit the enzyme (Tomioka et al. 1974). The enzyme is active down to about -29°C (cf. Castell et al. 1973, 1974; Dyer and Hiltz 1974; Dyer 1973; Hiltz et al. 1976). Unfortunately cold stores in this country don't usually go that low. In some species (at least in hake), the reaction can take place at temperatures somewhat above 0°C (Castell et al. 1973; Amano and Yamada 1964), but in other species it only seems to occur below 0°C.

It is not clear whether or not the reaction (or both reactions) in the frozen state is freeze- or cold-activated. It may simply have the normal temperature dependence of an enzyme, but only with frozen storage do we give the reaction enough time to occur to a measurable extent.

The enzyme is reported to be inactivated at 80°C. The pH maximum is around 6.1 in the enzyme from Alaska pollock at 26°C. The other points studied on either side of pH 6.1 were pH 5.4 and pH 7.0, thus making it hard to pinpoint the actual maxima (Yamada and Amano 1965).

An interesting set of experiments was reported by Svensson (1979) of the Swedish Food Institute. He confirmed that the kidney enzyme is destroyed at 80°C. However, if an aqueous muscle extract is then added, activity is restored, even though the extract itself has no activity. Fractionation of the extract indicates that the fraction that passes through a nominal 2000 MW cut-off ultrafiltration membrane has the restorative property. Furthermore, this enzyme-restoring property is lost by heating the extract fraction to 80°C. Other workers have reported a low molecular weight, non-heat denaturable cofactor. It has also been suggested that ferrous iron accelerates this reaction (Tomioka et al. 1974; Castell 1971).

The formaldehyde formed during the enzyme reaction is postulated to be involved in many reactions that lead to a crosslinking of the proteins. A typical reaction leading to a methylene bridge is

$$R\text{-}H + CH_2O \longrightarrow R\text{-}CH_2(OH)$$
$$R\text{-}CH_2(OH) + H\text{-}R' \longrightarrow R\text{-}CH_2\text{-}R' + H_2O$$

Much is known about the chemistry of formaldehyde and its reaction with individual amino acids (cf. Galembeck *et al.* 1977). It should be noted that malonaldehyde, a breakdown product from the oxidation of free fatty acids, may also react similarly with proteins.

The chemical changes of the proteins lead to a decrease in drip loss but to an increase in the expressible moisture of a system. The flesh has a dry and spongy feel. On cooking, the fish meat is unsatisfactory. Initially the material releases a large amount of water and then is very dry upon subsequent chewing. Panelists can identify this property, but unless special care is taken, some will call the material very juicy while others will call it very dry (Bremner 1977). (Our laboratory has tried to distinguish carefully between expressible moisture—moisture present that is removed by centrifugation or pressing—and water-holding capacity—water a material will hold in a centrifugal force when *excess* moisture has been added.)

In a recent paper, Gill *et al.* (1979) tried to show that formaldehyde added to fish muscle led to changes in the electrophoretic pattern of the fish muscle proteins that became similar to that found after prolonged storage. However, the experiment involved a complex extraction of the muscle so that the validity of the changes observed is difficult to determine.

Two papers at the Torry Conference dealt with the problem of the change in extractability of gadoid fish muscle proteins over time. Mathews and co-workers (1979) at Unilever, United Kingdom, looked at the whole muscle and Matsumoto and co-workers (Tsuchiya *et al.* 1979) from Japan looked at myosin and natural actomyosin. Taken together, their results suggested to us that the postmortem changes occur in three steps:

1. A series of "conformation–configurational" changes of an unspecified nature that leads to a decrease in the high salt extractable protein nitrogen. Although the extractability loss is in the myofibrillar protein fraction, it is not clear what changes in the muscle are responsible for this loss of extractability. An effort has been made to follow these changes electrophoretically, but without correcting for the amount of protein present, it is very difficult to interpret the observed patterns.
2. The formation of new disulfide bond crosslinks. These were suggested by the changes in the electrophoretic and solubility patterns in the presence and absence of mercaptoethanol.
3. The formation of a new conformation which required both mercaptoethanol and urea to restore the original pattern. This suggests that all of the covalent crosslinks are sulfhydryl bonds or that the formaldehyde crosslinks can be broken by either urea or mercaptoethanol. The latter seems highly unlikely.

A more detailed analysis of the changing gel patterns with time as was done by Rattrie and Regenstein (1977) may help clarify some of the ambiguity that exists at this time. It is also possible that these changes may not have been followed long enough. Independent measurements of the changes of both the texture and of the amines will have to be carefully correlated with the gel results.

It should be noted that a key basis for suggesting the participation of formaldehyde in the observed changes is that formaldehyde disappears long before DMA. The formation of modified amino acids even in the absence of crosslinking may be sufficient to explain the observed changes.

From a practical point of view, how does one stop this reaction? Clearly, very cold temperatures are one way. Another way, particularly with minced fish, might be to wash out the substrate TMAO. This can be done but requires extra processing and results in a loss of materials into the wash. The fish could be cooked first. We have successfully done this and the cooked product can be used in some further processing. One could also try to stop the enzyme or the reaction by chemical means, which is being studied in our lab. One could also try to modify the processing procedures so that the enzyme or substrate or their coming together is minimized. For example, a more extensive removal of the kidneys and the blood before mincing might help. One could also try to prevent the reaction of formaldehyde with the proteins. All of these are possible in principle; but more research, some of which we have begun, is needed in order to sort out the best possibilities from both economic and food quality standpoints. Thus, a better understanding of both the frozen storage and fresh changes in TMAO may make a significant contribution to the better utilization of our fisheries resources.

ACKNOWLEDGMENTS

The research work reported from our laboratory was carried out with the financial assistance of the New York Sea Grant Institute, Sea-Land Services, Inc. and Monsanto Industrial Chemicals, Inc. Material support was provided by the Cryovac Division of W.R. Grace and Co.

REFERENCES

AMANO, K., and YAMADA, K. 1964. A biological formation of formaldehyde in the muscle tissue of gadoid fish. Bull. Jpn. Soc. Sci. Fish. *30*, 430–435.

AMANO, K., and YAMADA, K. 1965. The biological formation of formaldehyde in cod flesh. *In* The Technology of Fish Utilization. Rudolph Kreuzer (Editor), pp. 73–78. Fishing News (Books) Ltd., London.

BREMNNER, H.A. 1977. Storage trials on the mechanically separated flesh of three Australian mid-water fish species. 1. Analytical Tests. Food Technol. (Aust.) *29*, 89–93.

CASTELL, C.H.   1971.   Metal-catalyzed lipid oxidation and changes of proteins in fish.   J. Am. Oil. Chem. Soc. 46, 645–649.

CASTELL, C.H., and GREENOUGH, M.F.   1957.   The action of Pseudomonas on fish muscle: 1.   Organisms responsible for odours produced during incipient spoilage of chilled fish muscle.   J. Fish. Res. Board Can. 14, 617–625.

CASTELL, C.H., SMITH, B., and NEAL, W.   1971.   Production of dimethylamine muscle of several species of gadoid fish during frozen storage, especially in relation to presence of dark muscle.   J. Fish. Res. Board Can. 28, 1–5.

CASTELL, C.H., NEAL, W.E., and DALE, J.   1973.   Comparison of changes in trimethylamine, dimethylamine, and extractable protein in iced and frozen gadoid fillets.   J. Fish. Res. Board Can. 30, 1246–1248.

CASTELL, C.H., SMITH, B., and DYER, W.J.   1974.   Simultaneous measurements of trimethylamine and dimethylamine in fish and their use for estimating quality of frozen-stored gadoid fillets.   J. Fish. Res. Board Can. 31, 383–389.

DYER, W.J.   1973.   New technical research on frozen fish.   Refrigeration (Tokyo) 48, 38–41.   (Transl. from Japanese by Fish. Mar. Serv. Transl. Ser. No. 2656, 1973).

DYER, W.J., and HILTZ, D.F.   1974.   Sensitivity of hake muscle to frozen storage.   Department of Environment, Halifax Lab., New Ser. Circ. 45.

FARBER, L.   1965.   Freshness tests.   In Fish as Food, Vol. IV.   Processing: Part 2.   Georg Borgstrom (Editor), pp. 65–126.   Academic Press, New York.

FEY, M.S., and REGENSTEIN, J.M.   1982.   Extending shelf-life of fresh red hake and salmon using CO_2–O_2 modified atmospheres and potassium sorbate ice at 1°C.   J. Food Sci.   In press.

GALEMBECK, F., RYAN, D.S., WHITAKER, J.R., and FEENEY, R.E.   1977.   Reaction of proteins with formaldehyde in the presence and absence of sodium borohydride.   J. Agric. Food Chem. 25, 238–245.

GILL, T.A., KEITH, R.A., and SMITH LALL, B.   1979.   Textural deterioration of red hake and haddock muscle in frozen storage as related to chemical parameters and changes in the myofibrillar proteins.   J. Food Sci. 44, 661–667.

HILTZ, D.F., SMITH, L.B., LEMON, D.W., and DYER, W.J.   1976.   Deteriorative changes during frozen storage in fillets and minced flesh of silver hake (Merluccius bilinearis) processed from round fish held in ice and refrigerated sea water.   J. Fish. Res. Board Can. 33, 2560–2567.

IKEDA, S.   1979.   Other organic components and inorganic components.   In Advances in Fish Science and Technology, J.J. Connell et al. (Editors), pp. 226–232.   (Jubilee Conf. Torry Res. Station, Aberdeen, Scotland, July 1979).   Fishing News Books Ltd., Farnham, Surrey, England.

LAYCOCK, R.A., and REGIER, L.Q.   1970.   Pseudomonads and Achromobacters in the spoilage of irradiated haddock of different pre-irradiation quality. Appl. Microbiol. *20*, 333–334.

LEE, J.S., WILLET, C.L., ROBINSON, S.M., and SINNHUBER, R.O.   1967. Comparative effects of chlortetracycline, freezing, and γ radiation on microbial population of ocean perch. Appl. Microbiol. *15*, 368–372.

LOVE, R.M.   1970.   The Chemical Biology of Fishes.   Academic Press, New York.

MATHEWS, A.D., PARK, G.R., and ANDERSON, E.M.   1979.   Evidence for the formation of covalent cross-linked myosin in frozen-stored cod minces. *In* Advances in Fish Science and Technology, J.J. Connell *et al*. (Editors), pp. 438–444.   (Jubilee Conf. Torry Res. Station, Aberdeen, Scotland, July 1979). Fishing News Books Ltd., Farnham, Surrey, England.

RATTRIE, N.W., and REGENSTEIN, J.M.   1977.   Action of crude papain on actin and myosin heavy chains isolated from chicken breast muscle.   J. Food Sci. *42*, 1159–1163.

REAY, G.A., and SHEWAN, J.M.   1949.   The spoilage of fish and its preservation by chilling.   Adv. Food Res., *2*, 348–392.

REGENSTEIN, J.M.   1979.   The Cornell experience with minced fish.   *In* Advances in Fish Science and Technology, J.J. Connell *et al* (Editors).   pp. 192–199.   (Jubilee Conf. Torry Res. Station, Aberdeen, Scotland, July 1979).   Fishing News (Books) Ltd., Farnham, Surrey, England.

SHAW, B.G., and SHEWAN, J.M.   1968.   Psychrophilic spoilage bacteria of fish.   J. Appl. Bacteriol. *31*, 89.

SPINELLI, J. and KOURY, B.   1979.   Nonenzymic formation of dimethylamine in dried fishery products.   J. Agric. Food. Chem. *27*, 1104–1108.

SVENSSON, S.   1979.   Stabilization of fish mince from gadoid species by pre-treatment of the fish.   *In* Advances in Fish Science and Technology, J.J. Connell *et al*. (Editors), pp. 226–232.   (Jubilee Conf. Torry Res. Station, Aberdeen, Scotland, July 1979).   Fishing News Books Ltd., Farnham, Surrey, England.

TOKUNAGA, T.   1974.   The effect of decomposed products of trimethylamine oxide on quality of frozen Alaska pollock fillet.   Bull. Jpn. Soc. Sci. Fish. *40*, 167–174.

TOMIOKA, K., OGUSHI, J., and ENDO, K.   1974.   Studies on dimethylamine in food. II. Concerning the enzymatic formation of dimethylamine. Bull. Jpn. Soc. Sci. Fish. *40*, 1021–1026.

TSUCHIYA,Y., TSUCHIYA, T., and MATSUMOTO, J.J.   1979.   The nature of the cross-bridges constituting aggregates of frozen stored carp myosin and actomyosin.   *In* Advances in Fish Science and Technology, J.J. Connell *et al*. (Editors).   pp. 434–438.   (Jubilee Conf. Torry Res. Station, Aberdeen, Scotland, July 1979).   Fishing News Books Ltd., Farnham, Surrey, England.

148 CHEMISTRY & BIOCHEMISTRY OF MARINE FOOD PRODUCTS

WATSON, D.W. 1939. Studies of fish spoilage. IV. The bacterial reduction of trimethylamine oxide. J. Fish. Res. Board Can. *4*, 252–266.

WEINBERG, E.D. 1978. Iron and Infection. Microbiol. Rev. *42*, 45–66.

YAMADA, K. and AMANO, K. 1965. Studies on the biological formation of formaldehyde and dimethylamine in fish and shellfish—V. On the enzymatic formation in the pyloric caeca of Alaska pollock. Bull. Jpn. Soc. Sci. Fish. *31*, 60–64.

12

Occurrence and Significance of Trimethylamine Oxide and Its Derivatives in Fish and Shellfish

Chieko E. Hebard[1], George J. Flick[1], and Roy E. Martin[2]

OCCURRENCE AND ORIGIN OF TMAO

Occurrence of TMAO

Species Differences. Trimethylamine oxide (TMAO) exists in a large number of fish and shellfish, generally in the largest amount in the elasmobranchs and in the negligible amount in freshwater fish (Dyer 1952; Groninger 1959; Ruiter 1971; Harada 1975). Shewan (1951) found that among ocean fishes he examined, elasmobranchs contained the most TMAO, flat fishes the least, with pelagic fishes and cod family in between. Elasmobranchs are known to contain extremely large amounts of TMAO, no less than 2.5% of the dry weight, for this compound plays a role in osmoregulation in these fish (Simudu 1961). Suyama (1960) and Suyama and Suzuki (1975) found 750–1480 mg% TMAO in the muscle of about 20 species of sharks and rays. The sum of urea and TMAO comprised 60–76% of the extractive nitrogen (Suyama and Suzuki 1975).

White-fleshed (demersal) fish generally contain larger quantities of TMAO than red-fleshed (pelagic) fish (Reay and Shewan 1949; Horie and Sekine 1956A). The demersal fishes studied include dogfish, skates, cod and its allied species, and flatfishes, while pelagic species include mackerel, sardines, and tunas. A compilation of data up to 1975 by Harada (1975) shows the difference in the average content of TMAO by family; from highest to lowest, Selachii (ca. 190 mg% TMAO-N), Rajida (ca. 99 mg%

[1] Department of Food Science and Technology, Virginia Polytechnic Institute and State University, Blacksburg, Virginia 24061
[2] National Fisheries Institute, Inc., Washington, DC. 20036

149

TMAO-N), Gadida (ca. 83 mg% TMAO-N), Cottida (ca. 54mg% TMAO-N), Lophiida (ca. 47 mg% TMAO-N), Pleuronectida (ca. 47 mg% TMAO-N), Clupeida (ca. 31 mg% TMAO-N), Percida (ca. 28 mg% TMAO-N), Tetraodontida (ca. 23 mg% TMAO-N), and Belonida (ca. 19 mg% TMAO-N).

Decapoda contain large amounts of TMAO. The mantle muscle of squid, for instance, contains as much as 100–200 mg/100 g TMAO-N, comparable to the amount present in elasmobranchs (Simidu et al. 1953; Konosu et al. 1958; Endo et al. 1962A; Takagi et al. 1976A; Harada et al. 1968). Octopus contains less TMAO than squid (Asano and Sato 1954; Sato 1960; Harada et al. 1972). Crustaceans also contain fair amounts of TMAO, including all the species of shrimp and crabs tested (Takagi et al. 1967A; Fujita et al. 1972; Hayashi et al. 1978).

TMAO was undetected in many mollusks by earlier workers. But in the last two decades, it has been found in oysters, mussels, clams, scallops, and others, though the amount is usually small (Simidu et al. 1953; Simidu and Hibiki 1957; Takagi and Simidu 1962; Harada et al. 1971). Only two of the bivalves, *Pecten albicans* and *Vasticardium burchard*, and one gastropod, *Tristichotrochus unicus*, are reported to contain significant amounts of TMAO (Harada et al. 1971). Of the arthropods, enchinoderms, and protochords examined, Harada et al. (1972) found that marine species contained fairly large amounts of TMAO and freshwater species small amounts. The only exception was crayfish *(Procambarus clarki)*, which, although a freshwater crustacea, contained a considerable amount of TMAO in the muscle.

It has been thought that TMAO is absent in marine algae though trimethylamine (TMA) and dimethylamine (DMA) are found in some species (Kapeller-Adler and Vering 1931; Steiner and Hartman 1968). In 1971, however, Fujiwara-Arasaki and Mino found significant amounts of TMAO, as well as TMA, in all of the 20 species of marine algae tested. They found that TMAO was low in the brown algae, intermediate in the green algae, and high in the red algae.

Many workers found no TMAO in freshwater fishes (Hoppe-Seyler 1930; Kutscher and Ackerman 1933; Smith 1936; Beatty 1939; Dyer 1952; Norris and Benoit 1945A; Johnson 1951). The occurrence of TMAO was first reported by Hoppe-Seyler (1933) in the tail muscle of river crab. Then Anderson and Fellers (1952) found TMAO in some of the freshwater species. Shewan (1951) noted that TMAO often occurred in freshwater fish but that the amount of TMAO is much smaller in freshwater species than in marine species. One exception was the pike, which contained 50 mg% TMAO (Shewan and Jones 1957). Absence of TMAO in food sources such as plants and zooplankton may be a reason for the low TMAO level in freshwater fishes (Kapeller-Adler and Vering 1931). Smith (1936) attributed the low TMAO level in freshwater fishes to rapid excretion of the compound, which is one of the nitrogenous waste products of methylation.

Thus, it has been established that variations in the amount of TMAO exist due to species difference. However, the difference in TMAO levels among individual fish of the same species may sometimes be greater than the difference among species.

Variation in TMAO Level. The TMAO level in fish varies with the season, size, and age of fish, as well as environmental conditions to which the animal is subjected. When samples are collected from distant parts of the world, the species or the family may not give much clue to the actual content of TMAO. For example, Atlantic sea cucumber, *Cucumaria frondosa*, contained 76–86 mg N/100 g TMAO, while Pacific and Japanese sea cucumbers (*Cucumaria miniata* or *Stichopus californicus* and *Stichopus japonicus*) contained none. TMAO was detected in Pacific and Indian oysters (*Crassostrea gigas* and *Ostrea cullata*), but not in Atlantic oyster (*Crassostra virginica*) or mussel (*Mytilus edulis*) (see Table 12.1 at end of chapter). Shewan (1951) found that Arctic cod and haddock had much higher TMAO levels than North Sea fish of the same species. This is in direct contrast to Dyer's (1952) finding of similar TMAO contents in the same or closely related species caught in different parts of the world (i.e., cod, halibut, haddock, salmon, and herring).

Futhermore, Dyer (1952) found no indication of seasonal variation with herring, yellowtails (*Limanda ferruginea*), haddock (*Melanogrammus aeglefinus*), or cod (*Gadus morhia*). This agreed with the finding of Shewan (1951) on cod, haddock, and whiting (*Gadus merlangus*). Perhaps, in some fishes, the TMAO content is constant throughout the year or changes so little that the change cannot be detected easily; but in other fishes, it appears to be related to seasonal changes in activity or metabolism. For instance, the TMAO content of herring (*Clupea harengus*) and spratt (*Clupea sprattus*) was lowest in summer and highest in winter and spring (Ronold and Jakobsen 1947; Hughes 1959). Killifish (*Fundulus heteroclitus*) contained more TMAO in winter, when the slowdown of metabolism occurred, than in summer (Ogilvie and Warren 1957). A TMAO increase occurred in winter in demersal fish (sea bream, *Pagrosmus major*) and in summer in pelagic fish (mackerel, *Scomber japonicus*, sardine, *Etrumeus micropus*) (Takada and Nishimoto 1958). A species of squid (*Ommastrephes sloani*) showed an increase in trimethylammonium compounds in summer and fall, while another species, *Sepia esculenta*, did so in fall and winter (Endo et al. 1962B).

Measuring the TMAO content of yellowtail (*Seriola quinqueradiata*), Endo et al. (1974) found that TMAO was higher in "wild-adult" specimens than in "cultured-adult" specimens and that there was a marked seasonal variation in "young" groups with a decrease in summer and an increase in late autumn. They surmised that a decrease in specific gravity of surrounding sea water in summer may have caused a TMAO decrease in young groups whose osmoregulatory function was not yet perfected. Konosu and Watanabe (1976) compared the TMAO levels of cultured and wild red sea bream (*Chrysophrys major*) from two localities in Japan. They found more TMAO in wild fish from both localities, but the difference was small.

The TMAO content was found to be higher in older and larger individuals of cod, yellowtail, haddock, and whiting (Dyer 1952; Shewan 1951). Similarly, sexually mature or aged herring contained more TMAO than did young ones (Hughes 1959). The TMAO content also increased with the length of fish in killifish (Ogilvie and Warren 1957). Furthermore, during the spawning period (end of July to beginning of August), female killifish contained larger amounts of TMAO than did males.

One note of caution is called for: The data obtained by earlier workers may not always be sufficiently accurate and thus not comparable with each other, owing to the use of different methods by different workers. No method gives 100% accuracy and some much less. The interference by other amines must also be considered, especially in the case of gadoid fish, which generally have high levels of secondary amines. This will be discussed more thoroughly later in the chapter.

Uneven Distribution of TMAO in the Body of Fish.   An uneven distribution of TMAO in the body of fish was suspected by Shewan (1951), who found that the dark lateral line of the flesh of herring and tuna had only half the TMAO as the rest of the skeletal muscle. In white-fleshed fishes such as seabass *(Lateolabrax japonicus)*, Japanese gurnard *(Chelidonichthys kumn)*, walleye pollock *(Theragra chalcogramma)*, Pacific saury *(Cololabis saira)*, and Japanese gizzard *(Konosirus punctatus)*, the TMAO content was found to be much larger in the ordinary muscle than in the bloody (dark) muscle (Takagi *et al.* 1967A; Tokunaga 1970A). On the other hand, in dark-fleshed fishes such as sardine *(Engraulis japonica)*, jack mackerel *(Trachurus japonicus)*, yellowtail *(Seriola quinqueradiata)*, yellowfin tuna *(Thunnus albacores)*, bigeye tuna *(Thunnus obsesus)*, skipjack *(Katsuwonus pelamis)*, and mackerel *(Scomber japonicus)*, it was large in the dark muscle while it was small and variable in the ordinary muscle (Takagi *et al.* 1967A; Tokunaga 1970A).

Moreover, comparing the TMAO content of bloody and ordinary muscles of mackerel, Tokunaga (1970A) found that the calculated TMAO nitrogen (including TMA and DMA) in the ordinary muscle was variable and increased with the size of the fish, while it was generally constant in the bloody muscle within the range of 20–40 mg N/100 g regardless of size. Amano (1971) speculated that the bloody muscles of fish may function in maintenance of the TMAO level.

In albacore, muscles near the tail contained several times more TMAO than muscles near the head (Koizumi *et al.* 1967). In yellowfin tuna, the TMAO level was higher in superficial muscles than deep muscles, and it was also high in the bloody muscles and muscles adjacent to fins (Yamagata *et al.* 1968, 1969). The TMAO value was correlated with the greening of canned tuna in these studies.

In elasmobranchs, TMAO is present in relatively high concentrations in the blood. It is absent in the blood of teleosts (Norris and Benoit 1945A). In sharks, high concentrations of TMAO were also found in the muscle, heart, and spleen, and low concentrations in the brain, liver, and kidney (Suyama

1960). Generally in marine fish, the TMAO level is lower in viscera than in muscle (Harada 1975). In several species of crabs, TMAO was highest in leg meat and hepatopancreas (Hayashi *et al.* 1978). The TMAO content in decapods is highest in the mantle muscle, intermediate in arm muscle, and lowest in midgut gland (Harada *et al.* 1968). In octopus, it is three times higher in the integument (foot and abdominal muscles) than in the visceral parts (Asano and Sato 1954). Bivalves have the highest TMAO levels in adductor, intermediate in foot and mantle, and lowest in viscera (Harada *et al.* 1970).

Origin of TMAO

Cowey and Parry (1963) found that Atlantic salmon *(Salmo salar)* at the parr and smolt stages contained no TMAO, while Norris and Benoit (1945A) found some TMAO in salmon in the sea. Benoit and Norris (1945) reported that young salmon *(Oncorhynchus tchawytscha)* raised in a marine environment accumulated some TMAO when fed a diet containing TMAO but accumulated none when fed a TMAO-free diet. Anderson and Fellers (1952) found that hatchery-raised brown trout *(Salmo trutta fario)* increased their TMAO deposit with age when fed a TMAO-containing diet, indicating a direct correlation between TMAO intake and its accumulation in the body.

Likewise the goldfish *(Carassius auratus)* and the eel *(Anguilla japonica)* contained no TMAO when they were fed a TMAO-free diet but accumulated it in their muscles when fed a TMAO-containing diet (Hashimoto and Okaichi 1958A,B). TMAO was confirmed to be entirely of exogenous origin in these latter studies.

The feeding experiment was extended to marine fishes by Okaichi *et al.* (1959). They reported that TMAO in the globefish *(Fugu niphobles)* and filefish *(Monacanthus cerrhifer)* increased when the fish were fed a diet containing TMAO and that it was maintained at a constant and fairly high level. On the other hand, the TMAO level in the tissue of jack mackerel *(Trachurus japonicus)* was not influenced by the ingestion of TMAO. The constant TMAO level in fish found in this study suggests the possibility of an endogenous synthesis of TMAO, which may play a certain role in the metabolic system of fish. This view was shared by Hegemann (1964) who found that perch *(Perca fluviatilis)* and pike *(Esox lucius)*, on transfer from brackish water to fresh water, secreted TMAO completely in 24 hr. At 10 and 20 days, after being returned to brackish water and fasting, the fish were transferred again to fresh water. They again secreted TMAO in amounts comparable to controls kept in brackish water throughout. In this case, TMAO was apparently endogenous in origin.

Quite different results were obtained with killifish by Ogilvie and Warren (1957). While the fish were on a TMAO-free diet, the TMAO content first rose, reaching the high in 35–45 days, then it fell, after which it rose again to its normal level. Those fish that had been starved showed a marked increase in the TMAO content. Suspecting the presence of TMAO to be the result of both exogenous and endogenous processing, Ogilvie and Warren interpreted their test results as the takeover of one process compensating for the absence of the other. When the exogenous supply of TMAO is cut off, the endogenous process carries on alone, raising the TMAO content. After a while, the lack of the exogenous source begins to show and the TMAO level falls. Then, the endogenous process again builds up TMAO, since a certain amount of TMAO must be maintained for metabolism of marine fish. The fasting fish probably underwent the first stage of the endogenous process only.

A primarily endogenous origin of TMAO was suspected with the spiny dogfish *(Squalus acanthias)*. Cohen *et al.* (1958) found that the TMAO concentration in the plasma of dogfish is maintained within the narrow range of 60–80 μmole/ml when the fish was subjected to prolonged fasting of up to 41 days. They also found that TMAO is freely filterable at the glomerulus but is avidly reabsorbed by the renal tubule at the average rate of 95–99%, with less than 10% of the filtered oxide appearing in the urine. Previously, Grollman (1929) reported 37% of the total nonprotein nitrogen in the urine of goosefish *(Lophius piscatorius)* to be TMAO. In the plasma of the same species, Brull and Nizet (1953A) found the main nonprotein constituents to be TMA and TMAO (11.34 mg N/100 ml).

As mentioned earlier, elasmobranchs are known to contain extremely high levels of TMAO, which appears to play a role in osmoregulation (Smith 1936). Forster and Goldstein (1976) transferred little skates *(Raja erinacea)* and stingrays *(Dasyatis americana)* from full strength to 50% seawater to study the change in intracellular concentrations of amino acids, urea, and TMAO. The concentrations of these compounds in both species fell in the 50% seawater, indicating that they clearly regulate the osmosis of the fish.

It was believed that TMAO in teleost fishes did not contribute to osmoregulation, since the osmotic pressure of teleost blood is lower than that of seawater. However, in 1965, Lange and Fugelli found a system of intracellular osmotic regulation, which exists in the euryhaline teleosts, namely, European flounder *(Pleuronectes flesus* L.) and three-spined stickle-back *(Gasterosteus aculeatus* L.). TMAO as well as the free ninhydrine-positive substances played an active role in this volume regulation of muscle cells with a concomitant adjustment of the number of intracellular osmotically active particles.

Daikoku (1977) found that a TMA-containing diet prolonged the survival time of the freshwater guppies *(Poecilia reticulata)* in salt water by 50%. The guppies fed a TMA-free diet also increased their TMAO content in the muscle when they were transferred from freshwater to seawater. It appeared that the adaptation of the fish to seawater, namely osmoregulation, was enhanced by TMAO.

Extending the osmoregulation hypothesis, Yamada (1967) suggested that TMAO was essentially a waste product, a detoxified form of TMA formed from choline, betaine, methionine, etc., in fish. He postulated that freshwater fish did not contain any significant amount of TMAO in their muscles because they excreted TMA promptly without having to store its detoxified form TMAO in their muscle. TMAO is detected in the muscle only when intake exceeds excretion and the difference must be stored in the body until it can be excreted, as in the case of the goldfish fed TMAO (Hashimoto and Okaichi 1958A). On the other hand, saltwater fish all contain varied amounts of TMAO. It is partly because they take in more TMAO in their food than freshwater fish, but mostly because they must limit their excretion to a lower level to counteract the higher osmotic pressure of seawater. Therefore, metabolically formed TMA is stored in the muscle in its oxidized form.

Occurrence of TMA

A number of workers have reported on the presence of TMA in freshly caught fish prior to the onset of bacterial growth (Hoppe-Seyler 1928; Suyama and Tokuhiro 1954; Suyama 1960; Takagi et al. 1967A; Harada et al. 1968, 1970, 1971, 1972; Ooyama 1973; Konosu et al. 1974). But in most cases, the TMA concentration is extremely low, normally under 1 mg N/100 g. The only exceptions are a few bivalves which contained ca. 20 mg N/100 g and a few species of Gastropodan Mollusca whose TMA levels were higher than the TMAO levels (Harada et al. 1970, 1971). Like TMAO, TMA generally is detected only in marine fish and not in freshwater fish (Harada 1975). Obata and Yamanishi (1951) found TMA in salmon caught at sea but not in salmon caught in rivers.

In elasmobranchs and marine teleosts, the viscera, especially the spleen, liver, and kidney contain the most TMA and the muscle the least (Suyama 1960; Amano et al. 1963A). The midgut gland has the highest level of TMA in squid (Harada et al. 1968). TMA has been found in the urine of some elasmobranchs and teleosts (Grollman 1929; Hoppe-Seyler 1930; Wood 1958).

Mechanism of TMAO formation

Enzymatic Oxidation. TMAO in the body of fish is believed to be the oxidation product of TMA (Amano 1971). In animals, TMA oxidation is the only known mechanism for the formation of TMAO (Strøm 1979). The enzyme catalyzing the reaction is a TMA monooxygenase:

$$(CH_3)_3N + NADPH_2 + O_2 \rightarrow (CH_3)_3NO + NADP + H_2O$$

The enzyme in the microsomal fraction of hog-liver homogenates was studied by Baker and Chaykin (1960, 1962) and Zeigler and Mitchell (1972). It has been known that the liver, kidney, and lung of mammals possess the monooxygenase (Lintzel 1934; Tarr 1941; Norris and Benoit 1945B). Baker et al. (1963) and Goldstein and Dewitt-Harley (1973) found it only in the liver of some vertebrates including elasmobranchs and freshwater and saltwater teleosts. It was not found in any invertebrates or zooplankton, the latter of which contained moderate amounts of TMAO. At about the same time, Bilinksi (1962) conducted an *in vivo* study of lemon sole and starry flounder with a number of ^{14}C-labeled compounds. He found [^{14}C]TMA to be the best precursor of TMAO. Goldstein and Funkhouser (1972) found that, *in vitro*, liver slices and liver homogenates of nurse sharks oxidized [^{14}C]TMA to [^{14}C]TMAO.

When exposed to dissolved ^{14}C-labeled TMA in seawater, zooplankton, mainly *Calanus finmarchicus* (Gunnerus) and some *Calanus hyperboreus* (Kroyer), oxidized TMA to TMAO, which accumulated in the organisms (Strøm 1979). This is the first time the monooxygenase activity was found in zooplankton. Some marine teleosts and elasmobranchs, which possess no detectable TMAO biosynthesis, may depend on their food, such as copecods, for their TMAO supply. And this may be a reason for variation in the TMAO values of fish.

The trimethylammonium group of choline and, to a lesser degree, the methyl group of methionine have been reported to be incorporated into TMAO in lobster and crab (Bilinski 1960, 1962). TMAO was also recovered when choline was injected intravenously to nurse sharks (Goldstein and Funkhouser 1972). The degree of incorporation of choline and methionine, however, is rather low compared with that of TMA.

It has not yet been determined whether TMAO is produced from choline in the digestive tract by bacteria or by fish enzymes. In rat, TMA was produced only when intestinal bacteria were present (Prentiss *et al.* 1961). Studies of the time and location of the first appearance of [^{14}C]TMAO after administration of labeled precursors could resolve this question.

Takada and Nishimoto (1958) reported that, in dead freshwater fish (carp, *Cyprinus carpio*) TMA was formed in the absence of TMAO. Considering the fact that choline was present and generally decreased as TMA increased, the precursor of TMA may be choline. TMA synthesis from choline may also be the reason for the presence of TMA in other freshwater fishes in the absence of TMAO (Ronold and Jakobsen 1947; Anderson and Fellers 1952). Takada and Nishimoto (1958) also found the choline formation to be caused by bacteria or bacterial enzyme. Tokunaga *et al.* (1977) also observed the formation of TMA and DMA in putrid carp muscle free of TMAO. The addition of betaine increased the formation of both TMA and DMA.

Microbial Oxidation. In mammals, TMA oxidation has been attributed to microbial activity in the digestive tract (Norris and Benoit 1945B; De La Huerga and Popper 1951; De La Huerga *et al.* 1952, 1953). Two pathways in the oxidation of TMA are presented in Fig. 12.1. One pathway involves an initial oxygen incorporation with the formation of TMAO (TMA monoxygenase, 1) and the demethylation of TMAO yielding DMA and FA (TMAO demethlyase, 2). The second nonenzymatic pathway involves an oxidative *N*-demethylation yielding DMA and FA directly from TMA (TMA dehydrogenase, 3).

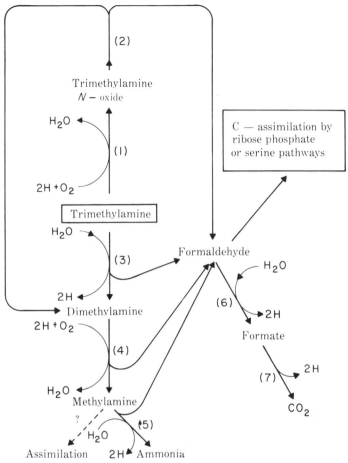

FIG. 12.1 OXIDATION OF TRIMETHYLAMINE BY OBLIGATE AND FACULTATIVE METH-
YLOTROPHS
(1) Large et al. (1972), Boulton et al. (1974), Boulton and Large (1975, 1977)—Pseudomonas
aminovorans; (2) Large (1971); (3) Colby and Zatman (1973, 1974)—Bacterium 4B6; (4) Eady
et al. (1971)—Pseudomonas aminovorans

TMA monooxygenase was found in succinate-grown *Pseudomonas
aminovorans* adapting to growth on TMA (Large *et al.* 1972; Boulton *et al.*
1974; Boulton and Large 1975, 1977). The enzyme was also found in cells of
bacterial strains 1A1, 1A2, 1A3, 1B1, 2B2, and *Pseudomonas* 3A2, all of
which were grown with TMA as the sole carbon source (Colby and Zatman
1973). Marine *Pseudomonas* sp. NCMB 1154 grown with TMA as the sole
nitrogen source also showed the TMA-oxidizing activity (Budd and Spencer
1968). However, the enzyme from the marine bacterium appeared to show
slight differences from the *P. aminovorans* enzyme (Boulton *et al.* 1974).
Boulton *et al.* (1974) suggested that the two pathways of TMA oxidation

may be mutually exclusive, since no organism has been found to have both TMA monooxygenase and TMA dehydrogenase.

TMAO REDUCTION

Two types of enzymes are considered to be responsible for the reduction of TMAO to TMA and to DMA and formaldehyde (FA); namely, endogenous enzymes in fish, and exogenous enzymes produced by bacteria in the course of spoilage. The enzyme activity of bacteria plays a major part in fish spoilage, and many studies have been undertaken to elucidate the relationship between the postmortem breakdown of TMAO to TMA and the presence and activity of bacterial enzymes.

Involvement of Bacteria in TMA Production

Bacteriology of Fish Spoilage. In some cases, no correlation is observed between bacterial growth and TMA production, because the number of TMA-producing bacteria is small compared with the total bacterial load or the percentage of spoilage bacteria (Tarr 1961; Shewan 1962A; Shaw and Shewan 1968). But in other cases, the two correlate well, for the percentage of TMA-producing bacteria is fairly constant despite the change in bacterial composition (Laycock and Regier 1971; Lerke *et al.* 1963; Adams *et al.* 1964).

The bacteriology of marine and freshwater animals has been extensively studied by many scientists, and only some of the works are cited in this chapter for the purpose of clarifying the relationship between bacterial activity and TMA formation. In newly caught, healthy fish, the flesh and body fluids generally are considered sterile. The external surfaces and, in the case of feeding fish, the digestive tract possess large, diverse populations of bacteria (Tarr 1954; Shewan 1961).

The bacterial flora of fish is derived essentially from a marine environment (Wood 1953). The total bacterial counts and the bacterial features of fish vary with season, place of catch, and other environmental factors (Griffiths 1937; Tarr 1939A; Reay and Shewan 1949; Shewan 1961, 1971). For example, fish from warm waters off India, Africa, and Australia have a high percentage of mesophiles such as *Bacillus* spp., coryneforms, and micrococci, and a low percentage of psychrophiles such as *Pseudomonas, Achromobacter*, and *Flavobacterium* spp. In fish caught in cold waters, psychrophilic bacteria are predominant (Shewan 1961, 1962A). In fresh fish, the predominant genera usually are *Pseudomonas, Achromobacter*, coryneforms, *Micrococcus*, and *Flavobacterium*. In the North Sea fish tested at Torry Research Station, pseudomonads generally consisted of *P. pellicudum* (40–50%), *P. geniculatum* (20–30%), brown-pigmented types (10–20%), green fluorescent strains (5–10%), and others. Achromobacters consisted of *A. alcaligenes* types (35–45%), types closely related to *A. liquefaciens* or *A. aquamarinus* (30%) (Shewan 1961).

When fish are stored in ice or at chill temperature, *Pseudomonas* spp. increase drastically while others decrease, except for *Acromobacter* spp.

which generally stay fairly constant in number (Reay and Shewan 1949; Wood 1953; Tarr 1954; Shewan *et al.* 1960B; Shewan 1961). After 12 days of storage, Shewan *et al.* (1960B) found that *Pseudomonas* spp. comprised 60–90% of the total population when the total bacterial count exceeded 10^6/g N of tissue. Fluorescent pseudomonads constituted up to 19.3% after 8 days of refrigerated storage (Chai *et al.* 1968).

The composition of bacterial flora differ with the type of storage or processing of fish. In haddock frozen at −12°C for 3 months, *Flavobacter* increased fourfold while *Pseudomonas* spp. disappeared and *Achromobacter* spp. were considerably reduced (Shewan 1962A). The lowest temperature for the growth of *Pseudomonas* in fish appears to be around −3°C (Shaw and Shewan 1968). In brined fish, the gram-positive types (micrococci and coryneforms) increased at the expense of gram-negatives (*Pseudomonas* and *Flavobacter* spp.) (Shewan 1962A). In dry-salted fish, micrococci comprised over 90% of the flora (Dussault 1958). Half of the cultures reduced TMAO to TMA.

Many *Pseudomonas* species are known to cause spoilage and odors (Castell and Greenough 1957, 1959; Cobb and Vanderzant 1971; Shaw and Shewan 1968; Herbert *et al.* 1971). All the species producing spoilage odors in cod muscle appeared to be *Pseudomonas* or allied species (Shewan 1971). Certain subgroups of *Achromobacter, Aeormonas* spp., and *Vibrio* spp. are also reported to be spoilers (Lerke *et al.* 1965; Sasajima 1973). Adams *et al.* (1964) found that the percentage incidence of spoilers in the bacterial population of raw press juice of English sole was fairly low, below 10% initially, with a slight increase (around 20%) followed by a decrease at the time of spoilage. Shaw and Shewan (1968) also reported that the proportion of active spoilers in the total viable bacterial population of fish did not alter markedly during spoilage and remained below 25%.

Bacteria That Produce TMA. The strains of bacteria capable of reducing TMAO to TMA have been found in most species of the Enterobacteriaceae including *Escherichia coli, Achromobacter, Micrococcus, Flavobacterium,* nonfluorescent *Pseudomonas, Clostridium, Alcaligenes,* and *Bacillus* spp.[1] Laycock and Regier (1971) found that there was a linear relationship between the number of *P. putrefaciens* and TMA production, 80% of all TMA-producing isolates belonging to this species. Pseudomonads have been known to be mainly responsible for the spoilage of fresh fish at low temperatures (Castell 1949A; Chai *et al.* 1968; Shewan 1971). Laycock and Regier (1971) also found that the percentage of TMA-forming achromobacters declined from the initial 60% to 32% of the TMA-producing flora after 13 days of storage. Coryneforms were the only group to show an increase in the percentage of TMA producers.

---

[1] See Tarr 1939A; Watson 1939A,B; Wood *et al.* 1943; Baird and Wood 1944; Castell 1946; Castell and Snow 1951; Tsuchiya *et al.* 1951; Robinson 1952; Suyama 1960; Krueger 1972; Miller *et al.* 1973.

Environmental Effects on Bacteria and TMA Production.   Spoilage proceeds more rapidly at room temperature than at chill temperature, and so does TMA production. The optimum temperature for the TMAO reduction by *Serratia marcescens, Achromobacter* spp., and *E. coli* was 37°C and above, whereas the optimum temperature for *Pseudomonas putrefaciens* was 25°C (Castell and Snow 1951). It was around 40°C for *P. myxogenes* and *A. tiogense* (Suyama 1960). Although TMA production is almost totally inhibited at subzero temperature, it occurs very slowly at chill temperature. Achrombacters reduced TMAO in cod muscle press juice at 2°C (Watson 1939A) and in shrimp at 4°C (Campbell and Williams 1952).

Sasajima's findings (1973) suggested the existence of a certain minimum number of viable cells of psychrotrophic bacteria for successful TMA production. For example, cell counts of $10^{7.5}$ to 10^8 were required to produce 16.2 μg of TMA. Using two strains of psychrotrophic bacteria resembling *Vibrio* sp. isolated from fresh fish, Sasajima (1974) then found that the minimum growth temperature for the bacteria was $-4°$ to $-5°C$. When the initial cell count was 10^6/ml, there was no increase in the number of bacterial cells nor TMAO-reducing activity at $-4°C$ during a 25-day storage. When the initial cell count was 10^8/ml under the same conditions, TMA was formed after 6 days and up to 30 μg of TMA N/ml after 22 days. At $-6°C$, no TMA formation occurred during 41 days of storage regardless of initial cell counts. Sasajima explained that TMA did not form in low temperatures because of the failure of bacteria to reach the necessary cell counts to start TMAO reduction.

Preservatives such as EDTA (ethylenediaminetetraacetic acid) and γ-irradiation selectively inhibit or reduce the growth of pseudomonads on fish and depress TMA production at the same time (Power *et al.* 1964; Miyauchi *et al.* 1966; Pelroy and Seman 1969). Laycock and Regier (1971) found that EDTA keeps TMA production low by inhibiting the growth of *P. putrefaciens* while allowing spoilage to occur. The usefulness of TMA production as an index of quality is therefore dependent on the presence of TMA-producing organisms such as *P. putrefaciens* in the spoilage flora.

Bacterial Enzyme.   Tomizawa (1951) was the first person to extract TMAO reductase from bacterial cells *(E. coli)*. He did so by using ultrasonic vibration to disrupt the cells. Others had previously failed to obtain the enzyme in a cell-free state (Tarr 1939A; Watson 1939A, B; Castell and Snow 1951). The enzyme is membrane bound in *Vibrio parahaemolyticus* (Unemoto *et al.* 1965) and *E. coli* cells (Sakaguchi and Kawai 1975B). Sagai and Ishimoto (1973) purified three amine oxide reductases 23-fold from *E. coli* cells using benzylbiologen (BV) as an electron donor in the enzymatic assay. Many earlier workers failed to purify the enzyme because, as an electron donor, they used NADH which is oxidized by hydrogenase earlier in the reaction. They found that BV could be replaced by FAD, FMN, or cytochrome *c*. The reduction was attributable to the action of a single enzyme.

Yamamoto and Ishimoto (1977) and Ishimoto and Shimokawa (1978) found that *E. coli* reduced TMAO in anaerobic respiration. Participation of cytochrome *c* as an intermediary electron carrier linked to amine oxide reductase was observed in the reduction. Phosphorylation coupled to the electron transport in anaerobic respiration was suspected on the basis of high molar growth yields.

Recently, Sakaguchi and Kawai (1978A) reported that formate and NADH could reduce cytochromes in membrane preparations of *E. coli*. The formate- and NADH-reduced cytochromes were gradually reoxidized by TMAO, suggesting the participation of cytochromes in TMAO reduction. Sakaguchi and Kawai (1978B) then found that the *c*-type cytochromes could properly be placed at the position just after the *b*-type in the electron transport system. The overall sequence of TMO reduction is summarized as follows:

Formate   ⟶   *b*-type   *c*-type   ⟶
NADH   ⟶   cytochromes   ⟶   cytochromes

                                         TMAO
                  TMO   ↓
                reductase   ⟶
                                         TMA

"Amine *N*-oxide reductase" was recently purified by Shimokawa and Ishikawa (unpublished data; Ishimoto and Shimokawa 1978). It is reported to be colorless and to reduce amine *N*-oxide with dithionite and BV as the electron donor system, with cytochrome *c* as the electron donor.

Kim and Chang (1974) found that TMAO, like nitrate, could support the anaerobic growth of *Salmonella* strain *his*G46 on glycerol. The extent of growth was proportional to the amount of TMAO reduced to TMA. They also noted that TMAO served as a terminal electron acceptor for anaerobic *Salmonella*.

Nonenzymatic Reduction of TMAO to TMA, DMA and FA.   TMAO at temperatures between 22° and 24°C was readily reduced by cysteine in the presence of iron or hemoglobin as a catalyst (Vaisey 1956). Larger amounts of iron (Fe^{2+}) could also reduce TMAO. TMA was the major product of this reduction, but appreciable amounts of DMA and FA were also formed.

Endogenous Enzyme.   In the dark muscle of freshly caught albacore [*Germo alalunga* (G.)] and frigate mackerel [*Auxis tapeinosoma* (Bleeker)], TMA increased markedly even under aseptic conditions (Kawabata 1953B). No such increase was observed in the white muscle of the same fish. The dark muscle reduced added TMAO during aseptic incubation but the white muscle did not. TMAO-reducing ability was strongly diminished or inhibited when muscle preparations were treated with heat or with dipyridyl or potassium cyanide, substances known to have an inhibitory influence on enzymes with heavy metal cofactor, especially iron. From these data, Kawabata (1953B) concluded that the dark muscle of pelagic fish contained an enzyme capable of reducing TMAO. Suyama (1960) also reported TMA formation under aseptic conditions in the dark muscle of *Mustelus manazo* and *Dasyatis akajei.* Addition of TMAO caused an increase of TMA in pyloric caeca of Pacific cod and in the midgut gland of squid *(Todarodes pacificus)* under aseptic conditions (Amano and Yamada 1964B; Harada and Yamada unpublished; Yamada 1968).

Tokunaga (1970B) observed that, during storage at 0° and −6°C, relatively large amounts of TMA and DMA were produced in the bloody muscle of several migratory fish, whereas neither of the amines was present in any significant amounts in the white muscle of the same fish. Although the samples were not kept under aseptic conditions, Tokunaga strongly suspected the formation of TMA and DMA to be caused by an endogenous enzyme in bloody muscle of fish rather than by bacterial enzyme. The reasons for this suspicion were that the amines began to form soon after the death of the fish, and that only negligible amounts were formed in white muscle. He further classified the fish tested according to presence or absence of the endogenous enzyme in the following manner:

1. the enzyme concentrated in bloody muscle only, e.g., tunas, skipjack, Japanese sardine.
2. the enzyme slightly active in white muscle as well as bloody muscle, e.g., mackerel, saury, Japanese grunt, jack mackerel.
3. the enzyme strongly active in white and bloody muscles, e.g., cod and other gadoid fishes.

Formation of DMA and FA from TMAO

Occurrence of DMA and FA.   DMA was first found by Beatty (1938) in cod muscle press juice. Reay (1938) and Shewan (1939A) also found small amounts of DMA in cod and haddock, respectively. DMA and FA have been isolated from Atlantic cod (Dyer and Mounsey 1945), haddock (Dyer and Mounsey 1945; Shewan 1939A), Alaska pollock (Amano *et al.* 1963B: Tokunaga 1964), Pacific cod (Amano *et al.* 1963B), *Eleginus gracilis* (Tokunaga 1964), *Lotella maximowiczi* and *L. phycis* (Yamada and Amano 1965C), herring (Hughes 1959), *Loligo formosa,* and *Todarodes pacificus* (Tokunaga 1964). Shewan noted that DMA began to form immediately after the death of fish preceding the production of TMA. Reay and Shewan (1949) stated that, while DMA was produced in haddock, cod, and whiting, it was not formed at all in freshwater perch and dogfish, and only in variable and small amounts in herring. The presence of FA in fresh fish had not been suspected until Amano *et al.* (1963A) extracted formol dimedone from cod. Yamada and Amano (1965C) found relatively high concentrations of FA in fresh crab, particularly in hepatopancreas. FA in canned crab had previously been considered to be derived solely from thermal decomposition of TMAO during processing (Hattori 1940). Amano *et al.* (1963A,B) noted that the quantities of DMA and FA were highest in the viscera of fish, intermediate in the skin, and lowest in the muscle. Miyahara (1960) found DMA in raw meats of teleosts *(Clupanodon thrissa, Pneumatophorus japonicus japonicus, Chrysophrys major)* and squid *(Loligo formosa).* Yamada and

Amano (1965A,C) found small amounts of DMA and FA in *Lepidion Oidema* and *Lotella phycis,* both related to the Gadidae, the hepatopancreas of abalone, Japanese oyster *(Crassostrea gigas),* Gazami crab *(Portunus tribuberculatus),* and *Ovalipes punctatus.*

Harada (1975) detected DMA in only Pacific cod and two squids *(Todarodes pacificus* and *Doryteuthis bleekeri),* although FA was found in 16 of 17 species of teleosts and shellfish.

Tokunaga (1970A) found DMA in the bloody muscle of all species of fish examined (both white-fleshed and dark-fleshed fish),[2] although only a few species contained DMA in the ordinary muscle. FA was found whenever DMA was present in measurable amounts. This led him to suspect strongly an enzymatic mediation of DMA synthesis. Tokunaga (1970B) further studied TMA decomposition products and found that, in Alaska pollock fillet, the largest amount of DMA was produced at $-10°C$ among the temperatures tested from $-5°$ to $-40°C$. In the dark muscle, DMA reached 30 mg/100 g after 10 days of storage at $-10°C$ while little or no TMA was detected. This corresponds with the results obtained by Castell *et al.* (1973); no measurable amount of TMA was formed in frozen cod, pollock *(Pollachius virens),* cusk *(Brosme brosme),* and silver hake *(Merluccius bilinearis)* stored at $-5°C$, whereas DMA was formed in large quantities under the same conditions. In iced storage, on the other hand, TMA was formed very rapidly with little or no DMA produced.

Studying the decomposition of TMAO in salted and frozen cod eggs, Usuki *et al.* (1971) found that a DMA-liberating enzyme in the eggs was active in the frozen state, whereas salting and freezing inhibited TMA formation. DMA and FA were also produced when fish flesh was heated for processing. The effect of heating on the production of DMA and FA is discussed later.

Tokunaga (1975A) found that the rate of thermal decomposition of TMAO varied, but generally was small in white-fleshed fish, high in red-fleshed fish, squid, and clams. He also found that the ratio of DMA to total decomposition products (DMA + TMA) was high in mollusks (0.7−0.9), medium in ordinary muscle (0.3−0.38), and low in dark muscle (0.15−0.20). The rate of TMAO decomposition below 100°C was lowest at 55°−60°C in dark muscle and 80°C in ordinary muscle.

Enzymic Formation of DMA and FA.   In a series of articles, Amano and his colleagues confirmed the enzymic formation of DMA and FA (Amano *et*

---

[2]Alaska pollock, alfonsino *(Beryx splendens),* southern kingfish *(Rexea solandri),* javelin fish *(Lepidorhynchus denticulatus),* ling *(Genypterus blacodes),* hoki *(Macruronus novaezelandiae),* barracuda *(Sphyraena picuda),* silver side *(Argentina semifasciata),* Japanese grunt *(Parapristipoma trilineatum),* Japanese dwarf barracuda *(Sphyraena pinguis),* jack mackerel *(Trachurus japonicus),* Japanese sardine *(Sardinops melanosticta),* mackerel *(Scomber japonicus),* southern bluefin *(Thunnus maccoyii),* skipjack *(Katsuwonus pelamis),* dolphin *(Coryphaena hippurus),* abalone *(Sulculus japonicus),* hard clam *(Meretrix lusoria),* arkshell *(Scapharca broughtonii),* kuruma prawn *(Penaeus japonicus),* spider crab *(Chinoecetes opilis),* squid *(Todarodes pacificus),* cuttlefish *(Sepia esculenta).*

al. 1963A,B; Amano and Yamada 1964A,B; Yamada and Amano 1965A, B,C). First, they detected FA in the skin, muscle, and organs of Pacific cod, Alaska pollock, and Japanese hake (*Hexagrammos stelleri,* later identified as *Lotella maximowiczi* by Yamada and Amano 1965B). FA was present in large amounts in pyloric caeca, stomach, gall bladder, and spleen, and in small amounts in the muscle. DMA was also present in most samples that contained FA, with the coefficient of the correlation being 0.89 (Amano *et al.* 1963A,B). During refrigerated storage of these fish, DMA and FA as well as TMA increased while TMAO decreased, though FA notably decreased after the spoilage of flesh took place (Amano and Yamada 1964A).

When TMAO was added to a suspension of the cod pyloric caeca in the presence of antiseptics, FA and DMA were formed. But neither was formed in a mixture of carp flesh homogenate and TMAO (Amano and Yamada 1964B). Yamada and Amano (1965A) then found that a specific enzyme in the pyloric caeca of Alaska pollock was involved in the reaction and that the precursor of DMA and FA was TMAO, not betaine or choline. The reaction was completely inhibited when the pyloric caeca suspension was heated at 100°C for 5 min. Yamada and Amano (1965C) then found that a minute amount of methylene blue enhanced the formation of DMA and FA by the enzyme in the pyloric caeca of Alaska pollock or the muscle and liver tissues of *Lotella phycis.* Moreover, in the presence of methylene blue, one molecule of TMAO produced one molecule each of FA and DMA. Castell *et al.* (1974) and Harada (1975) later asserted the equimolar production of DMA and FA. The participation of a heat-tolerant cofactor in the formation of DMA and FA from TMAO was then confirmed, and the cofactor was found to be present in the tissue of codlike fish and in the shark liver not having the enzyme (Yamada *et al.* 1969).

Harada (1975) studied the enzymatic formation of DMA and FA in the muscle, viscera, and liver of 239 species of marine animals and compiled data presented earlier by Harada and Yamada (1970, 1971A,B,C) along with his new data. The enzyme was detected in some but not all samples of three species of squid (*T. pacificus, Sepia esculenta,* and *Thysanotheuthis rhombus*). FA and DMA were identified in four species of bivalves (*Barbatia virescens, Cucullaea labiata granulosa, Septifer virgatus, Mytilus edulis*), three species of gastropods (*Babylonia japonica, Semisulcospira bensoni, Tristichotrochus uncus*) and one Coelenterata (*Alcyonium gracillimum*). Interestingly, the bivalves and gastropods that possessed the enzyme (except *T. uncus*) contained only small amounts of TMAO. Only *Portunus trituberculatus* was previously found to contain FA and DMA (Yamada and Amano 1965C). Of the 114 species of the *Myctophida* and one *Zeida,* the following species produced measurable amounts of FA and DMA; *Synodus hoshinonis, Trachinocephalus myops, Saurida undosquamis, Saurida tumbil,* and *Zeus japonicus.*

From the liver of lizardfish (*S. tumbil*), which had the greatest ability to produce FA and DMA from TMAO in the tissue, the TMAO-reducing enzyme was homogenized and purified 700 times. Harada found the cofactor to be a heat-stable, low molecular weight substance, and not a single unit. Tomioka *et al.* (1974) had found that (1) the enzyme was labile on heating at temperatures higher than 40°C; (2) the reaction was specific for tertiary amine *N*-oxide; (3) the optimum pH of the reaction was 5.0, but the enzyme was most stable at pH 6.2 on heating; and (4) the reaction was stimulated by Fe^{2+}, L-ascorbic acid, FMN, or betaine, and inhibited by Fe^{3+}, Cu^{2+}, EDTA, TMA, or choline. The enzyme is distributed in the liver and midgut gland of various species of marine animals.

Harada (1975) concluded that no TMA was formed in the enzymic reaction in fish. In the nonenzymatic reaction, however, significant amounts of TMA are known to form along with DMA and FA (Vaisey 1956; Craig *et al.* 1961; Ferris *et al.* 1967). Iron (II) and (III) have been used as catalysts in the nonenzymatic reaction. Harada found *tris*(hydroxymethyl)aminomethane-dibasic acid–sodium hydroxide (pH 10–11) to be the most active catalyst. From the data obtained, he postulated that a general base, as the electron donor, plays a role in the simultaneous formation of DMA and FA from TMAO. The reaction formula he presented is as follows:

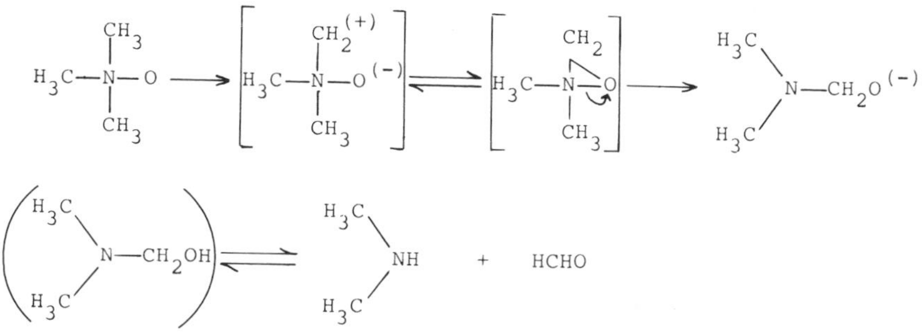

SPOILAGE INDICES

TMA as a Spoilage Index

Relation to Organoleptic Tests. Although it is associated with fishy odor, TMA by itself does not give off the odor, smelling rather like ammonia in its purified form. For instance, fresh halibut from which oil was removed had no fishy odor, whereas untreated halibut developed a strong odor (Stansby 1962). The fishy odor is produced when TMA reacts with fat in the muscle of fish (Davies and Gill 1936). In the course of spoilage, many off-odors are produced by bacteria, indicating the onset and development of spoilage (Reineccius 1979). Many workers therefore have conducted sensory tests, particularly those of off-odors, along with TMA determination to prove the correlation between the degree of spoilage and the TMA concentration in fish.

Beatty and Gibbons (1937) found that the TMA level in cod muscle press juice rose rapidly from the almost negligible level in fresh fish at the onset of spoilage and correlated with odors. Odors always appeared at a TMA level of 4–6 mg N/100 ml. At a level of 10 mg N/100 ml, there were definite off-odors. Subsequently, a number of experiments have correlated positively TMA levels and organoleptic test scores (Hess 1941; Dussault 1957; Castell *et al.* 1958; Collins *et al.* 1960; Koval'chuk and Moskalenko 1961; Spencer 1962; Farber 1965A; Magno-Orejana *et al.* 1971; Sen Gupta *et al.* 1972). However, it must be noted that TMA does not always correlate with flavor, odor, and other sensory tests (Botta and Shaw 1976).

Studying fishes from different parts of Northern European waters, Farber (1963A) found that correlations of the TMA content and sensory judgments for the white-fleshed fish were parallel with a correlation coefficient of 0.8–0.9, whereas the TMA value was not related to the progress of spoilage in herring. Spencer (1962) reported the raw odor score devised for commercial cod landed at Hull, Great Britain: Raw odor score (10 to 1 from freshest to putrid) = 6.20 − 1.46 TMA index, where the TMA index = log(1 + TMA content expressed as mg of TMA N/100 g of flesh). Shewan and Jones (1957) of Torry Research Station presented an equation for chilled cod:

$$\text{Raw odor score} + 0.47 \log 10(1 + \text{TMA N}/100 \text{ cm}^3) = 10.1.$$

Castell *et al.* (1958) and Castell and Greenough (1958) compared the grading of fish based on the organoleptic judgment by experienced plant foremen and fishery personnel and the TMA level of cod and haddock in the round, as gutted whole fish or in fillets. Generally, grade I fish contained 0–1 mg TMA N/100 g (0–5 mg TMA/100 g) in muscle and was judged to be of prime quality; grade II contained 1–5 mg N/100 g (5–26 mg/100 g) and were still marketable; grade III contained over 5 mg N/100 g and were judged unfit for processing as fresh or frozen fillets. Castell *et al.* (1958) also found that the TMA increase in iced fish was slow from the first to sixth day after landing, then accelerated through the ninth day, then became very rapid and almost linear around the tenth day. Shewan and Jones (1957) also found that there was a lag period of approximately 5 days, but that the increase was slower with linear stage of increase not starting till about fifteenth day. After this, TMA leveled off (Sigurdsson 1947; Hughes 1958). Cod and haddock with the TMA values of 10–20 mg/100 g were judged unacceptable by Dyer and Mounsey (1945). Also using cod and haddock, Hoogland (1958) devised the grade probability curve, showing the relation between the organoleptic grade and the TMA level as a linear regression equation. He suggested the TMA values (mg TMA N/100 g fillet) for grades I, II, and III to be 0.01–1.00, 1.01–7.00, and 7.01 and above, respectively. Castell *et al.* (1961) verified the accuracy of this curve with tests on more than 3000 samples.

When cod fillets were stored at various temperatures in the range of −2° and 4°C, TMA generally gave a constant value for the threshold of acceptability with the average value of 13 mg TMA N/100 g (Luijpen 1958). This is higher than the threshold value for iced, fresh fish reported by Reay and Shewan (1949) and Castell and Triggs (1955). Luijpen explained this difference by larger quantities of volatile bases detected in non-iced fish and fillets than iced ones of the same quality.

In the case of shrimp, limits of acceptability in some sectors of the Australian and Japanese markets are 5 mg TMA N/100 g (26 mg/100 g) shrimp muscle and/or 30 mg total volatile nitrogen (Montgomery et al. 1970), values similar to the threshold values for cod and haddock. In lobster tail (Panalirus laevicauda) significant correlation also was found between the organoleptic test and the TMA values whether or not the samples were treated with chlortetracyclin or spiramycin (Ogawa et al. 1970). Sen Gupta et al. (1972) found lower threshold values of TMA for a species of Indian fish. TMA values up to 1 mg/100 g indicated fresh fish, 1–5 mg, doubtful, over 5 mg, spoiling, to 8 mg indicating almost spoiled fish. Asano and Sato (1954) found that the ratio of TMAO/TMA is a good index of spoilage of three species of octopus tested.

In some species, the TMA value did not work as a spoilage index at all. One such species was the oyster, according to Lartigue et al. (1960). While the TMA content of gray cod correlated with spoilage as judged organoleptically and by bacterial counts, that of lemon flounder (Parophrys vetulus) or of defrosted lingcod was so small that it did not project the stale state of the fish (Tarr 1944).

It has been known that freshwater fish cannot be judged by their TMA values because they do not contain the precursor, TMAO, in sufficient amounts (Bligh 1971 among others). Furthermore, freshwater fish may spoil in a quite different manner than marine fish. Balakrishnan et al. (1971) found that, in iced freshwater fish, autolytic reactions appeared to be the dominant factor in determining quality rather than bacterial spoilage and accumulation of putrefactive products.

Species Difference in TMA Value. For a given TMA level, haddock showed greater deterioration than cod (Castell et al. 1961). In other words, TMA levels were higher for cod than for haddock of comparable quality as determined organoleptically (Castell and Triggs 1955). The problem of different thresholds of TMA in different species of fish was previously encountered by Sigurdsson (1947) and Koval'chuk and Moskalenko (1961). Sigurdsson proposed that, for herring that has higher initial concentrations of TMA than cod, the TMA values indicating spoiling and spoiled fish should be raised to 5–7 and 12 mg N/100 g, respectively, from 4–6 and 10 mg N/100 g suggested by Beatty and Gibbons (1937). Dussault (1957) found that rosefish (Sebastes marinus) was still edible with TMA levels higher than what would indicate spoilage in cod. Hillig et al. (1962A) also found that, among the fish of the same quality, cod contained the largest amounts of TMA, while haddock contained intermediate amounts and perch the smallest. The TMA value on the tenth day of storage on ice were much higher in scampi (Nephrops norvegicus) than in cod and haddock under similar conditions (Walker *et al.* 1970). It appears that shrimp spoil faster than many other species: *Pandalus hypsinotus* spoiled faster than squid *(Todarodes pacificus)* or teleost *(Sebastolobus macrochir)* at 4°, 10° and 20°C (Takagi *et al.* 1967B).

The TMA content during spoilage of fish and the amount of its precursor TMAO present at the time of death of fish appear to correlate in the two studies conducted to differentiate the spoilage patterns of elasmobranchs, marine teleosts, and freshwater teleosts. Shewan (1939A) found that perch, freshwater fish with little or no TMAO, contained only traces of TMA and DMA; haddock, representing marine teleosts, developed odors following the reduction of TMAO; dogfish, a representative of elasmobranchs, produced TMA in amounts similar to haddock. Haddock, however, produced larger amounts of DMA. These results agree with the known data. The relatively small rise of TMA in dogfish is due to a more rapid rise of ammonia and the resultant pH increase, which inhibits TMAO reduction (Suyama 1960). The other study used catfish *(Tachysurus spp.)* as marine fish, tilapia *(Tilapia mossambica)* as brackish water fish, and mrigal *(Cirrhina mrigala)* as freshwater fish (Pawar and Magar 1965). The most TMA increase was observed in catfish, the least in mrigal.

Variations.   Castell and Giles (1961) reported that seasonal fluctuations in the quality of landed Atlantic cod and haddock as determined by TMA values were confirmed by a careful organoleptic grading of the fillet. The percentage of grade I fish was 75% in late winter and spring when the mean TMA value was low, whereas it dropped to 25% or less in the summer and in November when the TMA value was high. Castell *et al.* (1961) also noted an interesting fact that, for a given level of TMA, fish caught in the summer and late fall usually showed more organoleptic deterioration than those caught in the spring and winter. This means that many of the fish caught in summer and late fall would be even poorer in quality than the observed rise in the TMA values would indicate (Castell and Giles 1961). Burt *et al.* (1976) also noted different rates of TMA increase in fish caught from different grounds at different seasons. Fish caught at Iceland in November accumulated TMA faster and spoiled faster than fish caught at North Sea in February, for instance. Ehrenberg and Shewan (1955) and Shewan and Ehrenberg (1957) also found the place of catch to affect the TMA value in iced white fish. In fact, the rate of spoilage differed from one catch to another, though it appeared that fish from North Sea and Iceland spoiled more slowly than fish from Spitzbergen and Lofoten (Shewan and Ehrenberg 1957).

TMA formation during spoilage was found to be greater and more regular in the ordinary muscle of white-fleshed fish than that of dark-fleshed fish (Horie and Sekine 1956). The former contained large amounts of TMAO (35–60 mg/TMAO N/100 g), whereas the latter contained small amounts (2–10 mg), which agrees with the findings reported earlier.

Frigate mackerel *(Auxis Thazard lacepeda)* spoiled faster in the head than in the tail and middle, the latter having the least amount of TMA (Magno-Orejana 1971). This is rather curious since TMAO, the precursor of TMA, is found in the reverse order of abundance in albacore and yellowfin tuna; the TMAO content is higher in the tail end muscle than in muscles near the head (Koizumi *et al.* 1967; Yamagata *et al.* 1968, 1969).

TMA in Relation to Bacterial Growth. Since postmortem bacterial growth is indicative of spoilage in fish, many efforts have been made to correlate the total bacterial count with the TMA value. Notevarp (1943) found that TMA values agreed with bacterial counts, with 10 mg TMA/100 g as a threshold value. Bailey *et al.* (1956) reported that a TMA N value of 1.5 mg/100 g in shrimp tissue and a bacterial count of 10×10^6 per gram or higher in headless, shell-on shrimp were indicative of unacceptable quality in most cases. Montgomery *et al.* (1970) reported that sensory assessment corresponded with bacterial counts and the volatile base content. Fish with a bacterial count in excess of 1×10^6/g and 5 mg TMA N were condemned unfit for human consumption. Sidhu *et al.* (1974B) found the correlation between bacterial counts and TMA in rock lobster *(Jasus novae-hollandiae)* previously immersed in a 3% sodium chloride solution for 4 minutes.

In fish stored at low temperatures, there is a lag period in TMA formation, and the lower the temperature, the longer the lag period (Anderson and Fellers 1949). Iyengar *et al.* (1960) found that a sudden increase in bacteria in iced shrimp at the end of 16 days coincided with the definite onset of spoilage. Horie and Sekine (1956) also found a sudden increase in TMA ($>$ 10 mg/100 g) to be concurrent with the onset of bacterial putrefaction. This is the linear stage of increase reported by Castell *et al.* (1958) when fish is already spoiling. Although bacterial growth begins immediately after the resolution of rigor, TMA formation does not for several days (Good and Stern 1955; Connell 1969). Quite often, the TMA test is inadequate in determining the onset of spoilage for this reason (Farber 1963; Laycock and Regier 1971). This problem is demonstrated by the findings that TMA showed a sudden increase only after the taste panel had rejected scallops *(Pecten gibbus)* and capelin *(Mallotus villosus)* stored in ice (Waters 1964; Shaw and Botta 1975, respectively). Also, TMA was of little value in iced shrimp since the TMA increase did not occur until shrimp had passed prime quality (Bethea and Ambrose 1962).

In fish stored at low temperatures, it is impossible to tell what stage of this lag period the fish has reached. Hess (1941) devised an experiment to determine the keeping quality of fish by subjecting the samples to 3 hr of incubation at 25°C and then comparing the TMA contents before and after incubation. If a 75% or higher increase in TMA occurs during the incubation period, the fish will spoil within 24−48 hr at 0.5°C. Farber (1965B) and Farber and Lerke (1961) also found the incubation technique to be of value. They determined the values of TMA N and volatile reducing substances

(VRS) before and after 5 hr of incubation at 31°C of various fish and shrimp. The reduction or disappearance of pigmented bacteria was also calculated. They concluded that these three tests coupled with incubation provided reliable criteria for evaluating the freshness of raw fish and estimating the keeping quality of fish in refrigerated storage.

Castell *et al.* (1948) found bacterial counts to be of little value as a measure of the degree of spoilage in fresh fillets. Instead, there was a very close correlation between the number of psychrophilic gram-negative organisms and the keeping time in cold storage. This is understandable in view of the fact that the TMA value was used as a spoilage index in this experiment, because many of psychrophilic gram-negative bacteria produce TMA from TMAO. The proliferation of species of *Pseudomonas* and *Achromobacter* was accompanied by offensive, putrid odors and rapid spoilage. Flavobacteria, most of micrococci, and all of microbacteria, however, did not cause such noticeable organoleptic changes. *Pseudomonas* and *Achromobacter* constitute the normal flora of the gut, skin, and gills of fish and are responsible for spoilage (Castell *et al.* 1948).

One exception was the study of Slabyj and True (1978), who found no increase in bacterial count corresponding to the TMA increase or organoleptic quality of sardine.

Effect of Storage and Processing on TMA Value.   The rate of increase in TMA during spoilage of fish varies with the storage temperature; quite pronounced at room temperature, but absent or negligible at subzero temperatures. When fish are stored at temperatures below 0, TMA formation is greatly retarded or totally inhibited, though spoilage continues (Anderson and Fellers 1949; Connell 1969; Karnicka and Jurewicz 1971; Uchiyama *et al.* 1974; Dingle and Hines 1975). Therefore, TMA is not a valid index of spoilage in frozen fish (Sigurdsson 1947; Castell and Triggs 1955).

Even in low temperature storage such as refrigeration above 0°, TMA formation slows down noticeably (Ishida *et al.* 1976). This alters the TMA threshold level at which fish are considered spoiled. In two fish of identical quality, the one stored at a lower temperature will show a lower TMA value (Anderson and Fellers 1949). Sasajima (1974) found that, at −4° to −5°C, TMA formation did not occur unless cell counts of psychrotrophic bacteria exceeded 10^8/ml. TMAO reduction did not occur because the cell count did not reach 7.5−8.0 in log count per milliliter, which was found to be necessary in his previous study (Sasajima 1973). At −6°C, no TMA was detected whatever the cell count.

Processing methods apparently affect the relationship between odor and TMA values. For example, organoleptic and TMA tests correlated in fresh silver salmon *(Oncorhynchus kisutch)* whereas no correlation was found in the canned product of the same species (Stansby 1962). Processing greatly increases TMA in fish because of the instability of TMAO to heat (Sigurdsson 1947; Castell 1949A). Tokunaga (1975A) reported that the rate of thermal decomposition of TMAO to TMA and DMA varied with species, but generally was low in white-fleshed fish and high in red-fleshed fish. It was low in the ordinary muscle and high in the dark muscle of fish. The difference in the rate of decomposition was due to the difference in the amount of hemoproteins such as hemoglobin and myoglobin, free amino acids, pH, and SH base. The high content of hemoproteins (myoglobin + hemoglobin) in the red muscle of skipjack, tuna, and mackerel was reported to be 2.04%, 3.91−5.09%, and 0.98%, respectively (Matsuura and Hashimoto 1954). It was also noted that the rate of TMA produced was highest in the dark muscle of fish, while mollusks and crustaceans produced most DMA from TMAO (Tokunaga 1975A). Rapid decomposition of TMAO occurred at temperatures above 55°−60°C in dark muscle and above 80°C in ordinary muscle.

Tokunaga (1975B) studied the relationship between the freshness of raw albacore and the quality of the canned product. He suggested that the ratio of TMAO remaining undecomposed to the total content of TMAO, TMA, and DMA might be an index for the freshness of raw fish. When the ratio was 90% or above, the fish was very fresh. When it was below 50%, the fish was organoleptically stale. To evaluate the quality of canned albacore, he suggested the use of the ratio of DMA to TMA; 50% indicated that good quality raw material was canned; 40%, fish was stored for 70 hr before canning; 30% or lower, fish was stored up to 116 hr. Ammonia and TMA could not be used as quality indices in canned products since considerable amounts of both were produced during heating in the canning process.

Sodium nitrite retarded TMA production in fresh, commercial cod fillet, while having no effect on the rate of bacterial growth (Castell 1949B; Dyer 1949). Benzoic acid also suppressed TMA development almost entirely without suppressing bacterial growth, and spoilage progressed without a significant TMA increase. Sodium chloride also slowed TMAO reduction to TMA by bacteria. Ishida et al. (1976) reported that, when more than 5% salt was added to mackerel homogenates, TMA concentration did not exceed the threshold value of spoilage.

The TMA values used to measure the quality of fresh fish do not apply to minced and processed fish because of the change in TMA concentration during processing. Minced fish meat normally contains larger amounts of TMA than do fillets because the process of mincing causes an immediate increase in TMA value (Babbitt et al. 1972). It was Kawabata (1953B) who first found the dark muscle of pelagic fish to possess the ability to reduce TMAO to TMA. Castell (1970) then found that blood pigments from cod and pollock frames catalyzed the formation of TMA. This was substantiated by the findings of Licciardello et al. (1979A) that unwashed mince from frames usually contained large amounts of blood pigments, causing high levels of TMA. Mince from pollock, a species with a high percentage of dark muscle, contained the second highest level of TMA, next to cod frame mince.

Despite all the data correlating the TMA value and the degree of spoilage in fish, TMA is by no means an absolutely reliable index of spoilage. Shewan and Ehrenberg (1957, 1959) stated that the relationship between quality and TMA differed from one catch of fish to another, even when the catches were made under very similar conditions and subsequent storage was carefully controlled, and that the TMA content was not consistently related to the quality as judged by the sensory test, except in broad approximation. There are many conflicting findings as to the validity of using TMA as a spoilage index. TMA is of little use in determining the quality of fish in some cases (Tarr 1961; Farber 1965A; Karnicka and Jurewicz 1971). Antonacopoulos (1971) suggested that TMA and total basic nitrogen (TVB) values should be used in capacities supplemental to sensory evaluation, though they should not be used as obligatory limits.

DMA as a Spoilage Index

As an increasing number of fish are being frozen, spoilage indices for frozen fish have become an important subject of study. Recently, many workers have chosen DMA instead of TMA as a spoilage index of gadoid fish. (DMA production during frozen storage is discussed further in the section Storage and Processing.) Castell *et al.* (1970) suggested that DMA be used as a measure of frozen storage deterioration for the gadoid species in the same way TMA has been used as a measure of microbial spoilage in unfrozen fish.

During frozen storage, production of DMA is much larger than production of TMA, which is minimal and negligible in most cases. But the obverse holds in unfrozen storage (Castell *et al.* 1973). Thus Castell *et al.* (1974) suggested that quality control of frozen gadoid fish will benefit greatly when DMA and TMA tests are used together; DMA as an index of enzymatic deterioration during frozen storage and TMA as an index of pre-freezing quality.

In nonfrozen storage, the formation of DMA precedes that of TMA in gadoid fish (Shewan 1938; Amano and Yamada 1964A). Martin *et al.* (1978) stated that the DMA test was most valuable in the early stages of spoilage, while TMA was more sensitive as an indicator of the later stages of spoilage. However, it is reported that, in the minced muscle of canary rockfish *(Sebastes pinniger)* stored at 0°C, the DMA content was extremely low for the first 14 days and increased only several days after TMA had begun a rapid climb, by which time the fish was already inedible (Miller *et al.* 1972B). In herring stored at ambient temperature (10°–12°C), only 8 mg/100 g DMA was produced while 100 mg/100 g TMA was produced in 90 hr (Hughes 1958).

The formation of DMA is accompanied by the equimolar formation of formaldehyde (FA) (Castell *et al.* 1973), which induces textural toughening of fish flesh through denaturation of myofibrillar proteins (Crawford *et al.* 1979, and references therein). But since FA is an unstable compound and difficult to extract from fish (Ota 1958A), DMA can be measured instead to determine the spoilage of frozen gadoid fish (Castell 1971B; Castell *et al.* 1974).

The problem with using DMA as a spoilage index of frozen fish is that it can be used only with gadoid fish, because other fishes do not develop DMA in sufficiently significant amounts during frozen storage. Castell *et al.* (1970, 1971) and Castell (1971B) found that, during frozen storage at −5°C, no DMA was formed in any fish tested except gadoid fish. The nongadoid species tested were halibut, flounders, plaice, redfish, wolffish, ocean perch, ocean catfish, shad, mackerel, muscle of lobster, shrimp, and scallops. However, Tokunaga (1970B) found that at −6° and 0°C, DMA was produced in the bloody muscle of various migratory fishes. In the case of skipjack and bigeye tuna, DMA was produced only at −6°C. Generally, the fish which produced large amounts of TMA also produced large amounts of DMA. After 7 days of storage at 0°C, the constant ratio of DMA:TMA = 1:2.5 was maintained, though the amounts of the amines varied with species or individual fish. At −6°C, more DMA was formed than at 0°C, while TMA formation was suppressed.

In other types of storage, several species other than the gadoid fishes were found to contain DMA (Walker *et al.* 1970). But its concentration is usually low and occurrence quite irregular even within the species (e.g., squid). At the present time, therefore, the DMA test appears to be applicable only to the gadoid fish whatever type of storage may be employed. One exception is canned fish which will be discussed later.

Of gadoid fishes, hake which spoils most rapidly contained more DMA than any other North Atlantic species tested (Dyer and Hiltz 1974; Licciardello *et al.* 1979A). Castell *et al.* (1971, 1973) found that DMA was lowest in haddock and increasingly higher in cod, pollock, cusk, and hake. Similar results were obtained by Hiltz *et al.* (1976): deterioration as measured by the DMA test was slowest in cod and haddock, intermediate in cusk and silver hake, and fastest in red hake *(Urophycis chuss)*. Seasonal variations in the DMA-producing activity of the muscle of fish was reported by Castell *et al.* (1971). Haddock, cod, and silver hake tested produced larger amounts of DMA more rapidly in the summer and fall than in the spring. Lall *et al.* (1975) also noted that DMA formation, hence deterioration, was faster in the summer (the spawning season) than in the winter in silver hake.

As is the case with TMA, DMA is produced more rapidly and in larger amounts in minced flesh than in intact flesh of gadoid fish (Tokunaga 1965, 1974; Castell 1971A; Lall *et al.* 1975). Dingle *et al.* (1977) found that when one part minced red hake muscle was added to four parts minced flatfish muscle stored at −10°C, protein denaturation caused by the formation of FA occurred as fast as in minced red hake alone. Under the same condition, minced flatfish was stable for 52 days.

Castell (1971B) commented that there appeared to be a close correlation between the amount of DMA formed and the amount of dark muscle in the hake fillets, and that the removal of the dark muscle from the fillets before freezing caused a marked reduction in the formation of DMA and FA during storage, resulting in less loss of extractable protein. Dyer and Hiltz (1974) did not find the removal of the red muscle to affect the rate of deterioration in red hake, although the red muscle contained several times more DMA than the ordinary muscle. Castell *et al.* (1971) suspected that DMA and FA formation in dark muscle and internal organs was catalyzed by the heme pigments present in these tissues.

Visceral organs are known to be most active in the formation of DMA and FA (series of publications by Amano, Yamada, and Harada). Dingle and Hines (1975) and Svensson (1977) found that kidney tissue is responsible for the high content of DMA and FA in minced flesh of gadoid fish. Dingle and Hines (1975) also found that the minced flesh of witch flounder *(Glypto-cephalus cynoglossus)* American plaice *(Hippoglossoides platessoides)* and Atlantic mackerel *(Scomber scombrus)* were relatively stable when mixed with homogenates of their own kidney tissues, but that the mixture of minced flounder and homogenated cod kidney caused changes similar to those observed in minced cod flesh. Irradiation of gadoid fish fillets with γ rays (0.6–5.6 Mrad) accelerated DMA and FA formation (Tozawa and Amano 1969A). Addition of a homogenate of the pyloric caeca of cod *(G. macrocephalus)* to horse mackerel muscle prior to γ irradiation at 3.0 Mrad further speeded the formation of DMA and FA (Tozawa and Amano 1969B). Svensson (1977) noted that, when the kidney tissues were removed prior to deboning, minces showed best storage stabilities.

Castell *et al.* (1971) reported the catalyst of DMA and FA production to be heat-stable. Precooking (steaming 5 min followed by autoclaving 10 min at 110°C) only slowed the formation of DMA in gadoid fish during subsequent frozen storage. But it was reported by Tokunaga (1964) that DMA formation was inhibited in Alaska pollock muscle by preheating for 30 min in a 50°C bath. Lall *et al.* (1975) attributed the inhibitory effect of heat in Tokunaga's report to the long heating time of small samples (30 g each). Lall *et al.* (1975) reported that preheating fillets and minced flesh of silver hake to temperatures up to 60°C had little or no effect on DMA formation during subsequent frozen storage at −10°C. But preheating to or above 80°C severely reduced, though did not inhibit, DMA formation.

STORAGE AND PROCESSING

Frozen storage

DMA appears to be a reliable index of spoilage as far as gadoid fish in frozen storage are concerned. Since FA, produced simultaneously with DMA, reduces extractable protein in fish muscle, textural change is more apparent and important than the change in taste or odor during frozen spoilage (Dyer *et al.* 1964). A decrease in extractable protein coupled with a proportional increase in DMA and FA was observed in Alaska pollock by Tokunaga (1974). Crawford *et al.* (1979) found a significant correlation between sensory evaluation and the DMA and FA levels of minced Pacific hake *(Merluccius productus)* frozen at −26°C.

It may be commercially unfeasible to keep the storage temperature low enough to effectively halt deterioration, but fish stored for long periods of time do deteriorate at higher temperatures even in frozen storage (Tozawa *et al.* 1971), and the lower the temperature, the less deterioration (Dyer *et al.* 1964; Connell 1969). The maximum DMA production occurred at -10°C in Alaska pollock fillets (Tokunaga 1974) and at -5°C in the gadoid species tested (Castell *et al.* 1973). Also at -10°C, minced red hake and a mixture of minced red hake and flatfish underwent a very rapid change in quality, while minced flatfish alone was stable for 52 days (Dingle *et al.* 1977). DMA (measured initially as TMA and later properly identified) slowly increased in cod stored at temperatures ranging from -3° to -26°C (Castell *et al.* 1968).

The highest temperature that reasonably ensures the quality of stored fish appears to be -26°C or thereabouts, for Castell (1970) found no increase in DMA in cod stored at -26°C during the storage period of 1347 days. Silver hake stored at -26°C for up to 6 months underwent little change (Hiltz *et al.* 1976.) Hiltz *et al.* (1977) additionally observed no loss of protein extractability in round frozen silver hake during 6 months of storage at -25°C, although some lipid hydrolysis occurred. Castell *et al.* (1974) reported that a storage temperature of approximately -29°C must be maintained to inhibit the formation of quality-degrading DMA and FA. Banks (1965) stated that -30°C was required to control deterioration. However, in the case of minced red hake, which spoils faster than any other fish, slow deterioration was observed even at -30°C (Dingle *et al.* 1977).

Lall *et al.* (1975) reported that preheating to 80°C of fillets and minced flesh of silver hake prior to freezing greatly retarded the development of DMA. Hiltz *et al.* (1976) reported that holding fish up to 6 days in refrigerated seawater at $0^\circ - 1^\circ$C before processing extended the frozen storage life of silver hake fillets, and that "firm texture and acceptable appearance was retained several days longer than in fish held in ice, where objectionable softening occurred." As mentioned previously, removal of dark muscle, kidney and other internal organs, and blood before deboning and mincing would help reduce the rate of DMA and FA increase.

Heat Treatment and Canning

Cooking causes an increase in the amounts of TMA and DMA in fish (Sasaki *et al.* 1953; Kawamura *et al.* 1971B, respectively). Moreover, the amount of amines produced is directly proportional to cooking time in herring (Hughes 1959) and horse mackerel (Shimomura *et al.* 1971). Short-time steam-heating does not enhance DMA formation (Ota 1958B). However, the thermal decomposition of TMAO to TMA and DMA takes place even at temperatures lower than 100°C, and it is strongly enhanced by the addition of sugars, especially xylose (Tokunaga 1975A). Distillation of TMA with glucose also is reported to promote the formation of DMA under acidic condition (Hayashi *et al.* 1974).

When fish is pressure-heated in the canning process, DMA as well as TMA is produced from TMAO, though large quantities of TMA remain unchanged after canning (Hughes 1959). In herring, the amount of DMA was approximately half that of TMA (Hughes 1958). Tokunaga (1975B) confirmed the ratio of DMA to TMA produced by thermal decomposition of TMA to be approximately 50% in the case of fresh fish.

Ota (1958B) found DMA in canned mackerel, salmon, and squid after pressure-heating at 115°C. The amount of DMA thus produced was almost proportional to the TMAO content of each species, being high in squid and low in salmon. Amano et al. (1968) detected DMA in canned mackerel, squid, king crab, smoked herring, fermented squid, and skipjack, but not in canned shrimp and pink salmon, while TMA was present in all samples. Kawamura et al. (1971A) found DMA in all canned foods tested including salmon and shrimp. Generally, the amount of DMA in canned products was higher than that in raw fish; sardines canned in oil had 30 times the amount of DMA found in raw fish.

In most fish, both TMA and DMA appear to be present. The DMA measured by the picrate method of Dyer as modified by Sasaki and Fujimaki (1953) was much larger than that measured by the dithiocarbamate method (Dyer 1945), indicating the presence of TMA (Ota 1958B). Sasaki et al. (1953) found that the TMA measured by the picrate method or steam distillation was larger than that measured by the modified aconitic acid method of Cromwell (1950). This, in turn, suggests the presence of DMA in the assay.

Farber and Ferro (1956) found that the TMA content varied with the species of fish canned, being high in Atlantic herring and low in tuna. But the TMA value did not reflect the organoleptic quality or condition of the fish tested. TMA cannot be used to evaluate the quality of canned fish because it is produced during heating in the canning process (Tokunaga 1975B). Slabyj and True (1978) suggested the TMA test be performed on raw sardines to estimate the quality of the canned products.

The rate of thermal decomposition is high in the red-fleshed fish, which contain small amounts of TMAO (mackerel, bluefin, skipjack). The rate is low in the ordinary muscle of white-fleshed fish which contain large amounts of TMAO (Alaska pollock, ling cod, alfonsino, Beryx splendens). Therefore much of the TMAO remains unchanged after canning and can act as a source of oxygen during subsequent storage (Hughes 1959). This is why fish with a high content of TMAO such as hake and other gadoid fish may easily discolor when TMAO is reduced to TMA, causing corrosion (Ronold and Jakobsen 1947). Hughes (1959) commented that TMAO as a potential oxygen supply was more important than the head space gas in the can. The former in a 14 oz can of herring is equivalent to 75−100 ml oxygen at S.T.P. as compared with 43−5 ml in the latter case. In canned herring pastes, residual TMAO is reduced within 3 months.

The green discoloration called "greening" appears in cooked tuna. It cannot be predicted from visual inspection of raw tuna flesh. Many studies

OCCURRENCE AND SIGNIFICANCE OF TRIMETHYLAMINE OXIDE   177

have been undertaken to find the cause of this quality degradation and to devise a test to predict it. Sasano *et al.* (1961) presented a high correlation between "green" tuna and the occurrence of "YS", which was detected as a yellow spot on paper chromatograms developed with ninhydrin. By paper chromatography, Koizumi and Hashimoto (1965A) identified this YS fraction as TMAO instead of a peptide as formerly supposed. Nagaoka and Suzuki (1964) found a correlation between the color and the TMA content of cooked meat, but not between the color and the TMA of raw meat. They then found that TMAO in raw meat correlated well with the color of cooked fish. Koizumi and Hashimoto (1965B) confirmed that TMAO itself participated in greening, not its heat degradation products such as TMA, DMA, FA, or monomethylamine. They further stated that TMAO probably acted as an oxygen donor since sodium hydrosulfide, a strong reducing substance, was effective in preventing the greening phenomenon.

Koizumi *et al.* (1967) noted that the degree of "greenness" was roughly proportional to the TMAO level in the raw muscle of albacore, with the TMAO-rich tail-end muscle being more prone to greening than other parts of the fish. It was also reported that the TMAO level in the muscle of green tuna was markedly higher than that in normal tuna (Yamagata *et al.* 1968). With the TMAO concentration below 13 mg% N, the occurrence of greening was unpredictable and erratic (Koizumi *et al.* 1967). Nagaoka *et al.* (1971) devised a special apparatus for easy determination of the sum content of TMAO and TMA as an indicator of greening.

Greening involves more than just TMAO. Koizumi and Matsuura (1967, 1968) and Koizumi and Nonaka (1970) found that the presence of metmyoglobin (MMb) and cysteine was a prerequisite to the development of greening. And greening occurred in the presence of specific levels of TMAO and MMb (Nagaoka *et al.* 1971). The deep-seated red muscle of tuna and bonito was found to contain large amounts of myoglobin (Mb), as much as 2% of wet weight (Matsuura and Hashimoto 1954). It is recommended by these studies that tuna with high concentrations of TMAO and Mb not be used for canning.

Irradiation Preservation

Low dosage ionizing irradiation as a means of preserving foods has become popular in recent years. It has been found that irradiation preservation is applicable to fresh fish. Gamma irradiation in a dosage high enough to sterilize fish meat (5.6 Mrad), however, is not recommended since it causes undesirable odor, flavor, and color changes (Shewan 1962B). Lower, pasteurization doses appear to extend shelf life sufficiently without any detrimental change in quality. Miyauchi *et al.* (1964) recommended 0.2–0.4 Mrad as the most effective range, whereas Power *et al.* (1964) found 0.075 Mrad to be an optimum level.

Pasteurization irradiation retards deterioration by reducing the number of spoilage microorganisms. Microbial reduction of TMAO is also slowed

(Power *et al.* 1964; Spinelli *et al.* 1965, 1969; Angelini *et al.* 1975). Irradiation also alters the makeup of the bacterial population in fish stored at chilled temperature. In unirradiated fish, pseudomonads and achromobacters become predominant in the course of spoilage. In fish irradiated at 0.1 Mrad and stored aerobically, however, the proportion of *Pseudomonas* is suppressed to only a few percent of the total bacterial flora, having been replaced mainly by *Achromobacter* (Laycock and Regier 1970; Pelroy *et al.* 1967; Licciardello *et al.* 1967). Pelroy *et al.* (1967) found that *Trichosporon* yeast as well as *Achromobacter* dominated in the flora of petrale sole.

In anaerobically stored irradiated fish such as vacuum-packed fillets, *Lactobacillus* becomes by far the predominant species (Laycock and Regier 1970; Pelroy and Eklund 1966; Licciardello *et al.* 1967). At a lower dosage of 0.1 Mrad, some growth of *Pseudomonas* is also observed (Pelroy and Eklund 1966).

Pelroy (Miyauchi *et al.* 1966) stated that the shelf life of irradiated fillets is related to both initial bacterial counts and the relative condition of the fish as reflected by objective chemical indices. In irradiated fish of poor initial quality, the number of *Pseudomonas* increases during storage accompanied by a TMA increase and ammoniacal putrid odor (Laycock and Regier 1970). Irradiated fish of good quality developed large quantities of TMA and putrid odors when it was inoculated with *Pseudomonas* (Licciardello *et al.* 1967). Sole inoculated with a pure culture of *Pseudomonas* sp. which had been isolated from fresh sole developed large quantities of TMA and a putrid odor when it was stored under anaerobic conditions but not under aerobic conditions (Miyauchi *et al.* 1966). In contrast, inoculation with an *Achromobacter* isolate resulted in more TMA under aerobic conditions and little under vacuum.

TMA production in king crab *(Paralithodes camtschatica)* was markedly reduced by irradiation, even when bacterial populations exceeded 1×10^8 per gram (Spinelli 1964). In unirradiated crab, significant sensory changes occurred with a bacterial count of 1×10^6/g. Spinelli *et al.* (1965) postulated that, since irradiated fish had a fairly select bacterial population, the number of bacteria required to induce sensory changes was considerably higher than it would be in unirradiated fish.

The amount of TMA produced in irradiated fish differs with a given dosage and the species of fish (Spinelli *et al.* 1969; Amano and Tozawa 1969). The maximum permissible dose and optimum dose also vary with the species (Shewan 1962B; Chung *et al.* 1976A,B). In Pacific cod stored at chill temperature, the TMA content in unirradiated samples at the stage of insipient spoilage was 11.4 mg/100 g after 2 weeks, while after 12 weeks the maximum TMA content in cod irradiated at 0.1 Mrad was 4.4 mg and that in cod irradiated at 0.2 Mrad was 0.8 mg (Miyauchi 1960). In most cases, 0.9 mg% TMA indicated borderline acceptability in king crab (Miyauchi *et al.* 1963). In dungeness crab *(Cancer magister)* the maximum TMA content in irradiated samples was 1.0 mg and 25.0 mg in unirradiated samples (Miyauchi *et al.* 1963).

Although the amount of TMA is extremely low in irradiated fish, it shows a rough correlation with spoilage (Miyauchi *et al.* 1963). Spinelli *et al.* (1969) stated that TMA as a quality index is applicable only to fish irradiated below the level of 0.2 Mrad. Over this level, TMA production is so small that it either does not correlate with sensory scores or is impractical to use as a criterion of quality (Spinelli *et al.* 1965). Tozawa and Amano (1969A), however, found that irradiation at 1.1 Mrad and above produced more TMA than irradiation at 0.6 Mrad. But the difference in the quantity of TMA formed was small among species or within a species of fish irradiated at different dosages.

Tozawa and Amano (1969A) found DMA and FA in irradiated fish; in fairly large quantities in gadoid fishes (cod and Alaska pollock), in small quantities in shark and cuttlefish, and in traces or absent in carp. The amount of DMA varied with a given dosage, species, and individual fish, increasing with higher dosage. Tozawa and Amano (1969B) considered the formation of DMA and FA to be enzymatic in nature, because the addition of the viscera of cod and Alaska pollock, especially cod pyloric caeca, known to contain the TMAO-reducing enzyme, markedly accelerated the formation of DMA in the flesh of cod, Alaska pollock, and horse mackerel during irradiation. Acceleration also occurred during irradiation in the mixture of the TMAO solution and cod pyloric caeca. Irradiation at 3.0 Mrad produced more DMA than 0.6 Mrad.

Heating pyloric caeca before mixing with fish flesh suppressed the "acceleration" of DMA formation. Mixing flesh with tissues possessing low or no enzyme activity, such as pyloric caeca of horse mackerel, skipjack, and gurnard, or hepatopancreas of carp, did not accelerate DMA formation. It was also noted that acceleration occurred only during irradiation and not after it.

Other Methods of Processing

Apparently, drying increases TMA and DMA in fish. Drum-drying caused accumulation of DMA in rockfish (Babbitt 1977) and shrimp and herring (Spinelli and Koury 1978). Drum-drying and freeze-drying increased the DMA content in hake considerably (Spinelli and Koury 1979). Freeze-dried products were reported to contain large quantities of DMA and small quantities of TMA, for most TMAO was converted to DMA (Kida and Tamoto 1976). When processed by drying DMA appears to accumulate in fishery products regardless of species. This is documented by Miyahara (1960), who found DMA as the result of processing in salted and dried Japanese sardine, and by Kawamura *et al.* (1971B) who found great accumulation of DMA in such species as plaice, mackerel, perch, and squid after drying and roasting.

Various factors seem to affect the amount of amines that accumulate in dried products. Ito *et al.* (1971B) reported that natural sun drying produced less DMA than propane or heavy oil drying in small sardines. The speed of drying affected the rate of TMA and DMA formation in Alaska pollock; the faster the drying, the less TMA and DMA formed (Kida and Tamoto 1976). In roasted mackerel, cuttlefish, and plaice, DMA peaked after 20 min of roasting, then gradually decreased (Ito et al. 1971B). The rate of TMA and DMA formation was found to be proportional to the freshness of the raw material; that is, the fresher the material, the less amine in dried products (Kida and Tamoto 1974). Spinelli and Koury (1979) related the amount of DMA to the water activity of the drum-dried and freeze-dried hake. Kida and Tamoto (1974) also reported that the TMA and DMA content was in inverse relation to the water content and TMAO content of the dried products. One additional point of interest is that dried fish may increase its amine content during storage too. Hamed and Adley (1974) found that the mean TMA N (mg/100 g dry weight) value in boiled, dried shrimp stored at room temperature was 7.0 initially, 56.1 after 4 months, 96.7 after 8 months, and 129.1 after 12 months of storage.

The data on the amines in cured or smoked fish are scant and inconclusive. TMA is found in much larger amounts in smoked and salted fish than in fresh fish (Dyer and Mounsey 1945). Light-salted cures, which naturally deteriorate faster than heavy-salted cures, were characterized by high concentrations of TMA and total volatile acids (Cardin et al. 1961). It has been shown, however, that when fish is salted, TMA formation is greatly suppressed and does not correlate with spoilage (Labrie and Gibbons 1937). Bilinski and Fougére (1959) found that TMA formation in cod muscle was inhibited by 10% NaCl for at least 15 days at 15° or 25°C. Yu and Cruess (1951) reported that, in smoked fish, TMA formation paralleled spoilage as evidenced by organoleptic examination. Spoilage was quite evident when the TMA value reached 50 mg/100 g of flesh.

A finding opposite to the above was reported by Velanker (1952), who used cured fish (salted and dried in the sun) stored at room temperature. He found that the TMA content of red discolored fish was lower than that of samples in good condition. He postulated that this was due to the loss of TMA in the spoiled samples during storage, rather than slow formation of TMA. Halophilic cocci were isolated from the surface of red discolored fish. Halophilic rods and cocci were also isolated from "pink" salt fish by Shewan (1971).

Fujii et al. (1974) found that the amount of TMA did not increase when molds grew abundantly on the surface of salted fish muscle homogenates, and that a penicillium isolated from the homogenates utilized TMA rapidly. They further discovered that, of 23 authentic strains of molds tested, 8 of 11 strains of Penicillium, 1 of 8 strains of Aspergillus, and none of Rhizopus, Mucor, Citromyces, or Alternaria utilized TMA. Therefore, it is quite possible that fish spoiled by molds contain less TMA than non-moldy fish. Ishida et al. (1976) also found that the TMA value was still quite low when salted fish was spoiled and molds and yeasts were present.

Certain antibiotics retard spoilage of fish. Watanabe (1965) found that round fish (pescada, *Microdon ancylodon*), dipped in a 30 ppm solution of chlortetracycline for 2 min and kept in ice, was edible for 19 days, while untreated fish lasted only 11–16 days in the same ice. Ogawa *et al.* (1970) also reported that the treatment of lobster tail with chlortetracycline retarded deterioration but that spiramycin had no effect. They noted a significant correlation between the organoleptic test and the TMA level. Several studies, however, found no correlation between the TMA content and organoleptic quality of fish stored in ice containing antibiotics, because TMA formation was not retarded (Tomiyama 1956; Bystedt and Liljemark 1956; Castell and Greenough 1957). Consequently, some fish in antibiotic ice is judged satisfactory organoleptically while having large amounts of TMA and other chemical indices of decomposition (Hillig *et al.* 1962B).

Sidhu *et al.* (1974B) found that rock lobster muscle immersed for 4 min in a 3% salt solution containing 15 ppm oxytetracycline showed low TMA production when stored at 20°, 15°, and 0°C, while the muscle dipped in a salt solution alone showed a rapid TMA increase at 20° and 15°C. Castell and Greenough (1957) commented that oxytetracycline did not itself inhibit the bacterial reduction of TMAO to TMA, but rather, a decrease in TMA formation was brought about by a selective reduction in the number of bacteria producing TMA.

One percent EDTA (ethylenediaminetetraacetic acid) solution used as a dip extends the shelf life of fish and suppresses TMA formation (Levin 1967; Pelroy and Seman 1969; Huss 1971). Although the number of bacteria is hardly reduced by the treatment, the growth of *Pseudomonas* spoilage organisms is markedly inhibited (Levin 1967; Pelroy and Seman 1969). *Achromobacter lipolyticum* was the only psychrophilic organism of the 20 tested that was insensitive to EDTA (Levin 1967). Power *et al.* (1968) found a good correlation between taste panel grades and TMA values of EDTA-treated haddock in spite of a rapid growth of bacteria. Spoilage as judged by the panel occurred when TMA reached 3–9.5 mg N/100 g.

Debevere and Voets (1971) found that more TMA was produced in packed fish than in unpacked fish. Also, the TMA value depended on the permeability of the packaging material used (Murray *et al.* 1971). A film with very low oxygen permeability (L film with oxygen permeability of ca. 500 ml/m^2/24 hr) prevented aerobic bacteria from proliferating (Debevere and Voets 1974), which resulted in anaerobic respiration by some bacteria of TMAO and a resultant increase in TMA. The use of the film promoted maximum spoilage.

The shelf life of cuttlefish fried with a plant oil was found to be longer than that of other fried foods. Ishikawa and Yuki (1974) and Ishikawa *et al.* (1978A,B) found it to be due to the presence in the cuttlefish of TMAO, which inhibited autoxidation of oil. TMAO may be an effective constituent for promoting the shelf life of fried marine products.

METHODS

Methods for estimating TMA have been reviewed and evaluated by She-wan *et al.* (1971). For the detailed procedure of each method, the original publications should be consulted. The numbers in parentheses after the headings refer to the Methods Used column in Table 12.1 starting on page 188.

Steam Distillation (Hjorth-Hansen 1952) (1)

Steam distillation takes up large space and requires the manpower of an experienced technician (Shewan *et al.* 1971). Venkataraman and Chari (1950) compared the results of this method with the microdiffusion method using three extracts for both; namely 96% ethanol extract, dry tricloroacetic acid crystal extract, and trichloroacetic acid solution–water extract. They preferred steam distillation under reduced pressure on an aliquot of 96% ethanol extract to Conway's microdiffusion estimation. The latter, they commented, was difficult to handle due to the "unwieldly volume of the final reduced extract."

Microdiffusion Method (2)

Shewan *et al.* (1971) stated that the Conway microdiffusion method (Conway and Byrne 1933; Conway 1947) as modified by Beatty and Gibbons (1937) was simple, inexpensive, fairly accurate, reproducible, and widely used. They also noted a few disadvantages. First, thorough cleaning of the apparatus that is essential for accuracy of data is troublesome and time-consuming. Incompletely cleaned glassware gives erroneously low TMA values (Spinelli 1964). Errors in titration can also affect the measurement as much as $10-20\%$ (Spinelli 1964). Montgomery (1956) suggested the use of potassium carbonate on the outer edge of the Conway unit as a seal instead of Vaseline or waxy materials commonly in use.

A second disadvantage is that DMA, if present, is not fixed by the added HCHO as does ammonia and monomethylamine, diffusing over with TMA (Shewan *et al.* 1971). Cobb *et al.* (1973) suggested that, instead of using saturated potassium carbonate as a releasing agent, saturated trisodium phosphate with KOH added should be used, because the latter lessens the interference of DMA and NH_3, allowing complete distillation of TMA N. A third disadvantage noted by Shewan *et al.* is the fact that the use of muscle juice requires determination of the moisture content of muscle before the TMA content can be expressed as mg N/100 g flesh.

A speedier determination of TMA N using the microdiffusion technique was devised by Montgomery (1956) and Yamagata *et al.* (1969). Montgomery's method involved partial absorptions over very short periods of time: the time it takes for the estimation of TMA, NH_3, and DMA is 2, 5, and 11 min, respectively, for 50% absorption.

Yamagata *et al.* (1969) found the Beatty and Gibbons modification of the microdiffusion method to be easier and simpler than the picric acid method as modified by Hashimoto and Okaichi (1957), though the TMA recovery rates of the two methods were equally good. Prior to microdiffusion, TMAO is reduced to TMA with titanous trichloride (TCT). Instead of leaving the solution containing TCT for 2 hr as practiced by Bystedt *et al.* (1959), Yamagata *et al.* (1969) heated the solution in an 80°C water bath until the red-purple color of TCT disappeared. This took only 1 to 1.5 min, greatly reducing the experiment time. This procedure has been widely used since (Cantoni and Ardemagni 1977).

Picrate Method (3)

TMA determination by Dyer's method (1943, 1945) using picric acid has been most widely evaluated. It has undergone a number of modifications for more accuracy and convenience.

Choice of the reducing agent affects the final outcome of TMAO determination whatever the method, because it is difficult to attain a complete reduction of TMAO to TMA for analysis, especially at low concentrations (Bystedt *et al.* 1959). The two most widely used reducing agents are Devarda's alloy and titanous chloride. Dyer *et al.* (1952) modified the method of Norris and Benoit (1945A) using Devarda's alloy and TCA or FA as extractant rather than hydrochloric acid for subsequent colorimetric determination. This made the procedure much simpler than Lintzel's original method (1934) and gave a recovery rate of approximately 96% down to about 0.4 mg N.

The reduction by Devarda's alloy, however, was found to be incomplete, especially with small quantities of TMA (Beatty 1938; Bystedt *et al.* 1959). Ronold and Jakobsen (1947) found titanous chloride to be a vastly superior reducing agent. This was confirmed by Bystedt *et al.* (1959), who reduced TMAO in a 5% TCA extract with $TiCl_3$ and determined the TMA colorimetrically as picrate. Barnes and Blackstock (1974) then came up with a scaled-down version of the procedure of Bystedt *et al.*, which, they found, could determine as little as 10 μg TMAO per gram of dry weight.

TCA as extractant was found to be better than hydrochloride or water extracts. Dyer (1959) used 7.5% TCA while Shewan *et al.* (1971) recommended 5% TCA. It minimized both volatilization and further reduction of amine (Murray and Gibson 1972A). Shewan *et al.* (1971) stated that extraction of TMA with tap water (Hoogland 1956) should be avoided because of the formation of emulsions, which made subsequent operations difficult to perform. Saito and Sameshima (1956A) also encountered turbidity, which made TMA determination impossible. They found that cadaverine was the cause of the turbidity (Saito and Sameshima 1956B), instead of ammonia and lecithin, which sometimes cause turbidity (Dyer 1945).

The most serious flaw in the original method of Dyer and that of Hoogland (1956) is the interference of other amines with TMA determination. Up to the level of approximately 60 mg TMA N/100 g of tissue, the values obtained by the picrate method and the microdiffusion procedure of Beatty and Gibbons (1937) agree fairly well. But above that level, the picrate reading gives much higher values, because picrate reacts with other amines that are produced at advanced stages of decomposition of fish (Dyer and Mounsey 1945). Even at very low levels of TMA, the picrate method may still give higher values than the microdiffusion method (Tozawa et al. 1970, 1971; Murray and Gibson 1972A,B). This is due to the interference of DMA, found for the first time in large quantities in frozen fish in 1964 (Tokunaga 1964). DMA gives 20% of the absorption of TMA in the colorimetric determination (Dyer and Mounsey 1945). Other volatile bases present in the early stage of spoilage, namely, ammonia and monomethylamine, are fixed by the FA used in the procedure and pose no problem.

To alleviate the problem of the interfering DMA, 50% K_2CO_3, used as alkali to liberate TMA by Dyer, was replaced by 25% KOH by Hashimoto and Okaichi (1957). These authors reported that the recovery rate of TMA using KOH at 30°C was over 97% down to 0.025 mg/100 g TMA N. The use of 25% KOH instead of 50% K_2CO_3, however, did not completely eliminate the problem of DMA. Tozawa et al. (1970, 1971) reported that, with KOH, DMA still produced sufficient color to give readable optical density values on the spectrophotometer. They also found that, when KOH was used, the color development of DMA was minimal with the addition of 1 ml of the 10% HCHO solution to the sample solution prior to dilution with H_2O and addition of base.

The modified method developed by scientists at Torry Research Station employed 45% KOH rather than the 25% KOH used by Japanese workers (Shewan et al. 1971; Murray and Gibson 1972A,B). The use of 45% KOH, which is equivalent in normality to 50% K_2CO_3, totally eliminated the interference by DMA. However, Castell et al. (1974) recommended 25% KOH on the basis that the correlation of color intensity of the picrate to the KOH concentration was linear up to 30% but leveled off above that with both TMA and DMA. For accurate estimation of TMA, elimination of DMA is particularly important in the case of gadoid fish, which are known to develop large quantities of DMA, especially during frozen storage (Tokunaga 1964; Castell et al. 1971; Murray and Gibson 1972B).

A modification was made on the wavelength, too. Instead of 420 nm used by Dyer (1945) and Hoogland (1956), 410 nm was chosen by Kawabata (1953A), Tozawa et al. (1970, 1971), Shewan et al. (1971), and Murray and Gibson (1972A,B), because maximum absorption of the color produced by DMA occurred at 410 nm.

Although the modified method using 45% KOH or 25% KOH with TCA and a wavelength of 410 nm appears to give an accurate estimation of TMAO and TMA, a few opposing views have been expressed. Botta and Shaw (1975) found that the TMA value in roughhead grenadier as determined by the method of Tozawa et al. (1971) was "anomalously high" compared with the TMA value obtained by Dyer's method. They speculated that a limited number of species may give completely false results when the method of Tozawa *et al.* is used.

TMA estimation is more accurate when Dyer's colorimetric procedure is applied to steam distillates obtained from the aqueous extracts of frozen cod and haddock (Bethea and Hillig 1965). Lartigue *et al.* (1960) used steam distillation to eliminate a nonvolatile component in oyster that interfered in the picrate determination.

cis-Aconitic Acid Method (4)

In 1950, Cromwell developed a method for microestimation of tertiary amines in plants. This method utilized reddish-purple colors produced by tertiary amines in the presence of *cis*-aconitic anhydride dissolved in acetic anhydride. It is specific for tertiary amines, since ammonia and primary and secondary amines do not react with aconitic acid. Sasaki and Fujimaki (1953) successfully applied this method to the TMA determination of meats and fish with certain modifications. They found that the deproteinization of the extract with TCA was better than steam distillation for extracting TMA, thus simplifying and speeding the procedure. The recovery rate of added TMAO was 98% at 0.1 mg TMAO (Sasaki *et al.* 1953). Sasaki *et al.* (1953) noted that, with the use of steam distillate, the aconite method gave a more accurate (lower) estimation of TMA in cooked fish than the picrate method did, although both estimations gave higher TMA values for cooked meat than raw meat. Sass *et al.* (1958) found that the aging of the reagent for 24 hr and a reaction time of 30 min for free tertiary amine gave a maximum repoducible color. This could replace the heating in Cromwell's procedure. In the case of the tertiary amine salt, 15-sec heating is sufficient.

Automated Method (5)

The automated method of Murray and Burt (1964) is an alternative to chromatographic methods. The Technicon autoanalyzer uses a TCA extract of fish muscle and colorimetric determination of TMA volatilized at 75°C by the addition of FA and KOH, before passage into the bromothymol blue solution. Accurate measurement of TMA is obtained with this method (Shewan *et al.* 1971). Kato and Uchiyama (1973) modified this method by changing the pH of the bromothymol blue solution from 6.0 to 5.0, and by using the Technicon CO_2 trap B_1 to liberate TMA from the reaction mixture. They also changed the temperature from 75° to 60°C to reduce interference by other volatile amines. With this modified automated method, the relation between optical density and TMA concentration was linear within the range of $3-50$ μg N/ml. The results agreed well, with a coefficient of 0.99, with those obtained by the picrate method as modified by Hashimoto and Okaichi (1957).

Ruiter and Weseman (1976) further improved the automated method to measure not only TMA but also DMA and ammonia. DMA determination was based on the formation of dimethyl dithiocarbamic acid as described by Dowden (1938). Since the reaction is specific for secondary amines, there was no interference from primary or tertiary amines. For TMA determination, Ruiter and Weseman found that a bath temperature of 70°C worked best, speeding up the operation and stabilizing the steady state better than 60°C. Replacing the KOH solution with a K_2CO_3 solution completely inhibited ammonia evaporation encountered at higher temperatures. Addition of 5% thiourea reduced the DMA interference brought about by the use of K_2CO_3. Ruiter and Weseman (1976) stated that the automated method of determining TMA and DMA was fast (30 samples per hour) and equaled gas chromatograhic determination in precision and accuracy. They recommended the automated method for routine use and gas chromatography for small experiments and for samples in which the presence of volatile bases other than TMA, DMA, and ammonia is expected.

Chromatographic Methods (6)

TMA, DMA, and other volatile amines in fish have been identified qualitatively and/or quantitatively by the use of paper chromatography (Obata and Matano 1952), gas chromatography (Mangan 1959; Sze and Borke 1963; Diemair 1965; Ritskes 1975), gas–liquid chromatography (James *et al.* 1952; Groninger 1958; Gruger 1972), gas–liquid–solid chromatography (Di Corcia *et al.* 1970), and thin-layer chromatography (Amano *et al.* 1968; Ito *et al.* 1971A).

Ritskes (1975) found that a Carbowax 400/polyethylene imine column completely separated TMA and DMA with hardly any tailing. A Graphon column was used by Di Corcia *et al.* (1970) and Miller *et al.* (1972A). A Dowfax 9N9-KOH column was used by Keay and Hardy (1972) who found gas chromatography to be a method vastly superior for determining TMA and DMA to the picrate method using either K_2CO_3 or KOH. Wong *et al.* (1967) combined mass spectrometry and gas chromatography to identify 18 volatile compounds. Mendelsohn *et al.* (1966) found the cryogenic GC to give best results.

In order to simplify procedures for practical use, Nonaka *et al.* (1967) used fish muscle extracted with *n*-heptane, which was directly injected into a gas chromatograph for TMA determination. They stated that the average recovery of TMA was estimated to be more than 90%, and that this method always gave better results than the picrate method did. Tokunaga *et al.* (1977) modified the simplified method of Nonaka *et al.* (1967) to determine not only TMA but also DMA, MMA, and other volatile amines. Perchloric acid was used as extractant and KOH as alkali. After shaking, the aliquot was gas-chromatographed.

It is generally agreed that the chromatographic determination of amines is more accurate than the picrate method, steam distillation, or microdiffusion. The complexity of the procedure, which is one of the drawbacks, is somewhat alleviated by simplified methods using extraction.

Enzymatic Method (7)

Large and McDougall (1975) found an enzymatic method for the micro-estimation of TMA using TMA hydrogenase from a bacterium *Hyphomicrobium vulgare* grown on TMA as the sole carbon source. They found that the calculation from the molar extinction coefficient of DCPIP (2,6-dichloro-phenolindophenol) was satisfactory with amounts of substrate (TMA) up to 140 nmoles, if the extrapolated extinction reading was used. The method is simple and inexpensive but not very rapid or sensitive. High concentrations of DMA interfere with the determination.

TMA-Specific Electrode (8)

Chang *et al.* (1976) developed a method for determining TMA with an electrode. An Orion ammonia electrode was made specific for TMA by replacing the inner filling solution with 0.01 M TMA hydrochloride in 0.04 M KCl. HCHO was added to the sample solution to reduce the response of the electrode to ammonia. This method is simpler, more rapid, and less expensive than other methods. It gives accurate measurements on aqueous solutions when compared with the results obtained by the picric acid method of Castell *et al.* (1974). When fish extracts are used, however, results are somewhat inaccurate. The electrode is not quite as selective for TMA over ammonia as is the picric acid method.

Simultaneous Determination of TMA and DMA (9)

The method for simultaneous measurement of TMA and DMA was devised by Castell *et al.* (1974). It is based on the combination of the picrate determination using KOH, which is fairly specific for TMA, and K_2CO_3, which reacts with both TMA and DMA. The DMA value is obtained by dividing by 0.5 (approximation for practical use) the difference between the values obtained by 50% K_2CO_3 and by 25% KOH. The DMA value thus obtained agreed well with the value obtained by the copper-dithiocarbamate method (Dyer and Mounsey 1945) on various gadoid fish with a correlation coefficient of 0.94. Therefore, this is a convenient and fairly accurate method for determining TMA and DMA.

Only when the fish is putrid at an advanced stage of spoilage does the picrate method give much higher values of DMA than the copper-dithiocarbamate method. As Castell *et al.* (1974) stated, this is only of academic interest, because, at such an advanced stage of deterioration, the fish is quite inedible and no test is necessary to determine quality.

The KOH value of DMA, however, is unreliable when DMA is predominant or when DMA alone is present, because DMA produces approximately 5% of the color produced by an equivalent amount of TMA with the use of KOH (Tozawa *et al.* 1970, 1971). One such case is frozen gadoid fillets. Castell *et al.* suggested that the following equation be used:

$$TMA = 1.1 \text{ KOH amine value} - 0.01 \text{ } K_2CO_3 \text{ amine value.}$$

TABLE 12.1. OCCURRENCE AND SIGNIFICANCE OF TRIMETHYLAMINE OXIDE

SCIENTIFIC NAME	COMMON NAME	TISSUE	TMAO (μM/100 g) RANGE	AVERAGE	TMA (μM/100g) RANGE	AVERAGE	DMA (μM/100g) RANGE	AVERAGE
Carcharhinidae								
Carcharhinus japonicus Glyphis glaucus		muscle	13133.33-19733.33	13133.33		2092.86		
Mustelus griseus Mestelus griseus		muscle		14533.33 13466.67, 14533.33		71.43		
Mustelus griseus Mustelus kanekonis Mustelus kanekonis Mustelus kanekonis		muscle		13466.67 16666.67 14800.00 14800.00, 16666.67		14.29 28.57 257.14		
Mustelus manago Mustelus manago	Requiem sharks	heart, liver, kidney, etc.	15333.33-19466.67	16400.00 9413.33 5080.00		121.43		
		Heart liver, kidney, etc.	6520-18133.33					
	Spotted shark	Muscle Heart liver kidney spleen brain ovary		249 222 167 151 177 120 215		13.57 200 268.57 254.29 452.86 97.86 24.29		
Mustelus manago				19642.86 5080.00		84.75		
		fetus		18533.33 19466.67 15333.33		15.71 13.57 25.00		
		pancreas spleen brain yolk liquid in eye chamber		14546.67 13426.67 98666.67 11240.00 13226.67		452.79 329.64 97.86 24.57 44.50		
		muscle (fetus) liquid in mucous lining cartilage muscle heart liver kidney fetus		17200.00 12853.33 10240.00 19493.33 18066.67 6520.00 12293.33 16066.67		44.64 38.00 104.43 13.43 200.14 268.36 254.43 29.29		
Prionace glaucus	Blue shark			19733.33 13133.33 13600.00 16666.67		442.86 4164.29 1592.86 814.29		
Triakas scyllia		muscle	18466.67-23133.33					
Triakas scyllium				23133.33 18733.33 18466.67		12.86 12.86 12.86		
Chimaeridae								
Hydrolaugus colliei	Ratfish	muscle blood serum		12714.29 714.29, 785.71				
Dasyatidae								
Dasyatis akejei Dasyatis akejei	Stingrays			16666.67 16666.67, 7506.66, 7600.00		64.29		
Dasyatis kuhlii				11133.33 11133.33		1678.57		
Dasyatis zugei				10000.00 10000.00		2750.00		
Urolophus aurantiacus Urolophus fuscus		muscle		14000.00 14000.00		17.86		
Heterodontidae								
Heterodontus japonicus	Blowhead shark	muscle		12800.00 12800.00		10.71		
Lamnidae								
Isurus glaucus Lamna cornubica Lamna ditropis Lamna masus	Sandshark Porbeagle	muscle muscle muscle		13333.33 17733.33 13293.33 10400.00 14285.71 14285.71		521.429		

NO.OF FISH EXAMINED	LENGTH OF FISH	BODY WEIGHT (g)	SEASON	METHOD USED	OTHER	REFERENCE
				3	Dry weight frozen	Suyama 1960
						Yamada 1967
				3	Dry weight frozen	Suyama 1960
						Yamada 1967
			5-10-60	3		Suyama 1960
			4-21-60	3		Suyama 1960
				3	Dry weight frozen	Suyama 1960
						Yamada 1967
				3	Dry weight frozen	Suyama 1960
						Yamada 1967
						Yamada 1967
						Yamada 1967
						Yamada 1967
				3		Suyama 1960
				3		Suyama 1960
				3		Suyama 1960
				3		Suyama 1960
				3		Suyama 1960
				3		Suyama 1960
				3		Suyama 1960
				3		Suyama/Tokuhiro 1954
				3		Sakaguchi/Simidu 1964
			3-15-60	3	All dry weight	Suyama 1960
			3-30-60	3	All dry weight	Suyama 1960
			5-15-60	3		Suyama 1960
				3		Suyama/Tokuhiro 1954
				3		Suyama/Tokuhiro 1954
				3		Suyama/Tokuhiro 1954
				3		Suyama/Tokuhiro 1954
				3		Suyama/Tokuhiro 1954
				3		Suyama/Tokuhiro 1954
				3		Suyama/Tokuhiro 1954
				3		Suyama/Tokuhiro 1954
				3		Suyama/Tokuhiro 1954
					Contains much blood	Suyama/Tokuhiro 1954
						Suyama/Tokuhiro 1954
						Suyama/Tokuhiro 1954
			5-15-60	3		Suyama 1960
				3		Suyama 1960
				3		Suyama 1960
				3		Suyama 1960
				3		Suyama 1960
				3		Suyama 1960
						Yamada 1967
			4-4-60	3		Suyama 1960
			4-4-60	3	Dry weight frozen	Suyama 1960
			4-5-60	3	Dry weight frozen	Suyama 1960
				3	Wet tissue	Norris/Penoit 1945
				3	Wet tissue	Norris/Benoit 1945
				3	Dry weight	Suyama 1960
						Yamada 1967
				3	Dry weight	Suyama 1960
						Yamada 1967
				3	Dry weight	Suyama 1960
						Yamada 1967
			4-20			Yamada 1967
				3	Dry weight	Suyama 1960
						Yamada 1967
			4-10-60	3	Dry weight	Suyama 1960
						Suyama 1960
			May 5	3	% water 70, 33	Suyama 1960
						Yamada 1967
						Yamada 1967
				3	Wet tissue	Dyer 1952
				3	Wet tissue	Dyer 1952

SCIENTIFIC NAME	COMMON NAME	TISSUE	TMAO (μM/100 g)		TMA (μM/100g)		DMA (μM/100g)	
			RANGE	AVERAGE	RANGE	AVERAGE	RANGE	AVERA
Mobulidae								
Mobula japonicus	Spinetail mobula	muscle		19000.00				
				19000.00		10.71		
Rajidae								
Raja batis	Skate			14714.29				
Raja clavata				1162.67				
Raja erinacea	Little skate			6142.86				
Raja hollandi	Skate			18142.86				
		muscle		18120.00		9.71		
		liver		8160.00		208.79		
		kidney		10373.33		124.93		
		spleen		12973.33		239.21		
		yolk		19493.33		6.79		
		shell gland		14640.0		352.79		
		liquid in eye chamber		14266.66		0		
				18133.33		10		
				8160.00		209.29		
				10373.33		125.00		
				12973.33		239.29		
	Atlantic skates & rays		3333.33-19066.67					
	Skates		4500.00-11428.57					
				6400.00				
				7200.00				
		liver, kidney, etc.	8160.00-19466.67					
			14400.00-18133.33					
				16266.67		15.714		
				14400.00		1042.86		
				19466.67		7.143		
				14666.67		356.43		
				14266.67		0		
Raja laevis	Barndoor skate			16714.29				
	Skate		840-2133.33					
	Barndoor skate							
				16.67				
				16714.29				
Raja scaberta	Prickly skate			3.60				
				5214.29				
	(Atlantic)			3642.86				
Raja senta	Smooth skate			7071.43				
				7.07				
				7071.43				
Raja sp.	Blue skate			14642.86				
Rays and Skates								
Chiloscyllium griscum				5928.57				
Rhyncoeatus djeddemsis				6214.29				
Scobiodon sp.				5142.86				
Tygron imbricata				3285.71				
	Skate			428.57				
Trygon microps				3500.00				
Trygon urnak				7428.57				
Scyliorhinidae								
Sephaloscyllium umbratile	Catshark			18933.33		20.00		
		muscle		19333.33				
Sphyrnidae								
Sphyrna mallius	Hammerhead shark			7642.86				
Sphyrna zygaena	Smooth hammerhead			5328.40		116.95		
				4924.13		427.12		
				2980.00		1762.71		
				799.20		3932.20		
				0		5294.24		
				51520.00		3035.71		
		muscle		11680.00,				
				14133.33				
Squalidae								
	Dogfish shark			12333.33				
				12400.00				
				2266.67-2773.33				
Squalus acanthius	Spiny dogfish			19.07				
		muscle		12333.33				
		muscle		13173.33				
		blood plasma		7428.57				
		muscle		13571.43				

NO.OF FISH EXAMINED	LENGTH OF FISH	BODY WEIGHT (g)	SEASON	METHOD USED	OTHER	REFERENCE
			4-20	3		Yamada 1967
						Suyama 1960
			4			
						Love et al 1959
				2		Cantoni/Ardemagni 1977
					Wet tissue	Dyer 1952
				3		Suyama/Tokuhiro 1954
				3		Suyama/Tokuhiro 1954
				3		Suyama/Tokuhiro 1954
				3		Suyama/Tokuhiro 1954
				3		Suyama/Tokuhiro 1954
				3		Suyama/Tokuhiro 1954
				3		Suyama/Tokuhiro 1954
				3		Suyama 1960
				3		Suyama 1960
				3		Suyama 1960
				3		Suyama 1960
				2		Shewan 1957
5				3		Castell 1949
5				2	Arctic	Shewan
						Yamada 1967
						Yamada 1967
			3-30	3	Dry weight	Suyama 1960
			4-30	3		Suyama 1960
				3		Suyama 1960
				3		Suyama 1960
				3		Suyama 1960
				3		Beatty/Gibbons 1937
				3		Castell 1949
				3		Beatty 1939
				3	Wet weight	Dyer 1952
				3	Wet weight	Beatty 1939
				3	Wet tissue	Dyer 1952
						Beatty/Gibbons 1937
						Beatty/Gibbons 1937
1				3	Wet weight	Beatty 1939
				3		Dyer 1952
					Wet tissue	Velankar/Govindan 1958
					Wet tissue	Velankar/Govindan 1958
					Wet tissue	Velankar/Govindan 1958
					Wet tissue	Velankar/Govindan 1958
					Wet tissue	Velankar/Govindan 1958
					Wet tissue	Velankar/Govindan 1958
			4-10	3	Dry weight	Suyama 1960
						Yamada 1967
				2	Wet tissue	Velankar/Govindan 1958
				3	0 hours	Takada/Nishimoto 1958
				3	24 hours	Takada/Nishimoto 1958
				3	48 hours	Takada/Nishimoto 1958
				3	72 hours	Takada/Nishimoto 1958
				3	120 hours	Takada/Nishimoto 1958
					Dry weight	Suyama 1960
						Yamada 1967
4				2		Shewan 1957
2				2		Shewan 1957
6				3		Beatty 1939
						Yamada 1967
						Yamada 1967
					Wet tissue	Cohen et al 1958
				3	Wet tissue	Dyer 1952

TABLE

SCIENTIFIC NAME	COMMON NAME	TISSUE	TMAO (µM/100 g)		TMA (µM/100g)		DMA (µM/100	
			RANGE	AVERAGE	RANGE	AVERAGE	RANGE	AVE
		kidney		11142.86				
		liver		1285.71				
		pancreas		714.29				
		spleen		6214.29				
		stomach		857.14				
	Atlantic dogfish			9466.66				
				19066.66				
				13571.43				
Squalus sp.	Dogfish			19.07				
Squalus suckleyi	Pacific dogfish		8800.00-13466.66					
				13571.43		1028.57		

NO.OF FISH EXAMINED	LENGTH OF FISH	BODY WEIGHT (g)	SEASON	METHOD USED	OTHER	REFERENCE
				3	Wet tissue	Norris/Benoit 1945
				3	Wet tissue	Norris/Benoit 1945
				3	Wet tissue	Norris/Benoit 1945
				3	Wet tissue	Norris/Benoit 1945
				3	Wet tissue	Norris/Benoit 1945
				2		Shewan 1957
				3	Wet weight	Dyer 1952
				3		Beatty 1939
				2		
				2		Shewan 1957
				2	Wet weight	Norris/Benoit 1945
				3	Dry weight	Suyama 1960

SCIENTIFIC NAME	COMMON NAME	TISSUE	TMAO (μM/100 g) RANGE	TMAO (μM/100 g) AVERAGE	TMA (μM/100g) RANGE	TMA (μM/100g) AVERAGE	DMA (μM/100g) RANGE	DMA (μM/100g) AVERAGE
ORDER -- ELOPIFORMES								
Elopidae								
Tarpon Atlanticus	Tarpon			3071.43				
ORDER -- ANGUILLIFORMES								
Congridae								
Astroconger myriaster		muscle		680 / 2186.67		1.69		
ORDER -- NOTACANTHIFORMES								
Notacanthidae								
Notacanthus nathus				9500.00				
ORDER -- CLUPEIFORMES								
Clupeidae								
Alosa sapidissima	American shad			3357.14 / 3214.29 / 277.33				
Clupea alosa				5285.714		357.14		
Clupea harengus	Atlantic herring			3428.57		285.71		
Clupea harengus	Herring	whole fish		4285.71		500.00		
				3428.57		357.14		
				3642.86		285.71		
				3642.86		428.57		
				3642.86		428.57		
				3642.86		285.71		
				3000.00		285.71		
				4071.43		285.71		
				3642.86		357.14		
				3285.71		500.00		
				3500.00		357.14		
				3000.00		285.71		
				3571.42		0		
				4571.43		285.71		
				3571.42		285.71		
				2714.29		428.57		
				3214.29		285.71		
				3000.00		214.29		
				3571.423				
	Atlantic herring			5285.71 / 6428.57 / 2571.43				
	Herring			6.4 / - / 3333.33				
	Atlantic herring			2866.67-4200.00				
	Herring			3333.33 / 1000.00 / 1071.43 / 578.67				
Clupea lile				2800.00				
Clupea harengus pallasi	Pacific herring	muscle		4928.57 / 4928.57				
Clupea sprattus	Herring	whole / entrails / milts / roe		666.67 / 0 / 5357.14 / 1285.71 / 1000.00				
Etremeus micropus		stomach, liver, pyloric caeca / others	66.67-1640 / 1333.33-4520					
Etremeus micropus	Sardine (Fish a)	pyloric caeca		4389.33		725.42		
	(Fish b)	pyloric caeca		1632.27		72.54		
	(Fish a)	generative organ		2400.00		542.37		
	(Fish b)	generative organ		1534.67		64.407		
	Fish A	ordinary muscle		1175.47		37.96		
		bloody muscle		1639.47		85.42		
	Fish B	ordinary muscle		68.27		16.27		
		bloody muscle		113.33		24.07		
	Fish A	stomach		3066.67		169.49		
	Fish B	stomach		1329.60		60.69		
	Fish A	liver		4517.33		1037.29		
	Fish B	liver		3066.67		76.271		
	Great herring			0		4357.14		
	Herring milts			2214.29		3785.71		
				5928.57		357.14		
				5428.57		642.86		

(Continued)

NO.OF FISH EXAMINED	LENGTH OF FISH	BODY WEIGHT (g)	SEASON	METHOD USED	OTHER	REFERENCE
				3		Dyer 1952
				3		Yamada 1967
						Takagi et al 1967
				3		Dyer 1952
				3		Dyer 1952
				3		Dyer 1952
				2		Dyer 1952
				2		Cantoni/Ardemagni 1977
7			12-3-45	3		Cantoni/Ardemagni 1977
20				3		Dyer 1952
				3		Ronold/Jakobsen 1947
			12-3-45	1		Ronold/Jakobsen 1947
			12-3-45	1		Ronold/Jakobsen 1947
			12-3-45	1		Ronold/Jakobsen 1947
			12-3-45	1		Ronold/Jakobsen 1947
			12-3-45	1		Ronold/Jakobsen 1947
			12-3-45	1		Ronold/Jakobsen 1947
			12-3-45	1		Ronold/Jakobsen 1947
			12-3-45	1		Ronold/Jakobsen 1947
			12-3-45	1		Ronold/Jakobsen 1947
				1	Specimen #11	Ronold/Jakobsen 1947
				1	Specimen #12	Ronold/Jakobsen 1947
				1	Specimen #13	Ronold/Jakobsen 1947
				1	Specimen #14	Ronold/Jakobsen 1947
				1	Specimen #15	Ronold/Jakobsen 1947
				1	Specimen #16	Ronold/Jakobsen 1947
				1	Specimen #17	Ronald/Jakobsen 1947
				1	Specimen #18	Ronold/Jakobsen 1947
				1	Specimen #19	Ronold/Jakobsen 1947
7				1	Specimen #20	Ronold/Jakobsen 1947
8				3		Dyer 1952
116				3		Dyer 1952
8				3		Dyer 1952
				11		Beatty 1939
				2		Kawamura et al 1971
						Shewan 1951
				2		Shewan 1951
				2		Shewan 1951
				2		Shewan 1951
				2		Shewan 1951
						Velankar 1958
				3		Yamada 1967
				3		Dyer 1952
				1		Dyer 1952
				1		Ronold/Jakobsen 1947
				1		Ronold/Jakobsen 1947
				1		Ronold/Jakobsen 1947
				3		Ronold/Jakobsen 1947
						Dyer 1952
						Yamada 1967
				2		Takada/Nishimoto 1958
				3		Takada/Nishimoto 1958
				3		Takada/Nishimoto 1958
				3		Takada/Nishimoto 1958
				3		Takada/Nishimoto 1958
				3		Takada/Nishimoto 1958
				3		Takada/Nishimoto 1958
				3		Takada/Nishimoto 1958
				3		Takada/Nishimoto 1958
				3		Takada/Nishimoto 1958
				3		Takada/Nishimoto 1958
				3		Takada/Nishimoto 1958
				3		Takada/Nishimoto 1958
				3		Takada/Nishimoto 1958
			12-2-44	1		Ronold/Jakobsen 1947
			12-2-44	1		Ronold/Jakobsen 1947
			9-2-45	1		
			12-2-45	1		

TABLE 1

SCIENTIFIC NAME	COMMON NAME	TISSUE	TMAO (μM/100 g)		TMA (μM/100g)		DMA (μM/100g)	
			RANGE	AVERAGE	RANGE	AVERAGE	RANGE	AVERAGE
	Herring roe			6857.14		214.29		
				6357.14		286.71		
				285.71		1428.57		
				1714.29		642.86		
				1857.14		214.29		
Pomolobus chrysochloris	Alewife			2500.00				
Pomolobus psiudoharengus	Alewife (gaspereau)			3142.86				
Sardinella albella				3857.14				
Sardinella albella		muscle		666.67				
Sardinops melanostica				506.67-				
				666.67				
Sardinops melanostica	Sardine			507.14				
				564.29				
Sardinops melanostica	Japanese sardine	ordinary		157.14		14.29		0
		bloody		2171.43		42.86		17
		ordinary		321.43		7.14		0
		bloody		1814.29		50.00		15
		ordinary		135.71		14.29		0
		bloody		2057.14		57.14		1
		ordinary		214.29		7.14		8
		bloody		1707.14		57.14		0
				1880.00		305.09		
				2560.00		1169.49		222
Sardinops sagax	Pacific sardine			-				
				2714.29				
Sardinella albella				725.33				
Sardinella longiceps				402.67				
Sardinella fimbriata				653.33				
Dorosomatidae								
Clupanodon thrissa				1160.00		1050.85		2
Engraulidae								
Engraulis encrasicholus		muscle		144.00				
Engraulis japonica				1373.33-				
				1506.67				
Engraulis japonica		ordinary muscle		366.67		27.12		
		dark muscle		902.67		40.68		
Engraulis japonica				2373.33		440.68		
Engraulis japonica								
ORDER --SALMONIFORMES								
Argentinidae								
Argentina silces	Argentine			8714.29				
Esocidae								
Esox lucius	Pike mackerel pike			214.29			320	55
Osmeridae								
Osmerus mordax	American smelt Smelt			1928.57				
				4533.33				
Salmonidae								
Leucichthys artedi	Shallow-water cisco			428.57				
Oncorhynchus keta		muscle		346.67				
Oncorhynchus kisutch	Silver salmon		642.86 714.29					
Oncorhynchus kisutch	Silver salmon		642.86- 857.14					
Oncorhynchus mason		muscle ordinary				266.67		
Oncorhynchus nerku		muscle dark	465.33			13.33		
Oncorhynchus tschawytscha	King salmon	muscle	416			5546.67		
						333.33		
Oncorhynchus tschawytscha	King salmon		666.67 500.00 642.86 714.29					
						333.33		
Oncorhynchus tschawytscha	King salmon		714.29- 857.143			1785.71		
Salmo salar	Atlantic salmon		714.29			1714.29		
Salmo salar	Atlantic salmon					1714.29		
Salvelinus fontinalis	Eastern brook trout					928.57		
ORDER - MYCTOPHIFORMES								
Cynodontidae								
Saurida tumbil				3928.57				
				3899.29				
ORDER -- CYPRINIFORMES								
Catostomidae								

NO.OF FISH EXAMINED	LENGTH OF FISH	BODY WEIGHT (g)	SEASON	METHOD USED	OTHER	REFERENCE
			15-2-45	1		Ronold/Jakobsen 1947
			2-3-45	1		Ronold/Jakobsen 1947
			12-2-44	1		Ronold/Jakobsen 1947
			9-2-45	1		Ronold/Jakobsen 1947
			15-2-45	1		Ronold/Jakobsen 1947
				3		Dyer 1952
				3		Dyer 1952
				2		Velankar/Govindan 1958
						Yamada 1967
				2		Velankar/Govindan 1958
				3		Horie/Sekine 1956
				3		Horie/Sekine 1956
	21.6	105	July 1969	3	Sample 1	Tokunaga 1970
	21.6	105	July 1969	3	Sample 1	Tokunaga 1970
	20.2	92	July 1969	3	Sample 2	Tokunaga 1970
	20.2	92	July 1969	11	Sample 2	Tokunaga 1970
	20.6	98	July 1969	11	Sample 3	Tokunaga 1970
	20.6	98	July 1969	11	Sample 3	Tokunaga 1970
	19.8	84	July 1969	11	Sample 4	Tokunaga 1970
	19.8	84	July 1969	11	Sample 4	Tokunaga 1970
	12			6		Mujahara 1960
				6		Mujahara 1960
				11		Kawamura et al 1971
				3		Horie/Sekine 1956
				2		Velankar 1958
				2		Velankar 1958
				2		Velankar 1958
	13			6		Mujahara 1960
				2		Cantoni/Ardemagni 1977
						Yamada 1967
				3		Takagi et al 1967
	10			6		Mujahara 1960
				3		Dyer 1952
				3		Dyer 1952
				11		Kawamura 1971
4				3		Dyer 1952
				2		Shewan 1951
				3		Dyer 1952
	3			3		Norris/Benoit 1945a
	3			3		Norris/Benoit 1945a
				3		Dyer 1952
						Yamada 1967
				3		Takagi et al 1967
				3		Takagi et al 1967
				2		Shewan 1951
				2		Shewan 1951
				3		Norris/Benoit 1945a
				3		Dyer 1952
				3		Dyer 1952
				3		Dyer 1952
				3		Dyer 1952
				2		Velankar/Govindan 1958
				2		Velankar/Govindan 1958

SCIENTIFIC NAME	COMMON NAME	TISSUE	TMAO (μM/100 g) RANGE	AVERAGE	TMA (μM/100g) RANGE	AVERAGE	DMA (μM/100) RANGE	AVE
Catostomus commersonnii	White sucker					0		
Moxostoma aureolum	Northern sucker					0		
Cobitidae								
Misgurnus anguillicaudatus						146.67		559.32
Cyprinidae								
Carassius auratus	Goldfish					3000.00		
Carassius carassius						240.00		457.63
Carassius carassius						226.67		2949.15
Cyprinus carpio	Carp					173.33		627.12
Cyprinus carpio	Carp	muscle				0	0	
Semotelus atromacalulatus	Creek chub					142.86		
ORDER -- SILURIFORMES								
Ariidae								
Arius dussumieri						1271.43		
Arius sona						2571.43		
Arius sona						2553.57		
Ictaluridae								
Ameirus nebulosis	Catfish					428.57		
Platycephalidae								
Platycephalus indicus			4400.00 3800.00					
Siluridae								
Parasilurus asotus						53.33		101.69
ORDER -- LOPHIFORMES								
Lophiidae								
Lophius litulon	Angler					2613.33		
Lophiomus setigerus						2560.00		
Lophius piscatorius	Goosefish		3000.00-5357.14			4214.29		
Lophius piscatorius	Monkfish		3000.00-5357.14			4214.29		
Torpedinidae								
Tetranarce occidentalis	Atlantic torpedo					8285.71		
ORDER -- GADIFORMES								
Gadidae								
	Gray rock cod							14.29 1514.29
Brosme brosme	Cusk					4642.86 4642.86		
	Cusk, Atlantic cod, haddock, whiting		1333.33-14400.00			4642.86		
Eleginus gracilis	Saffron cod	muscle				4213.33		
Gadus aeglefinus	Cod (Europe)		1357.14-3642.86			3142.86		
	Cod (arctic)		4285.71-10000.00			5785.71		
Gadus aeglefinus	Haddock					5733.33		
Gadus callarias	Cod (Europe)		2928.57-5214.29			4428.57		
Gadus callarias	Cod (arctic)		1357.14-1429.71			7357.14		
	Cod	muscle				4214.29		142.86
						3428.57		142.86
						3142.86		1000.00
						4214.29		642.86
						6142.86		428.57
						4785.71		255.71
						4571.43		0
	Ling					3142.86		0
	Pollack					3142.86		0
	Haddock					2642.86		142.86
	Haddock					3214.29		714.29
						3785.71		357.14
						3642.86		0
						2142.86		0
Gadus macrocephalus	Pacific cod	skin	10.40-7.87			8.93		
		surface						
		muscle				2928.57		14.29
		deep muscle				7571.43		21.43
						13071.43		35.71
		liver				500.00		100.00
		pyloric caeca				214.29		6.429

(Continued)   199

NO.OF FISH EXAMINED	LENGTH OF FISH	BODY WEIGHT (g)	SEASON	METHOD USED	OTHER	REFERENCE
2				3		Dyer 1952
				3		Dyer 1952
	5			6		Mujahara 1960
				3		Dyer 1952
	10			6		Mujahara 1960
				6		Mujahara 1960
	18			6		Mujahara 1960
						Yamada 1967
2				3		Dyer 1952
				2		Velankar/Govindan 1958
				2		Velankar/Govindan 1958
			.	2		Velankar/Govindan 1958
				3		Dyer 1952
						Yamada 1967
					-	
	15			6		Mujahara 1960
				3		Konosu et al 1974
2				3		Dyer 1952
2				3		Dyer 1952
				3	Wet weight	Dyer 1952
				2	Before storage	Horie/Sekine
				2	2 days at 7-16°C	Horie/Sekine
				3		Dyer 1952
				3		Dyer 1952[1]
				2		Shewan 1951
				3		Dyer 1952
				3		Dyer 1952
				3		Dyer 1952
135						Love et al 1959
136						Love et al 1959
				2		Shewan 1951
33						Love et al 1959
260						Love et al 1959
				3, 11		Amano/Yamada 1965
				3, 11		Amano/Yamada 1965
				3, 11		Amano/Yamada 1965
				3, 11		Amano/Yamada 1965
				3, 11		Amano/Yamada 1965

SCIENTIFIC NAME	COMMON NAME	TISSUE	TMAO (μM/100 g) RANGE	TMAO AVERAGE	TMA (μM/100g) RANGE	TMA AVERAGE	DMA (μM/100g) RANGE	DMA AVER
Gadus macrocephalus	Pacific cod	stomach		857.14		135.71		30
		stomach content		71.43		35.71		1
		ovary		1571.43		64.29		28
		gall bladder		-		-		85
		spleen						450
		gall bladder		-		-		
Gadus merlangus	Cod (Europe)		3142.86-4071.43	3642.86				
	Whiting			3133.33				
				3866.67				
				4040.00				
Gadus morhua	Atlantic cod			6785.714				
				8928.57				
				4357.14				
				1428.57				
				2714.29				
			4785.71-8214.29	6785.71				
			7857.14-10428.57	8928.57				
			3142.86-6142.86	4357.14				
				6266.67				
				6666.67				
				6096.67				
				7466.67				
				8066.67				
			7857.14-8214.29	8173.33				
				6785.71				
			7857.14-10428.57	8928.57				
			4785.71-5357.14					
			3571.43-6571.43	4714.29				
			2933.33-5200.00	4400.00				
Gadus aeglefinus	Haddock		1360.00-3666.67	3133.33				
Gadus morhua	Atlantic cod		1333.33-14400.00	1428.57				
			4266.67-1000.00	2714.29				
			4000.00-7000.00	7333.33				
Gadus virens	Coal fish			3285.71		0		
				2428.57		142.86		
				4285.71				
				3428.57		0		
				2571.43		142.86		
				2840.00				
				2857.14				
			4000-7000	5500.00				
				5533.33				
Gadus poulasson	Occhialone			1816.00				
Lotella maximowizi		liver, ovary, etc.		346.67				
		liver, ovary, etc.	13.33-186.67					
		skin		185.71	78.57	542.86		35
		muscle		342.86		485.71		109
		liver		14.29		235.71		133
Lotella maximowiczi	Japanese hake	ovary		142.86		257.14		133
		other visceral tissues		7.14		642.86		111
Lota lota	Burbot			1571.43				
Melanogrammus aeglefinus	Haddock			5000.00				
				5071.43				
				3071.43				
Merluccius merluccius	Merluzzo			780.00				
Melanogrammus aeglefinus	Haddock		3071.43-5928.57	5000.				
			4500-5714.29	5071.43				
			2142.86-3785.71	3071.43				
			3071.43-5928.57	5000.00				
			4500.00-5714.29	5071.43				
			2928.57-4000.00					
			2142.86-4142.86	3357.14				
Merluccius australis	New Zealand hake			6346.67				
Melanogrammus aeglefinus	Haddock		5.73-4.53	5.07				
			3071.43-5928.57					
Merluccius bilinearis	Silver hake		6357.14-7285.71					
Merluccius bilinearis	Silver hake		6357.14-8785.71	7571.43				

(Continued)

201

NO.OF FISH EXAMINED	LENGTH OF FISH	BODY WEIGHT (g)	SEASON	METHOD USED	OTHER	REFERENCE
				3, 11		Amano/Yamada 1965
				3, 11		Amano/Yamada 1965
				3, 11		Amano/Yamada 1965
				3, 11		Amano/Yamada 1965
				3, 11		Amano/Yamada 1965
70						Love et al 1959
						Love et al 1959
13						Love et al 1959
22	20-25			2		Shewan 1951
39	25-30			2		Shewan 1951
9	30-35			2		Shewan 1951
				1		Ronold/Jakobsen 1947
				1		Ronold/Jakobsen 1947
				1		Ronold/Jakobsen 1947
				1		Ronold/Jakobsen 1947
				1		Ronold/Jakobsen 1947
				1		Ronold/Jakobsen 1947
				1		Ronold/Jakobsen 1947
				1		Ronold/Jakobsen 1947
				1		Ronold/Jakobsen 1947
31	up to 50			2		Shewan 1951
69	50-60			2		Shewan 1951
102	60-70			2		Shewan 1951
40	70-80			2		Shewan 1951
20	80-100			2		Shewan 1951
25				3		Dyer 1952
50				3		Dyer 1952
				3		Dyer 1952
7				3		Dyer 1952
33				2	North Sea	Shewan 1951
135				2	North Sea	Shewan 1951
				2		Shewan 1951
				2		Shewan 1951
				2	Arctic Sea	Shewan 1951
				3, 1		Ronold/Jakobsen 1947
				3, 1		Ronold/Jakobsen 1947
				3, 1		Ronold/Jakobsen 1947
				1		Ronold/Jakobsen 1947
				1		Ronold/Jakobsen 1947
1				2	North Sea	Shewan 1951
				2	Arctic Sea	Shewan 1951
				2		Cantoni/Ardemagni 1977
				2	2nd amine	Kawamura et al 1971
						Yamada 1967
						Yamada 1967
				3,11		Amano/Yamada 1965
				3, 11		Amano/Yamada 1965
				3		Dyer 1952
				3		Beatty 1939
				1		Ronold/Jakobsen 1947
				2		Cantoni/Ardemagni 1977
9				3		Dyer 1952
8				3		Beatty 1939
5				1		Ronold/Jakobsen 1947
9				3		Dyer 1952
8				3		Dyer 1952
				3		Dyer 1952
5				3		Dyer 1952
8				3		Konosu et al 1978
				3	TMAO content of the muscle press juice	Beatty 1939
				3		Castell 1949
				3		Castell 1949

SCIENTIFIC NAME	COMMON NAME	TISSUE	TMAO (μM/100 g)		TMA (μM/100g)		DMA (μM/10(	
			RANGE	AVERAGE	RANGE	AVERAGE	RANGE	AV(
Micromesistius australis	Southern blue whiting			4240				
Pollachius virens	Pollock		2857.14- 5428.57	3928.57				
			5857.14- 6642.86	6428.57				
			6.67- 5.87	6.40				
Scomberomorus commersionii				2000.00				
Theragra chalcogramma	Walleye pollock	liver		2587.86				
Theragra chalcogramma	Walleye pollock	liver		502.14				
Theragra chalcogramma	Walleye pollock	liver		822.86				
Theragra chalcogramma	Walleye pollock	liver		345.71				
Theragra chalcogramma	Walleye pollock	liver		489.29				
Theragra chalcogramma	Walleye pollock	liver		511.43				
Theragra chalcogramma	Walleye pollock	liver		275.00				
Theragra chalcogramma	Walleye pollock	liver		698.57				
Theragra chalcogramma	Walleye pollock	liver		528.57				
Theragra chalcogramma	Walleye pollock	liver		272.14				
Theragra chalcogramma	Walleye pollock	liver		843.57				
Theragra chalcogramma	Walleye pollock	liver		1257.14				
Theragra chalcogramma	Walleye pollock	liver		476.43				
Theragra chalcogramma	Walleye pollock	liver		709.29				
Theragra chalcogramma	Walleye pollock	pyloric caeca		2020.71				
Theragra chalcogramma	Walleye pollock	pyloric caeca		1266.43				
Theragra chalcogramma	Walleye pollock	pyloric caeca		1506.43				
Theragra chalcogramma	Walleye pollock	pyloric caeca		425.00				
Theragra chalcogramma	Walleye pollock	pyloric caeca		2652.14				
Theragra chalcogramma	Walleye pollock	pyloric caeca		1218.57				
Theragra chalcogramma	Walleye pollock	pyloric caeca		2227.86				
Theragra chalcogramma	Walleye pollock	pyloric caeca		1267.86				
Theragra chalcogramma	Walleye pollock	pyloric caeca		1545.71				
Theragra chalcogramma	Walleye pollock	pyloric caeca		1305.71				
Theragra chalcogramma	Walleye pollock	pyloric caeca		1147.86				
Theragra chalcogramma	Walleye pollock	pyloric caeca		930.71				
Theragra chalcogramma	Walleye pollock	pyloric caeca		1111.43				
Theragra chalcogramma	Walleye pollock	pyloric caeca		1235.00				
Theragra chalcogramma	Walleye pollock	pyloric caeca		1439.29				
Theragra chalcogramma	Walleye pollock	gall blad		1090.00				
Theragra chalcogramma	Walleye pollock	gall blad		1258.57				
Theragra chalcogramma	Walleye pollock	gall blad		309.29				
Theragra chalcogramma	Walleye pollock	gall blad		289.29				
Theragra chalcogramma	Walleye pollock	gall blad		507.86				
Theragra chalcogramma	Walleye pollock	gall blad		805.00				
Theragra chalcogramma	Walleye pollock	gall blad		570.00				
Theragra chalcogramma	Wallaye pollock	gall blad		163.57				
Theragra chalcogramma	Walleye pollock	gall blad		1358.57				
Theragra chalcogramma	Walleye pollock	gall blad		118.71				
Theragra chalcogramma	Walleye pollock	gall blad		155.71				
Theragra chalcogramma	Walleye pollock	gall blad		211.43				
Theragra chalcogramma	Walleye pollock	intestine		1434.29				
Theragra chalcogramma	Walleye pollock	intestine		2627.86				
Theragra chalcogramma	Walleye pollock	intestine		2170.71				
Theragra chalcogramma	Walleye pollock	intestine		1550.71				
Theragra chalcogramma	Walleye pollock	intestine		1901.43				
Theragra chalcogramma	Walleye pollock	intestine		1712.86				
Theragra chalcogramma	Walleye pollock	intestine		2857.86				
Theragra chalcogramma	Walleye pollock	intestine		1800.71				
Theragra chalcogramma	Walleye pollock	intestine		573.57				
Theragra chalcogramma	Walleye pollock	intestine		1552.14				
Theragra chalcogramma	Walleye pollock	intestine		1882.14				
Theragra chalcogramma	Walleye pollock	intestine		1435.00				
Theragra chalcogramma	Walleye pollock	stomach		1875.00				
Theragra chalcogramma	Walleye pollock	stomach		1846.43				
Theragra chalcogramma	Walleye pollock	stomach		1780.71				
Theragra chalcogramma	Walleye pollock	stomach		1788.57				
Theragra chalcogramma	Walleye pollock	stomach		1589.29				
Theragra chalcogramma	Walleye pollock	stomach		2127.14				
Theragra chalcogramma	Walleye pollock	stomach		1727.86				
Theragra chalcogramma	Walleye pollock	stomach		3217.14				
Theragra chalcogramma	Walleye pollock	stomach		1590.00				
Theragra chalcogramma	Walleye pollock	stomach		1758.57				
Theragra chalcogramma	Walleye pollock	stomach		1514.29				
Theragra chalcogramma	Walleye pollock	stomach		1532.14				
Theragra chalcogramma	Walleye pollock	stomach		1908.57				
Theragra chalcogramma	Walleye pollock	stomach		1956.43				
Theragra chalcogramma	Walleye pollock	spleen		4570.71				
Theragra chalcogramma	Walleye pollock	spleen		2320.00				
Theragra chalcogramma	Walleye pollock	spleen		4888.57				
Theragra chalcogramma	Walleye pollock	spleen		5392.86				
Theragra chalcogramma	Walleye pollock	spleen		2320.00				
Theragra chalcogramma	Walleye pollock	spleen		12223.57				
Theragra chalcogramma	Walleye pollock	spleen		3887.14				

NO.OF FISH EXAMINED	LENGTH OF FISH	BODY WEIGHT (g)	SEASON	METHOD USED	OTHER	REFERENCE
12						
7				3		Dyer 1952
				3		Dyer 1952
7				3	TMAO content of the muscle press juice	Beatty 1939
				2		Velankar/Govindan 1958
				3	Sample 1	Tokunaga 1978
				3	Sample 2	Tokunaga 1978
				3	Sample 3	Tokunaga 1978
				3	Sample 4	Tokunaga 1978
				3	Sample 5	Tokunaga 1978
				3	Sample 6	Tokunaga 1978
				3	Sample 8	Tokunaga 1978
				3	Sample 9	Tokunaga 1978
				3	Sample 10	Tokunaga 1978
				3	Sample 11	Tokunaga 1978
				3	Sample 12	Tokunaga 1978
				3	Sample 13	Tokunaga 1978
				3	Sample 14	Tokunaga 1978
				3	Sample 15	Tokunaga 1978
				3	Sample 1	Tokunaga 1978
				3	Sample 2	Tokunaga 1978
				3	Sample 3	Tokunaga 1978
				3	Sample 4	Tokunaga 1978
				3	Sample 5	Tokunaga 1978
				3	Sample 6	Tokunaga 1978
				3	Sample 7	Tokunaga 1978
				3	Sample 8	Tokunaga 1978
				3	Sample 9	Tokunaga 1978
				3	Sample 10	Tokunaga 1978
				3	Sample 11	Tokunaga 1978
				3	Sample 12	Tokunaga 1978
				3	Sample 13	Tokunaga 1978
				3	Sample 14	Tokunaga 1978
				3	Sample 15	Tokunaga 1978
				3	Sample 1	Tokunaga 1978
				3	Sample 1	Tokunaga 1978
				3	Sample 2	Tokunaga 1978
				3	Sample 3	Tokunaga 1978
				3	Sample 4	Tokunaga 1978
				3	Sample 5	Tokunaga 1978
				3	Sample 6	Tokunaga 1978
				3	Sample 7	Tokunaga 1978
				3	Sample 8	Tokunaga 1978
				3	Sample 9	Tokunaga 1978
				3	Sample 11	Tokunaga 1978
				3	Sample 12	Tokunaga 1978
				3	Sample 15	Tokunaga 1978
				3	Sample 1	Tokunaga 1978
				3	Sample 2	Tokunaga 1978
				3	Sample 3	Tokunaga 1978
				3	Sample 4	Tokunaga 1978
				3	Sample 7	Tokunaga 1978
				3	Sample 8	Tokunaga 1978
				3	Sample 9	Tokunaga 1978
				3	Sample 10	Tokunaga 1978
				3	Sample 11	Tokunaga 1978
				3	Sample 12	Tokunaga 1978
				3	Sample 14	Tokunaga 1978
				3	Sample 15	Tokunaga 1978
				3	Sample 1	Tokunaga 1978
				3	Sample 2	Tokunaga 1978
				3	Sample 3	Tokunaga 1978
				3	Sample 4	Tokunaga 1978
				3	Sample 5	Tokunaga 1978
				3	Sample 6	Tokunaga 1978
				3	Sample 7	Tokunaga 1978
				3	Sample 8	Tokunaga 1978
				3	Sample 9	Tokunaga 1978
				3	Sample 10	Tokunaga 1978
				3	Sample 11	Tokunaga 1978
				3	Sample 12	Tokunaga 1978
				3	Sample 14	Tokunaga 1978
				3	Sample 15	Tokunaga 1978
				3	Sample 1	Tokunaga 1978
				3	Sample 2	Tokunaga 1978
				3	Sample 4	Tokunaga 1978
				3	Sample 5	Tokunaga 1978
				3	Sample 6	Tokunaga 1978
				3	Sample 7	Tokunaga 1978

TABLE 1

SCIENTIFIC NAME	COMMON NAME	TISSUE	TMAO (μM/100 g)		TMA (μM/100g)		DMA (μM/100g)	
			RANGE	AVERAGE	RANGE	AVERAGE	RANGE	AVERAGE
Theragra chalcogramma	Walleye pollock	spleen		2637.86				
Theragra chalcogramma	Walleye pollock	spleen		3465.71				
Theragra chalcogramma	Walleye pollock			3282.86				
Theragra chalcogramma	Walleye pollock			4772.86				
Theragra chalcogramma	Walleye pollock			457.14				
Theragra chalcogramma	Walleye pollock			1169.29				
Theragra chalcogramma	Walleye pollock			1067.86				
Theragra chalcogramma	Walleye pollock			1531.43				
Theragra chalcogramma	Walleye pollock			6572.14				
Theragra chalcogramma	Walleye pollock			6771.43				
Theragra chalcogramma	Walleye pollock			6820.71				
Theragra chalcogramma	Walleye pollock			7600.71				
Theragra chalcogramma	Walleye pollock			9210.00				
Theragra chalcogramma	Walleye pollock			8948.57				
Theragra chalcogramma	Walleye pollock			8716.43				
Theragra chalcogramma	Walleye pollock			1987.14				
Theragra chalcogramma	Walleye pollock			2542.86				
Theragra chalcogramma	Walleye pollock			4146.43				
Theragra chalcogramma	Walleye pollock			2865.71				
Theragra chalcogramma	Walleye pollock			2600.71				
Theragra chalcogramma	Walleye pollock	muscle		6250.71				
Theragra chalcogramma	Walleye pollock	muscle		8964.29				
Theragra chalcogramma	Walleye pollock	muscle		8816.43				
Theragra chalcogramma	Walleye pollock	muscle		7964.29				
Theragra chalcogramma	Walleye pollock	muscle		8378.57				
Theragra chalcogramma	Walleye pollock	muscle		10104.29				
Theragra chalcogramma	Walleye pollock	muscle		8510.00				
Theragra chalcogramma	Walleye pollock	muscle		8778.57				
Theragra chalcogramma	Walleye pollock	muscle		8664.29				
Theragra chalcogramma	Walleye pollock	muscle		10467.86				
Theragra chalcogramma	Walleye pollock	muscle		8645.00				
Theragra chalcogramma	Walleye pollock	muscle		8372.86				
Theragra chalcogramma	Walleye pollock	muscle		8763.57				
Theragra chalcogramma	Walleye pollock	liver				104.29		
Theragra chalcogramma	Walleye pollock	liver				25.00		
Theragra chalcogramma	Walleye pollock	liver				41.29		
Theragra chalcogramma	Walleye pollock	liver				62.14		
Theragra chalcogramma	Walleye pollock	liver				27.86		
Theragra chalcogramma	Walleye pollock	liver				25.71		
Theragra chalcogramma	Walleye pollock	liver				96.43		
Theragra chalcogramma	Walleye pollock	liver				37.14		
Theragra chalcogramma	Walleye pollock	liver				31.43		
Theragra chalcogramma	Walleye pollock	liver				27.14		
Theragra chalcogramma	Walleye pollock	liver				65.00		
Theragra chalcogramma	Walleye pollock	liver				85.71		
Theragra chalcogramma	Walleye pollock	liver				32.86		
Theragra chalcogramma	Walleye pollock	liver				50.00		
Theragra chalcogramma	Walleye pollock	pyloric caeca				108.57		
Theragra chalcogramma	Walleye pollock	pyloric caeca				96.43		
Theragra chalcogramma	Walleye pollock	pyloric caeca				100.71		
Theragra chalcogramma	Walleye pollock	pyloric caeca				52.14		
Theragra chalcogramma	Walleye pollock	pyloric caeca				135.71		
Theragra chalcogramma	Walleye pollock	pyloric caeca				122.86		
Theragra chalcogramma	Walleye pollock	pyloric caeca				210.00		
Theragra chalcogramma	Walleye pollock	pyloric caeca				97.14		
Theragra chalcogramma	Walleye pollock	pyloric caeca				115.71		
Theragra chalcogramma	Walleye pollock	pyloric caeca				96.43		
Theragra chalcogramma	Walleye pollock	pyloric caeca				87.14		
Theragra chalcogramma	Walleye pollock	pyloric caeca				78.57		
Theragra chalcogramma	Walleye pollock	pyloric caeca				88.57		
Theragra chalcogramma	Walleye pollock	pyloric caeca				98.57		
Theragra chalcogramma	Walleye pollock	pyloric caeca				107.86		
Theragra chalcogramma	Walleye pollock	gall blad.				71.43		
Theragra chalcogramma	Walleye pollock	gall blad.				96.43		
Theragra chalcogramma	Walleye pollock	gall blad.				81.43		
Theragra chalcogramma	Walleye pollock	gall blad.				69.29		
Theragra chalcogramma	Walleye pollock	gall blad.				22.14		
Theragra chalcogramma	Walleye pollock	gall blad.				60.71		
Theragra chalcogramma	Walleye pollock	gall blad.				67.14		
Theragra chalcogramma	Walleye pollock	gall blad.				79.29		
Theragra chalcogramma	Walleye pollock	gall blad.				27.14		
Theragra chalcogramma	Walleye pollock	gall blad.				90.71		
Theragra chalcogramma	Walleye pollock	gall blad.				71.43		
Theragra chalcogramma	Walleye pollock	gall blad.				67.14		
Theragra chalcogramma	Walleye pollock	intestine				113.57		
Theragra chalcogramma	Walleye pollock	intestine				14.29		
Theragra chalcogramma	Walleye pollock	intestine				12.14		
Theragra chalcogramma	Walleye pollock	intestine				72.86		
Theragra chalcogramma	Walleye pollock	intestine				60.71		
Theragra chalcogramma	Walleye pollock	intestine				60.71		
Theragra chalcogramma	Walleye pollock	intestine				40.00		

NO.OF FISH EXAMINED	LENGTH OF FISH	BODY WEIGHT (g)	SEASON	METHOD USED	OTHER	REFERENCE
				3	Sample 10	Tokunaga 1978
				3	Sample 12	Tokunaga 1978
				3	Sample 13	Tokunaga 1978
				3	Sample 15	Tokunaga 1978
				3	Sample 10	Tokunaga 1978
				3	Sample 12	Tokunaga 1978
				3	Sample 13	Tokunaga 1978
				3	Sample 15	Tokunaga 1978
				3	Sample 6	Tokunaga 1978
				3	Sample 7	Tokunaga 1978
				3	Sample 8	Tokunaga 1978
				3	Sample 9	Tokunaga 1978
				3	Sample 10	Tokunaga 1978
				3	Sample 11	Tokunaga 1978
				3	Sample 15	Tokunaga 1978
				3	Sample 2	Tokunaga 1978
				3	Sample 3	Tokunaga 1978
				3	Sample 4	Tokunaga 1978
				3	Sample 5	Tokunaga 1978
				3	Sample 13	Tokunaga 1978
				3	Sample 1	Tokunaga 1978
				3	Sample 2	Tokunaga 1978
				3	Sample 3	Tokunaga 1978
				3	Sample 4	Tokunaga 1978
				3	Sample 5	Tokunaga 1978
				3	Sample 6	Tokunaga 1978
				3	Sample 7	Tokunaga 1978
				3	Sample 8	Tokunaga 1978
				3	Sample 9	Tokunaga 1978
				3	Sample 10	Tokunaga 1978
				3	Sample 11	Tokunaga 1978
				3	Sample 12	Tokunaga 1978
				3	Sample 13	Tokunaga 1978
				3	Sample 1	Tokunaga 1978
				3	Sample 2	Tokunaga 1978
				3	Sample 3	Tokunaga 1978
				3	Sample 4	Tokunaga 1978
				3	Sample 5	Tokunaga 1978
				3	Sample 6	Tokunaga 1978
				3	Sample 8	Tokunaga 1978
				3	Sample 9	Tokunaga 1978
				3	Sample 10	Tokunaga 1978
				3	Sample 11	Tokunaga 1978
				3	Sample 12	Tokunaga 1978
				3	Sample 13	Tokunaga 1978
				3	Sample 14	Tokunaga 1978
				3	Sample 15	Tokunaga 1978
				3	Sample 1	Tokunaga 1978
				3	Sample 2	Tokunaga 1978
				3	Sample 3	Tokunaga 1978
				3	Sample 4	Tokunaga 1978
				3	Sample 5	Tokunaga 1978
				3	Sample 6	Tokunaga 1978
				3	Sample 7	Tokunaga 1978
				3	Sample 8	Tokunaga 1978
				3	Sample 9	Tokunaga 1978
				3	Sample 10	Tokunaga 1978
				3	Sample 11	Tokunaga 1978
				3	Sample 12	Tokunaga 1978
				3	Sample 13	Tokunaga 1978
				3	Sample 14	Tokunaga 1978
				3	Sample 15	Tokunaga 1978
				3	Sample 1	Tokunaga 1978
				3	Sample 2	Tokunaga 1978
				3	Sample 3	Tokunaga 1978
				3	Sample 4	Tokunaga 1978
				3	Sample 5	Tokunaga 1978
				3	Sample 6	Tokunaga 1978
				3	Sample 7	Tokunaga 1978
				3	Sample 8	Tokunaga 1978
				3	Sample 9	Tokunaga 1978
				3	Sample 11	Tokunaga 1978
				3	Sample 12	Tokunaga 1978
				3	Sample 15	Tokunaga 1978
				3	Sample 1	Tokunaga 1978
				3	Sample 2	Tokunaga 1978
				3	Sample 3	Tokunaga 1978
				3	Sample 4	Tokunaga 1978
				3	Sample 7	Tokunaga 1978
				3	Sample 8	Tokunaga 1978
				3	Sample 9	Tokunaga 1978

TABLE 12

206

SCIENTIFIC NAME	COMMON NAME	TISSUE	TMAO (μM/100 g) RANGE	AVERAGE	TMA (μM/100g) RANGE	AVERAGE	DMA (μM/100g) RANGE	AVERAGE
Theragra chalcogramma	Walleye pollock	intestine				41.43		
Theragra chalcogramma	Walleye pollock	intestine				75.00		
Theragra chalcogramma	Walleye pollock	intestine				55.00		
Theragra chalcogramma	Walleye pollock	intestine				41.43		
Theragra chalcogramma	Walleye pollock	intestine				52.86		
Theragra chalcogramma	Walleye pollock	stomach				35.00		
Theragra chalcogramma	Walleye pollock	stomach				192.14		
Theragra chalcogramma	Walleye pollock	stomach				9.29		
Theragra chalcogramma	Walleye pollock	stomach				87.14		
Theragra chalcogramma	Walleye pollock	stomach				57.86		
Theragra chalcogramma	Walleye pollock	stomach				42.86		
Theragra chalcogramma	Walleye pollock	stomach				92.86		
Theragra chalcogramma	Walleye pollock	stomach				29.29		
Theragra chalcogramma	Walleye pollock	stomach				77.14		
Theragra chalcogramma	Walleye pollock	stomach				33.57		
Theragra chalcogramma	Walleye pollock	stomach				95.00		
Theragra chalcogramma	Walleye pollock	stomach				62.14		
Theragra chalcogramma	Walleye pollock	stomach				110.71		
Theragra chalcogramma	Walleye pollock	stomach				23.57		
Theragra chalcogramma	Walleye pollock	stomach				56.43		
Theragra chalcogramma	Walleye pollock	heart				45.71		
Theragra chalcogramma	Walleye pollock	heart				120.00		
Theragra chalcogramma	Walleye pollock	heart				37.86		
Theragra chalcogramma	Walleye pollock	heart				71.43		
Theragra chalcogramma	Walleye pollock	testis				36.43		
Theragra chalcogramma	Walleye pollock	testis				17.86		
Theragra chalcogramma	Walleye pollock	testis				50.71		
Theragra chalcogramma	Walleye pollock	testis				26.43		
Theragra chalcogramma	Walleye pollock	testis				19.29		
Theragra chalcogramma	Walleye pollock	testis				42.86		
Theragra chalcogramma	Walleye pollock	testis				15.00		
Theragra chalcogramma	Walleye pollock	ovary				19.29		
Theragra chalcogramma	Walleye pollock	ovary				3.57		
Theragra chalcogramma	Walleye pollock	ovary				30.00		
Theragra chalcogramma	Walleye pollock	ovary				24.29		
Theragra chalcogramma	Walleye pollock	ovary				12.14		
Theragra chalcogramma	Walleye pollock	muscle				5.71		
Theragra chalcogramma	Walleye pollock	muscle				3.57		
Theragra chalcogramma	Walleye pollock	muscle				8.57		
Theragra chalcogramma	Walleye pollock	muscle				15.00		
Theragra chalcogramma	Walleye pollock	muscle				7.86		
Theragra chalcogramma	Walleye pollock	muscle				3.57		
Theragra chalcogramma	Walleye pollock	muscle				2.14		
Theragra chalcogramma	Walleye pollock	muscle				10.00		
Theragra chalcogramma	Walleye pollock	muscle				3.57		
Theragra chalcogramma	Walleye pollock	muscle				7.14		
Theragra chalcogramma	Walleye pollock	muscle				5.71		
Theragra chalcogramma	Walleye pollock	muscle				7.14		
Theragra chalcogramma	Walleye pollock	muscle				5.00		
Theragra chalcogramma	Walleye pollock	muscle				12.14		
Theragra chalcogramma	Walleye pollock	liver						5.
Theragra chalcogramma	Walleye pollock	liver						6.
Theragra chalcogramma	Walleye pollock	liver						12.
Theragra chalcogramma	Walleye pollock	liver						9.
Theragra chalcogramma	Walleye pollock	liver						2.
Theragra chalcogramma	Walleye pollock	liver						5.
Theragra chalcogramma	Walleye pollock	liver						10.
Theragra chalcogramma	Walleye pollock	liver						7.
Theragra chalcogramma	Walleye pollock	liver						5.
Theragra chalcogramma	Walleye pollock	liver						57.
Theragra chalcogramma	Walleye pollock	liver						12.
Theragra chalcogramma	Walleye pollock	liver						8.
Theragra chalcogramma	Walleye pollock	liver						15.
Theragra chalcogramma	Walleye pollock	liver						10.
Theragra chalcogramma	Walleye pollock	pyloric caeca						8
Theragra chalcogramma	Walleye pollock	pyloric caeca						16
Theragra chalcogramma	Walleye pollock	pyloric caeca						12
Theragra chalcogramma	Walleye pollock	pyloric caeca						1
Theragra chalcogramma	Walleye pollock	pyloric caeca						0
Theragra chalcogramma	Walleye pollock	pyloric caeca						4
Theragra chalcogramma	Walleye pollock	pyloric caeca						8
Theragra chalcogramma	Walleye pollock	pyloric caeca						0
Theragra chalcogramma	Walleye pollock	pyloric caeca						6
Theragra chalcogramma	Walleye pollock	pyloric caeca						
Theragra chalcogramma	Walleye pollock	pyloric caeca						
Theragra chalcogramma	Walleye pollock	pyloric caeca						
Theragra chalcogramma	Walleye pollock	pyloric caeca						10
Theragra chalcogramma	Walleye pollock	pyloric caeca						
Theragra chalcogramma	Walleye pollock	pyloric caeca						3
Theragra chalcogramma	Walleye pollock	gall blad.						19

NO.OF FISH EXAMINED	LENGTH OF FISH	BODY WEIGHT (g)	SEASON	METHOD USED	OTHER	REFERENCE
				3	Sample 10	Tokunaga 1978
				3	Sample 11	Tokunaga 1978
				3	Sample 12	Tokunaga 1978
				3	Sample 14	Tokunaga 1978
				3	Sample 15	Tokunaga 1978
				3	Sample 1	Tokunaga 1978
				3	Sample 2	Tokunaga 1978
				3	Sample 3	Tokunaga 1978
				3	Sample 4	Tokunaga 1978
				3	Sample 5	Tokunaga 1978
				3	Sample 6	Tokunaga 1978
				3	Sample 7	Tokunaga 1978
				3	Sample 8	Tokunaga 1978
				3	Sample 9	Tokunaga 1978
				3	Sample 10	Tokunaga 1978
				3	Sample 11	Tokunaga 1978
				3	Sample 12	Tokunaga 1978
				3	Sample 14	Tokunaga 1978
				3	Sample 15	Tokunaga 1978
				3	Sample 10	Tokunaga 1978
				3	Sample 12	Tokunaga 1978
				3	Sample 13	Tokunaga 1978
				3	Sample 15	Tokunaga 1978
				3	Sample 6	Tokunaga 1978
				3	Sample 7	Tokunaga 1978
				3	Sample 8	Tokunaga 1978
				3	Sample 9	Tokunaga 1978
				3	Sample 11	Tokunaga 1978
				3	Sample 12	Tokunaga 1978
				3	Sample 15	Tokunaga 1978
				3	Sample 2	Tokunaga 1978
				3	Sample 3	Tokunaga 1978
				3	Sample 4	Tokunaga 1978
				3	Sample 5	Tokunaga 1978
				3	Sample 13	Tokunaga 1978
				3	Sample 1	Tokunaga 1978
				3	Sample 2	Tokunaga 1978
				3	Sample 3	Tokunaga 1978
				3	Sample 4	Tokunaga 1978
				3	Sample 5	Tokunaga 1978
				3	Sample 6	Tokunaga 1978
				3	Sample 7	Tokunaga 1978
				3	Sample 8	Tokunaga 1978
				3	Sample 9	Tokunaga 1978
				3	Sample 10	Tokunaga 1978
				3	Sample 11	Tokunaga 1978
				3	Sample 12	Tokunaga 1978
				3	Sample 13	Tokunaga 1978
				3	Sample 14	Tokunaga 1978
				3	Sample 15	Tokunaga 1978
				3	Sample 1	Tokunaga 1978
				11	Sample 2	Tokunaga 1978
				11	Sample 3	Tokunaga 1978
				11	Sample 4	Tokunaga 1978
				11	Sample 5	Tokunaga 1978
				11	Sample 6	Tokunaga 1978
				11	Sample 8	Tokunaga 1978
				11	Sample 9	Tokunaga 1978
				11	Sample 10	Tokunaga 1978
				11	Sample 11	Tokunaga 1978
				11	Sample 12	Tokunaga 1978
				11	Sample 13	Tokunaga 1978
				11	Sample 14	Tokunaga 1978
				11	Sample 15	Tokunaga 1978
				11	Sample 1	Tokunaga 1978
				11	Sample 2	Tokunaga 1978
				11	Sample 3	Tokunaga 1978
				11	Sample 4	Tokunaga 1978
				11	Sample 5	Tokunaga 1978
				11	Sample 6	Tokunaga 1978
				11	Sample 7	Tokunaga 1978
				11	Sample 8	Tokunaga 1978
				11	Sample 9	
				11	Sample 9	
				11	Sample 10	Tokunaga 1978
				11	Sample 11	Tokunaga 1978
				11	Sample 12	Tokunaga 1978
				11	Sample 13	Tokunaga 1978
				11	Sample 14	Tokunaga 1978
				11	Sample 15	Tokunaga 1978
				11	Sample 1	Tokunaga 1978
				11	Sample 2	Tokunaga 1978

TABLE 1

SCIENTIFIC NAME	COMMON NAME	TISSUE	TMAO (µM/100 g) RANGE	AVERAGE	TMA (µM/100g) RANGE	AVERAGE	DMA (µM/100g) RANGE	AVERA
Theragra chalcogramma	Walleye pollock	gall blad.						246
Theragra chalcogramma	Walleye pollock	gall blad.						240
Theragra chalcogramma	Walleye pollock	gall blad.						94
Theragra chalcogramma	Walleye pollock	gall blad.						45
Theragra chalcogramma	Walleye pollock	gall blad.						636
Theragra chalcogramma	Walleye pollock	gall blad.						182
Theragra chalcogramma	Walleye pollock	gall blad.						2840
Theragra chalcogramma	Walleye pollock	gall blad.						192
Theragra chalcogramma	Walleye pollock	gall blad.						1320
Theragra chalcogramma	Walleye pollock	gall blad.						718
Theragra chalcogramma	Walleye pollock	intestine						4
Theragra chalcogramma	Walleye pollock	intestine						24
Theragra chalcogramma	Walleye pollock	intestine						33
Theragra chalcogramma	Walleye pollock	intestine						12
Theragra chalcogramma	Walleye pollock	intestine						5
Theragra chalcogramma	Walleye pollock	intestine						10
Theragra chalcogramma	Walleye pollock	intestine						59
Theragra chalcogramma	Walleye pollock	intestine						27
Theragra chalcogramma	Walleye pollock	intestine						80
Theragra chalcogramma	Walleye pollock	intestine						16
Theragra chalcogramma	Walleye pollock	intestine						14
Theragra chalcogramma	Walleye pollock	intestine						27
Theragra chalcogramma	Walleye pollock	stomach						13
Theragra chalcogramma	Walleye pollock	stomach						15
Theragra chalcogramma	Walleye pollock	stomach						12
Theragra chalcogramma	Walleye pollock	stomach						10
Theragra chalcogramma	Walleye pollock	stomach						7
Theragra chalcogramma	Walleye pollock	stomach						12
Theragra chalcogramma	Walleye pollock	stomach						24
Theragra chalcogramma	Walleye pollock	stomach						27
Theragra chalcogramma	Walleye pollock	stomach						47
Theragra chalcogramma	Walleye pollock	Stomach						14
Theragra chalcogramma	Walleye pollock	stomach						8
Theragra chalcogramma	Walleye pollock	stomach						9
Theragra chalcogramma	Walleye pollock	stomach						94
Theragra chalcogramma	Walleye pollock	stomach						22
Theragra chalcogramma	Walleye pollock	heart						9
Theragra chalcogramma	Walleye pollock	heart						17
Theragra chalcogramma	Walleye pollock	heart						55
Theragra chalcogramma	Walleye pollock	heart						26
Theragra chalcogramma	Walleye pollock	testis						5
Theragra chalcogramma	Walleye pollock	testis						5
Theragra chalcogramma	Walleye pollock	testis						3
Theragra chalcogramma	Walleye pollock	testis						3
Theragra chalcogramma	Walleye pollock	testis						4
Theragra chalcogramma	Walleye pollock	testis						6
Theragra chalcogramma	Walleye pollock	testis						5
Theragra chalcogramma	Walleye pollock	ovary						3
Theragra chalcogramma	Walleye pollock	ovary						3
Theragra chalcogramma	Walleye pollock	ovary						5
Theragra chalcogramma	Walleye pollock	ovary						53
Theragra chalcogramma	Walleye pollock	ovary						22
Theragra chalcogramma	Walleye pollock	spleen						56
Theragra chalcogramma	Walleye pollock	spleen						133
Theragra chalcogramma	Walleye pollock	spleen						126
Theragra chalcogramma	Walleye pollock	spleen						9
Theragra chalcogramma	Walleye pollock	spleen						69
Theragra chalcogramma	Walleye pollock	spleen						59
Theragra chalcogramma	Walleye pollock	spleen						7
Theragra chalcogramma	Walleye pollock	spleen						55
Theragra chalcogramma	Walleye pollock	spleen						226
Theragra chalcogramma	Walleye pollock	spleen						92
Theragra chalcogramma	Walleye pollock	muscle						1
Theragra chalcogramma	Walleye pollock	muscle						9
Theragra chalcogramma	Walleye pollock	muscle						12
Theragra chalcogramma	Walleye pollock	muscle						3
Theragra chalcogramma	Walleye pollock	muscle						0
Theragra chalcogramma	Walleye pollock	muscle						4
Theragra chalcogramma	Walleye pollock	muscle						6
Theragra chalcogramma	Walleye pollock	muscle						1
Theragra chalcogramma	Walleye pollock	muscle						5
Theragra chalcogramma	Walleye pollock	muscle						7
Theragra chalcogramma	Walleye pollock	muscle						5
Theragra chalcogramma	Walleye pollock	muscle						3
Theragra chalcogramma	Walleye pollock	muscle						7
Theragra chalcogramma	Walleye pollock	muscle						5
Theragra chalcogramma	Walleye pollock	muscle						4
Theragra chalcogramma	Walleye pollock	muscle, stomach, liver	4333.33-11000.00, 4080.00-1386.67					
Theragra chalcogramma	Walleye pollock	muscle, stomach, liver	66.67-1853.33					
Theragra chalrogramma	Walleye pollock	skin		8285.71		50.00		28.5
Theragra chalcogramma	Walleye pollock	surface muscle		13857.14		42.86		7.1
Theragra chalcogramma	Walleye pollock	deep muscle		13857.14		50.00		14.2
Theragra chalcogramma	Walleye pollock	liver		714.29		150.00		50.0
Theragra chalcogramma	Walleye pollock	pyloric caeca		142.86		185.7		935.7
Theragra chalcogramma	Walleye pollock	stomach		1071.43		100.00		1064.2
Theragra chalcogramma	Walleye pollock	stomach content		1857.14		50.00		21.4

NO.OF FISH EXAMINED	LENGTH OF FISH	BODY WEIGHT (g)	SEASON	METHOD USED	OTHER	REFERENCE
				11	Sample 3	Tokunaga 1978
				11	Sample 4	Tokunaga 1978
				11	Sample 5	Tokunaga 1978
				11	Sample 6	Tokunaga 1978
				11	Sample 7	Tokunaga 1978
				11	Sample 8	Tokunaga 1978
				11	Sample 9	Tokunaga 1978
				11	Sample 11	Tokunaga 1978
				11	Sample 12	Tokunaga 1978
				11	Sample 15	Tokunaga 1978
				11	Sample 1	Tokunaga 1978
				11	Sample 2	Tokunaga 1978
				11	Sample 3	Tokunaga 1978
				11	Sample 4	Tokunaga 1978
				11	Sample 7	Tokunaga 1978
				11	Sample 8	Tokunaga 1978
				11	Sample 9	Tokunaga 1978
				11	Sample 10	Tokunaga 1978
				11	Sample 11	Tokunaga 1978
				11	Sample 12	Tokunaga 1978
				11	Sample 14	Tokunaga 1978
				11	Sample 15	Tokunaga 1978
				11	Sample 1	Tokunaga 1978
				11	Sample 2	Tokunaga 1978
				11	Sample 3	Tokunaga 1978
				11	Sample 4	Tokunaga 1978
				11	Sample 5	Tokunaga 1978
				11	Sample 6	Tokunaga 1978
				11	Sample 7	Tokunaga 1978
				11	Sample 8	Tokunaga 1978
				11	Sample 9	Tokunaga 1978
				11	Sample 10	Tokunaga 1978
				11	Sample 11	Tokungag 1978
				11	Sample 12	Tokunaga 1978
				11	Sample 14	Tokunaga 1978
				11	Sample 15	Tokunaga 1978
				11	Sample 10	Tokunaga 1978
				11	Sample 12	Tokunaga 1978
				11	Sample 13	Tokunaga 1978
				11	Sample 15	Tokunaga 1978
				11	Sample 6	Tokunaga 1978
				11	Sample 7	Tokunaga 1978
				11	Sample 8	Tokunaga 1978
				11	Sample 9	Tokunaga 1978
				11	Sample 11	Tokunaga 1978
				11	Sample 12	Tokunaga 1978
				11	Sample 15	Tokunaga 1978
				11	Sample 2	Tokunaga 1978
				11	Sample 3	Tokunaga 1978
				11	Sample 4	Tokunaga 1978
				11	Sample 5	Tokunaga 1978
				11	Sample 13	Tokunaga 1978
				11	Sample 1	Tokunaga 1978
				11	Sample 2	Tokunaga 1978
				11	Sample 4	Tokunaga 1978
				11	Sample 5	Tokunaga 1978
				11	Sample 6	Tokunaga 1978
				11	Sample 7	Tokunaga 1978
				11	Sample 9	Tokunaga 1978
				11	Sample 10	Tokunaga 1978
				11	Sample 12	Tokunaga 1978
				11	Sample 13	Tokunaga 1978
				11	Sample 1	Tokunaga 1978
				11	Sample 2	Tokunaga 1978
				11	Sample 3	Tokunaga 1978
				11	Sample 4	Tokunaga 1978
				11	Sample 5	Tokunaga 1978
				11	Sample 6	Tokunaga 1978
				11	Sample 7	Tokunaga 1978
				11	Sample 8	Tokunaga 1978
				11	Sample 9	Tokunaga 1978
				11	Sample 10	Tokunaga 1978
				11	Sample 11	Tokunaga 1978
				11	Sample 12	Tokunaga 1978
				11	Sample 13	Tokunaga 1978
				11	Sample 14	Tokunaga 1978
				11	Sample 15	Tokunaga 1978
						Yamada 1967
						Yamada 1967
				11		Amano/Yamada 1965
				11		Amano/Yamada 1965
				11		Amano/Yamada 1965
				11		Amano/Yamada 1965
				11		Amano/Yamada 1965
				11		Amano/Yamada 1965
				11		Amano/Yamada 1965

TABLE 12.1

SCIENTIFIC NAME	COMMON NAME	TISSUE	TMAO (μM/100 g)		TMA (μM/100g)		DMA (μM/100g)	
			RANGE	AVERAGE	RANGE	AVERAGE	RANGE	AVERAGE
Theragra chalcogramma	Walleye pollock	ovary		1500.00		128.57		100.00
Theragra chalcogramma	Walleye pollock	gall blad				--		914.29
Theragra chalcogramma	Walleye pollock			8442.86		42.86		28.57
Theragra chalcogramma	Walleye pollock			8550.00		14.29		35.71
Theragra chalcogramma	Walleye pollock			7485.71		21.43		35.71
Theragra chalcogramma	Walleye pollock			7800.00		35.71		28.53
Theragra chalcogramma	Walleye pollock			7692.86		14.29		42.86
Theragra chalcogramma	Walleye pollock			4385.71		78.57		192.86
Theragra chalcogramma	Walleye pollock			4214.29		107.14		335.71
Theragra chalcogramma	Walleye pollock			3885.71		71.43		392.86
Theragra chalcogramma	Walleye pollock			4050.00		100.00		471.43
Theragra chalcogramma	Walleye pollock			3928.57		92.86		485.71
Theragra chalcogramma	Cod					107.14		
Theragra chalcogramma	Cod					107.14		
Theragra chalcogramma	Cod					114.29		
Theragra chalcogramma	Cod					50.00		
Theragra chalcogramma	Cod					50.00		
Theragra chalcogramma	Cod					35.71		
Theragra chalcogramma	Cod					107.14		
	Cod					114.29		
	Cod					85.71		
	Cod					64.29		
	Cod					42.86		
	Cod					100.00		
	Cod					235.71		
	Cod					150.00		
	Cod					171.43		
	Cod					149.29		
	Cod					71.43		
	Cod					307.14		
	Cod					235.71		
	Cod					485.71		
	Cod					92.86		
	Cod					157.14		
	Cod					107.14		
	Cod					114.29		
	Cod					271.43		
	Cod					1642.86		
	Cod					935.71		
	Cod					1264.29		
	Cod					314.29		
	Cod					114.29		
	Cod					278.57		
	Cod					450.00		
	Cod					428.57		
	Cod					600.00		
	Cod					71.43		
	Cod					257.14		
	Cod					1164.29		
	Cod					850.00		
	Cod					814.29		
	Cod					2707.14		
	Cod					1607.14		
	Cod					3614.29		
	Cod					3692.86		
	Cod					5221.43		
	Cod					1750.00		
	Cod					1057.14		
	Cod					1878.57		
	Cod					4621.43		
	Cod					4192.86		
	Cod					6564.29		
	Cod					4042.86		
	Cod					1421.43		
	Cod					4114.29		
	Cod					671.43		
	Cod					5800.00		
	Cod					2957.14		
	Cod					4835.71		
	Cod					3778.57		
	Cod					4700.00		
	Cod					5564.29		
	Cod					5221.43		
	Cod					3650.00		
	Cod					6357.14		
	Cod					3778.57		
	Cod					5600.00		
	Cod					5335.71		
	Cod					4064.29		
	Cod					4878.57		
	Cod					5042.86		
	Cod					487.57		
	Cod					250.00		
	Cod					464.29		
	Cod					335.71		
	Cod					264.29		
	Cod					107.14		
	Cod					564.29		
	Cod					478.57		
	Cod					678.57		
	Cod					557.14		
	Cod					371.43		
	Cod					378.57		
	Cod					364.29		
	Cod					5042.857		
	Cod					478.571		
	Cod					250.00		

NO.OF FISH EXAMINED	LENGTH OF FISH	BODY WEIGHT (g)	SEASON	METHOD USED	OTHER	REFERENCE
				11		Amano/Yamada 1965
				3		Amano/Yamada 1945
				3	Ordinary sample 1	Tokunaga 1970
				3	Ordinary sample 2	Tokunaga 1970
				3	Ordinary sample 3	Tokunaga 1970
				11	Ordinary sample 4	Tokunaga 1970
				11	Ordinary sample 5	Tokunaga 1970
				11	Bloody sample 1	Tokunaga 1970
				11	Bloody sample 2	Tokunaga 1970
				11	Bloody sample 3	Tokunaga 1970
				11	Bloody sample 4	Tokunaga 1970
				11	Bloody sample 5	Tokunaga 1970
					Fish Fish #1	Hillig et al 1958
					heavily Fish #2	Hillig et al 1958
					iced-- Fish #3	Hillig et al 1958
					1st pack Fish #4	Hillig et al 1958
					Age=0 days Fish #5	Hillig et al 1958
					Age=1 day Fish #1	Hillig et al 1958
					Age=1 day Fish #2	Hillig et al 1958
					Age=1 day Fish #3	Hillig et al 1958
					Age=2 days Fish #1	Hillig et al 1958
					Age=2 days Fish #2	Hillig et al 1958
					Age=2 days Fish #3	Hillig et al 1958
					Age=3 days Fish #1	Hillig et al 1958
					Age=3 days Fish #2	Hillig et al 1958
					Age=3 days Fish #3	Hillig et al 1958
					Age=4 days Fish #1	Hillig et al 1958
					Age=4 days Fish #2	Hillig et al 1958
					Age=4 days Fish #3	Hillig et al 1958
					Age=4 days Fish #4	Hillig et al 1958
					Age=4 days Fish #5	Hillig et al 1958
					Age=5 days Fish #1	Hillig et al 1958
					Age=5 days Fish #2	Hillig et al 1958
					Age=5 days Fish #3	Hillig et al 1958
					Age=6 days Fish #1	Hillig et al 1958
					Age=6 days Fish #2	Hillig et al 1958
					Age=6 days Fish #3	Hillig et al 1958
					Age=7 days Fish #1	Hillig et al 1958
					Age=7 days Fish #2	Hillig et al 1958
					Age=7 days Fish #3	Hillig et al 1958
					Age=8 days Fish #1	Hillig et al 1958
					Age=8 days Fish #2	Hillig et al 1958
					Age=8 days Fish #3	Hillig et al 1958
					Age=9 days Fish #1	Hillig et al 1958
					Age=9 days Fish #2	Hillig et al 1958
					Age=9 days Fish #3	Hillig et al 1958
					Age=10 days Fish #1	Hillig et al 1958
					Age=10 days Fish #2	Hillig et al 1958
					Age=11 days Fish #1	Hillig et al 1958
					Age=11 days Fish #2	Hillig et al 1958
					Age=11 days Fish #3	Hillig et al 1958
					Age=12 days Fish #1	Hillig et al 1958
					Age=12 days Fish #2	Hillig et al 1958
					Age=12 days Fish #1	Hillig et al 1958
					Age=12 days Fish #2	Hillig et al 1958
					Age=12 days Fish #1	Hillig et al 1958
					Age=13 days Fish #1	Hillig et al 1958
					Age=13 days Fish #2	Hillig et al 1958
					Age=13 days Fish #1	Hillig et al 1958
					Age=13 days Fish #1	Hillig et al 1958
					Age=13 days Fish #2	Hillig et al 1958
					Age=13 days Fish #3	Hillig et al 1958
					Age=14 days Fish #1	Hillig et al 1958
					Age=14 days Fish #2	Hillig et al 1958
					Age=14 days Fish #3	Hillig et al 1958
					Age=14 days Fish #1	Hillig et al 1958
					Age=14 days Fish #1	Hillig et al 1958
					Age=15 days Fish #1	Hillig et al 1958
					Age=15 days Fish #2	Hillig et al 1958
					Age=15 days Fish #3	Hillig et al 1958
					Age=15 days Fish #1	Hillig et al 1958
					Age=16 days Fish #1	Hillig et al 1958
					Age=16 days Fish #2	Hillig et al 1958
					Age=16 days Fish #3	Hillig et al 1958
					Age=16 days Fish #4	Hillig et al 1958
					Age=16 days Fish #5	Hillig et al 1958
					1st pack Fish #5	Hillig et al 1958
					Age=16 days Fish #1	Hillig et al 1958
					Age=16 days Fish #2	Hillig et al 1958
					Age=16 days Fish #3	Hillig et al 1958
					Age=16 days Fish #4	Hillig et al 1958
					Age=16 days Fish #5	Hillig et al 1958
					2nd pack Fish #1	Hillig et al 1958
					Age=0 days Fish #2	Hillig et al 1958
					Age=0 days Fish #3	Hillig et al 1958
					Age=0 days Fish #4	Hillig et al 1958
					Age=0 days Fish #5	Hillig et al 1958
					Age=2 days Fish #1	Hillig et al 1958
					Age=2 days Fish #2	Hillig et al 1958
					Age=2 days Fish #3	Hillig et al 1958
					Age=4 days Fish #1	Hillig et al 1958
					Age=4 days Fish #2	Hillig et al 1958
					Age=6 days Fish #1	Hillig et al 1958
					Age=6 days Fish #2	Hillig et al 1958
					Age=6 days Fish #3	Hillig et al 1958
					2nd pack Fish #1	Hillig et al 1958
					Age=0 days Fish #2	Hillig et al 1958

SCIENTIFIC NAME	COMMON NAME	TISSUE	TMAO (μM/100 g)		TMA (μM/100g)		DMA (μM/100g)	
			RANGE	AVERAGE	RANGE	AVERAGE	RANGE	AVER.
	Cod					464.286		
	Cod					335.714		
	Cod					264.286		
	Cod					107.143		
	Cod					564.286		
	Cod					478.571		
	Cod					678.571		
	Cod					557.143		
	Cod					371.429		
	Cod					378.571		
	Cod					364.286		
	Cod					1800.00		
	Cod					914.286		
	Cod					792.857		
	Cod					2878.571		
	Cod					2185.714		
	Cod					1800.00		
	Cod					914.29		
	Cod					792.86		
	Cod					2878.57		
	Cod					2185.71		
	Cod					1292.86		
	Cod					864.29		
	Cod					3821.43		
	Cod					1114.29		
	Cod					2921.43		
	Cod					3007.14		
	Cod					2342.86		
	Cod					3042.86		
	Cod					1850.00		
	Cod					3521.43		
	Cod					5178.57		
	Cod					3442.86		
	Cod					5571.43		
	Cod					4664.29		
	Cod					5814.29		
	Cod					5307.14		
	Cod					5600.00		
	Cod					3492.86		
	Cod					5664.29		
	Cod					478.57		
	Cod					250.00		
	Cod					464.29		
	Cod					335.71		
	Cod					264.29		
	Cod					621.43		
	Cod					--		
	Cod					542.86		
	Cod					664.29		
	Cod					885.71		
	Cod					4385.71		
	Cod					4435.71		
	Cod					4521.43		
	Cod					6357.14		
	Cod					6335.71		
	Cod					5471.43		
	Cod					5385.71		
	Cod					6650.00		
	Cod					6457.14		
	Cod					6078.57		
	Cod					292.86		
	Cod					478.57		
	Cod					642.86		
	Cod					364.29		
	Cod					857.14		
	Cod					1364.29		
	Cod					564.29		
	Cod					571.43		
	Cod					485.71		
	Cod					400.00		
	Cod					5385.71		
	Cod					5292.86		
	Cod					5957.14		
	Cod					5978.57		
	Cod					5485.71		
	Cod					3207.14		
	Cod					292.86		
	Cod					478.57		
	Cod					642.86		
	Cod					364.29		
	Cod					857.14		
	Cod					1364.29		
	Cod					564.29		
	Cod					571.43		
	Cod					485.71		
	Cod					400.00		
	Cod					300.00		
	Cod					492.86		
	Cod					764.29		
	Cod					478.57		
	Cod					1050.00		
	Cod					1357.14		
	Cod					292.857		
	Cod					478.571		
	Cod					642.857		
	Cod					364.286		

(Continued)

NO.OF FISH EXAMINED	LENGTH OF FISH	BODY WEIGHT (g)	SEASON	METHOD USED	OTHER	REFERENCE
					Age=0 days Fish #3	Hillig et al 1958
					Age=0 days Fish #4	Hillig et al 1958
					Age=0 days Fish #5	Hillig et al 1958
					Age=2 days Fish #1	Hillig et al 1958
					Age=2 days Fish #2	Hillig et al 1958
					Age=2 days Fish #3	Hillig et al 1958
					Age=4 days Fish #1	Hillig et al 1958
					Age=4 days Fish #2	Hillig et al 1958
					Age=6 days Fish #1	Hillig et al 1958
					Age=6 days Fish #2	Hillig et al 1958
					Age=6 days Fish #3	Hillig et al 1958
					Age=8 days Fish #1	Hillig et al 1958
					Age=8 days Fish #2	Hillig et al 1958
					Age=8 days Fish #3	Hillig et al 1958
					Age=10 days Fish #1	Hillig et al 1958
					Age=10 days Fish #2	Hillig et al 1958
					Age=8 days Fish #1	Hillig et al 1958
					Age=8 days Fish #2	Hillig et al 1958
					Age=8 days Fish #3	Hillig et al 1958
					Age=10 days Fish #1	Hillig et al 1958
					Age=10 days Fish #2	Hillig et al 1958
					Age=11 days Fish #1	Hillig et al 1958
					Age=11 days Fish #2	Hillig et al 1958
					Age=11 days Fish #3	Hillig et al 1958
					Age=12 days Fish #1	Hillig et al 1958
					Age=12 days Fish #2	Hillig et al 1958
					Age=12 days Fish #3	Hillig et al 1958
					Age=13 days Fish #1	Hillig et al 1958
					Age=13 days Fish #2	Hillig et al 1958
					Age=13 days Fish #3	Hillig et al 1958
					Age=14 days Fish #1	Hillig et al 1958
					Age=14 days Fish #2	Hillig et al 1958
					Age=14 days Fish #3	Hillig et al 1958
					Age=14 days Fish #4	Hillig et al 1958
					Age=14 days Fish #5	Hillig et al 1958
					Age=14 days Fish #1	Hillig et al 1958
					Age=14 days Fish #2	Hillig et al 1958
					Age=14 days Fish #3	Hillig et al 1958
					Age=14 days Fish #4	Hillig et al 1958
					Age=14 days Fish #5	Hillig et al 1958
					Fish Fish #1	Hillig et al 1958
					uniced-- Fish #2	Hillig et al 1958
					1st pack Fish #3	Hillig et al 1958
					Age=0 days Fish #4	Hillig et al 1958
					Age=0 days Fish #5	Hillig et al 1958
					Age=1 day Fish #1	Hillig et al 1958
					Age=1 day Fish #2	Hillig et al 1958
					Age=1 day Fish #3	Hillig et al 1958
					Age=1 day Fish #4	Hillig et al 1958
					Age=1 day Fish #5	Hillig et al 1958
					Age=2 days Fish #1	Hillig et al 1958
					Age=2 days Fish #2	Hillig et al 1958
					Age=2 days Fish #3	Hillig et al 1958
					Age=2 days Fish #4	Hillig et al 1958
					Age=2 days Fish #5	Hillig et al 1958
					Age=2 days Fish #1	Hillig et al 1958
					Age=2 days Fish #2	Hillig et al 1958
					Age=2 days Fish #3	Hillig et al 1958
					Age=2 days Fish #4	Hillig et al 1958
					Age=2 days Fish #5	Hillig et al 1958
					2nd pack Fish #1	Hillig et al 1958
					Age=0 days Fish #2	Hillig et al 1958
					Age=0 days Fish #3	Hillig et al 1958
					Age=0 days Fish #4	Hillig et al 1958
					Age=0 days Fish #5	Hillig et al 1958
					Age=1 day Fish #1	Hillig et al 1958
					Age=1 day Fish #1	Hillig et al 1958
					Age=1 day Fish #3	Hillig et al 1958
					Age=1 day Fish #4	Hillig et al 1958
					Age=1 day Fish #5	Hillig et al 1958
					Age=2 days Fish #1	Hillig et al 1958
					Age=2 days Fish #1	Hillig et al 1958
					Age=2 days Fish #2	Hillig et al 1958
					Age=2 days Fish #3	Hillig et al 1958
					Age=2 days Fish #4	Hillig et al 1958
					Age=2 days Fish #5	Hillig et al 1958
					Held ungut- Fish #1	Hillig et al 1958
					ted 18 hrs. Fish #2	Hillig et al 1958
					at 76°F. Gut- Fish #3	Hillig et al 1958
					ted & iced Fish #4	Hillig et al 1958
					Age=0 days Fish #5	Hillig et al 1958
					Age=1 day Fish #1	Hillig et al 1958
					Age=1 day Fish #2	Hillig et al 1958
					Age=1 day Fish #3	Hillig et al 1958
					Age=1 day Fish #4	Hillig et al 1958
					Age=1 day Fish #5	Hillig et al 1958
					Age=2 days Fish #1	Hillig et al 1958
					Age=2 days Fish #2	Hillig et al 1958
					Age=3 days Fish #1	Hillig et al 1958
					Age=3 days Fish #2	Hillig et al 1958
					Age=4 days Fish #1	Hillig et al 1958
					Age=4 days Fish #2	Hillig et al 1958
					Age=0 days Fish #1	Hillig et al 1958
					Age=0 days Fish #2	Hillig et al 1958
					Age=0 days Fish #3	Hillig et al 1958
					Age=0 days Fish #4	Hillig et al 1958

TABLE 12.

SCIENTIFIC NAME	COMMON NAME	TISSUE	TMAO (μM/100 g) RANGE	AVERAGE	TMA (μM/100g) RANGE	AVERAGE	DMA (μM/100g) RANGE	AVERAGE
	Cod					857.143		
	Cod					1364.286		
	Cod					564.286		
	Cod					571.429		
	Cod					485.714		
	Cod					400.00		
	Cod					300.00		
	Cod					492.857		
	Cod					764.286		
	Cod					478.571		
	Cod					1050.00		
	Cod					1357.143		
	Cod					678.571		
	Cod					535.714		
	Cod					685.714		
	Cod					678.57		
	Cod					535.71		
	Cod					685.71		
	Cod					900.00		
	Cod					635.71		
	Cod					1771.43		
	Cod					1957.14		
	Cod					5700.00		
	Cod					3142.86		
	Cod					2128.57		
	Cod					5407.14		
	Cod					5964.29		
	Cod					5585.71		
	Cod					3014.29		
	Cod					3178.57		
	Cod					6721.43		
	Cod					5671.43		
	Cod					6221.43		
	Cod					900.00		
	Cod					635.714		
	Cod					1771.429		
	Cod					1957.143		
	Cod					5700.00		
	Cod					3142.857		
	Cod					2128.571		
	Cod					5407.143		
	Cod					5964.286		
	Cod					5585.714		
	Cod					3014.286		
	Cod					3178.571		
	Cod					6721.429		
	Cod					5671.429		
	Cod					6221.429		
	Cod					5392.857		
	Cod					5585.714		
	Cod					5278.571		
	Cod					1642.857		
	Cod					5392.86		
	Cod					5585.71		
	Cod					5278.57		
	Cod					6142.86		
	Cod					6128.57		
	Cod							
	Cod					1642.86		
	Cod					1264.29		
	Cod					1164.29		
	Cod					850.00		
	Cod					814.29		
	Cod					2707.14		
	Cod					1607.14		
	Cod					1750.00		
	Cod					1057.14		
	Cod					671.43		
	Cod					1800.00		
	Cod					2878.57		
	Cod					2185.71		
	Cod					3821.43		
	Cod					2921.43		
	Cod					3007.14		
	Cod					5700.00		
	Cod					3142.86		
	Cod					2128.57		
	Cod							
	Cod		5000.00-8214.29					
Urophycis chuss	Red hake					8571.43		
						11857.14		
			7142.86-10000.00			8571.43		
			10500.00-12571.43			11857.14		
Urophycis sp.	Hake		13.07-10.40			11.87		
Macrouridae								
Macrourus berglax	Smooth spined rat tail					6071.44		
Macrouronus novaezelandiae	Hoki					1913.33		
	New Zealand whiptail					4733.33		
Ophididae								
Ophidion barbatum						930.67		

NO.OF FISH EXAMINED	LENGTH OF FISH	BODY WEIGHT (g)	SEASON	METHOD USED	OTHER	REFERENCE
					Age=0 days Fish #5	Hillig et al 1958
					Age=1 day Fish #1	Hillig et al 1958
					Age=1 day Fish #2	Hillig et al 1958
					Age=1 day Fish #3	Hillig et al 1958
					Age=1 day Fish #4	Hillig et al 1958
					Age=1 day Fish #5	Hillig et al 1958
					Age=2 days Fish #1	Hillig et al 1958
					Age=2 days Fish #2	Hillig et al 1958
					Age=3 days Fish #1	Hillig et al 1958
					Age=3 days Fish #2	Hillig et al 1958
					Age=4 days Fish #1	Hillig et al 1958
					Age=4 days Fish #2	Hillig et al 1958
					Age=4 days Fish #3	Hillig et al 1958
					Age=5 days Fish #1	Hillig et al 1958
					Age=4 days Fish #2	Hillig et al 1958
					Age=4 days Fish #3	Hillig et al 1958
					Age=5 days Fish #1	Hillig et al 1958
					Age=5 days Fish #2	Hillig et al 1958
					Age=5 days Fish #3	Hillig et al 1958
					Age=6 days Fish #1	Hillig et al 1958
					Age=6 days Fish #2	Hillig et al 1958
					Age=6 days Fish #3	Hillig et al 1958
					Age=7 days Fish #1	Hillig et al 1958
					Age=7 days Fish #2	Hillig et al 1958
					Age=7 days Fish #3	Hillig et al 1958
					Age=7 days Fish #1	Hillig et al 1958
					Age=7 days Fish #2	Hillig et al 1958
					Age=7 days Fish #3	Hillig et al 1958
					Age=8 days Fish #1	Hillig et al 1958
					Age=8 days Fish #2	Hillig et al 1958
					Age=10 days Fish #1	Hillig et al 1958
					Age=10 days Fish #2	Hillig et al 1958
					Age=10 days Fish #3	Hillig et al 1958
					Age=5 days Fish #3	Hillig et al 1958
					Age=6 days Fish #1	Hillig et al 1958
					Age=6 days Fish #2	Hillig et al 1958
					Age=6 days Fish #3	Hillig et al 1958
					Age=7 days Fish #1	Hillig et al 1958
					Age=7 days Fish #2	Hillig et al 1958
					Age=7 days Fish #3	Hillig et al 1958
					Age=7 days Fish #1	Hillig et al 1958
					Age=7 days Fish #2	Hillig et al 1958
					Age=8 days Fish #1	Hillig et al 1958
					Age=8 days Fish #2	Hillig et al 1958
					Age=10 days Fish #1	Hillig et al 1958
					Age=10 days Fish #2	Hillig et al 1958
					Age=10 days Fish #3	Hillig et al 1958
					Age=11 days Fish #1	Hillig et al 1958
					Age=11 days Fish #2	Hillig et al 1958
					Age=11 days Fish #3	Hillig et al 1958
					Age=11 days Fish #4	Hillig et al 1958
					Age=11 days Fish #1	Hillig et al 1958
					Age=11 days Fish #2	Hillig et al 1958
					Age=11 days Fish #3	Hillig et al 1958
					Age=11 days Fish #4	Hillig et al 1958
					Age=11 days Fish #5	Hillig et al 1958
					Grouping of * samples	Hillig et al 1958
					Age=7 days	Hillig et al 1958
					Age=7 days	Hillig et al 1958
					Age=11 days	Hillig et al 1958
					Age=11 days	Hillig et al 1958
					Age=11 days	Hillig et al 1958
					Age=12 days	Hillig et al 1958
					Age=12 days	Hillig et al 1958
					Age=13 days	Hillig et al 1958
					Age=13 days	Hillig et al 1958
					Age=14 days	Hillig et al 1958
					Age=8 days	Hillig et al 1958
					Age=10 days	Hillig et al 1958
					Age=10 days	Hillig et al 1958
					Age=11 days	Hillig et al 1958
					Age=12 days	Hillig et al 1958
					Age=12 days	Hillig et al 1958
					Age=7 days	Hillig et al 1958
					Age=7 days	Hillig et al 1958
					Age=7 days	Hillig et al 1958
				3		Castell 1949
				3		Dyer 1952
				3		Dyer 1952
				3		Beatty 1939
5				3		Beatty 1939
				3	TMAO Content of the musclepress juice	Beatty 1939
5				3		Beatty 1939
				3	TMAO Content of the musclepress juice	Beatty 1939
				3		Dyer 1952
				3		Tokunaga 1975
				3		Konosu et al 1978
				2		Cantoni/Ardemagni 1977

TABLE

SCIENTIFIC NAME	COMMON NAME	TISSUE	TMAO (μM/100 g) RANGE	TMAO (μM/100 g) AVERAGE	TMA (μM/100g) RANGE	TMA (μM/100g) AVERAGE	DMA (μM/100g) RANGE	DMA (μM/100g) AVER
Zoarcidae								
Macrozoardes americanus	Ellpout		4928.57-5214.29	5071.43				
Macrozoardes americanus	Ellpout			4214.29				
Zoarchius venefircus		muscle		2280				
ORDER -- ATHERINIFORMES								
Atherinidae								
Menidia notata	Atlantic silverside			2000.00				
				2000.00				
Cyprinodontidae								
Fundulus heteroclitus	Mummichog			1000.00				
Fundulus diaphanus	Banded killifish			0				
Oryziar latipes				785.70		305.09	0	
Exocoetidae								
Cypsilurus sp.				1785.71				
Cypsilurus spp.		ordinary		2342.86		7.14		
Cypselurus spp.		ordinary		2214.29		78.57		
		ordinary		2971.43		21.43		
		bloody		2071.43		78.57		
		ordinary		2657.14		14.29		
		bloody		1871.43		107.14		
		ordinary		2671.43		7.14	0	
		bloody		2328.57		57.14		
		ordinary		3142.86		14.29		
		bloody		2471.43		135.71		1
Cypsiturus sp.				1804.29				
Prognichthys agoo				840.00				
Hemiramphidae								
Hemiramphus sajori		muscle		1013.33				
Scombresocidae								
Belone belone	Aguglia			526.67				
Cololabis saira	Pacific saury		333.33-2773.33	1573.33				
	Saury			614.29				
				1614.29				
				328.57				
				2407.14				
				535.71				
				635.71				
				1300.00				
				1085.71				
				1200.00				
Cololabis saira	Pacific saury	ordinary		957.14		14.29		
		ordinary		671.43		14.29		
		ordinary		700.00		7.14		1
		ordinary		607.14		7.14		
		ordinary		721.43		7.14		2
		ordinary		700.00		0		2
		ordinary		807.14		0		
		ordinary		900.00		0		
		ordinary		1214.29				
		bloody		800.00		100.00		3
		bloody		614.29		78.57		2
		bloody		714.29		85.71		2
		bloody		714.29		71.43		3
		bloody		714.29		85.71		5
		bloody		729.86		57.14		3
		bloody		792.86		57.14		3
		bloody		871.43		50.00		2
		bloody		964.29		35.71		1
Scomberesox saurus	Atlantic saury					35.71		
	Saury					-		
						842.86		
						1042.86		
						1157.14		
						1185.71		
ORDER -- BERYCIFORMES								
Bericidae								
Beryx splendens	Red bream			2592				
ORDER -- GASTEROSTEIFORMES								
Gasterosteidae								
Gasterosteus aculeatus	Threespine stickleback			1000.00				

NO.OF FISH EXAMINED	LENGTH OF FISH	BODY WEIGHT (g)	SEASON	METHOD USED	OTHER	REFERENCE
2				3		Dyer 1952
				3		Dyer 1952
						Yamada 1967
				3		Dyer 1952
				3		Dyer 1952
				3		Dyer 1952
3				3		Dyer 1952
				6		Mujahara 1960
				2		Velankar/Govindan 1958
				3		Tokunaga 1970
				3		Tokunaga 1970
				3		Tokunaga 1970
				11		Tokunaga 1970
				11		Tokunaga 1970
				11		Tokunaga 1970
				11		Tokunaga 1970
				11		Tokunaga 1970
				11		Tokunaga 1970
				11		Tokunaga 1970
				2		Velankar 1958
						Yamada 1967
						Yamada 1967
				2		Cantoni/Ardemagni 1977
						Yamada 1967
						Yamada 1967
						Horie/Sekine 1956
						Horie/Sekine 1956
						Horie/Sekine 1956
						Horie/Sekine 1956
						Horie/Sekine 1956
						Horie/Sekine 1956
						Horie/Sekine 1956
						Horie/Sekine 1956
	33.0	127	July 1969	3, 11	Columns 1	Tokunaga 1970
	31.6	114	July 1969	3, 11	Columns 2	Tokunaga 1970
	30.2	105	July 1969	3, 11	Columns 3	Tokunaga 1970
	31.5	106	July 1969	3, 11	Columns 4	Tokunaga 1970
	30.5	108	July 1969	3, 11	Columns 5	Tokunaga 1970
	30.8	113	Oct 1969	3, 11	Columns 6	Tokunaga 1970
	29.8	103	Oct 1969	3, 11	Columns 7	Tokunaga 1970
	29.6	94	Oct 1969	3, 11	Columns 8	Tokunaga 1970
	33.0	127	July 1969	3, 11	Columns 1	Tokunaga 1970
	31.6	114	July 1969	3, 11	Columns 2	Tokunaga 1970
	30.2	105	July 1969	3, 11	Columns 3	Tokunaga 1970
	31.5	106	July 1969	3, 11	Columns 4	Tokunaga 1970
	30.5	108	July 1969	3, 11	Columns 5	Tokunaga 1970
	30.8	113	Oct 1969	3, 11	Columns 6	Tokunaga 1970
	29.8	103	Oct 1969	3, 11	Columns 7	Tokunaga 1970
	29.6	94	Oct 1969	3, 11	Columns 8	Tokunaga 1970
				3		Dyer 1952
				2	Storage 4-14°C 0 days	Horie/Sekine 1956
				2	1	Horie/Sekine 1956
				2	2	Horie/Sekine 1956
				2	3	Horie/Sekine 1956
				2	4	Horie/Sekine 1956
				2	5	Horie/Sekine 1956
				3		Tokunaga 1975
2				3		Dyer 1952

SCIENTIFIC NAME	COMMON NAME	TISSUE	TMAO (μM/100 g) RANGE	TMAO AVERAGE	TMA (μM/100g) RANGE	TMA AVERAGE	DMA (μM/100g) RANGE	DMA AVERA
ORDER -- PERCIFORMES								
Anarhichadidae								
Anarchias latifrons	Broadheaded catfish			4000.00				
Anarchias lupus	Common catfish		3785.71-4857.14	4500.00				
Anoplopomatidae								
Anoplopoma fimbria	Sablefish	ordinary		7500.00		14.29		2
		ordinary		8392.86		7.14		2
Anoplopoma fimbria		bloody		3214.29		42.86		71
		bloody		3500.00		21.43		85
Carangidae								
Caranx leptolepis				3851.43				
Caranx leptolipis				3857.14				
Cyttus traversi	Look-down dory	muscle		5466.67				
Decapterus macarellus	Mackerel scad					135.71		
						157.14		
						1371.43		
						1021.43		
						300.00		
Seriola brama	Warehow	muscle		2786.67				
Seriolella maculata	Silver warehow	muscle		4053.33				
Seriola quinqueradiata		ordinary						
		muscle		361.33		1.33		
		dark muscle		562.66		34.67		
Seriola quinqueradiate				123586.67				
				5293.33				
Seriola quinqueradiate	Yellowtail	ordinary		1707.14		0		(
		bloody		2107.14				8
		ordinary		1628.57		0		(
		bloody		2271.43		-		8
Seriola dumerili	Amberjack			4285.71				
Synagris japonicus				2857.14				
Synagris japonicus				2857.14				
Trachurus japonicus	Jack mackerel	ordinary		4014.29		21.43		2
		bloody		2814.29		78.57		1
		ordinary		3921.43		35.71		6
		bloody		2850.00		78.57		1
		ordinary		4800.00		28.57		6
		bloody		3042.86		121.43		15
		ordinary		4314.29		14.29		4
		bloody		2964.29		71.43		15
		ordinary		4850.00		35.71		11
		bloody		2814.29		157.14		1
Trachurus japonicus	Jack mackerel			4413.33				
Trachurus japonicus	Jack mackerel	ordinary						
		muscle		1373.33		16.0		
		dark muscle		1586.66		68.0		
				800.00		186.67		
				1346.67		trace		
	Horse mackerel			681.60		34.67		
				638.27		84.00		
				372.53		413.33		
				358.00		477.33		
				76.13		940.00		
				0		1050.67		
				1960,				
				2893.33,				
				3040,				
				2800				
				3146.66-4053.33				
				1346.67				
Trachurus symmetricus	Jack mackerel			4028.57				
				3142.86				
				4057.14				
						28.57		
						92.86		
						1514.29		
						1978.57		
						2350.00		
						3078.57		
Cottidae								
Hemitriptorus americanus	Sea raven			6214.29				
Myoxocephalus groenlandicus	Shorthorn sculpin			7000.00				
Moxocephalus octodecemspinosus	Longhorn sculpin	muscle		6500.00				
Scorpaenicthys marmoratus	Cabezoni (bull cod)			4642.86				
	Sculpin			5142.86-8000.00				
Hemitriptorus americanus	Sea raven			6214.29				
Scorpaenicthys marmoratus	Bullcod	muscle		46.00				
Cyclopteridae								
Cyclopterus lumpus	Lumpfish			3214.29				
Dactylopteridae								
	Gurnard	raw					180	
		roasted					630	

(Continued)

NO.OF FISH EXAMINED	LENGTH OF FISH	BODY WEIGHT (g)	SEASON	METHOD USED	OTHER	REFERENCE
				3	Wet weight	Dyer 1952
				3	Wet weight	Dyer 1952
				3, 11		Tokunaga 1970
				3, 11		Tokunaga 1970
				3, 11		Tokunaga 1970
				3, 11		Tokunaga 1970
				2		Velankar/Govindan 1958
				2		Velankar/Govindan 1958
				3		Konosu et al 1978
				3	Days elapsed 0	Horie/Sekine 1956
				3	Days elapsed 1	Horie/Sekine 1956
				3	Days elapsed 2	Horie/Sekine 1956
				3	Days elapsed 3	Horie/Sekine 1956
				3	Days elapsed 4	Horie/Sekine 1956
				3		Konosu et al 1978
				3		Konosu et al 1978
				3		Takagi et al 1967
				3		Takagi et al 1967
						Yamada 1967
	43.5	740	June 1967	3, 11	Fish #1	Tokunaga 1970
	43.5	740	June 1969	3, 11	Fish #1	Tokunaga 1970
	42.0	740	June 1969	3, 11	Fish #2	Tokunaga 1970
	42.0	680	July 1969	3, 11	Fish #2	Tokunaga 1970
				3		Dyer 1952
				2		Velankar/Govindan 1958
				2		Velankar/Govindan 1958
	21.8	680	July 1969	11	Fish #1	Tokunaga 1970
	21.8	115	July 1969	11	Fish #1	Tokunaga 1970
	21.8	115	July 1959	11	Fish #1	Tokunaga 1970
	21.8	115	July 1969		Fish #1	Tokunaga 1970
	21.3	115	July 1969	11	Fish #2	Tokunaga 1970
	21.3	108	July 1969	11	Fish #2	Tokunaga 1970
	22.0	108	July 1969	11	Fish #3	Tokunaga 1970
	22.0	114	July 1969	11	Fish #3	Tokunaga 1970
	21.3	114	July 1969	11	Fish #4	Tokunaga 1970
	21.3	110	July 1969	11	Fish #4	Tokunaga 1970
	21.6	110	July 1969	11	Fish #5	Tokunaga 1970
	21.6	115	July 1969	11	Fish #5	Tokunaga 1970
				3		Konosu et al 1974
				3		Takagi et al 1967
				3		Takagi et al 1967
				6		Mujahara 1960
				3		Sakaguchi/Simidu 1964
				3	Stored at $15^\circ\text{C}\pm2$ 0 hrs	Takada/Mishimoto 1958
					18 hrs	Takada/Mishimoto 1958
				3	27 hrs	Takada/Mishimoto 1958
				3	47 hrs	Takada/Nishimoto 1958
				3	71 hrs	Takada/Nishimoto 1958
				3	95 hrs	Takada/Nishimoto 1958
						Yamada 1967
						Yamada 1967
						Yamada 1967
3				3		Horie/Sekine 1956
3				3		Horie/Sekine 1956
3				3		Horie/Sekine 1956
				3	Days elapsed 1	Horie/Sekine 1956
				3	Days elapsed 2	Horie/Sekine 1956
				3	Days elapsed 3	Horie/Sekine 1956
				3	Days elapsed 4	Horie/Sekine 1956
				3	Days elapsed 5	Horie/Sekine 1956
4				3		Dyer 1952
				3		Dyer 1952
				3		Dyer 1952
				3		Dyer 1952
				3		Castell 1949
				3		Dyer 1952
				3		Norris/Benoit 1945
				3		Dyer 1952
				11		Kawamura et al 1971
				11		Kawamura et al 1971

SCIENTIFIC NAME	COMMON NAME	TISSUE	TMAO (μM/100 g) RANGE	AVERAGE	TMA (μM/100g) RANGE	AVERAGE	DMA (μM/100g) RANGE	AVER
Embiotocidae								
Ditrema temmincki				1165.33		15.25		
Ditrema temmincki				2693.33-				
				3373.33				
		Perch					30	540
		Surf perch				14.29		
						1042.86		
Taenitoca lateralis	Blue perch			4785.71				
	Surf perch			3371.43				
				2757.14				
				2685.71				
				2685.71				
Gerreidae								
Gerres sp.				2857.14				
Gerres sp.				2844.29				
Gobiidae								
Pterogobins elapoides				93.33		106.67		
Haemulidae								
Parapristipoma trilineatum	Japanese grunt	ordinary		1186.67		40.00		
				922.67		0		
				902.67		0		
				844.00		0		
		bloody		300.00		4.00		
				272.00		0		
				449.33		0		
				2280				
Hexagrammidae								
Hexagrammus otakii				1666.67		16		
Ophiodon elongatus	Lingcod			6000.00				
Pleurogrammus agonus				1493.33		5.33		
Pleurogrammus agonus		muscle		5813.33				
Labridae								
Labrus turdus	Wrasse			14.29				
	Wrasse			1042.86				
Leiognathidae								
Leiognathus mechalis				40.00		200.00		
Mugilidae								
Mugil aeur.				2750.00				
Mugil cephalus	Striped mullet	muscles		760.00				
				86.800				
Mugil cephalus				40.00		213.33		
Mugil sp.				1714.29				
Mugil sp.				1717.14				
Mullidae								
Mulloides flavolineatus	Goatfish			3642.86				
				3645.71				
Oplegnathidae								
Oplegnathus fasciatus				413.33		106.67		
Pampidae								
Pampus argentus				3927.86				
Pentacerotidae								
Pentaceros richardsoni		muscle		3146.67				
Perchichthyidae								
Morone americana	White perch			4214.29				
Roccus saxtilis	Striped bass			4428.57				
Percidae								
Perca flavescens	Yellow perch			0				
Pomadasyidae								
		Pigfish				14.29		
						2000		
Sciaenidae								
Argyrosomus argentatus				3000				
	Sea trout			1428.57				
Rexia solandri	Southern kingfish			1392				

NO.OF FISH EXAMINED	LENGTH OF FISH	BODY WEIGHT (g)	SEASON	METHOD USED	OTHER	REFERENCE
				3		Takagi 1967
				11		Yamada 1967
				3		Kawamura et al 1971
				3	Before storage	Horie/Sekine 1956
				3	2 days at 7-16°C	Horie/Sekine 1956
				3		Dyer 1952
				3		Horie/Sekine 1956
				3		Horie/Sekine 1956
				3		Horie/Sekine 1956
						Horie/Sekine 1956
				2		Velankar/Govindan 1958
				2		Velankar 1958
	7			6		Mujahara 1960
		372		6		Mujahara 1960
	30.6	372	Sept 1969	3, 11		Tokunaga 1970
	30.8	383	Sept 1969	3, 11		Tokunaga 1970
	30.6	372	Sept 1969	3, 11		Tokunaga 1970
	30.6	372		11		Tokunaga 1970
	30.8	383				Tokunaga 1970
	30.6	372				Yamada 1967
				3		Takagi et al 1967
				3		Dyer 1952
				3		Takagi et al 1967
						Yamada 1967
				2	Before storage	Horie/Sekine 1956
				2	2 days at 7-16°C	Horie/Sekine 1956
	7			6		Mujahara 1960
						Velankar 1958
						Yamada 1967
				2		Cantoni/Ardemagni 1977
	28			6		Mujahara 1960
				2		Velankar/Govindan 1958
				2		Velankar 1958
				2		Velankar/Govindan 1958
				2		Velankar Govindan 1958
	22			6		Mujahara 1960
				2		Velankar 1958
				3		Konosu et al 1978
				3		Dyer 1952
				3		Dyer 1952
5				3		Dyer 1952
				2	Before storage	Horie/Sekine 1956
				2	After 3 days at 7-16°C	Horie/Sekine 1956
						Yamada 1967
				3		Castell 1949
				3		Tokunaga 1975

SCIENTIFIC NAME	COMMON NAME	TISSUE	TMAO (μM/100 g) RANGE	TMAO (μM/100 g) AVERAGE	TMA (μM/100g) RANGE	TMA (μM/100g) AVERAGE	DMA (μM/100g) RANGE	DMA (μM/100g) AVER
Scombridae								
Auxis tapeinosoma	Frigate mackerel	dark meat		1135.71				
		white meat		114.29				
Auxis tapeinosome			106.67-1346.67	266.67				
Auxis tapeinosoma	Frigate mackerel	white muscle		128.57		10.71		
				-		10.71		
				100.00		12.86		
				150.00		12.14		
				107.14		15.00		
				100.00		12.14		
		dark muscle		1342.86		45.00		
				1307.14		63.57		
				1314.29		176.43		
				1092.86		220.71		
				821.43		140.00		
				957.14		209.29		
	Mackerel		2142.86-2642.86					
Auxis thayzard	Frigate mackerel		53.33-280					
				57.14				
				278.57				
				207.14				
Auxis thayzard	Frigate mackerel					21.43		
						28.57		
	Mackerel					128.57		
						64.29		
						107.14		
						85.71		
						128.57		
						135.71		
						164.29		
						14.29		
						-		
						-		
Katsuwonis pelamis	Katsuo			0		14.29		
	Mackerel roe - A							
	Mackerel roe - B							
Katsuwonis pelamis	Skipjack			214.29		21.43		
	Skipjack			135.71		7.14		
	Mackerel					660.71		
	Mackerel					603.57		
	Mackerel					285.71		
	Mackerel					403.57		
	Mackerel					321.43		
	Mackerel					123.57		
	Mackerel					797.14		
	Mackerel					944.29		
	Mackerel					342.86		
	Mackerel					549.29		
	Mackerel					214.29		
	Mackerel					357.14		
	Mackerel					214.29		
	Mackerel					61.43		
	Mackerel					607.14		
	Mackerel					566.43		
	Mackerel					236.43		
Neothunnus albacora (Lowe)	Yellowfin tuna					trace		
Pneumatophorus japonicus japonicus				2000.00		169.49		
				466.67		4593.22		
Scomberomorus comersonii	Chub			2010.71				
Scomber japonicus	Chub mackerel		426.67-3240					
			133.33-586.67	1426, 667,				
			293.33-480.00	2480, 306				
Scomber japonicus	Chub mackerel	ordinary muscle				61.07		
		bloody muscle				103.39		
		stomach				372.88		
		liver				1694.92		
		pyloric caeca				762.71		
		intestine				-		
		ordinary muscle				12.88		
		bloody muscle				25.76		
		stomach				81.36		
		liver				36.27		
		pyloric caeca				28.48		
		intestine				36.27		

NO.OF FISH EXAMINED	LENGTH OF FISH	BODY WEIGHT (g)	SEASON	METHOD USED	OTHER	REFERENCE
3				3		Dyer 1952
				3		Kawabata 1953
				3		Kawabata 1953 Yamada 1967
				3	Fish #1	Kawabata 1953
				3	2	Kawabata 1953
				3	3	Kawabata 1953
				3	4	Kawabata 1953
				3	5	Kawabata 1953
				3	6	Kawabata 1953
				3	Fish #1	Kawabata 1953
				3	2	Kawabata 1953
				3	3	Kawabata 1953
				3	4	Kawabata 1953
				3	5	Kawabata 1953
				3	6	Kawabata 1953
				3		Castell 1949
						Yamada 1967
				3		Horie/Sekine 1956
				3		Horie/Sekine 1956
				3		Horie/Sekine 1956
				2	Storage 4-14°C 4 Days	Horie/Sekine 1956
				2	5	Horie/Sekine 1956
				2	6	Horie/Sekine 1956
				2	7	Horie/Sekine 1956
				2	8	Horie/Sekine 1956
				2	0	Horie/Sekine 1956
				2	1	Horie/Sekine 1956
				2	2	Horie/Sekine 1956
				2	3	Horie/Sekine 1956
				2	4	Horie/Sekine 1956
				2	5	Horie/Sekine 1956
				2	6	Horie/Sekine 1956
				2	7	Horie/Sekine 1956
				2	8	Horie/Sekine 1956
				2	0	Horie/Sekine 1956
				2	1	Horie/Sekine 1956
				2	2	Horie/Sekine 1956
				2	3	Horie/Sekine 1956
						Yamada 1967
						Kawamura et al 1971
						Kawamura et al 1971
55		2930	June 1969	3		Tokunaga 1970
51		2460	June 1969	3		Tckunaga 1970
				1	96% ethanal extract	Venkatamaran/Chari 1950
				1	96% ethanal extract	Venkatamaran/Chari 1950
				1	96% ehtanal extract	Venkatamaran/Chari 1950
				1	96% ethanal extract	Venkatamaran/Chari 1950
				1	96% ethanal extract	Venkatamaran/Chari 1950
				1	96% ethanal extract	Venkatamaran/Chari 1950
				1	96% ethanal extract	Venkatamaran/Chari 1950
				1	96% ethanal extract	Venkatamaran/Chari 1950
				1	96% ethanal extract	Venkatamaran/Chari 1950
				2		Venkatamaran/Chari 1950
				2		Venkatamaran/Chari 1950
				2		Venkatamaran/Chari 1950
				2		Venkatamaran/Chari 1950
				2		Venkatamaran/Chari 1950
				2		Venkatamaran/Chari 1950
				2		Venkatamaran/Chari 1950
				3		Sakaguchi/Simidu 1964
		2		6		Mujahara 1960
		28		6		Mujahara 1960
				2		Velankar 1958
						Yamada 1967
				3	Fish a	Takada/Nishimoto 1958
				3	Fish a	Takada/Nishimoto 1958
				3	Fish a	Takada/Nishimoto 1958
				3	Fish a	Takada/Nishimoto 1958
				3	Fish a	Takada/Nishimoto 1958
				3	Fish a	Takada/Nishimoto 1958
				3	Fish b	Takada/Nishimoto 1958
				3	Fish b	Takada/Nishimoto 1958
				3	Fish b	Takada/Nishimoto 1958
				3	Fish b	Takada/Nishimoto 1958
				3	Fish b	Takada/Nishimoto 1958
				3	Fish b	Takada/Nishimoto 1958

TABLE 1

SCIENTIFIC NAME	COMMON NAME	TISSUE	TMAO (μM/100 g)		TMA (μM/100g)		DMA (μM/100g)	
			RANGE	AVERAGE	RANGE	AVERAGE	RANGE	AVERAG
Scomber japonicus	Chub mackerel					trace		
Scomber japonicus	Chub mackerel	ordinary muscle		346.67		6.67		
		dark muscle		754.67		26.67		
			426.67-3240	1426.67, 506.67				
			293.33-480, 133.33-586.67	2480.00,				
Scomber japonicus	Chub mackerel			306.67				
				626.67				
				300.00		3.39		
				70.67		3.39		
				186.67		23.73		
				117.33		27.12		
				198.67		30.51		
				150.67		37.29		
				200		40.68		
				1278.57		21.43		
				692.86		7.14		
				714.29		14.29		
Scomberomorus niphonius				1546.67				
				1546.67				
Scomber scombrus	Atlantic mackerel		2214.29 2714.29	2428.57				
Scomber scombrus	Atlantic mackerel	muscle	2920.57 3857.14	3428.57				
Scomber scombrus	Atlantic mackerel Mackerel			366.67	0	2164.29		
Scomber scombrus	Atlantic mackerel		3.867-2.93	3.47				
Scomber scombrus	Atlantic mackerel		2214.29 2714.29	2428.57				
	Atlantic mackerel		2928.57-3857.14	3428.57				
Thunnus alalunga (Germo alalunga G)	Albacore	white meat				228.57		
		dark meat				192.86		
Thunnus alalunga	Albacore		66.67-440					
Thunnus alalunga	Albacore	White Muscle surface layer				127.86		
		deep layer				62.86		
		dark muscle				362.14		
		white muscle of tail				44.29		
		ventral muscle				13.57		
		White Muscle surface layer				67.86		
		deep layer				45.71		
Thunnus alalunga	Albacore	dark muscle				469.29		
		white muscle of tail				148.57		
		ventral muscle				65.00		
		White Muscle surface layer				47.86		
		deep layer				39.29		
		dark muscle				480.00		
		white muscle of tail				54.29		
		ventral muscle				28.57		
		White Muscle surface layer				75.00		
		deep layer				55.71		
		dark muscle				510.71		
		white muscle of tail				438.57		
		ventral muscle				93.57		
		White Muscle surface layer				114.29		
		deep layer				46.43		
		dark muscle				480.71		

NO.OF FISH EXAMINED	LENGTH OF FISH	BODY WEIGHT (g)	SEASON	METHOD USED	OTHER	REFERENCE
				3		Sakaguchi/Simidu 1964
				3		Takagi 1967
				3		Takagi 1967
						Yamada 1967
						Yamada 1967
				3		Konosu et al 1974
	42.5	880	June 1969	3		Tokunaga 1970
	29.5	635	June 1969	3		Tokunaga 1970
	36.0	424	Sept 1969	3		Tokunaga 1970
	35.0	405	Sept 1969	3		Tokunaga 1970
	37.0	486	Sept 1969	3		Tokunaga 1970
	34.0	377	Sept 1969	3		Tokunaga 1970
	35.5	464	Sept 1969	3		Tokunaga 1970
	44.5	825	June 1969	3		Tokunaga 1970
	39.0	575	June 1969	3		Tokunaga 1970
	39.8	630	June 1969	3		Tokunaga 1970
						Yamada 1967
						Yamada 1967
3				3		Dyer 1952
10				3		Beatty/Gibbons 1937
				2		Cantoni/Ardemagni 1977
10				3		Horie/Sekine 1956
10				3		Dyer 1952
				3		Dyer 1952
				3		Kawabata 1953
				3		Kawabata 1953
						Yamada 1967
				3	Fish #21	Kawabata 1953
				3	21	Kawabata 1953
				3	21	Kawabata 1953
				3	21	Kawabata 1953
				3	21	Kawabata 1953
				3	22	Kawabata 1953
				3	22	Kawabata 1953
				3	Fish #22	Kawabata 1953
				3	22	Kawabata 1953
				3	22	Kawabata 1953
				3	24	Kawabata 1953
				3	24	Kawabata 1953
				3	24	Kawabata 1953
				3	24	Kawabata 1953
				3	24	Kawabata 1953
				2	25	Kawabata 1953
				2	25	Kawabata 1953
				2	25	Kawabata 1953
				2	25	Kawabata 1953
				2	25	Kawabata 1953
				2	26	Kawabata 1953
				2	26	Kawabata 1953
				2	26	Kawabata 1953

SCIENTIFIC NAME	COMMON NAME	TISSUE	TMAO (μM/100 g) RANGE	AVERAGE	TMA (μM/100g) RANGE	AVERAGE	DMA (μM/100g) RANGE	AVERA
		white muscle of tail				205.00		
		ventral muscle				105.00		
Thunnus alalunga	Albacore	White Muscle surface layer				171.43		
		deep layer				78.57		
		dark muscle				621.43		
		white muscle of tail				246.43		
		ventral muscle	initial	control	initial	control 81.43		
		dark muscle	435.71	329.29	235	435.71		
		white muscle	100.00	107.14	22.86	22.86		
		dark muscle	64.29	50.00	654.29	691.43		
		white muscle	300.00	350.00	27.14	28.57		
		dark muscle	192.86	114.29	614.29	705.71		
Thunnus albacares	Yellowfin tuna		146.67-1053.33, 693.33-7026.67	80.-				
Thunnus albacares	Yellowfin tuna					1342.86		
Thunnus albacares	Yellowfin tuna	muscle						
Thunnus albacares	Yellowfin tuna			371.43 371.43 142.86				
Thunnus albacares	Yellowfin tuna			350.00 142.86 342.86 257.14 1050.00 192.86 121.43		- - -		
Thunnus albacares	Yellowfin tuna						200.00 - - 171.43	
Thunnus albacares	Yellowfin tuna	Muscle of head region 10 cm above eye		1914.29		11.86		
		caudal fin		1821.43		33.90		
		dorsal fin		2850.00		40.68		
		anal fin		4214.29		84.75		
		pectoral fin		3285.71		54.24		
Thunnus albacares	Yellowfin tuna	Muscle of caudal fin		464.29		13.56		
		dorsal fin		578.57		10.17		
		anal fin		2385.71		20.34		
		pectoral fin		1464.29		40.68		
Thunnus albacares	Yellowfin tuna	Muscle of head region 10 cm above eye		2492.86		150.00		
		superficial muscle		-		-		
		interior muscle		1135.71		6.78		
		deep muscle		-		-		
		upper dorsal muscle		1242.86		-		
		belly muscle		3214.29		-		
		true red muscle		-		-		
		superficial muscle		1378.57		-		
		interior muscle		950.00		6.78		
		superficial muscle		1214.29		-		
		interior muscle		1157.14		3.39		
		deep muscle		714.29		-		
		upper dorsal muscle		814.29		67.80		

NO.OF FISH EXAMINED	LENGTH OF FISH	BODY WEIGHT (g)	SEASON	METHOD USED	OTHER	REFERENCE
				2	26	Kawabata 1953
				2	26	Kawabata 1953
				2	Fish #28	Kawabata 1953
				2	28	Kawabata 1953
				2	28	Kawabata 1953
				2	28	Kawabata 1953
				2	28	Kawabata 1953
				2	16	Kawabata 1953
				2	17 *-control-- aft. asceptic incubat'n	Kawabata 1953
				2	17 *-control-- aft. asceptic incubat'n	Kawabata 1953
				2	Fish #18	Kawabata 1953
				2	18	Kawabata 1953
9				2	2 days storage 7-16°C	Yamada 1967 Horie/Sekine
				3		Yamada 1967 Horie/Sekine 1956
				3		Horie/Sekine 1956
				3		Horie/Sekine 1956
				3		Horie/Sekine 1956
				3		Horie/Sekine 1956
				3		Horie/Sekine 1956
				3	Storage 4-14°C 5 days	Horie/Sekine 1956
				3	6	Horie/Sekine 1956
				3	7	Horie/Sekine 1956
				3	8	Horie/Sekine 1956
				3	0	Horie/Sekine 1956
				2	1	Horie/Sekine 1956
				2	2	Horie/Sekine 1956
				2	3	Horie/Sekine 1956
				2	4	Horie/Sekine 1956
				3	Green meat fish	Yamataga et al 1968
				3	Green meat fish	Yamataga et al 1968
				3	Green meat fish	Yamataga et al 1968
				3	Green meat fish	Yamataga et al 1968
				3	Green meat fish	Yamataga et al 1968
				3		Yamagata et al 1968
						Yamagata et al 1968
						Yamagata et al 1968
						Yamagata et al 1968
					* margin of gill cover	Yamagata et al 1968
					* margin of gill cover	Yamagata et al 1968
					* margin of gill cover	Yamagata et al 1968
					* margin of gill cover	Yamagata et al 1968
					* margin of gill cover	Yamagata et al 1968
					* margin of gill cover	Yamagata et al 1968
					* margin of gill cover	Yamagata et al 1968
					* anus	Yamagata et al 1968
					* anus	Yamagata et al 1968
					* anus	Yamagata et al 1968
					* anus	Yamagata et al 1968

TABLE 1

SCIENTIFIC NAME	COMMON NAME	TISSUE	TMAO (μM/100 g) RANGE	AVERAGE	TMA (μM/100g) RANGE	AVERAGE	DMA (μM/100g) RANGE	AVER...
Thunnus albacares	Yellowfin tuna	belly muscle		1521.43		20.34		
		true red muscle		292.86		247.46		
		superficial muscle		1328.57		-		
		interior muscle		1392.86		15.25		
		deep muscle		635.71		-		
		upper dorsal muscle		828.57		-		
		belly muscle		1257.14		-		
		true red muscle		357.14		240.68		
		deep muscle		1378.57		-		
		upper dorsal muscle		1628.57		-		
		belly muscle		1571.43		-		
		true red muscle		135.71		240.68		
		right side super-ficial		1221.43				
		right side interior		1178.57				
		right side deep		735.71				
		left side super-ficial		1207.14				
		left side interior		1171.43				
		left side deep		714.29				
		right side super-ficial		1214.29				
		right side interior		1100.00				
		right side deep		692.86				
		left side super-ficial		1214.29				
Thunnus albacares	Yellowfin tuna	left side interior		1171.43				
		left side deep		742.86				
		superficial muscle		-				
		interior muscle		42.86		30.51		
		deep muscle		-				
		upper dorsal muscle		150.00				
		belly muscle		850.00				
		true red muscle		528.57				
		superficial muscle		57.14				
		interior muscle		42.86		5.33		
		deep muscle		28.57				
		upper dorsal muscle		114.29				
		belly muscle		150.00				
		true red muscle		800.00				
		superficial muscle		100.00		-		
		interior muscle		21.43		10.17		
		deep muscle		7.14		-		
		upper dorsal muscle		50.00		3.39		
		belly muscle		392.86		18.64		
		true red muscle		500.00		254.24		
		superficial muscle		28.57		-		
Thunnus albacares	Yellowfin tuna	interior muscle		57.14		37.29		
		deep muscle		57.14		-		

NO. OF FISH EXAMINED	LENGTH OF FISH	BODY WEIGHT (g)	SEASON	METHOD USED	OTHER	REFERENCE
					* anus	Yamagata et al 1968
					* anus	Yamagata et al 1968
				3	* anus	Yamagata et al 1968
					* anus	Yamagata et al 1968
					7th spine of 1st dorsal fin	Yamagata et al 1968
					7th spine of 1st dorsal fin	Yamagata et al 1968
					7th spine of 1st dorsal fin	Yamagata et al 1968
					4th dorsal finlet	Yamagata et al 1968
					4th dorsal finlet	Yamagata et al 1968
					4th dorsal finlet	Yamagata et al 1968
					4th dorsal finlet	Yamagata et al 1968
					4th dorsal finlet	Yamagata et al 1968
					4th dorsal finlet	Yamagata et al 1968
					epaxial	Yamagata et al 1968
					epaxial	Yamagata et al 1968
					epaxial	Yamagata et al 1968
					epaxial	Yamagata et al 1968
					epaxial	Yamagata et al 1968
					epaxial	Yamagata et al 1968
					hypoxial	Yamagata et al 1968
					hypoxial	Yamagata et al 1968
					hypoxial	Yamagata et al 1968
				3	hypoxial	Yamagata et al 1968
					hypoxial	Yamagata et al 1968
					hypoxial	Yamagata et al 1968
					margin of gill cover	Yamagata et al 1968
					margin of gill cover	Yamagata et al 1968
					margin of gill cover	Yamagata et al 1968
					margin of gill cover	Yamagata et al 1968
					margin of gill cover	Yamagata et al 1968
					anus	Yamagata et al 1968
					anus	Yamagata et al 1968
					anus	Yamagata et al 1968
					anus	Yamagata et al 1968
					anus	Yamagata et al 1968
					anus	Yamagata et al 1968
					7th spine of 1st dorsal fin	Yamagata et al 1968
					7th spine of 1st dorsal fin	Yamagata et al 1968
					7th spine of 1st dorsal fin	Yamagata et al 1968
					7th spine of 1st dorsal fin	Yamagata et al 1968
					7th spine of 1st dorsal fin	Yamagata et al 1968
					7th spine of dorsal fin	Yamagata et al 1968
					4th dorsal finlet	Yamagata et al 1968
					4th dorsal finlet	Yamagata et al 1968

TABLE 1

SCIENTIFIC NAME	COMMON NAME	TISSUE	TMAO (μM/100 g) RANGE	AVERAGE	TMA (μM/100g) RANGE	AVERAGE	DMA (μM/100g) RANGE	AVERA
		upper dorsal muscle		128.57		-		
		belly muscle		142.86		-		
		true red muscle		-		-		
	Mackerel					557.14		
						-		
						-		
						285.71		
						297.14		
						87.14		
						1005.71		
						782.86		
						454.29		
						585.71		
						442.86		
						271.43		
						648.57		
						405.71		
						180.00		
						1250.00		
						869.29		
						495.71		
						342.86		
						392.86		
						171.43		
						200.00		
						240.00		
						37.14		
						611.43		
						537.14		
						362.86		
						364.29		
						428.57		
Thunnus albacares	Mackerel					150.00		
	Mackerel					428.57		
	Mackerel					250.00		
	Mackerel					80.71		
	Mackerel					1071.43		
	Mackerel					733.57		
	Mackerel					234.29		
	Small mackerel			714.29				
	Small mackerel			857.14				
	Small mackerel			642.86				
	Small mackerel			857.14				
	Small mackerel			214.29				
	Small mackerel			1000.00				
Thunnus albacares	Yellowfin tuna			41.33		1.70		
	Yellowfin tuna			40.00		1.70		
	Mackerel	Fillet		2642.86		214.29		
	Mackerel	Fillet		2071.43		357.14		
	Mackerel	fillet		1571.43		285.71		
	Small mackerel			1285.71		214.29		
	Small mackerel			285.71		428.57		
	Small makcerel			142.86		214.29		
	Small mackerel			428.57		214.29		
	Small mackerel			214.29		214.29		
Thunnus maccoyii	Southern bluefin					0.80		
	Southern bluefin	dark muscle				310.67		
Thunnus obesus	Bigeye tuna		240-1146.67					
Thunnus obesus	Bigeye tuna	muscle						
Thunnus obesus	Bigeye tuna					235.71		
						957.14		
						1157.14		
	Mackerel					428.57		
						864.29		
						907.14		
						992.26		
						1078.57		
						964.29		
						3242.86		
						671.43		
Thunnus obesus	Bigeye tuna					42.86		
						-		
						57.14		
						907.14		
						921.43		
						978.57		
						-		
						-		
Thunnus obesus	Bigeye tuna					42.67	6.78	
	Bigeye tuna					57.33	1.70	
Thunnus thynnus	Bluefin tuna					285.71		
Thunnus thynnus	Bluefin tuna		280					
						26.67		
						40		
Thunnus thynnus	Bluefin tuna	muscle						
Thunnus thynnus	Bluefin tuna					285.71		
	Mackerel	whole				2000.00	0	
	Mackerel	whole				2071.43	71.43	
	Mackerel	whole				1571.43	0	
	Mackerel	whole				1071.43	357.14	

(Continued)

NO.OF FISH EXAMINED	LENGTH OF FISH	BODY WEIGHT (g)	SEASON	METHOD USED	OTHER	REFERENCE
					4th dorsal finlet	Yamagata et al 1968
					4th dorsal finlet	Yamagata et al 1968
					4th dorsal finlet	Yamagata et al 1968
				1	Dry trichloracid/ crystal extract	Venkatamaran/Chari 1950
				1	Dry trichloracid/ crystal extract	Venkahamaran/Chari 1950
				1	Dry trichloracid/ crystal extract	Venkatamaran/Chari 1950
				1	Dry trichloracid/ crystal extract	Venkatamaran/Chari 1950
				1	Acid water extract	Venkatamaran/Chari 1950
				1	Acid water extract	Venkatamaran/Chari 1950
				1	Acid water extract	Venkatamaran/Chari 1950
				1	Acid water extract	Venkatamaran/Chari 1950
				1	Acid water extract	Venkatamaran/Chari 1950
				1	Acid water extract	Venkatamaran/Chari 1950
				1	Acid water extract	Venkatamaran/Chari 1950
				1	Acid water extract	Venkatamaran/Chari 1950
				1	Acid water extract	Venkatamaran/Chari 1950
				2	Dry trichloracid/ crystal extract	Venkatamaran/Chari 1950
				2	Dry trichloracid/ crystal extract	Venkatamaran/Chari 1950
				2	Dry trichloracid/ crystal extract	Venkatamaran/Chari 1950
				2	Dry trichloracid/ crystal extract	Venkatamaran/Chari 1950
				2	crystal extract	Venkatamaran/Chari 1950
				2	Acid water extract	Venkatamaran/Chari 1950
				2	Acid water extract	Venkatamaran/Chari 1950
				2	Acid water extract	Venkatamaran/Chari 1950
				2	Acid water extract	Venkatamaran/Chari 1950
				2	Acid water extract	Vankatamaran/Chari 1950
				2	Acid water extract	Venkatamaran/Chari 1950
				2	Acid water extract	Venkatamaran/Chari 1950
				2	Acid water extract	Venkatamaran/Chari 1950
			June 1969	3		Tokunaga 1970
			June 1969	3		Tokunaga 1970
			12-5-44	1		Ronold/Jakobsen 1947
			19-5-44	1		Ronold/Jakobsen 1947
			3-6-44	1		Ronold/Jakobsen 1947
			9-6-44	1		Ronold/Jakobsen 1947
			22-8-44	1		Ronold/Jakobsen 1947
			25-8-44	1		Ronold/Jakobsen 1947
			13-9-44	1		Ronold/Jakobsen 1947
			27-9-44	1		Ronold/Jakobsen 1947
				3		Tokunaga 1975
				3		Tokunaga 1975
						Yamada 1967
3						Yamada 1967
				3		Horie/Sekine 1956
				3		Horie/Sekine 1956
8				3		Horie/Sekine 1956
				3		Horie/Sekine 1956
				3		Horie/Sekine 1956
				3		Horie/Sekine 1956
				3		Horie/Sekine 1956
				3		Horie/Sekine 1956
				3		Horie/Sekine 1956
				3		Horie/Sekine 1956
				2	Storage 4-14°C 0 Days	Horie/Sekine 1956
					1	Horie/Sekine 1956
					2	Horie/Sekine 1956
					3	Horie/Sekine 1956
					4	Horie/Sekine 1956
					5	Horie/Sekine 1956
					6	Horie/Sekine 1956
					7	Horie/Sekine 1956
					8	Horie/Sekine 1956
			June 1969	3		Tokunaga 1970
			June 1969	3		Tokunaga 1970
				3		Dyer 1952
						Yamada 1967
			Analysed	3		Yamada 1967
			12-5-44	1		Ronold/Jakobsen 1947
			19-5-44	1		Ronold/Jakobsen 1947
			3-6-44	1		Ronold/Jakobsen 1947
			22-6-44	1		Ronold/Jakobsen 1947

SCIENTIFIC NAME	COMMON NAME	TISSUE	TMAO (μM/100 g) RANGE	TMAO (μM/100 g) AVERAGE	TMA (μM/100g) RANGE	TMA (μM/100g) AVERAGE	DMA (μM/100g) RANGE	DMA (μM/100g) AVERAGE
	Mackerel	whole		1571.43		500.00		
	Mackerel	whole		214.29		1785.71		
	Mackerel	whole		1785.71		71.43		
	Mackerel	whole		1357.14		214.29		
	Mackerel	whole		857.14		0		
Scorpaenidae								
Scorpaena porcus								
Sebastes baramenuke		muscle		640.00				
Sebastes inermis	Rockfish			1360.00				
	Scorpionfish					14.29		
	Scorpionfish					1514.29		
Sebastes inermis		muscle		1360.00				
Sebastes inermis	Japanese brown	ordinary		4585.71		14.29		50.0
	Japanese brown	ordinary		4621.43		28.57		35.7
	Pananese brown	ordinary		4857.14		35.71		21.4
	Japanese brown	bloody		2407.14		42.86		64.2
	Japanese brown	bloody		2142.86		85.71		57.1
	Japanese brown	bloody		2285.71		200.00		35.7
Sebastes marinus	Redfish			6571.43				
	Redfish			4785.71				
	Redfish			4142.86				
Sebastes vulpes				1666.67		11.86		
Sebastodes melanops	Black rockfish			6642.86				
Sebastodes sp.	Rockfish		1571.43-4785.71	3785.71				
Sebastodes sp.	Rockfish	muscle		1600.00				
		muscle		4000.00				
		muscle		4600.00				
		muscle		3800.00				
		muscle		4800.00				
		heart		2100.00				
		skin		700.00				
		liver		70.00				
				80.00				
Sebastolobus macrochir				3186.67		0		
				3173.33		1.70		
				3066.67		11.86		
				2746.67		277.97		
				2960.00		45.76		
				2893.33		176.27		
				2506.67		1096.61		
Sebastolobus macrochir		muscle	7200-9360					
				3160.00		0		
Sebastodes rubberimus	Yelloweye rockfish			6428.57				
Serranidae								
	Common sea bass					42.86		
	Common sea bass					307.14		
	Common sea bass					1492.86		
	Common sea bass					2292.86		
Lateolabrax japonicus	Common sea bass	muscle	3590-4373.33					
	Common sea bass			3957.14				
	Common sea bass			3735.71				
	Common sea bass			3614.29				
	Common sea bass			3521.43				
	Common sea bass			3900.00				
	Common sea bass			4371.43				
Lateolabrax japonicus	Japanese sea bass	ordinary		3671.43		0		0
	Japanese sea bass	ordinary		4300.00		0		0
	Japanese sea bass	ordinary		2964.29		0		0
	Japanese sea bass	bloody		2028.57		0		7.1
	Japanese sea bass	bloody		1771.43		0		0
	Japanese sea bass	bloody		1564.29		0		0
Lateolabrax japonicus				653.33		305.09		
Serranus diacanthus				5528.57				
Shyraenidae								
Thyrsites atun	Barracouta	muscle		1893.33				
Sillaginidae								
Sillago sihamer				1500.00				
Sillago sihama		muscle		1106.67				
Sillago japonica				840.00		67.80		0
Sillago sihama				1469.29				
Sparidae								
Chrysophyrus major	Red sea bream	muscle	1480.00-3440.00	2360.00, 120.00				
Chrysophyrus major	Red sea bream		26.67-53.33-293.33					
Chrysophyrus major	Red sea bream			1373.33		5.09		
Chrysophyrus major	Red sea bream			3280.00				
Chrysophyrus major	Sea bream			3466.67		389.83		88.
Chrysophyrus major	Sea bream	ordinary						
		muscle		3.2		28.48		

(Continued)

NO.OF FISH EXAMINED	LENGTH OF FISH	BODY WEIGHT (g)	SEASON	METHOD USED	OTHER	REFERENCE
			15-11-44	1		Ronold/Jakobsen 1947
			16-6-45	1		Ronold/Jakobsen 1947
			22-6-45	1		Ronold/Jakobsen 1947
			29-6-45	1		Ronold/Jakobsen 1947
			3-7-45	1		Ronold/Jakobsen 1947
				2		Cantoni/Ardemagni 1977
				3		Yamada 1967
				3	Before Storage	Sakaguchi/Simidu 1964
				2	After 2 days' storage	Horie/Sekine 1956
				2		Horie/Sekine 1956
1	26.5	280	Sept 1969	3		Yamada 1967
1	26.2	290	Sept 1969	3		Cantoni/Ardemagni 1977
1	27.1	298	Sept 1969	3		Cantoni/Ardemagni 1977
1	26.5	280	Sept 1969	3		Cantoni/Ardemagni 1977
1	26.2	290	Sept 1969	3		Cantoni/Ardemagni 1977
				3		Dyer 1952
				3		Dyer 1952
				3		Dyer 1952
				3		Takagi et al 1967
				3		Dyer 1952
				3		Dyer 1952
				3		Norris/Benoit 1945
				3		Norris/Benoit 1945
				3		Norris/Benoit 1945
				3		Norris/Benoit 1945
				3		Norris/Benoit 1945
				3		Norris/Benoit 1945
				3		Norris/Benoit 1945
				3		Norris/Benoit 1945
				3	0° Storage 0 hrs.	Takagi et al 1967b
				3	4 24	Takagi et al 1967b
				3	10 24	Takagi et al 1967b
				3	20 24	Takagi et al 1967b
				3	4 48	Takagi et al 1967b
				3	10 48	Takagi et al 1967b
				3	20 48	Takagi et al 1967b
						Yamada 1967
				3		Norris/Benoit 1945
				3		Dyer 1952
				2	Storage 4-14°C 0 Days	Horie/Sekine 1956
				2	2	Horie/Sekine 1956
				2	3	Horie/Sekine 1956
				2	4	Horie/Sekine 1956
				2		Yamada 1967
				2		Horie/Sekine 1956
				2		Horie/Sekine 1956
				2		Horie/Sekine 1956
				2		Horie/Sekine 1956
				2		Horie/Sekine 1956
				2		Horie/Sekine 1956
			Sept 1969	3, 11		Tokunaga 1970
			Oct 1969	3, 11		Tokunaga 1970
			Oct 1969	3, 11		Tokunaga 1970
			Sept 1969	3, 11		Tokunaga 1970
			Oct 1969	3, 11		Tokunaga 1970
28			Oct 1969	3, 11		Tokunaga 1970
				6		Mujahara 1960
				2		Velankar 1958
				3		Konosu et al 1978
				2		Velankar/Govindan 1958
16				6		Yamada 1967
				2		Mujahara 1960
						Velankar 1958
						Yamada 1967
				3		Yamada 1967
17				3		Konosu et al 1974
				6		Konosu et al 1974
						Mujahara 1960
			Jun 29 '58	3		Takada/Nishimoto 1958

234

TABLE 12.

SCIENTIFIC NAME	COMMON NAME	TISSUE	TMAO (μM/100 g) RANGE	TMAO AVERAGE	TMA (μM/100g) RANGE	TMA AVERAGE	DMA (μM/100g) RANGE	DMA AVERAGE
Chrysophyrus major	Sea bream	bloody muscle		5.33		61.02		
				21.33		.678		
Chrysophyrus major	Sea bream	stomach		6.44		8.81		
Chrysophyrus major	Sea bream	liver		10.67		13.56		
Chrysophyrus major	Sea bream	intestine						
Chrysophyrus major	Sea bream	generative organ		24.		16.95		
Chrysophyrus major	Sea bream	ordinary muscle		41.33		672.88		
Chrysophyrus major	Sea bream	bloody muscle		--		--		
Chrysophyrus major	Sea bream	stomach		78.67		157.63		
Chrysophyrus major	Sea bream	liver		92.00		377.97		
Chrysophyrus major	Sea bream	intestine		57.33		15.25		
Chrysophyrus major	Sea bream	generative organ		66.67		84.75		
Chrysophyrus major	Sea bream			1170.67		127.12		
Chrysophyrus major	Sea bream			838.67		501.70		
Chrysophyrus major	Sea bream			288.00		1121.86		
Chrysophyrus major	Sea bream			0		1666.10		
Chrysophyrus major	Sea bream			0		1567.80		
Erynnus japonica tanaka	Red sea bream					14.29		
Erynnus japonica tanaka	Red sea bream					292.86		
Erynnus japonica tanaka	Red sea bream					1928.57		
Erynnus japonica tanaka	Red sea bream					1271.43		
Mylio macrocephalus				1306.67		135.59		
Mylio macrocephalus		muscle		2280.00				
Pagellus eritoynus				641.33				
Pagellus mormyrus				630.67				
Taius tumifrons				360.00		271.19		0
Taius tumifrons		muscle		1613.33				
Sphyraenidae								
	Barracuda					35.71		
	Barracuda					107.14		
	Barracuda					742.86		
	Barracuda					1421.43		
	Barracuda					1800		
	Barracuda					14.29		
	Barracuda					1450		
	Barracuda					101.70		
Stromateidae								
	Lockiroton					310		
Palinurichthys perciformis	Black rudderfish			4214.29		11.30		
Porontus triacanthus	Butterfish			4142.86				
Stromateus cinerus				4700				
Stromateus niger				4871.43				
Trachinidae								
Trachinus draco				1049.33				
Trichiuridae								
Trichurius lepturus	Tachi-uo	muscle		4960, 2200				
Trichodontidae								
Arctoscopus japonicus				2000		123.73		
Triglidae								
Chelidonichthys spinosa				2706.67				0
Chelidonichthys kumn	Japanese gunard	ordinary		2707.14		21.43		0
	Japanese gunard	ordinary		3214.29		7.14		14
	Japanese gunard	bloody		1514.29		50.00		7.
	Japanese gunard	bloody		1714.29		357.14		7.
	Sea Bohen					0.4		
						26.3		
Lepidotrigla microptera				1480				
Lepidotrigla microptera				1733.33		1.70		
Trigla corax				920				
Uranoscopidae								
Uranoscopus scaber				1062.67				
Xiphiidae								
Xiphias gladius	Broadbill swordfish Swordfish			2214.29				1040
ORDER -- PLEURONECTIFORMES								
Bothidae								
Lepidorhynchus denticulatus	Javelin fish			1680				
Paralichthys olivaceus		muscle		246.66, 5600.00				
Paralichthys olivaceus				1166.66		4.00		
Paralichthyl olivaceus		flounder		4173.33				

NO.OF FISH EXAMINED	LENGTH OF FISH	BODY WEIGHT (g)	SEASON	METHOD USED	OTHER	REFERENCE
			Jun 29 '58	3		Takada/Nishimoto 1958
			Jun 29 '58	3		Takada/Nishimoto 1958
			Jun 29 '58	3		Takada/Nishimoto 1958
			Jun 29 '58	3		Takada/Nishimoto 195?
			Jun 29 '58	3		Takada/Nishimoto 1958
			Dec 6 '58	3		Takada/Nishimoto 1958
			Dec 6 '58	3		Takada/Nishimoto 1958
			Dec 6 '58	3		Takada/Nishimoto 1958
			Dec 6 '58	3		Takada/Nishimoto 1958
			Dec 6 '58	3		Takada/Nishimoto 1958
					Storage Temp. °C Storage Time/hrs.	
			Dec 6 '58	3	22 0	Takada/Nishimoto 1958
				3	24	Takada/Nishimoto 1958
				3	48	Takada/Nishimoto 1958
				3	60	Takada/Nishimoto 1958
				3	72	Takada/Nishimoto 1958
				2	4-14 Time 0 days	Horie/Sekine 1956
				2	2	Horie/Sekine 1956
				2	3	Horie/Sekine 1956
				2	4	Horie/Sekine 1956
17				6		Mujahara 1960
				6		Yamada 1967
				2		Cantoni/Ardemagni 1977
				2		Cantoni/Ardemagni 1977
17				6		Mujahara 1960
						Yamada 1967
					Storage Temp. °C Storage Time/days	
				2	0	Horie/Sekine 1956
				2	1	Horie/Sekine 1956
				2	2	Horie/Sekine 1956
				2	3	Horie/Sekine 1956
				2	4	Horie/Sekine 1956
				2	Before storage	Horie/Sekine 1956
				2	After 2 days at 7-16°C	Horie/Sekine 1956
				3		Konosu et al 1978
				6	Raw	Kawamura et al 1971
				6	Roasted	Kawamura et al 1971
				3		Dyer 1952
				3		Dyer 1952
				2		Velankar 1958
				2		Velankar 1958
				2		Cantoni/Ardemagni 1977
						Yamada 1967
				3		Takagi 1967
						Yamada 1967
	30.8	297	Sept 1969	3, 11		Tokunaga 1970
	37.5	310	Sept 1969	3, 11		Tokunaga 1970
	30.8	297	Sept 1969	3, 11		Tokunaga 1970
	37.5	310	Sept 1969			Tokunaga 1970
					1st reading	Horie/Sekine 1956
					2 days after 1st reading	Horie/Sekine 1956
						Yamada 1967
				3		Takagi et al 1967
				2		Cantoni/Ardemagni 1977
				2		Cantoni/Ardemagni 1977
				3		Dyer 1952
				11		Kawamura et al 1971
				3		Tokunaga 1975
						Yamada 1967
				3		Takagi et al 1967
				3		Konosu et al 1974

TABLE 1.

SCIENTIFIC NAME	COMMON NAME	TISSUE	TMAO (μM/100 g)		TMA (μM/100g)		DMA (μM/100g)	
			RANGE	AVERAGE	RANGE	AVERAGE	RANGE	AVERA
Cynoglossidae								
Cynoglossus bengalensis				2571.43				
Cynoglossus semifasciatus				2757.14				
Pleuronectidae								
Eucitharus inguatula				1122.67				
Glyptocephalus cynoglossus	Witch flounder		3071.43-7500.00	4142.86				
			3.07-7.47	4.133				
Glyptocephalus microcephalus	Lemon sole			2571.43				
	Flounder		2142.86-6428.57					
	Halibut		4642.86-5357.14					
	Flathead flounder			5320.00				
Glyptocephalus sp.			1928.57-2071.43					
Hippoglossoides dubius	Flathead flounder			2040.00				
	Atlantic plaice, sole, dabs, halibut, etc.		1466.67-8000.00					
	Pacific flounder		1866.67-2133.33					
				5320.00				
Hippoglossus hippoglossus	Atlantic halibut			5000.00				
Hippoglossus platessoides	American plaice			6642.86				
Hippoglossus stenolepis	Pacific halibut			4642.86				
Karieus bicoloratus	Stone flounder			4706.67				
Karieus bicoloratus	Stone flounder			697.33		27.12		
Karieus bicoloratus	Stone flounder			2426.67				
Limanda	Round flounder			400.00				
				3285.71				
				672.00				
Limanda ferruginea	Yellowtail flounder		1500.-6285.71	4428.57				
				5571.43				
Limanda ferruginea	Yellowtail flounder							
Limanda heryensteini			2184.86	697.33				
Limanda limand			840.91	2428.57				
				837.47				
				530.67				
Lopsetta grigorjuvi				1176.00				
Microstomus achne				2173.33				
Pleuronectes limanda	Dab		4933.33-7600.00	5866.67				
Pleuronectes platessa	Plaice		1466.67-1733.33	1600.00				
Pleuronectes platessa	Plaice		2533.33-4800.00	3733.33				
Pseudopleuronectes americanus	Winter flounder		3.33-7.2	50.67				
Pseudopleuronectes americanus	Winter flounder		4571.43-5857.14	5000.00				
ORDER -- TETRAODONTIFORMES								
Balistidae								
Stephanolepis cirrhifer		muscle		440, 3293.33, 946.67				
Molidae								
Mola mola	Sunfish			5000.00				
Tetraodontidae								
Fugu niphobles				1000.00				
Fugu niphobles				373.33		101.69		0
Fugu vermiculares porphyreum	Puffer			2080				
Fugu vermicularis				754.67		32.20		
Fugu vermicularis porphyreus				413.33				

NO.OF FISH EXAMINED	LENGTH OF FISH	BODY WEIGHT (g)	SEASON	METHOD USED	OTHER	REFERENCE
				2		Velankar/Govindan 1958
				2		Velankar/Govindan 1958
				2		Cantoni/Ardemagni 1977
				3		Beatty 1939
6				3		Beatty 1939
						Ronold/Jakobsen 1947
						Castell 1949
				3		Konosu et al 1974
				3		Konosu et al 1974
	3			3		Dyer 1952
				3		Sakaguchi/Simidu 1974
				2		Shewan 1951
				2		Shewan 1951
				3		Konosu et al 1974
				3		Yamada 1967
				3		Takagi et al 1967
				3		Konosu et al 1974
				3		Horie/Sekine 1956
				3		Horie/Sekine 1956
				3		Horie/Sekine 1956
				3		Dyer 1952
	5			3		Dyer 1952
				3		Dyer 1952
				3		Dyer 1952
				3		Beatty 1939
10				3		Dyer 1952
3						Love et al 1959
				3		Dyer 1952
				3		Takagi et al 1967
2				2		Shewan 1951
4				2		Shewan 1951
2				2	North Sea	Shewan 1951
3				2	Arctic	Shewan 1951
6				3	TMAO content of the musclepress juice	Beatty 1939
30				3		Dyer 1952
				3		Dyer 1952
	28			6		Yamada 1967
						Mujahara 1960
				3		Kcnosu et al 1974
				3		Takagi et al 1967
						Yamada 1967

TABLE 1.

SCIENTIFIC NAME	COMMON NAME	TISSUE	TMO (μM/100 g) RANGE	TMO (μM/100 g) AVERAGE	TMA (μM/100g) RANGE	TMA (μM/100g) AVERAGE	DMA (μM/100g) RANGE	DMA (μM/100g) AVERAGE
Before Processing	Brisling	whole		1214.29				
	Brisling	whole		642.86				
	Coal fish	fillet		3285.71				
	Coal fish	fillet		2428.57				
	Coal fish	fillet		2428.57				
	Cod	fillet		4214.29				
	Cod	fillet		4357.14				
	Crab			571.43				
	Haddock	fillet		2357.14				
	Haddock	fillet		2642.86				
	Herring, unsmoked	Fillet		4142.86				
	Herring	unsmoked		9285.71				
	Herring	smoked		4928.57				
	Herring	smoked		10642.86				
	Herring	unsmoked		3928.57				
	Herring	smoked		4642.86				
	Herring	smoked		4642.86				
	Herring, small	whole		1285.71				
	Lobster	muscle		3857.14				
	Mackerel	fillet		2642.86				
	Mackerel, small	whole		714.29				
	Shrimps	muscle		7142.86				
After Processing	Brisling	whole		0				
	Brisling	whole		0				
	Coal fish	fillet		2500.0				
	Coal fish	fillet		1428.57				
	Coal fish	fillet		1785.71				
	Cod	fillet		3357.14				
	Cod	fillet		3714.29				
	Crab			71.43				
	Haddock	fillet		857.14				
	Haddock	fillet				1642.86		
	Herring	whole		0				
	Herring, unsmoked	Fillet		3000.0				
		unsmoked		7928.57				
		smoked		3571.43				
		smoked		9571.43				
		unsmoked		2714.29				
		smoked		3642.86				
		smoked		3642.86				
	Lobster	muscle		1142.86				
	Mackerel	fillet		1071.43				
	Mackerel, small	whole		0				
	Shrimps	muscle		6500.0				
Difference	Brisling	whole		1214.29				
	Brisling	whole		642.86				
	Coal fish	fillet		785.71				
	Coal fish	fillet		1000.0				
	Coal fish	fillet		642.86				
	Cod	fillet		1571.43				
	Cod	fillet		642.86				
	Haddock	fillet		1500.0				
	Herring, unsmoked	Fillet		1142.86				
		unsmoked		1357.14				
	Herring	smoked		1357.14				
		smoked		1071.43				
	Herring	unsmoked		785.71				
		smoked		1000.0				
		smoked		1000.0				
	Mackerel	fillet		1571.43				
	Mackerel, small	whole		714.29				
Processing	California anchovies in tomato sauce				450.0-2657.14	1350.0		
					985.71-2657.14	1371.43		
	Pacific herring in tomato sauce				1292.86-2200.0	1692.86		
					1157.14-3071.43	1835.71		
	Atlantic herring in tomato sauce				1892.86-4714.29	3142.86		
					1714.29-4857.14	3192.86		
	California mackerel in brine				457.14-2200.0	1114.29		
					635.71-2278.57	1307.14		
	California sardines in brine				307.14-985.71	664.29		
					271.43-957.14	807.14		
	California sardines in tomato sauce				128.57-985.71	685.71		
					0-1092.86	714.29		
	Tuna in oil				0-721.43	242.86		
					85.71-542.86	328.57		

NO.OF FISH EXAMINED	LENGTH OF FISH	BODY WEIGHT (g)	SEASON	METHOD USED	OTHER	REFERENCE
				2	Cans are tinplate, unlacquered-78x16 mm	Ronold/Jakobsen 1947
				2	78 x 16 mm	Ronold/Jakobsen 1947
				2	78 x 16 mm	Ronold/Jakobsen 1947
				2	78 x 16 mm	Ronold/Jakobsen 1947
				2	78 x 16 mm	Ronold/Jakobsen 1947
				2	78 x 16 mm	Ronold/Jakobsen 1947
				2	78 x 16 mm	Ronold/Jakobsen 1947
				2	48 x 16 mm	Ronold/Jakobsen 1947
				2	78 x 16 mm	Ronold/Jakobsen 1947
				2	48 x 16 mm	Ronold/Jakobsen 1947
				2	78 x 16 mm	Ronold/Jakobsen 1947
				2	78 x 16 mm	Ronold/Jakobsen 1947
				2	78 x 16 mm	Ronold/Jakobsen 1947
				2	78 x 16 mm	Ronold/Jakobsen 1947
				2	78 x 16 mm	Ronold/Jakobsen 1947
				2	78 x 16 mm	Ronold/Jakobsen 1947
				2	1/2 oval	Ronold/Jakobsen 1947
				2	78 x 16 mm	Ronold/Jakobsen 1947
				2	48 x 16 mm	Ronold/Jakobsen 1947
				2	78 x 16 mm	Ronold/Jakobsen 1947
				2	78 x 16 mm	Ronold/Jakobsen 1947
				2	48 x 16 mm	Ronold/Jakobsen 1947
				2	Cans are tinplate, unlacquered-78x16 mm	Ronold/Jakobsen 1947
				2	78 x 16 mm	Ronold/Jakobsen 1947
				2	78 x 16 mm	Ronold/Jakobsen 1947
				2	78 x 16 mm	Ronold/Jakobsen 1947
				2	78 x 16 mm	Ronold/Jakobsen 1947
				2	78 x 16 mm	Ronold/Jakobsen 1947
				2	78 x 16 mm	Ronold/Jakobsen 1947
				2	48 x 16 mm	Ronold/Jakobsen 1947
				2	78 x 16 mm	Ronold/Jakobsen 1947
				2	48 x 16 mm	Ronold/Jakobsen 1947
				2	78 x 16 mm	Ronold/Jakobsen 1947
				2	78 x 16 mm	Ronold/Jakobsen 1947
				2	78 x 16 mm	Ronold/Jakobsen 1947
				2	78 x 16 mm	Ronold/Jakobsen 1947
				2	78 x 16 mm	Ronold/Jakobsen 1947
				2	1/2 oval	Ronold/Jakobsen 1947
				2	78 x 16 mm	Ronold/Jakobsen 1947
				2	48 x 16 mm	Ronold/Jakobsen 1947
				2	78 x 16 mm	Ronold/Jakobsen 1947
				2	78 x 16 mm	Ronold/Jakobsen 1947
				2	48 x 16 mm	Ronold/Jakobsen 1947
				2	Cans are tinplate, unlacquered-78x16 mm	Ronold/Jakobsen 1947
				2	78 x 16 mm	Ronold/Jakobsen 1947
				2	78 x 16 mm	Ronold/Jakobsen 1947
				2	78 x 16 mm	Ronold/Jakobsen 1947
				2	78 x 16 mm	Ronold/Jakobsen 1947
				2	78 x 16 mm	Ronold/Jakobsen 1947
				2	78 x 16 mm	Ronold/Jakobsen 1947
				2	78 x 16 mm	Ronold/Jakobsen 1947
				2	78 x 16 mm	Ronold/Jakobsen 1947
				2	78 x 16 mm	Ronold/Jakobsen 1947
				2	78 x 16 mm	Ronold/Jakobsen 1947
				2	78 x 16 mm	Ronold/Jakobsen 1947
				2	1/2 oval	Ronold/Jakobsen 1947
				2	78 x 16 mm	Ronold/Jakobsen 1947
				2	78 x 16 mm	Ronold/Jakobsen 1947
				2	271 cans	Farber/Ferro 1956
				2	40 cans	Farber/Ferro 1956
				2	5 cans	Farber/Ferro 1956
				2	8 cans	Farber/Ferro 1956
				2	44 cans	Farber/Ferro 1956
				2	17 cans	Farber/Ferro 1956
				2	50 cans	Farber/Ferro 1956
				2	82 cans	Farber/Ferro 1956
				2	37 cans	Farber/Ferro 1956
				2	38 cans	Farber/Ferro 1956
				2	148 cans	Farber/Ferro 1956
				2	250 cans	Farber/Ferro 1956
				2	180 cans	Farber/Ferro 1956
				2	17 cans	Farber/Ferro 1956

SCIENTIFIC NAME	COMMON NAME	TISSUE	TMAO (µM/100 g) RANGE	AVERAGE	TMA (µM/100g) RANGE	AVERAGE	DMA (µM/100g) RANGE	AVER.
Squillidae								
Squilla costata		muscle	6757.14- 7214.29	4492.86		135.71		
Squillis mantis	Mantis shrimp							
	Shako		7228.57 6750.0	1707.14				
Squilla mantis								
Squilla oratoria		muscle		3735.71		142.86		
Squilla oratoria				1706.67				
Penaeidae								
Metapenaeus affinis				1700.00				
Metapenaeopsis barbata		muscle		4142.86		150.00		
		viscera		1164.29		364.29		
Metapenaeus joyneri				4414.29				
Metapenaeus joyneri				4413.33				
Metapenaeus monoceros				5285.71				
Penaeus indicus				1400.00				
Penaeus japonica				2292.86				
Penaeus japonicus				2293.33				
Penaeus japonicus				5214.29				
Penaeus monodon				6071.43				
Penaeus monodon				1300.00				
Penaeus orientalis		muscle		2678.57, 2928.57				
Penaeus orientalis				2933.33, 2680.00				
Salenocera alticarinata		muscle		1242.86		285.71		
		viscera		585.71		535.71		
Trachypsenaeus curvirostris		muscle		3542.86 3546.67				
Pendalidae								
Pandalopsis japonica		muscle		4635.71				
Pandalopsis japonica				4640.		21.43		
Pandalopsis hypsinotus	Shrimp			3013.33		8.48		
				3000.		10.17		
				2906.67		106.78		
				2080.		1159.32		
				2626.67		267.80		
				2373.33		974.58		
				2013.33		1303.39		
				10428.57				
Pandalus danae	Shrimp			4785.71, 2785.71, 6285.71				
Pandalus danae	Shrimp			4800, 2800, 6300				
Pandalus hypsinotus		muscle		3014.29, 4235.71				
Pandalus hypsinotus				4240.		107.14		
Pandalus nipponensis				4840.				
Palaemonidae								
Leander pancidens				85.71				
Macrobranchium nipponensi		muscle		578.57		35.71		
Atelecyclidae								
Erimacrus isenbeckii	Crab			1864.29 1866.67				
Potamonidae								
Potamon dehaani	Crab	muscle		28.57		7.14		
		viscera		0		7.14		
Portunidae								
Charybdis japonica	Crab	muscle		1085.71		378.57		
		viscera		478.57		385.71		
Charybdis cruciata		muscle		3171.43		335.71		
Charybdis miles		muscle		5928.57		207.14		
		viscera		1128.57		271.43		
Portunus trituberculatus		muscle		871.43				
				866.67				
Portunus sanguinolentus		muscle		4764.29		78.57		
Xanthidae								
Liagore rubromaculata	Crab	muscle		4064.29		442.86		
		viscera		457.14		242.86		
Cancridae								
Cancer gracilis	Crab			2214.29				
Cancer gracilis	Crab		2200.00					
Cancer productus	Crab		1071.43					
Cancer productus	Crab		4600.00					

NO.OF FISH EXAMINED	LENGTH OF FISH	BODY WEIGHT (g)	SEASON	METHOD USED	OTHER	REFERENCE
				2, 3		Harada et al 1972
				2, 3		Harada et al 1972
				2, 3		Harada et al 1972
				2		Cantoni/Ardemagni 1977
				2, 3		Harada et al 1972
						Yamada 1967
				2		Velankar/Govindan 1958
				2, 3		Harada et al 1972
				2, 3		Harada et al 1972
				2, 3		Harada et al 1972
						Yamada 1967
				3		Fujita et al 1972
				2		Velankar/Govindan 1958
				2, 3		Harada et al 1972
						Yamada 1967
				3		Fujita et al 1972
				3		Fujita et al 1972
				2		Velankar/Govindan 1958
				2, 3		Harada et al 1972
						Yamada 1967
				2, 3		Harada et al 1972
				2, 3		Harada et al 1972
				2, 3		Harada et al 1972
						Yamada 1969
				3		Harada et al 1972
				3		Takagi et al 1967a
					$^{\circ}C$ 0 hrs.	Takagi et al 1967b
					4 24	Takagi et al 1967b
					10 24	Takagi et al 1967b
					20 24	Takagi et al 1967b
					4 48	Takagi et al 1967b
					10 48	Takagi et al 1967b
					20 48	Takagi et al 1967b
						Fujita et al 1972
				3		Harada et al 1972
				3		Norris/Benoit 1945
				3		Harada et al 1972
				3		Takagi et al 1967a
						Yamada 1967
				3		Harada et al 1972
				2		Harada et al 1972
				2, 3		Harada et al 1972
						Yamada 1967
				2, 3		Harada et al 1972
				2, 3		Harada et al 1972
				2, 3		Harada et al 1972
				2, 3		Harada et al 1972
				2, 3		Harada et al 1972
				2, 3		Harada et al 1972
				2, 3		Harada et al 1972
				2, 3		Harada et al 1972
				2, 3		Harada et al 1972
				3		Yamada 1967
				2, 3		Harada et al 1972
				2		Harada et al 1972
				3		Harada et al 1972
				2, 3		Harada et al 1977
				3		Norris/Benoit 1945
				2, 3		Harada et al 1977
				3		Norris/Benoit 1945

TABLE 12.

SCIENTIFIC NAME	COMMON NAME	TISSUE	TMAO (μM/100 g)		TMA (μM/100g)		DMA (μM/100g)	
			RANGE	AVERAGE	RANGE	AVERAGE	RANGE	AVERAGE
Grapsidae								
Eriocheir japonicus		muscle		378.57		7.14		
		viscera		7.14		14.29		
Hemigrapsus mudus	Shore crab			1071.43				
	Shore crab			1100.00				
Hemigrapsus sanguineus		muscle		314.29		192.86		
		viscera		242.86		100.		
Hemigrapsus penicillatus		muscle		1507.14		57.14		
		viscera		150.00		42.86		
Pachygrapus crassiper		muscle		2842.86		171.43		
		viscera		264.29		128.57		
Sesarma haematocheir		muscle		364.29		142.86		
		viscera		64.29		121.43		
Majidae								
Leptomithrax edwardsi		muscle		1614.29		192.86		
		viscera		342.86		250		
Oregona gracilis	Spider crab		1285.71					
Oregonia gracilis	Spider crab			1300				
Pugesta gracilis	Spider crab			928.57				
Pugettia gracilis	Spider crab			900				
Paguridae								
Pagurus alaskensis	Hermit crab			2571.43				
Pagurus alaskensis	Hermit crab			2600.00				
Pagurus ochotensis	Hermit crab			4714.29				
Pagurus ochotensis	Hermit crab			4700.00				
Pagurus samuelis		viscera		871.43		50.00		
Pagurus setosis	Hermit crab			4571.43				
Pagurus setosis	Hermit crab			4600.00				
Pagurus tenuimanus	Hermit crab			3000.00, 2785.71				
Pagurus tenuimanus	Hermit crab			3000.00, 2800.00				
Crabs								
	King crab	ovary		2080				
	Crab	muscle		1071.43		1214.29		
		muscle		1785.71		714.29		
		ovaries		142.86		714.29		
	Pacific crab		933.33, 4666.67					
	Zooplankton			3333.33				
	Crab			30.		680		
	King Crab	leg meat		3866.67				
		legmeat		4306.67				
	Snow crab	legmeat		4506.67				
		leg meat		2946.67				
		hepato- pancreas		5466.67				
		ovary		5066.67				
	Blue crab	leg meat		1866.67				
		leg meat		1813.33				
	Horsehair crab	leg meat		5226.67				
		leg meat		4453.33				
		hepato- pancreas		3253.33				
		ovary		3826.67				
Shrimp								
	Pacific shrimp		2800- 6266.67					
	Shrimps, crabs, lobsters		933.33- 8666.67					
	Shrimp			8000				
	Shrimp			7142.86		0		
	Shrimp			8928.57		357.14		
	Shrimp			8285.71		285.71		
	Shrimp			8785.71		785.71		
	Shrimp			9071.43		857.14		
	Shrimp			9928.57		428.57		
	Shrimp			9428.57		71.43		
Palaemon nipponensis de Haan				2428.57				
Ibacus ciliatus				3642.86				
Nephropsidae								
Homarus vulgaris	Lobster			2057.14, 4342.86				
Homarus vulgaris	Lobster	muscle, hepato- pancreas		7142.86- 7857.14, 1228.57				
Homarus vulgaris	Lobster	muscle 3		1466.67				
	Atlantic lobster		2000- 8666.67					
	Lobster	Muscle				571.43		
		tail		3857.14				
		claw		2285.71				
		tail		4142.86				
		claw		1500				
		tail		3000				

NO.OF FISH EXAMINED	LENGTH OF FISH	BODY WEIGHT (g)	SEASON	METHOD USED	OTHER	REFERENCE
				2, 3		Harada et al 1972
				2, 3		Harada et al 1972
				2, 3		Harada et al 1972
				3		Norris/Benoit 1945
				2, 3		Harada et al 1972
				2, 3		Harada et al 1972
				2, 3		Harada et al 1972
				2, 3		Harada et al 1972
				2, 3		Harada et al 1972
				2, 3		Harada et al 1972
				2, 3		Harada et al 1972
				2, 3		Harada et al 1972
				2, 3		Harada et al 1972
				2, 3		Harada et al 1972
				2, 3		Herada et al 1972
				3		Norris/Benoit 1945
				2, 3		Harada et al 1972
				2, 3		Harada et al 1972
				3		Norris/Benoit 1945
				2, 3		Harada et al 1972
				3		Norris/Benoit 1945
				2, 3		Harada et al 1972
				2, 3		Harada et al 1972
				2, 3		Harada et al 1972
				3		Norris/Benoit 1945
				2, 3		Harada et al 1972
				3		Norris/Benoit 1945
				3		Hayashi et al 1974
				2		Ronald/Jakobsen 1947
				2		Ronald/Jakobsen 1947
				2		Ronald/Jakobsen 1947
				2		Shewan 1951
				2		Shewan 1951
				3		Kawamura et al 1971
				3		Hayashi et al 1978
				3		Hayashi et al 1978
				3		Hayashi et al 1978
				3		Hayashi et al 1978
				3		Hayashi et al 1978
				3		Hayashi et al 1978
				3		Hayashi et al 1978
				3		Hayashi et al 1978
				3		Hayashi et al 1978
				3		Hayashi et al 1978
				3		Hayashi et al 1978
				3		Hayashi et al 1978
				2		Shewan 1957
				2		Shewan 1957
			25-2-44	2	Cooked	Ronold/Jakobsen 194/
			16-3-44	2		Ronold/Jakobsen 1947
			4-10-44	2		Ronold/Jakobsen 1947
			31-10-44	2		Ronold/Jakobsen 1947
			6-1-45	2		Ronold/Jakobsen 1947
			8-2-45	2		Ronold/Jakobsen 1947
			6-3-45	2		Ronold/Jakobsen 1947
				2		Ronold/Jakobsen 1947
				3		Fujita et al 1972
				2, 3		Harada et al 1972
				2, 3		Harada et al 1972
				2	2 hours	Kermack et al 1955
				2		Shewan 1951
			23-6-44	2		Ronold/Jakobsen 1947
			1-6-45	2		Ronold/Jakobsen 1947
			1-6-45	2		Ronold/Jakobsen 1947
			1-6-45	2		Ronold/Jakobsen 1947
			1-6-45	2		Ronold/Jakobsen 1947
			1-6-45	2		Ronold/Jakobsen 1947
			1-6-45	2		Ronold/Jakobsen 1947

TABLE 1

SCIENTIFIC NAME	COMMON NAME	TISSUE	TMAO (μM/100 g) RANGE	AVERAGE	TMA (μM/100g) RANGE	AVERAGE	DMA (μM/100g) RANGE	AVERA
	Lobster	Muscle claw		1928.57				
		tail		1714.29				
Homarus vulgaris	Lobster	muscle 3		-				
	Lobster	muscle 3		-				
	Lobster	muscle 4		186.67				
	Lobster	muscle 4		253.33				
	Lobster	muscle 4		346.67				
	Lobster	muscle 4		373.33				
	Lobster	muscle 4		480				
	Lobster	hepato-pancreas		213.33				
		hepato-pancreas		-				
		hepato-pancreas		373.33				
		hapato-pancreas		-				
	Lobster	hepato-pancreas		-				
	Lobster	muscle		1333.33				
	Lobster	muscle		1386.67				
	Lobster	muscle		1414.33				
	Lobster	muscle		1466.67				
	Lobster	hepato-		-				
	Lobster	pancreas		236.67				
	Lobster	hepato-pancreas		280				
	Lobster	muscle 1		1333.33				
	Lobster	muscle 1		1320				
	Lobster	muscle 1		1306.67				
	Lobster	muscle 1		1360				
	Lobster	muscle 1		-				
	Lobster	muscle 2		1386.67				
	Lobster	muscle 2		-				
	Lobster	muscle 2		1640				
	Lobster	muscle 2		1573.33				
	Lobster	muscle 2		-				
	Lobster	muscle 3		1413.33				
	Lobster	muscle 3		-				
Nephrops norvegicus	Norway lobster		8000-8500					
				8714.29				
Nephrops norvegicus	Norway lobster			8521.43				
				8007.14				
Palinuridae								
Panuliris dasypus				1484.0				
Panuliris japonicus	Lobster			2835.71				
				2840.0				
Panuliris japonicus				5000.0				
Potamobiidae								
Astacus fluviatitis	Crayfish			671.43,				
				178.57,				
				321.43				
Procambarus clarki	Crayfish	muscle		2250.0			78.57	
		viscera		0			85.71	

NO.OF FISH EXAMINED	LENGTH OF FISH	BODY WEIGHT (g)	SEASON	METHOD USED	OTHER	REFERENCE
			1-6-45	2		Ronold/Jakobsen 1947
			1-6-45	2		Ronold/Jakobsen 1947
				2	6 hours	Kermack et al 1955
				2	18 hours	Kermack et al 1955
				2	0 hours	Kermack et al 1955
				2	1 hour	Kermack et al 1955
				2	2 hours	Kermack et al 1955
				2	6 hours	Kermack et al 1955
				2	18 hours	Kermack et al 1955
				2	0 hours	Kermack et al 1955
				2	1 hour	Kermack et al 1955
				2	2 hours	Kermack et al 1955
				2	6 hours	Kermack et al 1955
				2	18 hours	Kermack et al 1955
						Kermack et al 1955
						Kermack et al 1955
						Kermack et al 1955
						Kermack et al 1955
						Kermack et al 1955
						Kermack et al 1955
					0 hours	Kermack et al 1955
					1 hour	Kermack et al 1955
					2 hours	Kermack et al 1955
					6 hours	Kermack et al 1955
					18 hours	Kermack et al 1955
					0 hours	Kermack et al 1955
					1 hour	Kermack et al 1955
					2 hours	Kermack et al 1955
					6 hours	Kermack et al 1955
					18 hours	Kermack et al 1955
					0 hours	Kermack et al 1955
					1 hour	Kermack et al 1955
				2, 3		Harada et al 1972
				2, 3		Harada et al 1972
				2		Velankar/Govindan 1958
				2, 3		Harada et al 1972
				3		Yamada 1967
						Fujita et al 1972
				2		Harada et al 1972
				2		Harada et al 1972
				2		Harada et al 1972

TABLE 12

SCIENTIFIC NAME	COMMON NAME	TISSUE	TMAO (μM/100 g) RANGE	TMAO AVERAGE	TMA (μM/100g) RANGE	TMA AVERAGE	DMA (μM/100g) RANGE	DMA AVERAGE
Haliotiidae								
Nordotis discus		muscle		7.14				
		viscera		21.43				
Nordotis discus		muscle		40.00				
Nordotis discus		muscle		42.86				
		muscle		114.29				
Nordotis discus hannai		muscle		0				
		viscera		0				
Nordotis giganteus sieboldii		muscle		7.14				
		viscera		0				
				4385.71				
				4386.67				
Nordotis gigantea		muscle		21.43				
		viscera		0				
Sulculus diversicolar aquatiles		muscle		7.14				
		viscera		7.14				
Haliotis gigantea				4385.71				
				2392.86				
Patellidae								
Cellana grata		muscle		7.14		157.14		
		viscera		28.57		121.43		
Cellana nigrolineata		muscle		7.14		242.86		
		viscera		42.86		107.14		
		muscle		0		150.0		
		viscera		28.57		114.29		
Cellana toreuma		muscle		7.14		78.57		
		viscera		7.14		57.14		
		muscle		0		128.57		
		viscera		0		64.29		
Pinnidae								
Atrina pectinata japonica		adductor muscle		960.0				
Atrina pectinata		adductor		928.57				
				960.0				
Pteriidae								
Pinctada fucata	Pearl oyster	adductor		100		314.29		
		foot & mantle		7.14		57.14		
		viscera		21.43		107.14		
		adductor		121.43		328.57		
		foot & mantle		7.14		85.71		
		viscera		14.29		57.14		
Solenidae								
Salen strictus	Razor clam	adductor		92.86		714.29		
		foot & mantle		100.00		557.14		
		viscera		57.14		650.00		
		adductor		200.00		2528.57		
		foot & mantle		14.29		871.43		
		viscera		64.29		971.43		
Tellinidae								
Macoma inquinata	Clam			0				
	Clam			0				
	Clam			0				
Myacidae								
Mya arenaria	Soft-shelled clam			0				
				0				
Mya arenadia oonogai		adductor		0		42.86		
		foot & mantle		0		42.86		
		viscera		0		71.43		
Mactridae								
Mactra veneriformes		muscle & viscera		35.71		692.86		
Mactra chinensis		adductor		71.43		1150		
		foot & mantle		28.57		650		
		viscera		7.14		571.43		
				142.86				
Spisula sachalinensis								
Spisula (Pseudocardium) sachalinansis				145.33		18.64		
Spisula solidissima	Surf clam			0				
Spisula solidissima	Surf clam			0				
Tresus keenae				0		685.71		
		adductor foot & mantle		0		407.14		
		viscera		42.86		485.71		

NO.OF FISH EXAMINED	LENGTH OF FISH	BODY WEIGHT (g)	SEASON	METHOD USED	OTHER	REFERENCE
					Initial	Simidu et al 1953
					After 6 days, incubated at 8-10°C	Simidu et al 1953
				3		Harada et al 1971
				3		Harada et al 1971
				3		Harada et al 1971
				3		Harada et al 1971
				3		Harada et al 1971
				3		Harada et al 1971
				3		Harada et al 1971
				3		Harada et al 1971
				3		Harada et al 1971
		1435	May 5	3		Takagi et al 1962
				2		Harada et al 1970
						Yamada 1967
				2, 3		Harada et al 1970
				2, 3		Harada et al 1970
				2, 3		Harada et al 1970
				2, 3		Harada et al 1970
				2, 3		Harada et al 1970
				2, 3		Harada et al 1970
				2, 3		Harada et al 1970
				2, 3		Harada et al 1970
				2, 3		Harada et al 1970
				2, 3		Harada et al 1970
				2, 3		Harada et al 1970
				2, 3		Harada et al 1970
				2, 3		Harada et al 1970
				3		Norris/Benoit 1945
				3		Dyer et al 1952
				2, 3		Harada et al 1970
				3		Dyer et al 1952
				2, 3		Harada et al 1970
				2, 3		Harada et al 1970
				2, 3		Harada et al 1970
				2, 3		Harada et al 1972
				2, 3		Harada et al 1970
				2, 3		Harada et al 1970
				2, 3		Harada et al 1970
				2, 3		Harada et al 1970
				3		Takagi et al 1967a
				2, 3		Harada et al 1970
				3		Dyer et al 1952
				2, 3		Harada et al 1970
				2, 3		Harada et al 1970

TABLE 12.

SCIENTIFIC NAME	COMMON NAME	TISSUE	TMAO (μM/100 g) RANGE	TMAO AVERAGE	TMA (μM/100g) RANGE	TMA AVERAGE	DMA (μM/100g) RANGE	DMA AVERAGE
Corbiculiidae								
Corbicula japonica		adductor		0		14.29		
		foot & mantle		0		14.29		
		viscera		0		14.29		
		adductor		0		7.14		
		foot & mantle		0		14.29		
		viscera		0		21.43		
Corbicula laena		soft part	14.29-28.57					
		soft part		13.33, 26.67				
		soft part		13.33		35.71		
		soft part		13.33				
		soft part		26.67				
Corbicula laena awajiensis		adductor		0		-		
		foot & mantle		0		7.14		
Corbicula laena awajiensis		viscera		0		14.29		
Veneridae								
Meretrix lusoria		adductor		0		1435.71		
		foot & mantle		28.57		407.14		
		viscera		35.71		707.14		
Meretrix lusoria				664.29, 666.67				
Meretrix lusoria		soft part		666.67				
Meretrix petechialis		adductor		42.86		235.71		
		foot & mantle		64.29		278.57		
		viscera		42.86		228.57		
Paphia staminea	Clam			0				
Paphia staminea	Clam			negligible				
Paphia staminea	Clam			0				
Prototheca jedsensis		muscle & viscera		0		135.71		
				0				
Saxidomus giganteus	Clam			negligible				
Saxidomus giganteus	Clam			0				
Saxidomus giganteus	Clam							
Tapes japonica		soft part		373.33				
				213.33				
				400.00				
				133.33				
				333.33				
				2320		203.39		0
				520		6813.56		44.4
Tapes philippinarum		soft part	13571.-400.					
Tapes philippinarum		adductor		42.86		1692.86		
		foot & mantle		14.28		578.57		
		viscera		28.57		392.86		
		adductor		42.86		2021.43		
		foot & mantle		7.14		464.29		
		viscera		21.43		371.43		
				14.29, 507.14, 2285.71				
Tapes philippinarum				13.33, 13.33, 400.00				
Carditidae								
Cardium californiense	Cockle			1071.43, 1285.71				
Cardium californiense	Cockle			1300, 1100				
Cardium corbis	Cockle			2285.71				
Cardium corbis	Cockle			2300				
Cardium corbis	Cockle			2300				
Vasticardium Burchardi		muscle		3971.43				
		viscera		1171.43				
Ischnochitonidae								
Liolophura japonica		muscle		185.71		878.57		
		viscera		114.29		700		
Mollusca Cryptoplacidae								
Cryptochiton stelleri	Giant chiton			negligible				
				negligible				
				0				
Katherina tunicata	Black chiton			negligible				
				negligible				
				0				
Pectinidae								
Chlamys ferreri				600.00				

NO.OF FISH EXAMINED	LENGTH OF FISH	BODY WEIGHT (g)	SEASON	METHOD USED	OTHER	REFERENCE
				2, 3		Harada et al 1970
				2, 3		Harada et al 1970
				2, 3		Harada et al 1970
				2, 3		Harada et al 1970
				2, 3		Harada et al 1970
				2, 3		Harada et al 1970
				2, 3		Harada et al 1970
				3		Yamada 1967
				3		Takagi et al 1967a
		835	June 10	3		Takagi et al 1962
		910	Jan 20	3		Takagi et al 1962
				2, 3		Harada et al 1970
				2, 3		Harada et al 1970
				2, 3		Harada et al 1970
				2, 3		Harada et al 1970
				2, 3		Harada et al 1970
				2, 3		Harada et al 1970
				2, 3		Harada et al 1970
			July 3	3		Yamada 1967
				3		Takagi et al 1962
				2, 3		Harada et al 1970
				2, 3		Harada et al 1970
				2, 3		Harada et al 1970
				2, 3		Harada et al 1970
				2, 3		Harada et al 1970
				3		Norris/Benoit 1945
				3		Dyer et al 1952
				2, 3		Harada et al 1972
				2, 3		Harada et al 1970
				3		Norris/Benoit 1945
				3		Dyer et al 1952
		1335	Jan 10	3		Takagi et al 1962
		1270	Mar 5	3		Takagi et al 1962
		1480	June 20	3		Takagi et al 1962
		1115	Sept 7	3		Takagi et al 1962
		2100	Nov 17	3		Takagi et al 1962
				6		Mujahara 1960
				6		Mujahara 1960
				3		Harada et al 1970
				2, 3		Harada et al 1970
				2, 3		Harada et al 1970
				2, 3		Harada et al 1970
				2, 3		Harada et al 1970
				2, 3		Harada et al 1970
				2, 3		Harada et al 1970
				2, 3		Harada et al 1970
				2, 3		Harada et al 1972
				3		Norris/Benoit 1945
				3		Dyer et al 1952
				2, 3		Harada et al 1972
				3		Norris/Benoit 1945
				3		Dyer et al 1952
				2, 3		Harada et al 1972
				2, 3		Harada et al 1972
				2, 3		Harada et al 1972
				3		Norris/Benoit 1945
				3		Dyer et al 1952
				2, 3		Harada et al 1972
				3		Norris/Benoit 1945
				3		Dyer et al 1952
				2, 3		Harada et al 1970

SCIENTIFIC NAME	COMMON NAME	TISSUE	TMAO (μM/100 g) RANGE	TMAO AVERAGE	TMA (μM/100g) RANGE	TMA AVERAGE	DMA (μM/100g) RANGE	DMA AVERA
	Pacific scallops		3000.00-7733.33					
	Atlantic scallops			6400.00				
Chlamys ferreri				600.00				
Chlamys nipponesis				605.33		96.61		
Patinopecten yessaensin				1586.67		42.37		
				693.33				
Patenopecten yessoensis				1571.43				
Pecten albicans		adductor		3585.71		392.86		
		foot &						
		mantle		1092.86		28.57		
		viscera		164.29		128.57		
Pecten albicans		adductor		692.86				
Pecten albicans				693.33				
Pecten albicans				693.33				
Pecten grandis	Scallop (Atlantic)		5642.86-6000.00					
Pecten grandis	Atlantic scallop		5642.86-6000.00					
Pecten hericus	Scallop		3214.29-5214.29					
	Scallop		214.29-428.57					
	Scallop	muscle	3214.29-5214.29					
		organs	221.43-457.14					
Pecten hericus	Scallop	muscle		4600, 5000, 3900, 5200, 4800, 4100, 4500, 5200, 3200				
		organs		460, 400, 220, 230				
Pecten hindsii	Scallop		3000.00-7857.14					
	Scallop		500.-857.14					
Pecten hindsii	Scallop	muscle	3000.00-7714.29					
		organs	500.00-928.57					
Pecten hindsii	Scallop	muscle		7700, 3000, 5600, 3800, 7100, 5100, 3800				
		organs		800, 500, 900				
Pecten jordani	Scallop	muscle		3214.29				
Pecten jordani		muscle		3214.29 3200.00				
Ostreidae								
	Oyster			.01		.02		
Crassostrea gigas	Pacific oyster	adductor		21.43		328.57		
		foot &						
		mantle		7.14		185.71		
		viscera		35.71		300.00		
		muscle		714.29				
		muscle		21.43				
		soft part		14.29				
Crassostrea gigas		soft parts		13.33				
				13.33				
				13.33				
Crassostrea gigas				13.33, 506.67				
Crassostrea nippona		adductor		14.29		21.43		
		foot &						
		mantle		50.00		28.57		
		viscera		21.43		100.00		
Ostrea cucullata		whole contents of shell		2365.71				
	Indian oyster			2357.14				
Ostrea japonica	Oyster (Pacific)			0				
	Pacific oyster			0				
Ostrea virginica	Oyster (Atlantic)			0				
	Atlantic oyster			0				
Naticidae								
Neverita didyma		muscle		21.43		707.14		
		viscera		21.43		528.57		
Polinices heros	Moonshell			0				
	Moonshell			0				

NO.OF FISH EXAMINED	LENGTH OF FISH	BODY WEIGHT (g)	SEASON	METHOD USED	OTHER	REFERENCE
				2		Shewan 1951
				2		Shewan 1951
				2, 3		Harada et al 1970
				3		Takagi et al 1967a
				3		Takagi et al 1967a
		820	Aug 26	3		Takagi/Shimidu 1962
				2, 3		Harada et al 1970
				2, 3		Harada et al 1970
				2, 3		Harada et al 1970
				2, 3		Harada et al 1970
				2, 3		Harada et al 1970
						Yamada 1967
				2, 3		Harada et al 1970
				3		Dyer et al 1952
9				3		Dyer et al 1952
4				3		Dyer et al 1952
				2, 3		Harada et al 1970
				2, 3		Harada et al 1970
				3		Norris/Benoit 1945
				3		Dyer et al 1952
				3		Norris/Benoit 1945
				3		Dyer et al 1952
				2, 3		Harada et al 1970
				2, 3		Harada et al 1970
				3		Norris/Benoit 1945
				3		Dyer et al 1952
				2, 3		Harada et al 1970
				3		Norris/Benoit 1945
				3		Norris/Benoit 1945
				6		Kawamura et al 1971
				2, 3		Harada et al 1970
				2, 3		Harada et al 1970
				2, 3		Harada et al 1970
				2, 3		Harada et al 1970
				2, 3		Harada et al 1970
				2, 3		Harada et al 1970
		1865	Apr 25	3		Takagi et al 1962
		2120	July 29	3		Takagi et al 1962
		1775	Dec 10	3		Takagi et al 1962
						Yamada 1967
				2, 3		Harada et al 1970
				2, 3		Harada et al 1970
				2, 3		Harada et al 1970
				2		Velankar/Govindan 1958
				2, 3		Harada et al 1970
				2, 3		Norris/Benoit 1945
				2, 3		Harada et al 1970
				3		Dyer et al 1952
				2, 3		Harada et al 1970
				2, 3		Harada et al 1971
				2, 3		Harada et al 1971
				2, 3		Harada et al 1971
				3		Dyer et al 1952

TABLE 12.

SCIENTIFIC NAME	COMMON NAME	TISSUE	TMAO (μM/100 g)		TMA (μM/100g)		DMA (μM/100g)	
			RANGE	AVERAGE	RANGE	AVERAGE	RANGE	AVERAGE
Mytilidae								
Mytilus corusus		adductor		50.00		564.29		
		foot & mantle		21.43		435.71		
		viscera		14.29		307.14		
Mytilus edulis	Blue mussel	soft part		0, 307.14- 321.43 306.67, 1714.29 negligible 320 306.67				
	Pacific mussel			0				
	Atlantic mussel			0				
Mytilus edulis	Blue mussel	adductor		35.71		78.57		
		foot & mantle		0		50.		
		viscera		28.57		7.14		
Septifer virgatus		adductor		14.29		50.		
		foot & mantle		0		7.14		
		viscera		7.14		50.00		
Mesodesmatidae								
Calcella chinensis		adductor		0		757.14		
		foot & mantle		0		728.57		
		viscera		0		914.29		

NO.OF FISH EXAMINED	LENGTH OF FISH	BODY WEIGHT (g)	SEASON	METHOD USED	OTHER	REFERENCE
				2, 3		Harada et al 1970
				2, 3		Harada et al 1970
				2, 3		Harada et al 1970
				2, 3		Harada et al 1970
						Yamada 1967
				3		Norris/Benoit 1945
		705	May 20	3		Takagi et al 1962
		800	Sept	3		Takagi et al 1962
				3		Dyer et al 1952
				3		Dyer et al 1952
				2, 3		Harada et al 1970
				2, 3		Harada et al 1970
				2, 3		Harada et al 1970
				2, 3		Harada et al 1970
				2, 3		Harada et al 1970
				2, 3		Harada et al 1970
				2, 3		Harada et al 1972
				2, 3		Harada et al 1970
				2, 3		Harada et al 1970

SCIENTIFIC NAME	COMMON NAME	TISSUE	TMAO (μM/100 g) RANGE	AVERAGE	TMA (μM/100g) RANGE	AVERAGE	DMA (μM/100) RANGE	AVE
Sepiidae								
Sepia afficinalis			9542.85-9900	10535.71	107.14-178.57			
Sepia esculenta				1944 2900, 3857.143-10714.29				
Sepia esculenta				3857.14				
Sepia esculenta			720-2000	2893.33-720				
Sepia officinalis				10428.57-10571.43				
Sepia peterseni				1500.00				
Sepiella japonica		mid-gut gland		314.29		221.43		
Sepiidae								
Sepia esculenta		upper half		7214.29		3.57		
		lower half		6500		3.57		
		arm		4857.14		40.00		
		mid-gut gland		0		15.00		
		epithelium, epithelium w/ tentacles		4571.43		228.57		
		arm		3571.43		157.14		
		mid-gut gland		407.14		178.57		
		upper half		16000.		85.71		
		lower half		16428.57		71.43		
		arm		110000		128.57		
		mid-gut gland		478.57		557.14		
Sepia esculenta		upper half		10142.86		22.86		
		lower half		9429.57		22.86		
		arm		5857.14		34.29		
		mid-gut gland		0		15.00		
Sepia kobiensis		upper half		6357.14		25.71		
		lower half		6357.14		27.14		
		arm		2928.57		28.57		
		mid-gut gland		335.71		371.43		
Sepia lycidas		upper half		10785.71		250		
		lower half		9571.43		214.29		
		arm		5857.14		200.00		
		mid-gut gland		407.14		250.00		
Sepia pardalis		upper half		10285.71		100.00		
		lower half		11142.86		100.00		
		arm		7928.57		157.14		
		mid-gut gland		1357.14		464.29		
Sepia peterseni		upper half		7785.71		128.57		
		lower half		8285.71		114.29		
		arm		3357.14		271.43		
Sepia peterseni		mid-gut gland		542.86		342.86		
Sepiella japonica		upper half		8214.29		85.71		
Sepiella japonica		lower half		7571.43		85.71		
		arm		2214.29		321.43		
		mid-gut gland		221.43		642.86		
		upper half		5857.14		157.14		
		lower half		7642.86		85.71		
		arm		4000		285.71		
Sepiola birostrata		mantle combined		7500		207.14		
		arm		5428.57		121.43		
		mid-gut gland		1214.29		178.57		
Squids								
	Pacific squid		10666.67 11066.67					
	Atlantic squid		4866.67-5200					
Thysanoteuthidae								
Thysanoteuthis rhombus	Squid	upper half		20357.14		62.86		
		lower half		-		-		
		arm		14857.14		31.43		
		mid-gut gland		200.00 18357.14 3426.67		78.57		

NO. OF FISH EXAMINED	LENGTH OF FISH	BODY WEIGHT (g)	SEASON	METHOD USED	OTHER	REFERENCE
				2		Cantoni/Ardemagni 1977
				2		Cantoni/Ardemagni 1977
				2		Cantoni/Ardemagni 1977
				2, 3		Harada et al 1968
				3		Endo et al 1962
						Yamada 1967
				2, 3		Harada et al 1968
				2, 3		Harada et al 1968
				2, 3		Harada et al 1968
				2, 3		Harada et al 1968
				2, 3		Harada et al 1968
				2, 3		Harada et al 1968
				2, 3		Harada et al 1968
				2, 3		Harada et al 1968
				2, 3		Harada et al 1968
				2, 3		Harada et al 1968
				2, 3		Harada et al 1968
				2, 3		Harada et al 1958
				2, 3		Harada et al 1968
				2, 3		Harada et al 1968
				2, 3		Harada et al 1968
				2, 3		Harada et al 1968
				2, 3		Harada et al 1968
				2, 3		Harada et al 1968
				2, 3		Harada et al 1968
				2, 3		Harada et al 1968
				2, 3		Harada et al 1968
				2, 3		Harada et al 1968
				2, 3		Harada et al 1968
				2, 3		Harada et al 1968
				2, 3		Harada et al 1968
				2, 3		Harada et al 1968
				2, 3		Harada et al 1968
				2, 3		Harada et al 1968
				2, 3		Harada et al 1968
				2, 3		Harada et al 1968
				2, 3		Harada et al 1968
				2, 3		Harada et al 1968
				2, 3		Harada et al 1968
				2, 3		Harada et al 1968
				2, 3		Harada et al 1968
				2, 3		Harada et al 1968
				2, 3		Harada et al 1968
				2, 3		Harada et al 1968
				2, 3		Harada et al 1968
				2, 3		Harada et al 1968
				2, 3		Harada et al 1968
				2, 3		Harada et al 1968
				2, 3		Harada et al 1968
				2		Shewan 1951
				2		Shewan 1951
				2, 3		Harada et al 1968
				2, 3		Harada et al 1968
				2, 3		Harada et al 1968
				2, 3		Harada et al 1968
				2, 3		Harada et al 1968
						Yamada 1967

TABLE 1

SCIENTIFIC NAME	COMMON NAME	TISSUE	TMAO (μM/100 g) RANGE	AVERAGE	TMA (μM/100g) RANGE	AVERAGE	DMA (μM/100g) RANGE	AVERAGE
Todarodidae								
Todarodes pacificus		arm		14357.14		34.29		
		mid-gut gland		785.71		135.71		
				3107.14,				
				6628.57,				
				15071.43				
				5192.86,				
				6757.14-				
				17071.43				
				9785.71-				
				13000,				
				5500-				
				7085.71				
				3106.67-				
				24142.86				
				6626.67,				
				15120,				
				52428.57-				
				13013.33				
				3186.67				
				1266.67				
				3186.67				
				10440.				
Todarodes pacificus		mid-gut gland		157.14		92.86		
		upper half		28428.57		150.00		
		lower half		33571.49		135.71		
		arm		13500.00		142.86		
		mid-gut gland		450.00		242.86		
		upper half		264.29		78.57		
		lower half		23071.43		78.57		
		arm		11928.57		65.71		
		mid-gut gland		435.71		285.71		
		upper half		22357.14		85.71		
		lower half		18714.29		92.86		
		arm		10000.00		100.00		
		mid-gut gland		34.29		300.00		
		upper half		17928.57		52.14		
		lower half		11500.00		37.14		
		arm		7714.29		47.86		
		mid-gut gland		571.43		114.29		
		upper half		28500.00		28.57		
		lower half		28357.14		28.57		
Todarodes pacificus		upper half		-		33.57		
		lower half		-		37.14		
		arm		-		37.14		
		mid-gut gland		-		100.00		
		upper half		15785.71		114.29		
		lower half		-		-		
		arm		10785.71		92.86		
		mid-gut gland		1214.29		378.57		
		upper half		19571.43		128.57		
		lower half		-		-		
		arm		12500.00		67.86		
		mid-gut gland		1571.43		407.14		
		upper half		22642.86		114.29		
		lower half		23428.57		171.43		
		arm		14642.86		164.29		
		mid-gut gland		114.29		328.57		
		upper half		20214.29		41.43		
		lower half		17928.57		37.14		
		arm		10857.14		32.14		
Loliginidae								
Loligo formosa	Squid			1866.67		305.09		44.4
Loligo formosa	Squid			53.33		3559.32		0
Loligo formosa	Squid			2933.33		271.19		88.8
Loliginidae								
Doryteuthis bleekeri	Squid			1480		68.48		
	Squid			453.33		1559.32		
	Squid			202.67		1915.25		
	Squid			0		3118.64		
	Squid			0		3203.39		
Doryteuthis bleekeri		mid-gut gland		507.14		357.14		
Doryteuthis bleekeri		upper half		22428.57		150		
		lower half		20714.29		157.14		
		arm		16928.57		171.43		
		mid-gut gland		707.14		714.29		
		upper half		20857.14		242.86		
		lower half		20142.86		235.71		
		arm		15000		250		

NO.OF FISH EXAMINED	LENGTH OF FISH	BODY WEIGHT (g)	SEASON	METHOD USED	OTHER	REFERENCE
				2, 3		Harada et al 1968
				2, 3		Harada et al 1968
				2, 3		Harada et al 1968
				2, 3		Harada et al 1968
				2, 3		Harada et al 1968
						Yamada 1967
						Yamada 1967
						Yamada 1967
						Yamada 1967
				3		Takagi et al 1967a
				3	$^{\circ}$C 0 hrs.	Takagi et al 1967b
				3	4 24	Takagi et al 1967b
				3	10 24	Takagi et al 1967b
				3	20 24	Takagi et al 1967b
				3	4 48	Takagi et al 1967b
				3	10 48	Takagi et al 1967b
				3	20 48	Takagi et al 1967b
				2, 3		Harada et al 1968
				2, 3		Harada et al 1968
				2, 3		Harada et al 1968
				2, 3		Harada et al 1968
				2, 3		Harada et al 1968
				2, 3		Harada et al 1968
				2, 3		Harada et al 1968
				2, 3		Harada et al 1968
				2, 3		Harada et al 1968
				2, 3		Harada et al 1968
				2, 3		Harada et al 1968
				2, 3		Harada et al 1968
				2, 3		Harada et al 1968
				2, 3		Harada et al 1968
				2, 3		Harada et al 1968
				2, 3		Harada et al 1968
				2, 3		Harada et al 1968
				2, 3		Harada et al 1968
				2, 3		Harada et al 1968
				2, 3		Harada et al 1968
				2, 3		Harada et al 1968
				2, 3		Harada et al 1968
				2, 3		Harada et al 1968
				2, 3		Harada et al 1968
				2, 3		Harada et al 1968
				2, 3		Harada et al 1968
				2, 3		Harada et al 1968
				2, 3		Harada et al 1968
				2, 3		Harada et al 1968
				2, 3		Harada et al 1968
				2, 3		Harada et al 1968
				2, 3		Harada et al 1968
				2, 3		Harada et al 1968
				2, 3		Harada et al 1968
				2, 3		Harada et al 1968
				6		Mujahara 1960
				6		Mujahara 1960
				6		Mujahara 1960
				3	Storage 15°C$\pm$2 0 hrs.	Takada/Nishimoto 1958
				3	24	Takada/Nishimoto 1958
				3	48	Takada/Nishimoto 1958
				3	72	Takada/Nishimoto 1958
				3	130	Takada/Nishimoto 1958
				2, 3		Herada et al 1968
				2, 3		Harada et al 1968
				2, 3		Harada et al 1968
				2, 3		Harada et al 1968
				2, 3		Harada et al 1968
				2, 3		Harada et al 1968
				2, 3		Harada et al 1968
				2, 3		Harada et al 1968

TABLE 12

SCIENTIFIC NAME	COMMON NAME	TISSUE	TMAO (μM/100 g) RANGE	AVERAGE	TMA (μM/100g) RANGE	AVERAGE	DMA (μM/100g) RANGE	AVERAGE
		mid-gut gland		928.57		700		
		upper half		34857.14		69.29		
		lower half		29857.14		78.57		
		arm		21928.57		69.29		
Doryteuthis bleekeri				7857.14, 1485.71				
Doryteuthis bleekeri				7853.33				
Doryteuthis kensaki			4746.67-6200					
Doryteuthis kensaki				493.33 8000, 4742.86-18642.86				
Loligo budo		upper half		11000		164.29		
		lower half		10071.43		150		
		arm		5428.57		250		
		mid-gut gland		1714.29		150		
		upper half		10714.29		142.86		
		lower half		10071.43		128.57		
		arm		6214.29		200		
		mid-gut gland		1714.29		150		
Loligo chinensis				9214.29				
Loligo chinensis				1720				
Loligo chinensis				9214.29				
Loligo edulis		upper half		12142.86		71.43		
		lower half		11071.43		70		
Loligo edulis		upper half		21462.86		67.86		
		lower half		22071.43		60.71		
		arm		14500		71.43		
		mid-gut gland		1000		214.29		
		upper half		18642.86		114.29		
		lower half		19428.57		114.29		
		arm		13642.86		135.71		
		mid-gut gland		407.14		478.57		
		arm		6714.29		71.43		
		mid-gut gland		672000. 6200		41.43		
Loligo kensaki				18664.29 4742.86				
Loligo opalescens			10714.29-11142.86					
Loligo formosa				1892.86				
Loligo japonica		upper half		9357.14		70		
		lower half		8714.29		78.57		
		arm		7500		78.57		
		mid-gut gland		4142.86		242.86		
		upper half		9714.29		53.57		
		lower half		8571.43		70.71		
		arm		8285.71		85.71		
		mid-gut gland		5214.29		228.57		
Loligo kensaki				8000				
Loligo opalescens	Squid			10700, 11100				
Loligo opalescens	Squid			10714.29 11142.86				
Loligo pealeii				7857.14, 8714.29				
Loligo pealeii				7857.14, 8714.29				
Loligo vulgaris			9300-11435.71	-	200-292.86			
Ommastrephes sloani				17071.43				
Ommastrephes sloani pacificus				5192.86				
Sepioteuthis arctipinnis				5924.29				
Sepioteuthis lessoniana				6571.43				
Sepioteuthis lessoniana				13950				
Sepioteuthis lessoniana		muscle		13933.33, 15142.86 6571.43				
Sepioteuthis lessoniana				2821.43, 6571.43 13928.57				
Sepioteuthis lessoniana		mid-gut gland		507.14		50		
		upper half		10000		34.29		
		lower half		8285.71		30		
		arm		7714.29		42.86		
		mid-gut gland		428.57		51.43		
		upper half		10428.57		57.14		
		lower half		8785.71		48.57		
		arm		8214.29		60		
Thysanoteuthis rhombus				18357.14				

NO.OF FISH EXAMINED	LENGTH OF FISH	BODY WEIGHT (g)	SEASON	METHOD USED	OTHER	REFERENCE
				2, 3		Harada et al 1968
				2, 3		Harada et al 1968
				2, 3		Harada et al 1968
				2, 3		Harada et al 1968
				2, 3		Harada et al 1968
				2, 3		Harada et al 1968
						Yamada 1967
						Yamada 1967
						Yamada 1967
						Yamada 1967
				2, 3		Harada et al 1968
				2, 3		Harada et al 1968
				2, 3		Harada et al 1968
				2, 3		Harada et al 1968
				2, 3		Harada et al 1968
				2, 3		Harada et al 1968
				2, 3		Harada et al 1968
				2, 3		Harada et al 1968
				2, 3		Harada et al 1968
				2, 3		Harada et al 1968
						Yamada 1967
				3		Endo et al 1962
				2, 3		Harada et al 1968
				2, 3		Harada et al 1968
				2, 3		Harada et al 1968
				2, 3		Harada et al 1968
				2, 3		Harada et al 1968
				2, 3		Harada et al 1968
				2, 3		Harada et al 1968
				2, 3		Harada et al 1968
				2, 3		Harada et al 1968
				2, 3		Harada et al 1968
				2, 3		Harada et al 1968
				2, 3		Harada et al 1968
			Aug 9			Simidu et al 1953
			Aug 30			Simidu et al 1953
			Sept 11			Simidu et al 1953
				2, 3		Harada et al 1968
				2, 3		Harada et al 1968
				2, 3		Harada et al 1968
				2, 3		Harada et al 1968
				2, 3		Harada et al 1968
				2, 3		Harada et al 1968
				2, 3		Harada et al 1968
				2, 3		Harada et al 1968
				2, 3		Harada et al 1968
				2, 3		Harada et al 1968
				2, 3		Harada et al 1968
				3		Endo et al 1962
				3		Norris/Benoit 1945
				3		Dyer et al 1952
				3		Dyer et al 1952
				2, 3		Harada et al 1968
				2		Cantoni/Ardemagni 1977
				3		Endo et al 1962
			Aug 30			Simidu et al 1953
				2		Velankar/Govindan 1958
				3		Endo et al 1962
				2, 3		Harada et al 1968
			Jul 28	3		Simidu et al 1953
						Yamada 1967
						Yamada 1967
				2, 3		Harada et al 1968
				2, 3		Harada et al 1968
				2, 3		Harada et al 1968
				2, 3		Harada et al 1968
				2, 3		Harada et al 1968
				2, 3		Harada et al 1968
				2, 3		Harada et al 1968
				2, 3		Harada et al 1968
				2, 3		Harada et al 1968
				2, 3		Harada et al 1968
				3		Endo et al 1962

TABLE 12

SCIENTIFIC NAME	COMMON NAME	TISSUE	TMAO (μM/100 g) RANGE	AVERAGE	TMA (μM/100g) RANGE	AVERAGE	DMA (μM/100g) RANGE	AVERAGE
Octopodidae								
Octopus dofleini		abdominal muscle foot		2882.14		182.86		
		muscle (basal) foot		1567.14		190		
		muscle terminal abdominal		2262.14		328.57		
		muscle foot		22.4		1.42		
		muscle (basal) foot		11.07		1.32		
		muscle terminal		16.		2.32		
Octopus fangsio		abdominal muscle foot		13.47		1.14		
		muscle (basal) foot		13.33		0.83		
		muscle terminal digestive		12.53		1.51		
		tract gonad		2.67		1.17		
		(ovary) salivary gland		3.27		0.42		
		posterior abdominal		3.33		0.36		
		muscle foot		1970		167.14		
		muscle (basal) foot		1954.29		122.86		
		muscle terminal digestive		1708.57		206.43		
		tract gonad		457.14		198.57		
		(ovary) salivary gland		647.86		83.57		
Octopus minor		posterior		1261.43		137.14		
		muscle		1171.43		100		
Octopus ocellatus		viscera		442.86		128.57		
		muscle		1307.14, 1707.14, 1971.43				
		others		457.14- 1264.29				
		muscle		600		92.86		
		viscera		428.571		157.14		
		muscle	453.33- 1266.67	1076.67- 1973.33	1306.67,			
Octopus vulgaris		abdominal muscle foot		846.43		27.14		
		muscle (basal)		781.43		20.71		
		abdominal muscle foot		704.29		34.29		
		muscle (basal) foot		989.29		22.14		
		muscle terminal gonad		742.14		60		
		(ovary) digestive tract		236.43		23.57		
		salivary gland posterior		116.43		32.86		
		abdominal muscle foot		200.71		32.14		
		muscle foot		720		84.29		
		muscle (basal) foot		1077.86		40.71		
		muscle terminal gonad		761.43		185		
		(ovary) digestive		205.71		11.43		
		tract salivary		277.14		87.14		
		gland posterior		137.14		nil		

NO.OF FISH EXAMINED	LENGTH OF FISH	BODY WEIGHT (g)	SEASON	METHOD USED	OTHER	REFERENCE
			Feb 1953	2, 3	mgN/100 g, wet weight	Asano/Sato 1954
			Feb 1953	2, 3	1 sample remarkably spoiled, landed at Shiwogama	Asano/Sato 1954
				2, 3	1 sample remarkably spoiled, landed at Shiwogama	Asano/Sato 1954
				2, 3		Asano/Sato 1954
			Feb 1953			Asano/Sato 1954
			Feb 1953			Asano/Sato 1954
		A - 1290	Feb 1953		Average of 3 samples, remarkably spoiled, landed at Shiwogama	Asano/Sato 1954
		B - 800				
		C - 718				Asano/Sato 1954
					Asano/Sato 1954	Asano/Sato 1954
						Asano/Sato 1954
						Asano/Sato 1954
						Asano/Sato 1954
3		A - 1290	Feb 1953	2, 3	mgN/100 g wet weight	Asano/Sato 1954
		B - 800			% - dry weight	
		C - 718	Feb 1953	2, 3	Average of 3 samples, remarkably spoiled, landed at Shiwogama	Asano/Sato 1954
				2, 3		
				2, 3	Average of 3 samples remarkably spoiled, landed at Shiwogama	Asano/Sato 1954
				2, 3	Average of 3 samples remarkably spoiled, landed at Shiwogama	Asano/Sato 1954
				2, 3	remarkably spoiled landed at Shiwogama	Asano/Sato 1954
					landed at Shiwogama remarkably spoiled	
				2, 3	landed at Shiwogama	Asano/Sato 1954
				2, 3		Harada et al 1972
				2, 3		Harada et al 1972
				2, 3		Harada et al 1972
				2, 3		Harada et al 1972
				2, 3		Harada et al 1972
				2, 3		Harada et al 1972
				2, 3		Harada et al 1972
						Yamada 1967
						Yamada 1967
3			Nov 1952	2, 3	mgN/100 g, wet, % dry weight	Asano/Sato 1954
				2, 3	Average of 3 samples	Asano/Sato 1954
			Dec 1952	2, 3	Average of 3 samples	Asano/Sato 1954
			Dec 1952	2, 3	Nov - Dec 1952	Asano/Sato 1954
						Asano/Sato 1954
			Dec 1952	2, 3	All very fresh, landed at Yuriage	Asano/Sato 1954
			Dec 1952	2, 3	All very fresh, landed at Yuriage	Asano/Sato 1954
			Dec 1952	2, 3	All very fresh, landed at Yuriage	Asano/Sato 1954
			Dec 1952	2, 3	All very fresh, landed at Yuriage	Asano/Sato 1954
			Jan 1953	2, 3	Average of 3 samples	Asano/Sato 1954
				2, 3	Slightly spoiled, landed at Yuriage	Asano/Sato 1954
				2, 3		Asano/Sato 1954

TABLE 12.1

SCIENTIFIC NAME	COMMON NAME	TISSUE	TMAO (μM/100 g) RANGE	TMAO (μM/100 g) AVERAGE	TMA (μM/100g) RANGE	TMA (μM/100g) AVERAGE	DMA (μM/100g) RANGE	DMA (μM/100g) AVERAGE
		abdominal muscle		4.67		0.15		
		muscle		2428.57		35.71		
		viscera		142.86		257.14		
		muscle		1786.67, 3714.29-1080.				
			200-280					
	Madako	muscle		1785.71, 692.86-1078.57				
		others		114.29-278.57				
		foot muscle (basal)		3.73		0.10		
		abdominal muscle		3.47		0.17		
		foot muscle (basal)		4.80		0.10		
		foot muscle terminal		3.87		0.32		
		gonad (ovary)		1.20		0.12		
		digestive tract		0.53		0.15		
		salivary gland posterior		0.67		0.10		
		abdominal muscle		4.0		0.46		
		foot muscle (basal)		6.27		0.24		
		foot muscle terminal		4.80		1.15		
		gonad (ovary)		1.20		0.07		
		digestive tract		1.47		0.48		
		salivary gland posterior		0.53		nil		
Poroctopus dofleini		muscle		1571.43-2878.57, 450-678.57				
Polypus longkongensis	Octopus			1714.29 1700 1714.29				

NO.OF FISH EXAMINED	LENGTH OF FISH	BODY WEIGHT (g)	SEASON	METHOD USED	OTHER	REFERENCE
				2, 3		Asano/Sato 1954
				2, 3		Asano/Sato 1954
			Nov 1952	2, 3	% = dry weight	Asano/Sato 1954
				2, 3		Harada et al 1972
				2, 3		Harada et al 1972
						Yamada 1967
						Yamada 1967
				2, 3		Harada et al 1972
				2, 3		Harada et al 1972
			Nov 1952	2, 3	%=dry weight. Average value of 3 samples	Asano/Sato 1954
		A - 3912	Dec 1952		Average value of 3 samples	
		B - 1690			Nov - Dec	Asano/Sato 1954
		C - 1120			1952, all very fresh, landed at Yunage	Asano/Sato 1954
					1952, all very fresh, landed at Yunage	Asano/Sato 1954
						Asano/Sato 1954
						Asano/Sato 1954
		A - 1140	Jan 1953		Average value of 2 samples, slightly spoiled, landed at Yunage	Asano/Sato 1954
		B - 834				Asano/Sato 1954
						Asano/Sato 1954
				2, 3		Harada et al 1972
				2, 3		Harada et al 1972
				3		Norris/Benoit 1945
				3		Dyer et al 1952

TABLE 1

SCIENTIFIC NAME	COMMON NAME	TISSUE	TMAO (μM/100 g) RANGE	TMAO (μM/100 g) AVERAGE	TMA (μM/100g) RANGE	TMA (μM/100g) AVERAGE	DMA (μM/100g) RANGE	DMA (μM/100g) AVER.
Nassariidae								
Niotha livescens		muscle		14.29		414.29		
		viscera		42.86		257.14		
Neritidae								
Heminerita japonica	Snail	muscle		7.14		142.86		
		viscera		0		107.14		
Philinidae								
Philine argentata	Snail	muscle		0		292.86		
		viscera		142.86		671.43		
Pleuroceridae								
Semisulcospira bensoni		muscle		0		21.43		
		viscera		14.29		50.0		
Potamididae								
Botillaria multiformis		muscle		0		235.71		
		viscera		0		185.71		
Cerithideopsilla cingulata		muscle		57.14		121.43		
		viscera		7.14		242.86		
Cerithidea rhigophorarum		muscle		14.29		192.86		
		viscera		0		192.86		
Bradybaenidae								
Acusta despecta	Snail	muscle		0		35.71		
		viscera		7.14		28.57		
		muscle		0		35.71		
		viscera		0		35.71		
Fasciolariidae								
Fasinus nigrirostratus		muscle		85.71		71.43		
		viscera		28.57		128.57		
Fasinus perplexus minor	Snail	muscle		50		214.29		
		viscera		28.57		150		
Ficidae								
Ficus subintermedia	Snail	muscle		371.43		914.29		
		viscera		257.14		257.14		
Trochidae								
Chlorostoma orgyrostoma lischkli	Snail	muscle		7.14		314.29		
		viscera		14.29		200.00		
Monodonta perplexa		muscle		0		1428.57		
		viscera		28.57		278.57		
Monodonta labio	Snail	muscle		21.43		500.00		
		viscera		14.29		300.00		
Omphalius rustica	Snail	muscle		50.00		107.14		
		viscera		50.00		128.57		
Omphalius pfeiffori carpenteri		muscle		7.14		207.14		
		viscera		14.29		164.29		
Tristichotrotus unicus	Snail	muscle		2157.14		128.57		
		viscera		600.00		307.14		
Turbinidae								
Batillus cornutus	Snail	muscle		21.43		264.29		
		viscera		7.14		221.43		
Batillus cornutus		muscle		250, 257.14, 1428.57				
Batillus cornutus	Snail	muscle		7642.86, 1285.71, 1357.14				
Lunella coronata	Snail	muscle		64.29		228.57		
		viscera		14.29		185.71		
Turbo cornutus		muscle		253.33 240.00 1428.57				
Vermetidae								
Superlorbis imbricatus		muscle		7.14		357.14		
		viscera		14.29		385.71		
Viviparidae								
Cipangopaludina chinensis malleata	Snail	muscle		-		21.43		
		viscera		-		21.43		
		muscle		-		42.86		
		viscera		7.14		28.57		
		muscle		7.14		28.57		
		viscera		28.57		35.71		
		muscle		92.86				
		muscle		93.33				
		muscle		93.33				

NO.OF FISH EXAMINED	LENGTH OF FISH	BODY WEIGHT (g)	SEASON	METHOD USED	OTHER	REFERENCE
				2		Harada et al 1971
				3		Harada et al 1971
				2		Harada et al 1971
				3		Harada et al 1971
				2, 3		Harada et al 1972
				2, 3		Harada et al 1972
				2, 3		Harada et al 1971
				2, 3		Harada et al 1971
				2, 3		Harada et al 1971
				2, 3		Harada et al 1971
				2, 3		Harada et al 1971
				2, 3		Harada et al 1971
				2, 3		Harada et al 1971
				2, 3		Harada et al 1971
				2, 3		Harada et al 1971
				2, 3		Harada et al 1971
				2, 3		Harada et al 1971
				2, 3		Harada et al 1971
				2, 3		Harada et al 1971
				2, 3		Harada et al 1971
				2, 3		Harada et al 1971
				2, 3		Harada et al 1971
				2, 3		Harada et al 1972
				2, 3		Harada et al 1972
				2, 3		Harada et al 1971
				2, 3		Harada et al 1971
				2, 3		Harada et al 1971
				2, 3		Harada et al 1971
				2, 3		Harada et al 1971
				2, 3		Harada et al 1971
				2, 3		Harada et al 1971
				2, 3		Harada et al 1971
				2, 3		Harada et al 1971
				2, 3		Harada et al 1971
				2, 3		Harada et al 1971
				2, 3		Harada et al 1971
				2, 3		Harada et al 1971
				2, 3		Harada et al 1971
						Yamada 1967
				2, 3		Harada et al 1971
				2, 3		Harada et al 1971
		2430	Sept 18	3		Takagi et al 1967
		2254	May 30	3		Takagi et al 1962
			Sept 22			Simidu et al 1953
				2, 3		Harada et al 1971
				2, 3		Harada et al 1971
				2, 3		Harada et al 1971
				2, 3		Harada et al 1971
				2, 3		Harada et al 1971
				2, 3		Harada et al 1971
				2, 3		Harada et al 1971
				2, 3		Harada et al 1971
				2, 3		Harada et al 1971
						Yamada 1967
		200	June 30	3		Takagi et al 1962

TABLE

SCIENTIFIC NAME	COMMON NAME	TISSUE	TMAO (μM/100 g) RANGE	TMAO (μM/100 g) AVERAGE	TMA (μM/100g) RANGE	TMA (μM/100g) AVERAGE	DMA (μM/10(RANGE	DMA AV\
Buccinidae								
Babylonia japonica		muscle		57.14		857.14		
		viscera		7.14		350		
Japeuthria ferrea		muscle		14.29		1407.14		
		viscera		57.14		635.71		
Neptunea arthritica		muscle		0				
Neptunus pelagicus				3866.43				
				4065				
Neptunea arthritica						0		
Siphonalia fusoides		muscle		92.86		1092.85		
		viscera		78.57		514.29		
Bucyconidae								
Hemifusus ternatanus	Snail	muscle		35.71		1292.86		
		viscera		50		1135.71		
Littorinidae								
Littorina brevicula		muscle		0		335.71		
		viscera		7.14		271.43		
Littorina silchana	snail			0				
Littorina silchana	snail	entire animal		negligible				
Littorina silchana	snail			0				
Muricidae								
Chicoreus asianus		muscle		21.43		178.57		
		viscera		7.14		200		
Rapanus thomasiana		muscle		14.29		857.14		
		viscera		14.29		664.29		
Thais bronni		muscle		14.29		535.71		
		viscera		14.29		252.94		
Thais clavigera		muscle		35.71		728.57		
		viscera		0		278.57		
Thais lamellosa	Snail			0				
	Snail			negligible				
	Snail			0				
Scalpellidae								
Mitella mitella	Barnacle	muscle		2214.29		1050		
		viscera		0				
Balanidae								
Balamus cariosus	Barnacle	entire animal		1714.29				
Balamus nubita	Barnacle	entire animal		5214.29,				
		entire animal		6285.71,				
		entire animal		4214.29,				
				7071.43				
Balamus cariosus	Barnacle	entire animal		1700				
Balamus nubita	Barnacle	entire animal		5200,				
				6300,				
				4200				
				7100				
Tetraelita squamosa japonica				300.00		757.14		
Asteriidae								
Asterias vulgaris	Starfish			1428.47				
	Starfish			0				
Asterinidae								
Asterias amurensis		viscera		0		100.00		
Asterina pectinifera		viscera		0		328.57		
Arcidae								
Anarda (Scapharca) Broughtonii				0				
Barbatia virescens		adductor foot		0		64.29		
		& mantle		0		121.43		
		viscera		7.14		121.43		
Scapharca broughtonii		adductor foot		21.43		128.57		
		& mantle		50.00		35.71		
		viscera		28.57		107.14		
		adductor foot		21.43		142.86		
		& mantle		0		28.57		
		viscera		21.43		142.86		
		adductor foot		14.29		135.71		
		& mantle		0		128.57		
		viscera		21.43		200.00		
Scapharca globsa arsus		adductor foot		35.71		250.00		
		& mantle		7.14		50.00		
		viscera		7.14		50.00		

NO.OF FISH EXAMINED	LENGTH OF FISH	BODY WEIGHT (g)	SEASON	METHOD USED	OTHER	REFERENCE
				2, 3		Harada et al 1971
				2, 3		Harada et al 1971
				2, 3		Harada et al 1971
				2, 3		Harada et al 1971
				2, 3		Takagi et al 1967a
				2		Velankar/Govindan 1958
				2		Velankar/Govindan 1958
				2, 3		Harada et al 1972
				2, 3		Harada et al 1972
				2, 3		Harada et al 1971
				2, 3		Harada et al 1971
				2		Harada et al 1971
				2		Harada et al 1971
				2		Harada et al 1971
				3		Norris/Benoit 1945
				3		Dyer et al 1952
				2, 3		Harada et al 1971
				2, 3		Harada et al 1971
				2, 3		Harada et al 1971
				2, 3		Harada et al 1971
				2, 3		Harada et al 1971
				2, 3		Harada et al 1971
				2, 3		Harada et al 1971
				2, 3		Harada et al 1971
				3		Norris/Benoit 1945
				3		Dyer et al 1952
				2, 3		Harada et al 1972
				2, 3		Harada et al 1972
				2, 3		Harada et al 1972
				2, 3		Harada et al 1972
				3		Norris/Benoit 1945
				3		Norris/Benoit 1945
				2, 3		Harada et al 1972
				2, 3		Harada et al 1972
				2		Shewan 1951
				2, 3		Harada et al 1972
				2, 3		Harada et al 1972
				3		Takagi et al 1967a
				3		Takagi et al 1967a
				2, 3		Harada et al 1970
				2, 3		Harada et al 1970
				2, 3		Harada et al 1970
				2, 3		Harada et al 1970
				2, 3		Harada et al 1970
				2, 3		Harada et al 1970
				2, 3		Harada et al 1970
				2, 3		Harada et al 1970
				2, 3		Harada et al 1970
				2, 3		Harada et al 1970
				2, 3		Harada et al 1970
				2, 3		Harada et al 1970
				2, 3		Harada et al 1970
				2, 3		Harada et al 1970

TABLE 12.

SCIENTIFIC NAME	COMMON NAME	TISSUE	TMAO (µM/100 g) RANGE	AVERAGE	TMA (µM/100g) RANGE	AVERAGE	DMA (µM/100g) RANGE	AVERAGE
Scapharca subcrenata		adductor foot & mantle viscera		14.29 28.57 21.43		400.00 614.29 214.29		
Aplysiidae								
Anisodoris nobilus	Sea slug			0 0 0				
Aplysia kurodai		muscle viscera		35.71 7.14		357.14 507.14		
Stichopodidae								
Cucumaria frondosa	Sea cucumber		5428.57-6142.86					
Cucumaria miaiata	Sea cucumber			negligible negligible				
Stichopus californicus	Sea urchin			negligible negligible				
Stichopus japonicus		muscle viscera muscle viscera		7.14 35.71 0 0		57.14 85.71 35.71 57.14		
	Pacific sea cucumber			negligible 0 0 trace amt.		0		
	Atlantic sea cucumber			34285.71				
Holothuriidae								
Holothuria monacaria	Sea cucumber	muscle viscera		7.14 7.14		71.43 50		
Centrechinidae								
Diadema petosum	Urchin	Viscera		64.29		64.29		
Echinidae								
Pseudocentrotus depressus	Urchin			0		207.14		
Toxopneustes pillolus		viscera		0		92.86		
Echinometridae								
Anthrocidaris crassipina		Viscera		28.57		107.14		
Strongylocentrotidae								
Hemicentrotus pulcherrimus		viscera		21.43		235.71		
Strongylocentrotus franciscanus	Sea urchin			negligible negligible				
Strongylocentrotus intermedius				42.67		11.87		
Order Amphipoda sp.								
	Sand-flea	entire animals		221.43				
	Sand-flea	entire animals		220.				
Subclass--Copepoda sp.								
Copepoda sp.		entire animals		1571.43 1500				
Mixture; largely corycaeus affinis, calanus finmarchius, tortanus discaudatis, epidabiocera amphrites				4500				
Mixture; nearly completely corycaeus affinis				1600				
	Pacific copepods		1600-6000					

(Continued)

269

NO.OF FISH EXAMINED	LENGTH OF FISH	BODY WEIGHT (g)	SEASON	METHOD USED	OTHER	REFERENCE
				2, 3		Harada et al 1970
				2, 3		Harada et al 1970
				2, 3		Harada et al 1970
				2, 3		Harada et al 1971
				3		Norris/Benoit 1945
				3		Dyer et al 1952
				2, 3		Harada et al 1971
				2, 3		Harada et al 1971
				2, 3		Harada et al 1972
				2, 3		Harada et al 1972
				3		Norris/Benoit 1945
				2, 3		Harada et al 1972
				3		Norris/Benoit 1945
				2, 3		Harada et al 1972
				2, 3		Harada et al 1972
				2, 3		Harada et al 1972
				2, 3		Harada et al 1972
				2, 3		Harada et al 1972
				3		Takagi et al 1967a
				2		Shewan 1951
						Yamada 1967
				2		Shewan 1951
				2, 3		Harada et al 1972
				2, 3		Harada et al 1972
				2, 3		Harada et al 1972
				2, 3		Harada et al 1972
				2, 3		Harada et al 1972
				2, 3		Harada et al 1972
				2, 3		Harada et al 1972
				2, 3		Harada et al 1972
				3		Norris/Benoit 1945
				3		Takagi et al 1967a
				3		Harada et al 1972
				3		Norris/Benoit 1945
				3		Harada et al 1972
				3		Norris/Benoit 1945
						Norris/Benoit 1945
				2		Shewan 1951

TABLE

SCIENTIFIC NAME	COMMON NAME	TISSUE	TMAO (µM/100 g)		TMA (µM/100g)		DMA (µM/100g)	
			RANGE	AVERAGE	RANGE	AVERAGE	RANGE	AVER
Algae								
Chondria crassicaulis	Red algae			1730.0		1500.0		
Chondria crassicaulis	Red algae			52800.		45700.0		
Grateloupia crassicaulis	Red algae			72800		63700.0		
Grateloupia elliptica	Red algae			2680.0		2340.0		
Grateloupia elliptica	Red algae			45800.0		63700.0		
Grateloupia filicina	Red algae			2340.0		3245.0		
Grateloupia filicina	Red algae			50700.0		45600.0		
Grateloupia turuturu	Red algae			2500.0		2240.0		
Grateloupia turuturu	Red algae			84500.0		76000.0		
Porphyrra suborbiculata	Red algae			64100.0		60900.0		
Porphyrra suburbiculata	Red algae			4765.0		4285.0		
Porphyrra tenera	Red algae			3320.0		3160.0		
Porphyrra tenera	Red algae							
Desmarestia viridis	Brown algae			553.0		1462.0		
Desmarestia viridis	Brown algae			18400.0		48500.0		
Dictyopteris divaricata	Brown algae			477.0		976.0		
Dictyopteris divaricata	Brown algae			22200.0		45400.0		
Eisenia bicyclis	Brown algae			229.0		2571.0		
Eisenia bicyclis	Brown algae			8800.0		98700.0		
Higikia fusiformis	Brown algae			517.0		1475.0		
Higikia fusiformis	Brown algae			30600.0		87200.0		
Sargassum thunbergii	Brown algae			30.0		2610.0		
Sargassum thunbergii	Brown algae			1600.0		139400.0		
Syctosiphon lomentarius	Brown algae			526.0		2289.0		
Syctosiphon lomentarius	Brown algae			11600.0		50100.0		
Undaria pinnatifida	Brown algae			15300.0		48000.0		
Undaria pinnatifida	Brown algae			464.0		1451.0		
Chaetomorphia crassa	Green algae			3085.0		2425.0		
Chaetomorphia crassa	Green algae			113000.0		89000.0		
Chamaedoris orientalis	Green algae			1460.0		1420.0		
Chamaedoris orientalis	Green algae			113200.0		109300.0		
Codium divaricatum	Green algae			1302.0		1828.0		
Codium fragile	Green algae			1102.0		1928.0		
Codium divaricatum	Green algae			74000.0		104000.0		
Codium fragile	Green algae			72500.0		126500.0		
Enteromorphia linga	Green algae			0		7340.0		
Enteromorphia linga	Green algae			0		202200.0		
Ulva pertusa	Green algae			580.0		7440.0		
Ulva reticulata	Green algae			0		3530.0		
Ulva pertusa	Green algae			9200.0		117300.0		
Ulva reticulata	Green algae			0		134200.0		
Other								
Calanus finmarchius	Female			1100.0				
	Copepodite V			1000.0				
	Copepodite V			500.0				
Calanus hyperboreus	Copepodite V			20.0				
	Female			600.0				
	Female			800.0				
	Copepodite V			1100.0				
	Copepodite V			300.0				

NO.OF FISH EXAMINED	LENGTH OF FISH	BODY WEIGHT (g)	SEASON	METHOD USED	OTHER	REFERENCE
				10	Dry weight	Fujiwara/Arasaki 1971
				10	Dry weight	Fujiwara/Arasaki 1971
				10	Dry weight	Fujiwara/Arasaki 1971
				10	Dry weight	Fujiwara/Arasaki 1971
				10	Dry weight	Fujiwara/Arasaki 1971
				10	Dry weight	Fujiwara/Arasaki 1971
				10	Dry weight	Fujiwara/Arasaki 1971
				10	Dry weight	Fujiwara/Arasaki 1971
				10	Dry weight	Fujiwara/Arasaki 1971
				10	Dry weight	Fujiwara/Arasaki 1971
				10	Dry weight	Fujiwara/Arasaki 1971
				10	Dry weight	Fujiwara/Arasaki 1971
				10	Dry weight	Fujiwara/Arasaki 1971
				10	Dry weight	Fujiwara/Arasaki 1971
				10	Dry weight	Fujiwara/Arasaki 1971
				10	Dry weight	Fujiwara/Arasaki 1971
				10	Dry weight	Fujiwara/Arasaki 1971
				10	Dry weight	Fujiwara/Arasaki 1971
				10	Dry weight	Fujiwara/Arasaki 1971
				10	Dry weight	Fujiwara/Arasaki 1971
				10	Dry weight	Fujiwara/Arasaki 1971
				10	Dry weight	Fujiwara/Arasaki 1971
				10	Dry weight	Fujiwara/Arasaki 1971
				10	Dry weight	Fujiwara/Arasaki 1971
				10	Dry weight	Fujiwara/Arasaki 1971
				10	Dry weight	Fujiwara/Arasaki 1971
				10	Dry weight	Fujiwara/Arasaki 1971
				10	Dry weight	Fujiwara/Arasaki 1971
				10	Dry weight	Fujiwara/Arasaki 1971
				10	Dry weight	Fujiwara/Arasaki 1971
				10	Dry weight	Fujiwara/Arasaki 1971
				10	Dry weight	Fujiwara/Arasaki 1971
				10	Dry weight	Fujiwara/Arasaki 1971
				10	Dry weight	Fujiwara/Arasaki 1971
				10	Dry weight	Fujiwara/Arasaki 1971
				10	Dry weight	Fujiwara/Arasaki 1971
			April	2, 6	Wet weight	Strom 1979
			May	2, 6	Wet weight	Strom 1979
			June	2, 6	Wet weight	Strom 1979
			March	2, 6	Wet weight	Strom 1979
			April	2, 6	Wet weight	Strom 1979
			May	2, 6	Wet weight	Strom 1979
			May	2, 6	Wet weight	Strom 1979
			June	2, 6	Wet weight	Strom 1979

Simultaneous Determination of TMA and TMAO (10)

Simultaneous determination of TMAO and TMA in marine algae was reported by Fujiwara-Arasaki and Mino (1972). TMAO determination was based on a colorimetric reading at 570 nm of FA condensed with chromotropic acid, released from a rearrangement product of TMAO, dimethylaminomethylol. One portion of the seaweed homogenate containing both TMAO and TMA was tested for TMAO with the above method. To this portion, sodium bisulfite was added to oxidize TMA to TMAO. Then the TMAO determination was performed. TMA was calculated by subtracting the TMAO value of the first homogenate from the second on the dry weight basis.

DMA Determination (11)

The colorimetric determination of DMA was devised by Dyer and Mounsey (1945) who measured DMA as copper dimethyldithiocarbamate according to the method of Dowden (1938). Uno and Yamamoto (1966) also developed a colorimetric method for estimating secondary amines. Ito and Tanimura (1971) improved this method by replacing EtOH with BuOH which increased the sensitivity by 1.5 times.

Ito et al. (1971B) found that steam distillation gave much better recovery (over 97%) and sensitivity than TCA extraction in both methods. Dyer's and Uno's methods using the steam distillation procedure gave similar results. The former is somewhat specific for methylamine and the latter reacts with TMAO. Kawabata et al. (1973) also noted the color produced by primary amines with the method of Dyer and Mounsey (1945).

REFERENCES

Some of the references listed here are not cited in the text. They are nevertheless important and relevant to the subject and make this chapter more comprehensive.

ADAMS, R., FARBER, L., and LERKE, P. 1964. Bacteriology of Spoilage of Fish Muscle II. Incidence of Spoilers During Spoilage. Appl. Microbiol. *12*:277—279.

AMANO, K. 1971. Selected Topics of TMAO (Trimethylamine Oxide) in Fish. Bull. Jpn. Soc. Sci. Fish. *37*(8):784—787.

AMANO, K. and TOZAWA, H. 1969. Irradiation Cleavage of Trimethylamine in Fish Muscle. In: Freezing and Irradiation of Fish. R. Kreuzer (Editor). Fishing News (Books) Ltd., London. pp. 467—471.

AMANO, K. and YAMADA, K. 1964A. A Biological Formation of Formaldehyde in the Muscle Tissue of Gadoid Fish. Bull. Jpn. Soc. Sci. Fish. *30*(5):430—435.

AMANO, K. and YAMADA, K. 1964B. Formaldehyde Formation from TMO by the Action of Pyloric Caeca of Cod. Bull. Jpn. Soc. Sci. Fish. *30*(8): 639–645.

AMANO, K. and YAMADA, K. 1965. The Biological Formation of Formaldehyde in Cod Flesh. In: Technology of Fish Utilization. FAO Symp. pp. 73–76.

AMANO, K., YAMADA, K., and BITO, M. 1963A. Detection and Identification of Formaldehyde in Gadoid Fish. Bull. Jpn. Soc. Sci. Fish. *29*(7): 695–701.

AMANO, K., YAMADA, K., and BITO, M. 1963B. Contents of Formaldehyde and Volatile Amines in Different Tissues of Gadoid Fish. Bull. Jpn. Soc. Sci. Fish. *29*(9):860–864.

AMANO, K., YAMADA, K., HARADA, K., and KAMIMOTO, Y. 1968. Separation and Identification of Volatile Amines From Some Marine Animals by Thin-Layer Chromatography. Bull. Tokai Reg. Fish. Res. Lab. *53*, 95–102.

AMU, L. and DISNEY, J.G. 1973. Quality Changes in West African Marine Fish During Iced Storage. Trop. Sci. *15*(2):125–138.

ANDERSON, D.W., JR. and FELLERS, C.R. 1949. Some Aspects of Trimethylamine Formation in Swordfish. Food Technol. *3*:271–273.

ANDERSON, D.W., JR. and FELLERS, C.R. 1952. The Occurrence of Trimethylamine and Trimethylamine Oxide in Fresh Water Fishes. Food Res. *17*:472–474.

ANDO, Y. and INOUE, K. 1957. Studies on Growth and Toxin Production of *Clostridium botulinum* Type E in Fish Products – I. On the growth in relation to the Oxidation-Reduction Potential in the Fish Flesh. Bull. Jpn. Soc. Sci. Fish. *23*(7,8):458–462.

ANGELINI, P., MERRITT, C., JR., MENDELSOHN, J.M., and KING, F.J. 1975. Effect of Irradiation on Volatile Constituents of Stored Haddock Flesh. J. Food Sci. *40*:197–199.

ANTONACOPOULOS, N. 1971. Comparison of Sensory and Objective Methods for Quality Evaluation of Fresh and Frozen Saltwater Fish. In: Fish Inspection and Quality Control. R. Kreuzer, (Editor). Fishing News (Books) Ltd., London. pp. 180–182.

ASANO, M. and SATO, H. 1954. Biochemical Studies on Octopus I. Trimethylamine and Trimethylamine Oxide Content of Octopus. Tohoku J. Agric. Res. *3*:191–195.

BABBITT, J.K. 1977. Personal communication.

BABBITT, J.K., CRAWFORD, D.L., and LAW, D.K. 1972. Decomposition of Trimethylamine Oxide and Changes in Protein Extractability During Frozen Storage of Minced and Intact Hake *(Merluccius productus)* Muscle. J. Agric. Food Chem. *20*:1052–1054.

BAILEY, M.E., FIEGER, E.A., and NOVAK, A.F. 1956. Objective Tests Applicable to Quality Studies of Ice Stored Shrimp. Food Res. *21*:611–619.

274 CHEMISTRY & BIOCHEMISTRY OF MARINE FOOD PRODUCTS

BAIRD, E.A. and WOOD, A.J. 1944. Reduction of Trimethylamine Oxide by Bacteria. J. Fish. Res. Bd. Can. 6(3):243–244.

BAKER, J. and CHAYKIN, S. 1960. The Biosynthesis of Trimethylamine-N-Oxide. Biochem. Biophys. Acta. 41:548–550.

BAKER, J.R. and CHAYKIN, S. 1962. The Biosynthesis of Trimethylamine-N-Oxide. J. Biol. Chem. 237(4):1309–1313.

BAKER, J.R., STRUEMPLER, A., and CHAYKIN, S. 1963. A Comparative Study of Trimethylamine-N-Oxide Biosynthesis. Biochem. Biophys. Acta 71:58–64.

BALAKRISHNAN NAIR, R., THARAMANI, P.K., and LAHIRY, N.L. 1971. Studies on Chilled Storage of Fresh Water Fish I. Changes Occurring During Iced Storage. J. Food. Sci. Technol. 8(6):53–56.

BANKS, A. 1965. Technological Problems in the Control of Deteriorative Changes in Frozen Fish Requiring More Knowledge from Fundamental Research. In: Technology of Fish Utilization; FAO Symp. pp. 89–91.

BARNES, H. and BLACKSTOCK, J. 1974. The Separation and Estimation of Free Amino Acids, Trimethylamine Oxide, and Betaine in Tissues and Body Fluids of Marine Invertebrates. J. Exp. Mar. Biol. Ecol. 16:29–45.

BARRETT, I., BRINNER, L., BROWN, W.D., DOLEV, A., KWON, T.W., LITTLE, A., OLCOTT, H.S., SCHAEFER, M.B., and SCHRADER, P. 1965. Changes in Tuna Quality, and Associated Biochemical Changes, During Handling and Storage Aboard Fishing Vessels. Food Technol. 19(12):108–117.

BEATTY, S.A. 1938. Studies of Fish Spoilage II. The Origin of Trimethylamine Produced During the Spoilage of Cod Muscle Press Juice. J. Fish. Res. Bd. Can. 4:63–68.

BEATTY, S.A. 1939. Studies of Fish Spoilage III. The Trimethylamine Oxide Content of the Muscles on Nova Scotia Fish. J. Fish. Res. Bd. Can. 4(4):229–232.

BEATTY, S.A. and COLLINS, V.K. 1939. Studies of Fish Spoilage VI. The Breakdown of Carbohydrates, Proteins and Amino Acids During Spoilage of Cod Muscle Press Juice. J. Fish. Res. Bd. Can. 4:412–423.

BEATTY, S.A. and COLLINS, V.K. 1940. Studies of Fish Spoilage VII. Dimethylamine Production in the Spoilage of Cod Muscle Press Juice. J. Fish. Res. Bd. Can. 5:32–35.

BEATTY, S.A. and GIBBONS, N.E. 1937. The Measurement of Spoilage in Fish. J. Biol. Bd. Can. 3:77–91.

BEDFORD, R.H. 1933. Marine Bacteria of the Northern Pacific Ocean. The Temperature Range of Growth. Contrib. Can. Biol. Fish. 7:433–438.

BENOIT, G.J., JR. and NORRIS, E.R. 1945. Studies on Trimethylamine Oxide II. The Origin of TMAO in Young Salmon. J. Biol. Chem. 158(2):439–442.

BETHEA, S. and AMBROSE, M.E. 1962. Comparison of pH, TMA Content, and Picric Acid Turbidity as Indices of Iced Shrimp Quality.   Commer. Fish. Rev. 24(3):7–10.

BETHEA, S. and HILLIG, F.   1965.   Determination of Trimethylamine-Nitrogen in Extracts and in Volatile Fraction of Fish.   J. Assoc. Off. Anal. Chem. 48(4):731–735.

BICKEL, M.H.   1969.   The Pharmacology and Biochemistry of N-Oxides. Pharmacol. Rev. 21(4):325–355.

BILINSKI, E.   1960.   Biosynthesis of Trimethylammonium Compounds in Aquatic Animals II.   Formation of Trimethlyamine Oxide and Betaine from C(14)-Labelled Compounds by Lobster (Homarus americanus). J. Fish. Res. Bd. Can. 17(6):895–902.

BILINSKI, E.   1961.   Biosynthesis of Trimethylammonium Compounds in Aquatic Animals II.   Role of Betaine in the Formation of Trimethylamine Oxide by Lobster (Homarus americanus).   J. Fish. Res. Bd. Can. 18(2): 285–286.

BILINSKI, E.   1962.   Biosynthesis of Trimethlyammonium Compounds in Aquatic Animals III.   Choline Metabolism in Marine Crustacea.   J. Fish. Res. Bd. Can. 19(3):505–510.

BILINSKI, E.   1964.   Biosynthesis of Trimethylammonium Compounds in Aquatic Animals IV.   Precursors of Trimethylamine Oxide and Betaine in Marine Teleosts.   J. Fish. Res. Bd. Can. 21(4):765–771.

BILINSKI, E. and FOUGERE, H.   1959.   The Effect of Sodium Chloride on Proteolysis and on the Fate of Amino Acids Present in the Muscle of Codfish (Gadus Callarias).   J. Fish. Res. Bd. Can. 16(5):747–754.

BLIGH, E.G.   1971.   Specific Problems in the Quality Assessment of Freshwater Fish.   In: Fish Inspection and Quality Control.   R. Kreuzer (Editor). Fishing News (Books) Ltd., London. pp. 81–85.

BOLAND, F.E. and PAIGE, D.D.   1971.   Collaborative Study of a Method for the Determination of Trimethylamine Nitrogen in Fish.   J. Assoc. Off. Anal. Chem. 54(3):725–727.

BOTTA, J.R. and SHAW, D.H.   1975.   Chemical and Sensory Analysis of Roughhead Grenadier (Macrourus berglax) Stored in Ice.   J. Food Sci. 40: 1249–1252.

BOTTA, J.R. and SHAW, D.H.   1976.   Chemical and Sensory Analysis of Roundnose Grenadier (Coryphaenoides rupestris) Stored in Ice.   J. Food Sci. 41:1285–1288.

BOULTON, C.A. and LARGE, P.J.   1975.   Oxidation on N-Alkyl- and NN-Dialkylhydroxylamines by Partially Purified Preparations of TMA Mono-Oxygenase from Pseudomonas aminovorans.   FEBS Lett. 55(1):286–290.

BOULTON, C.A. and LARGE, P.J.   1977.   Synthesis of Certain Assimilatory and Dissimilatory Enzymes During Bacterial Adaptation to Growth on Tri-methylamine.   J. Gen. Microbiol. 101:151–156.

BOULTON, C.A., CRABBE, M.J.C., and LARGE, P.J.   1974.   Microbial Oxidation of Amines: Partial Purification of a Trimethylamine Mono-Oxygenase from *Pseudomonas aminovorans* and its Role in Growth on Trimethylamine. Biochem. J. *140*:253–263.

BRULL, L. and NIZET, E. 1953. Blood and Urine Constituents of *Lophius piscatorius* L. J. Mar. Biol. Assoc. U.K. *32*: 321–328.

BRULL, L., NIZET, E., and VERNEY, E.B. 1953. Blood Perfusion of the Kidney of *Lophius piscatorius* L. J. Mar. Biol. Assoc. U.K. *32*:329–336.

BUDD, J.A. and SPENCER, C.P. 1968. The Utilization of Alkylated Amines by Marine Bacteria. Mar. Biol. 2:92–101.

BURT, J.R., GIBSON, D.M., JASON, A.C., and SANDERS, H.R. 1976. Comparison of Methods of Freshness Assessment of Wet Fish II. Instrumental and Chemical Assessments of Boxed Experimental Fish. J. Food Technol. *11*:73–89.

BYSTEDT, J. and LILJEMARK, A. 1956. FAO Interim Committee Rep. on Fish Handling and Processing, Ministry of Agriculture, Fisheries and Food, The Hague, The Netherlands, Meeting at Rotterdam, June 25–29.

BYSTEDT, J., SWENNE, L., and AAS, H.W. 1959. Determination of Trimethylamine Oxide in Fish Muscle. J. Sci. Food Agric. *10*:301–304.

CAMPBELL, L.L., JR. and WILLIAMS, O.B. 1952. The Bacteriology of Gulf Coast Shrimp IV. Bacteriological, Chemical, and Organoleptic Changes with Ice Storage. Food Technol. 6:125–126.

CANTONI, C. and ARDEMAGNI, A. 1977. Determination of Trimethylamine Oxide with Microdiffusion Technique. Arch. Vet. Ital. *28*(3,4):79–82.

CARDIN, A., BILINSKI, E., MALTAIS, F., BORDELEAU, M.A., and LAFRAMBOISE, A. 1961. Chemical Characteristics of Salted Cod. J. Fish. Res. Bd. Can. *18*(5):851–858.

CASTELL, C.H. 1946. Effect of Trimethylamine Oxide on the Growth of Bacteria. J. Fish. Res. Bd. Can. 6(7):491–497.

CASTELL, C.H. 1949A. The Several Characteristics of Trimethylamine and Their Effect on Sea Fish Spoilage. Food Can. 9(4):44–45.

CASTELL, C.H. 1949B. Effect of Nitrite on Reduction of Trimethylamine Oxide in Cod Fillets. J. Fish. Res. Bd. Can. 7(7):421–429.

CASTELL, C.H. 1971. Metal-Catalyzed Lipid Oxidation and Changes of Proteins in Fish. J. Am. Oil Chem. Soc. *48*:1645–1649.

CASTELL, C.H. and ANDERSON, G.W. 1948. Bacteria Associated with Spoilage of Cod Fillets. J. Fish. Res. Bd. Can. 7(6)370–377.

CASTELL, C.H. and GILES, J.G. 1961. Spoilage of Fish in the Vessels at Sea 7. Further Studies on Seasonal Variations in the Landed Quality of Gutted, Trawler-Caught Atlantic Cod and Haddock. J. Fish Res. Bd. Can. *18*(3):295–302.

CASTELL, C.H. and GREENOUGH, M.F. 1957. The Action of *Pseudomonas* on Fish Muscle I. Organisms Responsible for Odours Produced During Incipient Spoilage of Chilled Fish Muscle. J. Fish. Res. Bd. Can. *14*(4): 617–625.

CASTELL, C.H. and GREENOUGH, M.F. 1958. Grading Fish for Quality 3. Grading of Recently Cut Fillets. J. Fish. Res. Bd. Can. *15*(49):729–748.

CASTELL, C.H. and GREENOUGH, M.F. 1959. The Action of *Pseudomonas* on Fish Muscle 4. Relation Between Substrate Composition and the Development of Odours by *Pseudomonas fragi*. J. Fish. Res. Bd. Can. *16*(1): 21–31.

CASTELL, C.H. and MACCALLUM, W.A. 1953. Relative Importance of the Factors Causing Spoilage of Fish in Boats at Sea. Fish. Res. Bd. Can. Prog. Rep., Atl. Coast Stn. *55*:17–23.

CASTELL, C.H. and SNOW, J.M. 1951. Reduction of Trimethylamine Oxide by Bacterial Enzymes. J. Fish. Res. Bd. Can. *8*(4):195–206.

CASTELL, C.H. and TRIGGS, R.E. 1955. Spoilage of Haddock in the Trawler at Sea: The Measurement of Spoilage and Standards of Quality. J. Fish. Res. Bd. Can. *12*(3):329–341.

CASTELL, C.H., ANDERSON, G.W., and PIVNICK, H. 1948. Relation of Bacterial Counts to Quality of Cod Fillets. J. Fish. Res. Bd. Can. *7*(6): 378–388.

CASTELL, C.H., GREENOUGH, M.F., RODGERS, R.S., and MACFARLAND, A.S. 1958. Grading Fish for Quality 1. Trimethylamine Values of Fillets Cut from Graded Fish. J. Fish. Res. Bd. Can. *15*(4):701–716.

CASTELL, C.H., ELSON, M.F., and GILES, J.G. 1961. Grading Fish for Quality 4. Variations in the Relation Between Trimethlyamine Values and Grades for Gutted, Trawler-Caught Atlantic Cod and Haddock. J. Fish. Res. Bd. Can. *18*(3):303–310.

CASTELL, C.H., BISHOP, D.M., and NEAL, W.E. 1968. Production of TMA in Frozen Cod Muscle. J. Fish. Res. Bd. Can. *25*(5):921–933.

CASTELL, C.H., NEAL, W., and SMITH, B. 1970. Formation of Dimethylamine in Stored Frozen Sea Fish. J. Fish. Res. Bd. Can. *27*(10):1685–1690.

CASTELL, C.H., SMITH, B., and NEAL, W. 1971. Production of Dimethylamine in Muscle of Several Species of Gadoid Fish During Frozen Storage, Especially in Relation to Presence of Dark Muscle. J. Fish. Res. Bd. Can. *28*(1):1–5.

CASTELL, C.H., NEAL, W.B., and DALE, J. 1973. Comparison of Changes in Trimethylamine, Dimethylamine, and Extractable Protein in Iced and Frozen Gadoid Fillets. J. Fish. Res. Bd. Can. *30*(8):1246–1248.

CASTELL, C.H., SMITH, B., and DYER, W.J. 1974. Simultaneous Measurements of Trimethylamine and Dimethylamine in Fish, and Their Use for Estimating Quality of Frozen-Stored Gadoid Fish. J. Fish. Res. Bd. Can. *31* (4):383–389.

CHAI, T., CHEN, C., ROSEN, A., and LEVIN, R.E. 1968. Detection and Incidence of Specific Species of Spoilage Bacteria on Fish II. Relative Incidence of *Pseudomonas putrefaciens* and Fluorescent Pseudomonads on Haddock Fillets.   Appl. Microbiol. *16*(11):1738−1741.

CHANG, G.W. CHANG, W.L., and LEW, K.B.K.   1976.   TMA-specific Electrode for Fish Quality Control.   J. Food Sci. *41*:723−724.

CHUNG, J.R. and BYUN, S.M.   1977.   Radurization of Korean Horse Mackerel.   Final Rep for Oct. 1974 through Dec. 1976.   Int. Atomic Agency, IAEA Res. Contr. No. 1476/RB.

CHUNG, J.R., KIM, S.I., and LEE, M.C.   1976A.   Irradiation Preservation of Korean Shellfish.   Korean J. Food Sci. Technol. *8*(3):147−160.

CHUNG, J.R., KIM, S.I., and LEE, M.C.   1976B.   Irradiation Preservation of Korean Fishes.   Part II.   Korean J. Food Sci. Technol. *8*(3):161−171.

COBB, B.F., III. and VANDERZANT, C.   1971.   Biochemical Changes in Shrimp Inoculated with *Pseudomonas, Bacillus,* and a *Coryneform* Bacterium.   J. Milk Food Technol. *34*(11):533−540.

COBB, B.F., III., ALANIZ, I., and THOMPSON, C.A., JR.   1973.   Biochemical and Microbial Studies on Shrimp: Volatile Nitrogen and Amino Nitrogen Analysis.   J. Food Sci. *38*:431−436.

COHEN, J.J., KRUPP, M.A., and CHIDSEY, C.A., III.   1958.   Renal Conservation of Trimethylamine Oxide by the Spiny Dogfish, *Squalus acanthias.*   Am. J. Physiol. *194*(2):229−235.

COLBY, J. and ZATMAN, L.J.   1973.   Trimethylamine Metabolism in Obligate and Facultative Methylotrophs.   Biochem. J. *132*:101−112.

COLBY, J. and ZATMAN, L.J.   1974.   Purification and properties of the Trimethylamine Dehydrogenase of Bacterium 4B6.   Biochem. J. *143*: 555−567.

COLLINS, V.K.   1941.   Studies of Fish Spoilage VIII.   Volatile Acid of Cod Muscle Press Juice.   J. Fish Res. Bd. Can. *5*(3):197−207.

COLLINS, J., SEAGRAN, H., and IVERSON, J.   1960.   Processing and Quality Studies of Shrimp Held in Refrigerated Sea Water and Ice.   Commer. Fish. Rev. *22*(4):1−5.

CONNELL, J.J.,   1969.   Changes in the Eating Quality of Frozen Stored Cod and Associated Chemical and Physical Changes.   In: Freezing and Irradiation of Fish.   R. Kreuzer, (Editor). Fishing News (Books) Ltd., London. pp. 323−338.

CONNELL, J.J. and HOWGATE, P.F.   1968.   Sensory and Objective Measurements of the Quality of Frozen Stored Cod of Different Initial Freshness.   J. Sci. Food Agric. *19*:342−354.

CONWAY, E.J.   1947.   Microdiffusion Analysis and Volumetric Error. 2nd Edition.   Crosby Lockwood and Son Ltd., London.

CONWAY, E.J. and BYRNE, A.   1933.   LXI. An Absorption Apparatus for the Micro-Determination of Certain Volatile Substances.   I.   The Micro-Determination of Ammonia.   Biochem. J. *27*:419−429.

COWEY, C.B. and PARRY, G.   1963.   The Non-Protein Nitrogenous Constituents of the Muscle of Parr and Smolt Stages of the Atlantic Salmon

(Salmo salar). Comp. Biochem. Physiol. *8*:47–51.

CRAIG, J.C., DWYER, F.P., GLAZER, A.N., and HORNING, E.C. 1961. Tertiary Amine Oxide Rearrangements I. Mechanism. J. Am. Chem. Soc. *83*:1871–1878.

CRAWFORD, D.L., LAW, D.K., BABBIT, J.K., and MCGILL, L.A. 1979. Comparative Stability and Desirability of Frozen Pacific Hake Fillet and Minced Flesh Blocks. J. Food Sci. *44*(2):363–367.

CROMWELL, B.T. 1950. The Micro-Estimation and Origin of Trimethylamine in *Chenopodium vulvaria* L. Biochem. J. *46*:578–582.

DAIKOKU, T. 1977. Changes and Effects of Trimethylamine Oxide in Freshwater Fishes, the Guppies, *Poecilia reticulata* and the Goldfish, *Carassium auratus*. Annot. Zool. Jpn. *50*(4):203–211.

DAVIES, W.L. and GILL, E. 1936. Investigations on Fishy Flavor. J. Soc. Chem. Ind. *55*:141T–146T.

DEBEVERE, J.M. and VOETS, J.P. 1971. Microbiological Changes in Prepacked Cod Fillets in Relation to the Oxygen Permeability of the Film. J. Appl. Bacteriol. *34*(3):507–513.

DEBEVERE, J.M. and VOETS, J.P. 1974. Microbiological Changes in Prepacked Plaice in Relation to the Oxygen Permeability of the Film. Lebenism. Wiss. Technol. *7*(2):73–75.

DE LA HUERGA, J. and POPPER, H. 1952. Factors Influencing Choline Absorption in the Intestinal Tract. J. Clin. Invest. *31*:598–603. Chem. Abstr. *46* 9683B.

DE LA HUERGA, J., POPPER, H., and STEIGMANN, F. 1951. Urinary Excretion of Choline and Trimethylamine After Intravenous Administration of Choline in Liver Diseases. J. Lab. Clin. Med. *38*:904–910. Chem. Abstr. *46* 3646A, 1952.

DE LA HUERGA, J., GYORGY, P., WALDSTEIN, S., KATZ, R., and POPPER, H. 1953. The Effects of Antimicrobial Agents Upon Choline Degradation in the Intestinal Tract. J. Clin. Invest. *32*:1117–1120. Chem. Abstr. *48*, 1578H, 1954.

DI CORCIA, A., FRITZ, D., and BRUNER, F. 1970. Use of Graphitized Carbon Black for Linear Gas-Liquid-Solid Chromatography of Polar Low-Boiling Compounds. Anal. Chem. *42*(13):1500–1504.

DIEMAIR, W. 1965. Gas Chromatography in the Analysis of Volatile Odor and Flavor Components in Fish Flesh. In: Technology of Fish Utilization. FAO Symp. pp. 205–206.

DINGLE, J.R. and HINES, J.A. 1975. Protein Instability in Minced Flesh From Fillets and Frames of Several Commercial Atlantic Fishes During Storage at −5C. J. Fish. Res. Bd. Can. *32*:775–783.

DINGLE, J.R., KEITH, R.A., and LALL, B. 1977. Protein Instability in Frozen Storage Induced in Minced Muscle of Flatfishes by Mixture with Muscle of Red Hake. Can. Inst. Food Sci. Technol. J. *10*(3):143–146.

DOWDEN, H.C. 1938. The Determination of Small Amounts of Dimethylamine in Biological Fluids. Biochem. J. *32*:455–459.

DUSSAULT, H.P. 1957. TMA Test for Evaluating the Quality of Rosefish Fillets. Fish. Res. Bd. Can. Progr. Rep. Atl. Coast Stn. *67*.

DYER, F.E. and WOOD, A.J. 1947. Action of Enterobacteriaceae on Choline and Related Compounds. J. Fish. Res. Bd. Can. *7*(1):17–21.

DYER, W.J. 1943. A Color Test for the Measurement of Freshness of Sea Fish by Trimethylamine Estimation. Fish. Res. Bd. Can. Progr. Rep. Atl. Coast Stn. *34*:4–5.

DYER, W.J. 1945. Amines in Fish Muscle I. Colorimetric Determination of Trimethylamine as the Picrate Salt. J. Fish. Res. Bd. Can. *6*: 351–358.

DYER, W.J. 1949. Bacterial Reduction of Sodium Nitrite and Formation of Trimethylamine in Fish. J. Fish. Res. Bd. Can. *7*(8):461–470.

DYER, W.J. 1952. Amines in Fish Muscle VI. Trimethylamine Oxide Content of Fish and Marine Invertebrates. J. Fish. Res. Bd. Can. *8*(5): 314–324.

DYER, W.J. 1959. Report on Trimethylamine in Fish. J. Assoc. Off. Anal. Chem. *42*(2):292–294.

DYER, W.J. and HILTZ, D.F. 1974. Sensitivity of Hake Muscle to Frozen Storage. Fisheries and Marine Service. Halifax Lab. New Ser. Circ. No. 45.

DYER, W.J. and MOUNSEY, Y.A. 1945. Amines in Fish Muscle II. Development of Trimethylamine and Other Amines. J. Fish. Res. Bd. Can. *6*(5): 359–367.

DYER, W.J., DYER, F.E., and SNOW, J.M. 1952. Amines in Fish Muscle V. Trimethylamine Oxide Estimation. J. Fish. Res. Bd. Can. *8*(5): 309–313.

DYER, W.J., FRASER, D.I., MACINTOSH, R.G., and MYER, M. 1964. Cooking Method and Palatability of Frozen Cod Fillets of Various Qualities. J. Fish. Res. Bd. Can. *21*(3):577–589.

EADY, R.R. and LARGE, P.J. 1969. Bacterial Oxidation of Dimethylamine, a New Mono-Oxygenase Reaction. Biochem. J. *111*(5):37P–38P.

EADY, R.R., JARMAN, T.R., and LARGE, P.J. 1971. Microbial Oxidation of Amines. Partial Purification of a Mixed-Function Secondary Amine Oxidase System from *Pseudomonas aminovorans* that Contains an Enzymatically Active Cytochrome P-420-Type Hemoprotein. Biochem. J. *125*(2): 449–459.

EHIRA, S. and UCHIYAMA, H. 1974. Freshness-Lowering Rates of Cod and Sea Bream Viewed from Changes in Bacterial Count. Total Volatile Base and Trimethylamine-Nitrogen, and ATP Related Compounds. Bull. Jpn. Soc. Sci. Fish. *40*(5):479–487.

EHRENBERG, A.S.C. and SHEWAN, J.M. 1955. Volatile Bases and Sensory Quality-Factors in Iced White Fish. J. Sci. Food Agric. *6*: 207–217.

ELLIOTT, R.P. 1952. Reduction of Trimethylamine Oxide in Dogfish Flesh. Food Res. *17*:225–234.

ENDO, K., FUJITA, M., and SHIMIZU, W.   1962A.   Muscle of Aquatic Animals. XXX.   Free Amino Acids, Trimethylamine Oxide, and Betaine in Squids.   Bull. Jpn. Soc. Sci. Fish. 28:833–836.

ENDO, K., FUJITA, M., and SHIMIZU, W.   1962B.   Muscle of Aquatic Animals. XXXIII.   Seasonal Variation of Nitrogenous Extractives in Squid Muscle.   Bull. Jpn. Soc. Sci. Fish. 28:1099–1103.

ENDO, E., KISHIMOTO, R., YAMAMOTO, Y., and SHIMIZU, Y.   1974. Seasonal Variations in Chemical Constituents of Yellowtail Muscle—II Nitrogenous Extractives.   Bull. Jpn. Soc. Sci. Fish. 40(1):67–72.

FARBER, L.   1952.   A Comparison of Various Methods for the Determination of Spoilage in Fish.   Food Technol. 6:319–324.

FARBER, L.   1963.   Quality Evaluation Studies of Fish and Shellfish from Certain Northern European Waters.   Food Technol. 17:476–480.

FARBER, L.   1965A.   Freshness Tests.   In: Fish as Food.   George Borgstrom (Editor). Academic Press, New York. Vol. 4. pp. 65–126.

FARBER, L.   1965B.   Review of the VRS Method for the Determination of Spoilage of Fish.   In: The Technology of Fish Utilization.   FAO Symp., pp. 184–193.

FARBER, L. and FERRO, M.   1956.   Volatile Reducing Substances (VRS) and Volatile Nitrogen Compounds in Relation to Spoilage in Canned Fish. Food Technol. 10:303–304.

FARBER, L. and LERKE, P.   1961.   Studies on the Evaluation of Freshness and on the Estimation of the Storage Life of Raw Fishery Products. Food Technol. 25(4):191–196.

FERRIS, J.P., GERWE, R.D., and GAPSKI, G.R.   1967.   Detoxication Mechanisms. II.   The Iron-Catalyzed Dealkylation of Trimethylamine Oxide. J. Am. Chem. Soc. 89(20):5270–5275.

FORSTER, R.P. and GOLDSTEIN, L.   1976.   Intracellular Osmoregulatory Role of Amino Acids and Urea in Marine Elasmobranchs.   Am. J. Physiol. 230(4):925–931.

FUJII, T., ISHIDA, Y., and KADOTA, H.   1974.   Utilization of Trimethylamine by a Penicillium Strain Isolated from Salted Fish.   Bull. Jpn. Soc. Sci. Fish. 40(2):1309.

FUJIMOTO, K., MARUYAMA, M., and KANEDA, T.   1968.   Studies on the Brown Discoloration of Fish Products—I.   Factors Affecting the Discoloration.   Bull. Jpn. Soc. Sci. Fish. 34(6):519–523.

FUJITA, M., ENDO, K., and SIMIZU, W.   1972.   Studies on Muscle of Aquatic Animals—XXXXVI.   Free Amino Acids, Trimethylamine Oxide, and Betaine in Shrimp Muscle.   Kinki Daigaku Nogakubu Kiyo. 5:61–67.

FUJIWANA-ARASAKI, T. and MINO, N.   1972.   The Distribution of Trimethylamine and Trimethylamine Oxide in Marine Algae.   Proc. 7th Int. Seaweed Symp. Aug. 8–12, 1971. Sapporo, Japan. pp. 506–510.

GIBSON, D.M., HENDRIE, M.S., HOUSTON, N.C., and HOBBS, G. 1977.

The Identification of Some Gram Negative Heterotrophic Aquatic Bacteria. In: Aquatic Microbiology. F.A. Skinner and J.M. Shewan (Editors). Society for Applied Bacteriology. Symp. Ser. No. 6. Academic Press, New York. pp. 135–159.

GOLDSTEIN, L. and DEWITT-HARLEY, S. 1973. Trimethylamine Oxidase of Nurse Shark Liver and Its Relation to Mammalian Mixed Function Amine Oxidase. Comp. Biochem. Physiol. B 45(4):895–903.

GOLDSTEIN, L. and FUNKHOUSER, D. 1972. Biosynthesis of Trimethylamine Oxide in the Nurse Shark, *Ginglymostoma cirratum*. Comp. Biochem. Physiol. A 42:51–57.

GOLDSTEIN, L., HARTMAN, S.C., and FORSTER, R.P. 1967. On the Origin of Trimethylamine Oxide in the Spiny Dogfish, *Squalus acanthias*. Comp. Biochem. Physiol. 21:719–722.

GOOD, C.M. and STERN, J.A. 1955. The Effect of Iced and Frozen Storage Upon the Trimethylamine Content of Flounder *(Parophrys vetulus)* Muscle. Food Technol. 9:327–331.

GRIFFITHS, F.P. 1937. A Review of the Bacteriology of Fresh Marine Fishery Products. Food Res. 2:121–134.

GROLLMAN, A., 1929. The Urine of the Goose Fish *(Lophius piscatorius)*: Its Nitrogenous Constituents with Special Reference to the Presence In It of Trimethylamine Oxide. J. Biol. Chem. 781:267–278.

GRONINGER, H.S. 1958. Fish Spoilage I. Determination of Bacterial Metabolites by Gas Chromatography. Commer. Fish. Rev. 20(11):23–26.

GRONINGER, H.S. 1959. The Occurrence and Significance of Trimethylamine Oxide in Marine Animals. U.S. Fish and Wildl. Serv. Spec. Sci. Rep.—Fish. 333.

GRUGER, E.H., JR. 1972. Chromatographic Analyses of Volatile Amines in Marine Fish. J. Agric. Food Chem. 20(4):781–785.

HAMED, M.G.E. and ADLY, Z.S. 1974. A Contribution to the Study of Free Tyrosine, Trimethylamine, and Ammonia as Measures of the Degree of Deterioration of Dehydrated Shrimp. Egypt. J. Food Sci. 2(1):79–86.

HARADA, K. 1975. Studies on Enzyme Catalyzing the Formation of Formaldehyde and Dimethylamine in Tissues of Fishes and Shells. J. Shimonoseki Univ. Fish. 23(3):163–241.

HARADA, K. and YAMADA, K. 1970. Studies on the Production of Formaldehyde and Dimethylamine in Decapodan Mollusca. Suisan Daigakko Kenkyu Hokoku. 18(3):296–302.

HARADA, K. and YAMADA, K. 1971A. Studies on the Production of Formaldehyde and Dimethylamine in Bivalvian Mollusca. Suisan Daigakko Kenkyu Hokoku. 19(2–3):91–94.

HARADA, K. and YAMADA, K. 1971B. Some Properties of a Formaldehyde and Dimethylamine-Forming Enzyme Obtained from *Barbatia virescens*. Suisan Daigakko Kenkyu Hokoku.19(2–3):95–103.

HARADA, K. and YAMADA, K.   1971C.   Relation Between Trimethylamine Oxide Content and Formation of Formaldehyde and Dimethylamine in Gastropod.   Suisan Daigakko Kenkyu Hokoku. 20(1):35–40.

HARADA, K., ANAN, T., KII, K., and YAMADA, K.   1967.   Studies on the Separation and Quantitative Determination of Volatile Amines in Fish and Shellfish—I. Suisan Daigakko Kenkyu Hokoku. 16(1):11–15.

HARADA, K., FUJIMOTO, T., and YAMADA, K.   1968.   Distribution of Trimethylamine Oxide in Fish and Other Aquatic Animals I. Decapoda. Suisan Daigakko Kenkyu Hokoku. 17(2):87–95.

HARADA, K., TAKEDA, J., and YAMADA, K.   1970.   Distribution of Trimethylamine Oxide In Fishes and Other Aquatic Animals II.   Bivalvian Mollusca.   Suisan Daigakko Kenkyu Hokoku. 18(3):287–295.

HARADA, K., YAMAMOTO, Y., and YAMADA, K.   1971.   Distribution of Trimethylamine Oxide in Fishes and Other Aquatic Animals III.   Gastropodan Mollusca.   Suisan Daigakko Kenkyu Hokoku. 19:105–114.

HARADA, K., DEHIRA, T., and YAMADA, K.   1972.   Distribution of Trimethylamine Oxide in Fishes and Other Aquatic Animals—IV.   Arthropods, Echinoderms and Other Invertebrates.   Suisan Daigakko Kenkyu Hokoku. 20(3):249–264.

HASHIMOTO, Y. and OKAICHI, T.   1957.   A Modification of the Dyer Method.   Bull. Jpn. Soc. Sci. Fish. 23(5):269–272.

HASHIMOTO, Y. and OKAICHI, T.   1958A.   Trimethylamine Oxide in Fish Muscle I.   The Origin of TMAO in Goldfish Muscle.   Bull. Jpn. Soc. Sci. Fish. 24(8):640–644.

HASHIMOTO, Y. and OKAICHI, T.   1958B.   Trimethylamine Oxide in Fish Muscle II.   TMAO in the Muscle of Eels Kept in Fresh and Brackish Water. Bull. Jpn. Soc. Sci. Fish. 24(8):645–647.

HATTORI, Y.   1940.   Trimethylamine in Meats and Fishes IV. Mechanism of the Formation of Formaldehyde from Trimethylamine Oxide.   J. Pharm. Soc. Jpn. 60:24–45.

HAYASHI, J.   1969.   Raw Fish Flavor and Trimethylamine Oxide. Rinsho Eiyo 35(5):539.

HAYASHI, M., KUNISAKI, N., SAKAKIBARA, Y., and TAKEUCHI, T. 1974. Studies on Determination of Dimethylamine in Foods I.   On Possibility of Chemical Formation of Dimethylamine from Trimethylamine-N-Oxide Under Steam Distillation with Sodium Hydroxide.   Shokuhin Eiseigaku Zasshi. 15(1):48–50.

HAYASHI, T., YAMAGUCHI, K., and KONOSU, S.   1978.   Studies on Flavor Components in Boiled Crabs II.   Nucleotides and Organic Bases in the Extracts.   Bull. Jpn. Soc. Sci. Fish. 44(12):1357–1362.

HEGEMANN, M.   1964.   Endogenous Formation of Trimethylamine Oxide in Perch and Pike.   Naturwissenschaften. 51(14):343–344.   Chem. Abstr. 61, 13668D.

284   CHEMISTRY & BIOCHEMISTRY OF MARINE FOOD PRODUCTS

HERBERT, A. and SHEWAN, J.M.   1976.   Roles Played by Bacteria and Autolytic Enzymes in the Production of Volatile Sulphides in Spoiling North Sea Cod *(Gadus morhua)*.   J. Sci. Food Agric. 27:89–94.

HERBERT, R.A., HENDRIE, M.S., GIBSON, D.M., and SHEWAN, J.M. 1971. Bacteria Active in the Spoilage of Certain Sea Foods.   J. Appl. Bacteriol. 34(1):41–50.

HESS, E.   1934.   Effects of Low Temperatures on the Growth of Marine Bacteria.   Contrib. Can. Biol. Fish. 8:491–505.

HESS, E.   1941.   A Test to Estimate the Keeping Quality of Fresh Fish. Fish. Res. Bd. Can. Progr. Rep. Atl. Coast Stn. 30, 10–12.

HIGHLANDS, M.E. and WILLIAMS, O.B.   1944.   A Bacteriological Survey of Sardine Canning in Maine.   Food Res. 9:34–41.

HILLIG, F., SHELTON, L.R., JR., LOUGHREY, J.H., and EISNER, J. 1958. Chemical Indices of Decomposition in Cod.   J. Assoc. Off. Anal. Chem. 41(4): 763–776.

HILLIG, F., SHELTON, L.R., JR., and LOUGHREY, J.H.   1962A.   Summary of Chemical Data on Progressive Decomposition Studies of Cod, Haddock, and Perch.   J. Assoc. Off. Anal. Chem. 45(3):724–731.

HILLIG, F., SHELTON, L.R., JR., LOUGHREY, J.H., BETHEA, S., and CAMPBELL, C.M.   1962B.   Chemical Indices of Decomposition in Cod Stored in Natural Ice and in Chlortetracycline (CTC) Ice.   J. Assoc. Off. Anal. Chem. 45(3):694–724.

HILTZ, D.F., LALL, B.S., LEMON, D.W., and DYER, W.J.   1976.   Deteriorative Changes During Frozen Storage in Fillets and Minced Flesh of Silver Hake *(Merluccius bilinearis)* Processed from Round Fish Held in Ice and Refrigerated Sea Water.   J. Fish. Res. Bd. Can. 33:2560–2567.

HILTZ, D.F., NORTH, D.H., LALL, B.S., and KEITH, R.A.   1977.   Storage Life of Refrozen Silver Hake *(Merluccius bilinearis)* Processed as Fillets and Minced Flesh from Thawed, Stored, Round-Frozen Fish.   J. Fish. Res. Bd. Can. 34:2369–2373.

HJORTH-HANSEN, S.   1952.   Method for the Determination of the Oxide of Trimethylamine.   Anal. Chim. Acta. 6:438–441.   Chem. Abstr. 46:7940C.

HOLMOV, V.P.   1939.   Chemical Studies on the Deterioration of Fish. II. The Trimethylamine Content as Indicator of Spoilage.   Vopr. Pitan. 8(4): 73–80.

HOOGLAND, P.L.   1958.   Grading Fish for Quality 2.   Statistical Analysis of the Results of Experiments Regarding Grades and Trimethylamine Values. J. Fish. Res. Bd. Can. 15(4):717–728.

HOPPE-SEYLER, F.A.   1928.   The Identity of Carnirine with Trimethylamine Oxide.   Z. Physiol. Chem. 175:300–303.

HOPPE-SEYLER, F.A.   1930.   The Limitations and Significance of Biological Methylation Processes.   Z. Biol. 90:433:466.   Chem. Abstr. 25, 542, 1931.

HOPPE-SEYLER, F.A.   1933.   Trimethylamine Oxide and Other Nitrogen

Bases in Crab Muscles. Z. Physiol. Chem. *221*:45–50. Chem. Abstr. *28*, 216(9), 1934.

HORIE, S. and SEKINE, Y. 1956. Determination Method of Freshness of Fish Muscle with Trimethylamine. J. Tokyo Univ. Fish. *42*:25–31.

HUGHES, R.B. 1958. Volatile Amines of Herring Flesh. Nature. *181*: 1281–1282.

HUGHES, R.B. 1959. Chemical Studies on the Herring *(Clupea harengus)*. I. Trimethylamine Oxide and Volatile Amines in Fresh, Spoiling and Cooked Herring Flesh. J. Sci. Food Agric. *10*:431–436.

HUSS, H.H. 1971. Prepackaged Fresh Fish. In: Fish Inspection and Quality Control. R. Kreuzer (Editor). Fishing News (Books) Ltd., London. pp. 60–65.

INGRAHAM, J.L. and STOKES, J.L. 1959. Psychrophilic Bacteria. Bacteriol. Rev. *23*:97–108.

ISHIDA, Y., FUJII, T., and KADOTA, H. 1976. Microbiological Studies on Salted Fish Stored at Low Temperature I. Chemical Changes of Salted Fish During Storage. Bull. Jpn. Soc. Sci. Fish. *42*(3):351–358.

ISHIKAWA, Y. and YUKI, E. 1974. A Reaction Product from Butylated Hydroxyanisole and Trimethylamine Oxide. Agric. Biol. Chem. *38*(6): 1227–1233.

ISHIKAWA, Y., YUKI, E., KATO, H., and FUJIMAKI, M. 1978A. Synergistic Effect of Trimethylamine Oxide in the Inhibition of the Autoxidation of Methyl Linoleate by Gamma-Tocopherol. Agric. Biol. Chem. *42*(4): 703–709.

ISHIKAWA, Y., YUKI, E., KATO, H., and FUJIMAKI, M. 1978B. The Mechanism of Synergism Between Tocopherols and Trimethylamine Oxide in the Inhibition of the Autoxidation of Methyl Linoleate. Agric. Biol. Chem. *42*:711–716.

ISHIMOTO, M. and SHIMOKAWA, O. 1978. Reduction of Trimethylamine N-Oxide by *Escherichia coli* as Anaerobic Respiration. Z. Allg. Mikrobiol. *18*(3):173–181.

ITO, Y. and TANIMURA, A. 1971. Studies on Nitrosamines in Foods. II. Colorimetric Determination of Secondary Amines and Nitrosamines. Shokuhin Eiseigaku Zasshi *12*(3):177–184.

ITO, Y., SAKUTA, H., YOKOTA, S., AYUKAWA, I., and TANIMURA, A. 1971A. Studies on Nitrosamines in Foods III. Extraction and Identification of Secondary Amines in Foods. Shokuhin Eiseigaku Zasshi *12* (3): 185–191.

ITO, Y., SAKUTA, H., TAKADA, H., and TANIMURA, A. 1971B. Studies on Nitrosamines in Foods VI. Comparison of Trimethylamine Oxide Extraction and Determination Methods of Secondary Amines. Shokuhin Eiseigaku Zasshi *12*(5):399–403.

ITO, Y., SAKUTA, H., TAKADA, H., and TANIMURA, A. 1971C. Nitrosamines in Foods VII. Increment of Secondary Amines in Foods by Cooking or Processing. Shokuhin Eiseigaku Zasshi 12(5):404–407.

IYENGAR, J.R., VISWESWARIAH, K., MOORJANI, M.N., and BHATIA, D.S. 1960. Assessment of the Progressive Spoilage of Ice-Stored Shrimp. J. Fish. Res. Bd. Can. 17(4):475–485.

JAKOBSEN, F. 1944. Determination of Trimethylamine Oxide in Biological Materials. Tidsskr. Kjemi Bergves. Metall. 4:14. Chem. Abstr. 41, 494I, 1947.

JAKOBSEN, F. and MATHIESEN, E. 1948. Corrosion of Containers for Canned Foods. Skr. Nor. Vidensk. Akad. Oslo. 5:6–112. Chem. Abstr. 42, 994D.

JAMES, A.T., MARTIN, A.J.P., and HOWARD SMITH, G. 1952. Gas-Liquid Partition Chromatography: The Separation and Micro-Estimation of Ammonia and the Methylamines. Biochem. J. 52:238–242.

JARMAN, T.R. and LARGE, P.J. 1972. Distribution of the Enzymes Oxidizing Secondary and Tertiary Amines in Pseudomonas aminovorans Grown on Various Substances. J. Gen. Microbiol. 73:205–208.

JOHNSON, F. 1951. Determination of Nitrogen Bases, Especially Trimethylamine, in Meat of Fish According to Conway and Byrne's Method. VI. Nord. Veterinarmotet 1951:197–202.

KAPELLER-ADLER, R. and VERING, F. 1931. The Occurrence of Methylated Nitrogenous Compounds in Sea-Tangle and Some Feeding Experiments with Trimethylamine Performed on Cold-Blooded Animals. Biochem. Z. 243: 292–309.

KARNICKA, B. and JUREWICZ, I. 1971. Changes in the Contents of Trimethylamine Oxide, Trimethylamine, and Total Volatile Ammonium Bases in Fresh and Frozen Fish. Proc. Morsk. Inst. Rybackiego. Ser. B. 16: 193–203. Chem. Abstr. 82, 123485N, 1975.

KATO, N. and UCHIYAMA, H. 1973. An Automation Analysis of Trimethylamine in Fish Muscle. Bull. Jpn. Soc. Sci. Fish. 39(8):899–903.

KAWABATA, T. 1953A. Fundamental Studies on the Determination of Volatile Basic Nitrogen by Aeration Method III. Special Factors Affecting the Velocity Constant in Removing the Volatile Base. Bull. Jpn. Soc. Sci. Fish. 18(10):525–529.

KAWABATA, T. 1953B. Studies on the TMAO Reductase I. Reduction of TMAO in the Dark Muscle of Pelagic Migrating Fish Under Aseptic Condition. Bull.Jpn. Soc. Sci. Fish. 19:505–512.

KAWABATA, T., ISHIBASHI, T., and NAKAMURA, M. 1973. Studies on Secondary Amines in Foods I. Modified Co-Dithiocarbamate Colorimetric Method for the Determination of Secondary Amines. Shokuhin Eiseigaku Zasshi. 14(1):31–36.

KAWAMURA, T., SAKAI, K., MIYAZAWA, F., WADA, H., ITO, Y., and TANIMURA, A. 1971A. Studies on Nitrosamines in Foods IV. Distribution of

Secondary Amines in Foods (1). Shokuhin Eiseigaku Zasshi. *12*(3): 192–197.

KAWAMURA, T., SAKAI, K., MIYAZAWA, F., WADA, H., ITO, Y., and TANIMURA, A. 1971B. Studies on Nitrosamines in Foods V. Distribution of Secondary Amines in Foods (2). Shokuhin Eiseigaku Zasshi. *12*(5): 394–398.

KEAY, J.N. and HARDY, R. 1972. The Separation of Aliphatic Amines in Dilute Aqueous Solution by Gas Chromatography and Application of this Technique to the Quantitative Analysis of Tri- and Dimethylamine in Fish. J. Sci. Food. Agric. *23*:9–19.

KERMACK, W.O., LEES, H., and WOOK, J.D. 1955. Some Non-Protein Constituents of the Tissues of the Lobster. Biochem. J. *60*:424–428.

KIDA, K. and TAMOTO, K. 1974. Studies on the Development of Amines in Alaska Pollock Muscle by Drying. Hokusuishi Geppo *31*(12): 16–26.

KIDA, K. and TAMOTO, K. 1976. Studies on the Amines in Alaska Pollock Muscle II. Development of Trimethylamine and Dimethylamine by Drying. Hokusuishi Geppo *33*(3):44–61.

KIM, K.E. and CHANG, G.W. 1974. Trimethylamine Oxide Reduction by *Salmonella*. Can. J. Microbiol. *20*:1745–1748.

KISER, J.S. and BECKWITH, T.D. 1944. A Study of the Bacterial Flora of Mackerel. Food Res. *9*:250–256.

KOIZUMI, C. 1968. Green Tuna VI. Comparison of Green Tuna Pigment with Sulfmyoglobin and Cholehemochrome By Their Absorption Spectra. Bull. Jpn. Soc. Sci. Fish. *34*(9):810–815.

KOIZUMI, C. and HASHIMOTO, Y. 1965A. Studies on Green Tuna I. The Significance of Trimethylamine Oxide. Bull. Jpn. Soc. Sci. Fish. *31*(2): 157–160.

KOIZUMI, C. and HASHIMOTO, Y. 1965B. Studies on Green Tuna II. Discoloration of Cooked Tuna Meat due to Trimethylamine Oxide. Bull. Jpn. Soc. Sci. Fish. *31*(6):439–447.

KOIZUMI, C. and MATSUURA, F. 1967. Green Tuna IV. Effect of Cysteine on Greening of Myoglobin in the Presence of Trimethylamine Oxide. Bull. Jpn. Soc. Sci. Fish. *33*(9):839–842.

KOIZUMI, C. and MATSUURA, F. 1968. Studies on Green Tuna V. Spectral Properties of a Green Pigment Obtained from Myoglobin. Bull. Jpn. Soc. Sci. Fish. *34*(1):65–71.

KOIZUMI, C. and NONAKA, J. 1970. Green Pigment Produced from Tuna Metmyoglobin. Bull. Jpn. Soc. Sci. Fish. *36*(12):1258.

KOIZUMI, C., KAWAKAMI, H., and NONAKA, J. 1967. Green Tuna III. Relation Between Greening and Trimethylamine Oxide Concentration in Albacore Meat. Bull. Jpn. Soc. Sci. Fish. *33*(2):131–135.

KONOSU, S. and WATANABE, K. 1976. Comparison of Nitrogenous Extractives of Cultured and Wild Red Sea Breams. Bull. Jpn. Soc. Sci. Fish. *42*(11):1263–1266.

KONOSU, S., AKIYAMA, T., and MORI, T.   1958.   Muscle Extracts of Aquatic Animals. I.   Amino Acids, Trimethylamine, and Trimethylamine Oxide in the Muscle Extracts of a Squid, *Ommastrephes sloani pacificus*. Bull. Jpn. Soc. Sci. Fish. *23*:561–564.

KONOSU, S., WATANABE, K., and SHIMIZU, T.   1974.   Distribution of Nitrogenous Constituents in the Muscle Extracts of Eight Species of Fish. Bull. Jpn. Soc. Sci. Fish. *40*(9):909–915.

KONOSU, S., MATSUI, T., FUKE, S., KAWASAKI, I., and TANAKA, H. 1978. Proximate Composition, Extractive Components and Amino Acid Composition of Proteins of the Muscle of Newly Exploited Fish.   Eiyo To Shyokuryo. *31*(6):597–604.

KOVAL'CHUK, G.K. and MOSKALENKO, N.F.   1961.   Volatile Alkaline Matter and Trimethylamine in Meat of Various Fishes Caught in Azov-Black Sea Basin.   Rybn. Khoz. *37*(12):64–68. Chem. Abstr. *56*, 15894E, 1962.

KRUEGER, K.E.   1972.   Psychrotrophic Microorganisms in Fish. Arch. Lebensmittelhyg. *23*(12):275–277.   Chem. Abstr. *78*, 122887A.

KUNISAKI, N., MATSUURA, H., MATSUURA, K., and HAYASHI, M.   1976. Studies on Determination of Dimethylamine in Food II.   Dimethylamine Contents in Commercial Marine Fish and Products.   Shokuhin Eiseigaku Zasshi *17*(6):410–412.

KUTSCHER, F. and ACKERMANN, D.   1933.   The Comparative Biochemistry of Vertebrates and Invertebrates.   Annu. Rev. Biochem. *2*: 355–376.

LALL, B.S., MANZER, A.R., and HILTZ, D.F.   1975.   Preheat Treatment for Improvement of Frozen Storage Stability at −10C in Fillets and Minced Flesh of Silverhake *(Merluccius bilinearis)*.   J. Fish. Res. Bd. Can. *32*: 1450–1454.

LANGE, R. and FUGELLI, K.   1965.   The Osmotic Adjustment in the Euryhaline Teleosts, The Flounder, *Pleuronectes flesus* L. and the Three-Spined Stickleback, *Gasterosteus aculeatus* L.   Comp. Biochem. Physiol. *15*(3): 283–292.

LANGLEY, W.D.   1929.   Metabolism of Amines I.   Trimethylamine.   J. Biol. Chem. *84*:561–570.

LARGE, P.J.   1971.   Nonoxidative Demethylation of Trimethylamine *N*-Oxide by *Pseudomonas aminovorans*. Febs Lett. *18*(2):297–300.

LARGE, P.J. and MCDOUGALL, H.   1975.   An Enzymatic Method for the Microestimation of TMA.   Anal. Biochem. *64*:304–310.

LARGE, P.J., BOULTON, C.A., and CRABBE, M.J.C.   1972.   The Reduced Nicotinamide-Adenine Dinucleotide Phosphate- and Oxygen-Dependent N-Oxygenation of Trimethylamine by *Pseudomonas aminovorans*. Biochem. J. *128*:137–138.

LARTIGUE, D., NOVAK, A.F., and FIEGER, E.A.   1960.   An Evaluation of the Indole and Trimethylamine Tests for Oyster Quality.   Food Technol. *14*:109–112.

LAYCOCK, R.A. and REGIER, L.W.   1970.   Pseudomonads and Achromobacters in the Spoilage of Irradiated Haddock of Different Preirradiation Quality.   Appl. Microbiol. *20*(3):333–341.

LAYCOCK, R.A. and REGIER, L.W.   1971.   Trimethylamine-Producing Bacteria on Haddock *(Melanogrammus aeglefinus)* Fillets during Refrigerated Storage.   J. Fish. Res. Bd. Can. *28*(3):305–309.

LERKE, P., ADAMS, R., and FARBER, L.   1963.   Bacteriology of Spoilage of Fish Muscle. I.   Sterile Press Juice as a Suitable Experimental Medium. Appl. Microbiol. *11*:458–462.

LERKE, P., ADAMS, R., and FARBER, L.   1965.   Bacteriology of Spoilage of Fish Muscle. III.   Characterization of Spoilers.   Appl. Microbiol. *13*(4): 625–630.

LERKE, P., FARBER, L., and ADAMS, R.   1967.   Bacteriology of Spoilage of Fish Muscle. IV.   Role of Protein.   Appl. Microbiol. *15*:770–776.

LEVIN, R.E.   1967.   The Effectiveness of EDTA as a Fish Preservative. J. Milk Food Technol. *30*(9):277–283.

LICCIARDELLO, J.J. and HILL, W.S.   1978.   Microbiological Quality of Commercial Frozen Minced Blocks.   J. Food Prot. *41*(12):948–952.

LICCIARDELLO, J.J, RONSIVALLI, L.J., and SLAVIN, J.W.   1967.   Effect of Oxygen Tension on the Spoilage Microflora of Irradiated and Non-Irradiated Haddock *(Melanogrammus aeglefinus)* Fillets.   J. Appl. Bacteriol. *30*(1):239–245.

LICCIARDELLO, J.J., RAVESI, E.M., and ALLSUP, M.G.   1979A. Quality Aspects of Commercial Frozen Minced Fish Blocks.   J. Food Prot. *42*(1): 23–26.

LICCIARDELLO, J.J. RAVESI, E.M., ALLSUP, M.G., BROOKER, J.R., and KING, F.J.   1979B.   Frozen Storage Characteristics of Mixed Fillet-Mince Cod Blocks.   Lebensm. Wiss. Technol. *12*:290–292.

LINTZEL, W.   1934.   Studies on Trimethylammonium Bases III. Trimethylammonium Bases in Human Urine.   Biochem. Z. *273*:243–261.

LISTON, J.   1965.   Bacteriological Enzymes and Their Role in the Deteriorative Changes in Fish.   In: The Technology of Fish Utilization.   FAO Symp. pp. 53–57.

LOVE, R.M, LOVERN, J.S., and JONES, N.R.   1959.   Chemical Composition of Fish Tissues.   Food Investigation Spec. Rep. No. 69.   Food Investigation Board. Dept. of Scientific and Industrial Research, Great Britain. pp. 1–62.

LOVERN, J.A.   1952.   Chemistry and Advances in Fish Processing. Chem. Ind. *30*:948.

LUIJPEN, A.F.M.G.   1958.   Objective Spoilage Tests for Fish Stored Under Conditions Other than Normal Chilling in Ice.   J. Sci. Food Agric. *9*(7): 410–417.

290 CHEMISTRY & BIOCHEMISTRY OF MARINE FOOD PRODUCTS

MAGNO-OREJANA, F., JULIANO, R.O., and BANASIHAN, E.T. 1971. Trimethylamine and Volatile Reducing Substances in Frigate Mackerel *(Auxis thazard lacepede)*. Phillip. J. Sci. *100*(3–4):209–226.

MAHA, M., SOEDARMAN, H., SIAGIAN, E.G., and CHOSDU, R. 1978. Combined Gamma-Irradiation and Potassium Sorbate Treatment to Extend the Shelf Life of Precooked Chub Mackerel *(Rastrelliger* Species). At. Indones. *4*(1):1–12. Chem. Abstr. *90*, 136381R.

MALORNY, G. and RIETBROCK, N. 1965. Pharmacologically Effective Substances Occurring In Fish. In: The Technology of Fish Utilization. FAO Symp. pp. 79–83.

MANGAN, G.F., JR. 1959. Flavor and Odor of Fish—Progress Report. Commer. Fish. Rev. *21*:21–27.

MARQUES MENDES, H. and LAJOLO, F.M. 1975. Change of Total Volatile Bases and Trimethylamine in Fish and Their Use as Indicator of Quality. Rev. Farm. Bioquim. Univ. Sao Paulo. *13*(2):303–322. Chem. Abstr. *85*, 190963S.

MARTIN, R.E., GRAY, R.J.H., and PIERSON, M.D. 1978. Quality Assessment of Fresh Fish and the Role of the Naturally Occurring Microflora. Food Technol. *32*(5):188–192.

MATSUURA, F. and HASHIMOTO, K. 1954. Chemical Studies on the Red Hake Muscle *(Chiai)* of Fishes II. Determinations of the Content of Hemoglobin, Myoglobin and Cytochrome C in the Muscle of Fishes. Bull. Jpn. Soc. Sci. Fish. *20*(4):308–312.

MCPHAIL, M.E. 1957. A Selected Bibliography of Salted Cod. Fish. Res. Bd. Can. Halifax Technological Station. New Ser. Circ. No. 5.

MENDELSOHN, J.M., STEINBERG, M.A., and MERRITT, C., JR. 1966. Techniques for Collecting Volatile Components from Haddock Flesh for Gas Chromatographic Analysis. J. Food Sci. *31*:389–394.

MILLER, A., III., SCANLAN, R.A., LEE, J.S., and LIBBEY, L.M. 1972A. Quantitative and Selective Gas Chromatographic Analysis of Dimethyl- and Trimethylamine in Fish. J. Agric. Food Chem. *20*(3):709–711.

MILLER, A., III., SCANLAN, R.A., LEE, J. S., and LIBBEY, L.M. 1972B. Volatile Compounds Produced in Ground Muscle Tissue of Canary Rockfish *(Sebastes pinniger)* Stored on Ice. J. Fish. Res. Bd. Can. *29*(8):1125–1129.

MILLER, A., III., SCANLAN, R.A., LEE, J. S., and LIBBEY, L.M. 1973. Volatile Compounds Produced in Sterile Fish Muscle *(Sebastes melanops)* by *Pseudomonas putrefaciens, Pseudomonas fluorescens,* and an *Achromobacter* Species. Appl. Microbiol. *26*:18–21.

MILLER, A., III., SCANLAN, R.A., LIBBEY, L.M., PETROPAKIS, H., and ANGLEMIER, A.F. 1973. Quantitative Determination of Dimethyl- and Trimethylamine in Fish Protein Concentrate. J. Agric. Food Chem. *21*(3): 451–453.

MIYAHARA, S. 1960. Separation and Determination of Methylamines in

Fishes I. Chromatographic Separation and Determination of Methyl-amines. Nippon Kagaku Zasshi *81*:1158−1163.

MIYAUCHI, D.T. 1960. Irradiation Preservation of Pacific Northwest Fish I. Cod Fillets. Food Technol. *14*(2):379−382.

MIYAUCHI, D., EKLUND, M., SPINELLI, J., and STOLL, N. 1963. Application of Radiation-Pasteurization Processes to Pacific Crab and Flounder. Atomic Energy Commission Rep. No. Tid-19585.

MIYAUCHI, D., EKLUND, M., SPINELLI, J., and STOLL, N. 1964. Irradiation Preservation of Pacific Coast Shellfish I. Storage Life of King Crab Meats at 33 and 42F. Food Technol. *18*(6):928−932.

MIYAUCHI, D., SPINELLI, J., and PELROY, G. 1966. Application of Radiation-Pasteurization Processes to Pacific Crab and Flounder. Atomic Energy Commission Rep. No. Tid-23835.

MONTGOMERY, W.A. 1956. A Rapid Method for the Estimation of Volatile Bases in Fish Muscle. Fish Processing Technologists Meeting, Rotterdam, Symp. Paper No. 20. pp. 1−11.

MONTGOMERY, W.A., SIDHU, G.S., and VALE, G.L. 1970. The Australian Prawn Industry I. Natural Resources and Quality Aspects of Whole Cooked Fresh Prawns and Frozen Prawn Meat. Food Pres. Q. *30*:21−27.

MURATA, K. and OISHI, K. 1953. Studies on Fish Curing II. The Preservation Limits of the Dried and Salted Fish Meat. Bull. Jpn. Soc. Sci. Fish. *19*(4):579−580.

MURATA, M., SAKAGUCHI, M., and KAWAI, A. 1980. Formation of Trimethylamine and Dimethylamine in Bloody Muscle, Ordinary Muscle, and Liver of Yellowtail During Iced Storage. Kyoto Daigaku Shokuryo Kagaku Kenkyusho Hokoku *43*:18−23.

MURRAY, C.K. and BURT, J.R. 1974. An Automated Technique for Determining the Concentration of Trimethylamine in Acid Extracts of Fish Muscle. Torry Research Station, Aberdeen (Scotland) Mem. No. 225.

MURRAY, C.K. and GIBSON, D.M. 1972A. An Investigation of the Method of Determining Trimethylamine in Fish Muscle Extracts by the Formation of Its Picrate Salt−Part I. J. Food Technol. 7:35−46.

MURRAY, C.K. and GIBSON, D.M. 1972B. An Investigation of the Method of Determining Trimethylamine in Fish Muscle Extracts by the Formation of its Picrate Salt−Part II. J. Food Technol 7:47−51.

MURRAY, C.K., GIBSON, D.M, and SHEWAN, J.M. 1971. Quality Control Aspects of Prepackaged Fresh and Smoked Fish. In: Fish Inspection and Quality Control. R. Kreuzer (Editor). Fishing News (Books) Ltd., London. pp. 66−70.

NAGAOKA, C. and SUZUKI, N. 1964. Detection of Green-Meat Tuna Before Cooking. Food Technol. *18*(5):777−780.

NAGAOKA, C., YAMAGATA, M., and HORIMOTO, K. 1971. A Method for

Predicting Greening of Tuna Before Cooking.   In: Fish Inspection and Quality Control. R. Kreuzer (Editor). Fishing News (Books) Ltd., London. pp. 96–99.

NAGAOKA, T. and SUZUKI, N.   1962.   A Method for Predicting Green Meat of Tuna (Based on Relationship Between Trimethylamine, Trimethylamine Oxide, and Myoglobin of the Meat.)   Reito 37(414):11–19.

NEILANDS, J.B.   1945.   Factors Affecting Triamineoxidase I.   Inhibition of the Enzyme. J. Fish. Res. Bd. Can. 6(5):368–379.

NONAKA, J., MITANI, H., and KOIZUMI, C.   1967.   Determination of Volatile Amines in Fish Muscle by Gas-Liquid Chromatography I. Trimethylamine. Bull. Jpn. Soc. Sci. Fish. 33(8):753–757.

NORRIS, E.R. and BENOIT, G.J., JR.   1945A.   Studies on Trimethylamine Oxide I.   Occurrence of Trimethylamine Oxide in Marine Organisms.   J. Biol. Chem. 158:433–438.

NORRIS, E.R. and BENOIT, G.J., JR.   1945B.   Studies on Trimethylamine Oxide III.   Trimethylamine Oxide Excretion by the Rat. J. Biol. Chem. 158:443–448.

NOTEVARP, O.   1943.   The Contents of Ammonia and Trimethylamine in Fish and Storage Fish Muscles. Tidsskr. Kjemi, Bergves. Metall. 3:2–6.

NOZAWA, E., ISHIDA, Y., and KADOTA, H.   1979.   Combined Effect of NACl and Temperature on Trimethylamine Production by Some Bacteria Isolated from Chilled Salted Fish. Bull. Jpn. Soc. Sci. Fish. 45(11):1395–1399.

OBATA, Y. and MATANO, K.   1952.   The Flavor of Katsuobushi. II.   Identification of Volatile Substances by Paper Chromatography.   Nippon Nogei Kagaku Kaishi. 26:184–185.

OBATA, Y. and YAMANISHI, T.   1951.   Studies on the Substance of Fish Smell IV.   The Components of Mucilaginous Substances of Salmons Caught at Sea. Bull. Jpn. Soc. Sci. Fish. 16:361–362.

OGAWA, M., VIEIRA, G.H.F., and CALAND-NORONHA, M.DA. C.   1970.   Chlortetracycline and Spiramycin in the Preservation of Lobster Tails Panalirus laevicauda. Arg. Cienc. Mar. 10(2):165–169. Chem. Abstr. 78, 134603T.

OGILVIE, J.M.G. and WARREN, A.A.   1957.   The Occurrence of Trimethylamine Oxide in Fundulus heteroclitus. Can. J. Zool. 35:735–745.

OHSHIMA, H. and KAWABATA, T.   1978.   Mechanism of the N-Nitrosodimethylamine Formation from Trimethylamine and Trimethylamine Oxide. Bull. Jpn. Soc. Sci. Fish. 44(1):77–81.

OKAICHI, T., MANABE, M., and HASHIMOTO, Y.   1959.   Trimethylamine Oxide in Fish Muscle III.   The Origin of Trimethylamine Oxide in Marine Fish Muscle. Bull. Jpn. Soc. Sci. Fish. 25(2):136–142.

OOYAMA, S.   1973.   Odor of Canned Fish I.   Volatile Components from the Muscle of Fresh Fish. Kaseigaku Zasshi 24(8):694–698.

OTA, F. 1958A. Carbonyl Compounds in Fish as Related to the Deterioration I. Detection of Volatile Carbonyl Compounds Formed in Fish Flesh. Bull. Jpn. Soc. Sci Fish. 24(5):334–337.

OTA, F. 1958B. Carbonyl Compounds in Fish as Related to the Deterioration II. Thermal Production of Formaldehyde in Fish Flesh. Bull. Jpn. Soc. Sci. Fish. 24(5)338–341.

PAWAR, S.S. and MAGAR, N.G. 1965. Biochemical Changes in Catfish, Tilapia, and Mrigal Fish During Rigor Mortis. J. Food Sci. 30(1):121–125.

PAYNE, W.J. 1973. Reduction of Nitrogenous Oxides by Microorganisms. Bacteriol. Rev. 37(4):409–452.

PELROY, G.A. and EKLUND, M.W. 1966. Changes in the Microflora of Vacuum-Packaged, Irradiated Petrale Sole (Eopsetta jordani) Fillets Stored at 5C. Appl. Microbiol. 14(6):921–927.

PELROY, G.A. and SEMAN, J.P., JR. 1969. Effect of EDTA Treatment on Spoilage Characteristics of Petrale Sole and Ocean Perch Fillets. J. Fish. Res. Bd. Can. 26(10):2651–2657.

PELROY, G.A., SEMAN, J.P., and EKLUND, M.W. 1967. Changes in the Microflora of Irradiated Petrale Sole (Eopsetta jordani) Fillets Stored Aerobically at 5C. Appl. Microbiol. 15(1):92–96.

POWER, H.E., FRASER, D.I., NEAL, W., DYER, W.J., and CASTELL, C.H. 1964. Gamma Irradiation as a Means of Extending the Storage Life of Haddock Fillets. J. Fish. Res. Bd. Can. 21(4):827–835.

POWER, H.E., SINCLAIR, R., and SAVAGAON, K. 1968. Use of EDTA Compounds for the Preservation of Haddock Fillets. J. Fish. Res. Bd. Can. 25(10):2071–2082.

PRENTISS, P.G., ROSEN, H., BROWN, N., HOROWITZ, R.E., MALM, O.J., and LEVENSON, S.M. 1961. The Metabolism of Choline by the Germfree Rat. Arch. Biochem. Biophys. 94:424–429.

READ, L.J. 1968. Urea and Trimethylamine Oxide Levels in Elasmobranch Embryos. Biol. Bull. 135:537–547.

REAY, G.A. 1938. The Nitrogenous Extractives of Fish. Rep. of the Food Investigation Board for the Year 1937. Dept. Scientific and Industrial Research, Great Britain. pp. 69–71.

REAY, G.A. 1950. The Freezing and Cold-Storage of Fish. Food Investigation Leaflet No. 11. Dept. Scientific and Industrial Research, Great Britain.

REAY, G.A. and SHEWAN, J.M. 1949. The Spoilage of Fish and its Preservation by Chilling. Adv. Food Res. 2:343–398.

REAY, G.A., BANKS, A., and CUTTING, C.L. 1950. The Freezing and Cold-Storage of Fish. Food Investigation. Leaflet No. 11 Dept. Scientific and Industrial Research, Great Britain. pp. 1–17.

REINECCIUS, G.A. 1979. Off-Flavors in Meat and Fish–A Review. J. Food Sci. 44(1):12–24.

RITSKES, T.M. 1975. The Gas Chromatographic Determination of Trimethylamine and Dimethylamine in Fish, Fishery Products and Other Foodstuffs. J. Food Technol. 10:221-228.

ROBINSON, R.H.M., INGRAM, G.C., and EDDY, B.P. 1952. TMA-Producing Bacteria in Whalemeat. J. Sci. Food Agric. 3:175-179.

RONOLD, O.A. and JAKOBSEN, F. 1947. Trimethylamine Oxide in Marine Products. J. Soc. Chem. Ind. 66:160-166.

RUITER, A. 1971. Trimethylamine and the Quality of Fish. Voedingsmiddelen Technol. 2(43):1-10.

RUITER, A. and WESEMAN, J.M. 1976. The Automated Determination of Volatile Bases (Trimethylamine, Dimethylamine, and Ammonia) in Fish and Shrimp. J. Food Technol. 11:59-68.

SAGAI, M. and ISHIMOTO, M. 1973. An Enzyme Reducing Adenosine N-Oxide in Escherichia coli, Amine N-Oxide Reductase. J. Biochem. 73: 843-859.

SAITO, K. and SAMESHIMA, M. 1956A. Studies on the Putrefactive Products of Fish Tissues. I. Turbidity in Colorimetric Determination of Trimethylamine by Dyer's Method. Nippon Nogei Kagaku Kaishi 30: 531-534.

SAITO, K. and SAMESHIMA, M. 1956B. Studies on the Putrefactive Products of Fish Tissues. II. Isolation and Identification of Cadaverine. Nippon Nogei Kagaku Kaishi 30:535-537.

SAKAGUCHI, M. and KAWAI, A. 1975A. Induction of Trimethylamine N-Oxide Reductase in Escherichia coli. Bull. Jpn. Soc. Sci. Fish. 41(6): 661-665.

SAKAGUCHI, M. and KAWAI, A. 1975B. Trimethylamine N-Oxide Reductase: A Membrane-Bound Enzyme in Escherichia coli. Bull. Jpn. Soc. Sci. Fish.41(6):707.

SAKAGUCHI, M. and KAWAI, A. 1977. Electron Donors and Carriers for the Reduction of Trimethylamine N-Oxide in Escherichia coli. Bull. Jpn. Soc. Sci. Fish. 43(4):437-442.

SAKAGUCHI, M. and KAWAI, A. 1978A. The Participation of Cytochromes in the Reduction of Trimethylamine N-Oxide by Escherichia coli. Bull. Jpn. Soc. Sci. Fish. 44(5):511-516.

SAKAGUCHI, M. and KAWAI, A. 1978B. Presence of B- and C-Type Cytochromes in the Membrane of Escherichia coli Induced by Trimethylamine-N-Oxide. Bull. Jpn. Soc. Sci. Fish. 44(9):999-1002.

SAKAGUCHI, M. and KAWAI, A. 1981. Growth of Escherichia coli and the Associated Reduction of Trimethylamine N-Oxide in Fish Muscle Extracts. Bull. Jpn. Soc. Sci. Fish. 47(3):439.

SAKAGUCHI, M. and SHIMIZU, W. 1964. Studies on Muscle of Aquatic Animals XLIV. Amino Acids, Trimethylamine Oxide, Creatine, Creatinine and Nucleotides in Fish Muscle Extractives.   Bull. Jpn. Soc. Sci. Fish. *30*(12): 1003–1007.

SAKAGUCHI, M., KAN, K., and KAWAI, A.   1980.   Induced Synthesis of Membrane-Bound C-Type Cytochromes and Trimethylamine Oxide Reductase in *Escherichia coli*.   In: Advances in Fish Science and Technology. J.J. Connell (Editor).   Fishing News (Books) Ltd., Farnham, England. pp. 472–476.

SANO, Y. and HASHIMOTO, K.   1958.   Studies on the Discoloration in Fish Meat During Freezing Storage I.   A Spectrophotometric Method for the Simultaneous Determination of Ferrous and Ferric Forms of Myoglobin in Their Mixed Solution.   Bull. Jpn. Soc. Sci. Fish. *24*(6,7):519–523.

SANO, Y., HASHIMOTO, K., and MATSUURA, F.   1959.   Studies on the Discoloration in Fish Meat During Freezing Storage II.   A Spectrophotometric Method for the Simultaneous Determination of Ferrous and Ferric Forms of Myoglobin in Tuna Meat.   Bull. Jpn. Soc. Sci. Fish. *25*(6):285–289.

SASAJIMA, M.   1973.   Studies on Psychrotolerant Bacteria in Fish and Shellfish IV.   Relation Between the Number of Trimethylamine Oxide Reducing Psychrotrophic Bacteria and Their Activity.   Bull. Jpn. Soc. Sci. Fish. *39*(5):511–518.

SASAJIMA. M.   1974.   Studies on Psychrotolerant Bacteria in Fish and Shellfish V.   The Growth of Viability of Trimethylamine Oxide Reducing Psychrotrophic Bacteria and their Activity at Sub Zero Temperatures.   Bull. Jpn. Soc. Sci. Fish. *40*(6):625–630.

SASAKI, R. and FUJIMAKI, M.   1953.   Preservation and Preparation of Meats and Meat Products III.   Trimethylamine in Meats 1.   Methods of Colorimetric Estimation of Trimethylamine.   Nippon Nogei Kagaku Kaishi. *27*:420–424.

SASAKI, R., FUJIMAKI, M., and ODAGIRI, S.   1953.   Chemical Studies on Trimethylamine in Meats II.   On Trimethylamine Produced from Heating of Meats.   Nippon Nogei Kagaku Kaishi. *27*:424–428.

SASANO, Y., ONO, H., TAWARA, T., and HIGASHI, K.   1961.   Studies on the Green Meat of Albacore and Yellowfin Tuna.   Bull. Jpn. Soc. Sci. Fish. *27*(6):586–592.

SASS, S., KAUFMAN, J.J., CARDENAS, A.A., and MARTIN J.J.   1958.   Colorimetric Estimation of Tertiary and Quarternary Amines.   Anal. Chem. *30*:529–531.

SATO, Y.   1960.   Estimation of the Freshness of Bottom Fish.   Bull. Jpn. Soc. Sci. Fish. *26*:312–316.

SEN GUPTA, P., MONDAL, A., and MITRA, S.N.   1972.   Separation and Quantitative Estimation of Dimethylamine and Trimethylamine in Fish by Paper Chromatography.   J. Inst. Chem. Calcutta. *44*(2):49–50.

SHAW, D.H. and BOTTA, J.R.   1975.   Preservation Studies of Inshore Male Capelin *(Mallotus villosus)* Stored in Ice..   J. Fish. Res. Bd. Can. *32*(11): 2039–2046.

SHAW, B.G. and SHEWAN, J.M. 1968. Psychrotrophic Spoilage Bacteria of Fish. J. Appl. Bacteriol. 31:89-96.

SHEWAN, J.M. 1938. The Spoilage of Haddocks Stowed in Ice. Rep. of the Food Investigation Bd. for the Year 1937. Dept. Scientific and Industrial Research. Great Britain. pp. 75-78.

SHEWAN, J.M. 1939A. The Spoilage of Fish. Rep. of the Food Investigation Board for the Year 1938. Dept. Scientific and Industrial Research. Great Britain. pp. 79-87.

SHEWAN, J.M. 1939B. Trimethylamine Formation in Relation to the Viable Bacterial Population of Spoiling Fish Muscle. Nature 143:284.

SHEWAN, J.M. 1951. The Chemistry and Metabolism of the Nitrogenous Extractives in Fish. Biochem. Soc. Symp. 6:28-48.

SHEWAN, J.M. 1961. The Microbiology of Sea-Water Fish. In: Fish as Food. G. Borgstrom (Editor) Academic Press, New York. Vol. 1. pp. 478-560.

SHEWAN, J.M. 1962A. The Bacteriology of Fresh and Spoiling Fish and Some Related Chemical Changes. In: Recent Advances in Food Science. J. Hawthorn and J.M. Leitch (Editors). Butterworth, London. Vol. 1. pp. 167-193.

SHEWAN, J.M. 1962B. The Influence of Irradiation preservation on the Nutritive Value of Fish and Fishery Products. In: Fish in Nutrition. E. Heen and R. Kreuzer (Editors). Fishing News (Books) Ltd., London. pp. 207-219.

SHEWAN, J.M. 1971. The Microbiology of Fish and Fishery Products - A Progress Report. J. Appl. Bacteriol. 34(2):299-315.

SHEWAN, J.M. and EHRENBERG, A.S.C. 1957. Volatile Bases as Quality Indices of Iced North Sea Cod. J. Sci. Food Agric. 8:227-231.

SHEWAN, J.M. and EHRENBERG, A.S.C. 1959. Comparison of Certain Scottish and Canadian Experiments in Respect of Grading Fish for Quality. J. Fish. Res. Bd. Can. 16(4):555-557.

SHEWAN, J.M. and JONES, N.R. 1957. Chemical Changes Occurring in Cod Muscle During Chill Storage and their Possible Use as Objective Indices of Quality. J. Sci. Food Agric. 8(8):491-498.

SHEWAN, J.M., HOBBS, G., and HODGKISS, W. 1960A. A Determinative Scheme for the Identification of Certain Genera of Gram-Negative Bacteria, with Special Reference to the Pseudomonadaceae. J. Appl. Bacteriol. 23(3): 379-390.

SHEWAN, J.M., HOBBS, G., and HODGKISS, W. 1960B. The Pseudomonas and Achromobacter Groups of Bacteria in the Spoilage of Marine White Fish. J. Appl. Bacteriol. 23(3):463-468.

SHEWAN, J.M., GIBSON, D.M., and MURRAY, C.K. 1971. The Estimation of Trimethylamine in Fish Muscle. In: Fish Inspection and Quality Control. R. Kreuzer (Editor). Fishing News (Books) Ltd., London. pp. 183-186.

SHIMOMURA, M., YOSHIMATSU, F., and MATSUMOTO, F. 1971. Studies on Cooked Fish Odor of Cooked Horse Mackerel. Kaseigaku Zasshi 22(2):106−112.

SIDHU, G.S., MONTGOMERY, W.A., and BROWN, M.A. 1974A. Post Mortem Changes and Spoilage in Rock Lobster Muscle I. Biochemical Changes and Rigor Mortis in *Jasus Novae − Hollandiae*. J. Food Technol. 9:357−370.

SIDHU, G.S., MONTGOMERY, W.A., and BROWN, M.A. 1974B. Post Mortem Changes and Spoilage in Rock Lobster Muscle II. Role of Amino Acids in Bacterial Spoilage and Production of Volatile Bases in the Muscle of *Jasus Novae − Hollandiae*. J. Food Technol. 9:371−380.

SIGURDSSON, G.J. 1947. Comparison of Chemical Tests of the Quality of Fish. Anal. Chem. 19:892−902.

SIMIDU, W. 1961. Nonprotein Nitrogenous Compounds. In: Fish as Food. G. Borgstrom (Editor). Academic Press, New York. Vol. 1. pp. 353−375.

SIMIDU, W. and HIBIKI, S. 1954A. Studies on Putrefaction of Aquatic Products XII. On Putrefaction of Bloody Muscle. Bull. Jpn. Soc. Sci. Fish. 20(3):206−208.

SIMIDU, W. and HIBIKI, S. 1954B. Studies on Putrefaction of Aquatic Products XIII. Comparison on Putrefaction of Different Kinds of Fish (1). Bull. Jpn. Soc. Sci. Fish. 20(4):298−301.

SIMIDU, W. and HIBIKI, S. 1954C. Studies on Putrefaction of Aquatic Products XIV. Comparison on Putrefaction of Different Kinds of Fish (2). Bull. Jpn. Soc. Sci. Fish. 20(4):302−304.

SIMIDU, W. and HIBIKI, S. 1954D. Studies on Putrefaction of Aquatic Products XV. Comparison of Putrefaction for Round, Fillet, Minced and Denatured Fishes. Bull. Jpn. Soc. Sci. Fish. 20(5):388−391.

SIMIDU, W. and HIBIKI, S. 1954E. Studies on Putrefaction of Aquatic Products XVI. Consideration on Difference in Putrefaction for Various Kinds of Fish (1). Bull. Jpn. Soc. Sci. Fish. 20(5):392−395.

SIMIDU, W. and HIBIKI, S. 1957. Studies on Putrefaction of Aquatic Products XXIV. On Spoilage of Some Shellfishes. Bull. Jpn. Soc. Sci. Fish. 23(5): 255−259.

SIMIDU, W., HIBIKI, S., SIBATA, S., and TAKEDA, K. 1953. Studies on Muscle of Aquatic Animals XVI. Distribution of Extractive Nitrogens in Muscle of Several Kinds of Gastropod. Bull. Jpn. Soc. Sci. Fish. 19(8): 871−876.

SLABYJ, B.M. and TRUE, R.H. 1978. Effect of Preprocess Holding on the Quality of Canned Maine Sardines. J. Food Sci. 43(4):1172−1176.

SMITH, H.W. 1936. The Retention and Physiological Role of Urea in the Elasmobranchii. Biol. Rev. 11(1):49−82.

SOUDAN, F. 1962. The Natural Formal Content in Fisheries Products. In: Fish In Nutrition. E. Heen and R. Kreuzer (Editors). Fishing News (Books) Ltd., London. pp. 78−79.

SOUTHCOTT, B.A., MOYER, R., BAKER, E.G., and TARR, H.L.A. 1958. Experiments on Preservation of Fish with Tetracycline Antibiotics. Fish. Res. Bd. Can., Progr. Rep. Pac. Coast Stn. *110*, 16–18.

SPENCER, R. 1962. Odour and the Assessment of Fish Freshness. Soap Perfum. Cosmet. *35*:795–799.

SPINELLI, J. 1964. Evaluation on the Micro-Diffusion Method for the Determination of Tertiary Volatile Base in Marine Products. Fish. Ind. Res. *2*(3):17–19.

SPINELLI, J. and KOURY, B. 1979. Nonenzymatic Formation of Dimethylamine in Dried Fishery Products. J. Agric. Food Chem. *27*(5):1104–1108.

SPINELLI, J., EKLUND, M., and MIYAUCHI, D. 1964. Irradiation Preservation of Pacific Coast Shellfish II. Relation of Bacterial Counts, Trimethylamine and Total Volatile Base to Sensory Evaluation of Irradiated King Crab Meat. Food Technol. *18*, 933–937.

SPINELLI, J., EKLUND, M., STOLL, N., and MIYAUCHI, D. 1965. Irradiation Preservation of Pacific Coast Fish and Shellfish. Food Technol. *19*(6):126–130.

SPINELLI, J., PELROY, G., and MIYAUCHI, D. 1969. Quality Indices that Can Be Used to Assess Irradiated Seafoods. In: Freezing and Irradiation of Fish. R. Kreuzer (Editor). Fishing News (Books) Ltd., London. pp. 425–430.

SPINELLI, J., KOURY, B., GRONINGER, H., JR., and MILLER, R. 1977. Expanded Uses for Fish Protein from Underutilized Species. Food Technol. *31*:184–187.

STANLEY, J.G. and FLEMING, W.R. 1964. Excretion of Hypertonic Urine by a Teleost. Science. *144*:63–64.

STANSBY, M.E. 1962. Speculations on Fishery Odors and Flavors. Food Technol. *16*:28–32.

STEINER, M. and HARTMANN, T. 1968. The Occurrence and Distribution of Volatile Amines in Marine Algae. Planta (Berlin) *79*:113–121.

STROM, A.R. 1979. Biosynthesis of Trimethylamine Oxide in Calanoid Copepods. Seasonal Changes in Trimethylamine Monooxygenase Activity. Mar. Biol. *51*:33–40.

STROM, A.R. 1980. Biosynthesis of Trimethylamine Oxide in *Calanus finmarchicus*. Properties of a Soluble Trimethylamine Monooxygenase. Comp. Biochem. Physiol. B*65*:243–249.

STROM, A.R., and LARSEN, H. 1979. Anaerobic Fish Spoilage by Bacteria I. Biochemical Changes in Herring Extracts. J. Appl. Bacteriol. *46*: 531–543.

SUNDSVOLD, O.C., UPPSTAD, B., FERGUSON, G.W., MCLACHLAN, T., and FEELEY, D. 1969A. Trimethylamine Oxide Content of Norwegian Shrimps and Its Degradation to Methylamines and Formaldehyde I.

Presence of Formaldehyde in Canned Shrimps. Tidsskr. Hermetikind. 55(4): 94−95.

SUNDSVOLD, O.C., UPPSTAD, B., FERGUSON, G.W., MCLACHLAN, T., and FEELEY, D. 1969B. Trimethylamine Oxide Content of Norwegian Shrimps and its Degradation to Methylamines and Formaldehyde. II. Determination of Trimethylamine Oxide, Trimethylamine, Dimethylamine, and Formaldehyde, and the Effect of Catalysts on the Decomposition of Oxide. Tidsskr. Hermetikind. 55(4):96−97.

SUYAMA, M. 1960. Formation of Ammonia and Trimethylamine in Elasmobranch Fish. J. Tokyo Univ. Fish. Spec. Ed. III. 3(1):1−152.

SUYAMA, M. and SUZUKI, H. 1975. Nitrogenous Constituents in the Muscle Extracts of Marine Elasmobranchs. Bull. Jpn. Soc. Sci. Fish. 41(7): 787−790.

SUYAMA, M. and TOKUHIRO, T. 1954. Urea Content and Ammonia Formation of the Muscle of Cartilaginous Fishes III. The Distribution of Urea and Trimethylamine Oxide in Different Parts of the Body. Bull. Jpn. Soc. Sci. Fish. 19:1003−1006.

SVENSSON, S. 1977. Frozen Storage of Fish Mince III. Stabilization of Fish Mince from Gadoid Species by Pre-Treatment of the Fish. SIK-Rapp. 422. Chem. Abstr. 90. 102088K.

SZE, Y.L. and BORKE,M.L. 1963. Separation of Lower Aliphatic Amines by Gas Chromatography. Anal. Chem. 35(2):240−242.

TAKADA, K. and NISHIMOTO, J. 1958. Studies on the choline in Fish I. Contents of Choline and the Similar Substances in Fishes. Bull. Jpn. Soc. Sci. Fish. 24(8):632−635.

TAKAGI, M., MURAYAMA, H., and ENDO., S. 1967A. Trimethylamine and Trimethylamine Oxide Contents of Fish and Marine Invertebrates. Hokkaido Daigaku Suisan Gakubu Kenkyu Iho. 18(3):261−267.

TAKAGI, M., MURAYAMA, H., and ENDO, S. 1967B. Variation of the Volatile Basic Nitrogen, Trimethylamine and Trimethylamine Contents Accompanied by Loss of Freshness and Putrefaction of Fish and Marine Invertebrates. Hokkaido Daigaku Suisan Gakubu Kenkyu Iho. 18(3): 268−270.

TAKAGI, I. and SIMIDU. W. 1962. Studies on Muscle of Aquatic Animals XXXIV. Constituents and Extractive Nitrogens in a Few Species of Shellfish. Bull. Jpn. Soc. Sci. Fish. 28(12):1192−1198.

TARR, H.L.A. 1939A. The Bacterial Reduction of Trimethylamine Oxide to Trimethylamine. J. Fish. Res. Bd. Can. 4(5):367−377.

TARR, H.L.A. 1939B. The Bacterial Reduction of Trimethylamine Oxide to Trimethylamine. J. Soc. Chem. Ind. 58:253.

TARR, H.L.A. 1940. Specificity of Triamineoxidase. J. Fish. Res. Bd. Can. 5(2):187−196.

TARR, H.L.A. 1941. Fate of Trimethylamine Oxide and Trimethylamine in Man. J. Fish. Res. Bd. Can. 5:211–216.

TARR, H.L.A. 1944. Direct Bacterial Counts and Trimethylamine Tests as Criteria of Quality of British Columbia Flounders and Gray Cod. Fish Res. Bd. Can. Progr. Rep. Pac. Coast Stn. 59, 15–18.

TARR, H.L.A. 1954. Microbiological Determination of Fish Post Mortem. Its Detection and Control. Bacteriol. Rev. 18:1–15.

TARR, H.L.A. 1961. Some Observations Concerning Experimental Application of Objective Quality Tests to West Coast Fish. Can. Fish. Rep. Sept. 1961, pp. 27–31.

TARR, H.L.A. and NEY, P.W. 1949. Effect of Flesh Acidity on Bacterial Numbers and Trimethylamine in Spoiling Fish. Fish. Res. Bd. Can. Progr. Rep. Pac. Coast Stn. 78, 11–13.

TESHIMA, S., KANAZAWA, A., and KASHIWADA, K. 1968. Studies on the Volatile Fatty Acids and Volatile Bases in Shiokara II. Some Changes in the Process of the Ripening of Ika-Shiokara. Bull. Jpn. Soc. Sci. Fish. 34(2): 163–167.

TOKUNAGA, T. 1964. Studies on the Development of Dimethylamine and Formaldehyde in Alaska Pollack Muscle During Frozen Storage I. Suisan-Cho Hokkaido-ku Suisan Kenkyusho Kenkyu Hokoku 29:108–122.

TOKUNAGA, T. 1965. Studies on the Development of Dimethylamine and Formaldehyde in Alaska Pollack Muscle During Frozen Storage II. Factors Affecting the Formation of Dimethylamine and Formaldehyde. Suisan-Cho Hokkaido-ku Suisan Kenkyusho Kenkyu Hokoku 30:90–97.

TOKUNAGA, T. 1966. Studies on the Development of Dimethylamine and formaldehyde in Alaska Pollack Muscle During Frozen Storage III. On the Effect of Various Kinds of Additives. Suisan-cho Kokkaido-ku Suisan Kenkyusho Kenkyu Hokoku 31:95–111.

TOKUNAGA, T. 1970A. Trimethylamine Oxide and its Decomposition in the Bloody Muscle of Fish I. Trimethylamine Oxide, Trimethylamine, and Dimethylamine Contents in Ordinary and Bloody Muscles. Bull. Jpn. Soc. Sci. Fish. 36(5):502–509.

TOKUNAGA, T. 1970B. Trimethylamine Oxide and its Decomposition in the Bloody Muscle of Fish II. Formation of Dimethylamine and Trimethylamine During Storage. Bull. Jpn. Soc. Sci. Fish. 36(5):510–515.

TOKUNAGA, T. 1974. The Effect of Decomposed Products of Trimethylamine Oxide on Quality of Frozen Alaska Pollack Fillet. Bull. Jpn. Soc. Sci. Fish. 40(2):167–174.

TOKUNAGA, T. 1975A. On the Thermal Decomposition of Trimethylamine Oxide in Muscle of Some Marine Animals. Bull. Jpn. Soc. Sci. Fish. 41(5):535–546.

TOKUNAGA, T. 1975B. Studies on the Quality Evaluation of Canned Marine Products I. Determination of the Ratio of Dimethylamine to Trimethylamine in Canned Albacore. Bull. Jpn. Soc. Sci. Fish. *41*(5):547–553.

TOKUNAGA, T. 1978. Contents of Trimethylamine Oxide, Trimethylamine and Dimethylamine in Different Tissues of Live Alaska Pollack, *Theragra chalcogramma.* Tokai-ku Suisan Kenkyusho Kenkyu Hokoku *93*:79–85.

TOKUNAGA, T., IIDA, H., and MIWA, K. 1977. The Gas Chromatographic Analysis of Amines in Fish. Bull. Jpn. Soc. Sci. Fish. *43*(2):219–227.

TOMIOKA, K., OGUSHI, J., and ENDO, K. 1974. Studies on Dimethylamine in Foods II. Enzymatic Formation of Dimethylamine from Trimethylamine. Bull. Jpn. Soc. Sci. Fish. *40*(10):1021–1026.

TOMIYAMA, T., KUROKI, S., MAEDA, D., HAMADA, S., and HONDA, A. 1956. A Study of the Effects of Aureomycin-Containing Sea Water and Ices Upon the Storage Life of Round Herring. Food Technol. *10*:215–218.

TOMIZAWA, J. 1951. Trimethylamine Oxide Reductase. Jpn. Med. J. *4*: 21–31.

TOZAWA, H. and AMANO, K. 1969A. Studies on the Irradiation Cleavage of Trimethylamine Oxide in Fish Flesh I. Decomposition Products Found in Several Fishes. Bull. Jpn. Soc. Sci. Fish. *35*(4):391–396.

TOZAWA, H. and AMANO, K. 1969B. Studies on the Irradiation Cleavage of Trimethylamine Oxide in Fish Flesh II. Acceleration of Dimethylamine Formation by Addition of Gadoid Fish Viscera. Bull. Jpn. Soc. Sci. Fish. *35*(6):397–604.

TOZAWA, H., ENOKIHARA, K., and AMANO, K. 1970. Effect of Dimethylamine on the Value of Trimethylamine Determined by the Dyer's Method. Bull. Jpn. Soc. Sci. Fish. *36*(6):606–611.

TOZAWA, H., ENOKIHARA, K., and AMANO, K. 1971. Proposed Modification of Dyer's Methods for Trimethylamine Determination In Cod Fish. In: Fish Inspection and Quality Control. R. Kreuzer (Editor). Fishing News (Books) Ltd., London. pp. 187–190.

TSUCHIYA, Y. and ENDO, E. 1952. Enzymatic Reduction of Trimethylamine Oxide. Tohoku J. Agric. Res. *3*(1):127–133.

TSUCHIYA, Y., TAKAHASHI, I., and YOSHIDA, S. 1951. Studies on the Formation of Ammonia and Trimethylamine in Sharks. Tohoku J. Agric. Res. *2*:119–126.

UCHIYAMA, S., AMANO, R., KONDO, T., and TANABE, H. 1974. Studies on the Chemical Indexes and the Change of ATP and Related Compounds in Decomposition of Frozen Shrimps. Shokuhin Eiseigaku Zasshi *15*(4): 301–307.

UNEMOTO, T., HAYSHI., M.,MIYAKI, K., and HAYASHI, M. 1965. Intracellular Localization and Properties of TMA-N-O Reductase in *Vibrio parahaemolyticus.* Biochim. Biophys. Acta *110*:319–328.

UNO, T. and YAMAMOTO, M. 1966. Colorimetric Determination of Secondary Amines. Bunseki Kagaku *15*(9):958–961.

USUKI, M., NAKAMURA, M., and FUKUMI, T. 1971. Wholesomeness of

Fishery Products I. Fate of Amines During Storage of Codfish Eggs. Hokusuishi Geppo 28(11):2−7.

VAISEY, E.B. 1956. The Non-Enzymic Reduction of Trimethylamine Oxide to Trimethylamine, Dimethylamine, and Formaldehyde. Can. J. Biochem. Physiol. 34(6):1085−1090.

VANDERZANT, C., MROZ, E., and NICKELSON, R. 1970. Microbial Flora of Gulf of Mexico and Pond Shrimp. J. Milk Food Technol. 33:346−350.

VELANKAR, N.K. 1952. Moisture, Salt, Trimethylamine and Volatile Nitrogen Contents and Bacterial Counts of Salt-Cured Marine Fish. J. Sci. Ind. Res. Sect. A 11:359−360.

VELANKAR, N.K. and GOVINDAN, T.K. 1958. A Preliminary Study of the Distribution of Non-Protein Nitrogen in Some Marine Fishes and Invertebrates. Proc. Indian Acad. Sci. Part B. 47:202−209.

VELANKAR, N.K. and KAMASASTRI, P.V. 1956. The Bacterial Flora, Trimethylamine and Total Volatile Nitrogen of Fish Muscle at 0C (In Ice). Indian J. Fish. 3:269−289.

VENKATARAMAN, R. and CHARI, S.T. 1950. Studies on Fish Spoilage. Proc. Indian Acad. Sci. Part B. 31:54−59.

WALKER, P., CANN, D., and SHEWAN, J.M. 1970. The Bacteriology of Scampi (Nephrops norvegicus) I. Preliminary Bacteriological, Chemical and Sensory Studies. J. Food Technol. 5:375−385.

WATANABE, K. 1965. Technological Problems of Handling and Distribution of Fresh Fish in Southern Brazil. In: The Technology of Fish Utilization FAO Symp., pp. 44−46.

WATERS, M.E. 1964. Comparison of Chemical and Sensory Tests for Assessing Storage Life of Iced Calico Scallops (Pecten gibbus) Fish. Ind. Res. 2(3):5−10.

WATSON, D.W. 1939A. Studies of Fish Spoilage IV. The Bacterial Reduction of Trimethylamine Oxide. J. Fish. Res. Bd. Can. 4(4):252−266.

WATSON, D.W. 1939B. Studies of Fish Spoilage V. The Role of Trimethylamine Oxide in the Respiration of Achromobacter. J. Fish. Res. Bd. Can. 4(4):267−280.

WATTS, J.C.D. 1965. Some Observations on the Preservation of Fish in Sierra Leone. Bull. Inst. Fondam. Afr. Noire. Ser. A 27(1):339−396.

WONG, N.P., DAMICO, J.N., and SALWIN, H. 1967. Decomposition and Filth in Foods: Investigation of Volatile Compounds in Cod Fish by Gas Chromatography and Mass Spectrometry. J. Assoc. Offic. Anal. Chem. 50 (1):8−15.

WOOD, A.J. and BAIRD, E.A. 1943. Reduction of Trimethylamine Oxide by Bacteria 1. The Enterobacteriaceae. J. Fish. Res. Bd. Can. 6(2):194−201.

WOOD, A.J. and KEEPING, F.E. 1944 The Formation of Trimethylamine from Choline as a Characteristic of *Shigella alkalescens.*   J. Bacteriol. *47*, 309–310.

WOOD, A.J., SIGURDSSON, G.J., and DYER, W.J.   1942.   The Surface Concept in Measurement of Fish Spoilage.   J. Fish. Res. Bd. Can. *6*:53–62.

WOOD, A.J., BAIRD, E.A., and KEEPING, F.E.   1943.   A Primary Division of the Genus *Shigella* Based on the Trimethylamine Test.   J. Bacteriol. *46*:106–107.

WOOD, E.J.F.   1953.   Heterotrophic Bacteria in Marine Environments of Eastern Australia.   Aust. J. Mar. Freshwater Res. *4*:160–200.

WOOD, J.D.   1958.   Nitrogen Excretion in Some Marine Teleosts.   Can. J. Biochem. Physiol. *36*(12):1237–1242.

YAMADA, K.   1967.   Occurrence and Origin of Trimethylamine Oxide in Fishes and Marine Invertebrates.   Bull. Jpn. Soc. Sci. Fish. *33*(6):591–603.

YAMADA, K.   1968.   Post-Mortem Breakdown of Trimethylamine Oxide in Fishes and Marine Invertebrates.   Bull. Jpn. Soc. Sci. Fish. *34*(6):541–551.

YAMADA, K. and AMANO, K.   1965A.   Studies on the Biological Formation of Formaldehyde and Dimethylamine in Fish and Shellfish V.   On the Enzymatic Formation in the Pyloric Caeca of Alaska Pollock.   Bull. Jpn. Soc. Sci. Fish. *31*(1):60–64.

YAMADA, K. and AMANO, K.   1965B.   Studies on the Biological Formation of Formaldehyde and Dimethylamine in Fish and Shellfish VI.   Note on the Content of Formaldehyde and Dimethylamine in Two Species of Gadoid Fishes and Two Species of Marine Crabs.   Tokai Suisan Kenkyusho Kenkyu Hokoku. *41*(1):86–96.

YAMADA, K. and AMANO, K.   1965C.   Studies on the Biological Formation of Formaldehyde and Dimethylamine in Fish and Shellfish VII.   Effect of Methylene Blue on the Enzymatic Formation of Formaldehyde and Dimethylamine from Trimethylamine Oxide.   Bull. Jpn. Soc. Sci. Fish. *31*(12): 1030–1037.

YAMADA, K., HARADA, K., and AMANO, K.   1969.   Biological Formation of Formaldehyde and Dimethylamine in Fish and Shellfish VIII.   Requirement of a Cofactor in the Enzyme System.   Bull. Jpn. Soc. Sci. Fish. *35*(2): 227–231.

YAMAGATA, M., HORIMOTO, K., and NAGAOKA, C.   1968.   On the Distribution of Trimethylamine Oxide in the Muscles of Yellowfin Tuna.   Bull. Jpn. Soc. Sci. Fish. *34*(4):344–350.

YAMAGATA, M., HORIMOTO, K., and NAGAOKA, C.   1969.   Assessment of Green Tuna: Determining Trimethylamine Oxide and its Distribution in Tuna Muscles.   J. Food Sci. *34*:156–159.

YAMAMOTO, I. and ISHIMOTO, M.   1977.   Anaerobic Growth of *Escherichia coli* on Formate by Reduction of Nitrate, Fumarate, and TMA-N-Oxide.   Z. Allg. Mikrobiol. *17*(3):235–242.

YU, CHO-TENG and CRUESS, W.V. 1951. A Study of Several Factors in the Salting and Smoking of Fish. Canner *113*(6):12–14, (7):14,16,18.

ZEIGLER, D.M. and MITCHELL, C.H. 1972. Microsomal Oxidase IV. Properties of a Mixed-Function Amine Oxidase Isolated from Pig Liver Microsomes. Arch. Biochem. Biophys. *150*:116–125.

13

Irradiation of Seafoods

Joseph J. Licciardello and Louis J. Ronsivalli

HISTORICAL ASPECTS

Although some studies on food irradiation were being conducted in this country in the late 1940s, it was not until 1953 when President Eisenhower announced his Atoms for Peace Program that this area of research received a real impetus. The Department of the Army, probably because of its proven capability in food processing research and development during World War II, was assigned the task of coordinating a major national effort in food irradiation. The role of the Atomic Energy Commission (AEC) at this time was to supply radiation sources and technology.

In 1956 the Interdepartmental Committee on Radiation Preservation of Food was established. This committee was composed of representatives from various government agencies that had an active interest in the irradiation program. Its primary objectives were to provide broad guidance to the program, effect a transfer of program responsibility from the Department of the Army to other government agencies and private industry, and to report to the President on the progress of the Atoms for Peace Program (Anon. 1978).

During this early period, various foods were investigated for their reaction to radiation treatment at both sterilizing and sub-sterilizing doses, though the Army's principal interest seemed to be to develop a commercially sterile product suitable for military feeding. As it became evident that sterilizing doses, in most instances, produced undesirable side effects in many foods, the research thrust began to shift to low-dose irradiation coupled with subsequent refrigerated storage. Difficulties with the Surgeon General's animal feeding studies with irradiated foods in the late 1950s prompted the AEC to assume a more active role, and in 1960, the AEC initiated a food irradiation program with emphasis on low-dose application while the Department of the Army continued its involvement with emphasis on radiation sterilization.

Gloucester Laboratory, Northeast Fisheries Center, National Marine Fisheries Service, National Oceanic and Atmospheric Administration, Gloucester, Massachusetts 01930

Soon after this decision, Proctor *et al.* (1960) at Massachusetts Institute of Technology under a contract with the AEC surveyed the literature and published a report on the technical, economic, and practical feasibility of radiation preservation of fish. This was followed by a contract report by Nickerson *et al.* (1961) that contained an outline of projects and experimental protocol for determining the feasibility of radiation preservation of marine products. With this background information providing guidance, the AEC launched a national program on the low-dose irradiation of seafoods, drawing on the combined research efforts of universities, industry, and the technological laboratories of the Bureau of Commercial Fisheries (presently, the National Marine Fisheries Service). The AEC installed pool-type gamma sources of approximately 30 kilocuries (kCi) of cobalt-60 at MIT (Cambridge, MA), University of California (Davis, CA), University of Florida (Gainesville, FL), and University of Hawaii (Honolulu, HA) to provide some of its principal contractors with on-site irradiation facilities designed principally for research leading eventually to pilot plant studies. A Marine Products Development Irradiator of 250 kCi of cobalt-60 strength was installed at the Gloucester technological laboratory of the National Marine Fisheries Service for storage studies, shipping tests, and consumer tests on a pilot plant scale.

In the late 1960s the irradiation program received a severe setback. The clearance for radiation-sterilized bacon, which had previously been granted, was rescinded, and a more comprehensive set of guidelines for testing the wholesomeness of irradiated foods was issued by the Food and Drug Administration (FDA). In view of the time and expense required to initiate new wholesomeness studies, the AEC phased out its support for the low-dose food irradiation program. As a result of the de-emphasis by the United States on food irradiation, an international effort was initiated to study collectively the wholesomeness issue, and in 1970 the International Food Irradiation Project was established at Karlsruhe, Germany. This project is sponsored by the Organization for Economic Cooperation and Development (OECD), the International Atomic Energy Agency (IAEA), and the Food and Agricultural Organization (FAO) of the United Nations as well as 24 countries contributing to its support. Wholesomeness studies sponsored by this group have recently been completed on low-dose irradiated cod and ocean perch, and provisional approval has been granted.

In 1977 the Interdepartmental Committee on Radiation Preservation of Foods convened an expert panel on irradiation of fish and fish products to evaluate the benefits and prospects for use of low-dose radiation processing and to determine how the wholesomeness data already collected could be used and supplemented to obtain clearance for this process. In its final report published December 1978, the panel concluded that low-dose irradiation of seafoods would be beneficial, and recommendations and a plan of action for seeking clearance were set forth (Anon. 1978). This is the current status of low-dose irradiation of seafoods in this country.

OBJECTIVES

The objectives of food preservation by ionizing radiation can be divided into three categories (Hannesson 1972).

1. Sterilization (sometimes referred to as radappertization) for the purpose of inactivating spoilage and pathogenic microorganisms to a degree that microbial spoilage is arrested regardless of storage conditions. As in heat processing, complete sterility may not be attained with the usual radiation sterilizing dose, and the term commercial sterility, meaning viable microorganisms may be present but are incapable of multiplying, would be more appropriate.

The classical method for calculating processing times for canned foods is based on the time required for thermal inactivation of a population of 60 billion *Clostridium botulinum* spores or approximately a 12 log cycle reduction in count. The FDA stipulated that the radiation sterilization dose for foods should be calculated on a similar basis, that is, a dose that would effect a 12 log cycle reduction in spore count of *C. botulinum*. Under this condition the computed radiation sterilization dose would be in the range of 3.0–4.0 million rads. There are few, if any, species of fish or shellfish that would withstand such a high dose treatment without undergoing an undesirable change in color, flavor, or odor. Even if these changes could be averted by some process treatment such as irradiation in the frozen state, the seafood would have to be given a prior heat treatment to inactivate proteolytic enzymes that otherwise would rapidly destroy textural properties of the sterilized fish during room temperature storage. The thermal treatment, however, would invariably cook the fish and would nullify the advantage of using ionizing radiation, which is essentially a cold sterilization process. Thus, radiation sterilization is not generally applicable to seafoods.

2. Radiopasteurization or low-dose irradiation (sometimes referred to as radurization) is employed to reduce the total viable microbial population to such low numbers that, in conjunction with some inhibitory condition such as refrigerator storage, an extension of product shelf life is achieved. This particular treatment is regarded as the most feasible for radiation preservation of seafoods.

3. Radicidation is an irradiation treatment specifically intended to reduce or eliminate non-spore-forming pathogenic microorganisms in a food. This process could be employed to reduce salmonella in fish meal or shrimp. A dose of 500 krad (1 krad = 10 Gray) would result in approximately a 7 log cycle reduction in numbers. *Vibrio parahaemolyticus* is very radiosensitive and a dose of less than 200 krad should suffice to eliminate this pathogen from various seafoods (Matches and Liston 1971).

Benefits

What are the benefits to be derived from low-dose irradiation of seafoods? Seafoods are usually landed at coastal ports many miles from the large cities in the interior of the country, and the fish, when brought to port, may be anywhere from 1 to 4 days out of water. An additional 1–2 days may be added to the postmortem age at the primary processing plant. Under the best holding conditions, the shelf life of fresh fish on ice is approximately 10–14 days, and at warmer temperatures it is considerably less. Such a short remaining shelf life precludes the shipment of fresh fish to points beyond several hundred miles inland from the coast. The use of low-dose irradiation would permit the shipment of fresh New England haddock, for example, to points as far as the West Coast and shipment of fresh Gulf shrimp to northern states. This point has already been demonstrated. Miyauchi (1970) reported that cod fillets irradiated at Gloucester, MA, at 100–200 krad and shipped by rail to Seattle, WA, had an additional storage life of 7–14 days on ice, whereas the control fillets were spoiled on arrival.

Low-dose irradiation treatment of seafoods is unique in that it does not alter the physical characteristics. There is no other approved process for extending the storage life of fresh fish that compares with low-dose irradiation. Antibiotic treatment was effective, but approval was rescinded. Use of modified atmosphere storage looks promising. Freezing may be comparable to low-dose irradiation in its effects, but frozen seafoods do not enjoy the popularity of fresh seafoods. In addition, the energy requirements for freezing preservation are greater than low-dose irradiation treatment (Brynjolfsson 1978).

Irradiation of seafoods at the port of landing while the seafood is at top quality would assure a high quality product at point of retail sale, which, coupled with a potentially greater distribution channel across the country, should result in an expanded fresh seafood market. Irradiating the seafood at peak quality would also result in greater use of the seafood resource. Because of the high perishability of seafood and variability in quality, much of the merchandise is discarded in retail stores due to spoilage. Preservation of seafood by low-dose irradiation would extend the period during which its quality remains acceptable, thereby providing more time to sell it and thus reducing the amount of product lost to spoilage.

In an attempt to curb financial losses due to spoilage, most buyers for retail sales purchase less than their estimated amount of sale. This is particularly true when the wholesale price of fish is high due to short supply or toward the end of the week. This practice can result in a surplus of product which may be sold at a low price to a fish meal reduction plant. Similarly, the vagaries of weather, size and location of stocks, and other conditions can also affect supply and demand. With the quota system being instituted as a result of the Fisheries Conservation and Management Act, most of the allotted catch is usually taken in the first few weeks of the designated fishing period, resulting in a glut and low prices to the fisherman. Toward the end of this period the entire allocation may have already been taken and the fishery declared closed, resulting in a high demand and high prices. The use of radiation to preserve fish would help stabilize the supply by allowing processors to buy the large catches and to hold on short inventory the unsold portion, which could be released when the demand becomes favorable.

The principal disadvantage of the use of irradiation for preserving seafoods at this time is the word irradiation itself. It connotes radioactivity and other nuclear-related hazards to the general public. The recent incident at the nuclear power plant at Three Mile Island served to focus the public's distrust on the use of radiation. It will be necessary to educate and reassure the public as to the safety of irradiation as a food process for this treatment to be accepted.

WHOLESOMENESS

A joint FAO/IAEA/WHO Expert Committee on the Wholesomeness of Irradiated Foods has stated that the safety of irradiated foods for human consumption must be based on the following considerations (1977): (1) the absence of microorganisms and microbial toxins harmful to man; (2) the nutritional contribution of the irradiated food to the total diet; and (3) the absence of any significant amounts of toxic products formed in the food as a result of the irradiation process.

Microbiological Aspects

With the application of a radiation sterilizing dose, no public health problems are envisaged. With low-dose irradiation a shift in the microbial flora will usually result, but this will depend on the qualitative and quantitative composition of the initial microflora, the stage of the growth phase, the substrate, and the irradiation dose. The microbial flora of freshly caught marine fish taken from temperate waters consists principally of *Pseudomonas*, *Achromobacter* (*Moraxella* and *Acinetobacter*), *Micrococcus*, and *Flavobacterium* with minor proportions of *Corynebacterium*, *Vibrio*, *Bacillus*, *Proteus*, and yeasts (Dyer 1947; Liston 1960; Shewan and Hobbs 1967). Contamination aboard the fishing boats and in filleting plants causes a variation in the quantitative relationship of these bacterial species on a fish fillet. Spoilage of seafoods at refrigerator temperatures is caused eventually by overgrowth of psychrotrophs of the genus *Pseudomonas* (Shewan 1961). The extension of shelf life of seafoods with low doses of irradiation is due to the reduction of the initial pseudomonad component to an insignificant level.

The pseudomonads are among the most radiosensitive of microbial species (Thornley 1963). A dose range of 7–23 krad has been reported to result in 99% inactivation (Niven 1958). In general, rod-shaped cells are more radiosensitive than coccoid types, and the gram-negative species more radiosensitive than the gram-positives. Since a variation in radiation resistance has been found to exist among the different genera of microorganisms isolated from seafoods (yeast > *Micrococcus* > *Achromobacter* > *Flavobacterium* > *Pseudomonas*), the absorbed dose plays a role in the quantitative and qualitative aspects of the microflora after irradiation.

In most reported studies on seafoods, the microflora following a 100–300 krad treatment was predominantly *Achromobacter* (Shewan and Liston 1958; Corlett *et al.* 1965; Licciardello *et al.* 1967A; Kazanas and Emerson 1968). However, packaging under vacuum favors the selection and growth of lactic acid bacteria in low-dose irradiated seafoods, and eventually these microorganisms constitute a major portion of the spoilage microflora (Licciardello *et al.* 1967B). With samples irradiated at higher dose levels on the order of 500 krad, ultimate spoilage may be caused by yeasts.

The spores of *C. botulinum* are relatively radioresistant and treatment with a low-dose of ionizing radiation (~200 krad) would not effect a significant reduction in numbers. Thus, control of botulism in low-dose irradiated fish or shellfish would have to be achieved through temperature control or chemical inhibition. This would not be too difficult in the case of the proteolytic strains of *C. botulinum* types A and B since the spores do not germinate and grow at temperatures below 50°F (10°C); however, nonproteolytic strains of types B, E, and F could present a problem since they are capable of outgrowth and toxin production at a temperature as low as 38°F (3.3°C) (Schmidt *et al.* 1961; Hobbs 1968; Eklund and Poysky 1970).

The potential hazard attributed by some to low-dose irradiation of marine foods is that, with the extended shelf life resulting from a reduction of the natural microflora, particularly the spoilage-producing pseudomonads, spores of *C. botulinum* if present would have ample opportunity to grow and produce toxin without the product being recognizably spoiled. In assessing the potential botulism hazard the following variables would have to be considered: (1) initial concentration and strain of spores; (2) species of fish; (3) packaging method; (4) irradiation dose; and (5) storage temperature.

The initial concentration of spores governs the length of time required for toxin production at a given temperature and also the minimal temperature for growth. With regard to fish species, fatty fish are generally considered to be more botulinogenic than lean fish (Shewan and Hobbs 1970).

One effect of the irradiation dose is the selection of the spoilage microflora. At doses of approximately 100–150 krad or less, the spoilage flora of irradiated fish will most probably be pseudomonads. This group of microorganisms is usually responsible for the normal, fishy, putrid spoilage pattern of fish that is recognizable to most individuals. At dose levels in excess of 100–150 krad, the predominant spoilage microflora may be *Achromobacter* in an air-packed sample or lactobacilli in a vacuum-packed sample. The *Achromobacter* produce fruity or esteric odors at spoilage, whereas the lactobacilli produce odors of sour fish. Neither of these two spoilage forms produce changes as offensive as those caused by pseudomonads. Consequently, if toxin production and spoilage occur simultaneously in stored irradiated fish, samples irradiated at 100–150 krad or less may be rejected as inedible at spoilage, whereas samples receiving a higher dose may not. Another consequence of increasing the dose is the extension of refrigerated storage life, which increases the probability of toxigenesis before the occurrence of recognizable spoilage, provided the storage temperature is conducive to growth of *C. botulinum*. Two important factors that determine whether irradiated fish spoil before toxin production can occur are storage temperature and level of contamination. As the storage temperature and contamination level of spores increase, the safety margin between rejection due to spoilage and toxin development decreases (Hobbs 1967).

To determine whether irradiated seafoods present a greater botulism hazard than nonirradiated products, the following experiment was proposed (Ronsivalli *et al.* 1971)

1. Determine the spoilage time at various storage temperatures for irradiated and nonirradiated fish based on rejection by an inexpert panel

2. Measure the time required for toxin formation in inoculated packs of irradiated and nonirradiated samples and

3. Compare the times observed in steps 1 and 2 to obtain a measure of safety margin. Studies of this nature were carried out at MIT, NMFS Gloucester Laboratory, NMFS Seattle laboratory, and the Torry Research Station, Scotland (Eklund and Poysky 1970; Shewan and Hobbs 1970; Goldblith and Nickerson 1967, 1968). Spore inoculum levels ranged from about 10^2 to 10^6 per gram and storage temperatures varied from 38° to 50°F (3.3°–10°C). In general, the results indicated that, at higher storage temperatures and with a high spore challenge, there was either a very small or no margin of safety.

Based on inoculated pack studies at their respective labs, Eklund and Poysky (1970) at NMFS Seattle and Hobbs (1967) at Torry Research Station concluded that low-dose irradiation of fish would present no botulism hazard if the product were maintained at a storage temperature below 41°– 42°F (5°–5.6°C). In the provisional approval issued by the FAO/IAEA/WHO Joint Expert Committee for irradiation of cod and ocean perch (Anon. 1977), an irradiation dose range of 100–200 krad and storage temperature at or below 3°C (37.4°F) was specified. It should be pointed out that low-dose irradiation is not unique in its ability to alter the microflora. Other currently accepted processes such as thermal pasteurization of crabmeat have the same effect and, although a similar botulism hazard may be associated with such treatments, none has occurred in the many years of usage.

What little information is available on the natural quantitative level of contamination of seafoods with type E *C. botulinum* indicates the numbers to be low. In a survey of herring from Norwegian fishing grounds, the incidence of type E spores was estimated as 1 or less per 16 grams of fish (Cann *et al.* 1966). The highest level of type E cells found in haddock, cod, or flounder from the Gulf of Maine was 10 per 100 grams, and this occurred in the intestines (Nickerson *et al.* 1967). In a survey to determine the level of contamination of commercial haddock fillets, 24% of samples taken from five different plants in the Boston area were positive for type E *C. botulinum*

(Goldblith and Nickerson 1965). The highest concentration of cells found in any of the contaminated fillets was 17 per 100 grams. More survey data are needed as a guide for establishing a logical spore challenge in assessing the safety of low-dose irradiated seafoods. It is fortunate that the toxin of *C. botulinum* type E is heat-labile and, since fish is not usually consumed raw (except in some oriental countries), normal cooking would destroy any toxin that may have formed (Licciardello *et al.* 1967; Hobbs *et al.* 1969).

The application of ionizing radiation for control of botulism in cured or smoked fishery products appears promising. The smoke flavor permits the use of higher irradiation doses by masking irradiation off-flavors. The relatively high salt content of cured fish in conjunction with the radiation treatment may lessen the requirement for nitrite, which is normally used to prevent outgrowth of botulinum spores in cured products and whose usage is currently under investigation by FDA.

In tropical countries considerable losses occur in dried fish products due to insect damage. Treatment with chemicals can effectively eliminate the problem but is precluded because of toxic residues; however, a dose of radiation in the range of 15 to 25 krad was found to be adequate for sterilization of the insects. However, low-dose irradiation of lightly salted herring is ineffective in destroying anisakis larvae.

Quality Assessment

As was indicated previously, the natural microflora of fish comprises a variety of microbial genera each possessing a different range in metabolic activity. The pseudomonads are the most active, being capable of reducing trimethylamine oxide (a natural precursor in marine species) to trimethylamine, which is reputed to be responsible for the fishy odor of stale fish, producing hydrogen sulfide, ammonia, and a host of other compounds that collectively constitute spoilage. Chemical tests to measure the quality of fish are usually based on the concentrations of these metabolic products in the fish flesh. However, an irradiation treatment that eliminates the pseudomonads causes a shift in the spoilage microflora, which is usually less active metabolically. When this occurs, these metabolites either do not form or form to a lesser degree. Consequently, the results of certain chemical tests of such compounds as trimethylamine, total volatile bases, and total volatile acids have to be interpreted cautiously in quality assessment of irradiated fish (Spinelli *et al.* 1964, 1965, 1969; Power *et al.* 1964). The accumulation of hypoxanthine, which depends on nucleotide degradation by autolytic enzymes, is independent of the bacterial flora and has been found to be useful. Some preliminary tests in our laboratory have indicated that the Torrymeter[1] may have some application in measuring quality of

---

[1] Mention of trade names or commercial firms does not imply endorsement by the National Marine Fisheries Service, NOAA.

low-dose irradiated fish. Bacterial content (total plate count) as an indicator of spoilage is unreliable because, with nonirradiated fish, spoilage coincides with a count of approximately 10^6 per gram, whereas with low-dose irradiated fish, this numerical index at spoilage is of the order of 10^8 per gram. Organoleptic testing thus appears to be the most reliable method for measuring quality of refrigerated, radiopasteurized fish.

Nutritional Aspects

The effect of ionizing radiation on nutrients in foods has been reviewed (Josephson et al. 1976; Shewan 1962) and the general conclusion is that, at sterilizing doses, some losses to nutrients may occur, but that these losses are comparable to the losses incurred by other accepted processing methods such as thermal processing. Ley (1969) and Ley et al. (1972) reported excellent results with radiation-sterilized feed for germ-free rat and mouse colonies maintained for 5 years. The protein quality of haddock, crab, and flounder was not significantly changed as a result of radiation pasteurization (Reber et al. 1968). Brooke et al. (1966) concluded that low dose irradiation (250 krad) of haddock fillets had no deleterious effect on the essential amino acids. Other nutrients are not expected to be affected to any significant extent by low dose treatments.

Toxicological Aspects

The principal concern of the layman regarding ingestion of irradiated foods is that the product may be radioactive. Although some radionuclides have been detected in foods after irradiation with energy levels up to 24 MeV, the concentrations have not been significant. No induced radioactivity has been detected in matter irradiated at energy levels of 12 MeV or less. In foods or packaging materials thus far cleared for irradiation treatment, the maximum permissible energy level has been set at 10 MeV.

With regard to the potential problem of carcinogenicity or toxicity from ingesting irradiated seafoods, none was reported in the results of animal feeding studies involving irradiated cod (Alexander and Salmon 1959; Hickman 1966; Keplinger et al. 1974A,B, 1976), ocean perch (Keplinger et al. 1974A,B, 1976), tuna (Paynter 1959; Ross and Hood 1963), and shrimp (Maurer et al. 1961; Phillips et al. 1961). In these studies the irradiation dose was greater than 1 Mrad. Analyses of the radiolytic products of cod irradiated over a range of doses showed that the products were qualitatively similar, but that the concentrations increased with the irradiation dose (Taub et al. 1976). The FAO/IAEA/WHO Joint Expert Committee has envisaged that, for certain dose ranges up to 500 krad, all food might be cleared for irradiation. One of the principal reasons that enabled the Joint Expert Committee to reach this conclusion is that food irradiation was regarded as a process analogous to thermal processing, microwave processing, etc. In this country, however, food irradiation is defined as a food additive under the Food Additives Amendment of 1958 and, as such, has been subjected to extreme scrutiny involving lengthy, expensive wholesomeness testing. This has been a prime cause for the delay in granting clearance to this process in this country.

PROCESSING CONSIDERATIONS

Criteria for Selecting Optimum Dose

When selecting the optimum dose for low-dose irradiated foods, three fundamental criteria must be considered. The first is that the dose level selected does not cause any detectable organoleptic change. When testing for flavor change in fish, the method of preparation for tasting can influence the threshold level at which flavor changes are evident. Steaming or baking seafood are the methods of preparation most sensitive to irradiation off-flavors, whereas deep-frying tends to mask these off-flavors. The second criterion is the shelf-life extension desired at a particular storage temperature, and the third is the degree of safety desired from a potential botulism hazard. As was previously indicated, increasing the dose extends the shelf life, but it also increases the risk of botulism if the irradiated seafood is abused during storage.

Double-Dose Application

Liston and Matches (1968) reported that, when fish was irradiated with a low dose followed by about 1 week storage at refrigerator temperature and then given a second low dose, the extension in storage life exceeded that resulting from the administration of the equivalent dosage as a single dose. With strictly fresh fillets, the double-dose treatment was shown to be effective when the primary and secondary doses were as low as 50 krad each. However, the double-dose treatment lost its advantage when higher doses such as 100 and 100 krad were employed or when several-day-old fish were used.

The effectiveness of double-dose treatment raises the possibility that unsold irradiated fish could be reclaimed from retail stores, given an additional low-dose treatment, and then put back into distribution. This procedure would increase the risk of a botulism hazard and therefore, to prevent this practice, the labeling requirements for low-dose irradiated foods specify that wholesale packages and invoices of bulk shipment bear the statement "Treated with ionizing radiation—do not irradiate again."

SHIPBOARD IRRADIATION

The extended shelf life obtained with low-dose irradiation depends on a number of factors, one being the initial quality of the fish, which is optimal at the time of capture. From this fact it was deduced that it would be advantageous to irradiate fish on board ship immediately after capture. As a result of two independent trials conducted by the Bureau of Commercial Fisheries aboard vessels equipped with irradiation sources, the *M.V. Delaware* on the East Coast (Carver *et al.* 1969) and the *M.V. Miller Freeman* on the West Coast (Teeny and Miyauchi 1970), it was concluded that fish irradiated immediately after netting while still in pre-rigor had the longest storage life and best quality.

Shipboard irradiation offers certain advantages. It would allow the landing of high quality seafood and permit the vessels to remain at sea longer or travel to more distant fishing grounds. There are, however, some disadvantages, such as increased space requirement and shielding and inefficient use of the radiation source. But, most importantly, it is unlikely that fishing crew members in this country would be willing to remain at sea for more than several days.

Combination Treatments

Various processes or additives have been combined with irradiation either concurrently or as a pretreatment for the purpose of either effecting an additional extension of shelf life or of lessening or masking the development of irradiation off-odors and off-flavors. The combination of heating followed by low-dose irradiation was used to advantage with lobster and shrimp (Power *et al.* 1967; Kumta *et al.* 1970). It was shown that a greater reduction in microbial count of crab or lobster meat occurred when the thermal and ionizing energy were applied simultaneously (Goldblith and Nickerson 1966). A variety of chemical preservatives including sodium benzoate (0.1%), potassium sorbate (0.1%), sodium salts of methyl and propyl esters of parahydroxybenzoic acid (0.1%), and furyl furamide (0.002%) effectively extended the storage life of Dover sole, whale meat, or horse mackerel flesh when combined with low-dose irradiation (Shiflett 1965; Tomiyama *et al* 1969). Antibiotics such as chlortetracycline (5–10 ppm) or tylosin added to various seafoods have been demonstrated to exert a complementary effect when combined with low-dose irradiation (Shewan and Liston 1958; Tomiyama *et al.* 1969; Lerke *et al.* 1961). Flavoring agents such as spices or flavor enhancers (e.g., 5'-inosine monophosphate) were found to increase the acceptability of certain irradiated seafoods (Roy and Kaylor 1975; Spinelli and Miyauchi 1968).

EFFECT ON ORGANOLEPTIC PROPERTIES

A tremendous amount of research has been carried out on the effect of irradiation on organoleptic properties of seafoods. For a comprehensive review of the subject, the reader is referred to the forthcoming article by Nickerson *et al.* (1982). Low-dose irradiation treatment of seafoods usually does not induce an organoleptically detectable change in appearance or texture. With some products, a low-dose treatment may cause a slight loss of the typical flavor. But for each species, there is a threshold dose beyond which the odor of the raw product and the flavor and odor of the cooked product will be affected. Off-odor and off-flavor have been described as "burnt feathers" or "wet-dog." With most seafoods color is not affected to any great extent with low-dose treatment. Some light-fleshed fish may darken slightly, but still are acceptable. However, salmon does undergo a significant bleaching, and for this reason, may not be suitable for low-dose treatment. In salmon the astaxanthin pigment is dissolved in the lipid of the fish; in lobsters and certain crabs, the same pigment is present but in the nonlipid component, and is stable to low-dose irradiation.

The optimal dose, that which gives the longest shelf life without altering normal characteristics of the product, is shown in Table 13.1 for some selected seafoods. For most species this dose ranges from 150 to 250 krad. Smoked fish usually can tolerate higher doses. When one considers that the normal shelf life of most seafoods on ice (33°F) is about 10–14 days, the additional storage life gained by irradiation at the optimal dose becomes significant. It should be emphasized that this storage life extension is obtained only with a product of good initial quality. Low-dose irradiation of seafoods that have spent more than 7 days postmortem on ice is not recommended, not only because the shelf life extension will be less than that obtained with fresh fish, but because the irradiation treatment does not improve the quality of the product (Ampola and Ronsivalli 1969).

The temperature at which irradiated seafoods are stored is important in that it governs the storage life of the treated product. For maximum shelf life, irradiated seafoods should be maintained as near the freezing point as possible without freezing. The higher the temperature, the shorter the storage life, and little advantage is gained by irradiating seafoods and storing them at relatively high refrigerator temperatures. The shelf life of

TABLE 13.1. OPTIMAL RADIATION DOSE LEVELS AND SHELF LIFE AT 33°F (0.6°C) FOR FISH AND SHELLFISH AEROBICALLY PACKED IN HERMETICALLY SEALED CANS

Seafood	Optimal irradiation dose (Mrad)	Shelf life (weeks)
Oysters (shucked)	0.20	3–4
Shrimp	0.15	4
Smoked chub	0.10	6
Yellow perch fillets	0.30	4
Petrale sole fillets	0.20	2–3
Pacific halibut steaks	0.20	2
King crab meat (cooked)	0.20	4–6
Dungeness crab meat (cooked)	0.20	3–6
English sole fillets	0.20–0.30	4–5
Soft-shell clam meats	0.45	4
Haddock fillets	0.15–0.25	3–5
Pollock fillets	0.15	4
Cod fillets	0.15	4–5
Ocean perch fillets	0.15–0.25	4
Mackerel fillets	0.25	4–5
Lobster meat (cooked)	0.15	4

Source: Slavin *et al.* (1966).

cod fillets as a function of irradiation dose and storage temperature is presented in Table 13.2

Another requirement for maximum shelf life of irradiated fish is that the product be packaged in a hermetically sealed container impervious to microorganisms. In the case of low-fat fish such as cod and haddock, an oxygen-impermeable container such as a metal can or appropriate plastic bag, which also prevents moisture loss is suitable. Fish such as halibut, petrale sole, and ocean perch, which are higher in fat content, should be prepackaged under vacuum in the same type of container. Otherwise the irradiated product may become rancid during storage. If fish is to be irradiated only for the purpose of preventing spoilage during long distance shipping, the product may be bulk-packed in 10- or 20-pound rectangular tins with a friction lock cover, opened at the destination, and then handled and sold as freshly caught fish.

TABLE 13.2. THE MAXIMUM SHELF LIFE VALUE (IN DAYS) OF IRRADIATED AND NON-IRRADIATED COMMERCIAL-QUALITY COD FILLETS (EXPERIMENTS NOS. 1, 2, AND 3)

Radiation dose (krad)	Storage temperature (°F)				
	33 (0.6°C)	38 (3.3°C)	42 (5.6°C)	48 (8.8°C)	55 (12.8°C)
0	12–14	11	7– 8	5– 7	3– 4
75	23–40	11–27	9–11	8–11	6– 7
100	30–49	15–30	11–15	10–12	6– 9
200	45–50	29–32	22–23	13–15	8–10

Source: Ronsivalli et al. (1970).

CONCLUSION

If and when low-dose irradiation of seafoods is approved for human consumption in this country, it is not anticipated that this particular process will supersede all current handling methods for seafoods. Some products will continue to be marketed iced, frozen, or canned, and irradiation will find a niche among these different processes for those products for which this treatment provides a technological and economic advantage.

REFERENCES

ANON. 1978. Food irradiation in the United States. Food Irradiation Information 9, 69–93.

ANON. 1977. Wholesomeness of Irradiated Food. Joint FAO/IAEA/WHO Committee Rep. WHO Tech. Rep. Ser. 604—FAO Food and Nutrition Ser. 6. World Health Organization, Geneva.

ALEXANDER, H.D., and SALMON, W.D. 1959. Long-term rat and dog feeding tests on irradiated sweet potatoes and codfish. U.S. Army Contract No. DA-47-007-MD-543, Alabama Polytechnic Institute, Auburn, AL.

AMPOLA, V.G., and RONSIVALLI, L.J. 1969. Effect of preirradiation quality of eviscerated haddock on postirradiation shelf life of fillets. J. Food Sci. *34*, 27–30.

BROOKE, R.O., RAVESI, E.M., GADBOIS, D.F., and STEINBERG, M.A. 1966. Preservation of fresh unfrozen fishery products by low-level radiation. V. The effects of radiation pasteurization on amino acids and vitamins in haddock fillets. Food Technol. *20*, 99–102.

BRYNJOLFSSON, A. 1978. Energy and food irradiation. *In* Food Preservation by Irradiation, Vol. II, pp. 285–300. International Atomic Energy Agency, Vienna, Austria.

CANN, D.C., WILSON, B.B., SHEWAN, J.M., and HOBBS, G. 1966. Incidence of *Clostridium botulinum* type E in fish products in the United Kingdom. Nature (London) *211*, 205.

CARVER, J.H., CONNORS, T.J., and SLAVIN, J.W. 1969. Irradiation of fish at sea. *In* Freezing and Irradiation of Fish. R. Kreuzer (Editor), pp. 509–513. Fishing News (Books) Ltd., London.

CORLETT, D.A., JR., LEE, J.S., and SINNHUBER, R.O. 1965. Application of replicate plating and computer analysis for rapid identification of bacteria in some foods. II. Analysis of microbial flora in irradiated Dover sole *(Microstomus pacificus)*. Appl. Microbiol. *13*, 818–822.

DYER, F.E. 1947. Microorganisms from Atlantic cod. J. Fish. Res. Board Can. 7, 128–136.

EKLUND, M.W., and POYSKY, R.T. 1970. The significance of non-proteolytic *Clostridium botulinum* types B, E, and F in the development of radiation pasteurized fishery products. *In* Preservation of Fish by Irradiation, pp. 125–149. International Atomic Energy Agency,Vienna.

GOLDBLITH, S.A., and NICKERSON, J.T.R. 1965. The effect of gamma rays on haddock and clams inoculated with *Clostridium botulinum* type E. U.S. At. Energy Comm. Contract No. MIT03325, Mass. Inst. Technol., Cambridge, MA.

GOLDBLITH, S.A., and NICKERSON, J.T.R. 1966. Simultaneous radiation-heating treatment of precooked marine products. Final Rep. TID 4500 for Division of Isotopes Development, USAEC Contract No. AT(30-1)-3343, Mass. Inst. Technol., Cambridge, MA, Feb. 1, 1965 to Feb. 28, 1966.

GOLDBLITH, S.A., and NICKERSON, J.T.R. 1967. The effect of gamma rays on ocean perch inoculated with type E *Clostridium botulinum*. Final Rep. for Division of Biology and Medicine, U.S. At. Energy Comm. Contract No. AT(30-1)-3343. Mass. Inst. Technol., Cambridge, MA.

GOLDBLITH, S.A., and NICKERSON, J.T.R. 1968. The effect of gamma rays on marine finfish fillets inoculated with type E, *Clostridium botulinum*. Final Rep. for Division of Isotopes Development. U.S. At. Energy Comm. Contract No. AT(30-1)-3343, Mass. Inst. Technol., Cambridge, MA.

HANNESSON, G. 1972. Objectives and present status of irradiation of fish and seafoods. Food Irradiation Information No. 1, Int. Project in the Field of Food Irradiation, Karlsruhe, Germany.

HICKMAN, J.R. 1966. United Kingdom food irradiation programme—wholesomeness aspects. *In* Food Irradiation, Proc. International Symp., Karlsruhe, Germany, pp. 101–119. International Atomic Energy Agency, Vienna.

HOBBS, G. 1967. Toxin production by *Clostridium botulinum* type E in fish. *In* Microbiological Problems in Food Preservation by Irradiation, pp. 37–54. International Atomic Energy Agency, Vienna.

HOBBS, G. 1968. Prospects for the elimination of *Clostridium botulinum* from fish and fishery products by irradiation. *In* Elimination of Harmful Organisms from Food and Feed by Irradiation, pp. 101–107. International Atomic Energy Agency, Vienna.

HOBBS, G., CANN, D.C., and WILSON, B.B. 1969. An evaluation of the botulinum hazard in vacuum packaged smoked fish. J. Food Technol. *4*, 185–191.

JOSEPHSON, E.S., THOMAS, M.H., and CALHOUN, W.K. 1976. Nutritional aspects of food irradiation: An overview. Presented at the First Int. Congress on Engineering and Food, Boston, MA, Aug. 9–13, 1976.

KAZANAS, N., and EMERSON, J.A. 1968. Effect of gamma irradiation on the microflora of freshwater fish. III. Spoilage patterns and extension of re-frigerated storage life of yellow perch fillets irradiated to 0.1 and 0.2 megarad. Appl. Microbiol. *16*, 242–247.

KEPLINGER, M.L., KENNEDY, G.L., and SMITH, S. 1974A. International Project in the field of food irradiation, Rep. No. IFIP-R27.

KEPLINGER, M.L., KENNEDY, G.L., and SMITH, S. 1974B. International Project in the field of food irradiation, Rep. No. IFIP-R23.

KEPLINGER, M.L., KINOSHITA, F.K., KENNEDY, G.L., MARIAS, A.J., and OSCARSON, E. 1976. International Project in the field of food irradiation, Rep. No. IFIP-R38.

KUMTA, U.S., MAVINKURVE, S.S., CORE, M.S., SAWANT, P.L., CANGAL, S.V., and SREENIVASAN, A. 1970. Radiation pasteurization of fresh and blanched tropical shrimps. J. Food Sci. *35*, 360–363.

LERKE, P.A., FARBER, L., HUBER, W. 1961. Preservation of fish and shellfish by relatively low doses of beta radiation and antibiotics. Food Technol. *15*, 145–152.

LEY, F.J. 1972. The use of irradiation for the treatment of various animal feed products. Food Irradiat. Inform. *1*, 8.

LEY, F.J., BLEBY, J., COATES, M.E., and PETERSON, J.S. 1969. Sterilization of laboratory animal diets using gamma irradiation. Lab Animals *3*, 221–254.

LICCIARDELLO, JOSEPH, J., NICKERSON, J.T.R., RIBICH, C.A., and GOLDBLITH, S.A. 1967A. Thermal inactivation of type E botulinum toxin. Appl. Microbiol. *15*, 249.

LICCIARDELLO, J.J., RONSIVALLI, L.J., and SLAVIN, J.W. 1967B. The

320 CHEMISTRY & BIOCHEMISTRY OF MARINE FOOD PRODUCTS

effect of oxygen tension on the spoilage microflora of irradiated and nonirra-diated haddock *(Melanogrammus aeglefinus)* fillets. J. Appl. Bacteriol. *30*,239–245.

LISTON, J. 1960. The bacterial flora of fish caught in the Pacific. J. Appl.Bacteriol. *23*, 469–470.

LISTON, J., and MATCHES, J.R. 1968. Single and multiple doses in theradiation pasteurization of seafoods. Food Technol. *22*, 893–896.

MATCHES, J.R., and LISTON, J. 1971. Radiation destruction of *Vibrio**parahaemolyticus.* J. Food Sci. *36*, 339–340.

MAURER, F.D., ROSE, M.A., HOOD, E., and TUCKER, W.E. 1961. Radi-ation and sterilization of foods. Contract with Armed Forces Institute ofPathology, Washington, DC, Project No. 6x60-11-001, Virginia PolytechnicInst., Blacksburg, Va.

MIYAUCHI, D. 1970. Application of radiation pasteurization processes toPacific coast fishery products. U.S. At. Energy Comm. Contract No. AT(49-11)-2058. National Marine Fisheries Service, Seattle, WA.

NICKERSON, J.T.R., GOLDBLITH, S.A., MILLER, S.A., LICCIARDELLO,J.J., and KAREL, M. 1961. Outline of projects to determine the feasibilityof radiation preservation of marine products. U.S. At. Energy Comm. Con-tract No. AT(30-1)-2329, Mass. Inst. Technol., Cambridge, MA.

NICKERSON, J.T.R., GOLDBLITH, S.A., DIGIOIA, G., and BISHOP, W.W.1967. The presence of *Cl. botulinum* type E in fish and mud taken from theGulf of Maine. *In* Botulism 1966. M. Ingram and T.A. Roberts (Editors),pp. 25–34. Chapman and Hall, London.

NICKERSON, J.T.R., LICCIARDELLO, J.J., and RONSIVALLI, L.J. 1982.Radurization and radicidation. A. Fish and shellfish. *In* Preservation ofFood by Ionizing Radiation. E. Josephson and M. Peterson (Editors).C.R.C. Press, Inc., Cleveland, OH. In press.

NIVEN, C.F., JR. 1958. Microbiological aspects of radiation preservation offood. Annu. Rev. Microbiol. *12*, 507.

PAYNTER, O.E. 1959. Long-term feeding and reproduction studies on ir-radiated corn and tuna fish. U.S. Army Contract No. DA-49-007-MD-788.Final Rep. Hazelton Labs., Falls Church, Va.

PHILLIPS, A.W., NEWCOMB, H.R., and SHANKLIN, D. 1961. Long-termrat-feeding studies: Irradiated shrimp and oranges diet. U.S. Army Con-tract No. DA-49-007-MD-791. Final Rep., Biology Research Labs., SyracuseUniv. Res. Inst., Syracuse, NY.

POWER, H.E., FRASER, D.I., NEAL, W., DYER, W.J., CASTELL, C.H. 1964.Gamma irradiation as a means of extending the storage life of haddock fillets.J. Fish. Res. Board Can. *21*, 827–835.

POWER, H.E., FRASER, D.I., DYER, W.J., NEAL, W., and CASTELL, C.H.1967. Effect of pasteurizing doses of gamma radiation on storage life ofcooked lobster meat. J. Fish. Res. Board Can. *24*, 221–230.

PROCTOR, B.E., GOLDBLITH, S.A., NICKERSON, J.T.R., and FARKAS, D.S. 1960. Evaluation of the technical, economic and practical feasibility of radiation preservation of fish. U.S. At. Energy Comm. Contract No. AT (30-1)-2329, Mass. Inst. Technol., Cambridge, MA.

REBER, E.F., BERT, M.H., RUST, E.M., and KUO, E. 1968. Biological evaluation of protein quality of radiation-pasteurized haddock, flounder and crab. J. Food Sci. *33*, 335–337.

RONSIVALLI, L.J., KING, F.J., AMPOLA, V.G., and HOLSTON, J.A. 1970. Study of irradiated-pasteurized fishery products. Maximum shelf life study. B. Radiation chemistry. U.S. At. Energy Comm. Contract No. AT(49-11)-1889, Bureau of Commercial Fisheries Technological Laboratory, Gloucester, MA.

RONSIVALLI, L.J., SCHWARTZ, M.S., and NICKERSON, J.T.R. 1971. A proposed method for testing the possibility of a botulism hazard in radiation-pasteurized fish. Isot. Radiat. Technol. *8*, 211–217.

ROSS, M.A., and HOOD, E. 1963. Radiation and sterilization of foods. Armed Forces Institute of Pathology, Washington, D.C., Contract Project No. 6x60- 01-001-02, Hazelton Labs, Falls Church, Va.

ROY, A.N., and KAYLOR, J.D. 1975. Low level ionizing radiation and spice treatment of raw, headless, white shrimp. Marine Fish. Rev. *37*, 16–20.

SCHMIDT, C.F., LECHOWICH, R.V., and FOLINAZZA, J.F. 1961. Growth and toxin production by type E. *Clostridium botulinum* below 40°F. J. Food Sci. *26*, 626–634.

SHEWAN, J.M. 1961. The microbiology of sea-water fish. *In* Fish as Food, Vol. 1. G. Borgstrom (Editor), pp. 478–560. Academic Press, New York.

SHEWAN, J.M. 1962. The influence of irradiation preservation on the nutritive value of fish and fishery products. *In* Fish in Nutrition. E. Heen and R. Kreuzer (Editors), pp. 207–219. Fishing News (Books) Ltd., London.

SHEWAN, J.M., and HOBBS, G. 1967. The bacteriology of fish spoilage and preservation. *In* Progress in Industrial Microbiology. D.J.D. Hockenhull (Editor), Vol. 6, pp. 169–205. Lliffe Books Ltd., London.

SHEWAN, J.M., and HOBBS, G. 1970. The botulism hazard in the proposed use of irradiation of fish and fishery products in the United Kingdom. *In* Preservation of Fish by Irradiation, pp. 117–125. International Atomic Energy Agency, Vienna.

SHEWAN, J.M., and LISTON, J. 1958. Experiments on the irradiation of fish with 4 MeV cathode rays and cobalt-60 gamma rays. Proc. 2nd U.N. Int. Conf. Peaceful Uses At. Energy *27*, 377.

SHIFLETT, M.A. 1965. Preservation of Dover sole by low-dose radiation and antimicrobial agents. Masters thesis, Oregon State University, Corvalis, Oregon.

SLAVIN, J.W., NICKERSON, J.T.R., GOLDBLITH, S.A., RONSIVALLI, L.J., KAYLOR, J.D., and LICCIARDELLO, J.J. 1966. The quality and wholesomeness of radiation-pasteurized marine products with particular reference to fish fillets. Isot. Radiat. Technol. *3*, 365–381.

SPINELLI, J., and MIYAUCHI, D. 1968. Irradiation of Pacific coast fish and shellfish. 5. The effect of 5' inosine monophosphate on the flavor of irradiated fish fillets. Food Technol. *22*, 123–125.

SPINELLI, J., EKLUND, M., and MIYAUCHI, D. 1964. Irradiation preservation of Pacific coast shellfish. II. Relation of bacterial counts, trimethylamine and total volatile base to sensory evaluation of irradiated king crab meat. Food Technol. *18*, 143–147.

SPINELLI, J., EKLUND, M., STOLL, N., and MIYAUCHI, D. 1965. Irradiation preservation of Pacific coast fish and shellfish. III. Storage life of petrale sole fillets at 33° and 42°F. Food Technol. *19*, 126–130.

SPINELLI, J., PELROY, G., and MIYAUCHI, D. 1969. Quality indices that can be used to assess irradiated seafoods. *In* Freezing and Irradiation of Fish. R. Kreuzer (Editor), pp. 425–430. Fishing News (books) Ltd., London.

TAUB, I.A., ANGELLINI, P., and MERRITT, C., Jr. 1976. Irradiated food: validity of extrapolating wholesomeness data. J. Food Sci. *41*, 942–944.

TEENY, F.M., and MIYAUCHI, D. 1970. Irradiation of Pacific coast fish at sea. J. Milk Food Technol. *38*, 330–334.

THORNLEY, M.J. 1963. Radiation resistance among bacteria J. Appl. Bacteriol. *26*, 334–345.

TOMIYAMA, T., JENG, S.S., SHIRAISHI, E., HAMADA, M., and YAMADA, Y. 1969. Complementary effect of food preservative and gamma radiation of whale and horse mackerel flesh. *In* Freezing and Irradiation of Fish. R. Kreuzer (Editor), pp. 472–477. Fishing News (Books) Ltd., London.

14

Enzymatic Ammonia Production in Penaied Shrimp Held on Ice

Gunnar Finne

INTRODUCTION

Decomposition of shrimp held on ice is the result of the combined action of microbial growth and natural tissue enzymes (Nair and Bose 1964; Cobb and Vanderzant 1971; Flick and Lovell 1972). Early work on decomposition concentrated on total microbial numbers and variation in types of microorganisms present as time on ice increased (Campbell and Williams 1952; Carroll *et al*. 1968; Vanderzant *et al*. 1970; Cobb *et al*. 174). In order to express the quality of iced shrimp in terms of chemical parameters, a large number of reports have suggested the determination of a variety of chemical compounds. Changes in pH (Bethea and Ambrose 1962; Baily *et al*. 1956), trimethylamine (Iyengar *et al*. 1960; Fieger and Friloux 1954), total volatile nitrogen (TVN), nonprotein nitrogen (NPN), free amino acids (Velankar and Govidan 1957, 1958; Gagnon and Fellers 1957; Cobb *et al*. 1974), volatile acids (Fieger and Friloux 1954), indole (Duggan and Strasburger 1946), and carotenoid levels (Collins and Kelly 1969) have been either used or suggested as quality indices for shrimp held on ice. The importance of microbial metabolites, specifically volatile nitrogen compounds, is evident. Increase in total volatile nitrogen in shrimp tails during the postmortem storage period on ice has been reported by several investigators (Iyengar *et al*. 1960; Cobb and Vanderzant 1971; Cobb *et al*. 1973). The primary component included in the total volatile nitrogen fraction was shown by Vanderzant *et al*. (1973) to be ammonia.

Although most of the above indicators are considered to be microbial metabolites, ammonia can be produced by both microorganisms and tissue enzymes. Cobb and Vanderzant (1971) demonstrated this by showing a

Seafood Techology Section, Department of Animal Science, Texas A & M University, College Station, Texas 77843 progressive increase in total volatile nitrogen during storage of sterile shrimp extracts. Since ammonia contributes significantly to off-flavors characteristic of decomposing shrimp, it is important that every aspect of ammonia production is well understood. For this reason the Texas A & M University Seafood Laboratory has recently done extensive work on ammonia production in shrimp tails held on ice.

ENZYMATIC AMMONIA PRODUCTION

Microbial vs Enzymatic Ammonia Production

In an early study (Yeh *et al.* 1978), we investigated the ammonia produced in shrimp extracts with and without antibiotics at different temperatures. The levels of ammonia produced in the shrimp extracts are shown in Fig. 14.1. Ammonia is produced in the control samples by bacterial as well as tissue enzymes. It is evident that the difference in ammonia production between treated and nontreated extracts is markedly affected by incubation temperature. The large difference seen at 30°C is most probably due to the accelerated bacterial growth at this temperature. At 37°C, however, bacte-

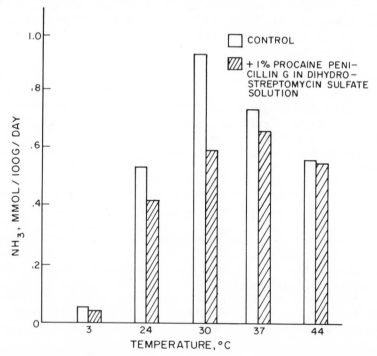

FIG. 14.1. AMMONIA PRODUCTION IN SHRIMP EXTRACTS AT DIFFERENT TEMPERATURES

rial ammonia production is reduced, since this temperature is above the maximum growth temperature of many of the organisms normally associated with shrimp spoilage. The importance of enzymatic ammonia production on initial postmortem quality deterioration is evident since, at every temperature tested, tissue enzyme production far exceeded bacterial enzyme production.

Chemical Properties of Enzymatic Ammonia Production

The effect of pH on enzymatic ammonia production, using different buffer systems, is shown in Figure 14.2. It appears that two tissue enzyme systems are responsible for the ammonia produced in postmortem shrimp muscle: one with a pH optimum around 6.0, and another with a pH optimum in the region of 8.4.

Rate of Ammonia Production in Sterile Muscle

Using optimum conditions of pH 9.6 and 24°C, the rate of ammonia production in sterile shrimp muscle is shown in Fig. 14.3. During the first 9 hr of storage, ammonia was produced at a linear rate of 0.045 mmol/hr/100 g. During prolonged storage, on the other hand, this rate was greatly reduced due, most probably, to enzyme denaturation or lack of substrate.

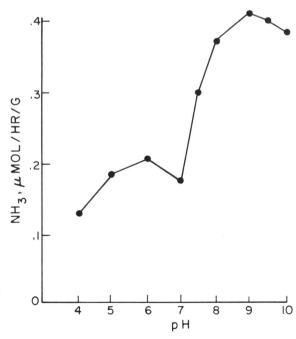

FIG. 14.2. EFFECT OF pH ON THE AMMONIA PRODUCING ENZYMES FROM SHRIMP MUSCLE TISSUE AT 37°C

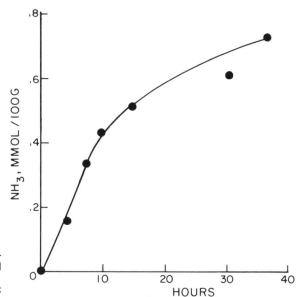

FIG. 14.3. RATE OF AM-
MONIA PRODUCTION IN
ANTIBIOTIC-TREATED
SHRIMP MUSCLE AT 24°C

Testing Individual Enzymes

In order to identify potential ammonia-producing tissue enzymes active during postmortem storage of iced shrimp tails, we tested a number of common enzymes. These included arginase, urease, adenase, adenosine deaminase, AMP-deaminase, and guanase together with a number of amino acid oxidases. Of all the potential enzymes tested, only arginase, adenosine deaminase, and AMP-deaminase were present at significant levels in antibiotic-treated shrimp muscle extracts. This is in close agreement with earlier works. Crustaceans have been shown to be devoid of all enzymatic activities associated with the urea cycle, except arginase (Chefurka 1965). Sisini (1953) reported that serine oxidase is the only amino oxidase that has been found in crustaceans. Finally, the lack of adenase and guanase in shrimp extracts is also in agreement with the results of Stone (1970), who failed to detect adenase in salmon, crab, and weathervane scallops, and the results of Tarr and Comer (1964) who reported that lingcod muscle possessed a very weak adenase activity and suggested that the deamination of the added substrate might be caused by the presence of adenosine deaminase.

Activity of Adenosine Deaminase and AMP Deaminase in Shrimp Stored on Ice

The activities of adenosine deaminase and AMP deaminase in muscle extracts from pink and brown shrimp as reported from our laboratory by

Cheuk *et al.* (1979) are shown in Fig. 14.4. As indicated, in all four cases tested there was a gradual loss in activity as storage progressed. Adenosine deaminases from pink and brown shrimp not only showed a higher activity than the corresponding AMP deaminases but also retained close-to-optimum activity during the early part of the storage period. In pink shrimp, for example, adenosine deaminase showed an initial activity of 0.29 µmole/g/min, 95% of which were retained after 6 days of iced storage. Although at a somewhat lesser activity, brown shrimp exhibited the same phenomenon as the adenosine deaminase from pink shrimp. Even though there was a marked reduction in activity of adenosine deaminase for both brown and pink shrimp during storage, the enzymes from both species retained activity throughout the entire storage period of 21 days.

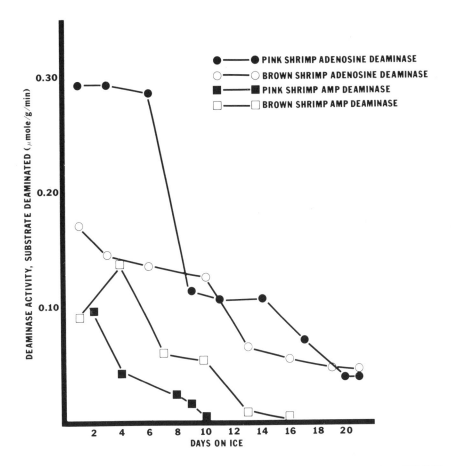

FIG. 14.4.   STABILITY OF ADENOSINE DEAMINASE AND AMP DEAMINASE ACTIVITY IN PINK AND BROWN SHRIMP HELD ON ICE

AMP deaminase activity was totally lost in pink shrimp after 10 days of storage. Even after 4 days on ice, only 50% of the original AMP deaminase activity was retained in pink shrimp. AMP deaminase from brown shrimp showed the same pattern as the corresponding enzyme from pink shrimp. The instability of AMP deaminase observed during these studies is in agreement with earlier work done on crustaceans (Dingle and Hines 1967; Flick and Lovell 1972). The loss in enzyme activity during iced storage can be due to a number of factors: the melting ice may wash out both enzymes and other compounds, a constant increase in bacterial population may cause enzyme degradation, or inhibitors may accumulate, causing a loss in enzyme activity. AMP deaminase has been shown to be inhibited by inorganic phosphate (Nikiforuk and Colowick 1955), seemingly due to the competition between free phosphate and the phosphate group on AMP for the binding site on AMP deaminase.

Nucleotide Breakdown Pathway in Gulf Shrimp

The nucleotide degradation pathway in shrimp has not been clearly established. Arai (1966) observed two pathways for the degradation of adenine nucleotides in Japanese prawn *(Pandalus hypsinotus)*. One involves the direct deamination of adenosine monophosphate (AMP) to inosine monophosphate (IMP), while the second involves dephosphorylation of AMP to adenosine, which is followed by deamination to inosine. Both pathways will eventually lead to hypoxanthine (Fig. 14.5). In Alaskan shrimp *(Pandalus borealis, Pandalus platyceros,* and *Pandalopsis dispar)* held on ice, the major pathway for adenine nucleotide degradation results in accumulation of IMP rather than inosine. Flick and Lovell (1972) showed the opposite to be true for white shrimp *(Penaeus setiferus)* from the Gulf of Mexico in which inosine instead of IMP was first detected after death.

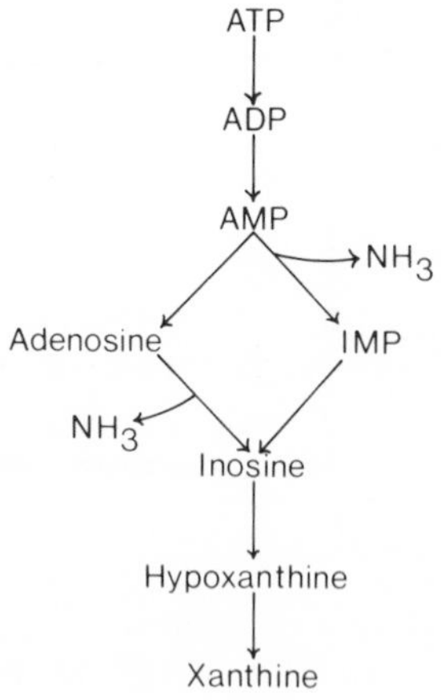

FIG. 14.5. DEGRADATION PATHWAY OF NUCLEO-TIDES IN SHRIMP

On the background of the simplified reaction sequence for the degradation of nucleotides in shrimp as shown in Fig. 14.5 (Flick and Lovell 1970), we suggested (Cheuk *et al.* 1979) that the principal nucleotide degradation in pink and brown shrimp held on ice is through adenosine rather than inosine monophosphate. The reason for this is the much higher initial activity observed of adenosine deaminase as compared with AMP deaminase and the rapid loss in AMP deaminase activity during the storage period. Both adenosine and AMP deaminases are principal ammonia-producing enzymes during early stages of ice storage, while adenosine deaminase is the sole ammonia producer during the later stages.

Ammonia Producing Enzyme Activity as Potential Quality Index for Fresh Shrimp

When correlating AMP and adenosine deaminase activities to a common chemical quality indicator (TVN) and sensory evaluations, there is a strong indication that the instability of AMP deaminase can be used as a quality parameter for shrimp held on ice. Our studies showed that AMP deaminase activity could not be detected after 10 days of ice storage. This time coincided with the point when the taste panel determined the shrimp to be no longer of prime quality. It also corresponded to the time when TVN values entered an accelerated phase. If a rapid and technically simple test for AMP deaminase activity can be developed, detection of activity can give a good indication of postharvest storage time. Since both AMP deaminase and adenosine deaminase gradually lose activity during the storage period, the rate of these enzymatic reactions can also give an indication of ice storage time.

When using ammonia-producing enzyme activities to test the quality of fresh shrimp landed on the Texas coast, we found that the enzyme activity data showed a close relationship with the length of storage in days after harvest. However, for these tests to find any usefulness as a quality control tool, methodology needs to be improved greatly since enzyme assays presently require well trained personnel and sophisticated instrumentation.

REFERENCES

ARAI, K. 1966. Nucleotides in the muscle of marine invertebrates. Bull. Jpn. Soc. Sci. Fish. *32*, 174.

BAILEY, M.E., FIEGER, E.A., and NOVAK, A.F. 1956. Objective tests applicable to quality studies of ice stored shrimp. Food Res. *21*, 611.

BETHEA, S., and AMBROSE, M.E. 1962. Comparison of pH, trimethylamine content, and picric acid turbidity as indices of ice shrimp quality. Commer. Fish. Rev. *24*, 7.

CAMPBELL, L.L., and WILLIAMS, O.B. 1952. The bacteriology of Gulf

Coast Shrimp. 4.   Bacteriological, chemical and organoleptic changes with ice storage.   Food Technol. 5, 125.

CARROLL, B.T., REESE, G.B., WARD, B.Q.   1968.   Microbiological study of iced shrimp.   Excerpts from the 1965 Iced-Shrimp Symposium.   U.S. Dept. Interior, Circ. 284, Washington, DC.

CHEFURKA, W.   1965.   Intermediary metabolism of nitrogenous and lipid compounds in insects.   In The Physiology of Insecta.   M. Rockstein (Editor), Vol. 2, p. 670.   Academic Press, New York.

CHEUK, W.L., FINNE, G., and NICKELSON, R.   1979.   Stability of adenosine deaminase and adenosine monophosphate deaminase during ice storage of pink and brown shrimp from the Gulf of Mexico.   J. Food Sci. 44, 1625.

COBB, B.F., III, and VANDERZANT, C.   1971.   Biochemical changes in shrimp inoculated with Pseudomonas, Bacillus and a coryneform bacterium.   J. Milk Food Technol. 34, 53.

COBB, B.F., III, ALANIZ, I., and THOMPSON, C.A., JR.   1973.   Biochemical and microbial studies on shrimp: Volatile nitrogen and amino nitrogen analysis.   J. Food Sci. 38, 431.

COBB, B.F., III, VANDERZANT, C., and HYDER, K.   1974.   Effect of ice storage upon the free amino acid contents of tails of white shrimp (Panaeus setiferus).   J. Agric. Food Chem. 22, 1052.

COLLINS, J., and KELLY, C.   1969.   Alaska pink shrimp, Pandalus borealis: Effects of heat treatment on color and machine peelability.   U.S. Fish. Wildl. Serv. Fish. Ind. Res. 5, 181.

DINGLE, J.R., and HINES, J.A.   1967.   Extraction and some properties of adenosine 5'-monophosphate aminohydrolase from pre-rigor and post-rigor muscle of cod.   J. Fish. Res. Board Can. 24, 1717.

DUGGAN, R.E., and STRASBURGER, L.W.   1946.   Indole in shrimp.   J. Assoc. Off. Anal. Chem. 29, 177.

FIEGER, E.A., and FRILOUX, J.J.   1954.   A comparison of objective tests for quality of Gulf shrimp.   Food Technol. 8, 35.

FLICK, G.J., and LOVELL, R.T.   1970.   Postmortem degradation of nucleotides and glycogen in Gulf shrimp.   Food Technol. 30, 1743-B.

FLICK, G.J., and LOVELL, R.T.   1972.   Postmortem biochemical changes in the muscle of Gulf shrimp (Penaeus aztecus).   J. Food Sci. 37, 609.

GAGNON, M., and FELLERS, C.R.   1957.   Biochemical methods for determining shrimp quality.   Food Technol. 12, 340.

IYENGAR, J.R., VISWESUARIAH, K., MOORJANI, M.N., and BHATIA, D.S.   1960.   Assessment of the progressive spoilage of ice-stored shrimp.   J. Fish. Res. Board Can. 17, 745.

NAIR, M.R., and BOSE, A.N.   1964.   Studies on postmortem biochemical changes in prawn.   In The Technology of Fish Utilization, FAO Symp. p. 58.

NIKIFORUK, G., and COLOWICK, S.P.   1955.   5'-Adenylic acid deaminase from muscle. *In* Methods in Enzymology. S.P. Colowick and N. Kaplan (Editors), Vol. 2, p. 469. Academic Press, New York.

SISINI, A. 1953. Metabolism of D- and L-serine in marine invertebrates. Bull. Soc. Ital. Biol. Sper. *39*, 1969.

STONE, F.E. 1970. Enzymatic deamination of adenosine monophosphate (AMP), adenosine and adenine by salmon, crab and scallop muscle extracts. J. Food Sci. *35*, 565.

TARR, H.L.A., and COMER, A.G. 1964. Deamination of adenine and related compounds and formation of deoxyadenosine and deoxyinosine by lingcod muscle enzymes. Can. J. Biochem. *42*, 1527.

VANDERZANT, C., MROZ, E., and NICKELSON, R., II. 1970. Microbial flora of Gulf of Mexico and pond shrimp. J. Milk Food Technol. *33*, 346.

VANDERZANT, C., COBB, B.F., III, THOMPSON, C.A., JR., and PARKER, J.C. 1973. Microbial flora, chemical characteristics and shelf life of four species of pond-reared shrimp. J. Milk Food Tech. *36*, 443.

VELANKAR, N.K. and GOVINDAN, T.K. 1957. The free α-amino acid nitrogen content of the skeletal muscle of some marine fishes and invertebrates. Curr. Sci. *26*, 385.

VELANKAR, N.K., and GOVINDAN, T.K. 1958. The free amino nitrogen content as index of quality of ice-stored prawns. Curr. Sci. *27*, 451.

YEH, C.S., NICKELSON, R., and FINNE, G. 1978. Ammonia-producing enzymes in white shrimp tails. J.Food Sci. *43*, 1400.

15

Effects of Processing on Clam Flavor Volatiles

George J. Flick,[1] Janis A. Hubbard,[1] Robert L. Ory,[2] Michael G. Legendre,[2] and A.J. St. Angelo[2]

INTRODUCTION

The sea is where seafood lives so, to get the freshest and most flavorful seafood, one should catch it, net it, dig it, trap it, or purchase it from local grocers or dockside fishermen as soon as possible after it is available. For most consumers, however, this is not possible unless costly means are used to retain the fresh quality. Usually the products must be processed by methods that can affect final product flavor. Simple and reliable methods for measuring seafood flavor and quality, such as the rapid unconventional gas chromatographic method of Dupuy and co-workers applied to salad oils and dressings (Dupuy *et al.* 1973, 1977), peanut products (Fore *et al.* 1976), soy protein products (Rayner *et al.* 1978), or oyster liquor and trout (Dupuy *et al.* 1978) are urgently needed.

Another factor to consider is economics. Seafoods have always been and always will be an important source of high quality protein throughout the world. Except for coastal areas, however, seafood is not readily available and in many cases, is not a low cost food item. Other animal proteins like beef, pork, and sausages are now being blended with vegetable protein (meat extenders) that do not lower nutritional quality of the product but do lower the cost to the consumer. In the United States and Europe, economics and functionality of vegetable proteins are increasing their use in manufacture of processed meats, cheese, and bakery products. Oil-seed proteins now offer similar opportunities to the seafood industry as functional aids during processing and as a means of improving finished product acceptability (Sipos *et al.* 1979). Unfortunately, however, there are very few nutrition studies on fish–vegetable protein products (or seafood–vegetable protein)

---

[1] Department of Food Science and Technology, Virginia Polytechnic Institute and State University, Blacksburg, Virginia 24061.
[2] Southern Regional Research Center, USDA-SEA, New Orleans, Louisiana 70179.

because this is still a relatively new area. Daley and Deng (1978) described "sea dogs" (hot dog analogues) made from fish and soy protein, but blends with other types of seafood should also be possible. Sipos *et al.* (1979) state that textured soy protein products have been increasingly advocated as seafood extenders; soy protein isolate may be a useful ingredient also for seafood applications, such as shrimp puffs, tuna salad, fish sticks and cakes, salmon patties, fish sausage, and clam products. They suggest use of textured soy protein concentrate as an alternative for clams in such items as canned minced clams or clam chowders. Vegetable proteins tend to absorb moisture or juices normally lost during processing and cooking.

In any type of seafood/vegetable protein blend or seafood-flavored vegetable protein product, the retention of fresh flavor and a simple accurate means of measuring the effects of processing and storage on the flavor (regardless of the particular seafood in question) is of major importance. The purpose of this research is to determine if the rapid, direct gas chromatographic method of Dupuy *et al.* (1978) could be used to measure the effects of processing on the flavor volatiles in clam juice that will be used ultimately for flavoring clam products as mentioned by Sipos *et al.* (1979), or for clam-flavored snack dips, a new product currently entering the consumer market.

MATERIALS AND METHODS

Types of Clam Juices Processed

Ocean quahogs *(Arctica islandica)* and surf clams *(Spisula solidissima)* were obtained within 24 hr of harvesting from the J.H. Miles Company in Norfolk, Virginia. In order to minimize any effects due to seasonal variation, the sampling frequency was conducted quarterly over a 2-year period. The juice was separated from the clams and analyzed fresh (without any processing) and juice from the quahogs was analyzed after several treatments. The clams were subjected to a brief heat treatment in a steam cooker. This heat shock procedure opened the shells prior to the mechanical shucking process and resulted in a liquid referred to as "extracted juice."

Part of the extracted juice was retained for direct analysis, freeze drying, and spray drying. The remainder was concentrated tenfold in a double-effect vacuum evaporator to obtain "concentrated juice" for direct analysis, freeze drying, and spray drying. Extracted and concentrated juices were obtained from ocean quahogs. Clam meats recovered from the retort vessel were washed during the commercial process and the effects of successive washings on volatiles carry-over into the wash water was determined.

EXPERIMENTAL METHODS

Analysis of volatiles by the rapid, direct gas chromatographic method of Legendre *et al.* (1979) was described earlier. This consists of an external closed inlet device for direct introduction of the entire sample into the gas chromatograph (GC), without prior steam distillation and concentration of the volatiles.

Approximately 200 mg of volatile-free glass wool is placed in one end of a 3 3/8 in. borosilicate glass tube. On top of this is added approximately 300 mg potassium carbonate followed by another 200 mg glass wool. A sample of clam juice, approximately 35 mg, is dripped onto the glass wool.

The upper pipe cap is removed from the inlet, the sample liner is put into the inlet assembly, the upper pipe cap reinstalled and hand-tightened, the Quick Connect fitting is attached for carrier gas, and the inlet is heated to 130°C via a heating tape. With the six-port valve in the inject position and the GC column at room temperature, the volatiles are swept from the sample and deposited at the head of the GC column. The column is 1/8 in. × 6 ft nickel tubing, Poropak Q packing. After a sweep time of 15 min, the six-port valve is put into the "Run/Purge" position, isolating the inlet from the GC column. The GC oven is heated to 100°C and, once there, the temperature is programmed to 200°C at 4°/min. While resolving the volatiles, the sample liner is removed and a blank liner installed to maintain the seal and flow of helium through the inlet. At this time the condenser assembly heater is activated to 150°C, and, with helium flow, the moisture from the sample is removed and swept to the atmosphere. After 20−30 min, the condenser heater is turned off and, with house air again flowing through the cooling coils, the external inlet is again ready for the next sample. Time for analysis of one sample is 70−80 min.

The condenser assembly and six-port rotary valve permits the removal of large amounts of water from samples such as clam juice, before the volatiles enter the chromatography column. By manipulation of the six-port rotary valve, water is condensed outside of the column and removed during GC analysis of volatiles. This device allows immediate introduction of subsequent samples with no loss of time or accuracy.

Conventional gas chromatographic analysis of clam juice concentrated volatiles (obtained by distillation and concentration; a 9 hr total process) was also performed. Concentrated samples were reconstituted before use. A total volume of 800 ml clam juice was distilled for each sample. The addition of a silicon antifoaming compound was necessary to prevent excessive foaming. Samples were distilled and volatiles isolated according to a procedure described by Sheldon (1979).

A modified rotary flash evaporator equipped with a spiral condenser was used in the distillation, which consisted of 1 hr at 60°C, 300 mm Hg; 1 hr at 75°C, 471 mm Hg; and 1 hr at 75°C, 500 mm Hg. A capillary leak of compressed air provided continuous agitation of the sample.

Methylnonadecanoate was added to the extracted volatiles as a standard to be used in determining peak areas. Volatiles were isolated by washing the extract with diethyl ether. Samples were concentrated using a rotary flash evaporator and then prepurified nitrogen before injection into the gas chromatograph.

Chromatograms were prepared using a micro-Tek 220 model gas chromatograph equipped with a flame ionization detector and fitted with a 52 cm × 2 mm i.d. glass column, 3% SP 2100 on 80/100 mesh Supelcoport. The column oven temperature program was increased from 50° to 250°C at 2°/min. Other operating conditions were injection port temperature, 180°C; detector port, 220°C; carrier gas, helium at 60 psi. Sample injection size was 2 µl. Data collection and normalization were made using a Perkin-Elmer M-2 calculating integrator.

GEL ELECTROPHORESIS OF PROTEINS

Sodium dodecyl sulfate (SDS) polyacrylamide gel electrophoresis was performed by the procedure of Weber *et al.* (1972).

RESULTS AND DISCUSSION

As a preliminary test of the system prior to analysis of clam juices, two samples of fish were analyzed by the direct GC system of Dupuy and co-workers (1977, 1978). Figure 15.1 illustrates the distinct differences between the volatile GC profiles of flounder and turbot fish in the major peaks at 3−6 min, 9 min, and 21 min. Flounder has more volatiles (flavor/aroma materials) than turbot in these areas and in the lesser peaks between 18 and 36 min. Polyacrylamide gel electrophoresis of proteins extracted from these fish are different (Fig. 15.2) with flounder exhibiting more intense protein bands than turbot. Protein profiles are not necessarily associated with flavor volatiles, however, gel electrophoresis is frequently employed to distinguish reliably between proteins or protein-containing foods. Dupuy *et al.* (1978) utilized the direct GC technique to compare volatiles profiles of trout fillets stored on ice for 2, 11, and 25 months. The chromatographic peaks in the profiles were similar, but the intensities increased dramatically with increased storage, and several new peaks appeared at 11 months (still more at 25) that were absent at 2 months. These results suggested that this method should be applicable to analyses of clam juice volatiles of different species, before and after processing treatments.

Volatiles concentrated from clam juice by the traditional scheme and analyzed by conventional long column GC did resolve many more minor peaks than does this unconventional GC method (unpublished results); however, upon analysis by mass spectroscopy, many of the peaks were found to be silicon derivatives rather than flavor compounds. These were due to the silicon antifoaming agent added to the samples as had been suggested in previous studies by other researchers (Labropoulos 1980). Sample preparation was very long and cumbersome (8−9 hr) and elution time for the long column required almost 3 hr compared to 70−80 min total time required for analysis of a sample by the rapid GC method.

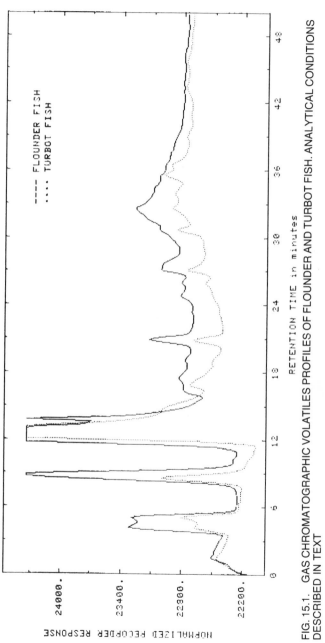

FIG. 15.1. GAS CHROMATOGRAPHIC VOLATILES PROFILES OF FLOUNDER AND TURBOT FISH. ANALYTICAL CONDITIONS DESCRIBED IN TEXT

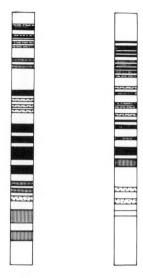

FIG. 15.2. GEL ELECTROPHORETIC PROTEIN
PATTERNS OF FLOUNDER AND TURBOT FISH   Flounder   Turbot

If fresh juices from quahog and surf clams are analyzed by the rapid GC method, noticeable differences are apparent in peaks at retention times of 3, 5–6, 9 21, 26–30, 33 (present in quahog but absent in surf clams), and 39 min (Fig. 15.3). This suggests that quahog juice should have a flavor distinctly different from surf clam juice, but, being an objective measurement, this method cannot label it as better or worse without concurrent subjective analysis by a trained taste panel. With the additional information, it should then be possible to utilize the rapid GC method alone to monitor the effects of processing on flavor of the juice.

With combined GC/MS analysis of the volatiles, many of the components of the profile could be identified (Table 15.1). Both species of clams contain essentially the same components, but, as seen in Fig. 15.3, the quantities are different. Changes in these components, particularly the 9 min (ethanol) peak, that are affected by various processing steps can therefore be monitored by the rapid GC procedure.

Figure 15.4 compares juice obtained from the retorting step, in which the clam shells are opened, to fresh clam juice. As expected, heating causes the loss of many flavor volatiles with peak retention times between 3 and 48 min. Interestingly, however, heat increases the 9 min peak (ethanol); it is much higher in extracted clam juice than in the fresh juices.

A comparison of the extracted versus concentrated clam juice is shown in Fig. 15.5. There is a striking difference in the 9 min peak only; much higher in extracted clam juice. This indicates that vacuum concentration of clam juice can cause slight increases of some of the flavor volatiles but sharply decreases the amount of ethanol.

Snack dips, a popular consumer product today, are available in several

EFFECTS OF PROCESSING ON CLAM FLAVOR VOLATILES 339

TABLE 15.1.   IDENTIFICATION OF PEAKS IN GAS CHROMATOGRAPHIC
VOLATILES PROFILES IN QUAHOG AND SURF CLAM JUICES[1]

Component	Quahog clam juice	Surf clam juice
Methyl mercaptan	+	−
Ethanol	+	+
Dimethyl Sulfide	+	+
Acetone	+	+
2-Propanol	+	+
Diacetyl	+	−
2-Butanone	+	−
Trimethylamine	+	−
Dimethyl disulfide	+	−
Pyridine	+	−
Benzaldehyde	+	−

[1] +; detected; −; undetected.

flavors. For flavoring either dairy- or nondairy-type (i.e., based on vegetable proteins) snack dips, it is more practical to add dried clam juice than to add the whole (or concentrated) juice, because of the high water content of fresh juice. The effects of freeze drying and spray drying on concentrated quahog juice are illustrated in Fig. 15.6. The two volatiles profiles curves are virtually identical, indicating that there is essentially no difference between the effects of freeze drying and spray drying on the volatiles. There also is a very small ethanol peak at 9 min, which seems to be effected by the vacuum concentration step (Fig. 15.5). Thus, a processor could select either method for drying clam juice; the choice being governed by the one that requires the least fuel energy and processing equipment. These same effects were obtained by GC analysis of freeze-dried and spray-dried extracted clam juices, indicating no apparent effect on volatiles caused by the longer drying times required for the more dilute juices. If the volatiles curves for freeze-dried extracted and concentrated clam juices and those for spray-dried extracted and concentrated clam juices were compared, these curves were also essentially the same. There was no loss of flavor volatiles by either method on both extracted and concentrated clam juices, confirming the results shown in Fig. 15.6. There was a slight variation in the first peaks (3−6 min) of spray-dried clam juices (slightly less volatiles in the concentrated juice), but this was not significant.

To examine the effects of successive washings on removal of flavor volatiles from clams, extracted clam juice volatiles were compared to those from the first five washings. Figure 15.7 compares only the first two washes and the extracted juice, since there are practically no volatiles remaining after the second (and subsequent) washes. There is only a slight removal of volatiles in the first wash, suggesting that the original clam juice retains essentially all of the flavor components. Thus, the extra washes (3 to 8) sometimes used by processors would not extract extra flavor.

Thermal processes employed in the industrial shucking or picking of clams, therefore, may result in very little destruction or in complete destruction of flavor volatiles, depending upon the amount of heat applied and the length of the heating period. Volatiles in clam juice can be affected by

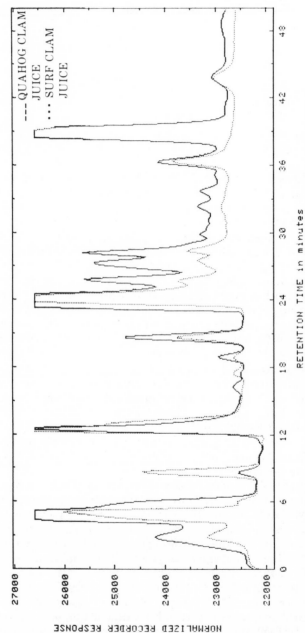

FIG. 15.3. GAS CHROMATOGRAPHIC VOLATILES PROFILES OF FRESH QUAHOG AND SURF CLAM JUICES

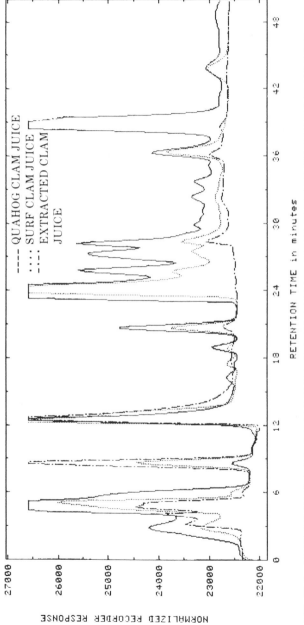

FIG. 15.4. EFFECTS OF HEATING ON GAS CHROMATOGRAPHIC VOLATILES PROFILES OF QUAHOG CLAM JUICE

341

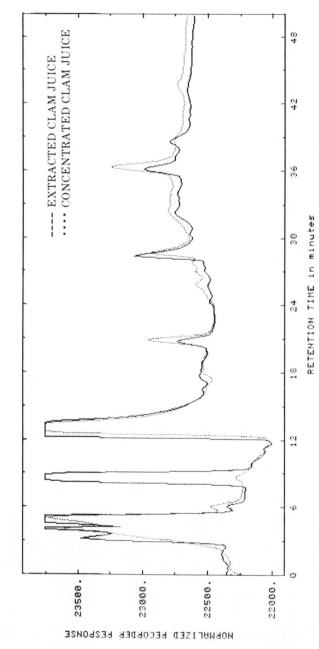

FIG. 15.5. EFFECTS OF HEAT ON GAS CHROMATOGRAPHIC VOLATILES PROFILES IN EXTRACTED AND CONCENTRATED QUAHOG CLAM JUICE

342

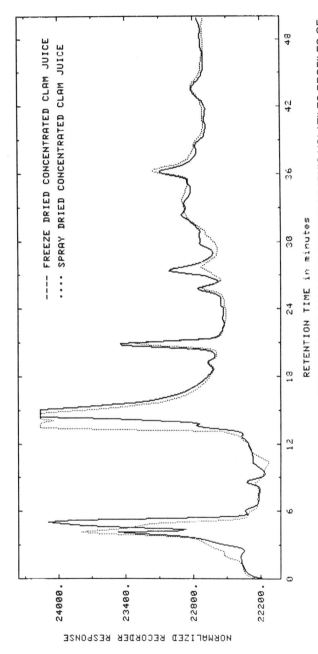

FIG. 15.6. EFFECTS OF FREEZE DRYING AND SPRAY DRYING ON GAS CHROMATOGRAPHIC VOLATILES PROFILES OF CONCENTRATED QUAHOG CLAM JUICE

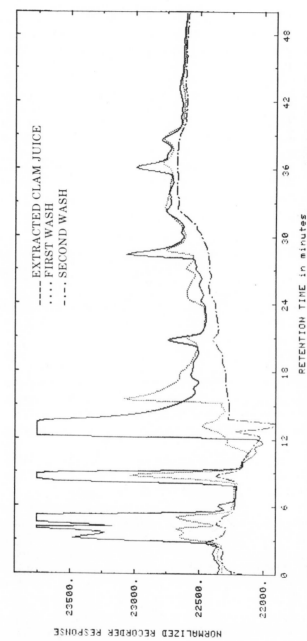

FIG. 15.7. EFFECTS OF SUCCESSIVE WATER WASHINGS ON GAS CHROMATOGRAPHIC VOLATILES PROFILES OF QUA-HOG CLAMS

these thermal processes. For drying clam juice, however, there seems to be little difference between the effects of freeze drying and spray drying on volatile profiles. Therefore, the most important consideration in choosing a drying process may be the fuel energy requirements of the system.

Current interest in increasing the quantity and quality of dietary protein supplies is centered on utilization of defatted oilseed meals, dairy whey by-products, and fish proteins (fish protein concentrate, fish flour). The protein ingredients market, worth $403 million in 1977, is projected to climb to $594.5 million in 1983 and $701.9 million by 1986 (Anon. 1979). Use of vegetable proteins is expected to increase in processed foods (due to pressures to cut ingredient costs, extend shelf life, and improve nutritional quality), in preparation of frozen fish with breaded or batter coatings, and in snack foods, as processors attempt to bolster nutritional quality and shed the "junk food" label. For clam flavoring of snack dips or vegetable protein clam-type analogues, therefore, freeze-dried or spray-dried clam juice appears to be appropriate for retention of the fresh clam flavor.

REFERENCES

ANONYMOUS 1979. Cereal Industry Newsletter: Market for protein ingredients to top $700 million by 1986. Cereal Foods World 24, 480.

DALEY, L.H., and DENG, J.C. 1978. "Sea Dog" made with minced mullet and textured soy flour. 3rd Annu. Trop. Subtrop. Fisheries Tech. Conf. Amer., New Orleans, p. 6 (Abstr.).

DUPUY, H.P., RAYNER, E.T., WADSWORTH, J.I., and LEGENDRE, M.G. 1977. Analysis of vegetable oils for flavor quality by direct gas chromatography. J. Am. Oil. Chem. Soc. 54, 445–449.

DUPUY, H.P., LEGENDRE, M.G., RAYNER, E.T., GRODNER, R.M., and NOVAK, A.F. 1978. Instrumental analysis of volatiles in seafood. Proc. 3rd Annu. Trop. Subtrop. Fisheries Tech. Conf. Amer., New Orleans, pp. 354–358.

FORE, S.P., DUPUY, H.P., and WADSWORTH, J.I. 1976. Correlation of volatile components of peanut products with flavor score. I. Shelf life studies of peanut butter. Peanut Sci. 3, 86–89.

LABROPOULOS, A.W. 1980. Process variables in a UHT system and their effects on psychophysics and rheology of yoghurt. Ph.D. dissertation. Virginia Polytechnic Institute and State University, Blacksburg, Va.

LEGENDRE, M.G., FISHER, G.S., SCHULLER, W.H., DUPUY, H.P., and RAYNER, E.T. 1979. Novel technique for the analysis of volatiles in aqueous and non-aqueous systems. J. Am. Oil Chem. Soc. 56 552–555.

RAYNER, E.T., WADSWORTH, J.I., LEGENDRE, M.G., and DUPUY, H.P. 1978. Analysis of flavor quality and residual solvent of soy protein products. J. Am. Oil. Chem. Soc. 55, 454–458.

SHELDON, B.W. 1979. Feed and intestinal microflora as factors in the flavor and quality of broiler meat. Ph.D. Dissertation. Virginia Polytechnic Institute and State University, Blacksburg, Va.

SIPOS, E.F., ENDRES, J.G., TYBOR, P.T., and NAKAJIMA, Y. 1979. Use of vegetable protein in processed seafood products. J. Am. Oil Chem. Soc. *56*, 320–327.

WEBER, K., PRINGLE, J.R., and OSBORN, M. 1972. Measurement of molecular weights by electrophoresis on SDS-acrylamide gel. *In* Methods in Enzymology. S.P. Colowick and N.O. Kaplan (Editors), Vol. XXVI, pp. 3–27. Academic Press, New York.

16

Biochemical Evaluation of Seafood

Lori F. Jacober and Arthur G. Rand, Jr.

INTRODUCTION

Criteria for evaluation of seafood quality have been an elusive goal for many years. There have been numerous attempts to find a reliable means of assessing seafood quality. While significant progress has been made, there has been no agreement on any one test procedure as completely acceptable for all types of seafood to describe total quality (Gould and Peters 1971; Martin *et al.* 1978). Total quality encompasses all important aspects from initial composition, nutritive value, freshness to the degree of spoilage, damage, and deterioration during catching, storing, processing, distributing, and sale (Connell 1975). Many quality tests do not find commercial application owing to a variety of limitations and the inability to measure true total quality.

The marker compounds measured routinely for the determination of fish quality, such as trimethylamine (TMA), total volatile bases (TVB), volatile acids, volatile reducing substances (VRS), and oxidized lipids (TBA) (Gould and Peters 1971; Hart and Fisher 1971; Pearson 1971), appear in significant amounts only in the later stages of the seafood quality period. Tests for these compounds are of limited value since they measure compounds that are indicative of advanced deterioration and spoilage and therefore do not reflect all the quality stages of seafood (Spinelli *et al.* 1964; Dugal 1967; Kassemsarn *et al.* 1962; Spinelli 1967; Fields and Richmond 1968; Burt 1977). The problem in the use of these compounds as criteria for the loss of quality, along with such indices as volume of drip loss and lactic acid build-up, is a consistent lack of reproducibility (Gould and Peters 1971). Requirements for any expensive and/or complicated equipment which permits only research utilization must also be considered (Burt 1977). Similarly, the Torrymeter or freshness tests measuring compounds such

---

[1]Department of Food Science and Technology, Nutrition and Dietetics, University of Rhode Island, Kingston, Rhode Island 02881

as hypoxanthine are indices of a single property or compound and do not include the incipiently spoiled phase of the total fish quality.

Another type of fish quality testing that has been utilized is sensory evaluation. Its inherent disadvantages as a single index of quality are obvious. The disadvantages range from standardization problems among laboratories to any personal prejudices a judge may have as to color, flavor, and odor. Therefore, trained and experienced judges must be used to increase objectivity and reduce error (Connell 1977; Gould and Peters 1971).

The ideal test should be a simple evaluation, which rapidly determines the quality status of a seafood product. It appears this cannot be accomplished with a single quality test. A combination of objective tests that are quick and simple to interpret and can integrate the freshness and spoilage phases of fish quality seems to be the optimum goal. The application of biochemical techniques for evaluation of seafood, though a recent development, has promise as the solution for total quality assessment. The problems associated with integrating two or more measurements can be minimized because of the specificity, rapidity, simplicity, and sensitivity that are characteristic of many biochemical analyses.

BIOCHEMICAL CHANGES AS POTENTIAL SEAFOOD QUALITY INDICES

The potential areas for application of biochemical evaluation in quality determination of fish muscle are illustrated in Fig. 16.1. Adapted from Eskin *et al.* (1971), this figure summarizes the post-harvest biochemical events, which can be classified as two phases: metabolic and microbial.

The metabolic changes are due to enzymes that remain active in the fish tissue after death. Metabolites from these inherent enzymatic changes could be used as indices of freshness through biochemical analyses. One of the first metabolites to appear is lactic acid. Lactic acid accumulates during postmortem changes because of the glycolytic conversion of storage glycogen in the fish muscle after the cessation of respiration (Fraser *et al.* 1965; Tarr 1966; Eskin *et al.* 1971; Gould and Peters 1971). Lactic acid build-up can cause a drop in pH, resulting in the liberation and activation of inherent acid cell proteases, cathepsins (Eskin *et al.* 1971; Chicester and Graham 1973; Connell 1975). The resulting proteolysis produces a second metabolite in the form of amino acids (Eskin *et al.* 1971; Gould and Peters 1971). Nucleotide degradation also commences with death and proceeds at a temperature-dependent rate (Beuchat 1973; Spinelli *et al.* 1964; Eskin *et al.* 1971; Jones *et al.* 1964; Spinelli 1967; Boyd and Wilson 1977; Murray *et al.* 1966; Martin *et al.* 1978; Jahns and Rand 1977). This results in the accumulation of a third metabolite hypoxanthine (Spinelli *et al.* 1964; Jones *et al.* 1964; Fraser *et al.* 1968B; Eskin *et al.* 1971; Beuchat 1973; Jahns *et al.* 1976; Burt 1977; Boyd and Wilson 1977; Jahns and Rand 1977; Martin *et al.* 1978; Jacober *et al.* 1978). It would appear that there should be a correlation between the post-harvest age of the fish and the levels of these compounds.

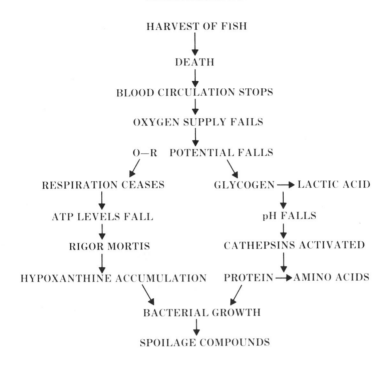

HARVEST OF FISH

DEATH

BLOOD CIRCULATION STOPS

OXYGEN SUPPLY FAILS

O—R POTENTIAL FALLS

RESPIRATION CEASES   GLYCOGEN —→ LACTIC ACID

ATP LEVELS FALL   pH FALLS

RIGOR MORTIS   CATHEPSINS ACTIVATED

HYPOXANTHINE ACCUMULATION   PROTEIN —→ AMINO ACIDS

BACTERIAL GROWTH

SPOILAGE COMPOUNDS

Adapted from Eskin et al. 1971

FIG. 16.1. POTENTIAL AREAS FOR APPLICATION OF BIOCHEMICAL EVALUATION IN QUALITY DETERMINATION OF FISH MUSCLE

The products formed by autolysis contribute to the support of bacterial growth (Eskin *et al.* 1971; Tomiyasu and Zenitani 1957; Fields and Richmond 1968; Chichester and Graham 1973). Combined with the loss of phagocyte action (Eskin *et al.* 1971), the bacteria present in the surface slime, gills, and intestinal tract invade the muscle tissue and multiply (Chichester and Graham 1973; Martin *et al.* 1978; Tomiyasu and Zenitani 1957; Connell 1975). Metabolites from microbial action can then be used in biochemical analyses as indices of the onset of spoilage. The main spoilage process involves bacterial metabolism of low-molecular-weight compounds in fish muscle to yield a variety of objectionable flavor and odor compounds. Microbial degradation of amino acids can yield volatile bases such as the diamines, cadaverine, and putrescine, as well as ammonia and the monoamine, histamine (Eskin *et al.* 1971; Tomiyasu and Zenitani 1957; Fields *et al.* 1968; Tabor and Tabor 1976; Mietz and Karmas 1977). Simultaneously, trimethylamine oxide and lactic acid can be metabolized by bacterial action to yield TMA and acetic acid (Fields *et al.* 1968; Tomiyasu and Zenitani 1957; Martin *et al.* 1978; Connell 1975; Eskin *et al.* 1971).

LACTIC ACID

The measurement of lactic acid in fish flesh as an index of quality has had little success due to apparent wide variation and difficulties in analysis (Eskin *et al.* 1971; Gould and Peters 1971). Most methods used for lactate detection are chemical procedures. Some procedures that have been used can be read spectrophotometrically, and many, especially AOAC methods, are lengthy and complicated, requiring expensive equipment (Hart and Fisher 1971; Pearson 1971; Fraser *et al.* 1965; Thomas and Chamberlain 1974). The measurement for lactic acid is not done specifically but is included as part of a titration for total volatile acids.

Recently, a prepackaged enzymatic analysis kit capable of determining L-lactic acid in a variety of foods has become available (Boehringer-Mannheim Co.). This simple and rapid analysis of lactic acid (Gutman and Wahlefeld 1974) was adapted to the neutralized perchloric acid fish extracts described by Jahns and Rand (1977) and Jacober *et al.* (1978). The procedure was tested on fresh trawl-caught winter flounder *(Pseudopleuronectes americanus)* stored on ice at 4°−6°C. The results are illustrated in Fig. 16.2. The graph compares L-lactic acid levels in flounder muscle with hypoxanthine development. While the hypoxanthine levels follow a normal path and appear to peak, the lactic acid levels are high initially and increase

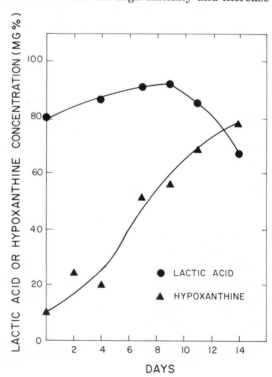

FIG. 16.2.   LACTIC ACID AND HYPOXANTHINE FORMATION IN WINTER FLOUNDER STORED ON ICE (0°C)

slightly for 9 days. As hypoxanthine concentration approaches peak values, lactic acid levels decline.

It would appear that enzymatic determination of lactic acid does not reflect any dramatic change in initial post-harvest quality. This may be explained by two factors. First, lactic acid formation is dependent on glycogen reserves in the fish muscle tissue. Any struggle prior to death will result in the depletion or loss of the endogenous substrate and the accumulation of lactic acid anaerobically by glycolysis (Eskin *et al.* 1971; Gould and Peters 1971; Tarr 1966; Fraser *et al.* 1965). Therefore, "rested" fish and those fish killed quickly would have more glycogen reserves, and glycolysis could continue with an apparent increase in lactate levels during storage (Eskin *et al.* 1971; Gould and Peters 1971; Tarr 1966; Fraser *et al.* 1965). The fish sampled in this study were allowed to struggle during capture and until death. Second, glycolytic changes are rapid and have been found to continue at a considerable rate at temperatures just below freezing (Gould and Peters 1971; Fraser *et al.* 1965). All fish in this study were placed on ice immediately after capture and samples were taken at the indicated time intervals and frozen until analysis could be completed. However, initial "zero" day samples were not taken and frozen until 5 to 6 hr after harvest. This series of events may explain the initially high levels of lactic acid and the relatively minor increase over time. These problems appear to preclude the use of lactic acid as an index of past-harvest quality. However, the decline or absence of lactic acid may be used to indicate or coincide with a loss in quality.

AMINO ACIDS

Since amino acids could be metabolites occurring during the autolytic changes in fish, this group of compounds might also reflect quality. Shenouda *et al.* (1979) adapted Folins reagent, widely used in amino acid analysis, to determine a tyrosine value in acid extracts of fish tissue as a possible quality index for ocean pout. This method was modified to use a perchloric acid extract (Jahns and Rand 1977; Jacober *et al.* 1978) and 0.4 M NaOH for neutralization. Any free tyrosine-equivalent material in the fish tissue extract was measured colorimetrically. As illustrated in Table 16.1, a study was conducted on winter flounder stored at $4°-6°C$, and the appearance of tyrosine was compared to the development of hypoxanthine, an index of freshness, and to the analysis for total volatile bases, an index of spoilage (Pearson 1971; Hart and Fisher 1971). Hypoxanthine followed the pattern of development as described previously, with a peak at 9 days. The TVB formation closely paralleled the pattern found in English sole by Spinelli *et al.* (1964); relatively constant initially with increases only in the later stages of storage. The development pattern of tyrosine was not significantly different from that of TVB. Thus, it would appear that amino acid analysis as a tyrosine value could be used to reflect the appearance of spoilage compounds in fish arising from bacterial action.

TABLE 16.1. COMPARISON OF TVB, TYROSINE, AND HYPOXANTHINE DEVELOP-
MENT IN WINTER FLOUNDER STORED AT 4°–6°C

Time (days)	Tyrosine (mg%)[1]		TVB[1] (mg% N)	Hypoxanthine[1] (mg%)
	Trial I	Trial II		
0	4	7	11	5
2	8	4	11	27
4	13	12	10	68
7	9	13	13	60
9	13	24	13	89
11	35	$(12.2)^2$	18	55
14	71	$(14.2)^2$	24	65

[1]Each value represents the average of two determinations on one fish.
[2]Insufficient data for determination.

The results obtained from the analysis of winter flounder indicated that significant proteolysis did not take place until bacterial spoilage had begun, as suggested by Gould and Peters (1971). Thus, amino acid analysis may not be sufficiently sensitive and specific to assess total fish quality.

HYPOXANTHINE

Postmortem dephosphorylation of nucleotides by autolytic processes in fish has been studied for a number of years as an index of quality. Adenine nucleotides are rapidly deaminated to inosine monophosphate (IMP) and degraded to hypoxanthine through inosine during storage (Eskin et al. 1971; Jones and Murray 1964; Fraser et al. 1968A; Kassemsarm et al. 1962; Boyd and Wilson 1977; Spinelli 1967; Fraser et al. 1968B). Unlike IMP, hypoxanthine increases as a result of autolytic changes and therefore has been the focus of much attention for many years as an index of fish freshness (Spinelli et al. 1964; Jones and Murray 1962; Jones et al. 1964; Murray et al. 1966; Dugal 1967; Spinelli 1967; Burt et al. 1968, 1969; Fraser et al. 1968A, B; Stone 1971; Beuchat 1973; Jahns et al. 1976; Jahns and Rand 1977; Boyd and Wilson 1977; Burt 1977; Connell 1975; Martin et al. 1978; Jacober et al. 1978). Colorimetric tests for detection of hypoxanthine employing the enzyme xanthine oxidase (EC 1.2.3.2) have been developed and tested on a number of different fish species (Burt et al. 1968, 1969, 1976A,B; Beuchat 1973; Jahns et al. 1976; Boyd and Wilson 1977; Jahns and Rand 1977; Burt 1977; Jacober et al. 1978). Figure 16.3 shows the general pattern of hypoxanthine development for all fish studied by Jahns et al. (1976), Jahns and Rand (1977), and Jacober et al. (1978): whiting, tautog, red hake, and winter flounder. In these cases, the hypoxanthine concentration increased to a maximum and then decreased. In general, it can be said that, if little or no hypoxanthine is present, the fish is fresh.

SPOILAGE COMPOUNDS—DIAMINES

Jahns and Rand (1977) suggested that a specific biochemical test was needed to indicate spoilage compounds produced by microbial action. It was

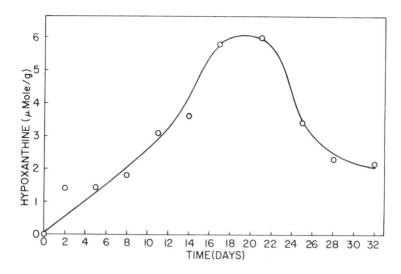

From Jahns and Rand 1977

FIG. 16.3.   GENERAL PATTERN OF HYPOXANTHINE DEVELOPMENT IN FISH AS IL-
LUSTRATED IN WHITING DURING ICED (0°C) STORAGE

felt that such a test could complement and be integrated with the enzymatic
test for hypoxanthine as a freshness index. Spinelli *et al.* (1964) compared
the pattern of hypoxanthine formation in English sole with the spoilage
indices of TVB and TMA. Their results indicated that the spoilage values
did not begin to increase until hypoxanthine had peaked, similar to the
results presented in Table 16.1. The procedures used to measure TVB and
TMA are complicated, lengthy, and require expensive equipment. The composition of TVB material includes amine compounds, which are produced by
microbial decarboxylation of amino acids (Eskin *et al.* 1971; Fields and
Richmond 1968; Tomiyasu and Zenitani 1957; Tabor and Tabor 1976).

Mietz and Karmas (1977) utilized high pressure liquid chromatography
to study the amine formation in tuna as a quality index. The development of
histamine and the diamines, putrescine and cadaverine, were followed with
storage time. These compounds increased in concentration as the fish became unacceptable. While this study validated the use of amines as a
specific indicator of fish spoilage, the procedure and equipment again were
lengthy and complicated. Therefore, diamines were selected as a rapid
fish spoilage indicator, since they could be detected by a simple, specific
enzymatic test employing diamine oxidase. Furthermore, amines have
been implicated as possible causative agents in human poisoning when
significant concentrations of mono- and diamines are present in scombroid
fish (Kim and Bjeldanes 1979; Bjeldanes 1977; Arnold and Brown 1978;

Lieber and Taylor 1978). Therefore, diamines would make a good index for incipient spoilage because of their potential toxicity.

Jahns and Rand (1977) developed a simple colorimetric test which could qualitatively represent diamine formation. As illustrated in Fig. 16.4, the diamine development, measured as putrescine equivalents, did not change significantly until hypoxanthine accumulation peaked. This was in total agreement with the theory described by Jahns and Rand (1977) as illustrated in Fig. 16.5. Jacober *et al.* (1978) quantified the test for diamines by modifying the procedure previously described (Jahns and Rand 1977). This method utilized the same perchloric acid extract of fish tissue as the hypoxanthine analysis and was a specific enzymatic test for diamines. However, the enzyme reaction was not rapid and the procedure developed was lengthy. The active site of diamine oxidase (EC 1.4.3.6), where the diamines physically complex with the enzyme, has been reported to contain pyridoxal-5'-phosphate (Davison 1956; Kawakita and Yamazaki 1978; Walsh 1979). Jacober *et al.* (1978) found that this compound by itself produced a color reaction with putrescine and cadaverine and, to a lesser extent, with histamine and several amino acids. This led to the development of a less specific but rapid and simple test for fish spoilage compounds.

These quantitative tests for diamines and fish spoilage compounds were evaluated against the enzymatic test for hypoxanthine in trials of winter flounder stored at 4°–6°C. As illustrated in Fig. 16.6, the hypoxanthine peaked at 10 days and declined at 15 days of storage. The spoilage marker compounds did not begin to develop until after 8 days of storage, with

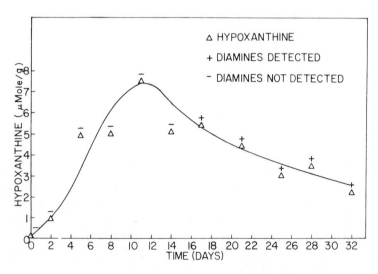

From Jahns and Rand 1977

FIG. 16.4.   HYPOXANTHINE CONCENTRATION AND QUALITATIVE DETERMINATION OF DIAMINE PRESENCE IN WINTER FLOUNDER DURING ICED (0°C) STORAGE

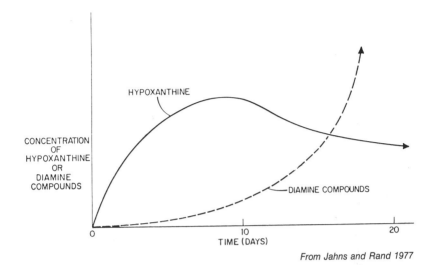

FIG. 16.5.   PATTERN OF HYPOXANTHINE AND DIAMINE DEVELOPMENT IN FISH

acceleration in formation after maximum hypoxanthine development. The pyridoxal-5'-phosphate indicated a higher baseline of reactive material, but closely paralleled the pattern followed by the specific diamine analysis. The integration of the relatively simple biochemical tests for diamines or spoilage compounds and hypoxanthine could reflect the freshness and incipiently spoiled phases of fish and more adequately evaluate total quality than any one procedure alone.

INTEGRATION OF BIOCHEMICAL TESTING PROCEDURES

The ultimate goal for seafood evaluation is a simple, rapid biochemical test that can discern the present quality status of a product, anywhere from fresh to incipient spoilage, preferably without the use of complex laboratory equipment. It must be a combination of tests, which easily detect seafood compounds associated with a loss of freshness and incipient spoilage, to present a single, meaningful value. Among marker compounds, hypoxanthine and diamines seem best suited for this (Jacober *et al.* 1978).

The first attempts to develop a rapid biochemical test for seafood quality were reported by Burt *et al.* (1968, 1969). They modified and adapted the hypoxanthine assay, using xanthine oxidase, to a colorimetric method employing the redox indicator dye 2,6-dichlorophenoindophenol (DIP). Visual estimates of hypoxanthine levels in perchloric acid fish extracts were correlated with the decolorization of the dye.

A new method for biochemical evaluation of fish was developed by Jahns *et al.* (1976) with the use of a hypoxanthine-sensitive paper strip impregnated with xanthine oxidase, buffer, gelatin and resazurin dye. The color development of blue to pink enabled this test to semiquantitatively distin-

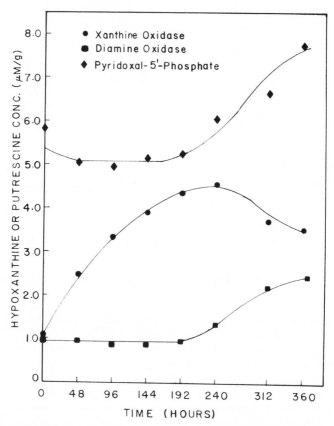

FIG. 16.6. FORMATION OF HYPOXANTHINE AND DEVELOPMENT OF SPOILAGE
COMPOUNDS, AS MEASURED BY THE DIAMINE PUTRESCINE, IN WINTER FLOUNDER
HELD AT 4°−6°C

guish between varying hypoxanthine levels. A blue strip color correlated
with little or no hypoxanthine and therefore exceptional fish freshness,
while a pink color indicated the presence of hypoxanthine and thus a fish of
inferior quality. This test was evaluated on neutralized perchloric acid
extracts of winter flounder stored on ice. The color of the test strip correlated
with the accumulation of hypoxanthine in fish muscle for up to 17 days. As
the fish tissue approached an age of 10−11 days, the strip turned pink. The
strip also reflected the expected decrease in hypoxanthine levels as storage
time was extended, yielding a blue color by 17 days of fish storage.
    Attempts were made to utilize this hypoxanthine strip directly on winter
flounder. A small slit was made along the spine and the dry hypoxanthine
test paper was inserted to absorb any free fluid. There was enough hypoxanthine present in the fish fluid following harvest to turn the test strip pink.

Hypoxanthine was also detected when test strips were moistened with fluid on the skin of fresh fish. The strip required some revisions for direct application to fish since the original unit was too sensitive for correct evaluation.

It was apparent that information was needed on the actual levels of the selected market compounds in fish fluids, as well as the potential interaction for quality assessment. Most of the available data had been obtained from perchloric acid extracts of fish muscle rather than pressed juice of the tissue, which was necessary for the ultimate adaptation of the visual test strip to a more simplified procedure of fish quality testing.

Hypoxanthine development in winter flounder was analyzed comparing the perchloric acid extraction and fish fluid procedures. Figure 16.7 illustrates the pattern of hypoxanthine accumulation in pressed juice and acid-extracted tissue. This study confirmed that the increase in hypoxanthine

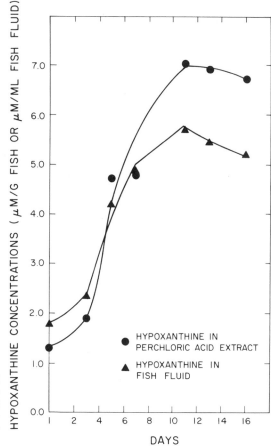

FIG. 16.7. HYPOXANTHINE DETERMINATIONS ON PERCHLORIC ACID EXTRACTS AND PRESSED JUICE SAMPLES FROM WINTER FLOUNDER STORED AT 4°–6°C

concentration to a maximum and the ultimate decrease could be accurately detected in fish fluid that had only been diluted 1–100 with potassium phosphate buffer. Hypoxanthine increased in the fish fluid for 10 days and then began to level off or decline. It is important to note that, in pressed juice and acid extracts, not only was the pattern of development comparable, but the peak and decline occurred at the same time of storage.

The goal has been to integrate the biochemical tests for rapid freshness and incipient spoilage evaluation of seafood and to adapt their relationship to visual test strips, such as the one described for hypoxanthine and one for spoilage compounds, as proposed by Jahns and Rand (1977). However, can these values be integrated and correlated to give a meaningful representation of the total fish quality? Spoilage compounds have been found to develop consistently after the hypoxanthine peak, but the numerical values of hypoxanthine, and probably diamines, are variable. The concentrations of these compounds vary not only by genus but within the same species owing to sampling inconsistencies (Spinelli 1967), seasonal differences, and environmental factors. The number of days it takes for maximum hypoxanthine development to occur also varies considerably among genera. Diamine spoilage values appear dependent on sampling procedure and, of course, are directly correlated with storage and handling. Therefore, single numerical values for freshness and incipient spoilage may not suffice as the true quality assessment in even one fish species.

As previously stated, there had been much research conducted on hypoxanthine in whole iced fish as determined in acid extracts. Many of the recent studies are summarized in Table 16.2. The average maximum hypoxanthine formation in seafood seems to be 5 μM or 68 mg%, with a range of 3.0–7.5 μM/g. The data on perchloric acid extracts of winter flounder analyzed after storage at 4°–6°C illustrate peak hypoxanthine concentrations which fall into this range. Standards for integrating these well-documented data with the quantitative biochemical analysis on spoilage compounds in winter flounder presented in this paper are presented in

TABLE 16.2.   COMPARISON OF THE MAXIMUM HYPOXANTHINE DEVELOPMENT REPORTED FOR A VARIETY OF SEAFOOD

Seafood	Development time (days)	Maximum Hypoxanthine concentration μM/g	Maximum Hypoxanthine concentration mg%	Reference
Winter flounder	8–10	5.0	68	Jahns et al. 1976
Winter flounder	11	7.5	102	Jahns and Rand 1977
Whiting	17–21	6.0	82	Jahns and Rand 1977
Tautog	12–14	3.0	41	Jahns and Rand 1977
Red Hake	17–18	4.0	54	Jahns and Rand 1977
English Sole	15	6.0	80	Spinelli et al. 1964
Ocean Perch	8–10	5.5	75	Spinelli et al. 1964
Redfish	2– 4	5.0	68	Fraser et al. 1968
Halibut	20	3.0	41	Spinelli 1967
Average		5.0	68	

Table 16.3. If this system is applied to Figs. 16.6 and 16.8, the following analyses are possible.

Figure 16.6: For the first 48 hr the fish is considered fresh or grade A. After 48 hr, but up to approximately 11 days, the fish is acceptable, but grade B. After 11 days, it is incipiently spoiled, and is either grade C or no longer acceptable.

Figure 16.8: For the first 48 hr, the fish is grade A. After 48 hr and up to approximately 192 hr (8 days), the fish can be classified grade B. Beyond 8 days, the fish reaches grade C and is progressively no longer acceptable.

Both results indicate incipient spoilage at or after the hypoxanthine peak. Application of this system to the results with iced winter flounder is found in Table 16.4. While this particular sample remained grade A or fresh for only 1–2 days, it had not yet reached incipient spoilage after 15 days. In the qualitative study of postmortem diamines on iced winter flounder by Jahns and Rand (1977), positive detectable diamine development did not occur until after 18 days of storage.

Therefore, integration of rapid and simple biochemical tests for hypoxanthine as a freshness index and diamines as general spoilage compounds is possible for winter flounder. The applicability of this integrated quality testing procedure to other fish species must be determined. If this integrated quality testing procedure is applicable to other fish species, the standards for a quick and inexpensive method of quality testing and possible grading as described by Jahns and Rand (1977) can be determined.

TABLE 16.3. PROPOSED INTEGRATED STANDARDS FOR THE EVALUATION OF SEAFOOD (FISH)

Proposed grade	Hypoxanthine[1]	Diamines[2]	Spoilage compounds[3]
A	<2.5	<1.5	<6.0
B	>2.5	<1.5	<6.0
C	>2.5	>1.5	>6.0
NA (or Reject)	<2.5	>1.5	>6.0

[1]Based on data in Table 16.2.
[2]Measured by diamine oxidase method.
[3]Measured by pyridoxal-5'-phosphate method.

TABLE 16.4. COMPARISON OF HYPOXANTHINE, DIAMINE, AND SPOILAGE COMPOUND ACCUMULATION, AS MEASURED BY ENZYMATIC AND PYRIDOXAL-5'-PHOSPHATE METHODS, RESPECTIVELY, IN WINTER FLOUNDER STORED ON ICE (0°C)

Time (days)	Hypoxanthine ($\mu M/g$)	Diamines[1] ($\mu M/g$)	Spoilage Compounds ($\mu M/g$)	Grade
1	2.0	0.6	4.5	A
3	3.6	0.6	4.1	B
5	5.3	0.6	4.5	B
8	7.4	<0.6	4.9	B
10	6.6	<0.6	3.5	B
12	5.3	0.8	4.8	B
15	6.0	0.6	4.5	B

[1]Approximate numbers due to the inability of the test to accurately distinguish very low diamine levels.

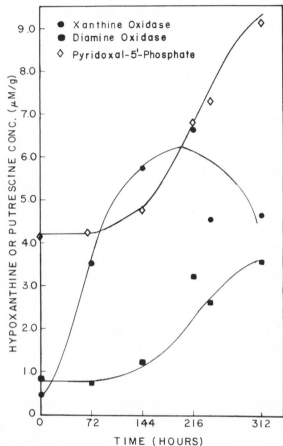

FIG. 16.8. FORMATION OF HYPOXANTHINE AND DEVELOPMENT OF SPOIL-AGE COMPOUNDS, MEA-SURED AS PUTRESCINE, IN A SECOND TRIAL OF WINTER FLOUNDER HELD AT 4°–6°C

The system of correlating hypoxanthine and diamines by biochemical means has only been accomplished on perchloric acid extracts of winter flounder. Therefore, a preliminary study was designed to measure both hypoxanthine and diamines directly in the pressed fluid of winter flounder stored at 4°–6°C. Initial dilutions of the fish fluid for hypoxanthine and diamine determinations were 1–100 and 1–50, respectively, with appropriate buffers (Jahns and Rand 1977; Jacober et al. 1978). As illustrated in Fig. 16.9, the development patterns of hypoxanthine and diamines or spoilage compounds as measured by enzymatic and pyridoxal-5'-phosphate tests, respectively, were very similar to those previously found in perchloric acid extracts of fish muscle. The diamine equivalents, as measured by the enzymatic and pyridoxal-5'-phosphate tests, began to accelerate after hypoxanthine had peaked. While the hypoxanthine level fell within the range discussed, the spoilage compounds exhibited a baseline that was higher

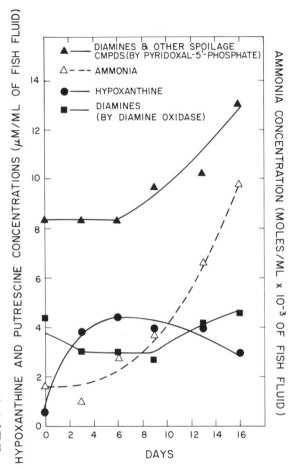

FIG. 16.9. MEASURE-
MENT OF HYPOXANTHINE,
DIAMINES, AND AMMONIA
IN JUICE PRESSED FROM
WINTER FLOUNDER
STORED AT 4°–6°C

than those documented in perchloric extracts of winter flounder. This may
have been due to the color imparted to the reaction mixture when the
diluted juice was added. The juice itself was brown and the indicator dye
developed from colorless to brown as the reaction proceeded. The problem
did not occur in the hypoxanthine analysis, perhaps because of a higher
initial dilution and the fact that the color readings were blue. An interesting addition was the application of a specific ion electrode analysis for
ammonia in pressed fish fluid. The pattern of development was similar to
diamine analysis, but the initial and final levels determined were significantly higher. This analysis could also be used as a rapid spoilage indicator
in laboratory situations.

More analyses of the hypoxanthine and diamine concentrations in fluid
are needed before it will be possible to adapt the proposed system of direct

quality evaluation of fish, utilizing only fluid. An example of application of revised standards to the results is presented in Fig. 16.9. The average hypoxanthine standard could remain at 2.5 $\mu M/g$ as proposed in Table 16.3, but the diamine and spoilage compound levels would have to be changed from 1.5 $\mu M/g$ and 6.0 $\mu M/g$ to 3.5 $\mu M/g$ and 9.0 $\mu M/g$, respectively. Then this fish, in refrigerated storage, could be graded A during the first 36 hr. After 36 hr and up to approximately 9–11 days, the fish would be graded B. After 11 days, it is grade C and probably unacceptable by day 16. This evaluation is consistent with grading suggested for the perchloric acid extracts from Figs. 16.6 and 16.8

The importance of the correlation of these values is not only in providing dependable biochemical procedures for evaluating quality but also in the final development of the test strips previously described. The hypoxanthine test strip has been revised by replacing gelatin with algin and increasing the dye level. It has been tested on samples of fish fluid (1–10 dilution with water) from winter flounder. The strips successfully followed the pattern of hypoxanthine formation through the blue to pink color development. A strip to detect spoilage compounds in fish using pyridoxal-5'-phosphate is now being developed. The feasibility of integrating these two strips for assessing total fish quality has been strengthened by the successful correlation of these compounds in analytical studies.

CONCLUSION

It is obvious that biochemical tests have found several applications in evaluation of seafood, and there are others with potential. Most are laboratory quality control measurements that could be superior to many chemical methods for routine analysis. Enzyme-based procedures are specific and can be adapted to simple visual analysis outside the quality control laboratory, such as on the dock or in the plant. Virtually all individual quality assessment procedures can only focus on one phase of the acceptable life for seafood. Combining test procedures to yield a single evaluation, such as the one proposed, can simplify quality evaluations and expand the applicability. With this approach, perhaps, it will be possible to avoid applying any specific number to the wide number of seafood varieties and their seasonal variations.

ACKNOWLEDGMENT

The authors would like to recognize the technical assistance of Susan Pettigrew, Nancy Miller, and Sonya Gartner and the 1979 Seafood Science class, who helped make this manuscript possible. The research reported in this paper was supported by the College of Resource Development, University of Rhode Island and by NOAA Office of Sea Grant, U.S. Department of Commerce under the grant 04-80M01-147. Contribution No. 1950 of the Rhode Island Agricultural Experiment Station.

REFERENCES

ARNOLD, S.H., and BROWN, W.D. 1978. Histamine (?) toxicity from fish products. Adv. Food Res. *24*, 113–154.

BEUCHAT, L.R. 1973. Hypoxanthine measurement in assessing freshness of chilled channel catfish *(Ictalurus punctatus)*. J. Agric. Food Chem. *21*, 453–455.

BJELDANES, L.F. 1977. Amine toxicity in fish products. Calif. Sea Grant Program Annu. Rep. 165–166.

BOYD, N.S., and WILSON, N.D.C. 1977. Hypoxanthine concentrations as an indicator of freshness of iced snapper. N. Z. J. Food Sci. *20*, 139–143.

BURT, J.R. 1977. Hypoxanthine: A biochemical index of fish quality. Process Biochem. *12*, 32–35.

BURT, J.R., Murray, J., and STROUD, G.D. 1968. An improved automated analysis of hypoxanthine. J. Food Technol. *3*, 165–170.

BURT, J.R., STROUD, G.D., and JONES, N.R. 1969. Estimation of hypoxanthine concentrations in fish muscle by a rapid, visual modification of the enzymatic assay. *In* Fishing and Irradiation of Fish. R. Kreuzer (Editor). Fishing News (Books) Ltd., London.

BURT, J.R., GIBSON, D.M., JASON, A.C., and SANDERS, H.R. 1976A. Comparison of methods of freshness assessment of wet fish. Part II. Instrumental and chemical assessment of boxed experimental fish. J. Food Technol. *11*, 73–89.

BURT, J.R., GIBSON, D.M., JASON, A.C., and SANDERS, H.R. 1976B. Comparison of methods of freshness assessment of wet fish. Part III. Laboratory assessment of commercial fish. J. Food Technol. *11*, 117–127.

CHICHESTER, C.O., and GRAHAM, H.D. (Editors). 1973. Microbial Safety of Fishery Products. Academic Press, New York.

CONNELL, J.J. 1975. Control of Fish Quality. Fishing News (Books) Ltd., London.

DAVISON, A.N. 1965. Pyridoxal phosphate as coenzyme of diamine oxidase. Biochem. J. *64* 546–548.

DUGAL, L.C. 1967. Hypoxanthine in iced freshwater fish. J. Fish Res. Board Can. *24*, 2229–2239.

ESKIN, N.A., HENDERSON, H.M., and TOWNSEND, R.J. 1971. Biochemistry of Foods. Academic Press, New York.

FIELDS, M.L., and RICHMOND, B.S. 1968. Food quality as determined by metabolic by-products of microorganisms. Adv. Food Res. *16*, 161–229.

FRASER, D.I., WEINSTEIN, H.M., and DYER, W.J. 1965. Postmortem glycolytic and associated changes in the muscle of trap- and trawl-caught cod. J. Fish. Res. Board Can. *22*, 83–100.

FRASER, D.I., PITTS, D.P., and DYER, W.J. 1968A. Nucleotide degradation and organoleptic quality in fresh and thawed mackeral muscle held at and above ice temperature. J.Fish. Res. Board Can. 25, 239–253.

FRASER, D.I., SIMPSON, S.G., and DYER, W.J. 1968B. Very rapid accumulation of hypoxanthine in the muscle of redfish stored in ice. J. Fish. Res. Board Can. 25, 817–821.

GOULD, E., and PETERS, J.A. 1971. On Testing the Freshness of Frozen Fish. Fishing News (Books) Ltd., London.

GUTMAN, I., and WAHLEFELD, A.W. 1974. L-Lactate determination with lactate dehydrogenase and NAD. In Methods of Enzymatic Analysis, H.U. Bergmeyer (Editor), 2nd Ed., Vol. 3, pp. 1464–1468. Academic Press, New York.

HART, F.L., and FISHER, H.J. 1971. Modern Food Analysis. Springer-Verlag, Berlin and New York.

JACOBER, L.F., JAHNS, F.D., and RAND, A.G., JR. 1978. A colorimetric test for fish spoilage compounds. 38th Annu. IFT Meeting, Dallas, TX., Abstr.

JAHNS, F.D., and RAND, A.G., JR. 1977. Enzyme methods to assess marine good quality. In Enzymes in Food and Beverage Processing. R.L. Ory and A.J. St. Angelo (Editors). ACS Symp. Ser. No. 47. AVI Publishing Co., Westport, CT.

JAHNS, F.D., HOWE, J.L., CODURI, R.J., JR. and RAND, A.G., JR. 1976. A rapid visual test to assess fish freshness. Food Technol. 30, 27–30.

JONES, N.R., and MURRAY, J. 1962. Degradation of adenine and hypoxanthine nucleotide in the muscle of chilled-stored trawled cod (Gadus callarias). J. Sci. Food Agric. 13, 475–480.

JONES, N.R., and MURRARY, J. 1964. Rapid measures of nucleotide dephosphorylation in iced fish muscle. Their value as indices of freshness and of inosine-5'-monophosphate concentration. J. Sci. Food Agric. 15, 684–689.

JONES, N.R., MURRAY, J., (in part) LIVINGSTON, E.I., and MURRAY, C.K. 1964. Rapid estimation of hypoxanthine concentrations as indices of the freshness of chill-stored fish. J. Sci. Food Agric. 15, 763–774.

KASSEMSARN, B., PEREZ, B.S., MURRAY, J., and JONES, N.R. 1962. Nucleotide degradation in muscle of iced haddock (Gadus aeglefinus), lemon sole (Pleuronectes microcephalus) and plaice (Pleuronectes platessa). J. Food Sci. 28, 28–35.

KAWAKITA, N., and YAMAZAKI, M. 1978. Allosteric properties of nucleotide diphosphatase. Activation by pyridoxal-5'-phosphate and specific modification of effector binding sites. Biochemistry 17, 3546–3550.

KIM, I.S., and BJELDANES, L.F. 1979. Amine content of toxic and wholesome canned tuna fish. J.Food Sci. 44, 922–923.

LIEBER, E.R., and TAYLOR, S.L. 1978. Thin-layer chromatographic screening methods for histamine. J. Chromatogr. 153, 143–152.

MARTIN, R.E., GRAY, R.J.H., and PIERSON, M.D. 1978. Quality assessment of fresh fish and the role of the naturally occurring microflora. Food

MIETZ, J.L., and KARMAS, E. 1977. Chemical quality index of canned tuna as determined by high-pressure liquid chromatography. J. Food Sci. *42*, 155–158.

MURRAY, J., JONES, N.R., and BURT, J.R. 1966. Hypoxanthine in the muscle of chilled-stored Atlantic salmon *(Salmo salar)*. J. Fish. Res. Board Can. *23*, 1795–1797.

PEARSON, D. 1971. The Chemical Analysis of Foods. Sixth Edition. Chemical Publishing Co., Inc., New York.

SHENOUDA, S., MONTECLAVO, J., JHAVERI, S., and CONSTANTINIDES, S.M. 1979. Technological studies on ocean pout, an unexploited fish species, for direct human consumption. J. Food Sci. *44*, 164–168.

SPINELLI, J. 1967. Degradation of nucleotides in ice-stored halibut. J. Food Sci. *32*, 38–41.

SPINELLI, J., EKLUND, M., and MIYAUCHI, D. 1964. Measurement of hypoxanthine in fish as a method of assessing freshness. J. Food Sci. *79*, 710–714.

STONE, F.E. 1971. Inosine monophosphate (IMP) and hypoxanthine formation in three species of shrimp held on ice. J. Milk Food Technol. *34*, 354–356.

TABOR, C.W., and TABOR, H. 1976. 1,4-Diaminobutane, (putrescine), spermidine, and spermine. Annu. Rev. Biochem. *45* 285–306.

TARR, H.L. 1966. Postmortem changes in glycogen, nucleotides, sugar phosphates and sugars in fish muscle—A review. J. Food Sci. *31*, 846–854.

THOMAS, I.C., and CHAMBERLAIN, G.J. 1974. Colorimetric Chemical Analytical Methods. Eighth Edition. Wiley and Sons, New York.

TOMIYASU, Y., and ZENITANI, B. 1957. Spoilage of fish and its preservation by chemical agents. Adv. Food Res. *7*, 41–82.

WALSH, CHRISTOPHER. 1979. Enzymatic Reaction Mechanisms, pp. 451–454, 776–780. W.H. Freeman and Co., San Francisco, California.

17

The Flavor Components in Fish and Shellfish

Shoji Konosu and Katsumi Yamaguchi

The palatability of fish and shellfish originates principally in the ingredients that are solubilized in water or in saliva when they are chewed. Of these, the proteins, polysaccharides, pigments, and vitamins are seldom involved in producing flavor; it is the other water-soluble low-molecular-weight components—that is, the extractive components—that are regarded as the principal flavor producers. The extractive components are more abundant in the muscles of mollusks and crustaceans than in the muscles of fish. This is consistent with the common experience that the flesh of clams, prawns, and crabs is more flavorful than that of fish.

In this chapter, the variety and content of compounds found in the muscle extracts of fish and shellfish are described, and the primary factors influencing the composition of the extracts are discussed. Recent studies in which the composition of the extracts has been almost completely elucidated are also reviewed.

EXTRACTIVE COMPONENTS

Extractive components may be divided into two broad groups: nitrogenous compounds, comprising free amino acids, low-molecular-weight peptides, nucleotides and related compounds, and organic bases; and nonnitrogenous compounds, comprising organic acids, sugars, and inorganic constituents. Although, in some cases, inorganic components are excluded from the extractive components, they are included in the nonnitrogenous extractives in this review.

Nitrogenous Compounds

Free Amino Acids. The free amino acid composition of the muscle extracts from approximately 60 species of commercially important fish and

---

Laboratory of Marine Biochemistry, Faculty of Agriculture, The University of Tokyo, Tokyo, Japan shellfish is given in systematic order in Table 17.1. The major characteristics found in each group are as follows.

Fishes. There is no obvious relationship between the phyletic position and the distribution of amino acids, not only among the teleosts but among the elasmobranchs as well. The high content of histidine in active migratory fishes, such as tuna and skipjack, may be a most notable feature. These active species are usually red-fleshed, but some white-fleshed freshwater fishes, e.g., carp and crucian carp, also show rather high contents of histidine. It should also be noted that a high taurine content is one of the characteristics of white-fleshed fishes, both marine and freshwater species.

Crustaceans. It is noteworthy that the free amino acid content in crustaceans is high when compared with that in fish. High levels of taurine, proline, glycine, alanine, and arginine are general characteristics found among crustaceans. A distinct difference between crabs and prawns is the remarkably high concentration of glycine in the latter, reaching more than 1% of the fresh muscle in most species. This led us to suspect that glycine may be related to the sweetness of prawn muscle (Hujita *et al.* 1972). It should also be pointed out that crabs have a tendency to accumulate more taurine.

Mollusks. Mollusks appear to lie between fishes and crustaceans as far as their free amino acid content is concerned. Commonly, mollusks are rich in taurine, proline, glycine, alanine, and arginine, but their levels fluctuate considerably from species to species in contrast to those of crustaceans. For instance, the content of glycine varied from 1455 mg (given in mg/100 g of raw muscle in this review, unless otherwise specified) in scallops to 10 mg in squids. It is also apparent that cephalopods and uni- and bivalves differ in their proline and glutamic acid content, the former having more proline and less glutamic acid than the latter.

As described above, the free amino acids in the muscle of fish and shellfish, for the most part, are composed of those amino acids found in muscle proteins. In addition to these, however, various amino acids and related compounds having the structures shown in Fig. 17.1 have also been detected. Taurine is a characteristic one and is found in almost every species. In abalone, there was nearly 1000 mg of taurine. Depending on the species, sarcosine, citrulline, α-amino-*n*-butyric acid, β-alanine, β-aminoisobutyric acid, γ-amino-*n*-butyric acid, ethanolamine, ornithine, 1-methylhistidine, and 3-methylhistidine have also been detected, though in small amounts. It has been pointed out that β-alanine and sarcosine are abundant in elasmobranchs, and β-alanine in fishes living in waters of low temperatures (Vul'fson 1961; Schaefer 1962). As shown in Table 17.1 they are also found in crustaceans such as the king crab, Alaska king crab, and krill, all of which are cold-water species.

In some species of fish, the occurrence of phosphoserine, phosphoethanolamine, serine ethanolamine phosphate, and threonine ethanolamine phosphate has been documented (Konosu 1971) (Fig. 17.2). The latter two were detected in the muscle of the rainbow trout and carp in small quantities (Porcellati *et al.* 1965).

Peptides. Since various free amino acids increase after hydrolysis of muscle extracts of fish and shellfish, it is evident that different kinds of low-molecular-weight peptides are present in the extracts. However, only a limited number of peptides, such as carnosine, anserine, balenine (Fig. 17.3), and glutathione, have been identified. The former three are dipeptides consisting of β-alanine and histidine or methylhistidine. Suyama *et al.* (1970A; Suyama and Yoshizawa 1973) and Lukton and Olcott (1958) investigated the distribution of these compounds in a wide variety of aquatic animals. In Table 17.2, their amounts in the muscle of fish and whales are given as reported by Suyama *et al.* (1970A; Suyama and Yoshizawa 1973).

Carnosine is abundant in the eel and skipjack. We have observed that the eel particularly accumulates a large amount of carnosine in the muscle (Konosu *et al.* 1964). Anserine is abundant in tuna, skipjack, and some species of sharks. Anserine (300–600 mg) was also found in salmon and trout (Cowey *et al.* 1962; Cowey and Parry 1963). Balenine has been detected only in small quantities in a limited number of species of tuna and sharks, but it makes up the major part of the extractive components of baleen whales, amounting to more than 1500 mg.

Small amounts of carnosine, anserine, and balenine can be found in the muscle of certain crustaceans and mollusks. Lukton and Olcott (1958) demonstrated the presence of carnosine in the muscle of prawns, squids, and crabs and anserine in oysters. On the other hand, Suyama *et al.* (1965, 1970A) analyzed 12 species of marine invertebrates including prawns, squids, crabs, and clams and only in the blue crab did they find about 3 mg of carnosine and anserine. We (Konosu *et al.* 1978A) also have analyzed the extracts of leg meat from five species of common edible crabs in Japan and detected a trace of carnosine only in the Alaska king crab. The presence of glutathione has been confirmed in the muscle of fish as well as terrestrial animals. Okada *et al.* (1953) reported the glutathione content of 4 mg in carp and Miyauchi (1937) detected 13–20 mg in salmon.

It has been known that fish muscle extracts liberate much more glycine than other amino acids when hydrolyzed with acid (Arakaki and Suyama 1966). In this connection, it has been shown that purine derivatives such as adenosine triphosphate (ATP), adenosine monophosphate (AMP), inosine monophosphate (IMP), inosine, and hypoxanthine, common in fish and shellfish muscle extracts, yielded nearly equimolar amounts of glycine when hydrolyzed with 6 N HCl at 110°C for 16 hr (Watanabe *et al.* 1974). This finding cautions us not to attribute the increase in glycine following the acid hydrolysis of muscle extracts wholly to peptides.

Nucleotides and Related Compounds. Nucleotides as biological constituents number over 100, having various biochemical functions (Suzuki 1963). From the food chemistry point of view, they serve as important

TABLE 17.1.   FREE AMINO ACIDS[1,2] IN THE MUSCLES OF FISH AND SHELLFISH

	Reference[3]	PE	Tau	Hyp	Asp	Thr	Ser	Asn	Gln	Sar	Pro	Glu	Cit	Gly	Ala
Angler (*Lophius litulon*)	*(1)*	–	75	4	2	23	12		8[4]		22	17		63	18
Puffer (*Fugu vermiculare*)	*(1)*	+	123	4	1	10	4		2[4]		13	4		20	22
Stone flounder (*Kareius bicoloratus*)	*(1)*	–	220	–	4	6	7		1[4]		2	7		28	19
Flathead flounder (*Hippoglossoides dubius*)	*(1)*	–	154	3	–	18	7		–		27	10		29	29
Flounder (*Paralichthys olivacus*)	*(1)*	–	171	–	+	4	3		1[4]		1	6		5	13
Triggerfish (*Stephanolepis cirrhifer*)	*(2)*		372		2	+	6				+	+		54	11
Cod (*Gadus morhua*)	*(3)*		81		5	5	10				4	15		75	36
Rockfish (*Sebastes inermis*)	*(4)*		30		5	3	1				+	2		7	6
Red sea bream (*Chrysophrys major*)	*(1)*	–	138	–	+	3	3		2[4]		2	5		12	13
Black sea bream (*Mylio macrocephalus*)	*(5)*				17	13	4				4	19		97	27
Rainbow runner (*Elagatis bipinnulata*)	*(6)*		61		1	4	2				4	13		3	12
Rudderfish (*Seriola purpurascens*)	*(6)*		53		1	5	6				2	6		24	18
Yellowtail (1) (*Seriola quinqueradiata*)	*(6)*		51		1	9	9				2	12		11	24
(2) (*Seriola aureovittata*)	*(6)*		21		2	7	11				24	20		9	15
Horse mackerel (*Trachurus japonicus*)	*(1)*	–	75	–	1	15	3		–		6	13		10	21
Black marlin (*Makaira mazara*)	*(6)*		7		3	9	7				3	2		17	15
Swordfish (*M. mitsukurii*)	*(6)*		77		1	7	5				10	6		10	17
Mackerel (*Scomber japonicus*)	*(1)*	–	84	–	–	11	6		7[4]		26	18		7	26
Frigate mackerel (*Auxis tapeinocephalus*)	*(6)*		55		2	16	9				8	22		10	32
Little tuna (*Euthunnus affinis yaito*)	*(6)*		65		3	10	6				8	20		10	26
Skipjack (*Katsuwonus pelamis*)	*(6)*		50		1	8	5				8	9		9	23
Yellowfin tuna (*Thunnus albacares*)	*(6)*		26		1	3	2				2	3		3	7
Big-eye tuna (*T. obesus*)	*(6)*		21		1	8	5				2	20		11	22
Southern bluefin (*T. maccoyii*)	*(6)*		63		2	7	5				4	11		12	20
Dolphin (*Coryphaena hippurus*)	*(6)*		53		1	8	6				9	16		21	26
Mullet (*Mugil cephalus*)	*(7)*		130		1	15	4				14	13		46	21
Saury (*Cololabis saira*)	*(8)*				2	1	1				1	3		1	1
Eel (*Anguilla japonica*)	*(7)*		35		1	3	3				–	5		13	12
Crucian carp (*Carassius carassius*)	*(2)*		96			10	14					16		62	26
Carp (*Cyprinus carpio*)	*(9)*				2	16	6				22	5		63	22
Ayu (*Plecoglossus altivelis*)	*(10)*		123	+	2	18	14				19	11		46	30
Salmon (*Salmo salar*)	*(11)*		24		1	7	5				6	15		22	31
Anchovy (*Engraulis japonicus*)	*(12)*		106		+	7	8				18	16		8	31
Herring (*Clupea harengus*)	*(13)*		124		+	12	5				+	7		20	22
Shark (1) (*Squalus acanthias*)	*(14)*				15	14	21			99		26		50	34
(2) (*Mustelus manazo*)	*(4)*		28		6	12	5				–	3		17	24
(3) (*M. kanekonis*)	*(15)*		35		6	10	9				7	12		28	21
(4) (*Lamma cornubica*)	*(15)*		44		7	7	10				7	12		21	19
Blue crab (*Portunus trituberculatus*)	*(16)*		214		15	24	23	147[4]		–	251	43	–	444	144
Horsehair crab (*Erimacrus isenbeckii*)	*(16)*		550		10	12	23	34[4]		–	383	22	–	894	158
Snowcrab (*Chionoecetes opilio*)	*(16)*		243		10	14	17	+		77	327	19	–	623	187
King crab (*Paralithodes brevipes*)	*(16)*		363		7	31	46	143[4]		–	319	75	+	741	176
Alaska king crab (*P. camtschaticus*)	*(16)*		372		10	35	17	255[4]		+	502	72	–	611	186
Prawn and shrimp (1) (*Ibacus ciliatus*)	*(17)*		89	–	5	4	78				36	21		1159	104
(2) (*Panulirus japonicus*)	*(17)*		68	–	–	6	107				116	7		1078	42
(3) (*Palaemon nipponensis*)	*(17)*		25	–	–	11	69				56	20		1167	100
(4) (*Pandalus hypsinotus*)	*(17)*		36	–	–	16	61				362	13		1079	60

ABA	Val	Cys	Met	Ile	Leu	Tyr	Phe	β-Ala	β-AIBA	γ-ABA	Orn	Lys	1-MeHis	His	3-MeHis	Trp	Arg
−	6		2	2	5	3	3	−	−	−	5	65	−	5	−	−	9
−	2	+	2	3	2	1		+	+	1	27	128	−	1	4	−	20
−	2	1	1	3	1	1		−	−	−	+	5	−	2	−	−	2
−	3	1	1	3	2	1		17	2	−	2	19	−	11	−	−	5
−	1	1	1	1	1	1		+	3	−	3	17	−	1	−	−	3
	1		1	1	2	1	4					75		17		3	3
	4	2	4	3	5	2	5	37				24		129			2
	+	−	1	1	4	4	4					8		3		+	8
+	3	+	3	4	2	2		−	−	−	+	11	−	4	−	−	2
	5	1	7	9	1	11						13		5		2	3
	3	3	2	3	2	2						22		709			1
	3	2	3	4	3	2						30		286			1
	4	3	3	5	5	3						42		1160			1
	6	4	4	8	7	5						73		732			1
1	6	1	1	5	1	1		−	−	−	5	54	−	289	−	−	3
	4	2	3	5	3	2						12		763			1
	5	4	4	7	4	3						30		831			1
−	16	2	7	14	7	4		−	−	−	5	93	−	676	−	−	11
	15	13	7	14	8	3						71		1460			+
	9	6	5	9	4	3						48		1090			+
	9	5	6	10	4	4						33		1340			+
	7	3	3	7	2	2						35		1220			1
	14	9	6	11	6	5						4		745			+
	7	4	3	7	8	4						16		667			+
	11	5	6	10	3	3						29		486			1
	3	−	3	3	2	+						52		206			4
	1	+	1	1	1	1	1					2		1		+	1
	5	−	2	3	5	2	2					13		7		−	2
	1	1	4	4								99		251			19
	3	2	2	4	13	+						76		127			17
4	5	−	3	5	5	3				3	4	24		45			8
	7		3	4	8	3	3	3				3		−			5
	9	1	4	6	10	4	3			−	1	27		481		−	3
	4	+	+	3	+	+						15		88		+	+
	+				42		−	22	105		25	+		−			50
	+	30	14	3	4	1	2					+		64		+	10
	5	−	5	5	8	2	4					4	−	11	−	−	7
	7	−	6	5	8	5	4					3	−	8	−	−	6
4	48		49	29	59	23	20	−	−	−		44	−	23	7	6	329
+	14		13	5	9	10	7	−	+	+		10	+	11	+	+	786
2	30		19	29	30	19	17	−		+	1	25	−	8	3	10	579
5	56		43	48	72	50	42	2		3	1	45	+	18	+	14	520
3	54		38	31	63	56	54	5		3	3	56	1	31	+	+	775
	28	−	12	10	11	2	2					14		13		−	658
	19	−	17	17	12	11	6					21		13		−	674
	1	−	7	4	9	6	4					30		12		−	603
	12	−	16	17	25	4	9					29		7		−	507

(Continued)

TABLE 17.1. *(Continued)*

	Reference[3]	PE	Tau	Hyp	Asp	Thr	Ser	Asn	Gln	Sar	Pro	Glu	Cit	Gly	Ala
(5) *(P. borealis)*	*(17)*	53	–	–	4	26					126	9		1127	30
(6) *(Metapenaeus monoceros)*	*(17)*	54	–	–	18	109					318	21		1553	126
(7) *(Penaeus japonicus)*	*(17)*	150	–	–	13	133					203	34		1222	43
(8) *(P. monodon)*	*(17)*	146	–	–	7	230					188	11		1145	26
(9) *(P. orientalis)*	*(17)*	58	–	–	36	115					493	59		566	129
(10) *(Sclerocrangon boreas)*	*(17)*	221	–	–	7	113					76	110		1476	80
Krill *(Euphausia superba)*	*(18)*		206		52	54	43	+23[4]			217	35		116	106
Octopus *(Polypus fangsiao)*	*(5)*				22	7	15				8	29		23	15
Squid (1) *(Ommastrephes sloani pacificus)*	*(19)*				+	23	16				479	26		42	75
(2) *(Tysanoteuthis rhombus)*	*(20)*	238	–	–	3	5					–	10		10	59
(3) *(Loligo kensaki)*	*(20)*	200	–	–	26	32					329	35		826	261
(4) *(L. chinensis)*	*(20)*	248	21	–	4	31	27				960	15		772	482
(5) *(Sepioteuthis lessoniana)*	*(20)*	160	–	–	9	134					747	3		829	182
(6) *(Sepia esculenta)*	*(20)*	480	49	–	57	24					596	34		63	150
Short-necked clam *(Tapes japonica)*	*(21)*				21	13	21				16	103		329	130
Hard clam *(Meretrix lusoria)*	*(22)*				32	44	–				17	249		265	573
Oyster *(Ostrea sp.)*	*(23)*				26	10	6				166	264		248	646
Scallop *(Pecten yessoensis)*	*(23)*				–	–	6				82	151		1455	1233
Mussel *(Mytilus sp.)*	*(23)*				200	31	–				29	317		399	340
Abalone *(Nordotis discus)*	*(24)*		946		9	82	95				83	109		174	98

[1] Key to amino acid abbreviations: PE, phosphoethanolamine; Tau, taurine; Hyp, hydroxyproline; Asp, aspartic acid; Thr, threonine; Ser, serine; Asn, asparagine; Gln, glutamine; Sar, sarcosine; Pro, proline; Glu, glutamic acid; Cit, citrulline; Gly, glycine; Ala, alanine; α-ABA, α-amino-*n*-butyric acid; Val, valine; Cys, cystine; Met, methionine; Ile, isoleucine; Leu, leucine; Tyr, tyrosine; Phe, phenylalanine; β-Ala, β-alanine; β-AIBA, β-aminoisobutyric acid; γ-ABA, γ-amino-*n*-butyric acid; Orn, ornithine; Lys, lysine; 1-MeHis, 1-methylhistidine; His, histidine; 3-MeHis, 3-methylhistidine; Trp, tryptophan; Arg, arginine.

[2] Values given in mg/100 g of raw muscle; + trace; –not detected.

[3] Key to references: *(1)* Konosu *et al.* 1974; *(2)* Simidu 1963; *(3)* Dambergs *et al.* 1968; *(4)* Sakaguchi and Simidu 1964; *(5)* Ito 1957; *(6)* Suyama and Yoshizawa 1973; *(7)* Konosu *et al.* 1964; *(8)* Oishi 1968; *(9)* Sakaguchi and Kawai 1971; *(10)* Suyama *et al.* 1970C; *(11)* Cowey *et al.* 1962; *(12)* Arakaki and Suyama 1966; *(13)* Hughes 1959B; *(14)* Konosu 1976; *(15)* Suyama and Suzuki 1975; *(16)* Konosu *et al.* 1978A; *(17)* Hujita *et al.* 1972; *(18)* Suyama *et al.* 1965; *(19)* Konosu *et al.* 1958; *(20)* Endo *et al.* 1962A; *(21)* Konosu *et al.* 1965; *(22)* Ito 1959; *(23)* Tsuchiya 1957; *(24)* Konosu 1973.

[4] Calculated as asparagine.

palatable taste *(umami)*-producing factors. Kuninaka (1960) demonstrated that 5′-nucleotides such as IMP and GMP show a distinct taste-enhancing effect in combination with glutamic acid. More than 90% of the nucleotides in the muscle of fish and shellfish are accounted for by purine derivatives, with small amounts of uracil and cytosine derivatives also being found (Seki 1971). Typical data are shown in Table 17.3, where the values cited from Jones and Murray (1957) and Arai (1966) are for live muscle, those from Hayashi *et al.* (1978B) are for boiled meat from fresh animals, and the others for fresh materials commercially available.

In the muscle of live animals ATP predominates under normal conditions. After death it is enzymatically degraded by the following pathway in fish:

$$ATP \longrightarrow ADP \longrightarrow AMP \longrightarrow IMP \longrightarrow \text{inosine} \longrightarrow \text{hypoxanthine}$$

ABA	Val	Cys	Met	Ile	Leu	Tyr	Phe	β-Ala	β-AIBA	γ-ABA	Orn	Lys	1-MeHis	His	3-MeHis	Trp	Arg
8	–		9	6	14	14	10					16		60		–	511
17	–		6	7	16	9	6					17		13		21	696
17	–		12	9	13	20	7					52		16		–	902
9	–		19	6	12	8	4					12		17		15	922
41	–		25	31	40	40	18					127		11		–	458
12	–		5	6	8	4	9					20		10		7	422
63	–		34	48	86	48	53	35			42	145		17			266
9			4	6	6	2	4					8		2		2	146
20			12	15	18	4	6					9		140		2	99
3	–		3	7	9	–	–					9		8		–	568
15		2	1	16	6	17	8					35		5		–	702
12	–		22	7	15	8	12					22		30		3	225
3		3	7	6	12	8	2					15		16		5	236
19		15	28	9	11	13	12					22		11		–	266
14		5	11	10	20	16	20					25		9		–	94
32			22	14	40	25	16					16		8		5	163
11			8	19	13	10	9					22		23		–	67
30			3	5	8	5	3					3		–		1	32
14			10	25	15	13	10					39		12		–	416
37			13	18	24	57	26					76		23		20	299

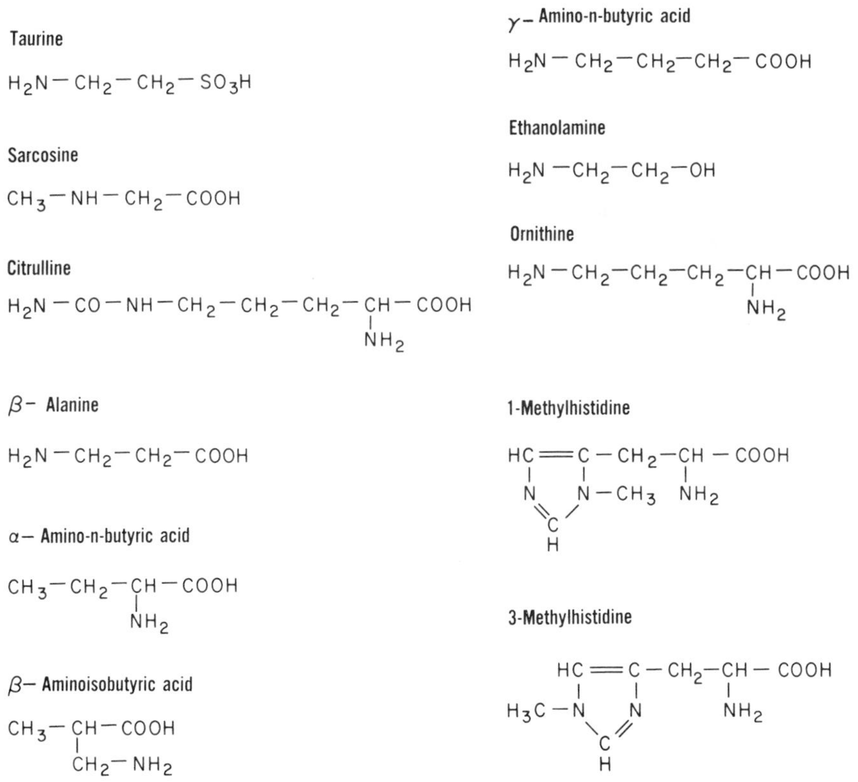

Taurine

$H_2N—CH_2—CH_2—SO_3H$

Sarcosine

$CH_3—NH—CH_2—COOH$

Citrulline

$H_2N—CO—NH—CH_2—CH_2—CH_2—CH—COOH$
  $\overset{|}{NH_2}$

β– Alanine

$H_2N—CH_2—CH_2—COOH$

α– Amino-n-butyric acid

$CH_3—CH_2—\overset{|}{CH}—COOH$
      NH_2

β– Aminoisobutyric acid

$CH_3—\overset{|}{CH}—COOH$
    $CH_2—NH_2$

γ – Amino-n-butyric acid

$H_2N—CH_2—CH_2—CH_2—COOH$

Ethanolamine

$H_2N—CH_2—CH_2—OH$

Ornithine

$H_2N—CH_2—CH_2—CH_2—\overset{|}{CH}—COOH$
                  NH_2

1-Methylhistidine

$HC=\!\!=C—CH_2—CH—COOH$
  $|$ $|$ $|$
  N $N—CH_3$ NH_2
   $\underset{H}{\overset{\diagdown}{C}{\diagup}}$

3-Methylhistidine

$HC=\!\!=C—CH_2—CH—COOH$
  $|$ $|$ $|$
$H_3C—N$ N NH_2
   $\underset{H}{\overset{\diagdown}{C}{\diagup}}$

FIG. 17.1.

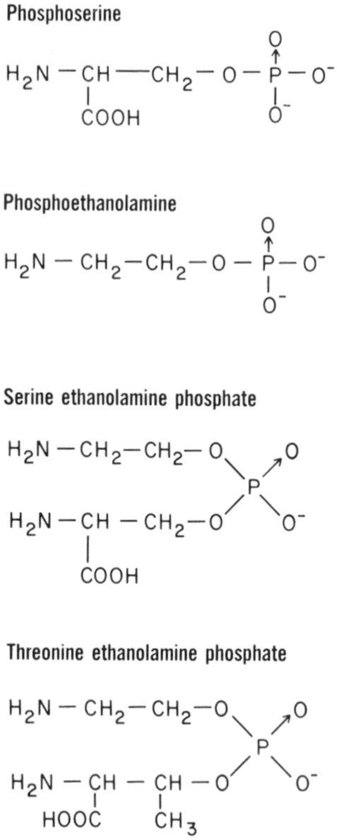

Phosphoserine

$$H_2N-\underset{\underset{COOH}{|}}{CH}-CH_2-O-\underset{\underset{O^-}{|}}{\overset{\overset{O}{\uparrow}}{P}}-O^-$$

Phosphoethanolamine

$$H_2N-CH_2-CH_2-O-\underset{\underset{O^-}{|}}{\overset{\overset{O}{\uparrow}}{P}}-O^-$$

Serine ethanolamine phosphate

$$H_2N-CH_2-CH_2-O\underset{H_2N-\underset{\underset{COOH}{|}}{CH}-CH_2-O}{\overset{\diagdown}{\diagup}}\underset{\diagdown O^-}{\overset{\diagup O}{P}}$$

Threonine ethanolamine phosphate

$$H_2N-CH_2-CH_2-O\underset{H_2N-\underset{\underset{HOOC}{|}}{CH}-\underset{\underset{CH_3}{|}}{CH}-O}{\overset{\diagdown}{\diagup}}\underset{\diagdown O^-}{\overset{\diagup O}{P}}$$

FIG. 17.2.

Since the reaction, IMP⟶ inosine, is rather slow, IMP usually accumulates in fresh fish muscle. In crustaceans, AMP tends to accumulate because of the low activity of AMP deaminase. Mollusks rarely have AMP deaminase, so that their major pathway of ATP degradation is assumed to be

ATP ⟶ ADP ⟶ AMP ⟶ adenosine ⟶ inosine ⟶ hypoxanthine

Table 17.3 clearly indicates the pathways of ATP degradation described above, but the amount of each component varies greatly depending on freshness.

With respect to nucleotides other than adenine derivatives, Jones and Murray (1960, 1961) noted the presence of small amounts of di- and tri-phosphopyridine nucleotide (DPN, TPN), guanosine triphosphate (GTP), and uridine triphosphate (UTP) and traces of guanosine 5'-mono- and diphosphates (GMP, GDP), uridine 5'-mono- and diphosphates (UMP, UDP), UDP-glucose, UDP-acetylglucosamine, and UDP-glucuronic acid in the muscle of resting codling. Most of these, however, decreased noticeably or disappeared entirely in struggling fish. Hayashi et al. (1978B) have detected

Carnosine (β-alanylhistidine)

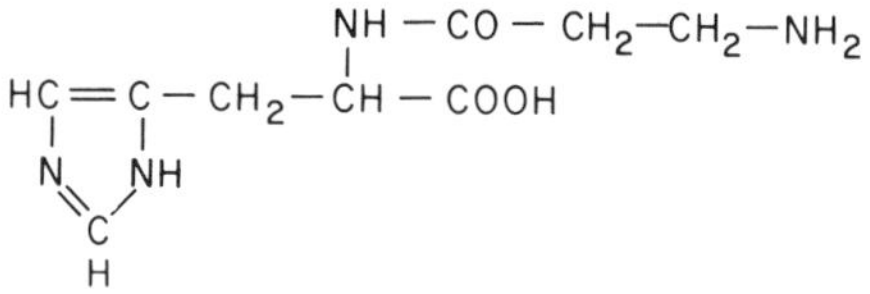

$$HC = C - CH_2 - \underset{\underset{NH - CO - CH_2-CH_2-NH_2}{|}}{CH} - COOH$$

(imidazole ring: N, NH, C, H)

Anserine (β-alanyl-l-methylhistidine)

$$HC = C - CH_2 - \underset{\underset{NH - CO - CH_2-CH_2-NH_2}{|}}{CH} - COOH$$

(imidazole ring: N, N—CH$_3$, C, H)

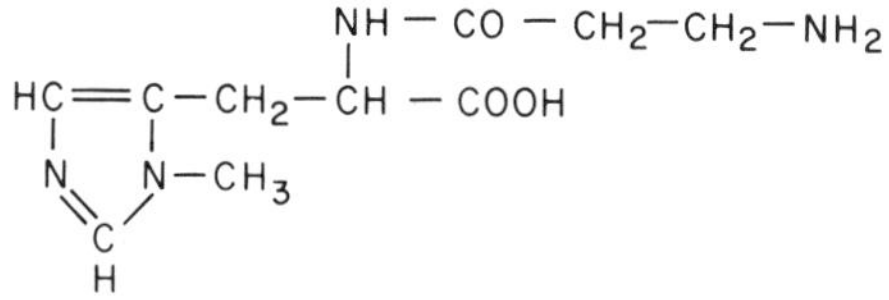

Balenine (β-alanyl-3-methylhistidine)

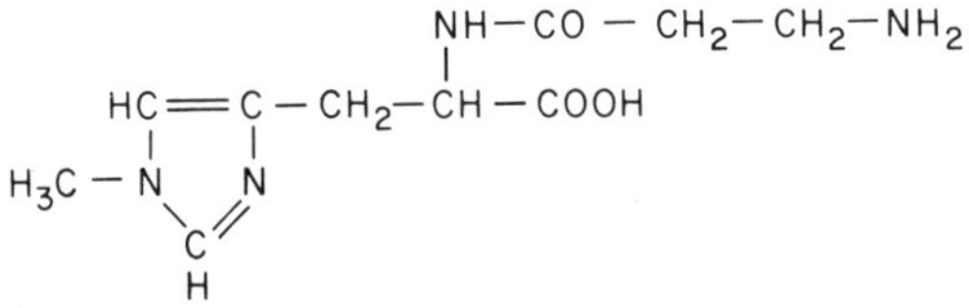

$$HC = C - CH_2 - \underset{\underset{NH-CO - CH_2-CH_2-NH_2}{|}}{CH} - COOH$$

(imidazole ring: H$_3$C—N, N, C, H)

FIG. 17.3.

AMP as a main component, about half as much CMP as AMP, and small amounts of ADP, IMP, GMP, and UMP in the leg meat extracts of boiled crabs.

Guanidino Compounds.   Guanidino compounds (Fig. 17.4) can be found in quite high amounts. Creatine and arginine predominate in fish and invertebrates, respectively. Both compounds occur mainly in the phosphorylated form in the muscle of live animals, playing an important role as phosphagens in the energy metabolism of the muscle. Creatinine, which is formed through dehydration of creatine, is also present, though in smaller amounts. The amounts of creatine and creatinine found in fish muscle is given in Table 17.4 (Konosu et al. 1974; Suyama and Yoshizawa 1973; Suyama et al. 1970C; Suyama and Suzuki 1975; Sakaguchi et al. 1964). No conspicuous differences are found either between red- and white-fleshed fishes or between teleosts and elasmobranchs, as has been observed by Sakaguchi and Simidu (1964).

Octopine is a guanidino compound peculiar to mollusks, making up 10–20% of the extractive nitrogen in cephalopods (Endo and Simidu 1963). Octopine increases strikingly with a decrease of arginine phosphate in the scallop (Grieshaber and Gaede 1977), nautiloids (Hochachka et al. 1977),

TABLE 17.2.   DIPEPTIDES IN THE MUSCLES OF FISH AND WHALES[1,2]

	Carnosine	Anserine	Balenine
Teleosts			
Stone flounder	—	—	—
Red sea bream	—	1.8	—
Sea perch			
(Lateolabrax japonicus)	0.1	—	0.4
Rainbow runner	91.6	81.4	—
Rudder fish	67.5	91.2	—
Yellowtail			
(1)	—	—	—
(2)	+	182	—
Horse mackerel	—	2.6	—
Black marlin	52.3	867	—
Swordfish	130	370	—
Mackerel	—	—	—
Frigate mackerel	144	387	—
Little tuna	+	72.1	—
Skipjack	252	559	—
Yellowfin tuna	9.5	1090	6.5
Big-eye tuna	—	1590	10.9
Albacore			
(Thunnus alalunga)	0.2	1570	—
Southern bluefin	—	735	—
Saury	—	—	—
Eel	542	—	—
Sardine			
(Sardinops melanosticta)	—	4.3	—
Elasmobranchs			
Ray			
(1) (Dasyatis akajei)	—	2.3	—
Shark			
(5) (Squalus mitsukurii)	0.4	1010	0.3
(6)(Carcharhinus longimanus)	50.3	284	29.9
(7) (Mustelus manazo)	—	—	—
(8) (Isrus glaucus)	—	872	2.9
Whales			
Baleen whales			
Fin whale	140	5.0	1500
(Balaenoptera physalus)			
Sei whale	131	6.4	1840
(B. borealis)			
Little piked whale			
(B. acutorostrata)	154	22.7	1930
Teethed whales			
Sperm whale			
(Physter catodon)	196	126	3.2
Pilot whale			
(Globicephala melaena)	227	39.0	515
Dolphin			
(Delphinus delphis)	447	92.7	489

[1]Values given as mg/100 g; + trace; — not detected.
[2]Refer to Table 17.1 for other scientific names.

squid (Gaede 1976; Grieshaber and Gaede 1976), and octopus (Gaede 1976) when subjected to vigorous exercise.

Urea.   The level of urea in the muscle of teleosts is usually below 50 mg. In elasmobranchs, however, it amounts to 1400–2000 mg and is the most prominent nitrogenous component of the extracts, serving not only for the detoxification of ammonia but also for osmoregulation. The urea content in the muscle of elasmobranchs is given in Table 17.5 (Konosu 1976; Suyama

TABLE 17.3.   ADENINE NUCLEOTIDES AND THEIR DERIVATIVES IN THE MUSCLE OF FISH AND SHELLFISH[1]

	ATP	ADP	AMP	IMP	HxR	Hx	Ref.[4]
Teleosts							
Angler	—	9	5	4	86[2]		(1)
Puffer	—	16	2	179	42[2]		(1)
Stone flounder	8	8	10	196	77[2]		(1)
Flathead flounder	8	+	6	—	171[2]		(1)
Flounder	21	—	+	188	74[2]		(1)
Cod[3]	271	25	24	44			(2)
Rockfish	—	3	7	191	36[2]		(3)
Red sea bream	11	6	10	342	15[2]		(1)
Horse mackerel	14	10	3	272	20[2]		(1)
Mackerel	7	4	7	282	64[2]		(1)
Yellowfin tuna	—	—	+	135	189[2]		(3)
Carp[3]	237	41	1	—	—[2]		(4)
Rainbow trout[3]	296	43	19	8	—[2]		(4)
Ayu			10	230	100[2]		(5)
Elasmobranchs							
Shark							
(2)	+	11	+	334	95[2]		(4)
(3)	1	11	21	265	41[2]		(6)
(4)	—	7	5	112	16[2]		(6)
Crustaceans							
Blue crab	—	2	63	2	19	5	(7)
Horsehair crab	—	3	82	—	1	2	(7)
Horsehair crab[3]	298	75	10	—	—	—	(4)
Snow crab	—	7	32	5	13	7	(7)
King crab	—	3	70	1	13	7	(7)
King crab[3]	178	70	9	6	—	—	(4)
Alaska king crab	—	3	46	1	+	4	(7)
Prawn (4)[3]	351	59	19	—	—	—	(4)
Squilla[3]							
(Squilla oratoria)	195	53	33	17	12	—	(4)
Mollusks							
Octopus[3]	203	44	7	—	—	—	(4)
Squid							
(1)	18	61	237	—	15		(8)
(1)[3]	379	65	19	—	—	+	(4)
Surf clam[3]							
(Spisula sachalinensis)	202	21	11	—	—	—	(4)
Scallop[3]	305	37	20	—	—	—	(4)
Abalone[3]							
(Haliotis discus hannai)	176	25	7	—	—	—	(4)

[1]Values in mg/100 g of raw muscle; + trace, — not detected.
[2]The sum of inosine (HxR) and hypoxanthine (Hx) calculated as HxR.
[3]Live muscle.
[4]Key to references: (1) Konous et al. 1974; (2) Jones and Murray 1957; (3) Sakaguchi and Simidu 1964; (4) Arai 1966; (5) Suyama et al. 1970C; (6) Suyama and Suzuki 1975; (7) Hayashi et al. 1978B; (8) Saito 1960.

and Suzuki 1975; Simidu and Oishi 1951). It is due mainly to urea and trimethylamine oxide that the level of muscle extractive nitrogen is markedly higher in elasmobranchs than in teleosts as will be mentioned below.

Quaternary Ammonium Bases.   Common bases found in the muscle of fish and shellfish are trimethylamine oxide (TMAO) and betaines. Numerous investigations have been done on the distribution of TMAO in aquatic animals, and the results were collected in reviews by Yamada (1967) and Harada (1975). The TMAO content of some principal edible species is

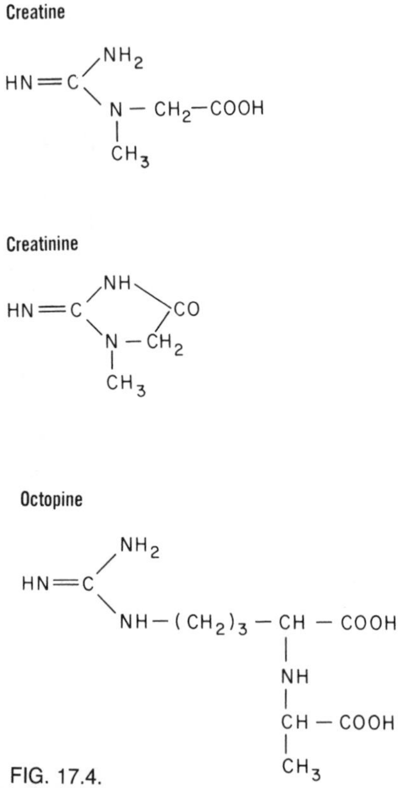

Creatine

$$HN = C\underset{\displaystyle N - CH_2 - COOH}{\overset{\displaystyle NH_2}{<}}$$

$$CH_3$$

Creatinine

$$HN = C\underset{\displaystyle N - CH_2}{\overset{\displaystyle NH}{<}}CO$$

$$CH_3$$

Octopine

$$HN = C\underset{\displaystyle NH - (CH_2)_3 - CH - COOH}{\overset{\displaystyle NH_2}{<}}$$

$$NH$$

$$CH - COOH$$

FIG. 17.4. $$CH_3$$

selected from Yamada's review (1967) and given in Table 17.6. The levels in marine teleosts are known to fluctuate greatly depending on season, size of fish, and environmental conditions. TMAO has not been detected or has been detected only in small amounts in freshwater teleosts (Kutscher and Ackermann 1933; Dyer 1952; Ronold and Jakobsen 1947; Norris and Benoit 1945; Beatty 1939; Suyama et al. 1958). Elasmobranchs contain much more TMAO in the muscle than teleosts, up to as much as about 1000 mg, and is regarded, like urea, as an important osmoregulator.

Among invertebrates squid appear to show a high content of TMAO; it varies widely, however, between 100 and 1000 mg from individual to individual (Yamada 1967). Trimethylamine, which is known as one of the principal producers of fish odor, is scarcely detected in fresh muscle but gradually increases with the postmortem bacterial reduction of TMAO.

Betaines (Fig. 17.5) are minor components in muscle extracts of fish, but are major compounds in extracts of crustaceans and mollusks (Konosu et al. 1965; Hayashi et al. 1978B; Konosu and Kasai 1961; Konosu and Maeda 1961; Beers 1967; Konosu and Hayashi 1975; Hayashi and Konosu 1977). The main compound is glycine betaine, whose distribution in crustaceans and mollusks is shown in Table 17.7 (Hujita et al. 1972; Suyama et al. 1965;

Endo *et al.* 1962A; Konosu *et al.* 1965; Hayashi *et al.* 1978B; Konosu and Hayashi 1975). It is present at levels of 400−900 mg in most species. Only a limited amount of earlier data is available on the glycine betaine content of

TABLE 17.4.   CREATINE AND CREATININE IN THE MUSCLES OF FISH[1,2]

	Creatine		Creatinine
Teleosts			
Angler	349		10
Puffer	561		21
Stone flounder	567		23
Flathead flounder	306		9
Flounder	464		11
Rockfish	508		12
Red sea bream	718		17
Rainbow runner		316^3	
Rudderfish		438^3	
Yellowtail			
(1)		196^3	
(2)		350^3	
Horse mackerel	488		11
Black marlin		243^3	
Swordfish		369^3	
Mackerel	475		13
Frigate mackerel		213^3	
Little tuna		281^3	
Skipjack		337^3	
Yellowfin tuna		372^3	
Big-eye tuna		435^3	
Southern blue fin		312^3	
Dolphin		372^3	
Ayu		410^3	
Elasmobranchs			
Shark			
(3)	485		48
(4)	507		33

[1]Values given in mg/100 g of raw muscle.
[2]Refer to Table 17.1 for scientific names.
[3]Creatine + creatinine

TABLE 17.5.   UREA IN THE MUSCLES OF ELASMOBRANCHS[1]

Mobula japonica	1830
Urolophus aurantiacus	2000
Dasyatis akajei	1810
Raja hollandi	2030
Dalatias licha	1900
Squalus mitsukurii	1530
Prionace glaucus	1600
Triakis scyllia	1730
Mustelus griseus	1420
Alopias vulpinus	1710
Lamna cornulica	1520
Isuropsis glauca	1410
Heterondontus japonicus	1830

[1]Values given in mg/100g of raw muscle.

TABLE 17.6.   TRIMETHYLAMINE OXIDE IN THE MUSCLES OF FISH AND SHELLFISH[1,2]

Teleosts		Elasmobranchs	
Angler	192	Ray	
Puffer	31	(1)	1250
Stone flounder	353	(2) *(Mobula japonica)*	1425
Flathead flounder	153	(3) *(Urolophus aurantiacus)*	1050
Flounder	420	(4)	1080−1360
Alaska pollack		Shark	
(Theragra		(1)	988
chalcogramma)	306−1040	(2)	1150−1460
Cod	412−980	(8)	1000
Rockfish	102	(9) *(Glyphis glaucus)*	985−1480
Red sea bream	258	(10) *(Triakis scyllia)*	1385−1735
Black sea bream	111−258	(11) *(Sphyraena zygaena)*	1060
Sea bream		(12) *(Heterodontus japonicus)*	960
(Taius tumifrons)	121	Crustaceans	
Perch		Blue crab	65
(Lateolabrax japonicus)	264−328	Horsehair crab	140
Yellowtail (1)	269−397	Prawn	
Horse mackerel	236−304	(2)	213
Mackerel	32−243	(7)	172
Frigate mackerel	8−101	Squilla	128
Yellowfin tuna	52−527	Mollusks	
Big-eye tuna	18−86	Octopus	134
Albacore	5−33	Squid	
Bluefin tuna	21	(1)	734−976
Mullet	57	(2)	257
Saury	25−178	(3)	356−465
Conger eel		(4)	129
(Astroconger myriaster)	51	(5)	1045
Carp	—	(6)	217
Trout		Fan-mussel	
(Oncorhynchus masou)	20	*(Atrina pectinata)*	72
Chum salmon		Scallop	52
(O. keta)	26	Abalone	3
Anchovy	113	Turban shell	
Sardine		*(Batillus cornutus)*	107
(Sardinops			
melanosticta)	38−50		
Herring	210		

[1]Values given in mg/100 g; — not detected.
[2]Refer to Tables 17.1, 17.2, and 17.3 for other scientific names.

fish muscle. However, Vyncke (1970) has analyzed the nitrogenous extractives of the spurdog *(Squalus acanthias)* and found the glycine betaine level to be 29−282 mg. Next to glycine betaine, homarine has been reported to be rather widely distributed among marine invertebrates (Hayashi *et al.* 1978B; Beers 1967; Gasteiger *et al.* 1960; Hirano 1975).

The occurrence of other betaines, such as γ-butyrobetaine, carnitine, trigonelline, and stachydrine, is also known, but they are present only in small quantities.

Other Nitrogenous Compounds.   Over 30 new nitrogenous compounds have been obtained from the extracts of marine animals in recent decades. Most of them have been reported from inedible species such as sea anemones, sea stars, and sipunculids (Konosu 1971; Weinheimer *et al.* 1973;

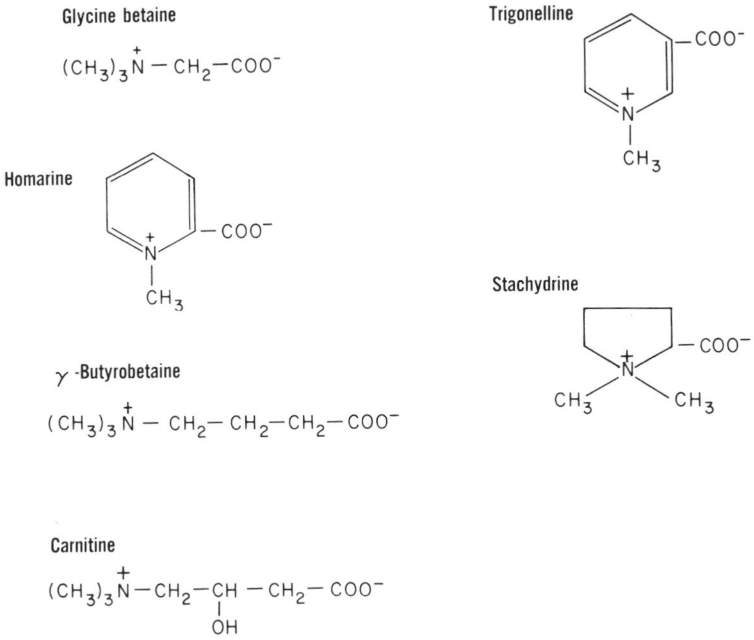

Glycine betaine

$$(CH_3)_3\overset{+}{N} - CH_2-COO^-$$

Trigonelline

Homarine

Stachydrine

γ -Butyrobetaine

$$(CH_3)_3\overset{+}{N} - CH_2- CH_2-CH_2- COO^-$$

Carnitine

$$(CH_3)_3\overset{+}{N}-CH_2-\underset{\underset{OH}{|}}{CH} -CH_2- COO^-$$

FIG. 17.5.

Howe and Sheikh 1975). In edible species, atrinine (Konosu *et al.* 1970) has been isolated from the fan-mussel, α-iminodipropionic acid (Sato *et al.* 1977A,B, 1978) from the squid and scallop, α-iminopropioacetic acid (Sato *et al.* 1978) from the scallop, and β-hydroxyaspartic acid (Sato *et al.* 1979) from the short-necked clam, each in rather small quantities (Fig. 17.6). β-Alanine betaine (β-homobetaine) was confirmed for the first time to be present in the fan-mussel (Konosu and Watanabe 1973), oyster (Abe and Kaneda 1975), scallop (Konosu and Hayashi 1975), krill (Konosu and Hayashi 1975), and certain species of fish (Konosu *et al.* 1978B).

Nonnitrogenous Compounds

The nonnitrogenous extractive components include the organic acids, sugars, and inorganic salts. Relatively few studies have been made of their distribution in fish and shellfish as compared with those of the nitrogenous compounds.

Organic Acids. Besides lactic acid, which is produced through glycolysis, propionic, acetic, pyruvic, succinic, oxalic acids and others have been detected (Osada and Okaya 1964; Osada 1966; Hayashi *et al.* 1979; Konosu *et al.* 1967). Their distribution is given in Table 17.8. Lactic acid is the main acid found in fish and crustaceans, and has been shown to accumulate in amounts up to 1000 mg or more in such active migratory fish as tuna and

TABLE 17.7. GLYCINE BETAINE IN THE
MUSCLES OF SHELLFISH[1,2]

Crustaceans	
Blue crab	646
Horsehair crab	711
Snow crab	357
King crab	476
Alaska king crab	417
Prawn	
(1)	677
(2)	961
(3)	251
(4)	385
(6)	744
(7)	752
(8)	635
(9)	401
Krill	106
Mollusks	
Octopus	
(Octopus vulgaris)	1434
Squid	
(1)	619
(2)	928
(3)	769
(4)	853
(5)	853
(6)	878
Short-necked clam	679
Hard clam	727
Oyster	805
Scallop	211
Fan-mussel	964
Abalone	668

[1]Values given in mg/100g of raw muscle.
[2]Refer to Tables 17.1 and 17.6 for other
scientific names.

skipjack (Tsuchiya 1962). In the short-necked clam and hard clam, the major component is succinic acid, which is claimed to be one of the taste-producing substances in clams. This idea, however, is still debatable (Konosu 1973; Takagi and Simidu 1962) and is in need of further study.

Sugars.   Glucose and ribose are the chief free sugars in the muscle of fish and shellfish. Jones and Burt (1960) found 8–32 mg of glucose in cod and herring. Other studies have shown that ribose increases in cod (Jones 1958) and plaice (Ehira and Uchiyama 1967) during the ice storage. Tsuchiya (1962) stated that glucose was present in most species of fish and shellfish and fructose occurred in some species of fish. We have found 3–86 mg of glucose together with traces of ribose, arabinose, and fructose in crabs (Hayashi et al. 1979). The occurrence of galactose in squids and prawns has also been reported (Tsuchiya 1962).

In addition to free sugars, a variety of sugar phosphates can be found in the muscle of fish and shellfish. Tarr (1949) indicated the presence of 2–61 mg of fructose 1,6-diphosphate, phosphoglyceric acid, glucose 1-phosphate

Atrinine

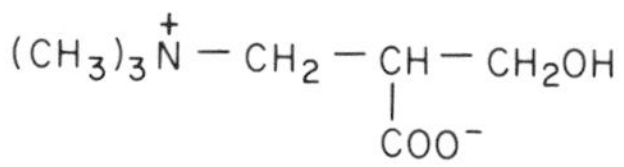

$$(CH_3)_3 \overset{+}{N} - CH_2 - \underset{\underset{COO^-}{|}}{CH} - CH_2OH$$

α-Iminodipropionic acid

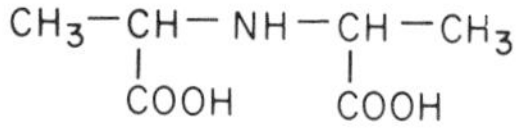

$$CH_3 - \underset{\underset{COOH}{|}}{CH} - NH - \underset{\underset{COOH}{|}}{CH} - CH_3$$

α-Iminopropioacetic acid

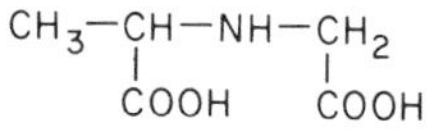

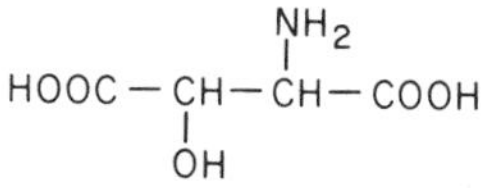

$$CH_3 - \underset{\underset{COOH}{|}}{CH} - NH - \underset{\underset{COOH}{|}}{CH_2}$$

β-Hydroxyaspartic acid

$$HOOC - \underset{\underset{OH}{|}}{CH} - \overset{\overset{NH_2}{|}}{CH} - COOH$$

β-Alanine betaine

$$(CH_3)_3 \overset{+}{N} - CH_2 - CH_2 - COO^-$$

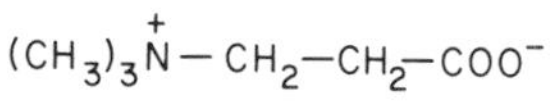

FIG. 17.6.

(G1P), glucose 6-phosphate (G6P), fructose 6-phosphate (F6P), and pentose phosphate in several species of fish. Yamanaka *et al.* (1974) detected tens of milligrams of G6P and F6P in the fresh muscle of skipjack. The analysis for G1P, G6P, and F6P was also performed on the hard clam and squids (Tsuchiya 1962). Inositol, a sugar alcohol, is also known to be distributed widely in the muscle of fish and mollusks (Tsuchiya 1962), and 5–10 mg of inositol was also detected in crab muscle (Hayashi *et al.* 1979).

In general, the content of free sugars and their derivatives in the muscle of fish and shellfish is fairly low, so it is doubtful that they contribute to the flavor. Jones (1961), however, stated that the sugar phosphates were "sweetish-salty" to most members of a taste panel when the compounds were tasted at the maximum concentration found in the fresh or chill-stored flesh of cod.

Inorganic Salts. A great number of papers have been published on the content of inorganic salts in the muscle of fish and shellfish, and the data for Na, K, Ca, Mg, P, and Cl on more than 160 species were collected in a review

TABLE 17.8.   ORGANIC ACIDS IN THE MUSCLES OF FISH AND SHELLFISH[1,2]

	Propionic	Acetic	Pyruvic	Fumaric	Succinic	Lactic	Pyro-glutamic	Malic	Oxalic	Citric	Tartaric
Yellowtail (1)	5	7	14		239	234					
Mackerel	11	9	10		15	684					
Snow crab	+	+			9	100			+		
Alaska king crab	+	+			4	130			+		
Prawn											
(2)	4	4	7		27	232	19		3		
(7)	7	5	7		6	130	8		3		
Short-necked clam	63	5	1	2	274	4		15			
Hard clam	5	9	8		80	26		5	9	22	2
Oyster	32	26	9		59	52		8		7	
Scallop				2	14	2		6		10	

[1]Values given in mg/100g of raw muscle; + trace.
[2]Refer to Table 17.1 for scientific names.

(Sidwell *et al*. 1977). These analyses were carried out exclusively from the standpoint of nutrition. Our analysis of the composition of the inorganic salts in crab muscle extract (Hayashi *et al*. 1979) may be the first instance where the study was made from the standpoint of flavor. Some of the data are given in Table 17.9. The major cations were Na^+ and K^+. The major anion was Cl^- with somewhat lower levels of PO_4^{3-} being present. It was shown that these ions made an indispensable contribution to the flavor (Hayashi *et al*. 1978A, 1981B).

FACTORS INFLUENCING THE NATURE OF THE EXTRACTIVE COMPONENTS

The factor having the greatest influence on the composition of extracts is, of course, the genetic makeup of the species. It is responsible for the various flavor characteristic of each species. Other factors, such as growth, season, spawning migration, environmental conditions, diets, parts and tissues of body, freshness, etc., can also cause changes in the composition of extracts, thus resulting in further diversification of the flavor of fish and shellfish.

Changes with Growth

Several papers have been published on the correlation between growth and the extractive components of fish (Cowey and Parry 1963; Vyncke 1970; Sakaguchi and Simidu 1965; Hibiki and Simidu 1959; Amano 1971). In addition, the relationship between the ecdysis of crab and changes in the extractive components was also investigated (Tucker and Costlow 1975).

Cowey and Parry (1963) observed a decrease of taurine and marked increases of anserine and creatine during the growth process from parr to smolt in the Atlantic salmon. Vyncke (1970) found significantly lower contents of α-amino nitrogen, alanine, glutamic acid, and glycine in sexually mature specimens of the spurdog than in immature ones and suggested the reason for this phenomenon to be the active participation of these amino acids in protein metabolism. On the other hand, Sakaguchi and Simidu (1965) observed that the amounts of extractive nitrogen and free histidine were lower in small-sized mackerel than in large-sized ones. This tendency has also been noticed in the yellowtail and horse mackerel (Hibiki and Simidu 1959). Also in this connection, it was reported that the levels of

TABLE 17.9.   INORGANIC CONSTITUENTS IN THE MUSCLES OF CRAB[1,2]

	Na^+	K^+	Ca^{2+}	Mg^{2+}	Cl^-	PO_4^{3-}
Blue crab	360	211	+	+	547	104
Horsehair crab	269	296	+	+	540	236
Snow crab	191	197	+	+	336	217
King crab	382	277	+	+	625	134
Alaska king crab	336	277	+	+	584	169

[1]Values given in mg/100g of raw muscle; + trace.
[2]Refer to Table 17.1 for scientific names.

creatine in salmon (Cowey and Parry 1963) and TMAO in mackerel (Amano 1971) both increased with growth.

Seasonal Variation

It is natural to consider that the seasonal variation in the extractive components of matured animals should relate closely to spawning. Simidu (1949) found that the levels of monoamino nitrogen in the muscle extract of tuna tended to increase in summer, the spawning season of this fish, and those of diamino nitrogen in winter. Oishi (1957) observed that the stone flounder accumulated glycine after spawning. On the basis of over 3 years of investigation on the fluctuation of free amino acids in the lemon sole, Jones (1959) concluded that the contents of glutamic acid, glycine, and taurine showed a distinct yearly variation and assumed that the reason for the rise of taurine in summer might be attributed to the elevated salt concentration of the seawater at the fishing ground.

Investigating the fluctuation in the contents of 10 free amino acids in herring living in British coastal waters, Hughes (1959) found a remarkable occurrence: histidine was highest in late May and lowest in October and November, as depicted in Fig. 17.7. No regular changes were observed for the other amino acids, and the levels of total amino acid exhibited a pattern

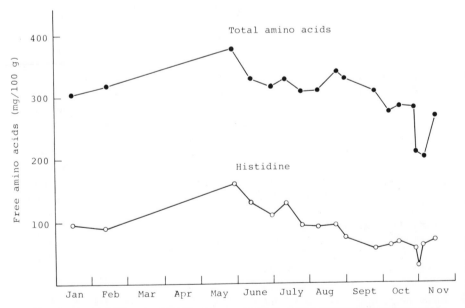

FIG. 17.7. SEASONAL VARIATION OF FREE AMINO ACIDS IN THE MUSCLE OF HERRING *Clupea harengus*

similar to that of histidine. There exist different populations among North Sea herring whose spawning seasons are discrete from each other. The spawning season of the herring concerned in the study is autumn, at which time the histidine content decreases considerably. In mackerel, too, specimens taken in winter are reported to have more extractive nitrogen, especially histidine and creatine, than those taken in spring, the spawning season (Sakaguchi and Simidu 1965). These findings lead us to propose that histidine, which is by far the predominant free amino acid, is metabolized actively during the spawning season in red-fleshed fishes. In this connection, it was observed that the content of histidine in the sockeye salmon decreased distinctly at an early stage of the anadromous movement for spawning (Wood et al. 1960). Such a change, however, was not recognized in the Atlantic salmon (Cowey et al. 1962). In the spurdog, the levels of free amino acids were not influenced by season either, though the peptides increased during the spring/summer period (Vyncke 1970).

With respect to components other than amino acids, several papers have been published on the seasonal variation of the creatine and TMAO contents in fish. The creatine content was found to decrease during the spawning migration of the sockeye salmon (Chang et al. 1960) and to be elevated during winter in the mackerel (Sakaguchi and Simidu 1965). Ronold and Jakobsen (1947) reported that the TMAO content in the herring species, Clupea harengus and C. sprattus, reached a minimum in summer and a maximum in winter/spring. This finding was confirmed by Hughes (1959A) for C. harengus. Takada and Nishimoto (1958) found that the TMAO content in the mackerel showed little difference between summer and winter but that in the round herring it was high in summer, and in the red sea bream it was high in winter. Dyer (1952), however, observed no distinct seasonal variation in herring, flounder, cod, and haddock.

Some papers have been published concerning the seasonal influence on the extractive components in invertebrates. Hujita (1961) undertook a study on seasonal variations in levels of free amino acids, betaine, and TMAO in the muscle extracts of prawns and obtained an interesting result as illustrated in Fig. 17.8. The content of glycine was at a level of around 1500 mg in January, and began to drop in May, reaching a minimum of about 700 mg from June to September. In contrast, the content of arginine showed an opposite change, so that the total of glycine and arginine remained almost constant throughout the year. On the basis of the fact that the periods of drop in glycine and rise in arginine were in line with the spawning season of the animal, the changes in both amino acids were believed to have a close relation to spawning.

Endo et al. (1962B) observed that the amounts of free amino acids decreased and those of TMAO and betaine increased in summer/autumn for squid and in autumn/winter for cuttlefish. Osada (1968) examined the seasonal variation of organic acids in short-necked clam and found that the contents of propionic, acetic, α-ketoglutaric, and citric acids scarcely

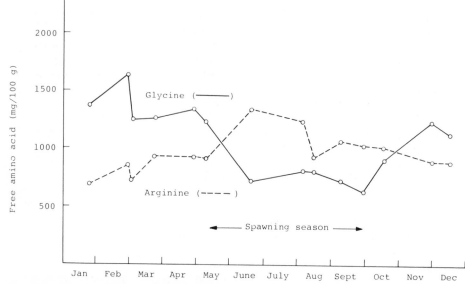

FIG. 17.8.   SEASONAL VARIATION OF FREE GLYCINE AND ARGININE IN THE MUSCLE OF PRAWN *Penaeus japonicus*

changed but that succinic acid reached the maximum quantity just before spawning and decreased again after spawning.

Influence of Salinity

It has been pointed out that free amino acids play a significant role in osmoregulation not only in fish but in many species of shellfish and that their amounts increase or decrease in accordance with the change in external salinity (Parry 1966; Huggins and Colley 1971; Colley *et al.* 1974; Forster and Goldstein 1976; Kaushik and Luquet 1977; Ahokas and Sorg 1977; Schoffeniels and Gilles 1970). During osmoregulation, fluctuations in the amount of taurine and glutamic acid, including glutamine, glycine, alanine, and proline, appear to be most striking (Cholette *et al.* 1970; Gilles 1970).

Differences between Cultured and Wild Fish

It is generally accepted that the flavor of cultured specimens of red sea bream, yellowtail, ayu, and eel is quite different from that of the corresponding wild ones. In recent years, the extractive components of both wild and cultured red sea bream (Konosu and Watanabe 1976), yellowtail (Shimizu *et al.* 1973; Endo *et al.* 1974), and ayu (Suyama *et al.* 1970C) have been analyzed. Some of the results obtained are compared in Table 17.10.

Our data (Konosu and Watanabe 1967) on cultured and wild red sea bream indicates that the composition of the extractive components is similar in spite of a somewhat lower content of taurine in the cultured specimen. Although a clear difference is obvious for anserine in the data given in Table 17.10, it may be due to individual variations because, in another case (Konosu and Watanabe 1967), very little difference was found in the anserine content. In the yellowtail also, Endo *et al.* (1974) could detect little

TABLE 17.10. NITROGENOUS CONSTITUENTS IN THE MUSCLE EXTRACTS OF CULTURED AND WILD FISHES OF THREE SPECIES[1]

	Red sea bream		Yellowtail		Ayu (Sweet smelt)	
	Cultured	Wild	Cultured	Wild	Cultured	Wild
Free amino acids						
Taurine	185	244	46	42	208	123
Hydroxyproline	2	1			+	+
Aspartic acid	+	−			2	2
Threonine	5	6	2	2	7	18
Serine	2	3	3	3	7	14
Asparagine + Glutamine[2]	7	1				
Sarcosine	−	+				
Proline	−	5	6	3	29	19
Glutamic acid	9	8	5	9	12	11
Citrulline	1	1				
Glycine	9	10	4	2	20	46
Alanine	11	16	17	18	12	30
α-Amino-n-butyric acid	+	+			+	4
Valine	2	4	6	2	4	5
Methionine	1	1	−	+	1	−
Isoleucine	2	2	3	1	2	3
Leucine	3	4	6	2	4	5
Tyrosine	2	+	−	1	2	5
Phenylalanine	2	1	−	1	2	3
β-Alanine	−	+				
γ-Amino-n-butyric acid					+	3
Ornithine	2	4			1	4
Ethanolamine	−	+			1	+
Lysine	82	74	34	14	27	24
Histidine	28	24	1237	1119	50	45
Tryptophan	−	−				
Arginine	8	10			3	8
Peptides						
Carnosine					+	−
Anserine	+	48			65	81
Nucleotides						
Inosine + hypoxanthine[3]	+	2			83	100
Inosine monophosphate	325	321			194	230
Adenosine monophosphate	−	−			11	10
Other bases						
Creatine	550	554			391[4]	410
Creatinine	38	37				
TMAO	158	175				
TMA	+	+				
NH3	17	15			11	12
Total extractive nitrogen	365	389	683	696	319	300

[1]Values given in mg/100g of raw muscle; + trace; − not detected.
[2]Calculated as asparagine.
[3]Calculated as inosine.
[4]Calculated as creatine.

difference between cultured and wild fish. In the case of the ayu, however, Suyama et al. (1970C) found a clear difference in the amount of taurine and anserine in cultured and wild specimens.

Generally, extracts from cultured and wild specimens of each species resemble one another in composition surprisingly well. Therefore, the difference in the flavor can be attributed to the higher fat content in the muscle of cultured specimens, a fact that has been confirmed in cultured fish irrespective of species (Suyama et al. 1970C; Konosu and Watanabe 1967; Shimizu et al. 1973). This in turn may be mainly attributable to differences in their diets.

Differences by Parts and Tissues

Unlike other animals, fish have a dark muscle that differs from ordinary muscle in physiological function as well as chemical composition. When the extractive components of dark muscle are compared with those of ordinary muscle, it can be shown that the content of histidine is lower in the dark muscle in various fishes (Ito 1957; Hughes 1964) and that the levels of taurine and alanine are higher in the anchovy (Arakaki and Suyama 1966). Saito et al. (1959) investigated postmortem changes in adenine nucleotides in both kinds of muscle in the rainbow trout and found that IMP disappears more rapidly in the dark muscle. Hughes (1964) found little difference in the histidine content of the fore, middle, and rear parts of the ordinary muscle of herring, whereas Koizumi et al. (1967) observed that TMAO in the ordinary muscle of the tail part of albacore is several times more abundant than in the head part.

Oishi et al. (1970) noticed a higher glycine content in the red (striated) part of the adductor muscle of the scallop than in the white (smooth) part. Harada et al. (1968) determined the amount of TMAO in individual tissues for 14 species of squid and found that the mantle muscle contained more TMAO than the arm muscle.

Freshness

Freshness is one of the principal factors influencing flavor. It is well known that some fish species taste better some time after death than immediately after death while others taste flatter with the lapse of time. This can be explained by a diversity in species-specific enzymatic actions, which bring about the rise and fall in the levels of free amino acids, nucleotides, etc., during postmortem storage.

Of the extractive components, changes in adenine nucleotides levels and their relationship to freshness have been investigated in detail. As already described in the foregoing chapter, the contents of IMP and AMP, which affect the flavor, change every moment, but aspects of their degradation are rather species-specific. For example, it has been shown that IMP in the cod or Alaska pollock disappeared almost completely after 1–2 days of chill storage but that the IMP levels in the red sea bream and black sea bream chill-stored for 2 weeks were still approximately 50% of the initial level (Uchiyama *et al.* 1974). Endo *et al.* (1963) observed that the content of AMP in the muscle of squid decreased rapidly during the first day of chill storage, producing inosine and hypoxanthine. It has been reported that both AMP and IMP accumulate in the flesh of crabs but that the former disappear more rapidly (Hiltz and Bishop 1975).

THE COMPOSITION OF EXTRACTS

In recent years, attempts have been made to elucidate the composition of extracts in full by exhaustively analyzing each sample. Most studies have dealt only with the nitrogenous components, but a few have also dealt with all the extractives including the nonnitrogenous ones.

Distribution of Nitrogenous Components

The extractive nitrogen in the muscle has been determined so far for a number of species of fish and shellfish (Table 17.11). Among fishes the extractive nitrogen levels are remarkably higher in elasmobranchs than teleosts. This is due to the abundance of urea and TMAO in the former, as already indicated. As far as teleosts are concerned, the extractive nitrogen of red-fleshed fishes such as the skipjack and tuna is appreciably higher than that of white-fleshed ones such as plaice and sea bream. This is attributable chiefly to the difference in histidine content. With the exception of the red-fleshed fishes having very large amounts of histidine, the quantity of the extractive nitrogen in invertebrates clearly exceeds that of teleosts. This supports the general opinion that shellfish are more flavorful than fish.

There are an increasing number of studies in which the total extractive nitrogen is accounted for by the sum of the nitrogen in individual nitrogenous components. Figure 17.9 shows examples in which more than 90% of the total extractive nitrogen has been elucidated (Konosu *et al.* 1965, 1974; Suyama *et al.* 1970C; Konosu 1971, 1976; Hayashi *et al.* 1978B). The figure depicts, with bar graphs, the nitrogen content of each group of compounds, which is calculated from the analytical data as percentage of total extractive nitrogen.

Creatine is one of the major components of teleosts, especially in white-fleshed fishes. But the total amount of free amino acids exceeds that of creatine in the mackerel because of histidine, the predominant amino acid. This may be true with red-fleshed fish in general. In addition to creatine, large amounts of nucleotides and TMAO occur in marine teleosts. However, it should be noted that freshwater teleosts lack TMAO almost completely. It has been found in the parr of salmon (Cowey and Parry 1963) that nearly all of the extractive nitrogen could be accounted for by free amino acids, anserine, creatine, creatinine, amido nitrogen, and volatile basic nitrogen.

TABLE 17.11. EXTRACTIVE NITRO-
GEN IN THE MUSCLES OF FISH AND
SHELLFISH

Teleosts	
Angler	253
Puffer	351
Stone flounder	339
Flathead flounder	320
Flounder	332
Rockfish	242
Red sea bream	396
Yellowtail (1)	474
Horse mackerel	423
Swordfish	564
Mackerel	524
Skipjack	802
Yellowfin tuna	614
Big-eye tuna	652
Eel	290
Ayu	300
Elasmobranchs	
Shark	
(2)	1010
(4)	1450
(8)	1400
Crustaceans	
Blue crab	564
Snow crab	618
Alaska king crab	863
Prawn	
(2)	846
(7)	820
Mollusks	
Squid	
(1)	728
(3)	884
(6)	728
Short-necked clam	593
Scallop	817

[1] Values given in mg/100g of raw
muscle.
[2] Refer to Tables 17.1 and 17.2 for scientific names.

In elasmobranchs, urea accounts for 50–60% of the extractive nitrogen, followed by creatine and TMAO. These three compounds account for 80–90% of the extractive nitrogen. The amount of amino acids and nucleotides, both important components in determining flavor, is fairly low despite the characteristically high levels of extractive nitrogen.

In strong contrast to elasmobranchs, the majority of mollusks and crustaceans have free amino acids as a predominant group of nitrogenous compounds in their extracts. Free amino acids and quaternary ammonium bases comprise nearly 90% of the extractive nitrogen. These components may well explain the rich flavor of crustaceans and mollusks.

The sum of the nitrogen of the individual nitrogenous compounds in the red sea bream, shark, snow crab, squid, and short-necked clam shown in

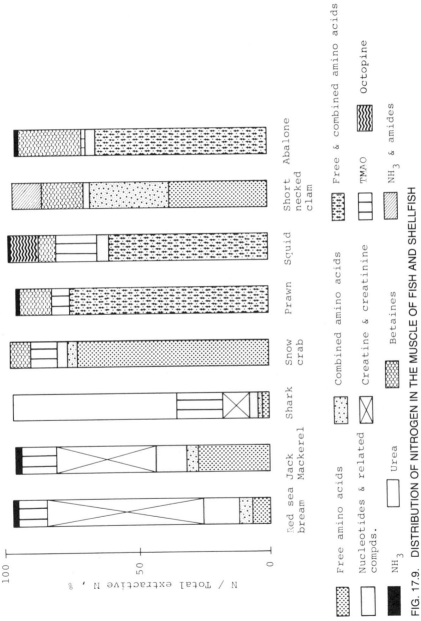

Red sea   Jack   Shark   Snow   Prawn   Squid   Short   Abalone
bream   Mackerel   crab   necked
                                                    clam

100 —

50 —

0 —

N / Total extractive N , %

Free amino acids   Combined amino acids   Free & combined amino acids

Nucleotides & related   Creatine & creatinine   TMAO   Octopine
compds.

NH₃   Urea   Betaines   NH₃ & amides

FIG. 17.9.   DISTRIBUTION OF NITROGEN IN THE MUSCLE OF FISH AND SHELLFISH

Fig. 17.9 is nearly 100%, indicating that the distribution of extractive nitrogen has been elucidated almost completely. In addition, the distribution of muscle extractive nitrogen has been determined almost completely in some species of deep sea fishes that have been newly developed as food resources in Japan by recent exploitation of new fishing grounds (Konosu *et al.* 1978C). Furthermore, more than 95% of the extractive nitrogen in the marine worm *(Perinereis brevicirrus)* (Konosu *et al.* 1966), and the gonads of sea urchins (Komata *et al.* 1962A,B; Komata and Eguchi 1962; Komata 1964; Hirano *et al.* 1978), has been accounted for. In a recent study (Suyama *et al.* 1979), approximately 90% of the nitrogen in the meat extract of freshwater softshell turtles has been identified.

Distribution of Extractive Components Including Nonnitrogenous Components

In order to trace the origin of flavor, analysis is required not only of nitrogenous compounds but also of nonnitrogenous components including organic acids, sugars, and inorganic constituents. Such an investigation, however, has not yet been done on fish, and our recent study on crab meat (Hayashi *et al.* 1979) may be the only study on shellfish. The distribution of

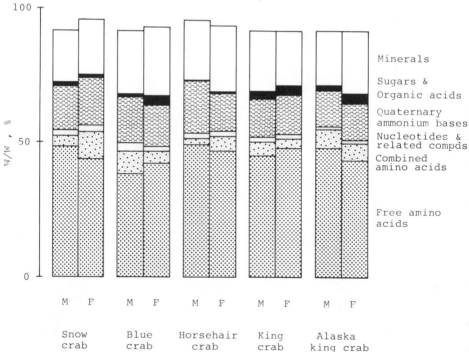

FIG. 17.10. DISTRIBUTION OF EXTRACTIVE COMPONENTS IN CRAB MUSCLE EXTRACTS

all the extractive components calculated as percentage of dry matter of the extracts from the meat of five species of crabs is given in Fig. 17.10. The dry matter consists of about 70% nitrogenous compounds, 20% inorganic matter, and small portions of sugars and organic acids. Through this analysis the composition of the crab extracts has been elucidated almost completely.

Another example of a very detailed analysis of extracts, though not of a fish or shellfish, is the analysis of the muscle extract of the sei whale performed by Suyama et al. (1970B), in which the analyzed constituents including the inorganic constituents accounted for 97.5% of the dry matter.

As has been mentioned above, considerable data have been accumulated on the composition of extracts of fish and shellfish, but how each component contributes to flavor remains largely unexplained. One of the effective means of solving this problem is the "omission test" that utilizes a synthetic extract prepared in accordance with analytical data. Using this method, the key flavor components in the meat of abalone, gonads of sea urchin, and whale meat have been identified (Konosu 1973).

Hayaski et al. (1978A, 1981A) prepared a synthetic extract of the snow crab leg meat with pure chemicals and confirmed that its flavor satisfactorily simulates that of the natural crab extract. The subsequent omission taste test revealed that glycine, glutamic acid, arginine, AMP, GMP, Na^+, and Cl^- contribute greatly to the characteristic flavor of boiled crab and that the essence of the crab flavor thus formed is elaborated on and enhanced by alanine, glycine betaine, K^+, and PO_4^{3-}, and possibly CMP. It should be stressed that Na^+ and Cl^- make very important contributions to the flavor. Interested readers are referred to a review by Konosu (1979) for detail. As is evident from this example, it is insufficient to draw inferences from the amounts of nitrogenous compounds alone, as has usually been done to date to elucidate the principles of flavor. A detailed analysis of the extractive components including inorganic constituents followed by organoleptic taste tests to correlate the analytical data directly with flavor is required.

ACKNOWLEDGMENT

The authors are indebted to Professor M. Ikawa, Department of Biochemistry, University of New Hampshire, for his assistance in the preparation of this manuscript.

REFERENCES

ABE, S., and KANEDA, T.   1975.   Studies on the effect of marine products on cholesterol metabolism in rats. X.   Isolation of β-homobetaine from oyster and betaine contents in oyster and scallop.   Bull. Jpn. Soc. Sci. Fish. *41*, 467–471.

AHOKAS, R.A., and SORG, G.   1977.   The effect of salinity and temperature on intracellular osmoregulation and muscle free amino acids in *Fundulus diaphanus*.   Comp. Biochem. Physiol. A *56*, 101–105.

AMANO, K. 1971. Selected topics of TMAO (trimethylamine oxide) in fish. Bull. Jpn. Soc. Sci. Fish. *37*, 784–787.

ARAI, K. 1966. Nucleotides in the muscle of marine invertebrates. Bull. Jpn. Soc. Sci. Fish. *32*, 174–179.

ARAKAKI, J., and SUYAMA, M. 1966. Free and conjugated amino acids in extracts of anchovy. Bull. Jpn. Soc. Sci. Fish. *32*, 74–79.

BEATTY, S.A. 1939. Studies on fish spoilage. III. The trimethylamine oxide content of the muscles of Nova Scotia fish. J. Fish. Res. Board Can. *4*, 229–232.

BEERS, J.R. 1967. The species distribution of some naturally occurring quaternary ammonium compounds. Comp. Biochem. Physiol. *21*, 11–21.

CHANG, V.M., TSUYUKI, H., and IDLER, D.R. 1960. Biological studies on sockeye salmon during spawning migration. XIII. The distribution of phosphorus compounds, creatine and inositol in the major tissues. J. Fish. Res. Board Can. *17*, 565–582.

CHOLETTE, C., GAGNON, A., and GERMAIN, P. 1970. Isoosmotic adaptation in *Myxine glutinosa*. I. Variation of some parameters and role of the amino acid pool of the muscle cells. Comp. Biochem. Physiol. *33*, 333–346.

COLLEY, L., FOX, F.R., and HUGGINS, A.K. 1974. Effects of changes in external salinity on the nonprotein nitrogenous constituents of parietal muscle from *Agonus cataphractus*. Comp. Biochem. Physiol. A *48*, 757–763.

COWEY, C.B., and PARRY, G. 1963. The nonprotein nitrogenous constituents of the muscle of parr and smolt stages of the Atlantic salmon. Comp. Biochem. Physiol. *8*, 47–51.

COWEY, C.B., DAISLEY, K.W., and PARRY, G. 1962. Amino acids free or as components of protein, and some B vitamins in the tissues of the Atlantic salmon during spawning and migration. Comp. Biochem. Physiol. *7*, 29–38.

DAMBERGS, N., ODENSE, P., and GUILBAULT, R. 1968. Changes in free amino acids in skeletal muscle of cod *(Gadus morhua)* under conditions simulating gillnet fishing. J. Fish. Res. Board Can. *15*, 935–942.

DYER, W.J. 1952. Amines in the fish muscle. VI. Trimethylamine oxide content of fish and marine invertebrates. J. Fish. Res. Board Can. *8*, 314–324.

EHIRA, S., and UCHIYAMA, H. 1967. Change in the ribose content of plaice muscle during ice storage. Bull. Jpn. Soc. Sci. Fish. *33*, 126–140.

ENDO, K., and SIMIDU, W. 1963. Muscle of aquatic animals. XXXVII. Octopine in squid muscle. Bull. Jpn. Soc. Sci. Fish. *29*, 362–365.

ENDO, K., HUJITA, M., and SIMIDU, W. 1962A. Muscle of aquatic animals. XXX. Free amino acids, trimethylamine oxide, and betaine in squids. Bull. Jpn. Soc. Sci. Fish. *28*, 833–836.

ENDO, K., HUJITA, M., and SIMIDU, W. 1962B. Muscle of aquatic animals. XXXIII. Seasonal variation of nitrogenous extractives in squid muscle. Bull. Jpn. Soc. Sci. Fish. *28*, 1099–1103.

ENDO, K., HUJITA, M., and SIMIDU, W.   1963.   Muscle of aquatic animals. XXXVIII.   Changes in nitrogenous extractives of squid muscle during storage.   Bull. Jpn. Soc. Sci. Fish. 29, 366–370.

ENDO, K., KISHIMOTO, Y., and SHIMIZU, Y.   1974.   Season variations in chemical constituents of yellowtail muscle. II.   Nitrogenous extractives. Bull. Jpn. Soc. Sci. Fish. 40, 67–72.

FORSTER, R.P., and GOLDSTEIN, L.   1976.   Intracellular osmoregulatory role of amino acids and urea in marine elasmobranchs.   Am. J. Physiol. 230, 925–931.

GAEDE, G.   1976.   Octopine dehydrogenase in the cockle Cardium edule. Biochem. Soc. Trans. 4, 433–436.

GASTEIGER, E.L., HAAKE, P.C., and GERGEN, J.A.   1960.   Investigation of the distribution and function of homarine (N-methyl picolinic acid).   Ann. N.Y. Acad. Sci. 90, 622–636.

GILLES, R.   1970.   Osmoregulation in the stenohaline crab Libinia emarginata.   Arch. Int. Physiol. Biochim. 78, 91–99.

GRIESHABER, M., and GAEDE, G.   1976.   The biological role of octopine in the squid.   J. Comp. Physiol. 108, 225–232.

GRIESHABER, M., and GAEDE, G.   1977.   Energy supply and the formation of octopine in the adductor muscle of the scallop, Pecten jacobaeus (Lamarck).   Comp. Biochem. Physiol. B 58, 249–252.

HARADA, K.   1975.   Enzyme system catalyzing the formation of formaldehyde and dimethylamine in tissues of fish and shellfish.   J. Shimonoseki Univ. Fish. 23, 163–241.

HARADA, K., FUJIMOTO, T., and YAMADA, K.   1968.   Distribution of trimethylamine oxide in fish and other aquatic animals. I.   Decapoda.   J. Shimonoseki Univ. Fish. 17, 87–95.

HAYASHI, T., and KONOSU, S.   1977.   Quaternary ammonium bases in the adductor muscle of fan-mussel.   Bull. Jpn. Soc. Sci. Fish. 43, 343–348.

HAYASHI, T., YAMAGUCHI, K., and KONOSU, S.   1978A.   Studies on flavor components in the extract of boiled snow crab meat.   Annu. Meeting of the Japanese Soc. of Scientific Fisheries, p. 122. Abstr.

HAYASHI, T., YAMAGUCHI, K., and KONOSU, S.   1978B.   Studies on flavor components in boiled crabs. II.   Nucleotides and organic bases in extracts.   Bull. Jpn. Soc. Sci. Fish. 44, 1357–1362.

HAYASHI, T., ASAKAWA, A., YAMAGUCHI, K., and KONOSU, S.   1979. Studies on flavor components in boiled crabs. III.   Sugars, organic acids, and minerals in the extracts.   Bull. Jpn. Soc. Sci. Fish. 45, 1325–1329.

HAYASHI, T., FURUKAWA, H., YAMAGUCHI, K., and KONOSU, S. 1981A.   Comparison of taste between natural and synthetic extracts of snow crab meat.   Bull. Jpn. Soc. Sci. Fish. 47, 529–534.

HAYASHI, T., YAMAGUCHI, K., and KONOSU, S.   1981B.   Sensory analysis of taste-active components in the extract of boiled snow crab meat. J. Food Sci. *46*, 479–483.

HIBIKI, S., and SIMIDU, W. 1959. Studies on putrefaction of aquatic products-27. Inhibition of histamine formation in spoiling of cooked fish and histidine content in various fishes. Bull. Jpn. Soc. Sic. Fish. *24*, 916–919.

HILTZ, D.F., and BISHOP, L.J. 1975. Postmortem glycolytic and nucleotide degradation changes in muscle of the Atlantic queen crab *(Chionecetes opilio)* upon iced storage of unfrozen and of thawed meat, and upon cooking. Comp. Biochem. Physiol. B *52*, 453–458.

HIRANO, T. 1975. On the distribution and season variation of homarine in some marine invertebrates. Bull. Jpn. Soc. Sci. Fish. *41*, 1047–1051.

HIRANO, T., YAMAZAWA, S., and SUYAMA, M. 1978. Chemical composition of the gonad extract of the sea urchin, *Strongylocentrotus nudus*. Bull. Jpn. Soc. Sci. Fish. *44*, 1037–1040.

HOCHACHKA, P.W., HARTLINE, P.H., and FIELDS, J.H.A. 1977. Octopine as an end product of anaerobic glycolysis in the chambered nautilus. Science *195*, 72–74.

HOWE, N.R., and SHEIKH, Y.M. 1975. Anthopleurine: a sea anemone alarm phermone. Science *189*, 386–388.

HUGGINS, A.K., and COLLEY, L. 1971. Changes in the non-protein nitrogenous constituents of muscle during the adaptation of *Anguilla anguilla* (eel) from freshwater to seawater. Comp. Biochem. Physiol. B *38*, 537–541.

HUGHES, R.B. 1959A. Chemical studies on the herring *(Clupea harengus)*. I. Trimethylamine oxide and volatile amines in fresh, spoiling, and cooked herring flesh. J. Sci. Food Agric. *10*, 431–436.

HUGHES, R.B. 1959B. Chemical studies on the herring *(Clupea harengus)*. II. Free amino acids of herring flesh and their behavior during postmortem spoilage. J. Sci. Food Agric. *10*, 558–564.

HUGHES, R.B. 1964. Chemical studies on the herring *(Clupea harengus)*. X. Histidine and free sugars in herring flesh. J. Sci. Food Agric. *15*, 293–299.

HUJITA, M. 1961. Studies on nitrogenous compounds in the muscle extract of prawn and shrimp. Ph.D. Dissertation, Kyoto University, Kyoto, Japan.

HUJITA, M., ENDO, K., and SIMIDU, W. 1972. Studies on muscle of aquatic animals. XXXXVI. Free amino acids, trimethylamine oxide and betaine in shrimp muscle. Mem. Fac. Agric. Kinki Univ. Kinki Daigaku Nogakubu Kiyo *5*, 61–67.

ITO, K. 1957. Amino acid composition of the muscle extracts of aquatic animals. I. Bull. Jpn. Soc. Sci. Fish. *23*, 497–500.

ITO, K. 1959. Amino acid composition of the muscle extracts of aquatic animals. II. The amounts of free amino acids in the muscle of shellfish and their variation during spoilage. Bull. Jpn. Soc. Sci. Fish. *25*, 658–660.

JONES, N.R. 1958. Free sugars in chilled-stored, trawled codling *(Gadus callarias)* muscle. J. Sci. Food Agric. *9*, 672–677.

JONES, N.R. 1959. Free amino acids of fish. II. Fresh skeletal muscle from lemon sole *(Pleuronectes microcephalus)*. J. Sci. Food Agric. *10*, 282–286.

JONES, N.R. 1961. Fish flavor. *In* Flavor Chemistry Symposium, p. 61. Campbell Soup Company. Camden, New Jersey.

JONES, N.R., and BURT, J.R. 1960. The separation and determination of sugar phosphates with particular reference to extracts of fish tissue. Analyst (London) *85*, 810–814.

JONES, N.R., and MURRAY, J. 1957. Nucleotides in the skeletal muscle of codling *(Gadus callarias)*. Biochem. J. *66*, 5.

JONES, N.R., and MURRAY, J. 1960. Acid-soluble nucleotides of codling *(Gadus callarias)* muscle. Biochem. J. *77*, 567–575.

JONES, N.R., and MURRAY, J. 1961. Nucleotide concentration in codling *(Gadus callarias)* muscle passing through rigor mortis at 0°. Z. Vgl. Physiol. *44*, 174–183.

KAUSHIK, S., and LUQUET, P. 1977. Study of free amino acids in rainbow trout in relation to salinity changes. II. Muscle free amino acids during starvation. Ann. Hydrobiol. *8*, 375–387.

KOIZUMI, C., KAWAKAMI, H., and NONAKA, J. 1967. Green tuna. III. Relation between greening and trimethylamine oxide concentration in albacore meat. Bull. Jpn. Soc. Sci. Fish. *33*, 131–135.

KOMATA, Y. 1964. The extractions of uni. IV. Taste of each component in the extractives. Bull. Jpn. Soc. Sci. Fish. *30*, 749–756.

KOMATA, Y., and EGUCHI, H. 1962. The extractives of uni. II. Nucleotides and organic bases. Bull. Jpn. Soc. Sci. Fish. *28*, 630–635.

KOMATA, Y., KOSUGI, N., and ITO, T. 1962A. The extractives of uni. I. Free amino acid composition. Bull. Jpn. Soc. Sci. Fish. *28*, 623–629.

KOMATA, Y., MUKAI, A., and OKADA, Y. 1962B. The extractives of uni. III. Organic acids and carbohydrates. Bull. Jpn. Soc. Sci. Fish. *28*, 747–750.

KONOSU, S. 1971. Distribution of nitrogenous constituents in the extracts of aquatic animals. Bull. Jpn. Soc. Sci. Fish. *37*, 763–770.

KONOSU, S. 1973. Tastes of fish and shellfish with special reference to taste-producing substances. J. Jpn. Soc. Food Sci. Technol. *20*, 432–439.

KONOSU, S. 1976. Extracts of fish muscle. J. Fish Sausage *206*, 24–37.

KONOSU, S. 1979. The taste of fish and shellfish. *In* Food Taste Chemistry. J.C. Boudreau (Editor). ACS Symp. Ser. *115*, 185–203.

KONOSU, S., and HAYASHI, T. 1975. Determination of β-alanine betaine and glycine betaine in some marine invertebrates. Bull. Jpn. Soc. Sci. Fish. *41*, 743–746.

KONOSU, S., and KASAI, E. 1961. Muscle extracts of aquatic animals. III.

Determination of betaine and its content of the muscle of some marine animals. Bull. Jpn. Soc. Sci. Fish. 27, 194–198.

KONOSU, S., and MAEDA, Y. 1961. Muscle extracts of aquatic animals. IV. Distribution of nitrogenous constituents in the muscle extracts of an abalone, Haliotis gigantea discus REEVE. Bull. Jpn. Soc. Sci. Fish. 27, 251–254.

KONOSU, S., and WATANABE, K. 1973. Occurrence of β-alanine betaine in the adductor muscle of fan-mussel. Bull. Jpn. Soc. Sci. Fish. 39, 645–648.

KONOSU, S., and WATANABE, K. 1976. Comparison of nitrogenous extractives of cultured and wild red sea breams. Bull. Jpn. Soc. Sci. Fish. 42, 1263–1266.

KONOSU, S., AKIYAMA, T., and MORI, T. 1958. Muscle extracts of aquatic animals. I. Amino acids, trimethylamine, and trimethylamine oxide in the muscle extracts of a squid Ommastrephes sloani pacificus. Bull. Jpn. Soc. Sci. Fish. 23, 561–564.

KONOSU, S., OZAY, M., and HASHIMOTO, Y. 1964. Free amino acids in the muscle of a few species of fish. Bull. Jpn. Soc. Sci. Fish. 30, 930–934.

KONOSU, S., FUJIMOTO, K., TAKASHIMA, Y., MATSUSHITA, T., and HASHIMOTO, Y. 1965. Constituents of the extracts and the amino acid composition of the protein of short-necked clam. Bull. Jpn. Soc. Sci. Fish. 31, 680–686.

KONOSU, S., CHEN, Y.N., and HASHIMOTO, Y. 1966. Constituents of extracts of a marine worm, Perinereis brevicirrus. Bull. Jpn. Soc. Sci. Fish. 32, 881–886.

KONOSU, S., SHIBOTA, M., and HASHIMOTO, Y. 1967. Concentration of organic acids in shellfish, with particular reference to succinic acid. J. Jpn. Soc. Food Nutr. 20, 186–189.

KONOSU, S., CHEN, Y.N., and WATANABE, K. 1970. Atrinine, a new betaine isolated from the adductor muscle of a fan-mussel. Bull. Jpn. Soc. Sci. Fish. 36, 940–944.

KONOSU, S., WATANABE, K., and SHIMIZU, T. 1974. Distribution of nitrogenous constituents in the muscle extracts of eight species of fish. Bull. Jpn. Soc. Sci. Fish. 40, 909–915.

KONOSU, S., YAMAGUCHI, K., and HAYASHI, T. 1978A. Studies on flavor components in boiled crabs. I. Amino acids and related compounds in the extracts. Bull. Jpn. Soc. Sci. Fish. 44, 505–510.

KONOSU, S., MURAKAMI, M., HAYASHI, T., and FUKE, S. 1978B. Occurrence of β-alanine betaine in the muscles of New Zealand whiptail and southern blue whiting. Bull. Jpn. Soc. Sci. Fish. 44, 1165–1166.

KONOSU, S., MATSUI, T., FUKE, S., KAWASAKI, I., and TANAKA, H. 1978C. Proximate composition, extractive components and amino acid composition of proteins of the muscles of newly exploited fish. J. Jpn. Soc. Food Nutr. 31, 597–604.

KUNINAKA, A.   1960.   Studies on taste of ribonucleic acid derivatives. Nippon Nogei Kagaku Kaishi *34*, 489–492.

KUTSCHER, F., and ACKERMANN, D.   1933.   Comparative biochemistry of vertebrates and invertebrates.   Annu. Rev. Biochem. *2*, 355–376.

LUKTON, A., and OLCOTT, H.S.   1958.   Content of free imidazole compounds in the muscle tissue of aquatic animals.   Food Res. *23*, 611–618.

MIYAUCHI, S.   1937.   On the glutathione content of salmon.   Jpn. J. Med. Sci. II. Biochem. *3*, 267. (German).

NORRIS, E.R., and BENOIT, G.J., JR.   1945.   Trimethylamine oxide. I.   Occurrence of trimethylamine oxide in marine organisms.   J. Biol. Chem. *158*, 433–438.

OISHI, K.   1957.   Extracts of fish muscle.   In Extracts of Marine Products. pp. 20–29.   Japanese Soc. Scientific Fisheries Symp., Hokkaido Univ. Fac. Fish., Hokadate, Japan.

OISHI, K.   1968.   Extractive components of fish and shellfish muscle.   New Food Ind. *10*, 1–12.

OISHI, K., IIDA, A., and YOSHIMURA, A.   1970.   Amino acid composition and phosphorus content in the extracts of scallop adductor muscle.   Bull. Jpn. Soc. Sci. Fish. *36*, 1226–1230.

OKADA, I., OSAKABE, I., KURATOMI, Y., and SEKINE, E.   1953.   Glutathione in carp.   J. Tokyo Inst. Fish. *39*, 185–191.

OSADA, H.   1966.   Studies on the organic acids in marine products—I.   Distribution of the organic acids in marine products.   Toyo Shokuhin Kogyo Tanki Daigaku, Toyo Shokuhin Kenkyusho Kenkyu Hokoku 7, 271–274.

OSADA, H.   1968.   Studies on the organic acids in marine products—II.   Variation of the amounts of organic acids in baby clam with seasons.   Toyo Shokunhin Kogyo Tanki Daigaku, Toyo Shokuhin Kenkyusho Kenkyu Hokoku 8, 293–296.

OSADA, H. and OKAYA, C.   1964.   Chemical studies of baby clam, *Venerupis semidecusata* Deshayes—III.   The organic acid content in baby clam.   Toyo Shokuhin Kogyo Tanki Daigaku, Toyo Shokuhin Kenkyusho Kenkyu Hokoku 6, 54–59.

PARRY, G.   1966.   Osmotic adaption in fishes.   Biol. Rev. Cambridge Philos. Soc. *41*, 392–444.

PORCELLATI, G., FLORIDI, A., and CIAMMARUGHI, A.   1965.   The distribution and the biological significance of L-serine ethanolamine and L-threonine ethanolamine phosphates.   Comp. Biochem. Physiol. *14*, 413–418.

RONOLD, O.R., and JAKOBSEN, F.   1947.   Trimethyamine oxide in marine products.   J. Soc. Chem. Ind. *66*, 160–166.

SAITO, T.   1960.   Tastes of fishes. Fishery products and inosinic acid. Kagaku (Kyoto) *15*, 101–107.

SAITO, T., ARAI, K., and YAJIMA, T.   1959.   Changes in purine nucleotides of red lateral muscle of rainbow trout.   Nature *185*, 1415.

SAKAGUCHI, M., and KAWAI, A.   1971.   Occurrence of histidine in the muscle extractives and its metabolism in fish tissues.   Bull. Res. Inst. Food Sci. Kyoto Univ. *34*, 28–51.

SAKAGUCHI, M., and SIMIDU, W.   1964.   Muscle of aquatic animals.XLIV. Amino acids, trimethylamine oxide, creatine, creatinine and nucleotides in fish muscle extractives.   Bull. Jpn. Soc. Sci. Fish. *30*, 1003–1007.

SAKAGUCHI, M., and SIMIDU, W.   1965.   Muscle of aquatic animals—XXXXV.   Variation with season and growth in nitrogenous exractives of mackerel muscle.   Bull. Jpn. Soc. Sci. Fish. *31*, 72–75.

SAKAGUCHI, M., HUJITA, M., and SIMIDU, W.   1964.   Creatine and creatinine contents in fish muscle extractives.   Bull. Jpn. Soc. Sci. Fish. *30*, 999–1002.

SATO, M., SATO, Y., and TSUCHIYA, Y.   1977A.   Studies on the extractives of molluscs. I.   α-Iminodipropionic acid isolated from the squid muscle extracts. (1)   Bull. Jpn. Soc. Sci. Fish. *43*, 1077–1079.

SATO, M., SATO, Y., and TSUCHIYA, Y.   1977B.   Studies on the extractives of molluscs. II.   α-Iminodipropionic acid isolated from squid muscle extracts. (2)   Bull. Jpn. Soc. Sci. Fish. *43*, 1441–1444.

SATO, M., SATO, Y., and TSUCHIYA, Y.   1978.   D-α-Iminopropioacetic acid isolated from the adductor muscle of a scallop.   Bull. Jpn. Soc. Sci. Fish. *44*, 247–250.

SATO, M., SATO, Y., and TSUCHIYA, Y.   1979.   L-*threo*-β-hydroxyaspartic acid isolated from the muscle of short-necked clam.   Bull. Jpn. Soc. Sci. Fish. *45*, 635–638.

SCHAEFER, H.   1962.   Free amino acids and related compounds in the trunk muscles of freshly caught marine teleosts.   Free amino acids and related compounds in the muscle of chimaera and some elasmobranchs and invertebrates.   Helgol. Wiss. Meeresunters. *8*, 257–275, 280–286.

SCHOFFENIELS, E., and GILLES, R.   1970.   Osmoregulation in aquatic arthropods.   *In* Chemical Zoology, (Vol. V, 255–286.) M. Florkin and B.T. Scheer (Editors).   Academic Press, New York.

SEKI, N.   1971.   Nucleotides in aquatic animals and seaweeds.   Bull. Jpn. Soc. Sci. Fish. *37*, 777–783.

SHIMIZU, Y., TADA, M., and ENDO, K.   1973.   Seasonal variations in chemical constituents of yellowtail muscle. I.   Water, lipid and crude protein. Bull. Jpn. Soc. Sci. Fish. *39*, 993–999.

SIDWELL, V.D., BUZZELL, D.H., FONCANNOU, P.R., and SMITH, A.L. 1977.   Composition of the edible portion of raw (fresh or frozen) crustaceans, finfish, and mollusks. 2.   Macroelements: sodium, potassium, chlorine, calcium, phosphorus, and magnesium.   Mar. Fish. Rev. *39*, 1–11.

SIMIDU, W.   1949.   Muscle of the aquatic animals—VI.   Distribution of extractive nitrogens in the muscle of tuna, *Thunnus orientalis*. Bull. Jpn. Soc. Fish. *15*, 28–31.

SIMIDU, W.   1963.   Nitrogenous extracts of marine animals.   *In* The Lecture Abstract on Extracts of Marine Animals.   Japanese Society of Scientific Fisheries Symp. pp. 26–40.

SIMIDU, W., and OISHI, K.   1951.   Putrefaction of aquatic products. V. Urea in elasmobranchiate fishes.   Bull. Jpn. Soc. Sci. Fish. *16*, 31–33.

SUYAMA, M., and SUZUKI, H.   1975.   Nitrogenous constituents in the muscle extracts of marine elasmobranchs.   Bull. Jpn. Soc. Sci. Fish. *41*, 787–790.

SUYAMA, M., and YOSHIZAWA, U.   1973.   Free amino acid composition of the skeletal muscle of migratory fish.   Bull. Jpn. Soc. Sci. Fish. *39*, 1339–1343.

SUYAMA, M., KOIKE, J., and SUZUKI, K.   1958.   The buffering capacity of fish muscle. IV.   Buffering capacity of muscles of some marine animals.   Bull. Jpn. Soc. Sci. Fish. *24*, 281–284.

SUYAMA, M., NAKAJIMA, K., and NONAKA, J.   1965.   Nitrogenous constituents of Euphausia.   Bull. Jpn. Soc. Sci. Fish. *31*, 302–306.

SUYAMA, M., SUZUKI, T., MARUYAMA, M., and SAITO, K.   1970A.   Determination of carnosine, anserine and balenine in the muscle of animal.   Bull. Jpn. Soc. Sci. Fish. *36*, 1048–1053.

SUYAMA, M., MARUYAMA, M., and TAKEUCHI, S.   1970B.   Chemical composition of the extracts of whale meat and its change during condensation.   Bull. Jpn. Soc. Sci. Fish. *36*, 1250–1257.

SUYAMA, M., HIRANO, T., OKADA, N., and SHIBUYA, T.   1970C.   Quality of wild and cultured ayu—I.   On the proximate composition, free amino acids and related compounds.   Bull. Jpn. Soc. Sci. Fish. *43*, 535–540.

SUYAMA, M., HIRANO, T., SATO, K., and FUKUDA, H.   1979.   Nitrogenous constituents of meat extract of fresh-water softshell turtle.   Bull. Jpn. Soc. Sci. Fish. *45*, 595–599.

SUZUKI, S.   1963.   Chemistry of acid soluble nucleotides.   Seikagaku *35*, 737–752.

TAKADA, K., and NISHIMOTO, J.   1958.   Studies on the choline in fish. I. Content of choline and the similar substances in fishes.   Bull. Jpn. Soc. Sci. Fish. *24*, 632–635.

TAKAGI, I., and SIMIDU, W.   1962.   Muscle of aquatic animals. XXXIV. Constituents and extractive nitrogen in a few species of shellfish.   Bull. Jpn. Soc. Sci. Fish. *28*, 1192–1198.

TARR, H.L.   1949.   The acid-soluble phosphorus compounds of fish skeletal muscle.   J. Fish. Res. Board Can. 7, 608–612.

TSUCHIYA, Y.   1957.   Extracts of invertebrates.   *In* Extracts of Marine Products, Japanese Society of Scientific Fisheries Symp., pp. 40–50.

TSUCHIYA, Y.   1962.   Fishery Chemistry (Suisan Kagaku), p. 447. Koseisha Koseikaku Publishing Co., Tokyo, Japan. (Japanese).

TUCKER, R.K., and COSTLOW, J.D., JR.   1975.   Free amino acid changes in normal and eyestalkless megalopa larvae of the blue crab, *Callinectes sapidus*, during the molt cycle. Comp. Biochem. Physiol. A *51*, 75–78.

UCHIYAMA, H., EHIRA, S., and KATO, N. 1974. Relationship between postmortem changes in fish muscle nucleotides and the freshness. Suisangaku Ser. *4*, 81–103.

VUL'FSON, P.L. 1961. Nitrogenous extractives in fish muscles. Biokhimiya *26*, 300–304.

VYNCKE, W. 1970. Influence of biological and environmental factors on nitrogenous extractives of the spurdog *Squalus acanthias*. Mar. Biol. *6*, 248–255.

WATANABE, K., SHIMIZU, T., and KONOSU, S. 1974. Formation of glycine from purine derivatives in the fish muscle extracts during acid hydrolysis. Bull. Jpn. Soc. Sci. Fish. *40*, 731.

WEINHEIMER, A.J., METZNER, E.K., and MOLE, M.L., JR. 1973. New marine betaine, norzooanemonin, in the gorgonian *Pseudopterogorgia americana*. Tetrahedron *29*, 3135–3136.

WOOD, J.D., DUNCAN, D.W., and JACKSON, M. 1960. Biochemical studies on sockeye salmon during spawning migration. XI. The free histidine content of the tissues. J. Fish. Res. Board Can. *17*, 347–351.

YAMADA, K. 1967. Occurrence and origin of trimethylamine oxide in fishes and marine invertebrates. Bull. Jpn. Soc. Sci. Fish. *33*, 591–603.

YAMANAKA, H., BITO, M., and YOKOSEKI, M. 1974. Orange discolored meat of canned skipjack—III. Changes in amounts of glycolytic intermediates in skipjack meat during thawing and cooking. Bull. Jpn. Soc. Sci. Fish. *40*, 941–947.

18

The Effect of Heat Processing on Color Characteristics in Crustacean Blood

Terushige Motohiro

The value of heat-processed seafood, like any other food, depends to a great extent on nonnutritional characteristics of the product; namely, flavor, color, taste, and texture. Color and flavor, because of their nature, are the most important factors influencing subjective assessment of food quality by consumers. Discoloration of canned seafood, therefore, is a serious quality problem.

Discoloration usually causes an undesirable appearance resulting in downgrading of the product. Considerable effort has been made to alleviate the problem of discoloration in canned seafood. For many years, "blackening," which occurs in a large variety of canned fish and shellfish, has been the primary concern. However, many of the recent investigations have dealt with "green" tuna and the "brown" or "blue" meat in canned crab, both of which are of commercial importance.

This author has investigated the cause and mechanism of blue discoloration of canned crab with respect to the chemistry of crustacean blood. Reported in this chapter are findings on the effect of heat processing on hemocyanin, a biochemical component in crustacean blood, which is significant to the discoloration process.

CHEMICAL PROPERTIES OF BLUE MEAT

Studies have found that blue discoloration of canned crab is due to the copper in the crab meat and that the degree of blue discoloration depends on the copper content of the meat (Gordievskaya 1966). The average copper level is higher in blue meat (2.80 mg% wet wt.) than in normal meat (0.49 mg% wet wt.) (Fig. 18.1). Levels of volatile basic nitrogen, total nitrogen,

Laboratory of Food Environmental Engineering, Faculty of Fisheries, Hokkaido University, Hakodate, Hokkaido, Japan

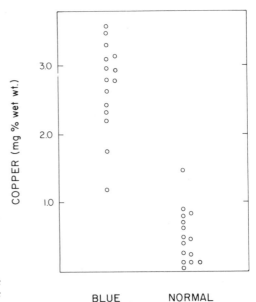

FIG. 18.1.   COPPER CONTENT OF
BLUE AND NORMAL MEATS OF   BLUE   NORMAL
CANNED KING CRAB   MEAT   MEAT

iron, hydrogen sulfide, and ash are similar in normal and blue meats (Table 18.1). Meat that frequently develops blue discoloration, that of the shoulder, surface of the first leg, claw, and near the joints, has been found to contain comparatively large amounts of copper (Table 18.2). The copper level remains high when this meat is canned, and blue discoloration can occur whenever the copper level reaches over 2 mg% (Table 18.3).

Hemocyanin reaction is positive in sodium hydroxide extracts of blue meat, while it is negative in extracts of the normal meat. The solution of the normal meat extract becomes brown when left for several hours. The blue meat hemocyanin and the heat-coagulated hemocyanin also give a positive reaction, while the normal meat gives a negative reaction. The joint meat of boiled crab contains a large amount of hemocyanin as witnessed by a marked reaction.

TABLE 18.1.   CHEMICAL ANALYSIS OF BLUE AND NORMAL MEATS IN CANNED KING CRAB

	Blue meat	Normal meat
pH	6.95	6.89
Volatile basic nitrogen (mg%)	23.3	22.4
Total nitrogen (%)	4.36	4.23
Copper (mg%)	3.52	0.41
Iron (mg%)	0.74	0.81
Hydrogen sulfide (mg%)	2.01	1.80
Ash (%)	2.34	2.16

TABLE 18.2. AMOUNT OF COPPER IN MEAT FROM
DIFFERENT PARTS OF KING CRAB[1]

Parts	Copper content
Shoulder meat	2.15
First leg meat	1.25
First leg meat (cut)	2.10
First leg meat (surface)	3.16
Second leg meat	1.04
Second leg meat (broken)	1.30
Third leg meat	0.83
Third leg meat (cut)	2.05
Third leg meat (broken)	1.22
Claw meat	2.15
Claw meat (Immovable finger)	1.26

[1]Value in milligrams per 100 g of wet weight of meat.

TABLE 18.3. AMOUNT OF COPPER IN
CANNED MEAT FROM DIFFERENT PARTS OF
KING CRAB[1]

Parts	Copper content
Shoulder meat	1.64
First leg meat	1.14
First leg meat (surface)	1.19
Second leg meat (broken)	1.09
Third leg meat (cut)	1.61
Third leg meat (broken)	1.15
Claw meat	1.51

[1]Value in milligrams per 100 g wet weight of
meat.

Blue discoloration can be prevented by using a method called the low temperature and fractional heating process (Osakabe 1958). Based on the theory that hemocyanin is the causative agent in the bluing reaction, this method utilizes a temperature differential. Blood protein of crab coagulates at 69°–70°C, whereas meat protein coagulates at 59°–60°C. When the carcass is heated to 59°–60°C, the meat coagulates but the blood remains fluid and runny. Since hemocyanin is detected in portions of crab with higher levels of copper, blue discoloration appears to be caused by hemocyanin contained in the hemolymph.

CAUSATIVE SUBSTANCE OF BLUE MEAT

The following procedure for isolation of the causative substance for blue meat is recommended by Inoue and Motohiro (1970):

After separating blue meat from normal meat, the blue meat portion of commercially packed king crab *(Paralithodes camtschatica)* is dried under vacuum and ground in a mortor. A suspension prepared by mixing 15.8 g of dried blue meat with 350 ml distilled water and 0.63 g proteinase ("Prozyme B," Kyowa Hakko Kogyo Co., Ltd.) is incubated at 40°C for 24 or 48 hr, then diluted with an equal volume of 10% TCA and centrifuged at 1500 g for 20 min. The precipitate is washed with 20 ml 95% ethanol for 5 min, and the alcoholic solution is discarded after centrifuging at 1500 g for 20 min. Washing and precipitation is repeated several times until the precipitate forms a dark green crystal. The yield of the blue pigment by this procedure is approximately 4.56%.

The chemical composition of blue substance I is similar to that of hemocyanin (Table 18.4). The result suggests that blue substance I is derived from hemocyanin. The amount of total nitrogen in 1 mg of blue substance I is less and the amount of copper is more than those in blue meat. This fact might be due to the removal of impurities contained in blue meat (Table 18.5).

The sulfide contained in organic materials such as cysteine, oxidized or reduced glutathione, insulin, and bovine serum albumin cannot be estimated by the method of Lovenberg et al. (1963). However, sulfide bound with iron in artificial nonheme iron proteins derived from bovine serum albumin (protein–iron–sulfide complex) and ferredoxin can be measured by the methods of McCarthy and Lovenberg (1968) and Lovenberg et al. (1963). Therefore, the sulfide in hemocyanin probably is different from that in the protein–iron–sulfide complex and ferredoxin with respect to its mode of binding. Sulfide in blue substance I can be measured after incubation for 48 hr at 40°C by the same method. This fact suggests that sulfide in blue substance II might become detectable after some protein breakdown. The reduction of sulfide in blue substance III may be due to its release during the enzymatic process. Thus the blue substance I is the cause of blue discoloration and is a sulfide complex that cannot be measured properly by the method of Lovenberg et al. (1963).

Although hemocyanin and hydrogen sulfide are involved in blue discoloration of heat-processed crab meat, more detailed knowledge of the caus-

TABLE 18.4. ANALYTICAL DATA OF BLUE SUBSTANCE AND HEMOCYANIN OF KING CRAB (Paralithodes camtschatica)

	Blue substance I[1]	Hemocyanin
Copper (μg/mg)	1.49	1.20
Total nitrogen (mg/mg)	0.10	0.11
Crude protein (mg/mg)	0.63	0.69
Iron (μg/mg)	0.0	0.0
Inorganic sulfide (μg/mg)	0.0	0.0

[1] Blue meat was incubated with protease at 40°C for 24 hr.

TABLE 18.5. PURIFICATION OF BLUE SUBSTANCE AND ITS ANALYTICAL DATA

	Total nitrogen (mg/mg)	Copper (μg/mg)	Inorganic sulfide μg/mg
Blue meat	0.14	0.27	0.0
Blue substance I[1]	0.10	1.49	0.0
Blue substance II[2]	0.11	3.94	1.07
Blue substance III[3]	0.09	5.00	0.37

[1] Blue meat was incubated with protease at 40°C for 24 hr.
[2] Blue meat was incubated with protease at 40°C for 48 hr.
[3] Blue substance II was incubated with protease at 40°C for additional 24 hr.

ative substance is required in order to elucidate the mechanism of the reaction of copper and sulfide including the chemical binding of copper in hemocyanin.

Isolation and purification of the blue substance is carried out by the procedure shown in Fig. 18.2. Fraction B from the blue meat extract contains a high level of copper and shows a remarkable hemocyanin-like reaction (Table 18.6), while fractions A and C show slight reactions. Fractions D and E contain no copper and show negative hemocyaninlike reactions. Paper electrophoresis indicates that fraction B contains a much slower material than the other fractions. The protein and copper contents and the extent of the hemocyaninlike reaction of the blue substance purified from fraction B of blue meat are shown in Table 18.7. The blue substance contains more copper than fraction B, though less of it is free. Most of the copper in the blue substance and in king crab hemocyanin dialyzed in the presence of EDTA can be removed by treating with 10 μmoles of diazobenzenesulfonic acid per milligram of protein (Table 18.8).

It is possible to remove over 90% of the copper in hemocyanin by treating it this way. Imidazole groups probably participate in the binding of copper in hemocyanin. However, since the copper in the blue substance and king crab hemocyanin can be removed in the presence of EDTA, the copper in the blue substance must be combined in a hemocyanin derivative. The high

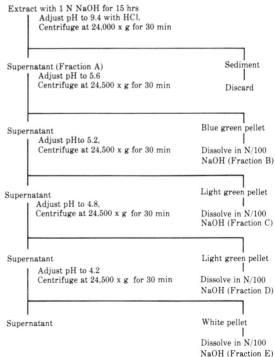

FIG. 18.2. A FLOW DIAGRAM FOR FRACTIONATION OF THE EXTRACT FROM BLUE MEAT

TABLE 18.6.   PROTEIN AND COPPER CONTENTS AND HEMOCYANIN-LIKE REACTION
OF FRACTIONS EXTRACTED BY 1 *N* SODIUM HYDROXIDE FROM BLUE AND NORMAL
MEATS

	Fraction	Protein (mg)	Copper (μg/mg)	Hemocyanin-like reaction[1]
	A	2303	0.21	+
	B	49.5	7.03	+ +
Blue meat	C	385.0	0.30	+
	D	800.0	0.0	−
	E	255.0	0.0	−
	B	26.3	0.0	−
	C	182.0	0.0	−
Normal meat	D	1055	0.0	−
	E	397.5	0.0	−

[1] + + Hemocyanin-like reation is very clear; + hemocyanin-like reaction is slight; −
hemocyanin-like reaction is negative.

TABLE 18.7.   PROTEIN AND COPPER CONTENTS AND HEMOCYANIN-LIKE REACTION
OF FRACTION B AND THE BLUE SUBSTANCE

	Protein (mg)	Copper (μg/mg)	Free copper (μg/mg)	Hemocyanin-like reaction[1]
Fraction B	49.5	7.03	1.67	+ +
Blue substance	19.5	7.52	0.12	+ +

[1]See Table 18.6.

TABLE 18.8.   EFFECT OF DIAZOBENZENESULFONIC ACID ON
THE BLUE SUBSTANCE AND KING CRAB HEMOCYANIN

	Percentage copper remaining in	
EDTA[1]	Blue substance	King crab hemocyanin
With	18.8	23.3
Without	75.8	82.2

[1]Dialysed against 0.1 *M* phosphate buffer (pH 7.0) with or without
the addition of 0.01 *M* EDTA. The amount of diazobenzenesulfonic acid: 10 μmoles/mg protein. Duration of experiment; 10 min
at 24°C.

level of copper in the blue substance indicates that the structure of hemocyanin might be destroyed during the extraction procedure with 1 *N* sodium
hydroxide. Therefore, it is suggested that the causative substance of blue
discoloration is a hemocyanin derivative.

Crab hemocyanins show varied electrophoretic patterns on starch gel
depending on species (Inoue and Motohiro 1969). However, differences in
electrophoretic patterns of crab hemocyanins do not directly affect their
chemical binding affinity with hydrogen sulfide.

SULFIDE REACTION OF CRAB HEMOCYANIN

The hemocyanin solution turns brown after treating with hydrogen sulfide, and produces a white coagulum on heating. Characteristic absorption
bands at 338 nm and 570 nm of oxyhemocyanin disappear after adding
hydrogen sulfide (Fig. 18.3). The white coagulum formed by heating hemo-

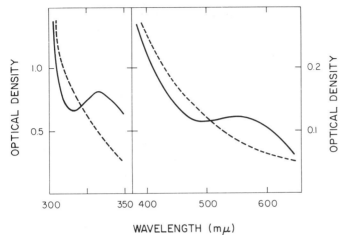

WAVELENGTH (mμ)

FIG. 18.3. ABSORPTION SPECTRA OF OXYHEMOCYANIN AND HEMOCYANIN TREATED WITH HYDROGEN SULFIDE

——, Oxyhemocyanin; - - - - hemocyanin treated with hydrogen sulfide.

cyanin changes to light brown initially, then gradually turns blue-green within 10 min. When ammonium sulfide is added to the hemocyanin solution, the color changes to brown. This solution does not coagulate by heating, but coagulates and turns blue-green when neutralized with hydrochloric acid. This coagulum is similar to that produced by hydrogen sulfide.

When heated without any sulfides, the hemocyanin solution produces a whitish coagulum. Similar coagula are obtained by heating the hemocyanin solution with trimethylamineoxide hydrochloride or with cysteine hydrochloride. When dipping heat-coagulated hemocyanin into a hydrogen sulfide solution, the color changes to bluish-green on reheating for 15 min. This fact suggests that heat-coagulated hemocyanin causes blue coloring in the presence of hydrogen sulfide. Oxyhemocyanin is denatured when left at 37°C for 20 hr, and its color changes from blue to brown. However, even denatured hemocyanin turns blue-green after heating with hydrogen sulfide. Hemocyanin with or without oxygen becomes blue after heating with hydrogen sulfide. There is not change of color when heating ground crab leg meat with hydrogen sulfide. From these results, it is obvious that, apart from hemocyanin, no compound in crab muscle produces blue discoloration.

In canning, cooked crab meat is usually packed in a tin container and processed. Thus, hemocyanin that has been coagulated is still chemically active and can react with hydrogen sulfide to produce bluing.

Under reducing conditions with hydroxylamine, most of the copper in heat-coagulated hemocyanin is detected as cuprous copper. No cuprous copper is detected with EDTA. This suggest that the copper in heat-coagulated hemocyanin is chelated with EDTA, and that copper hemocyanin or heat-coagulated hemocyanin may be masked with other chelating reagents. When heat-coagulated hemocyanin is not added to reducing or chelating reagents, one-half of the copper is detected in the cuprous state (Table

18.9). A small amount of residual copper remaining after cuprous copper estimation is assumed to be associated with inactivated sites during preparation of heat-coagulated hemocyanin. The serum of horseshoe crab *(Limulus polyphemus)* contained a material capable of reducing copper (Felsenfeld 1960).

Cupric copper is also reduced by proteins (Needham 1961). One-half of the copper in heat-coagulated hemocyanin is detectable as cuprous copper, and the remainder is cupric copper. A small change in the amount of cuprous ion is detected by increasing the *p*-chloromercuribenzoate concentration (Table 18.10). Cuprous copper in heat-coagulated hemocyanin with *p*-chloromercuribenzoate is found to be 36% of the total copper (Table 18.11). As for the hemocyanin–sulfide complex, very little free cuprous copper of heat-coagu-

TABLE 18.9. THE STATE OF COPPER IN HEAT-COAGULATED HEMOCYANIN IN VARIOUS CONDITIONS

	Cuprous copper (μg/mg)	Cupric copper (μg/mg)
No addition	0.49	
Hydroxylamine	0.97	
EDTA	0.00	
Residue after cuprous copper estimation		0.17
Total copper		1.17

TABLE 18.10. THE EFFECT OF *p*-CHLOROMERCURIBENZOATE (PCMB) CONCENTRATION ON CUPROUS ION CONCENTRATION MEASURED BY BIQUINOLINE–GLACIAL ACETIC ACID REAGENT

Concentration of PCMB (moles PCMB/mole of Total Cu)	Cuprous copper (μg/mg)
5	0.44
10	0.41
15	0.42
20	0.42

TABLE 18.11. COPPER IN THE HEMOCYANIN–SULFIDE COMPLEX

	Cuprous copper (μg/mg)	Cupric copper (μg/mg)
Free cuprous copper with hydroxylamine	0.11	
Total copper		1.23

TABLE 18.12. SULFIDE CONTENT IN HEAT-COAGULATED HEMOCYANIN AND THE HEMOCYANIN–SULFIDE COMPLEX

	Sulfide (μg/mg)		Number of determinations
	Average	Range	
Heat-coagulated hemocyanin	3.33	2.90–3.44	4
Hemocyanin–sulfide complex	3.61	3.29–3.90	4

lated hemocyanin is combined, presumably, with sulfide. The content of sulfide in the hemocyanin−sulfide complex is 0.28 μg/mg more than that in heat-coagulated hemocyanin (Table 12.12). The copper combined with sulfide in the hemocyanin−sulfide complex is 1.12 μg/mg of dry matter. The contents of copper and sulfide combined with copper are 17.6×10^{-3} and 8.7×10^{-3} μM/mg, respectively.

REFERENCES

FELSENFELD, G.   1960.   The determination of cuprous ions in Cu proteins. Arch. Biochem. Biophys. *87*, 247−251.

GORDIEVSKAYA, V.S.   1966.   Reasons for crab meat turning blue.   Chem. Abstr. *64*, 1265e.

INOUE, N., and MOTOHIRO, T.   1969.   Starch gel electrophoresis of crab haemocyanins.   Bull. Jpn. Soc. Sci. Fish. *35*, 559−561.

INOUE, N., and MOTOHIRO, T.   1970.   A cause and mechanism of blue discoloration of canned crabmeat. VI.   The mechanism of copper and sulfide reaction in heat coagulated haemocyanin.   Bull. Jpn. Soc. Sci. Fish. *36*, 1044−1047.

LOVENBERG, W., BUCHANAN, B.B., and RABINOWITZ, J.C.   1963.   The chemical nature of clostridial ferredoxin.   J. Biol. Chem. *238*, 3899−3913.

MCCARTHY, K., and LOVENBERG, W.   1968.   Optical properties of artificial nonheme iron proteins derived from bovine serum albumin.   J. Biol. Chem. *243*, 6436−6441.

NEEDHAM, A.E.   1961.   Methemocyanin.   Nature *189*, 308−309.

OSAKABE, I.   1958.   A study on prevention of blue discoloration in the meat of canned crab by low temperature and fractional heating process.   Canners J. *37*, 72−103.

19

Utilization of Shellfish Waste for Chitin and Chitosan Production

E. Lee Johnson and Q.P. Peniston[†]

INTRODUCTION

In the past 10 years research activities on chitin and chitosan, largely promoted and sponsored by the National Sea Grant Program, NOAA, Department of Commerce, have generated great and widespread interest in the possibilities of these materials (Muzzarelli and Pariser 1978). In spite of the voluminous research that has been conducted and the many uses that have been proposed, commercial development of a chitin/chitosan industry has not yet occurred to any appreciable extent, except in Japan. It now appears, however, that the growing demand for these products and the pressing need for a practical solution to the waste disposal problems of the shellfish industry will shortly result in a substantial production activity. For this reason it seems desirable to consider some of the problems associated with chitin/chitosan production that have become apparent through research, process development, and pilot scale manufacturing by the Kypro Company.

The Kypro Company was established in 1972 following preliminary research and process design initiated in 1967 by Food, Chemical and Research Laboratories, Inc. of Seattle, Washington. A pilot plant capable of producing about two tons per month of chitin or chitosan was constructed at Tukwila, near Seattle, in 1973, and has been in operation continuously to date. During this period many process modifications have been studied and many of the problems associated with actual production have been experienced.

The projection of pilot scale operation to full scale, economically viable, commercial production has been one of our prime considerations. Such projection requires consideration of several factors including raw material supply, standards for product quality, process design, plant location, by-

Kypro Company, Seattle, Washington 98004
[†]Deceased

product recovery, economical use of energy and process chemicals, and quality control.

RAW MATERIALS

While the occurrence of chitin is widespread in nature, the only practical source for consideration in the near future is the shell of the commercially harvested crustacea species such as crab, shrimp, lobster, and crayfish. The shell of these animals is not only the richest source of chitin—in general 20–30% on a dry basis—but also the only source presently available in quantities sufficient to support a chitin/chitosan industry. Thus, if a production of one million pounds per year of chitin is to be accepted as a minimum viable size for a production facility (Johnson and Peniston 1978), raw material requirement can be estimated as follows.

Shellfish on a live weight basis, in general, contain about 25% solids, 20–25% edible meat, and 50–60% recoverable waste, the rest being lost as solubles and fines in processing. The waste, also at 25% solids, may contain 25% chitin on a dry basis. The raw material requirement for the minimum plant is thus

$$\frac{1 \times 10^6}{.25 \times .25 \times .55}$$

or 29 million pounds on a live weight basis.

There are several localities in the United States and elsewhere in the world where this annual production of shellfish is met or exceeded. These include Chesapeake Bay, the New Orleans area, the Oregon and Washington coasts, Southeastern Alaska, Kodiak, Alaska, and Dutch Harbor, Alaska. Outside the United States, important shellfisheries occur in India, Malaya, Australia, South America, South Africa, and Iceland. The immediate problem is not the quantity of shellfish waste available but its preservation and transport to a chitin/chitosan producing facility in suitable condition at allowable cost. The present world supply could possibly support a chitin/chitosan production of 50 to 100 million pounds of chitosan per year, but the world's supply of shellfish waste is not unlimited. So at least for the near future, chitosan production should not be based on uses requiring many times the potential production.

Shellfish waste is a highly perishable material. Within hours of initial recovery, bacterial and/or enzymatic degradation processes begin and attach chitin and protein—both adventitious and intimately associated with chitin—in the shell matrix. Effects of degradation on the protein are destruction of its nutritional quality and molecular cleavage, resulting in poor recovery by isoelectric precipitation from extract solutions. Effects on chitin are cleavage and deamination, resulting in chitosan of poor solubility and lowered molecular size.

Consequently, such degradative changes must be minimized in a raw material for chitin/chitosan production. This can be accomplished in several ways. First, the chitosan plant could be located at or near the primary shellfish processing facility, thus permitting rapid recovery of chitin from the waste. Second, the waste material could be dried or frozen for transport to the chitosan plant. And third, the waste could be treated at the point of origin to prevent degradation. We have found that grinding the waste and covering it with a dilute solution of sodium hydroxide is effective in preventing spoilage for up to several days, depending on weather conditions. The alkali is not wasted since the first step in our chitin isolation process is protein extraction. Another way in which preservation can be accomplished for longer periods is to extract the protein at the primary shellfish processing facility. When the protein is reduced to a low percentage of the shell residue, the chitin is much more resistant to bacterial attacks and can be held for several weeks or even months without significant damage. This, of course, would require installation and operation of extraction and protein recovery equipment at or near the shellfish processing plant, which may be undesirable unless large quantities of waste are involved.

Another problem in shell supply is the fluctuation in shellfish production. Many fisheries operate on a seasonal basis depending on species availability and fishing restrictions. This problem may be partially offset by processing different species in different seasons. Thus a chitosan plant might find it desirable to process shrimp, crab, or lobster waste as determined by seasonal availability. In other fisheries, day-to-day fluctuations in production occur due to weather conditions, migration of shellfish populations, and other factors. Therefore, considerable shell storage capacity at a chitosan plant would be desirable. Stored waste could be dried, frozen, or preserved shell, depending on the circumstances of the individual plant and the characteristics of the particular fishery involved. Obviously, the economics of shell supply, transport, and storage should receive thorough analysis as an essential part of the design of a chitin/chitosan production facility.

As far as variation in chitin quality with species is concerned, we believe that good quality chitin or chitosan can be prepared from all commercial crustacea species. Minor variations in molecular weight, solubility, attainable purity, and other characteristics are probably more dependent on processing details than on true chitin variability. There are, however, physical differences among species which require modification of processing procedures. Some crab species have highly calcified and dense claw tips, which are resistant to extraction and demineralization. Shrimp shell is generally more papery in texture than crab shell and poses other problems in filtration and centrifugation. Flexibility in the design of a processing plant is thus desirable to permit economical handling of different species.

PROTEIN EXTRACTION AND RECOVERY

One of the components of shellfish waste that has not received due consideration from a practical standpoint is the protein associated with chitin and calcium carbonate in the shell matrix. This protein can amount to 30–40% of the organic matter in the shell (Richards 1951; Tofon 1948) and, together with the adventitious protein generally associated with shellfish waste, can be equal in yield to the chitin obtained. We have found that the protein recoverable from shrimp and crab waste by mild alkaline extraction and isoelectric precipitation has an amino acid profile similar to casein except for a lack of cystine and methionine. Feeding tests on rats and mink indicate it to be of good nutritional value when supplemented with a small amount of methionine. It is recovered in 85–90% yield as a dry light tan powder containing upwards of 90% protein. This protein has a ready market in the pet food industry and can be used as a high grade additive to livestock starter feeds.

Protein recovery has not been considered by other investigators of chitin manufacturing processes. We believe that, at a price comparable to casein, it would alleviate a large part of the manufacturing burden for chitin and chitosan and contribute significantly to the profitability of a chitin/chitosan enterprise. It also represents a resource already harvested which, under current disposal methods, is either wasted or utilized in such a way that its nutritional value is not taken advantage of. Also, if the protein is not recovered, it poses a disposal problem to the chitin/chitosan plant with a consequent increase in manufacturing cost.

The protein recovery process is quite simple. The extraction of the waste with 1 or 2% sodium hydroxide at 60–70°C is conducted in two or more stages concurrently to build up a sodium proteinate concentration in the extract of 6% or higher. The extract is clarified if necessary to remove extraneous solids, cooled in a heat exchanger, and treated with dilute hydrochloric or sulfuric acid to reduce the pH to the isoelectric point, generally about pH 4.5. The protein precipitates in granular curds, which, with proper controls, can be washed by decantation or centrifugal means. The washed protein slurry can be dewatered to 15–20% solids and dried using either a roll or a spray drier. The product can contain 90% or more protein with ash at 5% or below.

DEMINERALIZATION

Crustacean shell generally contains 30–50% mineral matter on a dry basis depending on species and other factors. It is mostly calcium carbonate but may contain calcium phosphate in amounts up to 8 or 10% of the total inorganic matter. It is generally removed by dissolution with dilute acids. While hydrochloric acid is used most commonly, other acids such as sulfurous acid may be preferable under some circumstances (Peniston and Johnson 1978). Other investigators have usually conducted demineralization before protein extraction. We prefer the reverse order, however, to take advantage of the stabilizing value of alkali on the raw shell, to maximize protein yield and quality, and to avoid protein contamination of demineralization liquors.

The ground, deproteinized shell is slurried in cold water or spent brine, to which acid is added. It is maintained at as low a concentration as is practical to accomplish demineralization in reasonable time. With good agitation, demineralization can usually be done in 2 to 3 hr. We find it advantageous to recycle spent brines to the demineralization process, thus completely utilizing the acid and higher brine concentrations for recovery purposes. When dissolution of the calcium carbonate is complete, the brine is drained and the chitin is washed by reslurrying in water and transferred to centrifugal equipment.

There is evidence in the literature (Austin 1979) and in our own experience that considerable damage can be done to the chitin during demineralization by hydrolytic cleavage catalyzed by too drastic conditions. We believe that much of this damage results from residual absorbed acid during drying of the chitin product. Chitin can contain some free amino groups either by slight deacetylation during processing or incomplete acetylation in formation. Free amino groups will also be associated with residual protein. These can bind acid and associate under drying conditions. There may also be occluded acid in the interstices of the chitin structure, which diffuses only slowly in the washing process. We find it desirable to finish washing with addition of a small amount of alkali to insure a pH of over 7 in the moist chitin. In this way, deterioration during drying can be minimized. When chitin is to be converted directly to chitosan, complete drying of the chitin is not necessary, though partial dewatering is recommended to avoid dilution of the alkali used.

Recovery of by-products from demineralization brines may be economical in areas where ready markets can be found. In the Pacific Northwest limerock is used to neutralize waste hydrochloric acid from manufacture of chlorinated compounds, and the calcium chloride brines are used by the pulp and paper industry. Markets may be found for calcium chloride in the cement industry and for road dust control. Using sulfurous acid for demineralization calcium sulfite is a possible by-product.

DEACETYLATION

Chitin is considerably more resistant to deacetylation by treatment with alkalis than might normally be expected of an N-acetyl substance. This is probably due to the dense nature of the unit cell in the chitin crystalline structure and the extensive hydrogen bonding between nitrogen atoms and carboxyl groups of adjacent chains (Muzzarelli 1979). Consequently, high concentrations of sodium hydroxide (40−50%) and high temperatures (100°−150°C) exclusive of air have generally been used by previous investigators to effect conversion of chitin to chitosan. These drastic conditions require corrosion-resistant vessels for the reaction to combat the effects of severe caustic embrittlement. With today's prices of nickel and highly corrosion-resistant steel alloys, the equipment cost for deacetylation would greatly increase the capital requirements of a chitosan plant. Also, at high temperatures and short reaction times, agitation is necessary to obtain uniformity in reaction. This requires a high degree of fluidity in the reaction mixture, i.e., high rates of sodium hydroxide solution to chitin solids (about 10 to 1). This results in larger vessels and the use of larger quantities of alkali.

We have found that deacetylation can be accomplished at lower temperatures (70°–80°C) using plastic-lined equipment and a quiescent system with much lower liquor-to-solid ratios. While reaction times are much longer, the cost of equipment, power, and alkali is much smaller. Also, the possibilities for recycling the alkali in the deacetylation process are improved at lower temperatures, for there is less contamination of the recovered liquor with degradation products. Most of the alkali liquor can be recovered full-strength by pressing or centrifugation, except for actual conversion to sodium acetate in the deacetylation reaction. By countercurrent washing much of the remaining alkali liquor can be recovered at intermediate concentrations for recycling after fortification or evaporation, and dilute washings can be used in the protein extraction process. It is thus possible to reduce the alkali used for deacetylation nearly to the stoichiometric quantity which is 0.2 pounds of sodium hydroxide per pound of chitin. Recovery of sodium acetate is also possible from the deacetylation liquors. The stoichiometric amount of sodium acetate trihydrate is 0.67 pounds per pound of chitin.

In any deacetylation process, oxidative degradation must be avoided if high-molecular-weight chitosan is desired. This can be accomplished by nitrogen blanketing or in a quiescent system by deaeration of the reaction mixture with vacuum and covering with a layer of alkali during the reaction.

QUALITY CONTROL

If high quality products are to be constantly prepared and chemical costs are to be minimized, the entire manufacturing process from raw shell to finished materials must be routinely monitored by quality control procedures. Raw shell must be inspected for evidence of putrefaction and for absence of extraneous materials such as rubber gloves, plastic, foil, wood, and paper. The prime products chitin and chitosan remain in the solid state throughout the process. And while some extraneous materials such as sand can be removed by density differences, others are not easily separated.

In the protein extraction process, free caustic alkali concentrations must be held to minimum effective levels in order to avoid protein damage. Residual protein in the extracted shell can be estimated on site by washing the sample, extracting with 5% alkali at boiling temperature, and applying the buiret reaction using a colorimeter. Protein concentration in the sodium proteinate liquor can also be determined with the buiret reaction. Protein concentration in the supernatant from protein precipitation can be estimated in the same way. Finished protein should be monitored by laboratory analysis for moisture, nitrogen, ash, and fat contents.

In the demineralization step, acid levels and temperatures should be held to minimum levels to avoid chitin damage. pH control and on-site titrations can be used. Residual calcium in chitin can be estimated by boiling a washed sample with stronger acid, adding oxalate to the neutralized supernatant, and turbidimetric measurement. Neutrality of washed chitin should be assured before drying. Finished chitin should be checked by laboratory analysis for moisture, ash, nitrogen, and residual protein contents.

Chitosan should be checked on-site for solubility at the end of the deacetylation treatment. Finished chitosan should be analyzed in the laboratory for solubility, moisture, pH, ash, total nitrogen, free amino nitrogen, and viscosity.

EFFLUENT CONSIDERATIONS

It should be possible to operate a chitosan manufacturing facility with very little of the organic material originally present in the raw material from being discharged into process effluents. Protein recovery of 85–90% can be attained with careful extraction procedures. Chitin losses as fines in screening operations can be minimized by centrifugal collection from wash liquors. Fats can be separated from sodium proteinate extracts by partial neutralization and centrifugal separation before protein precipitation.

Discharge of inorganic materials can be cut down by product recovery. The practicality of this will depend on economic factors at individual plant locations and requirements of local pollution control authorities. Effluent discharges should be collected and neutralized before they are discharged into sewers or receiving waters. Fortunately, the process balance between acidic and alkaline effluents should make little adjustment necessary.

ENERGY AND CAPITAL CONSIDERATIONS

The chitin/chitosan manufacturing process is not energy-intensive. Principal heat requirements are in the protein extraction process in which shell slurries at 8–10% solids must be heated to 60°–70°C and in drying of chitin or chitosan and protein. The former can be minimized by the use of heat exchangers between sodium proteinate extract and fresh extraction liquor and the latter by efficient dewatering of chitin or chitosan to 35–40% solids before drying.

Power requirements are moderate. They include power for materials, transfer equipment, grinding, screening, centrifugal operations, and agitation in the steps of protein extraction, protein precipitation, and demineralization.

Capital requirements also are nonintensive for a chemical separation process. Most of the processing steps can be conducted in plastic-lined steel milk vessels. The only high cost equipment items are centrifuges, presses, and driers.

CONCLUSION

The production of industrial quality chitin and chitosan from crustacean shell can be economically accomplished if strict attention is paid to obtaining unputrefied raw materials and subjecting them to mild chemical treatment under controlled conditions utilizing standard unit operations and quality control.

REFERENCES

AUSTIN, P.R.   1979.   Personal communication, University of Delaware.

JOHNSON, E.L., and PENISTON, Q.P.   1978.   The production of chitin and chitosan.   Proc. First International Conference on Chitin/Chitosan, pp. 80–87. MIT Sea Grant 78-7, Cambridge, MA.

MUZZARELLI, R.A.A.   1979.   Chitin, pp. 45–58.   Pergamon Press, New York.

MUZZARELLI, R.A.A., and PARISER, E.R. (Editors).   1978.   Proc. First International Conference on Chitin/Chitosan.   MIT Sea Grant 78-7. Cambridge, MA.

PENISTON, Q.P. and JOHNSON, E.L.   U.S. Patent No. 4066735.   Dated Jan. 3, 1978.

RICHARDS, A.G.   1951.   The Integument of Arthropods, pp. 110–111. University of Minnesota Press, Minneapolis, MN.

TOFON, MAX.   1948.   Nouvelles recherches biochinique et physiologiques sur le squellette legumentaire des crustaces.   Bull. Inst. Oceanogr. *45.*

20

Blueing Discoloration of Dungeness Crabmeat

Jerry K. Babbitt

Despite almost a century of study, general agreement has not been reached on the causes of or cures for discoloration of processed crabmeat (Boon 1975). A common problem with processed crabmeat is a discoloration usually called blueing, although the actual color may range from light blue to blue-gray to black.

Generally, the blueing of thermal-processed crabmeat is localized on the surface of the meat and in the coagulated blood that is released from the meat. The blueing has been observed in king crab (Groninger and Dassow 1964), blue crab (Waters 1971), queen crab (Dewberry 1970), and dungeness crab (Elliot and Harvey 1951). Several plausible explanations have linked the blueing to the formation of copper–protein and biuret complexes (Groninger and Dassow 1964), copper sulfide (Inoue and Motohiro 1970A, B), and iron sulfide and iron complexes (Waters 1971). Several studies have demonstrated a relationship between the presence of blood and the occurrence of blueing in processed crabmeat see Chapter 18, this volume. These studies have led several investigators to suggest procedures for the reduction of residual blood prior to or during processing (Elliot and Harvey 1951; Farber 1953; Osakabe 1957). The crab industry has, for a number of years, advocated and practiced handling and processing of only live, vigorous crabs. This practice has stemmed from practical experience and is supported by the studies of Elliott and Harvey (1951), Farber (1953), and Dewberry (1970). Waters (1971) found that the condition of the crab did not lead to blueing but that the condition may be contributing when other factors are present.

Commercially, chemicals have been used to minimize the blue discoloration and the method used generally employs rinsing or packing the picked crabmeat in approximately a 1% solution of an acid such as citric, acetic, lactic, or tartaric acid. Farber (1953) stated that these acid treatments

Northwest and Alaska Fisheries Center, National Marine Fisheries Service, National Oceanic and Atmospheric Administration, Seattle, Washington 98112 worked fairly well and that a product reasonably free from marked blueing can be prepared. However, acid treatment causes denaturation of the meat proteins. The crabmeat usually found in commercial packs often is rubbery and stringy with little resemblance to the texture or flavor of fresh cooked crabmeat. Farber (1953), using sodium citrate and citric acid neutralized with disodium phosphate, and Waters (1971), using a patented phosphate buffered citric acid solution, have reported reducing the incidence of blueing in canned crabmeat while maintaining the quality of meat. These studies indicate that a system more complex than sulfide formation is involved in the blueing discoloration since the formation of iron and copper sulfides is independent of pH.

From observations of the blueing occurring in whole cooked dungeness crab, it was felt that perhaps the blueing in thermal-processed crabmeat may be similar to the formation of "black spot" in shrimp *(Penaeus setiferus)*. Baily *et al.* (1960) have related the formation of black spot to the formation of melanins by phenolases. Pinhey (1930) has related the blackening of blood in clots of wounds in spider crab *(Maia squinado)* to the oxidation of tyrosine to melanin by tyrosinase. The phenolase system (Summers 1967) involved in the hardening and darkening (sclerotization) of the cuticle of fiddler crab *(Uca pugnax)* appears to be very similar to systems present in insects (Malek 1961) and amphibians (Miller *et al.* 1970). The blueing of thermal-processed crabmeat has not been considered an enzymatic reaction since the temperatures used during retorting would destroy the enzymes. However, tyrosinases and phenol oxidases present in live crabs may initiate the oxidation of phenols to melanins (Pinhey 1930; Summers 1967). The subsequent oxidation and polymerization of these intermediate phenolic derivatives in canned crabmeat may proceed non-enzymatically to form colored chromophores, particularly in the presence of metals (Mathew and Parpia 1971).

Thus, the following scheme for blueing in dungeness crabmeat has been developed.

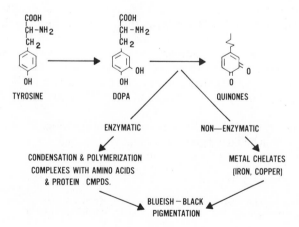

The key to this scheme is the presence of phenolases capable of oxidizing tyrosine to blueish-black melanins. A monophenolase (tyrosinase) was found in dungeness crab, particularly in the crab blood (Babbitt et al. 1973A). After 1 hr at 37°C, the formation of melanins from tyrosine was visually detected by the development of a blue-black color in the reaction mixture and a decrease in total phenols. Heating the enzyme at 100°C for 20 min completely destroyed its activity. However, there was only a slight loss in enzymatic activity after 2 min at 85°C.

The phenolases in crab are inhibited by antioxidants (ascorbic acid) and metal chelating-substances (phenylthiourea). Apparently, phenylthiourea blocks tyrosinase activity completely by chelating copper that is required as its prosthetic group (Mathew and Parpia 1971). The increase in dopa by tyrosinase in the presence of ascorbic acid suggests that the oxidation of tyrosine to melanin is blocked by the smaller oxidation–reduction potential of ascorbic acid, which keeps dopa in the reduced state (Mason 1957).

The presence of phenolic compounds in crab tissue and blood was confirmed using thin-layer silica gel chromatography (Babbit et al. 1973A). Of the more than nine chromatographic spots, tyrosine, dopa (3,4-dihydroxyphenylalanine), and 3-hydroxytyramine were tentatively identified when compared to known standards. Also, it was found that the phenolic content (Babbitt et al. 1973B, 1975) of live crab held at 1°–3°C for 4 days increased very rapidly (Table 20.1).

When crabs in "excellent" condition, freshly caught, and those in "poor" condition, held 4 days, were processed in a manner simulating the production of whole cooked crabs (Babbitt et al. 1973A), both the length of holding and cooking times were apparent factors in the formation of blue discoloration (Table 20.2).

TABLE 20.1.   CHANGES IN PHENOLIC CONTENT AND pH OF LIVE CRAB HELD AT 1°–3°C

Days held at 1°–3°C	Phenolic content[1] (μg/g)	pH[1]
0	140.8 ± 15.1	6.65 ± 0.30
1	169.5 ± 37.5	7.05 ± 0.07
2	188.3 ± 37.7	7.10 ± 0.28
3	194.9 ± 54.2	7.19 ± 0.01
4	322.5 ± 80.6	7.65 ± 0.21

[1] Mean ± standard deviation from five crabs.

Cooking the whole crab at 100°C for 30 min was adequate for inactivating the polyphenolases and preventing blueing, while cooking for 15 min was not. However, cooking the crab in "poor" condition for even 30 min at 100°C could not prevent the blue discoloration.

Experiments designed to determine the stability of some of the phenolic intermediates demonstrated that they were very unstable. Using dopa, pyrocatechol, and 3-hydroxytyramine, it was found that they easily polymerized to form colored chromophores particularly under alkaline conditions and in the presence of metals (copper and iron).

TABLE 20.2. EXTENT OF BLUE DISCOLORATION IN WHOLE COOKED CRAB HELD FOR 72 HR AT 1°–3°C AFTER COOKING BEFORE EXAMINATION[1]

Cooking time (min)	Holding time of live crab before cooking	
	16 hr	96 hr
15	Moderate	Extensive
30	None–slight	Moderate

[1] Extent of blueing: Extensive: dark blue-black discoloration of gills, body cavity and meat; Moderate: blue to blue-black discoloration of gills, some discoloration in body cavity and meat; None: no discoloration.

The question that still remained was whether or not this scheme could be used to explain why thermal-processed canned crabmeat turns blue. To solve this question, crabmeat was extensively extracted with acetone and dialyzed against distilled water to remove all traces of phenolic compounds and metals (Babbitt et al. 1973B). The extracted and dialyzed crabmeat was then used in a model system to study the blueing phenomenon.

It is well documented that copper (Elliot and Harvey 1951; Groninger and Dassow 1964) and iron (Waters 1971) are involved in the blueing of canned crabmeat. When copper or iron was added to untreated crabmeat, pronounced blueing occurred. However, the addition of iron or copper to the treated (extracted and dialyzed) crabmeat did not produce blueing.

The addition of phenolic compounds (dopa, 3-hydroxytyramine, dopamine) to the treated crabmeat produced blueing. Under alkaline conditions, the blueing was much darker and intense. Furthermore, the addition of the phenolic compounds and copper or iron to the treated crabmeat resulted in blueing after canning even under acidic conditions.

As illustrated in Table 20.1, the pH and phenolic compounds increased during chilled storage of live crabs. Table 20.3 summarizes the effect of storage on the phenolic content and pH of crabmeat after thermal processing (Babbitt et al. 1973B). The low levels of phenolic compounds detected in the canned crabmeat indicate that most of the phenols had undergone polymerization to blueish-black chromophores during retorting.

Thus, the changes in phenolic compounds in crabs appear to have a significant role in causing the blueing observed in processed crabs and crabmeat. Once the oxidation of phenols is enzymatically initiated, further oxidation and polymerization of phenols may proceed nonenzymatically, particularly under alkaline conditions and in the presence of metals.

TABLE 20.3. PHENOLIC CONTENT, pH, AND EXTENT OF BLUEING OF RETORTED CRAB MEAT

Days held prior to processing	Phenolic content (μg/g)	pH	Visual evaluation of blueing
0	157.5	7.3	None–slight
2	163.0	7.5	Slight–moderate
4	161.0	7.8	Moderate–extensive

How then can the blueing discoloration be prevented? Industry, by trial and error, has developed several practices to reduce the incidence of blueing. Only crabs that are alive and in good condition are processed. Crabs that have been held in a cooler (1°–3°C) even for up to 4 days are edible if properly cooked. However, the chances of blueing occurring in the cooked crab are greatly increased, particularly if the cooking times and temperatures are not adequate to inactivate the phenolases. Certainly, care must be taken to properly cook the crab, since underprocessing will result in blueing.

Molting is a factor in the blueing reaction, since the phenolic compounds are involved in the formation of the new shell (sclerotization) of the crab. So, during times of molting, extra care must be used in handling and processing crab to prevent blueing.

If the crabmeat is to be thermal-processed, the cooking time and temperatures of the raw crab are not as critical. However, as soon as the crab is cooked, the meat from the shell must be removed and thermal-processed. Regardless of how long the live crab are cooked, any delay in thermal-processing the crabmeat will result in a higher incidence of blueing. Using frozen crab sections to produce canned crabmeat will also increase the risk of blueing. Whole crab or crab sections should be thoroughly cooked before freezing to reduce the risk of blueing. Finally, avoid any contact of copper or iron with the crab since these metals can greatly intensify the blueing discoloration.

REFERENCES

BABBITT, J.K., LAW, D.K., and CRAWFORD, D.L.   1973A.   Phenolases and blue discoloration in whole cooked dungeness crab *(Cancer magister)*.   J. Food Sci. *38*, 1089–1090.

BABBITT, J.K., LAW, D.K., and CRAWFORD, D.L.   1973B.   Blueing discoloration in canned crab meat *(Cancer magister)*.   J. Food Sci. *38*, 1101–1103.

BABBITT, J.K., LAW, D.K., and CRAWFORD, D.L.   1975.   Effect of precooking on copper content, phenolic content and blueing of canned dungeness crab meat.   J. Food Sci. *40*, 649–650.

BAILEY, M.E., FIEGER, E.A., and NOVAK, A.F.   1960.   Physico-chemical properties of the enzymes involved in shrimp melanogenesis.   Food Res. *25*, 557–564.

BOON, D.D.   1975.   Discoloration in processed crabmeat. A Review.   J. Food Sci. *40*, 756–761.

DEWBERRY, E.B.   1970.   Speed is the essence.   Food Proc. Ind. *39*, 50–53.

ELLIOTT, H.H., and HARVEY, E.W.   1951.   Biological methods of blood removal and their effectiveness in reducing discoloration in canned dungeness crab meat.   Food Technol. *5*, 163–166.

FARBER, L.   1953.   Observations on the canning of Pacific coast or dungeness crab meat.   Food Technol. *7*, 465–468.

GRONINGER, H.S., and DASSOW, J.A. 1964. Observations of the "blue-ing" of king crab, *Paralithodes camtschatica*. Fish. Ind. Res. *2*, 47–52.

INOUE, N., and MOTOHIRO, T. 1970A. A cause and mechanism of blue discoloration of canned crab meat–I. Chemical analysis and histological observation of blue meat. Bull. Jpn. Soc. Sci. Fish. *36*, 588–591.

INOUE, N., and MOTOHIRO, T. 1970B. A cause and mechanism of blue discoloration of canned crab meat—VI. The mechanism of copper and sulphide reaction in heat-coagulated haemocyanin. Bull. Jpn. Soc. Sci. Fish. *36*, 1044–1047.

MALEK, S.R.A. 1961. Polyphenols and their quinone derivatives in the cuticle of the desert locust, *Ichistocerca gregaria* (forskal). Comp. Biochem. Physiol. *2*, 35–50.

MASON, H.S. 1957. Mechanism of oxygen metabolism. Adv. Enzymol. *19*, 79–233.

MATHEW, A.G., and PARPIA, H.A.B. 1971. Food browning as a polyphenol reaction. Adv. Food Res. *19*, 75–145.

MILLER, L.O., NEWCOMBE, R., and TRIPLETT, E.L. 1970. Isolation and partial characterization of amphibian tyrosine oxidase. Comp. Biochem. Physiol. *32*, 555–567.

OSAKABE, I. 1957. Low cook produces high quality in Kegani crab. Pac. Fisherman *55*, 48.

PINHEY, K.O. 1930. Tyrosinase in crustacean blood. J. Exp. Bio. *7*, 19–36.

SUMMERS, N.M. 1967. Cuticle sclerotization and blood phenol oxidase in the fiddler crab, *Uca pugnax*. Comp. Biochem. Physiol. *23*, 129–138.

WATERS, M.E. 1971. Blueing of processed crab meat. II. Identification of some factors involved in the blue discoloration of canned crab meat *(Callinectes sapidus)*. Spec. Sci. Rep. Fisheries No. 633. U.S. Dept. Comm. NOAA-NMFS. Washington, DC.

21

Vitamins and Minerals in Seafoods of the Pacific Northwest

Dennis T. Gordon[1] and Roy E. Martin[2]

A substantial amount of work was accomplished during the period 1930 to the mid-1960s on the nutrient composition of marine products. The earliest studies, some prior to 1930, dealt with minerals. Determination of the vitamins in seafoods kept pace with their discovery. Many of the large surveys were of rather small numbers of samples analyzed that had been obtained throughout the world. An alternative approach was to measure the level of a limited number of vitamins or minerals from a more defined geographical region. Some of the more comprehensive reviews have been done by very active researchers in the fisheries area (Braekan 1962A,B; Love 1970; Higashi 1961; Stansby 1962).

The 1970s witnessed a resurgence of interest in nutrition and a call for additional information on the nutrient content of all foods (U.S. Senate Select Committee on Nutrition and Human Needs 1977). To accommodate this need in seafoods, a project was undertaken by Sea Grant[3] to evaluate the nutritional profile of marine products common to the Pacific Northwest. Initial objectives were to bring together available information and to determine analytically quantities of nutrients in products for which there was a paucity of data. A long range goal, which will not be presented here, was to simplify this information for use by the lay public (Gordon 1980).

As with any undertaking of this nature, certain limitations were imposed. It was impossible to analyze every species or to take fully into consideration variables such as size, age, and sex. However, some of these variables may not be as important as previously believed and this will be discussed later. To help simplify the discussion of available data, the mean content of each nutrient will be presented for all white fish as one common

[1] Seafoods Laboratory, Oregon State University, Astoria, Oregon 97103
[2] National Fisheries Institute, Inc., Washington, D.C. 20036
[3] Oregon State University Sea Grant College Program, National Oceanic and Atmospheric Administration, U.S. Department of Commerce, with support from the National Fisheries Institute, Inc.

entity. Since many white fish species of various size, age, and sex were examined, this consolidation of information will help overcome the lack of sampling variability. The primary purpose of this work is to provide seafood nutrient compositional information. Further use of this knowledge in the 1980s and beyond is intended to be helpful to those interested in gaining a further understanding of marine life.

There exists a voluminous amount of information on the nutrient content of whole fish, offal, and selected organs (Jacquot 1961; Causeret 1962; Cruickshank 1962). Comparison of these values with those obtained on edible portions of fish from different geographical regions are avoided for the most part. Emphasis has been placed on reviewing the available literature pertinent to the Pacific Northwest.

Most of the common seafoods have been analyzed in the Seafoods Laboratory, Oregon State University, Astoria, Oregon (Table 21.1). Based on their volume and economic value, these marine foods represent a major portion of the Pacific Northwest's annual harvest (Fishery Statistics of the United States 1973). Some major exclusions are acknowledged, e.g., Alaska pollock, king crab, chum, coho, and pink salmon, Pacific herring, and Pacific halibut. Samples reported herein were drawn from the Pacific Northwest and all represent products that are commonly consumed. Except for some canned items, cooked shrimp, and cooked crab, all products were raw.

TABLE 21.1. COMMON SEAFOODS OF THE PACIFIC NORTHWEST FOR WHICH VITAMIN AND MINERAL LEVELS HAVE BEEN OBTAINED[1]

	Species
Low-fat fish; <5%	
Butter sole	*Isopsetta isolepis*
Dover sole	*Microstomus pacificus*
English sole	*Parophrys vetalus*
Ling cod	*Ophiodon elongatus*
Pacific cod (True cod)	*Gadus macrocephalus*
Pacific hake	*Merluccius productus*
Petrale sole	*Eopsetta jordani*
Rex sole	*Glyptocephalus zachirus*
Rockfish, black	*Sebastodes melanops*
Rockfish, orange	*Sebastodes pinniger*
Rockfish, yellowtail	*Sebastodes flavidus*
Starry flounder	*Platichthys stellatus*
High-fat fish; >5%	
Black cod (Sablefish)	*Noplopoma fimbria*
Albacore tuna	*Thunnus alalunga*
American shad	*Alosa sapidissima*
Chinook salmon	*Oncorhynchus tshawytscha*
Sockeye salmon	*Oncorhynchus nerka*
Mollusks	
Oysters	*Crassostrea gigas*
Geoduck	*Panope generosa*
Crustacea	
Pacific shrimp	*Pandalus jordani*
Dungeness crab	*Cancer magister*

[1]Seafoods Laboratory, Oregon State University, Astoria, Oregon 97103.

One cause of variability that must be considered in attempting to obtain accurate nutrient levels is analytical methodology. Emission spectroscopy had previously been used to measure phosphorus (Gordon and Roberts 1977). An alternative approach was to use a colorimetric assay and measure the concentration of this element in the same freeze-dried composites originally analyzed. The result was a significantly higher (12.7%; $P <$ 0.001) cumulative phosphorus value by the colorimetric method (Table 21.2). A lack of multiple observations by emission spectroscopy prevented statistical comparison of individual samples. The method giving the most accurate result cannot be currently assigned, but results obtained employing the Fiske−Subbarow (1925) method are presented. Phosphorus averaged 188 ± 22 mg/100 g in white fish with a high of 390 mg/100 g in canned salmon (Table 21.2).

A certified standard (i.e., food) for phosphorus would have helped resolve which method is best. If available, a certified standard for all nutrient

TABLE 21.2. PHOSPHORUS IN SEAFOODS AS DETERMINED BY TWO ANALYTICAL METHODS[1]

	Emission spectroscopy[1]		Colorimetric[2]	
	Dry weight[3,4] (%)	Wet weight[3] (mg/100 g)	Dry weight[3,5,6] (%)	Wet weight (mg/100 g)
Dover sole	0.88	137	0.96	154
English sole	0.90	163	0.97	176
Ling cod	1.00	201	1.11	223
Pacific cod	0.96	174	0.97	176
Pacific hake	0.97	162	1.05	175
Petrale sole	0.88	182	0.97	200
Rockfish, black	0.87	187	0.94	204
Rockfish, orange	0.87	178	0.93	200
Albacore tuna, canned	0.75	221	0.98	292
American shad	0.80	272	0.86	202
Sockeye salmon, fresh	0.67	175	0.88	230
Sockeye salmon, canned	0.88	293	1.17	390
Oysters I	1.04	194	1.06	197
Oysters II	0.86	130	1.14	173
Pacific shrimp, fresh	0.64	137	0.77	166
Pacific shrimp, canned	0.52	129	0.58	143
Dungeness crab, body	0.56	112	0.61	130
Dungeness crab, leg	0.60	127	0.70	139
Round steak	0.75	184	1.00	246
Bovine liver, SRM[7]	1.08	—	1.01	—
Wheat bran, AACC[8]	1.03	—	0.90	—

[1] Christensen et al. (1968) and Gordon and Roberts (1977).
[2] Fiske and Subbarow (1925).
[3] Freeze-dried material analyzed and converted to wet weight based on moisture content of original samples.
[4] Single observation of one freeze-dried composite sample.
[5] Mean value of four composite samples.
[6] Gordon, D.T., unpublished data.
[7] U.S. National Bureau of Standards (NBS) Standard Reference Material 1577, Bovine liver, no P value reported.
[8] American Association of Cereal Chemists. Certified Food Grade Wheat Bran; noncertified phosphorus value of 1.04%.

analyses would greatly facilitate standardizing results between laboratories. A certified reference material exists for some elements, e.g., iron (Standard Reference Material, Bovine Liver 1577, National Bureau of Standards). Use of this material indicated that iron levels in seafoods determined by atomic absorption spectrophotometry (AAS) were most accurate. Iron values obtained by a colorimetric procedure using ferrozine (Gordon 1978) were lower by 7.7% ($P < 0.005$) compared with values obtained by AAS.

There is the possibility that phosphorus levels could increase in seafood products. Phosphates are occasionally used in the processing of fish and are being evaluated with shrimp on the Pacific Coast (Crawford 1980). Phosphate dips have been reported to increase the phosphorus content of fish muscle by 50–100 mg/100 g (Gibson and Murray 1973).

The mean levels of five macro- and four microminerals in marine products are indicated in Table 21.3. The potassium/sodium ratio in white fish was 6.8 based on mean potassium and sodium concentrations of 351 ± 45 and 52 ± 15 mg/100 g, respectively. This ratio appeared to be typical of all seafoods except oysters and those products processed with salt. The potassium levels in Table 21.3 are similar to those previously reported by Thurston (1958, 1961) and Nelson and Thurston (1964). However, the sodium content of fish was lower than that reported. The sodium content of marine products can be expected to increase if refrigerated sea water systems were used at sea. These systems, while constantly being evaluated, have not gained acceptance on the Pacific Coast. Calcium levels in white fish muscle reported in Table 21.3 are low, averaging 9 ± 3 mg/100 g with 2 to 4 times this amount in crustacea. A plausible explanation is that more calcium is needed in crustacea for muscle function and/or shell growth (i.e., chitin). A surprising uniformity was found in the magnesium level among all marine products. This element averaged 25 ± 4 mg/100 g with a range of 16.9 – 3.6 mg/100 g. Sulfur is another mineral having a fairly uniform level in all products with a mean of 225 ± 43 mg/100 g. The amino acids cystine, cysteine, and methionine are the chief sources of this mineral. Iron is low in white fish, averaging 0.31 ± 0.08 mg/100 g. Similar concentrations were found in crustacea. It has been reported that most of the iron in fish is held in complexes of ferritin and hemosiderin (Martinez-Torres et al. 1975). However, this observation is believed to be due to a larger amount of dark lateral muscle rich in these iron chelates that have been extracted by these investigators. Myoglobin is considered the primary form of iron complex in white fish muscle. The zinc content of white fish averaged 0.28 ± 0.04 mg/100 g with 4 and 14 times this amount in Pacific shrimp and dungeness crab, respectively. Copper and manganese averaged 29 ± 7 and 19 ± 8 μg/100 g in white fish. Crustacea had high copper levels, and much of this is believed to be associated with the highly active polyphenoloxidase system. This enzyme is responsible for the undesirable blue discoloration observed in improperly cooked crustacea (Babbitt et al. 1973). The significance of high zinc levels in crustacea, especially crab, is unknown.

TABLE 21.3. MINERAL LEVELS IN SEAFOODS OF THE PACIFIC NORTHWEST[1,2]

	K	Ca	Mg	Na	S	Fe	Zn	Cu	Mn
Dover sole	299	7.0	19.7	75.0	151	0.23	0.21	22.8	11.5
English sole	305	9.4	21.5	49.8	212	0.30	0.34	24.1	25.5
Ling cod	434	13.9	26.3	42.0	215	0.32	0.30	32.6	19.5
Pacific cod	370	7.3	24.3	64.6	213	0.25	0.29	20.2	12.2
Pacific hake	328	8.7	23.7	66.3	152	0.41	0.26	27.1	14.4
Petrale sole	333	10.8	29.3	46.4	211	0.19	0.31	28.8	16.8
Rockfish, black	384	5.0	31.3	32.0	205	0.33	0.23	32.4	34.6
Rockfish, orange	352	9.2	26.3	36.5	241	0.43	0.27	44.7	15.9
Albacore tuna, canned[3]	267	2.1	28.8	370.4	303	0.49	0.40	27.3	15.4
American shad	437	47.2	30.1	48.9	243	0.96	0.27	78.7	42.1
Sockeye salmon, fresh	299	5.5	24.1	42.7	181	0.62	0.26	47.0	13.9
Sockeye salmon, canned[3]	279	251.5	28.7	479.6	287	0.98	0.76	115.6	33.7
Oysters I	192	8.2	23.8	143.4	298	8.20	14.97	1220.2	784.5
Oysters II	144	8.4	20.8	68.9	223	5.45	11.89	869.4	501.1
Pacific shrimp, fresh[3]	114	39.2	33.6	479.4	203	0.32	0.93	193.2	33.8
Pacific shrimp, canned[3]	81	31.4	22.5	567.9	237	0.37	1.17	179.8	30.4
Dungeness crab, body[3]	109	17.9	16.9	879.2	225	0.35	4.00	366.6	17.9
Dungeness crab, leg[2]	154	25.1	20.9	805.2	253	0.35	4.23	977.1	17.1

[1] Gordon and Roberts (1977).
[2] Mean levels reported in mg/100 g except for Cu and Mn which are given in μg/100 g.
[3] Salt added during processing.

Mineral levels were determined in two composite oyster samples (i.e., I and II, Table 21.3) obtained at different time periods. With mollusks, seasonal and geographical differences among samples, even within the Northwest, appear to have a great influence on the amount of minerals present. It is fair to assume that oysters are one of the food sources very rich in microminerals (e.g., Fe, Cu, Zn, Mn). Another general statement offered is that, among all seafoods, mollusks may be the richest in a broad spectrum of both vitamins and minerals.

The aluminum, boron, and strontium present in various seafoods previously analyzed (Gordon and Roberts 1977) are reported in Table 21.4. Aluminum and boron are highest and strontium intermediate in oysters compared with other products. Canned salmon containing bone and crustacea are high in strontium compared with white fish muscle. The mercury, lead, and cadmium levels in fish of the Oregon coast are indicated in Table 21.5. Hall et al. (1976A,B) extensively examined the mercury content of Pacific halibut and sablefish (black cod) and found a majority with less than 0.5 μg/g. The range of halogens in seafoods, not necessarily from the Pacific Northwest, has been reviewed by Causeret (1962). The range in concentration of halogens found in marine products include chlorine, 60–250 mg/100 g; iodine, 0.01–0.2 mg/100 g; and fluorine, 0.5–1 mg/100 g. Although not being specific as to the samples they analyzed, Vought and London (1964) stated that seven seafoods were found to contain 0.066 ± 0.018 mg iodine/ 100 g. Kidd et al. (1974) reported that cod, shrimp, and canned tuna con-

TABLE 21.4. ALUMINUM, BORON AND, STRONTIUM IN SEAFOODS OF THE PACIFIC NORTHWEST[1] BY EMISSION SPECTROSCOPY[2]

	Al	B	Sr
		$(\mu g/g)^3$	
Dover sole	*[4]	2.84	2.15
English sole	*	2.64	2.18
Ling cod	*	2.97	1.65
Pacific cod	*	2.32	1.06
Pacific hake	*	2.27	1.45
Petrale sole	*	2.64	**
Rockfish, black	*	2.45	**
Rockfish, orange	*	3.23	**
Albacore tuna, canned	*	1.75	**
American, shad	*	2.70	1.57
Sockeye salmon, fresh	*	2.34	**
Sockeye salmon, canned	17.3	3.21	28.0
Oysters, sample I	93.2	8.62	5.08
Oysters, sample II	97.9	12.80	5.0
Pacific shrimp, fresh	*	1.60	32.0
Pacific shrimp, canned	*	**	31.4
Dungeness crab, body	*	3.21	18.1
Dungeness crab, leg	*	4.38	35.6

[1] See Gordon and Roberts (1977) for description of samples; Gordon D.T., unpublished data.
[2] Christensen et al. (1968).
[3] Dry weight; single observation of one freeze-dried composite.
[4] Lower than limit of detection: * < 10 ppm; ** < 1 ppm.

TABLE 21.5.   MERCURY, LEAD, AND CADMIUM CONTENT OF FISH HARVESTED OFF THE OREGON COAST

	Hg[1]	Pb[2]	Cd[2]
		μg/g (wet weight)	
Dover sole	0.122 ± 0.076[3]	0.075 − 0.105[4]	0.011 − 0.014[4]
English sole	0.108 ± 0.032	0.033 − 0.130	0.007 − 0.013
Ling cod	0.351 ± 0.240	0.036 − 0.070	0.009 − 0.224
Pacific hake	0.102 ± 0.035	0.044 ± 0.009	0.014 ± 0.002
Petrale sole	0.114 ± 0.045	0.044 − 0.091	0.008 − 0.012
Rex sole	0.199 ± 0.050	0.114 − 0.229	0.012 − 0.0260
Rockfish, Canary[5]	0.197 ± 0.123	—	—
Rockfish, flag[6]	0.136 ± 0.091	—	—
Rockfish, orange	0.136 ± 0.091	0.069 − 0.092	0.014 − 0.088
Rockfish, rougheye[7]	0.080 ± 0.012	—	—
Rockfish, yellowtail	0.371 ± 0.095	—	—
Sand sole	0.083 ± 0.036	0.047 ± 0.014	0.014 ± 0.003
Starry flounder	0.235 ± 0.102	0.048 ± 0.004	0.008 ± 0.002
Arrowtooth flounder[8]	0.154 ± 0.089	—	—
Black cod	0.138 ± 0.148	—	—
Spiny dogfish[9]	0.602 ± 0.275	—	—

[1] Childs and Gaffke (1973).
[2] Childs and Gaffke (1974).
[3] Mean ± SE.
[4] Range of mean values between Southern and Northern Oregon Coast.
[5] Sebastodes pinniger.
[6] Sebastodes rubrivinctus.
[7] Sebastodes aleutianus.
[8] Atheresthes stomias.
[9] Squalus acanthias.

tained 0.1 mg, 0.04 mg, and 0.02 mg/100 g of iodine, respectively. No additional information was given on the species examined. Without fluoridation of water and iodization of common table salt, these nutrients, along with certain other constituents in the human diet, are greatly influenced by the proportion of seafoods consumed. The extent to which seafoods contribute to man's dietary needs may not be fully understood or appreciated. It has also been reported by Causeret (1962) that fish contain less than 0.5 mg arsenic per 100 g. Another report states haddock has 0.22 mg, oysters 0.28 mg, and shrimp 0.15 mg arsenic per 100 g (Schroeder and Balassa 1966). There does not appear to be any danger due to the ingested arsenic from seafoods. This element is believed to be organically bound, and although readily absorbed, it is excreted in quantity (Chapman1926; Coulson et al. 1935). The physical and/or chemical forms of most nutrients in marine products are not adequately known. By far, the most extensive determination of minerals in seafoods was accomplished by the Russian scientist Vinogradov (1953). Nilson and Coulson (1939) were the last to report on the minerals in Pacific fishery products. A comprehensive review on six minerals in crustacea, finfish, and mollusks was prepared by Sidwell et al. (1977).

The thiamin, riboflavin and niacin content of Northwest marine products are reported in Table 21.6. Thiamin averaged 0.04 ± 0.01 mg/100 g in white fish with approximately equal amounts in Pacific shrimp and dungeness crab. Oysters have about twice the level of thiamin found in fish. Geoducks are believed to contain thaiminase because of the low level of thiamin

TABLE 21.6.   THIAMIN, RIBOFLAVIN, AND NIACIN LEVELS IN SEAFOODS OF THE PACIFIC NORTHWEST[1]

	Thiamin	Riboflavin (mg/100 g)[2]	Niacin
Butter sole	0.038 ± 0.012[3]	0.051 ± 0.005	1.17 ± 0.18
Dover sole	0.073 ± 0.006	0.038 ± 0.003	1.60 ± 0.34
English sole	0.043 ± 0.002	0.042 ± 0.007	2.88 ± 0.63
Ling cod	0.030 ± 0.011	0.114 ± 0.016	1.90 ± 0.31
Pacific cod	0.022 ± 0.005	0.042 ± 0.003	2.04 ± 0.43
Pacific hake	0.052 ± 0.010	0.061 ± 0.008	2.19 ± 0.16
Rockfish, black	0.053 ± 0.009	0.079 ± 0.007	2.85 ± 0.62
Rockfish, orange	0.044 ± 0.011	0.056 ± 0.011	2.69 ± 0.33
Rockfish, yellowtail	0.037 ± 0.006	0.076 ± 0.014	3.35 ± 0.91
Starry flounder	0.143 ± 0.046	0.114 ± 0.016	3.49 ± 0.73
Albacore tuna, raw	0.044 ± 0.009	0.045 ± 0.006	15.75 ± 1.15
Albacore tuna, canned	0.043 ± 0.003	0.060 ± 0.003	13.43 ± 0.64
Chinook salmon, raw	0.037 ± 0.010	0.114 ± 0.036	8.42 ± 0.94
Chinook salmon, canned	0.012 ± 0.005	0.129 ± 0.034	7.25 ± 0.76
Oysters	0.067 ± 0.012	0.233 ± 0.032	2.01 ± 0.19
Geoducks	0.005 ± 0.001	0.290 ± 0.069	1.71 ± 0.05
Pacific shrimp, raw	0.034 ± 0.006	0.034 ± 0.004	1.58 ± 0.27
Pacific shrimp, cooked	0.023 ± 0.002	0.020 ± 0.007	0.99 ± 0.20
Pacific shrimp, canned	0.011 ± 0.002	0.015 ± 0.004	0.78 ± 0.03
Dungeness crab, sample I, cooked	0.037 ± 0.005	—	2.26 ± 0.07
Dungeness crab, sample II, raw	0.047 ± 0.017	0.167 ± 0.086	3.14 ± 0.14
Dungeness crab, sample III, cooked	0.059 ± 0.017	0.127 ± 0.059	243 ± 0.30

[1] Gordon et al. (1979).
[2] Wet weight edible portion.
[3] Mean ± SD, duplicate determinations on three fish or three composites.

observed in them (0.005 mg/100 g); but this has not been confirmed (Greig 1971). White fish averaged 0.07 ± 0.01 mg/100 g riboflavin, but levels were two to three times higher in mollusks. Niacin is fairly high in all seafoods, averaging over 3.8 mg/100 g, especially in such fish as salmon and tuna. These two fish were found to contain 8.4 and 15.8 mg/100 g, respectively. Canning of these fish lowers the amount of niacin by approximately 15%. Fatty fish have been reported to contain larger amounts of niacin in body tissue (Higashi 1961). The average niacin content of white fish was 2.4 ± 0.8 mg/100 g. Dungeness crab contained about the same amount, while mollusks and Pacific shrimp contained slightly less. The thiamin and riboflavin values of white fish presented in Table 21.6 are in agreement with values reported by Sautier (1946A,B).

The effect of processing on the water-soluble vitamins thiamin, riboflavin, and niacin also is illustrated in Table 21.6. Pacific shrimp is used as an example. Thiamin, riboflavin, and niacin levels dropped 32, 41, and 37%, respectively, in shrimp after they were cooked in an automatic peeling operation. Further processing of the cooked shrimp by retorting to produce a canned product lowered thiamin by 51%, riboflavin by 25%, and niacin 21%. These reductions should not be considered to result from vitamin destruction. During the first cooking cycle, the large amount of water used to move the shrimp in the peeling operation is believed to have washed the nutrients away. Since the liquid was drained from the canned product prior to analysis, this accounts for the second reduction. Loss of water-soluble vitamins by diffusion into brine of canned seafoods can amount to 30 – 35% (Bramsnaes 1962). Tarr (1962) provided one of the most comprehensive reviews on the changes in nutrient value of seafoods due to handling and processing. Also, the stability of nutrients during food processing has been reviewed by Harris (1975), and this information can be considered relevant to seafoods.

Levels of ascorbic acid, vitamin A, and vitamin E in the edible portion of fishery products have not been examined extensively. Only low levels of vitamins A and E are believed to be present in muscle tissue, whereas large amounts are found in offal and, especially, liver (Butler 1946). To obtain some idea as to the amount of these nutrients in various seafoods, a limited number of individual samples were screened. Vitamins A and E and ascorbic acid levels are reported in Table 21.7.

The ascorbic acid found in white fish muscle averaged 333 ± 187 µg/100 g with slightly more in oysters and 1.7 mg/100 g in salmon. Hastings and Spencer (1952) found canned albacore tuna to have 5.1 mg, silver salmon 1.3 mg, and Pacific oysters 38.1 mg of ascorbic acid per 100 g. If correct, these latter values are extremely high. An early observation (Hoygaard and Rasmussen 1939) found cod *(Gadus callarias)* to contain 2 mg/100 g and mussel *(Mytilus edulis)* 6 mg/100 g of ascorbic acid. Vitamin A, as retinol equivalents (RE), averaged 6 ± 1 µg/100 g in Pacific Coast white fish (Table 21.7). One sample of black cod contained 142 µg RE/100 g, and three oyster composites had 75 ± 25 µg RE/100 g. An extensive survey of vitamin A in fish fillets was accomplished by Junker (1956). Pennock et al. (1962) could not detect any vitamin A in cod *(Gadus callarias)* but did find 0.33 mg/100 g α-tocopherol. Vitamin E averaged 0.53 mg/100 g in Pacific Northwest white

TABLE 21.7. ASCORBIC ACID, VITAMIN A, AND VITAMIN E IN SEAFOODS OF THE PACIFIC NORTHWEST

	Ascorbic acid[1-3] (µg/100 g)		Vitamin A, RE[1,2,4]		Vitamin E[2,5] (mg/100 g)	
English sole	155	(1)[6]			0.57	(1)
Ling cod			7.4 ± 0.3	(3)	0.16	(1)
Pacific cod	688	(2)			0.20	(1)
Petrale sole	192	(1)			0.32	(1)
Rex sole	291 ± 142	(4)	5.9 ± 0.4	(3)	0.35	(3)
Rockfish, orange	213 ± 166	(4)	7.0 ± 1.2	(3)	0.79	(3)
Rockfish, yellowtail	311 ± 106	(3)	4.7	(2)	1.34	(3)
Starry flounder	460	(1)				
Block cod	161	(1)	142	(1)		
Albacore tuna	290	(1)				
Chinook salmon	1,712	(1)	28	(1)	0.53	(1)
Oysters	565 ± 94	(3)	75 ± 25	(3)	1.05	(1)
Shrimp, cooked	275	(1)	20	(1)		
Shrimp, frozen	324	(1)	22	(1)		
Shrimp, canned	0	(1)	18	(1)		

[1] Gordon (1980).
[2] Gordon, D.T., unpublished data.
[3] Fluorometric assay using o-phenylenediamine (AOAC, 1970).
[4] Trifluoroacetic acid colorimetric assay (Neeld and Pearson, 1963).
[5] Emmerie–Engle reaction after isolation of tocopherol by thin-layer chromatography (Biere, 1967).
[6] Number in parenthesis indicates individual samples analyzed in duplicate.

fish, and the levels observed in salmon and oysters fell within the range established with these finfish (Table 21.7). α-Tocopherol is the principal type of tocopherol in marine animals (Brown 1953A,B; Nazir and Magar 1964). Examining Eastern seafoods, Ackman and Cormier (1967) found cod *(Gadus morhua)* to range from 0.17 to 0.24 mg α-tocopherol per 100 g. Sablefish *(Anoplopoma fimbria)* had 4.4 mg/100 g.

The vitamin A and vitamin E levels reported in Table 21.7 were determined colorimetrically using the method of Neeld and Pearson (1963) and the Emmerie–Engel reaction (Bieri 1969), respectively. Considering the very low levels of both vitamins found in seafoods and the possible chance of artifacts, analysis by high pressure liquid chromatography of these vitamins would seem more appropriate. With the low levels of all fat-soluble vitamins and ascorbic acid in seafoods, it is easy to understand why food nutrient tables in general report their content as zero.

Independent questions related to the endogenous amounts of ascorbic acid and α-tocopherol in seafoods are "How long do they remain in tissue after harvest from the sea?" "What are the kenetics of their interaction?" and "For how long do they protect against oxidation and contribute to product shelf life?"

Oyster and other mollusks in particular are considered to be some of the richest food sources of the provitamins D, especially 7-dehydrocholesterol (Bergmann 1952), which has been found in oysters *(Crassostrea gigas)* to average 22 ± 8 mg/100 g (Gordon 1979). Crustacea and most finfish do not contain this precursor of vitamin D. Bailey (1952) found Pacific salmon to range in vitamin D content from 240 to 540 IU/100 g. Generally, fish having a high oil content are good sources of this vitamin (e.g., sardines, herring, and slid). Levels in smelt, shad, and black cod are unknown. Currently available literature indicates that white fish contain negligible amounts.

Other vitamins in marine products which have received relatively little investigative attention are vitamin B_6, folacin, biotin, and pantothenic acid. Tarr *et al.* (1950) extensively evaluated the vitamin B_{12} in various fish and their offal. Table 21.8 presents those levels reported in the literature for the edible portion of fish from the Pacific Northwest. The blanks in Table 21.8 indicate a lack of information. Attempting to place an estimate on the amount of the five vitamins mentioned above in white fish muscle, the following values are offered: vitamin B_6, 0.02–1.20 mg/100 g; folacin, 0.5–2.5 μg/100 g; biotin, 0.1–8 μg/100 g; pantothenic acid, 0.15–0.80 mg/100 g; and vitamin B_{12}, 1–10 μg/100 g. These ranges are based on available data in the literature for white fish with global distribution. Similar range estimates have been offered by Stansby (1962) and Murray and Burt (1975), the latter for fish harvested in Britain. Addressing the question of what form in which some vitamins exist in seafoods, Hayashi *et al.* (1945) stated that pyridoxamine is the predominant form of vitamin B_6 in fish, mollusks, and crustacea.

The normal variation that can exist between any two biological samples is realized and must always be addressed. Accurate mean nutrient levels

TABLE 21.8. VITAMIN B₆, FOLACIN, BIOTIN, PANTOTHENIC ACID, AND VITAMIN B₁₂ LEVELS REPORTED IN THE LITERATURE OF SOME PACIFIC SEAFOODS

	Vitamin B_6		Folacin (mg/100g wet weight)		Biotin		Pantothenic acid		Vitamin B_{12}	
Ling cod									180 µg/g dry weight	(3)[4]
Ocean perch[1]	0.34	(2)			0.001	(1)	0.36	(1)	0.01 µg/g wet weight	(1)
Pacific cod	0.02–0.09	(5)					0.15	(1)	0.0009 µg/g wet weight	(1)
Pacific halibut[2]	0.03–0.05	(5)								
Pollock, Alaska[3]	0.13	(5)			0.0032	(1)	0.25–0.42	(1)	0.01 µg/g wet weight	(1)
Rockfish (Sebastodes sp.)			0.06–0.12	(6)			0.08–0.10	(6)	120 µg/g dry weight	(3)
Starry flounder									0.11 µg/g wet weight	(6)
Albacore tuna, canned	0.44	(2)	0.0006	(2)	0.003	(1)	0.42	(2)	0.0017 µg/g wet weight	(1)
Salmon, canned	0.45	(2)	0.0005	(2)	0.015	(2)	0.58	(2)	0.021 µg/g wet weight	(4)

[1] Specie unknown.
[2] Hippoglossus sp.
[3] Gadus pollachius.
[4] Number in parenthesis refers to original reference: (1) Stansby and Hall (1967); (2) Neilands et al. (1947); (3) Tarr et al. (1950); (4) Teesi et al. (1957); (5) Yanase (1956); (6) Higashi (1961).

TABLE 21.9. COMPARISONS OF PHYSICAL CHARACTERISTICS AND PROXIMATE COMPOSITION ON VITAMIN[1] AND MINERAL[2] LEVELS IN SELECTED SEAFOODS

	Weight (kg)	Length (cm)	Protein (%)	Lipid (%)	Thiamin	Riboflavin	Niacin	K (mg/100g)	Ca	Mg	Na	Fe	Zn	Cu (μg/100 g)
Ling cod, raw	1.15	20.5	18.8	0.93	0.026	0.041	1.86	274	11.1	17.1	36.1	0.36	0.45	70
	2.85	27.5	17.0	0.89	0.021	0.045	1.63	322	6.9	17.2	31.2	0.44	0.42	30
	4.85	31.0	19.3	1.12	0.021	0.041	2.20	363	6.0	18.3	28.6	0.56	0.50	49
Starry flounder, raw	0.70	16.0	16.2	—	0.138	0.125	3.09	—	—	—	—	—	—	—
	1.35	19.0	17.8	1.21	0.109	0.108	3.81	321	3.3	15.8	37.8	0.60	0.53	75
	2.55	23.0	17.8	1.08	0.220	0.111	3.58	253	4.6	14.5	34.3	0.41	0.54	45
Albacore tuna, raw	2.80	21.0	24.3	1.57	0.040	0.041	17.12	—	—	—	—	—	—	—
	5.15	24.0	24.8	8.31	0.056	0.045	15.36	—	—	—	—	—	—	—
	9.60	30.0	22.7	12.9	0.037	0.050	14.8	—	—	—	—	—	—	—
Chinook salmon, raw	4.35	30.0	20.7	5.52	0.038	0.085	9.39	273	7.1	25.6	81.9	1.60	0.35	96
	9.10	35.0	19.2	7.76	0.037	0.143	7.39	244	9.2	26.2	70.9	1.01	0.68	95
	12.50	37.0	20.6	14.8	0.037	0.114	8.47	253	6.6	25.3	54.8	1.30	0.38	62

[1] Gordon et al. (1979).
[2] Gordon D.T., unpublished data.

require continual efforts to survey sample populations using up-to-date methodology. Many nutrients in fish are so low in concentration that extensive analyses may not be warranted. The degree of standard deviation in a population mean or the range of nutrient levels is important and dependent on variables previously discussed. From our studies and those of Braekkan (1959), size and proximate composition appear to be unimportant variables within a species. Comparisons of the physical characteristics and proximate composition of four species with selected vitamin and mineral levels suggest a total lack of correlation among these parameters (Table 21.9). Size variability in ling cod and starry flounder and both size and lipid differences in albacore tuna and chinook salmon resulted in little difference in nutrient amounts per unit mass. A similar lack of correlation was found by Braekkan (1959) between the levels of the four vitamins, niacin (2.28 ± 0.07), pantothenic acid (0.173 ± 0.009), riboflavin (0.085 ± 0.005), and vitamin B_{12} (0.0011 ± 0.0004), in 19 cod *(Gadus morhua)* ranging in size from 0.5 to 7.7 kg. Mean values ± SD for each vitamin in mg/100 g are indicated for comparison with Pacific cod *(Gadus macrocephalus)* previously presented (Tables 21.6, 21.8, and 21.9). Since the age of fish has no significant effect on nutrient content, examination of any size fish would suffice to give information for comparative purposes. Just how different the nutrient levels are in similar species ranging throughout the world's oceans remains to be accurately determined. A possible source of difference in vitamin and mineral levels among fresh fish samples is the amount of lateral dark muscle removed with a fillet prior to analysis. Since dark muscle is comparatively rich in nutrients (Braekkan 1959), failure to obtain representative samples may cause larger differences in compositional values than season or geographical location.

REFERENCES

ACKMAN, R.G., and CORMIER, M.G. 1967. α-Tocopherol in some Atlantic fish and shellfish with particular reference to live-holding without food. J. Fish. Res. Board Can. *24*, 357–373.

ASSOCIATION OF OFFICIAL ANALYTICAL CHEMISTS. 1970. Official Methods of Analysis, 11th Ed. p. 778, 39.056. Washington, D.C.

BABBITT, J.K., LAW, D.K., and CRAWFORD, D.L. 1973. Phenolases and blue discoloration in whole cooked dungeness crab *(Cancer magister)* J. Food Sci. *38*, 1089–1090.

BAILY, B.E., CARTER, N.M. and SWAIN, L.A. 1952. Marine oils with particular reference to those of Canada. Fish. Res. Board Can. Bull. *89*, 1–413.

BERGMANN, W. 1962. Sterols: Their structure and distribution. *In* Comparative Biochemistry. M. Florkin and H.S. Mason (Editors), pp. 103–162. Academic Press, New York.

BIERI, J.G. 1969. Chromatography of tocopherols. *In* Lipid Chromatographic Analyses. G.V. Marinerri (Editor), Vol. 2, pp. 460–478. Marcel Dekker, New York.

BRAEKKAN, O.R. 1959. A comparative study of vitamins in the trunk muscles of fish. Reports on Technological Research Concerning Norwegian Fish Industry, Vol. III, No. 8, 5–42. A.S. John Griegs, Boktrykkeri, Bergen, Norway.

BRAEKKAN, O.R. 1962A. B-vitamins in fish and shellfish. *In* Fish in Nutrition. E. Heen and R. Kreuzer (Editors), pp. 132–140. Fishing News (Books) Ltd., London.

BRAEKKAN, O.R. 1962B. B-vitamins in some fish products. *In* Fish in Nutrition. E. Heen and R. Kreuzer (Editors), pp. 141–145. Fishing News (Books) Ltd., London.

BRAMSNAES, F. 1962. The influence of refrigeration and canning on the nutritive value of fish. *In* Fish in Nutrition. E. Heen and R. Kreuzer (Editors), pp. 153–160. Fishing News (Books) Ltd., London, England.

BROWN, F. 1953A. The occurrence of α-tocopherol in seaweed. Chem. Ind. London *21*, 174.

BROWN, F. 1953B. Occurrence of vitamin E in cod and other fish-liver oils. Nature *171*, 790–791.

BUTLER, C. 1946. Vitamin A and D in fish liver and viscena. Commer. Fish. Rev. *8*, 13–19.

CAUSERET, J. 1962. Fish as a source of mineral nutrition. *In* Fish as Food. G. Borgstorm (Editor), Vol. II. pp. 205–234. Academic Press, New York.

CHAPMAN, A.C. 1926. On the presence of compounds of arsenic in marine crustaceas and shell fish. Analyst *51*, 548–563.

CHILDS, E.A., and GAFFKE, J.N. 1973. Mercury content of Oregon ground fish. Fish. Bull. *71*, 713–717.

CHILDS, E.A., and GAFFKE, J.N. 1974. Lead and cadmium content of selected Oregon ground fish. J. Food Sci. *39*, 853–854.

CHRISTENSEN, R.E., BECKMAN, R.M., and BIRDSALL, J.J. 1968. Some mineral elements of commercial species and herbs as determined by direct reading emission spectroscopy. J. Assoc. Off. Anal. Chem. *51*, 1003–1010.

COULSON, E.J., REMINGTON, R.E., and LYNCH, K.M. 1935. Metabolism in the rat of the naturally occurring arsenic of shrimp as compared with arsenic trioxide. J. Nutr. *10*, 255–270.

CRAWFORD, D.L. 1980. Personal communication. Seafoods Laboratory, Asotria, Oregon.

CRUICKSHANK, E.M. 1962. Fat soluble vitamins. *In* Fish as Food. G. Borgstrom (Editor), Vol. II. pp. 175–203. Academic Press, New York.

FISHERY STATISTICS OF THE UNITED STATES. 1973. Statistical Digest, No. 67. U.S. Department of Commerce, Washington, D.C.

FISKE, C.H., and SUBBAROW, Y. 1925. The colorimetric determination of phosphorus. J. Biol. Chem. *66*, 375–400.

GIBSON, D.M., and MURRAY, C.K. 1973. Polyphosphates and fish: some chemical studies. J. Food Technol. *8*, 197–204.

GORDON, D.T. 1978. Atomic absorption spectrometric and colorimetric determination of iron in seafoods. Assoc. Off. Anal. Chem. *61*, 715–719.

GORDON, D.T. 1979. Quantification of steroids in mollusks. Presented at the American Oil Chemists Society Meeting, San Francisco, Calif., April 29–May 3, 1979.

GORDON, D.T. 1980. Nutritional labeling of fish as a fresh commodity. Presented at the 40th Annual Meeting of the Institute of Food Technologists, New Orleans, LA, June 8–10, 1980.

GORDON, D.T., and ROBERTS, G.L. 1977. Mineral and proximate composition of Pacific Coast fish. J. Agric. Food Chem. *25*, 1262–1268.

GORDON, D.T., ROBERTS, G.L., and HEINZ, D.M. 1979. Thiamin, riboflavin and niacin content and stability in Pacific Coast seafoods. J. Agric. Food Chem. *27*, 483–490.

GREIG, R.A., and GNOLDINGER, F.H. 1971. U.S. Department of Commerce, Spec. Scie. Rep. Fisheries No. 631, pp 1–7. National Marine Fisheries Service, NOAA, U.S. Dept. Comm., Washington, D.C.

HALL, A.S., TEENY, F.M., LEWIS, L.G., HARDMAN, W.H., and GAUGLITZ, E.J., Jr. 1976A. Mercury in fish and shellfish of the Northeast Pacific. I. Pacific halibut, *Hippoglossus stenolepis*. Fish. Bull. *74*, 783–789.

HALL, A.S., TEENY, F.M., and GAUGLITZ, E.J., JR. 1976B. Mercury in fish and shellfish of the Northwest Pacific. II. Sablefish, *Anoplopoma fimbria*. Fish. Bull. *74*, 791–797.

HARRIS, R.S. 1975. General discussion on the stability of nutrients. *In* Nutrition Evaluation of Food Processing. R.S. Harris and E. Kassmas (Editors), 2nd Ed., pp. 1–4. Avi Publishing Co., Inc., Westport, CT.

HASTINGS, W.H., and SPENCER, S.F. 1952. Determination of free and bound ascorbic acid in fishery products. J. Mar. Res. *11*, 241–244.

HAYASHI, K., SUZUKI, K., and MIYAKI, M. 1945. Studies on vitamin B_6 in marine products, II. The distribution of vitamin B_6 group in aquatic animals. Rep. Fac. Fisheries, Prefect. Univ. Mie *2*, 33–38.

HIGASHI, H. 1961. Vitamins in fish with special reference to edible parts. *In* Fish as Food. G. Borgstrom (Editor), Vol. I, pp. 411–486. Academic Press, New York.

HOYGAARD, A., and RASMUSSEN, H.W. 1939. Vitamin C sources in Eskimo food. Nature *143*, 943.

JACQUOT, R. 1961. Organic constituents of fish and other aquatic animal foods. *In* Fish as Food. G. Borgstrom (Editor), Vol. I, pp. 174–209. Academic Press, New York.

JUNKER, M. 1956. Vitamin A in fish, crustaceans, and mollusks. Arch.

Fischereiwiss. 7, 248–272.

KIDD, P.S., TROWBRIDGE, F.L., GOLDSBY, J.B., and NICHAMAN, M.Z. 1974. Sources of dietary iodine. J. Diet. Assoc. 65, 420–422.

LOVE, R.M. 1970. The Chemical Biology of fishes. Academic Press, New York.

MARTINEZ-TORRES, C., LEETS, I., and LYRISSE, M. 1975. Iron absorption by humans from fish. Arch. Latinoam. Nutr. 25, 199–210.

MURRY, J., and BURT, J.R. 1975. The composition of fish. Torry Advisary Note No. 38, pp. 3–16. Torry Res. Stn. Aberdeen, Scotland.

NAZIR, D.J., and MAGAR, N.G. 1964. Determination of ubiquinone and α-tocopherol in some tissues of shark (Carcharias elioti Day). Biochem. J. 90, 268–270.

NEELD, J.B. JR., and PEARSON, W.N. 1963. Macro- and micromethods for the determination of serum vitamin A using trifluoroacetic acid. J. Nutr. 79, 454–462.

NEILANDS, J.B., STRONG, F.M., and ELVEHJEM, C.A. 1947. The nutritive value of canned foods. XXV. Vitamin content of canned fish products. J. Nutr. 34, 633–643.

NELSON, R.W., and THURSTON, C.E. 1964. Proximate composition, sodium, and potassium of dungeness crab. J. Am. Diet. Assoc. 45, 41–43.

NILSON, H.W., and COULSON, E.J. 1939. The mineral content of the edible portions of some American fishery products. Investigated Rep. No., 41, pp. 1–7. U.S. Dept. of Comm. Bureau of Fisheries, Washington, D.C.

PENNOCK, J.F., MORTON, R.A., LAWSON, D.E.M., and LAIDMAN, D.L. 1962. Quinones and related compounds in fish tissue. Biochem. J. 84, 637–640.

SAUTIER, P. 1946A. Thiamine assays of fishery products. Commer. Fish. Rev. 8, 17–19.

SAUTIER, P. 1946B. Riboflavin assays of fishery products. Commer. Fish. Rev. 8, 19–21.

SCHROEDER, H.A., and BALASSA, J.J. 1966. Abnormal trace metals in man: Arsenic. J. Chronic Dis. 19, 85–106.

SIDWELL, V.D., BUZZEL, D.H., FONCANNON, P.R., and SMITH, A.L. 1977. Composition of the edible portion of raw (fresh or frozen) crustaceans, finfish and mollusks. II. Macroelements: sodium, potassium, chlorine, calcium, phosphorus and magnesium. Mar. Fish Rev. 39, 1–11.

STANSBY, M.E. 1962. Proximate composition of fish. In Fish in Nutrition. E. Heen and R. Kreuger (Editors), pp. 55–60. Fishing News (Books) Ltd., London.

STANSBY, M.E., and HALL. A.S. 1967. Chemical composition of commercially important fish of the United States. Fish. Ind. Res. 3, 29–46.

TARR, H.L.A. 1962. Changes in nutritive value through handling and processing procedures. *In* Fish as Food. G. Borgstrom (Editor), Vol. II, pp. 235–236. Academic Press, New York.

TARR, H.L.A., SOUTHCOTT, B.A., and IVEY, P.W.   1950.   Vitamin B_{12}-active substances in fish products. Food Technol. *4*, 354–358.

TEERI, A.E., LOUGHLIN, M.E., and JOSSELYN, D.   1957.   Nutritive value of fish. I.   Nicotinic acid, riboflavin, vitamin B_{12}, and amino acids of various salt water species. Food Res. *22*, 145–149.

THURSTON, C.E.   1958.   Sodium and potassium content of 34 species of fish. J. Am. Diet. Assoc. *34*, 396–399.

THURSTON, C.E.   1961.   Proximate composition and sodium potassium contents of four species of commercial bottom fish.   J. Food Sci. *26*, 495–498.

UNITED STATES SENATE SELECT COMMITTEE ON NUTRITION AND HUMAN NEEDS.   1977.   Dietary Goals for the United States.   95th Congress 1st Session.   U.S. Government Printing Office, Washington, D.C.

VINOGRADOV, A.P.   1953.   The elementary chemical composition of marine organisms.   Sears Foundation for Marine Research.   Yale University, New Haven, CT.

VOUGHT, R.L., and LONDON, W.T.   1964.   Dietary sources of iodine.   Am. J. Clin. Nutr. *14*, 186–192.

YANASE, M.   1956.   The vitamin B_6 content of fish meat.   Bull. Jpn. Soc. Sci. Fish. *22*, 51–55.

22

Enzyme Modifications of Fishery By-Products

George M. Pigott

A by-product, "a material derived secondarily in the manufacture of another," would be better defined in the fishing industry as a "secondary raw material." It is well known that a relatively small portion of the total resources from the sea are being directly consumed by humans. However, much of the so-called by-product volume is wholesome and nutritious and certainly warrants efforts to upgrade its utilization above that of low grade animal feed or waste. Secondary raw materials capable of more efficient utilization include not only the waste from processing of edible fish but also the discarded by-catches from specific fisheries and industrial fish that can be upgraded to products of higher value than conventional fish meal.

Perhaps we have been trying too hard to solve the problem in hand. Past programs for upgrading low grade fish or fishery by-products have been carried out on a grandiose "save the world" scale and often have created more problems than they solved. Witness the birth, public life, and demise of solvent-extracted fish protein concentrate (FPC). Conceived in an atmosphere of dire predictions regarding world food shortages when it was politically popular to push programs involving gigantic improvements in animal protein production, the destiny of FPC was removed from the hands of capable scientists. We are no closer to our ultimate goal of "total utilization" of food from the sea today then we were 20 years ago.

A practical technique for upgrading the use of seafood must encompass several important, often neglected, areas.

1. Simple, inexpensive procedures for handling and holding on shipboard when separation or collection is to be made at sea. This includes not only materials from processing or preprocessing but by-catch that is often too small, too bony, or too oily for direct economic use.

College of Fisheries, Institute for Food Science and Technology, University of Washington, Seattle, Washington 98195

2. Procedures that allow fairly long-term, inexpensive holding of material with minimum nutritional loss prior to or during processing. This allows collection at sea as well as in small processing plants that do not have sufficient material for continuous processing.
3. Processing techniques that allow small and large companies to continually process large volumes or periodically process small batches of material.

Whether or not processes are available to upgrade secondary raw materials to high quality animal feed or human food is immaterial when considering the impact of the above factors on the overall economic feasibility.

There are many potential techniques for extracting protein from animal or fish. These include the use of aqueous and organic solvents; the conventional processes of cooking, pressing, and drying; chemical hydrolysis; hot oil extraction; and biological processes utilizing endogenous or added enzymes and bacteria. Of these, the biological processes offer the best potential for producing protein concentrates that can be used widely in formulated foods, the basic use for such products. Extracted proteins resulting from biological action can be made to retain their functionality and, when properly concentrated or dried, can be cheaper than and equal to or better than milk proteins as nutritious components of a prepared formula. The object of this discussion is to review the status of extracting or modifying whole or by-product seafoods by enzymes.

ACCELERATED ENZYMATIC PROCESSES

Development Research

The length of time required for processing and the low yields from natural fermentations led researchers to investigate means of accelerating and improving biological FPC methods, which centered on the addition of various proteolytic enzymes. The basic principle involved is the rapid hydrolytic breakdown of the long-chain protein molecules by the enzymes added. Proteolytic enzymes are either exo or endo peptidases. Exo refers to enzymes that split terminal amino acids from one end of the chain of the peptide bond by hydrolysis. The endo peptidases hydrolize peptide bonds within the molecule, usually at specific residues, to produce relatively large peptide chains. Pepsin-like enzymes attack peptide bonds adjacent to residues with free carboxyl groups, while trypsin-like enzymes attack those adjacent to residues with free amino groups. Enzymes such as the vegetable enzymes, papain and bromelain, or the microbial proteases have broader specificities (Mackie 1974). The fish proteins are broken into shorter peptides and polypeptides and individual amino acids that are water-soluble. The lipid from the fish flesh is also released during hydrolysis and can be physically separated by centrifugation. The hydrolysate product can be used as a concentrated paste or as a dried powder (Hale 1974).

The earlier research on this type of process is exemplified by Murayama (1962), who added proteolytic enzymes to fish sauce fermentation and succeeded in reducing the process time from 6 months to 2 months. Since then, a variety of enzymes and processes have been proposed. McBride *et al.* (1961) tested three enzymes to accelerate fish silage. They found pepsin to have the highest activity, followed by bromelain and rhozome B-6. Hale (1969) measured the relative activity of 20 commercially available proteolytic enzymes on fish protein. The microbial enzyme pronase exhibited the greatest activity per unit weight, but in general, microbial enzymes ranked low in relative activity with moderate cost. Aasmundrud (1974) investigated ficin, an enzyme with its maximum activity near neutral pH. He found, however, that the natural cathepsins in the fish flesh made the reaction very difficult to control.

Iseki *et al.* (1969) used commercial enzymes in a process to produce a high quality functional product. Digestion temperatures of 50°–60°C for 4 hr with 0.3% enzyme (based on fish weight) were used, giving yields of over 80% of the original protein. They found, however, that activated carbon was necessary to remove off-colors and steam distillation to remove odor.

Enzymatic Processes

Perhaps the most successful enzyme processes to date are those developed by French workers (Mackie 1974). Eijssalet (1974) describes the apparent success of the French company Nacoma in producing a milk replacer. A shipboard operation has been developed where whole fish and fish waste are processed directly into the hydrolysate. The protein hydrolysate is stored in tanks at 0°C on board until the ship returns to port, where, after separation of oil and solids, it is finally dried. The enzyme used is not specified, but Heggelund (1975) concluded that it is papain. Other French groups have also investigated enzyme digestions. Gattino *et al.* (1972) were awarded a French patent for a process to produce a fish protein powder from whole fish or fish fragments and viscera. An unspecified enzyme is used at pH 3.5–4.5 and 35°–60°C until the fish is liquefied. The slurry is centrifuged and the liquid portion dried. Nestlé S. A. was awarded a U.S. Patent (Bosund and Gengtsson 1976) for a similar process. The Nestlé process utilizes the insoluble protein fraction as well as the soluble fraction to provide protein isolates.

Pigott *et al.* (1978) have shown that a high quality fish protein hydrolysate can be commercially produced from whole fish or fish waste economically and with relatively simple engineering. This product produced by pepsin hydrolysis has excellent emulsification and foam formation qualities which make it useful in many formulations.

There has been a considerable amount of research work to develop or modify enzyme processes for specific applications or to overcome certain disadvantages of the final product. Protein hydrolysates characteristically have a bitter taste owing to the production of certain peptides. Lalasides and Sjöberg (1978) have reviewed this problem and have shown that azeo-tropic secondary butyl alcohol (SBA) extraction of enzymatic protein hydro-lysates removes the bitter compounds. However, up to 10% of the hydroly-sate is removed by total removal of the bitter compounds. Adler-Nissen (1976) has prepared an excellent review paper that shows the requirement for concentrated proteins having high solubility. He points out that enzy-matic hydrolysis is the best means of preparing products meeting this requirement but that the formation of bitter peptides is the main problem.

Fujimaki et al. (1971, 1973) have been leaders in investigating the cause of bittering and other off-tastes and the methods for removing them. They have reported that a method of enzymatic hydrolysis followed by enzymatic resynthesis to produce a new substance called plastein results in an insolu-ble product that has a bland odor and taste. Yamashita et al. (1976) have used the plastein reaction to produce a low-phenylolanine, high-tyrosine dietetic food for curing phenylketonuria.

Heveia and Olcott (1977) have shown that the off-flavors in fish protein hydrolysates prepared by proteolytic enzymes bromelain, ficin, or pronase were due to bitterness and glutamic acid taste. Hence, the general draw-back to enzyme hydrolysates is the off-flavors. Techniques are becoming available for removing these flavors, particularly bitterness, when it is essential for the end use. On the other hand, Pigott et al. (1978) have determined that the bitterness can be reduced by controlled processing to the degree that is acceptable for many applications.

Enzyme Digested FPC

In a related development, a number of researchers have investigated the possibilities of enzymatically digesting solvent-extracted FPC to improve the functional characteristics of that product (Spinelli et al. 1975). The VioBin Corporation carried out extensive hydrolyses of VioBin FPC (ex-tracted with ethylene dichloride) with a wide variety of enzymes. They found the resulting products to be of excellent nutritional quality, as dem-onstrated by animal feeding (E. Levin 1978 personal communication). Cheftel (1972) studied the effects of pH, temperature, substrate, and en-zyme concentration on the hydrolysis of FPC by pronase and monzyme. Continuous systems with some recycling of enzyme were developed on a laboratory scale. Archer et al. (1973) studied the kinetics of the enzymatic solubilization of FPC. Their work revealed that the enzyme is first adsorbed to the surface of the substrate, with the initial rate of reaction being proportional to the surface area of substrate exposed to the aqueous phase. The overall kinetics were described by a sequence of two first-order pro-cesses—an initial, fast reaction in which loosely bound polypeptides chains are cleaved from an insoluble protein particle, and a second, slower reaction in which a more compacted core protein is digested. Heveia et al. (1976) reported rates of solubilization of FPC with bromelain, pronase, and ficin. Like the other work in this area, Heveia used very dilute solutions (19%

weight of FPC by volume of water). These dilutions are required for the optical density measurements used to determine reaction rates. Pronase at 1% (by weight of FPC) and activated ficin at 4% showed the best rates of solubilization and gave yields of 51% and 53%, respectively, of the original protein after 1-hr digestion. The gain in solubility was only about 20% when the hydrolysis time was increased from 1 to 7 hr.

At the University of Washington, we have continued to refine a pepsin process (Pigott *et al.* 1978) and to develop uses for the product. The fish protein hydrolysate has been used in experimentally formulated foods and animal feeds. Of particular interest is the ability to bind fish larval feeds while contributing significantly to a desired high protein level. Efforts are being made to develop a manufacturing process that combines the plastein reaction during the formulation and processing, thus minimizing the bitter taste associated with hydrolysates.

SUMMARY

Numerous processes and techniques for enzyme hydrolyzing fish flesh have been developed. The modification of fish flesh certainly is developing into a practical technique for upgrading or recovering the larger amount of animal protein that is currently being wasted or used in low value products. Present research directed toward eliminating the adverse off-flavors caused by hydrolysis of the protein is encouraging. Elimination of the major detriment to the use of hydrolysis processes should result in widespread use of this most desirable form of protein food.

REFERENCES

AASMUNDRUD, O. 1974. Enzymatic processing of fish raw materials. Tidsskr. Hermetikind. *60*, 224–228.

ADLER-NISSEN, J. 1976. Enzymatic hydrolysis of proteins for increased solubility. J. Agric. Food Chem. *24(6)*, 1090–93.

ARCHER, M.C., RAGNARSSON, J.O., TANNENBAUM, S., and WANG, D. 1973. Enzymatic solubilization of an insoluble substrate, fish protein concentrate: Process and kinetic considerations. Biotechnol. Bioeng. *15*, 181–196.

BOSUND, S.L.W., and GENGTSSON, B.L. 1976. Fish protein isolate, U.S. Patent 3,924,005.

CHEFTEL, C. 1972. Continuous enzymatic solubilization of fish protein concentrate. Ann. Technol. Agric. *21*, 423–433.

EIJSSALET, R.J. 1974. L'utilisation du faus-poisson ramene por les crevettiers de l'atlantic. Rep. Technical Conf. Fishery Products. FAO Fisheries Rep. No. 146.

FUJIMAKI, M., ARAI, S., and YAMASHITA, M. 1971. Enzymatic protein hydrolysis and plastein synthesis: Their application to producing acceptable proteinaceous food materials. Presented at the Symposium of Microbial Foods, Kyoto, Japan.

FUJIMAKI, M., ARAI, S., YAMASHITA, M., KATO, H., and NAGUCHI, M. 1973. Taste peptide fractionation from a fish protein hydrolysate. Agric. Biol. Chem. *37*, 2891–2898.

GATTINO, J., HURM, A. and LAMOTTE, G. 1972. Process for cytolysis of fish, French Patent 2097636.

HALE, M.B. 1969. Relative activities of commercially available enzymes in hydrolysis of fish protein. Food Technol. *23*, 107.

HALE, M.B. 1974. Using enzymes to make fish protein concentrates. Mar. Fish. Rev. *36*, 15.

HEGGELUND, P.O. 1975. Studies to upgrade the pepsin digestion of fish waste for high quality protein recovery. M.S. Thesis, University of Washington, Seattle, WA.

HEVEIA, P., and OLCOTT, H.S. 1977. Flavor of enzyme-solubilized fish protein concentrate fractions. J. Agric. Food Chem. *25*, 772–774.

ISEKI, S., WATANABE, T., and KINUMAKI, T. 1969. Studies on "liquefied fish protein." IV—Examination of processing conditions for industrial production. Tokai-ku Suisan Kenkyusho Kenkyu Hokoku *59*, 81–99.

LALASIDES, G., SJÖBERG, and LARS-BÖRJE. 1978. Two new methods of debittering protein hydrolysates and a fraction of hydrolysates with exceptionally high content of amino acids. J. Agric. Food Chem. *26*, 742–749.

MACKIE, T.M. 1974. Proteolytic enzymes in recovery of proteins from fish waste. Process Biochem. *9*, 12.

MCBRIDE, J.R., IDLER, D.R., and MACLEOD, R.A. 1961. The liquefaction of British Columbia herring by ensilage, proteolytic enzymes and acid hydrolysis. J. Fish. Res. Board Can. *18*, 93.

MURAYAMA, D., CALVEZ, L., and NITAYACHIN, P. 1962. Production of fish sauce. I. Effect of commercial protein proteolytic enzymes on the production of fish sauce. Tokai-ku Suisan Kenkyusho Kenkyu Hokoku *23*, 155–163.

PIGOTT, G., BUCOVE, G., and OSTRANDER, J. 1978. Engineering a plant for enzymatic production of supplemental fish protein. J. Food Process. Preserv. *2*, 33–54.

SPINELLI, J., GRONINGER, H., KOURY, B., and MILLER, R. 1975. Functional protein isolates and derivatives from fish muscle. Process Biochem. *10*, 31–6, 42.

YAMASHITA, M., ARAI, S., and FUJIMAKI, M. 1976. A low phenylalanine, high-tyrosine plastein as an acceptable dietetic food. J. Food Sci. *41*, 1029–1032.

23

Preservation of Seafood
with Modified Atmospheres

Kirk L. Parkin and W. Duane Brown

INTRODUCTION

Fresh seafood products, as well as other fresh muscle foods, are savored by American consumers. Moreover, the fresh forms of these foods are generally considered to be superior in quality to their frozen or processed counterparts. Nevertheless, in 1977, only about 3% of the total United States commercial seafood landing was marketed as a fresh product (U.S. Dept. Commerce 1978). In addition, most of the fresh seafood market is confined to the coastal areas of the country. Owing to the existing limitations of contemporary transportation and shipping facilities with respect to product quality, fresh seafood is infrequently, if ever, available to landlocked regions. Or, consumers in one coastal region rarely enjoy the fresh seafood that is unique to other coastal locations for obvious economic reasons alone. Fresh seafood marketing is also limited by the fact that the harvesting of marine food resources is often a seasonal event. At the time of harvest, therefore, it is likely that a bulk of the harvest cannot be handled swiftly enough to market it as fresh product.

The limitations that exist in the marketing of fresh seafood are inherent in the foods themselves. Animals harvested from the sea as food sources possess a natural microbial flora on their exterior surfaces and in their digestive tracts. At the time of processing, the product receives a relatively high degree of bacterial loading, even when the best sanitary and processing conditions are observed. This renders the product very susceptible to bacterial spoilage. Chemically, normal metabolites and other molecular constituents of marine animal tissues are sensitive to undesirable deteriorative reactions, resulting in the production of off-flavors and/or off-odors. One such example is the oxidation of polyunsaturated fatty acids and the subsequent development of rancidity.

Institute of Marine Resources, Department of Food Science and Technology, University of California, Davis, CA 95616

MODIFIED ATMOSPHERE SYSTEMS

Modified atmosphere (MA) systems appear to possess great potential for becoming a valuable technological tool for fresh seafood processing, handling, and distribution. Such systems may be instituted through a simple redistribution of atmospheric gases in the immediate storage environment of the product. It is primarily the enrichment of carbon dioxide (CO_2) into the storage atmosphere as a means of controlling microbial growth that results in the preservation of the product. The gases used for these systems are produced inexpensively, being natural components of the environment. Also, these systems are generally simple to administer and maintain.

This report reviews the use of modified atmospheres, particularly those employing high levels of carbon dioxide, for the preservation of seafoods, and explores the mechanism of action of such atmospheres. No attempt was made here to summarize all literature pertaining to the use of atmospheres with red meats and poultry, but selected references are included when appropriate.

Mermelstein (1979) summarized the use and potential of hypobaric conditions in food preservation, and so we will not review this in the present chapter. It may be appropriate to note, however, that hypobaric systems may be less effective with seafood products than MA applications. Haard *et al.* (1979) observed that the optimal shelf life of eviscerated herring and cod was 3 days longer than that of fish stored in air. They also found that whole herring could not be successfully held by means of a hypobaric process because of "bellyburn" caused by accelerated proteolysis. Also, since equipment and operating costs are likely to be significantly higher with hypobaric systems than those employing modified atmospheres, the latter approach should be the more economical of the two.

Almost a century has passed since Kolbe (1882) first investigated and discovered the preservative effect of CO_2 on meats. Other early work included that of Moran *et al.* (1932), which looked at mold-inoculated chilled beef stored in MA of $20-100\%$ CO_2. They found that the meat held as air control samples suffered extensive mold growth by 8 days, while no growth was observed on meats stored for 18 days in MA. However, $60-100\%$ CO_2 atmospheres induced serious surface browning on the meat. These investigators obtained similar results with $10-30\%$ CO_2 atmospheres using molds in pure culture of strains commonly found in beef. Callow (1932) found that the use of 100% CO_2 atmospheres extended the shelf life of pork and bacon well beyond that observed in those products stored in normal air atmospheres. He observed that this preservative effect was not due to the exclusion of oxygen, since an essentially 100% nitrogen atmosphere offered no advantage over normal air storage. The same microbial growth-inhibitory properties of CO_2 and N_2 atmospheres that were observed in the studies with meats were again displayed in cultures of microorganisms isolated from spoiled pork. Haines (1933) demonstrated that concentrations of CO_2 as low as $10-20\%$ of the atmosphere were sufficient to inhibit effectively the growth of *Achromobacter* (now *Acinetobacter/Moraxella*) and *Pseudo-*

monas cultures, those bacteria associated with the spoilage of fresh meats. In this study, it was also found that the inhibition by CO_2 was manifest in an increased lag phase and a slower rate of growth during the logarithmic growth phase. Inhibition by CO_2 was found to be more effective when the product was stored at the lower range of refrigeration temperatures.

Coyne (1932, 1933) was one of the first investigators to apply the use of modified atmosphere systems to fishery products. In a preliminary study dealing with several pure cultures of bacteria isolated from fish products, CO_2 atmospheres were found to inhibit the growth of bacteria markedly, whereas normal growth patterns were observed under air or N_2 atmospheres (Coyne 1932). It was also observed that, in several cases, bacterial growth was inhibited even after the cultures were removed from the CO_2 atmosphere and transferred to an air environment. This observation is interpreted as a residual effect of CO_2 treatment. In this same study, it was noted that 25% CO_2 was distinctly inhibitive of bacterial growth and that growth was almost nonexistent under higher CO_2 concentrations for 4 days at 15°C. Twenty to 100% CO_2 atmospheres were found to be very effective for the preservation of fresh haddock, cod, sole, whiting, and plaice, in the round and as fillets, with optimal conditions observed under the 40–50% CO_2 systems (Coyne 1933). Higher CO_2 concentrations caused browning of tissues associated with the circulatory system of the fishes (e.g., the gills), apparently due to the formation of metmyoglobin. Some tissue softening was induced in fillets held at the higher CO_2 concentrations. These findings corroborated an earlier study (Killeffer 1930) which involved a variety of foods, including fish, held under CO_2, but in less well-controlled environments. Stansby and Griffiths (1935) in a careful study found that whole haddock stored under 25% CO_2 had a shelf life approximately twice that of products handled by conventional methods.

Shewan (1950) encouraged further research and suggested the use of 30–40% CO_2 atmospheres for optimal benefits of MA storage. Tarr (1954) reflected views similar to those of Shewan and advocated CO_2 contents on the order of 50%, indicating that its preservative effect may be negligible below concentrations of 40%. Yokoseki et al. (1956) found CO_2 atmospheres to be beneficial for the storage of fish cakes.

Pohja et al. (1967) concluded that, for red meats, the preservative capacity of modified atmosphere systems increased linearly with the amount of CO_2 included, but that above 20% CO_2, the meat discolored. These workers also found that the exclusion of O_2 by substitution of N_2 for air was of little value, verifying the conclusions reached in earlier studies. It was found in many laboratories that good beef color could be maintained when using systems of low O_2 tension (Ledward 1970) or high O_2 tension (Daun et al. 1971; Clark and Lentz 1973; Taylor and MacDougall 1973; Ordonez and Ledward 1977) in conjunction with CO_2 concentrations of up to 25%. When attempts were made to use higher CO_2 levels, Silliker and co-workers (1977) found that 20 or 60% CO_2 induced severe discoloration on beef cuts, even in the presence of 20–25% O_2. However, these investigators found no adverse color changes when storing pork cuts in a 50% CO_2 : 25% O_2 : 25% N_2 atmosphere, presumably due to the lower myoglobin content of pork as compared to beef. Other studies also indicated that pork was less suscepti- ble to discoloration when stored in 20–25% CO_2 using high or low O_2 tensions (Ordonez and Ledward 1977; Adams and Huffman 1972). Further advances led to the use of high (50%) CO_2 systems containing 1% carbon monoxide (CO) to provide maximal preservation along with good color stability for beef (Wolfe et al. 1976; Gee and Brown 1978A,B). As is well known, in the presence of carbon monoxide, the carboxymyoglobin pigment is formed. For reasons that are not well understood, this pigment is much more resistant to oxidation in the presence of high levels of carbon dioxide than oxymyoglobin.

The preservative effect of CO_2 has been applied to the holding of fresh seafood in refrigerated seawater (RSW). The National Marine Fisheries Service in Seattle, Washington, was primarily responsible for the develop- ment of the CO_2-saturated refrigerated seawater (CO_2–RSW) system when it was demonstrated that this medium was effective in extending the storage life of whole halibut *(Hippoglossus hippoglossus)*, yellowtail rock- fish *(Sebastes flavidus)*, pink shrimp *(Pandalus jordani* and *Pandalus borealis)*, and dressed chum salmon *(Oncorhynchus keta)* (Nelson and Barnett 1971; Barnett et al. 1971). Other laboratories followed with reports describing the preservation of whole pink shrimp *(Pandalus* spp.) through the use of CO_2-saturated brines (Bullard and Collins 1978; Barnett et al. 1978) and of ocean perch *(Sebastes marinus)* in the round (Longard and Reiger 1974). Hiltz and co-workers (1976) found that whole silver hake *(Merluccius bilinearis)* maintained good quality longer when held in CO_2– RSW in comparison to RSW or ice. It was also observed in this study that frozen minced flesh appeared to deteriorate chemically at a slower rate when the raw material was initially stored in CO_2–RSW than when it was held in RSW alone or on ice prior to processing.

The National Marine Fisheries Service in cooperation with Whirlpool Corporation has studied the preservation of fresh seafood through the use of CO_2 in gaseous storage (Nelson and Tretsven 1975). In this investigation, the storage life of fresh dressed salmon *(Oncorhynchus kisutch)* was ex- tended by 4–6 days under an 11.5% CO_2 : 1.5% O_2 : 87% N_2, in comparison to salmon held in air. When a continuous flow of this gas mixture was employed, the shelf life extension was increased by 7–9 days. It should be noted that the use of a continuous flow of a given gas mixture provides "controlled" atmospheres rather than "modified" ones. The latter usually applies to a situation in which an initial gas mixture is provided, then the container is sealed. Such atmospheres may change during storage, whereas controlled atmospheres should remain the same. Windsor and Thoma (1974) looked at the preservation of fish products using CO_2 and propionic acid. Williams and co-workers (1978) demonstrated that 100% CO_2 atmo- spheres markedly inhibited growth of bacteria in pure cultures. These bacteria were those common to a variety of meat products including beef, poultry, and fish. Brown and co-workers (1980) looked at the feasibility of holding rockfish *(Sebastes miniatus)* fillets and silver salmon *(Oncorhynchus kisutch)* steaks under modified atmospheres with or without the inclusion of 1% CO to prevent any possible discoloration problems. In this study, sensory panelists indicated that the products held under a 20 or 40% CO_2 were superior to those held in air over extended periods of time. Chemically and microbiologically, the 40% CO_2 was more effective in controlling undesirable changes in these products. The inclusion of 1% CO in the storage environment was somewhat effective in preventing discoloration of the rockfish fillets. Fey and Regenstein (1979) reported that a 60% CO_2 atmosphere was very advantageous in extending the quality shelf life of fresh red hake *(Urophycis chuss)* packed in gas impermeable bags. Further shelf life extension was observed when the 60% CO_2 atmosphere was employed together with a 1% sorbate dip treatment.

Since many fish and shellfish are practically void of myoglobin, it is conceivable that very high levels of CO_2 could be used to effect maximal bacteriostatic properties with little risk of discoloration. The implementation of this concept was previously suggested by Tarr (1954) and from the experimental results of others (Coyne, 1933). High levels of CO_2 appear to be very promising indeed. On a commercial scale, over 2 million pounds of fresh, dressed salmon were shipped from Anchorage, Alaska, to Seattle, Washington, in the summer of 1978 under TransFresh Corporation's patented system. Shipping times involved periods of up to 10 days and all of the product arriving in Seattle was of very high quality (Veranth and Robe 1979).

Recent work in our own laboratory has shown that a modified atmosphere of 80% CO_2 and 20% air was very effective in extending the shelf life of fresh rockcod fillets *(Sebastes* spp.) well past that observed under conventional storage conditions. Aerobic plate counts and tissue trimethylamine levels were significantly lower in samples held in modified atmospheres than samples held in air controls. A decline in surface pH was observed on the fillets stored under CO_2, presumably due to absorption of CO_2 and its conversion to carbonic acid. Trained sensory panelists could not detect differences in surface color between fresh samples and those stored in MA for 13 days, while both groups were significantly different in appearance from air controls. Odor comparisons yielded similar findings. Other studies in our laboratory dealing with MA storage of fresh cooked dungeness crab *(Cancer magister)* indicate a significant extension of shelf life of this product compared to that held under conventional conditions; i.e., refrigerated in air. Again, the product held in MA displayed lower aerobic plate counts as well as lower tissue ammonia levels and surface pH values compared to air controls. Also, the residual effect of CO_2 on bacterial growth was apparent when the product was removed from the MA. Unfortunately, with prolonged storage, the crabmeat developed an uncharacteristic "flat" or acidic taste as a result of the high CO_2 treatment, as indicated by the panelists. This taste could be eliminated by subjecting the crabmeat to a mild steam treatment prior to sensory evaluation.

Additional research projects dealing with the use of MA for preservation of seafood products should be initiated. Patterns of change in the microbial flora should be examined using a variety of products held under MA environments. Potential changes in flora could lead to spoilage patterns that are unfamiliar to consumers, possibily removing a valuable food quality safeguard that exists for products held under conventional storage conditions. Chemical methods for quality assessment of products held under MA should be reexamined for the reasons just mentioned. The quality and shelf life of products held under MA should be evaluated after removal from the MA, in simulation of actual marketing practices. Finally, many scientists express concern about using MA systems having low levels of O_2 because of fear of *Clostridium botulinum* type E and toxin production. Although the toxin problem can be controlled by proper refrigeration practices alone, the concern over the *C. botulinum* microorganism is legitimate. It is recommended that studies of inoculated products be initiated to examine this potential hazard in products held in MA storage. At the time of this writing, we have informal reports that such studies are being conducted. However, to our knowledge, no publications subject to citation have appeared as of this date.

POSSIBLE MECHANISM OF ACTION OF CARBON DIOXIDE

Carbon dioxide has been found to exhibit major effects on various tissues. Of these perhaps the most important is the lowering of the internal pH (pH_i) of the tissue. This has been found to be true for crab muscle fibers (Aickin and Thomas 1975), snail giant neurons (Thomas 1974), sheep heart cells (Thomas and Ellis 1976), squid giant axons (Boron and DeWeer 1976), and *Xenopus* embryos (Turin and Warner 1977). In all cases, exposure of the tissues to the external CO_2 present resulted in a rapid acidification of the internal cellular environment, the extent of which was found to be dependent on the type of tissue, membrane permeability, the level of CO_2 present in the surrounding environment, and the presence or absence of bicarbonate. In all of these studies, it was observed that the rapid internal acidification by CO_2 (drop in pH ranging from 0.06 to 1.06 units, depending on the tissue involved and the conditions employed) was followed by a slow alkalization that resulted in total recovery of pH_i to the initial value, often leading to a pH_i value greater than the initial value. In the squid giant axons study, it was found that this tissue alkalization resulted in the acidification of the extracellular environment. With respect to the MA storage of seafood products, the acidification of the extracellular environment, if operable in this case, could have some effect on bacterial growth patterns. The authors suggested that this "proton extruding pump" required CO_2/HCO_3 and found that the tissue alkalization was reversibly blocked by cyanide and dinitrophenol. This active transport system could be the movement of H^+ (or OH^- or HCO_3) across the membrane.

Somewhat contradictory to the theory of an active transport system, however, is the Donnan effect, proposed as a result of other similar CO_2 exposure experiments with rat and crab muscle tissue (Paillard 1972). In this study, a pH_i gradient of 6.11 at the surface tissue to 6.68 in the deep zones of rat muscle tissue was observed. The pH_i gradient of the surface tissue could be explained by the Donnan equilibrium, whereas the correlation could not be made with the deep zone tissue pH_i. However, when the pH_i of the surface tissue was measured, it was noticed that a sensitive portion of the microelectrode used remained extracellular during the pH_i determination.

It was found in most of these previous studies that membrane potential and external pH (pH_e) had little, if any, effect on pH_i, indicating a direct effect by CO_2. Crab muscle fibers with a pH_i of 7.27 were exposed to a Tris-buffered Ringer solution at pH 6.5, and the observed drop in pH_i was only 0.05 units (Aicken and Thomas 1975). In this experiment, the membrane potential remained at -64.9 mV and the buffer contained no HCO_3^-. In this same study, exposure of the tissue to 1.2 mmoles of potassium resulted in a drop of membrane potential of approximately 8 mV and the pH_i remained unaffected. Depolarization of the membrane of this tissue through exposure to 24 mmoles of potassium for 10 min produced a pH_i change of only 0.1 unit, which was suggested to be due to a calcium-hydrogen ion exchange caused by contraction. Exposure of this tissue to the Fatt and Katz crab Ringer equilibrated with 100% CO_2 resulted in a fall in membrane potential from -64.9 to -55 mV, which was reversible upon removal of the 100% CO_2 medium. In studies done with *Xenopus* embyro, a drop in membrane potential of 10 mV was observed when the tissue was exposed to a medium equilibrated with 100% CO_2, consistent with results obtained from crab muscle fibers (Turin and Warner 1977). Similar observations of the negligible effect of a change in pH_e on membrane potential and the lack of influence of either pH_e or membrane potential on pH_i were made in studies with sheep heart cells (Thomas and Ellis 1976). The major concern with the cell membrane potential in respect to pH_i, pH_e, and %CO_2 is that a change in membrane potential may alter certain transport processes and/or permeability, electrochemical gradients, or ionic communication between cells (Turin and Warner 1977), all of which could greatly affect the metabolism of the cell itself.

With regard to the MA storage of fresh seafood using CO_2, the intracellular or extracellular acidification of tissues could have several important effects. It has long been known that CO_2 is an effective antimicrobial agent, but little is known about the nature of its antimicrobial properties or mechanisms of its action. In studies done with *Pseudomonas aeruginosa* suspensions, pH was found to have a direct effect on the rate of growth of the organism (King and Nagel 1967). In this study, optimal pH for growth was

6.5 to 7.0, with increases in generation time of up to 50% at pH values of 5.0 and 7.5. But since bacteria can grow over a fairly wide pH range (pH 5–8) (Munro 1970), the range of acidities that occur in most foodstuffs is usually conducive to growth of many bacterial species. This wide range of pH in which bacteria can grow is due to the relative impermeability of the cytosolic membrane in bacteria to H^+/OH^-. Rather than an extracellular pH inhibition of bacterial growth, CO_2 more likely inhibits bacterial growth through an intracellular acidification of bacteria, if indeed the bacteriostatic mechanism of CO_2 involves a pH effect. This intracellular acidification could have a marked effect on many specific enzymatic activities that play an integral part in bacterial growth processes.

Another consequence of an intracellular acidification of microbial cells is that a H^+/K^+ transport system is activated in order to relieve the imposed stress (Ryan and Ryan 1972; Harold et al. 1970). In yeast an intracellular pH of 5.70 was found to result in the highest amount of K^+ uptake. In the bacterium Streptococcus faecalis, a transmembrane pH gradient was investigated (Harold et al. 1970). Glycolyzing cells maintained an internal pH slightly more alkaline than the pH_e value. It was suggested that this pH gradient is maintained by an energy-requiring proton extrusion process that also generates a membrane potential. The intracellular acidification by CO_2 could very well activate this ion transport system and produce an accumulation of K^+ ions inside the cell. The stimulation of an ionic transport system would tend to draw from the energy reserves of the cell due to the energy-requiring nature of such systems. This could lead to a misdirection of energy usage, with the cell having to sacrifice the maintenance of other metabolic or growth processes.

The accumulation of K^+ ions could affect many different enzymatic activities, since K^+ ions are known to be an important regulator for many enzymes. Active transport processes, as well as other cellular mechanisms at or near the surface, can be affected by an extracellular pH change. For example, the cytochrome oxidases, which can exert control on the respiratory processes of the cell, could easily be controlled through surface changes at the cell membranes. These membrane effects are elaborated upon on the next page.

Another possible mode of action of CO_2 is that CO_2 itself may act directly as a metabolic regulator. In studies done on microbial growth in fresh beef, where the effect of CO_2 was considered to be under constant pH, it was found that CO_2 alone directly inhibited microbial growth (King and Nagel 1975). Specifically, these authors looked for changes in the metabolism of Pseudomonas aerugionosa that would affect the growth pattern of the organism. They observed that there was a greater lag time of growth of the organism in CO_2 in comparison to a normal air atmosphere. However, it was found that the concentrations of many of the metabolic intermediates decreased when the organism was grown in the presence of CO_2, and that the enzymatic activities of isocitrate dehydrogenase and malate dehydrogenase decreased linearly with an increasing amount of CO_2 comprising the atmosphere. It was suggested that the effect of CO_2 on growth of this and other organisms is due to a shift in equilibrium of the decarboxylating enzymes (such as isocitrate dehydrogenase), making them rate-limiting and thus promoting an overall effect of retarded growth. In another study, using an atmosphere of 100% CO_2 in the storage of beef, it was found that anaerobic as well as aerobic bacterial growth was negligible after 27 days' storage at 1.1°C (Huffman et al. 1975). These authors also noticed that an atmosphere of 100% CO_2 used for storage of beef was much more effective in preventing microbial growth than atmospheres of air, 100% O_2, 100% N_2, or a mix of 70% N_2, 25% CO_2, and 5% O_2. Gill and Tan (1979) have recently reported on the effect of carbon dioxide on growth of Pseudomonas fluorescens. The same workers (Gill and Tan 1980) have studied the effect of carbon dioxide on growth of meat spoilage bacteria and conclude that, while the basis of inhibition of microbial growth is not yet known, inhibition of specific enzymes may be involved.

Membrane properties can be greatly affected by the presence of HCO_3^- and CO_2 (Sears and Eisenberg 1961). In a membrane model system, it was found that HCO_3^- in the absence of CO_2 caused a marked decrease in the interfacial surface tension of the membrane. Bicarbonate also caused a hydration of the membrane and changes in the intermolecular spacings of the membrane components, reflecting a change to a more ionic-permeable membrane. In the presence of CO_2, a smaller decrease in surface tension is observed because CO_2 tends to dehydrate the surface, increasing the continuity of the membrane and making it less permeable to ions. The importance of the phenomenon is that, upon dissolution and hydration of CO_2 in tissues, bicarbonate may be formed and may then increase the permeability of microbial membranes. This increased permeability could allow passage or leakage of certain ionic species and may thus alter the metabolic processes of the microorganisms, inhibiting their growth. Loss of integrity of the cell membrane may also have an effect on membrane processes. Although only 0.26% of the dissolved CO_2 (in aqueous solution) forms bicarbonate and/or acid, the conversion in biological systems may be greatly enhanced by the absorption of CO_2 by the muscle tissues and bacterial cells. Also, cell membranes are very permeable to CO_2. As stated earlier, exposure of biological tissues to CO_2 has a marked effect on the membrane potential. This could produce drastic alterations in membrane enzymatic processes that are dependent on the oxidation reduction potential of the system. These membrane metabolic processes are often those associated with supplying the cell with energy to carry out other cellular anabolic processes. Another interesting observation was that environmental CO_2 stimulated rat liver mitochondrial ATPase activity (Fenestil et al. 1963). Moreover, it was suggested that increasing CO_2 concentrations had an uncoupling effect on oxidative phosphorylation. If this type of situation exists in bacteria as well, then the uncoupling by CO_2 would lead to a partial loss of the cell's energy source (i.e., ATP), which would presumably result in a much retarded rate of growth.

In summary, there have been many studies of the effects of CO_2 on tissues and microorganisms, but there is little direct evidence dealing with the mechanism of action. The following appear to be salient points.

1. Carbon dioxide lowers the intra- and extracellular pH of tissues and possibly that of microorganisms.
2. The carbon dioxide/bicarbonate ratio has an observed effect on the permeability of membranes.
3. Carbon dioxide may affect the membrane potential of microorganisms.
4. Carbon dioxide may have a direct influence on the equilibrium of decarboxylating enzymes of microorganisms.

The use of modified atmospheres for the storage and transport of seafoods appears to offer great potential. While considerable work remains to be done to establish ideal parameters for individual products, the evidence to date is sufficiently promising to warrant major efforts toward developing this technology further.

ACKNOWLEDGMENT

That portion of the work described herein as being done in our own laboratories was supported by NOAA Office of Sea Grant, Department of Commerce; the Resources Agency, State of California; and by the Trans-Fresh Corporation.

REFERENCES

ADAMS, J.R., and HUFFMAN, D.L. 1972. Effect of controlled gas atmospheres and temperatures on quality of packaged pork. J. Food Sci. *37*, 869–872.

AICKIN, C.C., and THOMAS, R.C. 1975. Microelectrode measurement of the internal pH of crab muscle fibers. J. Physiol. *252*, 803–815.

BARNETT, H.J., NELSON, R.W., HUNTER, P.J., BARNES, S., and GRONINGER, H. 1971. Studies on the use of carbon dioxide dissolved in refrigerated brine for the preservation of whole fish. Fish. Bull. *69*, 433.

BARNETT, H.J., NELSON, R.W., HUNTER, P.J., and GRONINGER, H.S. 1978. Use of carbon dioxide dissolved in refrigerated brine for the preservation of pink shrimp *(Pandalus spp.)*. Mar. Fish. Rev. *40*, 24–28.

BORON, W.F., and DE WEER, P. 1976. Active proton transport stimulated by carbon dioxide/bicarbonate, blocked by cyanide. Nature *259*, 240–241.

BROWN, W.D., ALBRIGHT, M., WATTS, D.A., HEYER, B., SPRUCE, B., and PRICE, R.J. 1980. Modified atmosphere storage on rockfish *(Sebastes miniatus)* and silver salmon *(Oncorhynchus kisutch)*. J. Food Sci. *45*, 93–96.

BULLARD, F.A., and COLLINS, J. 1978. Physical and chemical changes of pink shrimp, *Pandalus borealis*, held in carbon dioxide modified refrigerated seawater compared with pink shrimp held in ice.   Fish. Bull. *76*, 73–78.

CALLOW, E.H.   1932.   Gas storage of pork and bacon. I.   Preliminary experiments.   J. Soc. Chem. Ind. *51*, 116T–119T.

CLARK, D.S., and LENTZ, C.P.   1973.   Carbon dioxide for extending shelf life of prepackaged beef.   Can. Inst. Food Sci. Technol. J. *6*, 175–178.

COYNE, F.P.   1932.   The effect of carbon dioxide on bacterial growth with special reference to the preservation of fish. I.   J. Soc. Chem. Ind. *51*, 119T–121T.

COYNE, F.P.   1933.   The effect of carbon dioxide on bacterial growth with special reference to the preservation of fish. II.   J. Soc. Chem. Ind. *52*, 19T–24T.

DAUN, H., SOLBERG, M., FRANKE, W., and GILBERT, S.   1971.   Effect of oxygen-enriched atmospheres on storage quality of packaged fresh meat.   J. Food Sci. *36*, 1011–1014.

FENESTIL, D.D., HASTINGS, A.B., and MAHOWALD, T.A.   1963.   Environmental CO_2 stipulation of mitrochondrial adenosine triphosphatase activity.   J. Biol. Chem. *236*, 836–842.

FEY, M., and REGENSTEIN, J.M.   1979.   Shelf life extension of fresh fish.   Presented at the Atlantic Fisheries Technological Conference, Danvers, MA.

GEE, D.L., and BROWN, W.D.   1978A.   Stability of carboxymyoglobin in refrigerated ground beef.   J. Agric. Food Chem. *26*, 273–274.

GEE, D.L., and BROWN, W.D.   1978B.   Extension of shelf life in refrigerated ground beef stored under an atmosphere containing carbon dioxide and carbon monoxide.   J. Agric. Food Chem. *26*, 274–276.

GILL, C.O., and TAN, K.H.   1979.   Effect of carbon dioxide on growth of *Pseudomonas fluorescens*.   Appl. Environ. Microbiol. *38*, 237–240.

GILL, C.O., and TAN, K.H.   1980.   Effect of carbon dioxide on growth of spoilage bacteria.   Appl. Environ. Microbiol. *39*, 317–319.

HAARD, N.F., MARTINS, I., NEWBURY, R., and BOTTA, R.   1979.   Hypobaric storage of Atlantic herring and cod.   Can. Inst. Food Sci. Technol. J. *12*, 84–87.

HAINES, R.B.   1933.   The influence of carbon dioxide on the rate of multiplication of certain bacteria, as judged by viable counts.   J. Soc. Ind. Chem. *52*, 13T–17T.

HAROLD, F.M., PAVLASOVA, E., and BAARDA, J.R.   1970.   Transmembrane pH gradient in *Streptococcus faecalis*: Origin and dissipation by proton conductors and *N, N'*-dicyclohexylcarbodiimide.   Biochim. Biophys. Acta *196*, 235–244.

HILTZ, D.F., LALL, B.S., LEMON, D.W., and DYER, W.J.   1976.   Detriorative changes during frozen storage in fillets and minced flesh of silver hake *(Merluccius bilinearis)* processed from round fish held in ice and refrigerated sea water.   J. Fish. Res. Board Can. *33*, 2560–2567.

HUFFMAN, D.L., DAVIS, K.A., MARPLE, D.N., and MCGUIRE, I.A.   1975.   Effect of gas atmospheres on microbial growth, color and pH of beef.   J. Food

Sci. *40*, 1229−1231.

KILLEFFER, D.H. 1930. Carbon dioxide preservation of meat and fish. Ind. Eng. Chem. *22*, 140−143.

KING, A.D., and NAGEL, C.W. 1967. Growth inhibition of a *Pseudomonas* by carbon dioxide. J. Food Sci. *32*, 575−579.

KING, A.D., and NAGEL, C.W. 1975. Influence of carbon dioxide upon the metabolism of *Pseudomonas aeroginosa*. J. Food Sci. *40*, 362−366.

KOLBE, H. 1882. Antiseptiche eigneschaften der Kohlensäure. J. Prakt. Chem. *26*, 249−255.

LEDWARD, D.A. 1970. Metmyoglobin formation in beef stored in carbon dioxide enriched and oxygen depleted atmospheres. J. Food Sci. *35*, 33−37.

LONGARD, A.A., and REIGER, L.W. 1974. Color and some composition changes in ocean perch *(Sebastes marinus)* held in refrigerated sea water with and without carbon dioxide. J. Fish. Res. Board Can. *31*, 456−460.

MERMELSTEIN, N.H. 1979. Hypobaric transport and storage of fresh meats and produce earns. Food Technol. *33*, 32−35, 38−40.

MORAN, T., SMITH, E.C., and TOMKINS, R.G. 1932. The inhibition of mold growth on meat by carbon dioxide. J. Soc. Chem. Ind. *51*, 114−116.

MUNRO, A.L.S. 1970. Measurement and control of pH values. *In* Methods of Microbiology, Vol. 2, Chapter II. J.R. Norris and D.W. Ribbons (Editors). Academic Press, New York.

NELSON, R.W., and BARNETT, H.J. 1971. Fish preservation in refrigerated sea water modified with carbon dioxide. *In* Progress in Refrigeration Science and Technology, Proc. XIIIth Int. Cong. Refrig. Vol. III, pp. 57−62 AVI Publishing Co., Westport, CT.

NELSON, R.W., and TRETSVEN, W.I. 1975. Storage of Pacific salmon in controlled atmosphere. Proc. XIVth Int. Congress on Refrigeration, Moscow, U.S.S.R. (In press).

ORDONEZ, J.A., and LEDWARD, D.A. 1977. Lipid and myoglobin oxidation in pork stored in oxygen- and carbon dioxide-enriched atmospheres. Meat Sci. *1*, 41−48.

PAILLARD, M. 1972. Direct intracellular pH measurement in rat and crab muscle. J. Physiol. *223*, 297−319.

POHJA, M.S., ALIVAARA, A., and SORSAVIRTA, O. 1967. Influence of carbon dioxide and nitrogen atmospheres on shelf life of refrigerated meat. Proc. Meeting of European Meat Research Workers, Rotterdam, The Netherlands, *B8*, 1−37. (German).

RYAN, J.P., and RYAN, H. 1972. Role of intracellular pH in the regulation of cation exchanges in yeast. Biochem. J. *128*, 138−146.

SEARS, D.F., and EISENBERG, R.M. 1961. A model representing a physiological role of carbon dioxide at the cell membrane. J. Gen. Physiol. *44*, 869−887.

SHEWAN, J.M. 1950. Improving the quality of white fish by the use of gas storage. Fish. News *1946*, 14−15.

SILLIKER, J.H., WOODRUFF, R.E., LUGG, J.R., WOLFE, S.K., and BROWN, W.D. 1977. Preservation of refrigerated meats with controlled atmospheres: Treatment and post-treatment effects of carbon dioxide on pork and beef. Meat Sci. *1*, 195−204.

STANSBY, M.E., and GRIFFITHS, F.P. 1935. Carbon dioxide in handling fresh fish. Ind. Eng. Chem. *27*, 1452−1458.

TARR, H.L.A. 1954. Microbiological deterioration of fish post mortem, its detection and control. Bacteriol. Rev. *18*, 1−5.

TAYLOR, A.A., and MACDOUGALL, B.D. 1973. Fresh beef packed in mixtures of oxygen and carbon dioxide. J. Food Technol. *8*, 453−461.

THOMAS, R.C. 1974. Intracellular pH of snail neurons measured with a new pH-sensitive glass micro-electrode. J. Physiol. *238*, 159−180.

THOMAS, R.C. and ELLIS, D. 1976. Micro-electrode measurement of the intracellular pH of mammalian heart cells. Nature *262*, 224−225.

TURIN, L., and WARNER, A. 1977. Carbon dioxide reversibly abolishes ionic communication between cells of early amphibian embryo. Nature *270*, 56−57.

U. S. DEPARTMENT OF COMMERCE 1978. Current Fisheries Statistics No. 7500. NOAA, Washington, DC.

VERANTH, M.F., and ROBE, K. 1979. CO_2-enriched atmosphere keeps fish fresh more than twice as long. Food Process. *40*, 76−79.

WILLIAMS, A.P., BLOOD, R.M., and JARVIS, B. 1978. The effects of carbon dioxide on the growth of bacteria isolated from meat, poultry and fish. J. Appl. Bacteriol. *45*, xxvi.

WINDSOR, M.L, and THOMA, T. 1974. Chemical preservation of industrial fish. J. Sci. Food Agric. *25*, 993−1005.

WOLFE, S.K., BROWN, W.D., and SILLIKER, J.H. 1976. Transfresh shipping of meat. Proc. Meat Ind. Res. Conf., Chicago, pp. 137−148.

YOKOSEKI, M., UCHIYAMA, H., and AMANO, K. 1956. Preservation of fish cakes. IV. Factors involved in preservative effect of carbon dioxide. Bull. Jpn. Soc. Sci. Fish. *22*, 35−40.

Index